Volume Three

THE REEF AQUARIUM
Science, Art, and Technology
by J. Charles Delbeek and Julian Sprung

Book Design by Daniel N. Ramirez

Published by Ricordea Publishing
Coconut Grove, Florida 33133 USA

The Reef Aquarium Volume Three: Science, Art, and Technology
by J. Charles Delbeek and Julian Sprung

First Printing: 2005
10 9 8 7 6 5 4 3 2

Published and distributed by
Two Little Fishies, Inc.
d.b.a. Ricordea Publishing
4016 El Prado Blvd., Coconut Grove
Florida, 33133 USA

Printed and bound by Mondadori Printing, Verona, Italy
Design and production by Daniel N. Ramirez
Cover photograph is a composite image, realized in Adobe
Photoshop™ by Elliot Sprung, using images from Christy Falkenberg
(of a portion of the aquarium of Jamie Cross, British Columbia),
Marko Haaga (of a portion of his aquarium), and Julian Sprung.
Back cover photographer: Lie Ken Delbeek

ISBN 1-883693-14-4

Table of Contents

Acknowledgements

Any undertaking of this size is rarely possible without the help of countless others. We would like to thank the following people for helping us make this book:

Andy Aiken, Eduard Aulov, Marj Awai, Dominique Barthelemy, Frank Baensch, Rick Bell, Mirko Belosevic, Stuart Bertram, Joe Biesterfeld, Dr. Craig Bingman, Eric Borneman, Robert Brons, Rob Brynda, Anthony Calfo, Mitch Carl, Dr. Bruce Carlson, Kevin Carpenter, Andy Case, Norton Chan, Phil Cooper, Alex Correia, Jamie Cross, Kevin Curlee, Dr. Dan DiResta, Dan B. Dalke, Lie Ken Delbeek, Dustin Dorton, Dr. Phillip Dustan, Jean-Jacques Eckert, Karen and Bob Elder, Kiyoshi Endo, Paul R. Endtricht, Christy Falkenberg, Dr. A-Y. Fan, Ann Fielding and the crew of the Spirit of Solomons, Harvey Feinberg, Svein Fosså, Tom Frakes, David Fridman and family, Kevin Gaines, Joe and Jan Genero, Warren Gibbons, Tim Goertemiller, Jorge Gomezjurado, Marko Hagga, Richard Harker, Bill Hoffman, Randy Holmes-Farley, Takushi Horita, George Houthoff, Dr. Markus Huettel, Dorothy Hurley, Lance and Miki Ichinotsubo, Dr. Jean Jaubert, Steve Jackson, Max Janse, Jef with one F, Sanjay Joshi, Johannes Kirchhauser, Dave Keeley, Jason Kim, Suk Choo Kim, Daniel Knop, Kevin Kohen, Rand Kollman, Marc Langouet, David Lazenby, Rich Lerner, Morgan Lidster, Rick and Terry Loewen, Jeff Macare, Koji Matzusaki, Scott W. Michael, Yoshi Mizuno, Martin A. Moe Jr., Michael G. Moye, Kirk Murakami, Dr. Vorathep Muthuwan, Alf Nilsen, Masanori Nonaka, Grant Norton, Fernando Nosratpour, Des Ong, Dr. Nadia Ounais, Mike Paletta, Joe Pecorelli, Dirk Peterson, Vince Rado, Dr. Jack Randall, Markus Resch, Barry Reynolds, Dana Riddle, Nancy Sabina Rivadeneira, Greg Schiemer, Habib Sekha, Ed Seidel, Bart Shepherd, Terry Siegel, François Seneca, Walt Smith, Elliot Sprung, Leng Sy, Sandy Trautwein, Dr. Rob Toonen, Andrew Trevor-Jones, Axel Tunze, Steve Tyree, Hitoshi Ueno, Tony Vargas, D. Wachenfeld, Koji Wada, Dr. Kirsten Michalek-Wagner, Peter Wilkens, and last, but never least, Joe Yaiullo.

We would also like to thank the various manufacturers, distributors, pet stores, public aquariums, and publishers for providing and/or giving permission to use their figures and/or photos.

About the Authors

J. Charles Delbeek graduated from the University of Toronto in 1981 with an honors bachelor's degree in biology, a master's in zoology in 1986 and a bachelor's in education in 1986. After enduring one winter too many in his native Toronto, he moved to Hawaii and took a position with the Waikiki Aquarium in 1995. He has been caring for marine organisms in closed systems for over 30 years and currently maintains ten exhibits at the Waikiki Aquarium ranging from a 12 gallon live coral exhibit to a 5500 gallon living reef tank. Charles' latest projects included the construction of 5500 and 1200 gallon living reef displays opened in June of 2002 at the Waikiki Aquarium, and a 4000 gallon coral farm completed in the summer of 2004. A certified SCUBA diver since the age of 14, Charles has made over 300 dives in locations throughout the world including Canada, Fiji, Hawaii, Indonesia, Japan, south Korea, the Marshall Islands, Palau, the Solomon Islands, Thailand, the Florida Keys, Bonaire, St. Kitts, and St. Maartin. Charles has lectured at over 40 aquarium-related conferences and meetings, and published over 60 articles in the popular aquarium literature in the last 15 years. In addition to writing a monthly reef aquarium column for Aquarium Fish Magazine since 1997 and a bi-monthly column for Advanced Aquarist Online, he has with this book now co-authored three popular aquarium books with Julian Sprung.

Julian Sprung is an author, photographer, aquarium design consultant, and Vice President of Two Little Fishies, Inc., an aquarium industry manufacturing and publishing company. Julian has a bachelor of science degree in zoology from the University of Florida, and has been keeping marine aquariums for nearly 30 years. He currently maintains 5 marine aquariums and two freshwater planted aquariums. Julian's love of marinelife has resulted in many friendships with other coral reef researchers and reef keeping hobbyists around the world. He has dived on reefs in Australia, the Bahamas, Mexico, the Mediterranean, Panama, Puerto Rico, Fiji, Florida, Hawaii, Japan, Israel, Egypt, and the Solomon Islands. Julian's other books include *The Reef Aquarium*, volumes one and two, which he co-authored with J. Charles Delbeek, *Reef Notes Revisited and Revised* (volumes 1, 2, 3, and 4), *Corals: A Quick Reference Guide*, *Invertebrates: A Quick Reference Guide*, and *Algae: A Problem Solver Guide*.

Introduction

Ever since we published the second volume in this series in 1997, marine aquarists have been asking us when volume three would be finished. The hunger for our next book was certainly gratifying, but after spending several years preparing the first two books we needed a chance to rest! Furthermore, what would we put in the third volume? With each year new methods and equipment came on the scene, but it has never been our intention to merely catalogue the aquarium market. Nor was it our intention to repackage the ideas we already had presented in our first two books. Our goal has always been to present the state of the art of reef aquarium husbandry in its most practical modes. In addition, we intend to inspire the development of new directions, to share our own enthusiasm about areas less well studied, and demonstrate emerging technology that has potential useful application in aquariums. We also believe that aquarists should see exhibits featuring unusual scale, creatures, or aquascaping technique, and we have assembled some nice examples for this book.

Volume three took shape as the hobby evolved to embrace more simple and natural approaches to duplicating tropical reef ecosystems. Even as we completed the second volume, we could see the trend toward an interest in some of the special habitats associated with coral reefs, and interest in the biology of these ecosystems and their inhabitants. In this third volume we explore ways to duplicate these habitats and incorporate them as part of a tropical reef aquarium display.

The technological devices used to manage a reef aquarium evolved almost to the point of non-existence following the trend toward natural systems, but there have also been exciting developments in the essential systems used to move the water, illuminate the aquarium, and maintain the necessary chemical and physical water parameters. The *techniques* discussed in this book are its core. We can speculate that techniques will continue to evolve, but the reefkeeping hobby has matured to a point where much of the existing methods are so well accepted and so easily managed that future changes are likely to be subtler than previous ones.

This is your brain under actinic light. A colourful example of the brain coral, *Leptoria phrygia*.
J. Sprung

In addition to the technological advances of the past ten years, much attention has also focused on the chemical and biological needs of a coral reef aquarium. The scientific and aquarium literature offer new information about subjects directly related to the husbandry of aquariums such as nutrition, feeding modes, and trace elements. In this volume, we discuss these new findings and their implications for reef aquariums.

Why we need reef aquariums

The widespread popularity of reef aquariums has made them a fixture at numerous research institutions, universities, and high schools. Thus, they have become a tool for introducing students to coral reef ecology. For the coral reef researcher they have become a valuable in-house workstation that makes it possible to observe the effects of manipulating various physical and chemical parameters, something that cannot be done on natural reefs. A reef aquarium therefore offers the possibility to study whole ecosystem questions as well as the affects that manipulating the environment can have on corals or any other living part of the reef.

The study of whole ecosystems in closed aquariums is not merely the folly of hobbyists, public aquariums, and researchers wishing to understand coral reefs. It is also the seed of a new branch of science, *biospherics* that studies the maintenance of living ecosystems with the goal of creating self-sustaining habitats separate from the planet Earth, so-called *biospheres*. It might seem like an idea taken from the pages of a science fiction novel, but this discipline is not something restricted to the imagination. It is an active pursuit of numerous scientific institutions. This is because the maintenance of life on distant moons, planets, space ships, space stations, or even here on earth in cities underground, or under the sea, will depend on functioning living ecosystems full of microbes and a diversity of life, not on invented

This reef aquarium managed by student Benjamin West is in Dr. Dan DiResta's undergraduate marine biology department at the University of Miami.
J. Sprung

10

A portion of one of the coral labs at the Oceanographic Museum in Monaco. J. Sprung

This *Stylophora pistillata* tissue grown on a glass slide in Professor Jean Jaubert's lab in Monaco provides the unique opportunity to observe and study calcification mechanisms. J. Sprung

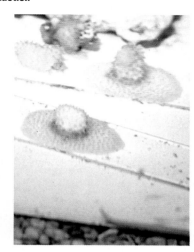

The middle section of the beautiful reef display at Penn State University. S. Joshi.

This reef aquarium lab set up by Dan Dalke is located at a private high school called the Lovett School, located near Atlanta, Georgia. D. Dalke

mechanical filtration machines. It has even been proposed that this human pursuit of creating and cultivating living ecosystems is the means by which the living earth, *Gaia* reproduces, a way that life moves from Earth into space (Sagan, 1990). That notion puts a completely new perspective on the evolution of humans…and gives a great deal of importance to this *hobby* of reef aquarium keeping!

The commercial culture of ornamental marinelife has blossomed in the past decade, including advances in both the culture of ornamental marine fishes and of other coral reef animals and plants. The reef aquarium hobby has been a big part in making this happen, because reef aquarium hobbyists have largely devised invertebrate culture techniques, and because the ready market for aquacultured products is the aquarium industry with its environmentally conscious and enthusiastic reefkeeping element.

Amphiprion clarkii clownfish raised at *Oceans Reefs and Aquariums*, Ft. Pierce, Florida. J. Sprung

Amphiprion percula clownfish raised at *Oceans Reefs and Aquariums*, Ft. Pierce, Florida. J. Sprung

Pseudochromis aldabraensis raised at *Oceans Reefs and Aquariums*, Ft. Pierce, Florida. J. Sprung

Pseudochromis springeri raised at *Oceans Reefs and Aquariums*, Ft. Pierce, Florida. J. Sprung

Pseudochromis sankeyi raised at *Oceans Reefs and Aquariums*, Ft. Pierce, Florida. J. Sprung

Pseudochromis fridmani raised at *Oceans Reefs and Aquariums*, Ft. Pierce, Florida. J. Sprung

A butterflyfish harvested from the plankton as a postlarva and reared in captivity for the aquarium trade by the company *EcoOcean*® (www.ecocean.fr). This new technique can produce hardy fishes from species that normally are difficult to feed in captivity. O. Andromede

A tank full of Green Chromis (*Chromis viridis*) raised in captivity by *EcoOcean*® from postlarvae attracted to floating artificial reef structures. O. Andromede

The first tank-raised lemonpeel angelfish in the world. F. Baensch

A mix of three tank-raised pygmy angelfish species.
F. Baensch

The marine aquarium hobby has entered a new phase where
aquaculture is providing a larger proportion of the creatures kept
compared with wild harvest. Interest in the aquaculture of
ornamental marinelife has been promoted by several factors,
including higher wholesale prices for marinelife, higher quality
aquacultured animals due to improvements in diet and grow-out
techniques, increased demand for aquacultured products, and
sharing of information at international congresses such as the
biannual Marine Ornamentals conference. At the same time the
formation of organizations like the Marine Aquarium Council
(MAC) has promoted the sustainable harvest of marinelife and
improvements in husbandry and handling practices, with the goals
of keeping the aquarium industry healthy, promoting coral reef
conservation and ethical treatment of marinelife.

Furthermore, the techniques developed by coral farms for culturing
corals and other reef life can be employed for reef restoration
projects. Having farms in the region where reefs occur allows for
the conservation of genetic diversity, and provides an opportunity
for governments to employ local people to actively improve the
marine habitat. In the eco-tourist business, it is also possible that
reef restoration could be an activity offered for the visitor to not
only see but also actively become involved in. Seaside hotels could
coordinate programs for tourists to visit the coral farms, get trained
about coral reef ecology and restoration techniques, and then plant
coral cuttings on a designated *house reef* behind the hotel, or
nearby. Such hands-on experience is invaluable for educating the
public about coral reefs and inspiring concern for their
conservation. The farming of reef corals and other marinelife used
for restoration is also a more tangible way to enhance the natural
resource, compared to purely analytical research. Although such

Coral propagation system at *C.V. Dinar*, Bali, Indonesia. K. Wada

schemes may seem fantasy to some, we are aware of many such programs currently in operation- in Florida (Ken Nedimyer), in Fiji (*Walt Smith International*), Japan (*C.P. Farm*, Ishigaki Island), Indonesia (numerous entities), and the Philippines (Thomas Heegar, pers. comm.).

Ethical and ecological concerns about our hobby

The marine aquarium hobby is challenging and rewarding, but it involves much more than just putting together an aquarium and hoping for success. The hobby begins with a supply of mostly wild-caught marinelife from the tropical and subtropical oceans of the world, and it brings important income to people in many countries. Since the harvest is mostly taken from the wild, it has the potential to disturb the natural environment on a small local scale. The marine aquarium hobby conversely has the potential to protect

Walt Smith International provides economic benefit to Fijians who both harvest and cultivate marinelife for the aquarium trade. Photo courtesy of Walt Smith International.

These *polyp rocks* have been available for several years, having been produced in Indonesia by clever reef farmers who cement together cuttings of many different but compatible species. J. Sprung

vast areas of wild habitat when the economic incentive of a thriving fishing industry is matched with a conservation ethic that promotes the use of environmentally sustainable harvest practices. People involved in the marine aquarium hobby, reef aquarium keepers in particular, are very conscious of the natural environment and are concerned about how their hobby might affect it.

Once taken from the wild, the harvested creatures are transported great distances and must be maintained under conditions that insure their survival, good health, and minimize stress. This *chain of custody* must follow guidelines that insure the health of the marinelife along the way.

Some marine ornamentals are also raised in aquaculture. This activity is commonly touted as preferred since it minimizes harvest or so-called *environmental impact*. However, taking the source of marinelife away from the wild has the potential to reduce income from the people in the countries where the marinelife is normally harvested. This removes an important economic incentive to protect the natural resource, especially if the wild harvest is banned. The aquarium trade provides the most value to local people for their renewable coral reef resources. For example, Wabnitz *et al.*, (2003) notes that a kilogram (about 2 pounds) of aquarium fish from the Maldives is worth $500, while food fish there are worth $6 per kilo. Limestone is harvested from the sea for construction material (e.g. cement making, road building) in many island nations at a value of $40-$60 per ton. The same material, sold as *live rock* for aquariums brings $4000 to $8000 per ton. The aquaculture of ornamental marinelife is a positive activity that should be supported, but not in exclusivity of wild harvest.

Construction workers use an abundant and renewable natural resource, coral rock washed ashore by storms, to build a breakwater to protect the shoreline in Tuvalu, an island threatened by rising sea levels. K. Warne

Walt Smith International not only farms live corals but also manufactures realistic artificial corals. J. Sprung

Where to locate the farms

Remote aquaculture (across the globe from the origin) of a natural resource that is an important source of income to indigenous peoples is sometimes referred to a *bio-piracy*. Aquaculture activity can also be employed locally in the countries where marinelife is harvested. Such reef farming industries have numerous positive features. They can be used to conserve and propagate rare varieties of corals or other invertebrates, retaining their value as a resource locally. Keeping the resource local can also make aquaculture facilities instrumental in preventing loss of diversity due to storms, bleaching, or other natural disasters. Ideally, farming industries should be established both in the aquarium hobby regions and in the countries of origin for the marinelife. This way the aquarium hobby has a steady supply of aquacultured marinelife without removing the income from the countries of origin.

Artificial corals, anemones, clams, plants, etc.

Numerous companies have developed realistic looking corals and other sea creatures made from epoxies, resins, textiles, plastics, or silicone. These creations have become very popular for aquarium decoration in marine aquariums, where once the only decorating items widely available were bleached coral skeletons from the curio trade. Some of the fake corals are so realistic and so life-like that they can easily be mistaken for living corals. These artificial decorating items are marketed as being an eco-friendly alternative to harvest from the wild. We agree that using them in fish aquariums is in some respects better than promoting the removal and bleaching of large coral heads for decoration in a fish tank. The eco-friendly idea is a bit hard to defend on other levels, however. Surely, the manufacture of these things produces pollution, as does the

17

An artificial anemone manufactured by *Marineland Aquarium Products* providing habitat for tank raised hybrid clownfish (*Amphiprion ocellaris* x *Premnas biaculeatus*) produced by *Proaquatix*, Ft. Pierce, Florida. J. Sprung

The shape of things to come? Artificial fluorescent corals in a micro aquarium. J. Sprung

For those who don't care if it's live this fluorescent coral display offers a consistent view. J. Sprung

A trade show display of artificial coral produced by *Living Color* looks like a slice of the reef. J. Sprung

packaging. Furthermore, the items themselves are not easily biodegradable. Of course, the world is not black and white with respect to eco-friendliness, and the choice of *paper or plastic* bags at your local grocery is likewise not easily answered if you think too much about the ecological significance.

Artificial live rock made from cement and coral sand, clay, or epoxy resins has also become a popular alternative to collection of the naturally occurring live rock still commonly used to build reef structures in aquariums. Chapters 2 and 9 discuss the various types of live rock, including artificial and farmed varieties. The *artificial* rocks offer the aquarist or public aquarium a special opportunity to build unique aquascapes, something we delve into in chapter 9.

Renewable resource?

Much of the effort to make the harvest of marinelife an ecologically sustainable activity concerns the issue of how renewable is a resource taken from the reef. Reefs, we are told by so many publications, grow slowly over millennia. They may increase in size a few millimeters per year. Using that fact, the average person assumes that a coral of say, 15 cm (6 in.) in diameter must be about 50 years old (6 inches is about 152 mm. At 3 mm per year that would be 50 years old). Following this time scale, a coral of 60 cm (24 in.) in diameter might be 200 years old. It was this kind of logic that led to the well-intentioned but misguided display we saw at the *British Museum of Natural History* in London. A small colony of *Pocillopora damicornis* had a label stating it was less than 10 years old. While this was correct, the scale used led the observer to believe that it was

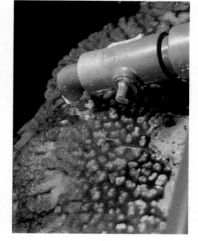

A well-intentioned but misleading display. This coral could easily represent just 10 months of growth. J. Sprung

A few years growth of *Pocillopora damicornis* in a reef display at the *Loebbecke Museum* in Dusseldorf, Germany. J. Sprung

This display at the *British Museum of Natural History* is supposedly composed of illegally harvested black corals (Antipatharia). In fact they are gorgonian skeletons, which are often washed ashore naturally by storms. J. Sprung

Santiago Gutierrez of Puerto Rico showed us this stretch of beach with a meter-wide band of gorgonian skeletons washed ashore by storm waves and wind. J. Sprung

Coral farming allows for the mass vegetative propagation of colourful and hardy species. This *Acropora* sp. is cultivated at *Oceans Reefs and Aquariums* (*ORA*) J. Sprung

Small polyped reef corals cultured at *ORA* in Ft. Pierce, Florida. Note that cuttings are taken from cuttings to mass-produce a maximum number of colonies. J. Sprung

nearly 10 years old. In fact, a colony of this size could easily be only about one year old, or only several months old in the right conditions. A demonstration of this fact can be seen in the image taken at the *Lobbecke Museum and Aquazoo* in Dusseldorf.

Reefs may indeed grow only a few millimeters per year, but the corals on them can grow much faster. This separation of the forest from the trees is essential to understanding the renewability of corals and the live rock that forms when they die. Just how much solid substrate (live coral, live rock, shells, sand, gravel) can be removed from a given area of reef in a sustainable manner? The answer is not easy to give, as it depends on many factors. However, we would like to demonstrate examples from some aquarium reefs. At the *Birch Aquarium at Scripps* in La Jolla, California, there is a reef aquarium with an area of 3.6 square metres. A small brown colony of *Acropora* sp. placed in the aquarium in 1995 was monitored by assistant aquarium curator Fernando Nosratpour for eight years as it grew. During that time it was pruned numerous times, producing additional colonies in several other aquariums and these have grown into substantial specimens. It also spawned on August 15, 2000, October 24, 2001 and September 14, 2002, demonstrating an ability to complete its life cycle in captivity. On September 25, 2003 the large colony was removed from the aquarium, killed and bleached (see photo, opposite). This *death* did not eliminate the coral, however, as daughter colonies now exist in other aquariums, including the one from which the large colony was taken. One could make a rough approximation to show the rate of harvest of this one coral in kilograms per year per square meter. If you extend this out to the scale of a coral reef, the quantity seems to become absurdly large. Of course, this would only apply to this particular species of coral and reefs are not homogeneous surfaces, so such extrapolation is full of error. It does nevertheless point to the fact that a substantial harvest of certain genera is possible without significant long-term impact. We want to furthermore point out that Fernando Nosratpour commented that he could not give this coral away as quickly as it could have been harvested since it was just a plain brown species. The desirability of colourful species produces higher demand and thus a better match of the ratio of potential yield to growth rate.

The mother colonies of colourful *Acropora* spp. maintained at *Ocean Reefs and Aquariums* in Ft. Pierce, Florida demonstrate this well. They are maintained in a state of constant harvest and rapid growth, with a yield that would far exceed the figure for the coral from the *Birch Aquarium*. Since live rock is made up of the skeletons of dead corals and coralline algae, among other contributors, the rapid growth of these corals is also a demonstration of the renewability of live rock, in regions where

Top left, the *Birch Aquarium* coral on September 8, 1995. M. Conlin

Top right, the *Birch Aquarium* coral on November 2, 1995. M. Conlin

Right, the *Birch Aquarium* coral in May 1997. F. Nosratpour.

Fernando Nosratpour and his home grown coral, removed and killed September 25, 2003. Though this colony is dead, its genes aren't. It now exists in several aquariums from which colonies like this one could be harvested. M. Ball.

21

corals are actively growing. In other non-coral reef habitats, the formation of live rock from consolidated sand and coralline algae can also be quite rapid, but there is little scientific literature showing the rate of its formation.

Wild harvest of corals

However large the resource may be, there must be a clear demonstration of the method of harvest, and that the harvest is done in a manner that is sustainable. For example, the size of the specimens harvested must be considered, as well as the practice of removing specimens in such a way that the void space left is quickly re-grown by surrounding coral branches or colonies of the same species. In effect, it is like pruning out branches from trees without taking out the trees themselves. An education program for collectors with specific rules about the proper way to harvest

A shallow back reef zone in Fiji dominated by a fast-growing soft coral in the genus *Sinularia*. Harvest of small colonies for aquariums from such sites is a harmless activity that provides income to Fijian families. Photo courtesy of *Walt Smith International*.

A small intact colony extracted by a diver from the mass of *Sinularia*, which reproduces prolifically by vegetative growth and division. Photo courtesy of *Walt Smith International*.

Note: In sps corals the points of fragmentation often produce several new axial polyps or growing tips. Therefore periodic pruning also results in an exponential increase in the number of branches.

would be a positive effort. It would also be extremely valuable to photograph (with video) harvest in a fixed location and show, over months, the re-growth of the coral. For example, in *Euphyllia* spp, if one photographed a colony of one square meter size and the harvest of numerous small colonies from it, the growth in six to twelve months should produce a return to the original skeletal mass. This technique can also be used, in a short time, to increase the size of the resource. It is a fact that artificial propagation by fragmentation can produce a larger quantity of coral than simply leaving the coral to grow *as mother nature intended*. The reason is that upper branches shade lower branches, reducing the growth of the whole colony. Removing some branches lets in the light and opens the opportunity for rapid growth of all branches.

The gorgeous red form of *Cynarina deshayesiana*, a solitary coral that could become locally overharvested unless size limits are followed. J. Sprung

Trachyphyllia geoffroyi is a common solitary species that is harvested in large quantities for aquariums. J. Sprung

Catalaphyllia jardinei is a popular solitary coral in the aquarium trade that is generally uncommon, but locally abundant in some regions. Size limits imposed on their harvest would help to assure that they are not locally over-harvested. J. Sprung

The agencies that wish to limit or end the harvest of corals need to be shown that the harvest is sustainable in order to change their point of view. It is difficult to make a convincing argument without showing sustainable working techniques. Merely showing an apparently limitless resource is not sufficient. Agencies opposed to coral collection believe the aquarium industry demand is larger than the resource, and they believe that collectors clear-cut the coral forests. This perception needs to be changed with documented evidence, not simple assurances.

Specific examples exist where a type of coral could become locally over-harvested. Solitary species of corals such as *Trachyphyllia* and *Cynarina* are collected as whole colonies, and though locally abundant at times, they live only in specific types of habitats and could be over-harvested on a local scale to meet demand by the aquarium market. Because of this fact, limits on their harvest have been proposed. Size restrictions would be another option that would have the added benefit of leaving colonies distributed throughout the collection areas. With harvest quotas but no size limits, it remains possible to remove all colonies from a small locality. Furthermore, the harvest of even the fast growing abundant small polyped stony (sps) corals in a region might be subject to the health of reefs in the region. If a mass die-off occurs, as when high temperatures cause mass bleaching events, the commercial harvest of affected species could have an impact on their recovery, as there would be far fewer live colonies from which to choose. Therefore, the monitoring of mass bleaching events should be coordinated with the permitting of coral harvest.

Publications on the trade

Misleading information has been written about the aquarium trade, from the point of view of conservationists and from the aquarium industry side as well. Recently, however, serious efforts have been made to quantify the size of the trade in various types of marinelife from various regions. The result is a very informative paper by Colette Wabnitz, Michelle Taylor, Edmund Green and Tries Razak of the World Conservation Monitoring Center entitled *From Ocean to Aquarium: The global trade in marine ornamental species* (Wabnitz *et al.*, 2003). Organizations such as the World Conservation Monitoring Centre and Marine Aquarium Council (MAC) continue to report the information about our hobby as accurately as possible.

Disease

The husbandry of fishes and invertebrates in captivity involves more than just management of water quality, knowledge of how the equipment works or even understanding the requirements of the individual species. Various pathogenic diseases commonly affect fishes and invertebrates, and they can produce failure with marine aquarium keeping despite *perfect conditions* and *proper handling*. How can you prevent this? Disease management remains a stumbling point for both the individual aquarist and the companies that import or sell fishes and invertebrates. Since we are dealing with living creatures mainly harvested from the wild, this issue will continue to need careful attention, see chapter 11 for more details.

Ever since the announcement of the formation of the Marine Aquarium Council we have been excited about the positive direction it has taken. MAC is a non-profit organization dedicated to reef conservation. It brings together the marine aquarium industry and hobbyists, public aquariums and conservation organizations, and sets standards for the global trade in marine aquarium organisms. MAC actively works to educate consumers in the demand countries (esp. USA, Europe and Japan) about responsible aquarium keeping, issues involved in the trade, and their role as consumers in supporting reef conservation through their purchasing choices. MAC certified organisms come from managed reefs, are collected by trained fishermen using non-destructive methods, and move through MAC certified exporters, importers and retailers. They are marketed with the *MAC Certified* label. MAC works with numerous entities such as government agencies, environmental and conservation groups, collectors, importers and dealers. Their aim is to protect the natural environment, promote sustainable harvest of marinelife, and create a system of guidelines, standards, and quality practices. These guidelines and practices insure the proper care and handling of marinelife in the chain of custody from the point of collection to the retailer. MAC also has helped to promote objective, accurate data on the marine ornamental trade. MAC's goals benefit marinelife, the natural habitat, the collectors and their communities, and the marine aquarium hobby. Hobbyists and industry professionals can locate certified facilities on the MAC website www.aquariumcouncil.org.

Other ecological concerns about aquariums

Release of non-native *exotic* or *invasive* species

The aquarium hobby has been the focus of attention with regard to a potential ecological consequence other than harvest impact. In this case, it is the release of captive creatures that has the potential to do harm. The history of invasive aquatic species research does not begin and end with aquariums, however. At various times government agencies have, with good intentions, altered native habitats by releasing plants, fishes, or other creatures into a habitat for the purpose of enhancing it or controlling some pest. The released non-native organism sometimes turns out to be a pest that out-competes native species. In Florida, this can be seen clearly in the effect of the Australian Pine tree *Casuarina* that overshadows and kills mangroves, and the Australian tea tree *Malelluca*, that has dominated and dried up vast areas of wetlands in the Everglades. In the water, the Brazilian aquatic plant, water hyacinth, can be found completely covering some nutrient enriched lakes and canals in Florida. Non-native freshwater fishes are also common in Florida's waterways, some released by government agencies, some released by aquarists. Non-native marinelife becoming established is less typical, but there have been numerous examples, mostly due to transport on ship hulls or with ship ballast water. The Asian green mussel (*Perna viridis*) was found in Tampa Bay, Florida in late 1999, having been introduced into the Gulf of Mexico about ten years earlier, presumably as larvae in the seawater ballast tanks of a large ship. The popular orange cup coral, *Tubastraea coccinea*, is another example. It was introduced to the Southern Caribbean region in the early 1900's (Cairns, 2000), presumably via boats passing through the Panama Canal. It now occurs throughout the Caribbean and along the Florida Coast. Its presence, however, does not appear to have caused any harm.

The peacock grouper (*Cephalopholis argus*) and the bluestripe snapper (*Lutjanus kasmira*) were released in large numbers off Hawaii in the 1950's to establish them as food fishes there. The introductions were successful and these species now occur in large numbers on the reefs off the Kona coast, where many ornamental fishes are harvested for the aquarium trade. Unfortunately, the grouper is a source of the fish toxin ciguatera and is avoided by fishermen, and the snapper is not commercially desirable as a food fish due to its low market value. It is felt that since the snappers are now found at considerable depths they are outcompeting the more valuable native deepwater snappers for food, and are the cause of their decline in recent years. It is interesting to contemplate the impact these predators may also have on the populations of marine ornamentals, compared to the impact of collectors.

Some ecological issues surrounding the introduction of an exotic species:

1. Can the exotic species alter the predator and prey relationship of the new environment?

2. Will the exotic species out-compete native species, displace native species, and/or alter the biological diversity of the new environment?

3. Will the exotic species cross breed with closely related species and alter the genetic history of the local population?

4. Will the exotic species introduce new diseases or parasites?

5. Will there be any economic effect?

6. Is the exotic species a direct human health threat?

7. Even if the species is not an exotic (i.e. it is native) has it been in an aquarium with exotics? In that case number 4 applies.

The recent very popular Disney Film *Finding Nemo* has, as an important message, the idea that captive marinelife wants to return home to the sea, and shows flushing fish down the toilet as a quick route back to the ocean! This was an unfortunate bit of artistic license for numerous reasons! Marinelife flushed down the toilet quickly dies in the freshwater and doesn't end up being routed directly to a storm drain that dumps into the sea as depicted in the movie. Furthermore, sending the message to viewers that releasing fish (or other marinelife) is the right thing to do is completely counter to the efforts of organizations such as MAC, the Reef Environmental Education Foundation (R.E.E.F.), and others who have worked to get the message out to never release any aquarium pets. This of course has to be taken in context with the fact that releasing marinelife from an aquarium is illegal, and several states in the US require that pet stores must accept fish brought in by hobbyists, in an effort to reduce intentional releases. The uninformed aquarist may wonder why releasing a fish or other creature is such a bad idea.

One risk of establishing a non-native fish in a new location is that it could out-compete and eliminate native species, altering the balance of the ecosystem. Another risk is that some popular non-native fishes, lionfish for example, are venomous. Non-native species could carry non-native pathogens, so releasing even one fish could introduce a disease against which local species may have little or no resistance. Such an introduction could wipe out many fish or affect a whole food fishery. There are no reports of such a thing ever happening because of the release of an aquarium pet, but it is theoretically possible. The potential for disease transmission from captive to wild populations has been highlighted in the salmon and prawn aquaculture industries in North America, Asia, Europe and elsewhere.

The risk is not limited to fishes of course. The invertebrates and algae we keep also must not be released, as they can easily become established due to their simpler vegetative propagation. Released non-native invertebrates and algae may also carry disease-causing organisms that could harm many other creatures. For all of these reasons even the water used to house non-native marinelife should not be allowed to flow back to the sea, or into a stormwater drain that dumps into a natural body of saltwater. An apparent oversight in this regard may have led to the introduction of *Caulerpa taxifolia* in the northern Mediterranean by the aquarium in Monaco. It is also possible that *C. taxifolia* was accidentally planted there by scientists as part of attempts to mitigate lost seagrasses by planting *Caulerpa* spp. in the vacant mud where the seagrasses had died, but we will never know for sure.

On the other hand…in many instances, the introduction of a foreign species has little measurable impact upon native communities (Nolan 1994; Reise *et al.* 1999; Jaubert *et al.* 2003; Theodoropoulos 2003). Theodoropoulos (2003) examines the nature of *invasive species* dispersed by man, and debunks much of the popular fear of *invaders* and hysteria surrounding the subject. He demonstrates that contrary to the claims of nativists, research shows that man-dispersed species increase biodiversity and benefit ecosystems. In his view, proliferation of invasive species is symptomatic of ecosystem damage rather than an indication that the invaders inherently are harmful. His book points conservation biology in a new direction - incorporating dispersal as an essential strategy. In that case, aquariums and aquaculture could be viewed as tools that could be used for the enhancement of biodiversity. We find this concept compelling, though it is hard to argue the point when it comes to foreign pathogens that can be introduced with non-native species. Also it is an apples to oranges discussion when you compare biodiversity of the ecosystem on the one hand to the preservation of all the species that are native to it on the other. If the former is the goal then indeed it could benefit all ecosystems to incorporate exotic species. Ecosystems and the creatures in them can and do evolve, whether or not man is involved with

Caulerpa taxifolia has gotten a bad rap due to its proliferation in polluted harbors in the northern Mediterranean (Meinesz, 1999). Recent data shows that its presence is not as damaging as reported by Meinesz. Jaubert *et al.*, (2003) shows that it benefits the habitat where it occurs, and furthermore it is not as widespread as had been reported, even now 15 years after the initial discovery that it had been released there.

initiating the changes. We must nevertheless reiterate that one should never release marinelife from home aquariums, whether native species or not. This is our position, and it is backed up by laws concerning the subject.

The discovery of *Caulerpa taxifolia* in a boat harbor in southern California brought the subject of release of exotics to the center spotlight, and drew unfavorable media attention to the aquarium hobby, the presumed source of the plant. Similarly, the occurrence of Volitan lionfish (*Pterois volitans*) on shipwrecks and at other locations along the east coast of the USA prompted a flurry of articles in the popular press and some scientific journals, suggesting that this species had been introduced by aquarists and was successfully breeding (Whitfield, *et al.*, 2002). In fact, newly settled juveniles of this venomous fish have been collected in the summer of 2002 and 2003 from various locations in Long Island, New York (J. Yaiullo and Matt Gannon, pers. comm.). Clearly there is at least one breeding pair somewhere along the Atlantic coast. Genetic studies of the juveniles collected will establish whether they come from more than one pair.

Lionfish collected off Long Island! Jaws who?
J. Yaiullo

The Reef Environmental Education Foundation (R.E.E.F.), www.reef.org, is a non-profit organization of recreational divers who regularly conduct fish biodiversity and abundance surveys during their dives. With funding from PADI® project AWARE, R.E.E.F. created and distributed to Florida aquarium wholesalers and retail stores an informative pamphlet regarding the harm of releasing non-native marine species. R.E.E.F. also initiated a program to identify and record the locations of exotic marinelife based on diver reports. Their effort goes a long way toward preventing people who don't know better from releasing their pets. The Pet Industry Joint Advisory Council (PIJAC) has also advanced a program, in partnership with U.S. Fish and Wildlife Service and NOAA's Sea Grant, for increasing public awareness of this issue (www.Habitattitude.net).

Such education programs are valuable to the prevention of this problem, but there are other areas that prevention programs need to consider. One is that having an easy to find, secure home for unwanted marinelife would help prevent releases. Such a solution could be achieved quite simply on one of the Internet discussion forums. Aquarists could advertise their unwanted specimens free to a good home, and the buyer/adopter would pay for shipping.

A simple system could also be established to remove marine exotics. In South Florida, where R.E.E.F. collects data for sightings of non-native marinelife, the data could be shared with designated local marinelife collectors so that specimens could be harvested as soon as they are sighted. Such a plan was used successfully when a few Indo-Pacific species of batfish that had been repeatedly sighted in the Florida Keys were removed as a team effort involving R.E.E.F., the Florida Keys National Marine Sanctuary, the New England Aquarium, and local marine life collectors. The potential problem with this idea is that it could encourage the release of non-native marines in order to establish breeding populations so they could be harvested for profit. This has been the accusation made over the lemonpeel and non-local flame angels found in Kaneohe Bay, Hawaii. It is also why the state of Hawaii has banned the export of Jackson's chameleons, an exotic introduction to Hawaii; they do not want to encourage people breeding and importing other non-native species of chameleon.

Since marinelife collectors in Florida make their living from collecting native marinelife, and they do so at the mercy of the weather, it does not seem likely that they need to add to their list of species, only that they need more days with good diving conditions to do their work. In Hawaii, the situation is a little different because a place like Kaneohe Bay is sheltered from the affects of the weather, so having new high-value fish available to collect year-round is potentially a motivating factor.

Why people might release aquarium pets

There are a few common reasons why people might release their aquarium pets. Some examples include when fish such as the panther grouper or orbiculate batfish outgrow their aquarium. Another cause is the need to *dispose* of *disposable* aggressive starter fishes such as damsels. The whole notion of disposable fishes never made sense to us. It was promoted 30 years ago as the way to start the nitrogen cycle. The aquarist bought hardy and inexpensive damselfish to *cycle* the tank and returned them to the dealer when the ammonia and nitrite levels dropped. If dealers don't take the fish back and hobbyists no longer want such aggressive fishes, the potential exists for them to be released as an act of kindness to the fish. Another case is unmarketable (by pet dealers and wholesalers) fishes with lateral line erosion. This problem appears to be the source of purple tangs, sailfin tangs, emperor and other non-native angelfish in south Florida waters. There may even be a religious/cultural factor involved in some examples of released aquatic life. Some cultures may still practice a tradition-based activity that involves purchasing and then ceremonially releasing fish, turtles, birds, or other animals. The main purpose of this practice and ceremony is to save lives that are in danger and to pray for their ultimate enlightenment as well as for that of all sentient beings. Finally, another possible motivation to release aquarium pets was that movie about a little clownfish called Nemo…

The role of public aquariums

When discussing public aquariums it is important to make a distinction between for-profit private and public aquariums versus non-profit aquariums. Most non-profit aquariums operate from a primarily educational perspective whereas for-profit facilities often compromise educational activities for other, more profitable programs. The average aquarium going public is often unaware of this distinction but it can make a significant difference in the messages these institutions send to their customers concerning conservation as well as any actual conservation activities they undertake.

Public aquariums serve many purposes beyond mere entertainment. Since they have such a large audience, they provide an opportunity to expose people to creatures and habitats that they may not otherwise ever see. This raises public awareness of the environment, a key goal of most public aquariums. Displays in public aquariums also have been tending to include a broader range of the whole habitat rather than just a few animals in an artificial simulated *background*. While the latter is in some respects easier to create, the former is in many ways easier to maintain and is far more educational and interesting to see. Public aquariums may feature creatures from aquatic habitats of various types, but the displays that feature ornamental marinelife provide the greatest opportunity to raise public awareness about coral reefs, mangrove habitats, seagrass beds, and their special associated creatures.

Some public aquariums have taken the opportunity to promote the Marine Aquarium Council, promoting the purchase of organisms that are MAC certified, and being involved in the development of certification and labeling. In this way, the public aquariums play a part in promoting a sustainable and environmentally sound marine ornamentals trade.

However, there are still public aquariums that don't wish to promote the *hobby* of aquarium keeping in the home, by non-professional aquarists. It seems to us though, that the reef-keeping hobby especially, has resulted in a greater connection being made between the aquarists at public aquariums, hobbyist reefkeepers, and the scientists who study reefs. The increased ease of communication provided by the Internet and e-mail surely has played a role. These new links are a positive trend that helps promote good aquarium husbandry practices by all involved. Furthermore, many aquarists now employed in public aquariums began as reef hobbyists and this is reflected by the improved quality, and the increased quantity and size of living reef displays, especially in North American and Japanese aquariums. It is now common to see reef displays filled with

A view from above the coral farm exhibit at the Waikiki Aquarium gives the impression of looking over shallow reef in the Western Pacific. The front viewing window and the rare Clipperton angel, endemic to Clipperton Island in the Eastern Pacific, make it clear this is an aquarium scene. J. Sprung

The large tropical reef exhibit at the Long Beach Aquarium of the Pacific is among the most beautiful public aquarium reef displays. J. Sprung

living corals all the way up to 3,800,000 liters (100,000+ gallons) in today's newer public aquariums.

Public aquariums typically employ trained veterinarian staff who, given the exposure to problems affecting aquariums, can develop and publish information about novel disease treatment methods for both fishes and invertebrates such as corals. Sharing this information can benefit aquarium hobbyists and other public aquariums alike.

Public aquariums today also have a special opportunity: with their funding, permitting and drive to make unique exhibits, they can explore ways to keep and display rare or delicate marinelife. In doing so they open the door to new opportunities for biological reasearch, excite public interest, and promote conservation.

Chapter One

The Basics of Aquarium Selection and Design

Before selecting an aquarium to hold your vision of a reef, there are a few issues to consider. One of these is the type of inhabitants that you wish to keep. This influences the aquarium you choose since some of these inhabitants may have specific requirements regarding the size of aquarium in which they will feel most comfortable and behave most naturally. Some corals for example will grow so rapidly that they can quickly overrun a small system. Another issue is aquascaping. Certain aquarium shapes and dimensions lend themselves better to a particular aquascape that you may want to recreate. Aquarium shape and dimension also come into play when it comes to deciding where you want to place the aquarium. You may have a location in mind that would require a certain shape or size to compliment the existing décor or architecture.

Finally, you must realize that maintaining a reef aquarium is a major commitment. You will be keeping animals that come to you directly from the wild in many cases. Therefore, you must be prepared to do what ever it takes to keep them in the best possible health. A reef aquarium is not something you can just set up and then walk away from, though a well-planned one does not require constant attention either. Reef aquariums require time, nurturing and patient planning to reach their full potential.

A turquoise patterned *Tridacna squamosa* in one of Julian Sprung's reef aquariums. J. Sprung

In this chapter, we will discuss the basics of aquarium selection, design and placement, and discuss common elements of aquascaping and filtration. A more detailed discussion of individual system designs and philosophies will be presented in chapters 6 and 9.

The aquarium

The first step in setting up a reef aquarium is purchasing the aquarium itself. There are two options for acquiring an aquarium: purchase one or purchase the materials to build one. There are pros and cons to each; the most obvious is that building an aquarium takes skill, experience, patience and the right equipment to do the job successfully. We will not go into any detail on building your own aquarium in this volume as there are several online guides to doing so (see http://saltaquarium.about.com as a starting point) and lets face it, most of us buy our aquariums ready-made.

Figure 1.1 Typical arrangement of aquarium, surface skimming overflow and sump.

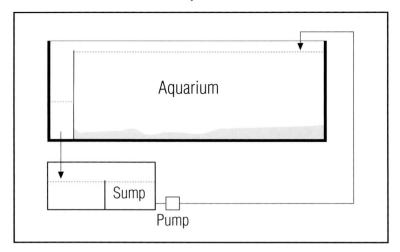

Today several manufactures offer setups that already have overflows and bulkheads installed, and include all the necessary fittings for passing water to a sump and for returning water to the tank. Many of these systems already include a sump as well. Setups can be purchased in glass or acrylic, but are often limited in the sizes and shapes available. Those who want odd sizes or shapes will have to modify existing designs or have a custom designed aquarium made.

Glass tanks

When buying a glass aquarium, observe the quality of the workmanship and construction. If clear silicone is used, the joints should be clear, with very few bubbles. The pieces of glass should fit evenly at all joints so that no piece sticks out beyond the others. Large aquariums and tall ones have top braces installed to prevent bowing of the glass, and some large custom aquariums also have bottom strips of glass inside, to provide additional bracing and prevent leaks from the bottom joints. These bottom strips are also helpful in preventing leaks caused by polychaete worms that can sometimes bore through silicone. It is also possible to have custom glass aquariums made that include curved surfaces, and newer off-the-shelf designs include solid rounded corners with no silicone glued seams, but these can be expensive compared to standard tanks of the same size.

The primary advantage of glass tanks is that they tend to be cheaper on a gallon-by-gallon basis versus other materials. This is especially true in areas where manufactured glass panes are readily available. Glass also tends to be more scratch resistant and is therefore easier to clean aggressively without damaging the surface. Today's glass tanks can be more stylish than those of ten or twenty years ago as beveled edges and the use of black silicone adhesive techniques first popularized in Europe have become more mainstream. Glass is also structurally stronger than acrylic, fiberglass or wood and is therefore less prone to

Normally glass aquariums have braces on the top to prevent bowing. Braces also help prevent fish from jumping out of the aquarium, but they gather dust and salt crystals that block light and add to maintenance chores. J. Sprung

Using thicker glass than is required for the aquarium dimension makes it possible to eliminate the support braces on the top. A flat polished edge and trimmed black silicone give a nice finish to the construction. J. Sprung

bending or warping under pressure. Aquariums made from tempered glass further resist bowing and can be made of thinner glass with less bracing required, so they are lighter and cheaper than aquariums made from un-tempered glass. Tempered glass cannot safely be drilled, however. Finally, with glass aquariums it is relatively easy to glue in partitions or overflows using silicone glue sold for aquarium or potable water uses.

There are some drawbacks to glass aquariums. The primary one is that drilling holes in glass is difficult and is best left to those with the necessary equipment and experience. Even then, there are no guarantees when it comes to drilling glass and a shattered pane can be the result. Furthermore, as mentioned above, tempered glass cannot be drilled, so it is unsuitable for special modifications. Although glass tanks are more scratch resistant, once they do scratch, it is very difficult for the average hobbyist to remove those scratches. Although it is transparent, glass in not colourless. If you look along any cut edge of glass, you will note that it has a green cast to it. This is not a problem in tanks with thin sheets of glass, but once you get over 1.25 cm (half an inch) in thickness, you will notice a greenish tinge to the view. There are special grades of glass that have less colour but these are much more expensive (e.g. *Starfire* glass). Finally, for any given tank volume or shape, glass tanks are much heavier than acrylic or fiberglass, and this must be taken into account when building a support for the tank and estimating the floor strength required underneath it. The heavy weight puts an upper limit on the practical size of all-glass aquariums.

Acrylic tanks

Acrylic aquariums are rapidly gaining in popularity, especially in the tank maintenance segment of the market in the United States. They have strong appeal due to the rounded, seamless corners, interesting shapes and brilliant view afforded by the nature of acrylic. There are

Concrete tanks can last many years but eventually degrade over time. This tank at the Waikiki Aquarium has been in service since 1955. J.C. Delbeek

Fiberglass tanks can be made in any shape but commonly have only one viewing opening. Waikiki Aquarium. J.C. Delbeek

Fiberglass tank in service at the Waikiki Aquarium. J.C. Delbeek

several advantages offered by acrylic the most important of which is the ease with which modifications can be made. Holes for overflows and returns are easily drilled using readily available equipment. However, gluing in partitions and overflows requires special solvents and is more difficult than working with glass and silicone glue. Luckily, most acrylic aquariums come with overflows already installed. Acrylic is a naturally clear material unlike glass, which has a slight greenish tint. This is not very noticeable in small aquariums but larger, thicker pieces of glass cast a definite greenish hue whereas an identical thickness of acrylic would be colourless. Acrylic tanks are much lighter than equal size glass tanks. This makes them easier to handle and they require a less robust support than glass tanks. Check the joints to make sure there are no bubbles or any fine spidery cracks running from the edges of the joint. This is called *hazing* and is often found in older tanks or in tanks that have undergone a lot of stress in that area.

Since acrylic is more flexible than glass, acrylic tanks need supports along the top edge along with cross braces, especially for tanks of any length. These restrict access and can hamper tank maintenance and aquascaping. Cross braces also impair light penetration and accumulate salt, and therefore need to be kept clean on a regular basis. By far the biggest drawback to acrylic is its softness compared to glass. This means it scratches easily and it is therefore more difficult to clean easily than glass. Make sure that any material you use to clean the viewing windows will not scratch acrylic. Even products that claim to be acrylic safe should be tested in an unobtrusive spot before use on the front panel of the aquarium. To make matters worse, coralline algae have an affinity for plastics, including acrylic. The coralline algae in particular create a problem because the calcium they deposit will scratch the acrylic when you try to remove them to keep the viewing window clear, if you are not careful. This makes keeping a reef aquarium in an acrylic tank more problematic than a glass tank, but not impossible. For larger tanks, acrylic windows offer the best view due to their colourless nature. They are also lighter than similarly sized glass panels. Acrylic is more prone to scratching, but scratches can be buffed out easily (see chapter 11). Materials can also be placed along the top front edge of the window to shade it, and the tank lights can be angled so as not to shine directly on the front window, thereby cutting down on algal growth and minimizing cleaning.

Other options

Fiberglass tanks are commonly used in research institutions and commercial aquaculture operations. They are simply fiberglass tubs with one large piece of glass or acrylic bonded or secured on one side to serve as a window. One advantage is that plumbing holes can be incorporated with relative ease, and another is that the tank is lightweight, yet strong. For tanks over 1900 L (500 gal) fiberglass becomes a cost effective alternative to glass or acrylic. The best use of a

Construction of the basic framework of a large wood aquarium. K. Carpenter

Here is how to convert your basement into a reef. K. Carpenter

The completed aquarium. K. Carpenter

fiberglass tank is when only one viewing angle will be possible. For example, when installing a large tank in a wall, the single viewing opening is not an issue. Of course, larger tanks mean more weight and this means the tank support needs to be well constructed. In some cases, simple concrete blocks can be used or more elaborate fiberglass or wooden stands can be constructed.

Wooden tanks have been popular among freshwater aquarists for years. They are relatively easy to make and, if well constructed, can last a long time. They are easy to drill should you require drainage or return holes. Drawbacks include their heavy weight, construction time and cost. Small wood tanks can cost more than similar sized all-glass aquariums. For large exhibits though (> 500 gallons, 1900 L), they can be cost effective.

Concrete allows for the construction of very large, cost effective aquariums such as this 11400 L (2000 gallon) aquarium belonging to Richard Harker, Raleigh, NC, USA. R. Harker

The inside of Harker's concrete aquarium prior to sealing with epoxy paint. R. Harker

The finished inside. R. Harker

Concrete tanks are used by public aquariums for large displays, typically with thick acrylic sheets for the viewing windows. Aquaculture facilities also use concrete to make long, raceway style tanks. Concrete is not typically used for home aquariums, but it is a good material for making big tanks when weight is of no concern. If you wish to use concrete to build that giant aquarium of your dreams, we suggest that you contact an exhibit design company that works with public aquariums.

Dimensions
When it comes to what size of tank is best to purchase, the most common recommendation people are given is to purchase the largest aquarium they can afford. Larger aquariums have additional costs in set up and maintenance, so factor these costs when deciding how much you can afford; not only monetarily but time wise too.

There are two schools of thought regarding the recommended size of the first reef aquarium for a beginning hobbyist. The *old school* recommends as large an aquarium as possible. A newer approach is to initiate the novice with a small aquarium of limited scope, minimizing the initial investment, and allowing a gradual introduction to the requirements of the hobby. Keeping small *nano reef* aquariums of less than 19 L (5 gal) is possible, and is becoming very popular due to the high costs of much larger systems. Small systems require special effort or proper design to prevent wide temperature swings, low oxygen levels, or changes in specific gravity due to evaporation. Another negative feature regarding small aquariums concerns the fish. Most fish available for marine aquariums are not suitable to be housed in an aquarium smaller than 76 L (20 gal). Nevertheless, some types of fish are perfectly suitable for aquariums between 19 and 57 L (5 and 15 gal). While

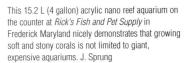

This 15.2 L (4 gallon) acrylic nano reef aquarium on the counter at *Rick's Fish and Pet Supply* in Frederick Maryland nicely demonstrates that growing soft and stony corals is not limited to giant, expensive aquariums. J. Sprung

On the other end of the scale there are large reef aquariums such as this 130,000 L (35,000 gallon) display at the Oceanographic Museum in Monaco. Only the upper portion of this deep aquarium is visible in this photo. J. Yaiullo

some invertebrates are not suitable for aquariums of 76 L (20 gal) or less, most are, albeit with the caveat that they may not be compatible with a large number of other invertebrates within such a small space. Therefore, for small tanks the problem is mainly the fish. The funny thing is, the problem with large tanks is also the fish. Many marine fish are delicate, and most are very prone to getting parasitic diseases, no matter what the size of the aquarium.

Starting with a tank of at least 190 L (50 gal) capacity is an option that gives you a system large enough to be stable with respect to water chemistry changes, yet small enough to fit into a small space. This size is also reasonably inexpensive to set up and maintain. Of course, a common epidemic in the reef aquarium hobby is that undeniable desire to have a larger tank as soon as your present tank becomes overcrowded. Unfortunately, there is no cure for this syndrome and we all are afflicted by it. Fortunately, but not always, sanity and limited budgets prevail.

Ideally, you should choose a tank with a wide dimension, instead of a tall, narrow tank. The majority of the so-called *standard-sized* aquariums in North America are not well designed with respect to their dimensions. An aquarium is a living, breathing organism. It must interact with its environment in order to absorb and release gases. To best achieve this, it must have a favourable ratio of surface area to volume. Simple math tells us that as the volume of an object increases, it does so as the cube, while the surface area increases only as a square of itself. Therefore, as an object gets larger, its volume increases much faster than its surface area. Since the ratio between area and volume decreases as an object gets larger, it becomes harder for that object to absorb or release gases. One way to alleviate this in an aquarium is to ensure that the height of an aquarium does not exceed its front to back depth by too much. This is the problem with commercial aquariums: the height of the aquarium is often substantially greater than its front to back depth. This decreases the amount of surface area available for gas exchange. In addition, taller tanks are more difficult to clean, more difficult to aquascape in a pleasing and interesting way, and require stronger lighting to provide adequate light at the bottom. Furthermore, the position of corals on a reef is not like books on a vertical wall of shelves. It is more like bushes growing in a field. Taller tanks force aquascapes that look like the former, while wider tanks allow the correct installation of aquascapes that look like the latter. The importance of the difference in these aquascapes lies not just in the style and aesthetics. It also relates to the lighting requirements for the corals, which tend to orient perpendicular to the angle of lighting. Wall structures have limited surface for ideal coral placement. For this reason growth of reef-building stony corals on reef walls in nature is limited to the uppermost surfaces, with a few small encrusting growths occurring lower down, where the reefs become dominated by non-photosynthetic flexible soft corals. In chapter 9, we discuss aquascaping aesthetics and the biological significance of the shape of the reef.

There are standard commercial aquariums with wider dimensions and we recommend these. In North America these tanks often have square cross sections of 30 cm x 30cm, 45 cm x 45 cm, 60 cm x 60 cm (12" x 12", 18" x 18" or 24" x 24"). Of course, if it is within your budget, you can have a custom aquarium built.

Preparing the aquarium

Before an aquarium is ready to hold its inhabitants, it must be prepared. This involves cleaning, the installation of bulkheads for removing and returning water, as well as the installation of overflows.

Drilling holes

As we mentioned previously, drilling holes into an aquarium can be a very intimidating task for most of us, especially when it comes to a glass tank. In our opinion, the best option when it comes to glass tanks is to have the holes drilled by a professional. However, you still have to prepare the tank to make the hole drilling go smoothly. The first step is to decide how many holes and what size you want them. For drains, use the largest bulkhead you can, for most tanks this would be 3.75 cm (1.5 in.). The reason is that you do not want to restrict a drain. It is much easier to reduce the size of the drain by using reducing fittings than to enlarge a hole once you find out it is too small. Sight the drain hole using the bulkhead you intend to use and make sure there is enough room around on all sides so that the upper ring of the bulkhead is free from the sides of the overflow box. Make sure the hole is not too close to any edges as well. Mark the spot by tracing the opening onto the glass. For returns, smaller bulkheads of 2.5 cm (1 in.) or less can be used depending on the number of returns, size of the tank and desired turnover rate. Again, using bulkheads slightly larger than you think you may need is prudent since they can be easily reduced if needed.

The above advice can also be used when drilling holes into acrylic tanks. As with glass, drilling holes in acrylic is not for everyone and is best left to professionals. However, unlike glass, you can drill the holes in acrylic if you feel adventuresome. Make sure that you purchase a new hole saw since you want the sharpest bit possible; old, dull bits will tend to melt and even burn the acrylic. The use of a variable speed drill is also important as you can easily control the rate at which the hole is cut. Choose a hole saw that is slightly larger than the outside diameter of the bulkhead you want to use. Test drill a hole in a piece of wood and make sure the bulkhead fits snugly and the hole is not so large that the gasket won't seal properly.

The key to cutting holes in acrylic is patience. If you try to rush the drilling process by putting too much pressure on the drill, you run the risk of heating the acrylic to the point where it will begin to melt. This can result in discolouration and distortion of the surrounding acrylic. You also need to keep the drill bit teeth parallel to the surface of the acrylic. If you do not, the drill will begin to drill more deeply on one side and the bit may bind causing the acrylic to crack or more dangerously, result in a broken or badly sprained wrist. You may need to gently rock the drill back and forth to regain a parallel cut. This is especially important when drilling acrylic more than 1.25 cm (0.5 in.) thick.

If you are hiring someone to drill the holes for you, mark the center points of the holes and make sure you explain exactly where you want the holes drilled with the person who will be doing the actual drilling.

Also, provide them with the fittings you want installed so that they can select the proper bit sizes and test fit the holes once they are drilled.

The overflow

Most reef aquariums today use an overflow of some sort to remove water from the surface of the system and pass it to a sump and/or filtration system located either beneath or behind the aquarium. There are several overflow variations and they all work. The type of overflow that's best to use depends greatly on the design and size of the aquarium. We do not recommend that the overflow be used as a mechanical filter by placing floss or sponge material on the top. This impedes water flow and if it clogs this can lead to water overflowing on the ground. It is better to place any such mechanical filtration in the sump area at the point where the water enters from the overflow and is easily accessible.

Figure 1.2
Typical surface skimming overflow arrangements.
A. Corner or end partition forming an overflow box.
B. A PVC 90° fitting inserted into the bulkhead to form a surface drain. Note the air vent provided by the standpipe in A, and the external open top *T* in B.

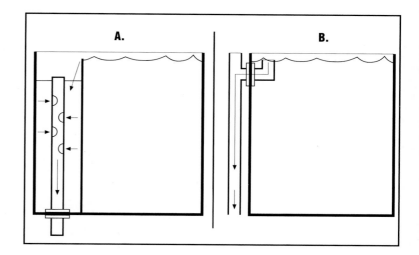

Corner partitions

Building a partition in one of the rear corners of an aquarium is a universal standard for the construction of an *overflow box* and this simple design in our opinion, works the best. The partition may be a single pane forming a triangular overflow box or two pieces forming a square or rectangular box. We recommend that glass aquariums use glass partitions, since silicone will not permanently seal an acrylic partition. Such a break in the seal on the partition wall is not a problem if the drain has a solid standpipe installed. Without a standpipe (or if the standpipe is perforated to the bottom), a broken seal on the overflow wall would result in more water on the floor than should naturally be there, in other words a flood. Installing an overflow partition in an acrylic aquarium is more difficult given the nature of bonding acrylic. This type of work is best left to those experienced in working with acrylic and

This corner box overflow has a removable toothed strainer and lid that effectively prevent fishes from going over the falls. Being able to remove the strainer facilitates cleaning it to keep it free of algae growth and trapped matter. Note air vent on top. Also note how the lid is alligned with the glass braces to reduce the chance of fish jumping out of the aquarium. J. Sprung

solvents that liberate fumes that are toxic to humans. For both glass and acrylic aquariums, the best options are to request the overflow and bulkhead drain be installed when the aquarium is first built, or purchase a ready-made system.

Inside the overflow, a standpipe is placed in the bulkhead at the bottom such that it reaches to just below the top of the overflow; this reduces the sound of falling water and if the overflow were to leak or fail the display tank would only lose a small amount of water to the sump. The sump should be sized to handle this extra amount of water draining down when the power shuts off, about an inch over the length and width of the aquarium plus the volume of the overflow partition to avoid spilling water onto the floor. See the formula used to calculate this volume, under the topic *Sump design* in this chapter. It is common to have perforations in the standpipe to improve water entry into the drain and allow air to vent out of the top of the standpipe. For a clever way to reduce the noise produced by water draining through an overflow partition see our description of the Durso overflow design that follows.

Two or more overflows

Aquariums over 2 m (> six feet) in length often use two overflows to facilitate the removal of surface water from both ends of the tank, which helps to prevent stagnant patches from forming in the corners. Some aquariums utilize more than one overflow simply to increase the gallon per hour flow through the aquarium filter. In the latter case, an alternative to having more than one overflow is to install more than one drain in a single overflow chamber if the overflow surface area is great enough to handle the increased flow without raising the water level too high in the aquarium.

Multi-level overflow

Overflows that remove water from both the surface and deeper in the aquarium are also common. In this design, slots or other small openings are placed into the lower sides of standard overflows. The slots are of a size and number such that water cannot enter fast enough to prevent the water level from rising in the aquarium, therefore water will also still flow over the top providing surface skimming. Inside the overflow a standpipe reaches to the top of the overflow so that the tank won't drain if the return pump is shut off.

Wall mounted strainers

It is possible to create an overflow drain by simply inserting a strainer in a bulkhead drilled in the back wall of the aquarium. The strainer is best attached to a 90° elbow inserted in the bulkhead, which gives

A notched length of PVC pipe with a piece of PVC sheet glued on the end turns a bulkhead fitting into an effective overflow. The flat piece of PVC turns the bulkhead into a smaller weir. Waikiki Aquarium. J.C. Delbeek

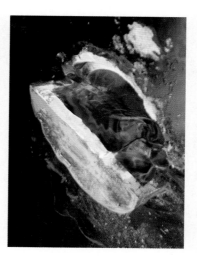

the ability to modify the water level. Simply inserting a strainer directly into the bulkhead cuts down the surface area of the overflow, further reducing the water flow it can handle. An option is to partially block the bulkhead with a section of PVC sheeting to create a weir for the water to flow over. A strainer can be then be placed in front of the weir. A variation on this design is to use a large bulkhead and attach a short length of PVC pipe capped at the end and cut to form a trough along the top edge. Coarse plastic mesh can then be added inside the pipe to act as a strainer to prevent material from going into the sump. Another variation is to place a 90 degree elbow in the bulkhead fitting to create more surface area.

The drawback to this design is that as the strainer becomes clogged the flow is reduced, which can raise the water level in the aquarium and lower the level in the sump located below the tank.

A simple overflow can be created by inserting a 90 degree elbow into a bulkhead, in this case a 5 cm (2 in.) diameter fitting is used with a wide mesh screen. Waikiki Aquarium. J.C. Delbeek

Anemones do wander, so they cannot safely be placed in an aquarium with a simple strainer/overflow arrangement. The result can be disastrous: caught early you have an injured anemone and possibly a flood on the floor. Caught late you have a real mess. J. Sprung

This can be particularly problematic for systems that use level sensors for automatic freshwater top-off. In practice, we have rarely had this happen, but checking and cleaning the strainer must be a part of any regular maintenance routine. Another drawback to the design is that it can be noisy, particularly when a strainer becomes clogged and slurps air.

Bulkhead and overflow box

This is a variation of the above example. In this case, a bulkhead fitting is placed partway down the side or back of a tank and fitted with a 90-degree elbow. An overflow box is then attached via another bulkhead to the top of the elbow. You can also attach the overflow box directly to the bulkhead on the tank wall but this limits you in that you cannot adjust the water height as easily by moving the box. The advantage of this system is that you do not need to drill a hole in the bottom of your tank. If the bulkhead or overflow fails, the tank will only drain to the level of the bulkhead, not to the bottom of the tank as in the case of an overflow based around a bottom drain. Another advantage has to do with noise. The shorter overflow box means the water does not fall a long distance to the bottom of the overflow, lessening the noise of splashing or gurgling water.

A variation on this method is to place one or more bulkheads along one side or along the back of the aquarium such that they are just below the intended water level. An overflow is then constructed by gluing a partition along the entire side or back of the tank at a 45-degree or shallower angle. This effectively forms a trough and allows surface skimming along the entire length of the side or back of the tank.

Using a 5 cm (2 in.) bulkhead fitting, a corner overflow box is attached in the upper corner of this aquarium, hidden from view behind the live rock and corals. Waikiki Aquarium. J. C. Delbeek

Weir overflow

In some cases, it is not desirable to have an overflow box inside the aquarium. For example, you may want to maximize the space in the tank, or you may not like the look of them, or the tank is simply too large and the water flow too great for an interior overflow to handle. In these cases, a weir overflow may be the answer. This consists of a section of the top edge of the tank pane being removed creating an area where the water will then pass over before it reaches the top. An overflow box is then glued to the outside of the tank and the water then flows from here via one or more bulkheads to the sump via plumbing. The slot can be completely cut away and plastic mesh used as a strainer or *teeth* can be cut in the pane instead, forming a natural strainer. On very large systems, the sump can be attached directly to the side of the aquarium where the weir is located and the water simply cascades over it and into the sump. This method is also

Above: An overflow box mounted to the outside of the tank with two standpipes. Collapsible pool hose carries water from the overflow box to the sump below and helps to evacuate air, while coarse mesh screening prevents fish from passing into the box. Waikiki Aquarium. J.C. Delbeek

Right: With the sump attached to the side of the tank, a screened weir makes an effective overflow on the coral farm exhibit at the Waikiki Aquarium. J.C. Delbeek

used in smaller systems that have a built-in sump and filtration system on the end of the aquarium or along the back. As with any strainer, the strainer over the weir must be kept clean of algae and other debris to prevent water backing up in the aquarium and the sump level falling.

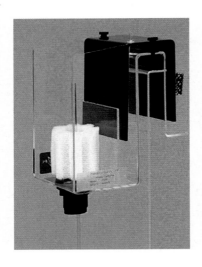

An acrylic hang-on overflow design manufactured by *CPR* Inc. S.C. Kim

Hang-on overflow

In some cases, hobbyists want to modify an existing aquarium into a reef aquarium without tearing it down, or they simply want to add a filtration accessory such as a small protein skimmer. In this case, various hang-on overflow box designs are available that rely on siphon tubes or a broad siphon section. Alternatively, a small powerhead placed in a box in the tank can be used to move the water out of the aquarium for overhead accessories only. These work well when used for the purpose they were intended for, but have some drawbacks. With designs that use siphon tubes, the tank can overflow if the return of water back to the tank is too great, or if the siphons become clogged or blocked by air bubbles. If a sump is not used and water is pumped from an overflow box to a filtration apparatus such as a protein skimmer, then the overflow box will act as a sump. In other words, the water level in this small box will rapidly fall due to evaporation. The water loss must be topped off daily to prevent air being sucked into and stopping the powerhead.

Durso Standpipe™ noise reduction system

An inventive and avid reef aquarist named Richard Durso designed a simple device that practically eliminates the gurgling sounds commonly associated with surface skimming overflow chambers.

With a low water level in the overflow chamber, water entering a tall chamber has a large drop that can produce a lot of noise. Water bringing large air bubbles with it down the drain also creates a gurgling noise. As noted on Durso's website (www.dursostandpipes.com) a colleague, Mark Lanett, suggested the problem could be solved by using a solid standpipe with a submerged intake instead of the perforated standpipe commonly employed. The result was the Durso Standpipe, which offers several favourable features. This design results in very little *waterfall* effect, depending on the height of pipe used and the overflow depth, resulting in less splashing and the elimination of gurgling noises. A Durso Standpipe system is self-priming and will not allow the overflow chamber to drain during a power outage. As a result, the overflow chamber can also act as a refugium.

The system consists of a solid standpipe placed in the overflow bulkhead. At the top of the standpipe a T-fitting is placed. On the sideout of the T-fitting, a 90-degree street-ell elbow is placed facing downwards. On the top of the T-fitting a short section of pipe is placed along with an end-cap fitting that has a small hole drilled in it. Water enters the pipe via the street-ell fitting and the hole in the end cap allows air to enter. Since the end of the street-ell is below the water line, it cannot suck air (figure 1.3).

The construction of this type of overflow siphon is simple but it does need some attention to detail to work properly. The diameter of the overflow pipe (6) depends in the size of the bulkhead fitting in the overflow (1) and the amount of room available in the overflow. Generally, the diameter of this pipe is 3.63 cm (1.25 in.) for bulkhead diameters of 3.63 cm (1.25 in.) or less. Larger pipes and their fittings will not fit in most overflows. If the bulkhead is 2.5 cm (1 in.) then a reducing fitting needs to be used. This consists of a 3.63 cm (1.25 in.) coupling fitting (5) glued onto the pipe with a 3.63 cm (1.25 in.) to 2.5 cm (1 in.) reducing bushing (4) glued into the other end of the

Figure 1.3 Durso Standpipe

A modified Durso Standpipe design produced by *All-Glass Aquarium Co.* J. Sprung

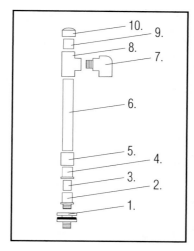

coupler. A short piece of 2.5 cm (1 in.) PVC pipe (3) is then glued into the bushing and the other end is fitted into the overflow bulkhead fitting (1). DO NOT GLUE the 2.5 cm (1 in.) pipe into the bulkhead fitting, instead use several turns of Teflon tape on the pipe to ensure a snug, watertight fit into the bulkhead. If the overflow bulkhead has an internal thread then you need to use a 2.5 cm (1 in.) threaded male adaptor (2). Glue this fitting onto the end of the 2.5 cm (1 in.) pipe coming from the bushing, apply Teflon tape to the male adapter thread and then screw this into the bulkhead (1). An alternative to the above is to use a reducing male adapter that can be threaded directly into the bulkhead while the pipe is glued directly into the adapter; this eliminates a couple of fittings.

On top of the PVC pipe a 3.63 cm (1.25 in.) PVC T-fitting (8) is placed and held in place using Teflon tape. Not gluing this piece allows you to easily adjust the height of the pipe if necessary. A short piece of PVC pipe (9) is glued into the top of the T-fitting and then a PVC end cap (10) is placed on top of this section of pipe and held in place with Teflon tape. This PVC cap should have a very small (2 mm) hole drilled into the top of it. In the side of the T-fitting is placed the street-ell fitting (7) pointed straight down; this can be glued in place. This is the water intake and should always be submerged. Since it is submerged, it cannot suck in air. If the street-ell has a female threaded end, a strainer can be inserted to prevent fishes or snails from being drawn into the standpipe. The water level should be somewhere around the middle of the street-ell if constructed correctly. If the water level is slightly higher, it should not be a problem but if the water level is lower, at the opening of the street-ell you will get a sucking noise. If this should happen, make the hole in end-cap (10) larger. If the hole is too large then the water level in the overflow will rise too high and the hole size will need to be decreased. One way to get around the hole size problem is to drill a small hole through the side of both the end cap and the PVC pipe, then you can decrease or increase the size of the hole by twisting the cap and overlapping the two openings giving you control on how much air can be sucked in. This hole is very important as the air it allows in prevents the standpipe from becoming a siphon.

The overall length of the Durso Standpipe should be such that when the water level is in the mid-point of the street-ell, it is about 5 cm (2 in.) from the top of the overflow chamber. This is low enough to allow for good gas exchange and remove the surface film from the water in the tank, and high enough to prevent the sound of falling water.

Tip: To prevent the water level in the overflow from oscillating up and down, ensure that the discharge pipe from the overflow does not extend too far under the water level in the sump.

Detailed assembly instructions and diagrams, as well as several design details can be found on Mr. Durso's website along with several modifications and improvements to the initial design that allows this concept to work in a variety of internal and external overflow chambers. A commercially manufactured molded system based on this design has also been produced by the All Glass Aquarium company in the USA.

The sump
The sump is one of the simplest yet most important components of a reef aquarium today. Originally employed on aquariums as a part of wet/dry (trickle) filters, the sump has been retained in most modern reef aquarium designs. The sump is the most convenient way to

make full use of surface overflows, equipment concealment and to incorporate various filtration aids. In its simplest form, the sump is a container that sits below or adjacent to the main aquarium. We have seen budget rate sumps made from buckets or other common household objects that hold a sufficient amount of water. Water travels from the overflow system to the sump from where it is pumped back into the aquarium. This ensures that the water level in the main display remains the same and any drop in water level due to loss of water from evaporation is only apparent in the sump. However, the water level may change in the aquarium as the surface skimmer develops growths of algae and other marinelife that impede the flow of water through strainers or over a weir.

Some sump designs incorporate various baffles and plates to slow water flow or direct it in certain directions such as towards heaters, pump intakes or accessory filtration. Generally, the volume of the sump is less than the main aquarium, but some aquarists make sumps of the same volume, or greater than the main display. This allows for the use of a plenum, refugium or settling chamber in the sump. Larger sumps also increase the total volume of the system, and help to prevent rapid changes in water quality and especially temperature. Temperature control of small aquariums utilizing natural sunlight can be achieved by simply attaching them to a large sump not exposed to the light or source of heat.

The same factors described above for tank construction and installation also apply to the sump. It can be made from glass or acrylic, or may be as simple as a garbage can when aesthetics are not a concern, e.g. when the filtration system is in a basement or behind a wall. The ease with which holes can be drilled and bulkheads installed makes acrylic sumps the most common choice.

We will discuss sump designs in more detail in chapter 6.

Tip: When designing a sump, make sure that it is large enough to handle the overflow of water from the aquarium that occurs when the main pump is turned off. To calculate this volume of water use the following formula:

$$\frac{\text{Tank length (inches) x Tank Width (inches) x 1}}{231}$$

= volume drained to sump when the main pump is shut off

Add 40% to this calculation for the extra volume of your sump to cover a rise in the tank's water level due to gradual blockage of the drain.

The aquarium of Michael G. Moye shows how well a reef tank can be integrated into a room's décor. M.G. Moye

Aquarium location

In conjunction with choosing the size and shape of aquarium you should also consider where you are going to place it. Aside from the aesthetic aspect of placing an aquarium where it will enhance the appearance of the room or house, there are numerous considerations, mostly physical, but some biological, that relate to the position of the tank. Even proponents of the spiritual discipline of Feng Shui have something to say about the location of an aquarium in the home.

Physical Considerations

Weight

One gallon of saltwater weighs approximately 3.9 kg (8.5 lbs.), therefore a standard 250 L (65 gal.) aquarium full of water will weigh at least 251 kg (553 lbs.), not including the weight of the aquarium itself. Remember, the bottom material, rocks, corals, lights, filtration equipment and sumps will add even more weight if they are placed on or underneath the tank. Therefore, the floor underneath the aquarium must be strong enough to support this weight. This ability should not be compromised in the event that a large quantity of water is spilled on the floor. The floor should be level and rigid for large aquariums. Flexible floors may allow too much vibration when people walk by the aquarium, and this can translate to stress on the tank wall bonds as well as an unsteady aquascape and excessive nail biting by onlookers (and nervous diarrhea in dogs or cats?). It would be wise to consult with a structural engineer when deciding where to place a particularly large aquarium to be sure the floor underneath can handle the weight. For such systems, the stand should be designed so that weight is spread out as evenly as possible over the entire floor and not just concentrated in a few areas.

Electrical and water supply access considerations

Keep in mind the location and distance of water sources and electrical outlets when choosing a location. Running lengths of hose through a house or apartment, or carrying buckets of water up and down stairs, can be a messy proposition. Fire departments frown upon the excessive use of extension cords and multiple electric cords plugged into other electric cords. You may need to have some additional electrical outlets placed close enough to the aquarium to avoid the need for extension cords and overcrowded power strip outlets.

In addition, depending on the power consumption needs of your aquarium, it may be necessary to have an electrician install a dedicated line for the aquarium or increase the power supply to the house. Some HQI lighting systems may easily be tripped off by the use of a vacuum cleaner or other high power consumption appliance on the same electrical circuit. In that case, a dedicated circuit may be recommended. Aquarium chillers have special power requirements that may result in them not cooling even though they appear to be operating. In that case, a dedicated circuit or an increased power supply to the home may be needed. See chapter 3 for a more detailed discussion of electrical considerations.

The stand

The support under the aquarium, commonly called the stand, must be rigid and able to support the weight of the aquarium and its contents. The stand should allow for easy access to any equipment that will be installed underneath the tank e.g. sump, pumps, meters, dosers, filters, etc. In enclosed cabinets, the stand should be designed such that air can flow through easily, usually via a system of vents and fans that will allow air to be pulled in via fans and forced out the vents. This is especially critical if you place a chiller in the cabinet. Unless some method of forced airflow is included, the excess heat that accumulates in the cabinet will severely affect the operation of the chiller and will shorten its life. Increased airflow will also increase the evaporation rate in systems that use sumps under the tank (see chapter 4, cooling). This aids in evaporative cooling and allows for a greater addition of saturated kalkwasser solution for evaporative top off.

The stand should not be made of a material that would be damaged by water or salt. Pressboard, for example, which may be used for small aquarium stands, is ultimately not an ideal aquarium stand construction material and is dangerous to use for large aquariums because it can soak up water and swell, which weakens it structurally over time. Stands are best made from solid woods that have been specially coated to withstand moisture. We have found that marine grade plywood that has been coated with a marine epoxy based paint works well as a platform to place the aquarium on.

Consulting with a professional carpenter is always a wise step when designing or selecting a stand for your aquarium. There are dozens of designs and instructions for building a wooden aquarium stand on the Internet. Performing a web search using the keywords AQUARIUM STAND with any Internet search engine will yield hundreds of hits. For example, English search engines will pull up such sites as: http://www.garf.org/stand.html, http://www.fishandtips.com/index.php, and http://www.brouhaha.com/~ellis/aquarium/stand.html.

Metal (iron) stands offer the best strength if they are designed properly for the size of load. However, metal surfaces easily corrode from salt spray or water drips. To prevent this they should be properly coated. Any damage to this coating can lead to corrosion problems that will weaken the stand over time. Care must be taken not to

A stand made from extruded aluminum by Porsa Italy SRL. J. Sprung

Another aquarium stand style made from extruded aluminum by Porsa Italy SRL. J. Sprung

damage this coating when installing the tank and stand. The most effective coating consist of a process called *powder coating* where a thin layer of powdered material is sprayed on to the metal, bonding with it to form a tight seal. Most commercially made aquarium stands are already coated in this manner. If you have a custom metal stand built, be sure to ask that it be powder coated, while adding to the expense, it will greatly extend the life of the stand. Stands made from lengths of extruded aluminum tube connected by special connection unions offer strength, rigidity, and a very lightweight design. They resist corrosion and have a contemporary appearance.

Concrete blocks can also be used as support structures for large aquariums. These need to be coated with a water proof sealant first to prevent moisture penetration, and then painted if desired, or else the blocks will begin to crumble over time and will need to be

Greg Schiemer used this simple, inexpensive solution to support his 10 foot long reef aquarium. I-beams and cinder blocks. G. Schiemer

replaced; not an easy task with a tank full of water on top of them. Such sealants are commonly sold in hardware or masonry stores.

Cushioning the aquarium

We recommend placing a thin sheet of Styrofoam, rubber matting or other cushioning material between the aquarium and stand. The cushion will compress slightly, which helps to correct slight errors in level. The cushion should be thick enough to prevent any irregularity in the stand surface from putting pressure on the bottom of the aquarium. This cushion will prevent cracks and leaks from developing. If there are support ribs on the upper frame upon which the aquarium will sit, and they are not level with the rest of the frame, the sheet of Styrofoam or rubber matting must be sufficiently thick to *absorb* the difference in level. This will prevent the ribs from exerting pressure on the bottom of the aquarium, which would

Make sure the stand and aquarium are level before filling with water. J. Sprung

Stands that incorparate adjustable leveling feet make the job of leveling the aquarium much easier. Otherwise shims must be used. J. Sprung

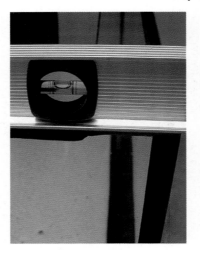

cause it to crack. An aquarium (or sump) placed directly on the floor or on a shelf inside a stand should also have such a cushion to prevent a high spot from pressing against the bottom.

Leveling the stand

Once the stand has been installed in the desired location, use a carpenter's level to check all sides. It is desirable for the stand to have adjustable feet to make leveling simpler and compensate for an uneven floor surface. Adjustments can be made with shims under portions of the stand or by using the adjustable feet. Once the stand has been leveled, add the cushion and aquarium to the stand and again check all sides of the aquarium with the level, making adjustments as necessary with the leveling feet or with shims.

Water spills & splashes, proximity to a wall, other practical considerations

The area where the aquarium is located should be able to tolerate periodic drips and spills of saltwater on the floor. Saltwater will corrode metal feet of an aquarium stand, and this corrosion will leave a permanent rust stain on carpet and porous flooring in contact with the stand. Placing tiles under the tank itself, extending out beyond the footprint can help to preserve the floor covering beneath the tank, but the tiles must not compromise the stability of the stand nor cause one to stub ones toes or trip when walking by the aquarium. When locating an aquarium against a wall, one should allow sufficient room between the aquarium and wall for plumbing and electrical lines and for modifications that may be added later on. While it is a natural thing to locate the aquarium in front of wall outlets, there is a danger involved with this. If the aquarium is too close to the wall, water may splash into the outlet(s) and cause a short, which could start a fire. For this reason hang on style filters should never be located directly above a wall outlet. See our discussion of GFI's in chapter 3. In addition, the maintenance of the house must be considered. If the aquarium is too

Important Notes: A large, open topped reef aquarium will increase the humidity in your home. Normally this is managed by running the air conditioning system, which collects and conducts the excess water out of the home. The drain lines for the AC unit may need extra maintenance to prevent clogging so they can handle the extra water. In homes without air conditioning or during cooler months, the use of a dehumidifier may become necessary to keep the humidity in the home at a comfortable level. It is also essential because the high humidity can promote the development of molds in the walls! Some aquarists simply ventilate the living space with dry air from the outside, or use extractors to draw out the humid air from a basement or fish room. In small rooms, salt spray emitted from the aquarium by splashing or by popping bubbles can lead to widespread corrosion problems. When salt spray is located near the intake of a home central AC unit, the corrosion problems can be transported throughout the house! Designing a system that reduces or eliminates the formation of salt spray is essential to protecting your home. See our discussion of plumbing and pumping systems in chapter 3.

close to the wall, it may be impossible to pass a mop behind it, or vacuum the area behind it. Positioning the aquarium too close to the wall leads to a gradual accumulation behind it of dust, salt flakes, dried fish carcasses (jumpers), dead insects (attracted to the high intensity lights and subsequently fried), small dog toys, spare change, screws, pencils, paper clips, and other things that fall out of hand and gravitate to places where you can't reach. In addition, the humidity from the aquarium and any saltwater splash will cause the paint on the wall to blister up and peel, and the sheetrock or plaster will eventually begin to erode after a couple of years. All of this can be prevented by leaving sufficient space between the aquarium and the wall. One can also fasten material such as clear acrylic sheeting against the wall directly behind the aquarium to protect it from water splashes and high humidity. Reef aquariums are also best located away from central air conditioner thermostats and air intakes. The heat from high intensity lighting will cause the air conditioner to cycle on more frequently than necessary if the lamps are near the thermostat. If located less than 3 m (10 ft.) away from the AC air intake, the salt spray from the aquarium can travel with air currents into the intake and damage the coil as well as corrode the metal stand the air handler sits on.

Biological Considerations

Carbon dioxide

Locating the aquarium in a small room, office or basement sometimes leads to problems with pH (Jordan, 2002). The chronic low pH relates to the fact that a small volume of air in the space surrounding the aquarium can accumulate carbon dioxide to well above normal atmospheric levels. The problem is easily remedied if a ventilation system is installed to flush out the stale air. Such a system will help vent excess heat too (see chapter 4).

Algal filters can also be employed to scrub carbon dioxide from the water in an aquarium that has a chronic low pH problem. Such a system can be managed with a pH controller that senses the drop in pH that occurs in the water when there is excess carbon dioxide in the air. The drop in pH is sensed by a pH probe, and when a set point is reached, it causes a switch in the controller to turn on the light over the algal filter. In the light phase of photosynthesis the algae take up the carbon dioxide from the water, elevating the pH in addition to producing oxygen. When the pH rises to the second set point, the controller switches the lights off again. A similar carbon dioxide scavenging system could be installed with a pH controller and dosing pump for administering kalkwasser (a saturated solution of calcium hydroxide) based on the pH, taking advantage of kalkwasser's ability to combine with carbon dioxide. Please refer to chapters 4 and 5 for a detailed description of carbon dioxide, alkalinity and pH.

Temperature

Locating an aquarium close to a source of heat or chilling can lead to problems if steps are not taken to assure temperature stability. The problem can be intermittent, for example, if the aquarium is located in a room where the afternoon sun causes a temperature rise at certain times of the year, or northerly winds and lack of proper insulation cause excessive chilling. In northern climes, a tank located near a drafty door or window can also cause temperature instabilities in the winter, which can lead to disease outbreaks in the aquarium.

The photoperiod and its timing can also have a dramatic impact on the aquarium temperature. For example, if the photoperiod begins at actual dawn and ends at actual dusk, the aquarium will be heated at the same time that the house is heated by the sun. This will make the aquarium hotter, make the home cooling system work harder, make the aquarium chiller (if present) work more, and result in a higher power bill. If the aquarium photoperiod is skewed so that it begins much later in the day and extends later into the night, the heating effect will not be in sync with the sun, so less power will be consumed and the aquarium will be cooler. In colder climes, or in the winter, taking advantage of natural sunlight and the heat it creates can actually help to keep the aquarium from becoming too cold, and the later photoperiod will keep the aquarium warm when the sun has set. On the subject of photoperiod and temperature, the photoperiod can be about 8 to 13.5 hours, as in the natural setting, but with multiple lamps used, the high intensity lights may be run for a shorter period, for example 4 to 6 hours, thus reducing electrical consumption, extending bulb life, and reducing heat input into the aquarium.

Sunlight

Older reference books suggest that aquariums should not be placed where they would receive direct sunlight from a window. The reasoning was that such sun exposure could heat the aquarium excessively or the extra illumination could promote problems with algae. Since modern reef aquariums commonly have both temperature control and nutrient management systems, the need to *stay out of the sun* is reduced, and in fact, many aquarists build skylights or even sunrooms to encourage the sun to shine in their aquariums for a portion of the day. The photosynthetic corals appreciate the extra light intensity, and the aquarist can view the aquarium under natural light, which makes the corals and fishes look especially colourful. Of course, the temperature needs to be controlled to prevent rapid increases when the sun shines directly onto the aquarium. One drawback to sunlight use is that algae may grow more quickly on the windows of the tank. The use of thick sand beds, refugiums and/or plenum systems seems to curb this effect, as the bacteria growing in the bottom sediments compete with the algae for the same nutrients, as do the macroalgae in the refugium.

Cleaning the aquarium

Once the aquarium has been completely assembled, the final step in preparing it is to thoroughly clean it. Simply rinsing out the aquarium or wiping it down with cold water and a sponge should suffice. However, before you do so it is best to vacuum the tank to remove any debris left over from drilling holes or the installation of overflows because small sand grains or shards of plastic or glass can get picked up by the sponge and scratch a viewing window. If you purchase a system that has already been assembled, it should have been cleaned already but it never hurts to clean it one more time. For any greasy spots, a mild dishwashing liquid is fine to use, but the tank should be well rinsed with freshwater afterwards.

When cleaning acrylic aquariums the same procedures can be followed but be careful not to use a sponge if there is any sand in the tank, and don't use any abrasive materials to wipe the tank or, if you vacuum it, don't touch the viewing windows with the end of the vacuum hose. Also, don't use stiff brush attachments with the vacuum, since these can cause fine scratches. You can use rubbing alcohol to remove any greasy spots or residue from glues used to hold protective papers. Whenever using any material to rub acrylic, remember that grains of sand attached to the sponge, pad, etc. will scratch the acrylic. It is wise to inspect empty acrylic tanks closely for any scratches that may be present (especially on the inside) and remove these using 3-step acrylic polishes designed for light scratches or abrasive cloths (micromesh) for deeper scratches. Never, ever use any solvents such as acetone on or near an acrylic surface. This will cause the acrylic to cloud or craze, and can severely damage bonded surfaces. We have seen clear bonds turn milky white within a few minutes of exposure to the fumes of chemical solvents used a short distance away from a tank. Rubbing alcohol is, however, safe and can be used to remove residues left behind from protective coverings.

The reef aquarium of Dr. Hitoshi Ueno in Osaka, Japan has its own dedicated sunroom.
J.C. Delbeek

The Common Elements

According to Chinese astrology, the universe consists of five basic elements: metal, water, wood, fire and earth. These aren't literal *elements* in the sense we commonly think of them, but qualities in a continuous cycle of constant change. Other cultures, some religions, and mystic texts discuss these *elements*, and include related ones such as wind, space, and ether. The concept of *basic elements* was included in writing even as far back as the ancient civilization of Sumeria. Greek theories of four basic elements (earth, water, air, fire) were originally developed by Empedocles and later expanded by Aristotle. From a macroscopic point of view, the biosphere of the planet Earth consists of land, sea, atmosphere and sun *elements*. Our aquariums can also be thought of from this point of view.

Regardless of the type of reef aquarium you are planning, there are common elements. All (so far!) are contained in a vessel called *the aquarium*, all have water, all have light, and all have solid substrates. Chapter 1 covers features of the aquarium. In this section, we will examine the water and earth elements common to reef aquariums: water, seawater, live rock and bottom substrata (sand, gravel, mud). Other *common elements* such as light and motion are treated separately in this book.

Closeup view of the surface of an *Acropora* sp. coral, showing polyps and skeletal structure. J. Sprung

Water

All aquariums need water. Water is the medium on which all life in the aquarium depends. As such, the type and quality of seawater and freshwater used to run the aquarium is of critical importance. The freshwater can be taken from a well, from the faucet (tapwater), or it can be purified by various methods. Freshwater is used both for the mixing of new seawater and for the replenishment of water that evaporates from the aquarium. Since only freshwater evaporates, leaving the salt behind, replacing evaporated water must be done with freshwater, not with seawater, since the latter would lead to an increase in specific gravity. There are two types of seawater that can be used, natural and artificial.

Natural seawater

Many people believe that using natural seawater is unsafe. This belief most likely developed from older hobby references that recommended against using natural seawater, combined with the general perception that natural waters are polluted. Indeed, coastal seawater in some areas is not suitable for reef aquarium use due to high nutrient levels, pesticides, fertilizers, oils and other chemical contaminants. Any seawater collection areas that are located close to sewage outlets, river mouths, industrial areas, harbours, and estuaries should be avoided. However, properly selected areas, even bays, can yield surprisingly good quality water suitable for use in aquariums. The best time to collect water near shore is when high tides bring in generally cleaner and clearer offshore waters.

Disease causing pathogens can be brought in with natural seawater, but you can lessen the risk of disease introduction by filtering the water through an ultraviolet sterilizer or a diatomaceous earth filter before using it. It is of course also possible to collect seawater and use it immediately without any filtration. If the seawater stays stagnant in a container for more than a day, some of the plankton it contains will die and the decomposing of this plankton produces ammonia and bacterial blooms that cloud the water and quickly make it toxic. After a few weeks, the bacteria convert the ammonia to nitrate and their populations drop so that the water is clear again. For this reason older texts recommend storing the water in the dark without aeration for a few weeks. The clear water from the surface is then decanted or siphoned into another container where the water is aerated until needed. The detritus that settles at the bottom of the storage containers is discarded. Another method is to use a mild chlorine bleach solution to sterilize the water. The chlorine is added and left to stand for 24 hours and then a dechlorinator (e.g. sodium thiosulfate) is added, in combination with heavy aeration for a few days, to remove any residual chlorine. Moe (1982) offers further instructions for collecting and sterilizing natural seawater for aquarium use.

Haulover inlet, just north of Miami Beach, is a popular place for aquarists to collect seawater on incoming tide. J. Sprung

An alternative to collecting your own seawater is to use commercially available natural seawater. Some companies are now offering bottled natural seawater that has been collected offshore and sterilized with ozone or ultraviolet light.

It is ironic that some people are paranoid about introducing diseases with natural seawater, whereas they think nothing of adding fish, corals, live sand and live rock without any quarantine procedures at all. In our opinion, these additions to the aquarium are much more likely to introduce diseases than natural seawater, due to the much greater density of possible disease causing organisms in these sources.

Artificial seawater

Most reef aquarium hobbyists do not have the luxury of using natural seawater and must rely on artificial seawater mixes. These consist of the major, minor and trace chemical constituents of seawater in dry powdered form. The seawater mix is added to the proper volume of water, the solution is vigorously aerated for a few days, allowing adequate time for the solution to reach chemical equilibrium, and the solution is then ready to use. Using a powerhead does a better job of mixing than an airstone but does not help with dissolved gas equilibrium. The best technique is to use both. Aeration will also correct both high and low pH problems. However, if the salt mix is not properly buffered, the pH may not reach the proper level.

Often one will find a white precipitate at the bottom of the mixing container. This can be undissolved calcium carbonate and is often a result of salts that mix to a higher than normal pH value, have higher than normal calcium and bicarbonate buffer levels, or have been contaminated with moisture while in the packaging. Excess moisture allows calcium chloride and sodium bicarbonate to react and create calcium carbonate particles and carbon dioxide gas, which is liberated. The net effect is to reduce the calcium level, reduce the bicarbonate level (buffer) and increase the pH of the newly mixed product (often to 9.0+). The seawater will actually have a lower buffer level in spite of the higher pH (T. Frakes, pers. comm.). Aeration will help correct the pH imbalance but will not redissolve the calcium carbonate. If there is a large amount of precipitate, it is best to remove the water from the mixing tank, leave the precipitate behind, and then gradually correct the calcium and bicarbonate levels before adding organisms and/or live rock, especially if the water is being used to set up a new aquarium. If the water is being used for a small partial water change, the discrepancy of calcium and alkalinity is not likely to be significant, or at least it can be corrected in the aquarium with the addition of calcium and buffer, or with a balanced ion two-part calcium and alkalinity supplement. Do not add any of the precipitate to established reef aquariums as this can lead to irritation of the animals if it lands on them. It is harmless otherwise, and it won't dissolve anyway unless the tank pH is lower than 7.8.

Tip: A good method to rapidly dissolve a batch of salt mix was first described by Bingman (1997). Use a special polypropylene-clad shaft and propeller driven with a household drill in a water-filled vat to rapidly mix the solution and dissolve the salt in small volumes. An alternative is to use plastic paint mixer shafts, though these are not usually long enough to serve large vats of seawater. Use a battery-operated hand-held drill to reduce the risk of electric shock.

This brings up the question of where best to mix the salt with the water. When setting up a new aquarium you can first add freshwater, start up the filtration and circulation system, and then add the salt to the bare system (no live rock, no bottom material, etc.), and let the salt dissolve over the course of a few days. However, we still prefer to use separate containers for mixing the seawater since it is easier to adjust for salinity and pH problems and avoid adding precipitates. The water can then be decanted or pumped into the system when ready. After the aquarium has been running for some time you will need to mix seawater for water changes in a separate container anyway. It is also a good idea to have a system in place that will allow you to make up saltwater to do at least a 50% water change in case problems develop in the tank such as disease outbreaks or leaks.

For small water changes (5 to 10 percent), it is acceptable to use newly mixed seawater immediately, only checking first to be sure that the salinity is correct. Simply add the salt to the water in a clean pail (not the other way around) and mix until it clears. There is no need to wait for the pH to adjust for such a small water change since it won't have a significant impact on the pH of the aquarium.

Today there are over a dozen salt mixes available, all with wondrous claims as to their abilities. There have been numerous online and published articles comparing the various salts available, some conducted by the product companies, others by hobbyists or scientists (e.g. Atkinson and Bingman, 1999). Most of these are aimed at outlining the difference between the various brands and then trying to come to some conclusion about which is best. The bottom line is, are they able to keep your animals alive or not? The vast majority do, and you can't really go wrong with any of the brands available on the market today. There are of course differences and one should be on the look out for a few signs that indicate a good quality mix for reef aquariums. For example, once the salt has been thoroughly aerated, mixed and totally dissolved over a few days check the pH, alkalinity, magnesium and calcium levels. These should all be within the normal ranges considered appropriate for reef aquariums. You should also measure the specific gravity or salinity and make sure this is also within the required range (see chapter 4).

There has been much written about the levels of minor and trace elements in salt mixes, how these could build-up to potentially toxic levels in aquariums, and that this may explain difficulties in keeping some marine life (see Shimek 2002a,b,c,d). However, even though these elements show up in chemical analyses, they are naturally bonded with organic or inorganic complexes in the seawater in aquariums and so the dangerous concentrations are simply not biologically available (Sekha, 2003). In addition, while an assay of a dry salt mix may show excesses in some trace elements, the product produced when the salt is mixed with water may not have such high concentrations of these elements in solution. They may simply precipitate out. Furthermore, the marinelife in the aquarium may quickly respond to excesses of some metals by secreting chelating substances that render them biologically unavailable (Sekha, 2003). Finally, the suitability of the testing methodology used in these studies (e.g. Shimek 2002a,b) has been brought in to question and at this time it is still not clear how much a problem trace element accumulation really is in an aquarium (see Harker, 2003 and Harker, 2004 a,b,c). Harker (2004 b,c) demonstrates that the levels of some heavy metals in natural seawater collected from coral reef regions are consistent with the elevated, supposedly toxic levels, reported by Shimek (2002 a,b) for aquariums. It is not clear whether this fact is an erroneous artifact of the testing method (ICP analysis) used by both Shimek and Harker, or whether Harker has discovered a unique feature of the coral reef environment, namely that it may naturally have higher levels of heavy metals than the open sea.

Tip: Always store unused salt mix in an airtight container. Failure to do so will cause moisture in the air to mix with the salt and precipitate calcium carbonate. It will also cause the salt to become rock solid. A few tyvek enclosed packages containing moisture absorbing silica gel beads placed on top of the salt in a sealed container can help to prevent excess moisture from ruining the salt.

Freshwater preparation

While the quality of the salt mix you use is important, the quality of the freshwater you use to make your saltwater is equally, if not more important. Contact the local water works department to ask for a print out of what is in the tapwater in your area. Examine the levels of ammonia, nitrite, nitrate, phosphate, iron, silicate, calcium, magnesium, pH, alkalinity and organics. They should all be within the normal accepted ranges for reef aquariums (see chapter 4). Many treatment plants add chemicals to the water to sterilize it as well as to cut down on the amount of hard water scale that can develop in pipes. These usually consist of compounds containing chlorine, chloramines, ammonia and phosphate. In some areas, you must treat the water first to remove these compounds before the water can be used in a reef aquarium. In other areas, even after the water is treated, it will still contain unacceptable levels of the elements we mentioned. Most hobbyists err on the side of caution and always process their tap water before using it. Another potential problem concerns the water mains in the home, or those supplying the home. In many homes these can be copper or even lead in older homes. It

A reverse osmosis filter with carbon and fine particulate prefiltration stages, near right, and a combination reverse osmosis and deionization unit, far right. Manufactured by *Spectrapure®*

is not unusual for tapwater to have copper levels high enough to be toxic to invertebrates but for it to be otherwise acceptable for aquarium use. Therefore, if you plan to use untreated tapwater make sure you test it for copper levels first.

There are several methods available today to process tap water to make it as pure as possible. However, the most common and effective method is to use a combination of reverse osmosis and deionization filters. Reverse osmosis units use a porous membrane that allows small molecules, such as water, to pass through but blocks the passage of larger molecules such as phosphate. These blocked molecules then pass out of the filter along with rejected water. Reverse osmosis filters block up to 95% of many compounds but for every 3.8 L (gallon) of pure water produced about 30 L (8 gal.) of rejected water is released. This can be somewhat improved by increasing the pressure of the incoming water, which is done with *booster* pumps and recirculation loops on more efficient units that can achieve much closer to a 1:1 product to rejection ratio.

Tip: One should periodically check the efficacy of the R.O. filter by using a conductivity meter. The raw tapwater value is compared to the filtered product water. The product water should have a conductivity at least 90-95 percent lower than the raw tap water.

Deionization resins consist of tiny beads that function to adsorb certain types of compounds. Due to this ability, deionization columns can be filled with a variety of resin types or can be custom designed to target one type of compound for removal. Passing the reverse osmosis water through a deionization column further purifies the water and produces extremely pure freshwater. Several companies produce these units so it is best to consult with them to determine what combination of resins and reverse osmosis membranes would best suit the water chemistry of the tapwater in your area. This pure water should also be used to replace freshwater lost to evaporation.

Tip: Store your pure freshwater in airtight, inert containers. Such pure water is very aggressive, it will rapidly absorb contaminants from the air and any surface it meets. Contrary to popular belief that it should be neutral, reverse osmosis/deionized water often has an acidic pH between 5 and 7 due to the presence of excess dissolved CO_2.

Live rock photographed on a reef in the Solomon Islands. Turf algae, coralline algae, sponges, zoanthids, snails, foraminiferans and crustaceans are some of the obvious colonizers of the surface. Inside it the porous structure houses sponges, bacteria, worms, and a host of other creatures, forming a stable community. J. Sprung

Live rock

The one element that every reef aquarium philosophy has in common is the use of live rocks in the construction of the aquascape of the system. Live rocks are pieces of old coral skeletons and shells that have become encrusted with coralline algae and a variety of other plants and invertebrates. In some locations live rocks are composed of fused sand grains coated by coralline algae and other marinelife, and in some locations the bulk of the calcium carbonate rock mass is produced entirely by fast-growing coralline algae, not corals. Worms, large and small crustaceans, clams, and sponges inhabit the holes in its porous structure. It also carries heterotrophic, nitrifying and denitrifying bacteria, and other microorganisms. Due to the microscopic and macroscopic life that good quality live rock contains, it performs a number of important functions. The bacteria on and in the rocks provide the bulk of the biological filtration in the aquarium; no other biological filters are required. The micro-crustaceans (e.g. amphipods and copepods) and worms in the rocks spread throughout the aquarium and their larvae contribute to the food chain in the system. Finally, the algae on the rock also spread throughout the system, helping to maintain the water quality and contributing to the food chain. The highly desirable pink and purple coralline algae also quickly spread to cover exposed surfaces, lending a very natural appearance to any established reef aquarium. We discuss the roles of live rock in filtration and how to best aquascape with it in chapters 6 and 9 respectively.

Types

Live rocks are collected in a variety of locations and the sources vary every year as legislation restricts the harvest in one place and new locations open up. Most live rock is collected as loose

A view of a section of dried Fiji live rock shows that it is composed principally of coralline algae. J. Sprung

A view of a section of live rock harvested from the Gulf of Mexico prior to the ban on collection of live rock in Florida , shows that it is composed mainly of fused quartz and calcium carbonate sand grains, with a coating of coralline algae. J. Sprung

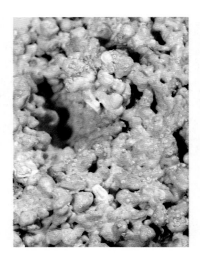

lightweight pieces from offshore rubble zones or reef flats adjacent to reefs, where it is a plentiful and renewable resource. In the last ten years, a second source for live rock has emerged. Aquacultured live rock is becoming more common in the trade and is gaining favor with environmentally conscious aquarists. In some cases, calcareous rock from terrestrial sources is used (e.g. Florida aquacultured rock) in others live rocks are made from mixes containing calcareous rubble and concrete (e.g. Fiji, Hawaii). The reason for this is that local government regulations often require that the aquacultured live rock not resemble local live rock to dissuade the poaching of illegal local sources. In other cases, it is more economical to make rock using local supplies than to import non-native dried rocks. An advantage to man-made live rock is that it can be made into various shapes and sizes, and it can be branded, making it easy to distinguish it from natural live rock.

Aquacultured sources

Fiji

Some suppliers of live rock in Fiji are now turning to producing artificial live rock (e.g. *Walt Smith International*). These rocks vary in size and surface texture, and come in irregular shapes. During the manufacture of the rock, a reddish color is imparted to the cement material, which makes it look like natural coralline algae. The rocks are placed in offshore reef areas and become indistinguishable from wild live rock within six to eight months. Encrusted with coralline algae, sponges and algae these rocks make a fine substitute for natural live rock.

Making artificial live rock at *Walt Smith International*, Suva, Fiji. M. Awai

Palettes of artificial Fiji live rock ready for deployment in the ocean. M. Awai

Artificial Fijian live rock after six months in the ocean, *Walt Smith International*, Suva, Fiji. M. Awai

Florida

Several companies in Florida now offer cultured live rock. Some of them are located on the Gulf of Mexico and others in the Florida Keys. Most of these companies use terrestrial limestone that is porous and with nice shapes or solid smoother chunky pieces. The rocks are placed on special bottom leases permitted by the state of Florida, and harvested a year or more later when they are encrusted by marinelife. One special feature of this aquacultured rock is that it can have several Atlantic stony coral species on it that would not otherwise be legal to collect. Other organisms found on Florida aquacultured rock include very colourful coralline algae, hardy encrusting sponges, tunicates, and some nice red seaweeds.

This colony of *Acropora cervicornis* is growing on live rock planted by Ken Nedimyer on a bottom lease site in the Florida Keys. It represents the first time that this species can legally be harvested for commercial sale to the aquarium trade. K. Nedimyer

Agaricia agaricites growing on Ken Nedimyer's cultured live rock. K. Nedimyer

An overview of Ken Nedimyer's bottom lease live rock farm. K. Nedimyer

The fire coral *Millepora alcicornis* grows prolifically on Florida aquacultured live rock. K. Nedimyer

Hawaii

It has been illegal to collect and sell live rock from Hawaii since the early 1990s. Anyone offering live rocks from Hawaii other than aquacultured is most certainly doing so illegally. However, *Indo Pacific Sea Farms* (*IPSF*) on the Kona coast of Hawaii uses a concrete and calcareous gravel mixture to make live rocks that are held in land-based raceways using ocean water supplied by offshore pumps or saltwater wells. In addition to *IPSF*, there are several groups looking to produce aquacultured live rock in inshore areas and native Hawaiian fishponds on the island of Molokai and elsewhere in Hawaii.

Purchasing live rock

Live rock can be purchased in a number of ways. Purchasing through retailers is the most common option, either local or online. In some cases, it is possible to order aquacultured rock directly from the supplier. It is also possible to order wild live rock from the source via transhippers.

When live rock first arrives, usually after 24-48 hours of extremely stressful shipping conditions, the rock needs time to cleanse away excess nitrogenous wastes produced by the decay of various worms, algae, sponges and clams etc. on and in the rock, that have died as a result of the transport. This process, known as *curing*, *cycling*, or *seeding*, parallels the conditioning of an external biological filter in that bacteria populations need time to develop in order to handle the increase in nitrogenous wastes, particularly ammonia.

One of the advantages of purchasing live rock from a retailer is that this *seeding* process has already been performed if the rock was held by the retailer for more than a couple of weeks. This allows you to use the rock to set up a reef aquarium complete with fish and corals within a few days. However, this type of rock also tends to be the most expensive. Live rock that has been cultured *ex-situ* (in raceways) often has a lower biological load than wild rock or rock aquacultured in the ocean and tends to require a much shorter *seeding* time as well.

At *Walt Smith International*, live rock is held in long raceways, wetted only with seawater spray from spray-emitting outlets. This rinses off sediment, assures that the rocks are supersaturated with oxygen, and maintains the life on them in excellent condition. J. Sprung

Seeding live rock

The vast majority of imported live rock needs to be seeded, by either the retailer or the hobbyist. *Seeding* can be accomplished either in the aquarium or in a holding system. Most aquarists only have facilities for the latter option, but holding the rock in a separate vessel allows the decay and sloughing of detritus to occur outside the aquarium, and the rock is therefore much cleaner when it is finally arranged in the display tank. Housing the rock separately first, also allows the opportunity to remove unwanted hitchhikers such as mantis shrimp, crabs, worms, nudibranchs and carnivorous snails. Whether done in the tank or in storage containers, strong water movement, aeration, the use of activated carbon and protein skimming, are all used to cycle the rock as quickly as possible with the minimum amount of die-off. We wish to emphasize that although many organisms on and in the rock are killed during shipping and handling, the individual losses are minor, and the vast majority of micro and macro-organisms do survive, grow and reproduce. With live rock, it is possible to have ecosystem level complexity of food webs, especially in large aquariums.

Tip: There is a nifty solution that your local retailer may be willing to help you with to eradicate all mantis shrimp during the quarantine and *seeding* of the rocks. Add a hungry octopus to the live rock holding tank, and the result is lots of shrimp and crab shells accumulating on the bottom of the tank (R. Bull, pers. comm.). Then remove the octopus and return it to the retailer. This technique is meant for new set-ups only, before the fish are introduced, because octopus may feed on fish. Caution: The aquarium or vat must have a secure lid when the octopus is inside, to keep it from escaping. There is also a risk of the octopus going over the overflow and getting into the drain.

Live rock preparation

When live rock is first received, it should be rinsed in saltwater in order to remove such goodies as newspaper ink (from the paper used to wrap it and keep it moist), algae leachates, sand, muck and ammonia that have been released by the rock inhabitants during transport. Saltwater in a bucket is fine for this rinse. Excessive sponge and algae growth should be removed also, if this has not already been done for you by the supplier. CAUTION HERE! The average hobbyist is poorly able to distinguish between sponge, coral, and meatloaf. A rare, desirable specimen could be lost to aimless cleaning. Experience prepares the hobbyist to judge what's good and what's not.

The white film on this newly imported piece of live rock indicates that sponges that lived within its inner porous spaces have died. The film is a type of bacteria called *Beggiatoa*, and it is associated with a characteristic rotten egg smell. J. Sprung

Normally we do not advise scrubbing the rock with a brush. Though the practice is not ultimately harmful, it is needless work and potentially removes many desirable creatures. However, rocks with obvious signs of fouling (i.e. white sloughing film, black, sulfur-smelling areas) should be thoroughly scrubbed and rinsed. These necrotic areas represent regions where organisms on or in the rock have died. Large mats of algae should also be removed since the rock will be stacked in such a way that it will be crushed or shaded anyway. The algae will grow back when the rock is illuminated, and it can be controlled with herbivores.

Cycling the live rock

The procedures for cycling the rock are the same regardless if it is done in the aquarium or in a separate container. Once the rock has been cleaned and placed into the system, activated carbon should be used to adsorb organic leachates given off by decaying sponges and plants. Some carbon dust from the fresh carbon will inevitably be released in the water. Within an hour, depending on the turnover rate of the aquarium, the water will be crystal clear and the carbon dust, with the adsorbed organics, will have been trapped in the mechanical filter. This filter can then be simply thrown away and replaced with fresh material or left empty depending on your design. The protein skimmer is shut off during this period, as the carbon dust would quickly coat the skimmer tube. A few hours after installation of the carbon, the protein skimmer should be re-started. See chapter 6 for descriptions of how to install activated carbon effectively.

It is good practice to leave the lights off during the cycling process, since it is during this period that algae nutrients will be at their highest level, and high intensity lighting can stimulate excessive algae growth. In addition, the growth of nitrifying bacteria is inhibited by light. The use of granular iron based phosphate adsorbing media can be initiated right at the onset to adsorb the excess phosphate produced by new rock, and eliminate the typical algae bloom that results from it. Stacking of the rock in a loose arrangement, with plenty of gaps and open spaces, will facilitate the circulation of oxygen rich water throughout the reef structure and aid seeding. Do not create a tight brick wall! Chapter 9 includes more detail about aquascaping possibilities.

If one has to purchase live rock in small amounts due to budget constraints, and the aquarium contains fish and valued invertebrates, then it is essential that the rocks be well *seeded* in a separate container or aquarium before they are placed in the display aquarium. Operate your protein skimmer from day one, but caution: it will be pulling out excessive amounts of material during the *seeding* process. Make sure you empty the collection cup regularly and clean the skimmer tube frequently to maintain peak efficiency.

Ammonia and nitrite levels should be monitored weekly and once acceptable levels are reached (usually within two to three weeks) then the rock can be used to set up the aquarium if cycled outside the system. This period is highly variable and sometimes a tank will show very little ammonia at all, or very high amounts for a longer period. As the rock cycles, detritus should be siphoned from the rocks and tank as frequently and possible. During this period, a powerhead can also be used to blast in and around the rocks to help dislodge pockets of detritus so that it can be removed by the filtration system. Once the rock as cycled it can be added to the system, or if the rock was cycled in the system, the bottom substrata (if used) can now be added. Generally, animals can be introduced after about two weeks as long as there are no white filmy areas on the rock and there is no measurable ammonia or nitrite. As soon as ammonia and nitrite parameters reach acceptable levels, you can add a number of herbivores to the tank. In our opinion, the various turban snails (*Trochus, Astraea, Turbo* spp.) are ideal, and we recommend approximately one snail per 3.8 L (gallon), initially for aquariums between 38 L (10 gal.) and 760 L (200 gal.), half this amount later. Snails are introduced as soon as possible after the ammonia level has declined, effectively limiting the development of microalgae. Some *Turbo* sp. snails are very large, so fewer of them are needed, and their size and habit of *bowling* over invertebrates can be a problem in smaller aquariums. Other snails that are useful herbivores for reef aquariums include *Trochus, Nerita, Neritina, Vittina* and various *Ceriths* (Sprung, 2002).

It must be understood that the most successful exhibits are created as much with patience as with skill. Therefore waiting longer before adding specimens other than herbivores is highly recommended. It should also be apparent that a completed nitrogen cycle is not an indication that all of the rock is completely *seeded*, only that the bacteria colonies have developed sufficiently to handle the ammonia released into the water by the fouling rocks. Again, the longer one waits before adding any specimens, the better. Some hobbyists may wait as long as six months before adding any fish, though it is not essential to be so extremely patient. Generally, it is safe to add fish after one month of *seeding* the tank. Delaying the introduction of fish allows the populations of various creatures and algae to increase and strengthen such that they will provide a constantly available food source once the fish are added. In systems that employ well-developed refugia, this is less of a factor since they will provide abundant microcrustaceans to the system too (see chapter 6). While it is possible to create a balanced environment rather quickly, it is always best to be patient and proceed slowly. In the goal of achieving a wonderfully beautiful and educational natural ecosystem, it would be a shame to risk killing organisms needlessly because of a lack of patience.

The bottom material

One of the greatest changes in reef keeping in the last ten years has been the use of bottom substratum materials. In the late 1980's, recommendations in North American reef aquarium literature discouraged the use of sand or gravel on the bottom, as it was perceived as a detritus trap that could promote the proliferation of undesirable algae. These partly factual notions resulted in an unfortunate proliferation of tanks with nothing at all on the bottom!

In *The Reef Aquarium* volume one (Delbeek and Sprung, 1994) we pointed out that sand or gravel beds in an reef aquarium could play a very important role in nutrient cycling and act as a refuge for various micro-organisms, worms, and crustaceans. Living in the sand, they would digest detritus settling there and their reproduction in this refuge would generate food for filter feeders and fish. Since that time, there has been a proliferation of methods for keeping reef tanks based on a variety of bottom material sizes and bed thickness.

Bottom material can be placed in the aquarium right from the beginning, but it is also possible to wait a month or so after adding live rock before adding it. After the rocks have *seeded*, the initial heavy release of detritus can be siphoned away. At this point one may add bottom media to the aquarium. Another consideration for adding the rocks before the bottom substratum is that a rock arrangement supported by the hard bottom of the aquarium is structurally sounder than one on a foundation of sand, which can shift easily. The *Jaubert method* described later in this book can have the rocks suspended over the bottom rather than resting directly on it, or it uses so little rock that the structural stability is not an issue if the rocks are laying on the gravel. *Deep sand bed* setups often use non-living limestone base rocks resting on the bottom to form a stable base within the sand bed to support rocks positioned higher up and prevent shifting. See chapter 9 for more details on the techniques used.

Sand and gravel

Sizes
The particle or grain sizes for bottom substrates ranges from so-called *sugar fine* aragonite to coarse coral gravel fragments 1 cm (3/8 in.) or more in length. These different substrates have different uses in a reef aquarium system, based on the biotope created, and some of them have been adopted specifically for a type of filtration system employed.

Calcium carbonate affects on the water
Aragonite and other calcium carbonate sands are considered beneficial because they can dissolve, which adds calcium and carbonate to the water. This is especially true of aragonite, which dissolves at a pH level slightly below the normal level in aquariums. Other forms of calcium carbonate dissolve only at much lower pH. While the long-term effect of aragonite dissolving may supply some calcium and carbonate alkalinity, initially the introduction of *new* calcium carbonate substratum to an aquarium produces a drop in the calcium and alkalinity levels (Spotte, 1992). Therefore, if you are starting with dead, dry calcium carbonate, after rinsing it with freshwater it is a good idea to soak it in seawater (or artificial

seawater) for at least 24 hours before adding it to the aquarium, using a volume ratio of 3:1, saltwater to gravel or sand. After soaking it, discard the water. This allows magnesian calcite to precipitate onto the surfaces of the sand/gravel, and prevents it from significantly depleting alkalinity and calcium level of the display aquarium (Spotte, 1992). It is a minor point for reef aquariums, and many successful aquariums have been established without this first step. In reef aquariums it is normal to use calcium and alkalinity increasing supplements, which would counter the affects of adding raw calcium carbonate to the water (see chapter 5).

Coral sand

Coral sand consists of a mix of mainly small coral fragments, oolites, foraminiferan tests, and mollusk shells. It is mainly harvested from shorelines in the Philippines and Indonesia, but other sources are certainly possible. The legal status of this harvest was established by resolution 9.6 of the 12th Conference of the Parties (CoP12) of CITES (the Convention on International Trade in Endangered Species) convention. Coral sand (pieces of 2 mm or less) and fragments (gravel and rubble) between 2 and 30 mm in diameter) are not covered by CITES restrictions since they are not considered readily recognizable (http://www.cites.org/eng/resols/9/9_6.shtml). Coral sand comes in a variety of grades (sizes) ranging from 1 to 10 mm in diameter. Often a mix of grades is best as this provides the best substratum for burrowing organisms and allows shrimp and fishes to make effective burrows.

Grades of Coral Sand

Coral sand and gravel from the Philippines, Indonesia and other Pacific nations is sold in several different sizes that have use in different types of reef aquarium set-ups. The differences are not just aesthetic, as they relate to some important physical and biological considerations. Coral gravel and sand from the Bahamas and Caribbean are also available in different sizes for different types of displays.

Sugar fine aragonite

Powdery fine white oolitic sand (naturally precipitated calcium carbonate spheres of approximately 0.25 mm in diameter) collected from the Bahama Bank is a popular bottom substratum in the USA for the *deep sand bed* (DSB) method (see Adey, 1991; Shimek, 1999; Shimek, 2001). A nice feature of this material is that it is almost a pure white color. This makes it reflect light upwards, to the benefit of corals that can use upwelling light. It is claimed that extremely fine sand grains prevent detritus from seeping into the sand bed, keeping it on top only, where it can be re-suspended and removed by the skimmer or mechanical filtration. To some extent, this is true, but not so much that it really prevents the sandbed from getting dirty eventually. Over time, a sand bed made from sugar fine aragonite accumulates detritus just as any other sand bed does.

Basic considerations and preparation

Depending on the source, there may also be a high content of extremely fine dust in sugar fine sand. This is problematic at initial installation of the substrate, since it will produce cloudy water for a couple of days and will coat surfaces in the aquarium. Therefore, some aquarists prefer to rinse away the bulk of the fine dust by putting the sand in a bucket outside or in a utility sink and running a stream of water from a garden hose through it until the water *clears* up. Washing sugar fine sand can be a frustrating task. It is so easily suspended that some sand is easily lost in the wash water, and it is impossible to get the wash water to clear. Otherwise, the dust is considered a benefit as it provides a special habitat for microorganisms. Some aquarists don't bother washing it, saying that the fine dust it contains adds to the calcium level. In fact, while theoretically logical, the calcium carbonate dust may have the opposite effect, at least when initially added to the water (Spotte, 1992). Afterwards the dust will dissolve over time.

Special considerations

The sand grains are so small that they are easily suspended by strong currents. This quality changes with time as bacterial films make it more stable.

number 0 mm and 1mm

Slightly larger than the sugar fine aragonite from the Bahamas, number 0 size sand is available from the Pacific. It washes much easier and cleaner than sugar fine aragonite, but is darker. Either of these coral sand sizes can be used for a thin 2.5-7.5cm (1-3 inch) sand layer, as in Berlin system aquariums.

3 mm

Coral sand of 3mm size is the minimum size recommended for Jaubert system filtration. It is easily rinsed and installed.

5 - 6 mm

Coral sand of 5 or 6 mm nominal size is ideal for Jaubert systems, and is used as bottom material in Berlin system aquariums. When used in Berlin system aquariums it is important to include the convict blenny, *Pholidichthys leucotaenia*, which burrows through the sand and prevents the development of detritus buildup.

1 cm and larger coral fragments

Gravel composed of broken coral branches and shells of a size 1 cm or larger is very useful in coral propagation tanks, where it is an ideal attachment point for small soft coral fragments. It is also an attractive substratum for Berlin style reef aquariums because it soon becomes coated with coralline algae, lending a different appearance to the aquarium bottom, compared to otherwise

A fragmented polyp of *Duncanopsammia axifuga* is supported by large gravel and shells on top of fine sand. J. Sprung

In aquariums with live rock, strong water flow, and high alkalinity and calcium levels, large gravel pieces soon become coated with coralline algae, like mini live rocks. J. Sprung

Different sizes for coral gravel from Indonesia. J. Sprung

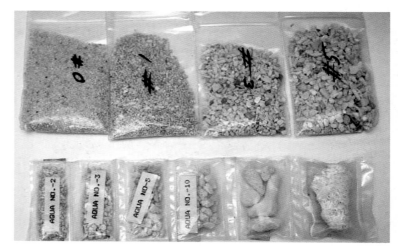

whitish sand or gravel bottoms. A nice feature of larger gravel sizes is that fungiid corals are less likely to become partially buried by them. Fungiids can inflate their tissues to escape burial, but sometimes they are covered too quickly, and if it happens at night, the low oxygen level can cause the buried tissue to suffocate. Placing small piles of 1cm coral fragments here and their on top of fine sand provides a footing for corals placed on the bottom, but does not protect them in the event a *Pholidichthys* or other burrowing fish dumps a huge amount of substrate over them. These larger fragments also allow burrow-creating animals such as pistol shrimp and jawfish to create stable burrows within the sand bed.

Basic considerations and preparation

As with fine sands, it is a good idea to thoroughly rinse coral sand to remove impurities such as bits of wood and other organic matter, as well as fine sediment that may have accumulated at the bottom of the bag due to abrasion of the coral sand grains. There is often a mixture of sizes in coral sand mixes, even though they are usually graded in size. This is not a bad thing, in fact, depending on the types of organisms to be kept, it is often a good idea to mix various grades to create a more heterogeneous mixture since fishes and invertebrates that construct burrows will use the larger pieces to reinforce their tunnels.

Foraminiferan sand

A special calcareous gravel exists that is comprised almost entirely of foraminiferan tests with a spherical shape and grain size of about 2mm. It is harvested from Indonesia and marketed by several aquarium industry suppliers, and it is an interesting media for biological filtration, among other possibilities. From an aesthetic point of view, its uniform grain size makes it look a bit artificial, but otherwise it works extremely well as a bottom substrate. Furthermore, no significant washing in necessary to prepare it.

Black sand

Throughout the world, there are various reefs located in areas that are of volcanic origin. In these areas, darker sands are the norm. There are now mixtures available that have various amounts of black sand added to them to recreate these areas. Often combined with calcareous sands to provide some buffering, these darker sands can create a unique look for a reef tank. Mitch Carl at the Omaha Zoo's Scott Aquarium in Omaha, Nebraska, has used black sand to create a 98,421 L (26,000 gal.- this volume also includes off-exhibit sumps) exhibit that mimics the volcanic sand habitat of the Lembeh Strait region of Sulawesi, Indonesia to great effect. The main drawback to this type of bottom material is that it is not calcareous in nature and does not provide any buffering ability or calcium replenishment (see chapter 5).

Basic considerations and preparation

Aside from the usual thorough rinsing of the sand to remove foreign particles and fine sediments, there are no other special preparations. Since many of these black sands are silicaceous in nature, we strongly advise wearing a dust mask when handling this material in its dry state to avoid inhaling any dust.

Live Sand

Several sources of *live* sand are available in the aquarium industry. Some are marketed pre-packaged in bags or containers through the

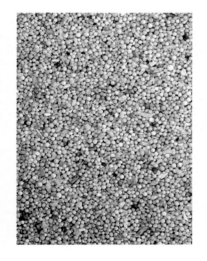

This special bottom substrate from Indonesia is composed mainly of the tests of a spherical foraminiferan. J. Sprung

Left and right sections of the black sand bottom Sulawesi beaches and shores exhibit at the Scott Aquarium, Henry Doorly Zoo, Omaha, NE. M. Carl

pet industry dry goods distribution channels; other types are merely harvested and sold by the pound as livestock. Various grain sizes are available. Live sand is usually purchased more as an accessory for seeding sand beds than as the primary bottom coverage due to its cost and the fact that inert sand beds will eventually become fully colonized once inoculated by a percentage of live sand.

Basic considerations, and preparation

Live sand should not be rinsed in any way, as rinsing would wash away the living creatures that give it its name. We recommend adding the live sand after adding the live rock and any other bottom material. This allows the live rock to discharge its initial load of detritus and prevents a large initial loading on to an unconditioned/unseeded sand bed.

Mud

The use of mud or clays for a bottom substratum in the aquarium has become popularized for refugia but not for the main display. In refugia, it is treated as a growing medium that supports vigorous health in *Caulerpa* spp., as part of the *Ecosystem Aquarium® method* of aquarium keeping introduced by Leng Sy. Ecosystem or *mud system* aquariums are described in chapter 6. The use of soft fine substrates in a display aquarium is a possibility not well explored, but it offers some opportunities to create habitats rarely duplicated in aquariums.

Basic considerations

Aquariums with mud bottoms cannot have strong water movement since the soft fine mud is easily suspended in the water column when disturbed. Therefore, a mud bottom aquarium must have no water currents and little or no surge. This restriction does not preclude significant water turnover rates, however. It is entirely possible to have a turnover rate of 10 tank volumes per hour or higher without producing any current in the aquarium. Using a surface skimming overflow and a water output divided into numerous ports, or a slotted pipe, the flow velocity can be minimized while retaining the same volume. It is also possible to have a tidal system in an aquarium with a mud bottom.

A special consideration for mud-bottomed tanks is the oxygen level, which is easily depleted by biological activity in the mud. The low velocity of water also promotes oxygen depletion, but this is countered by maintaining a high water turnover rate, which effectively brings oxygen depleted water to the surface where it can pick up more oxygen. A surge device that gently creates a to and fro motion without causing high velocity of the water can help to promote higher oxygen levels by causing the water within the substratum to move, but it is no substitute for surface skimming and water turnover. The addition of a refugium using reverse daylight photosynthesis is another option for boosting dissolved oxygen at night, see chapters 4 and 6 for a description of this method.

Preparing the tank with a mud bottom.

If the mud is dry to begin with, spread about two thirds of it over the bottom of the aquarium. After the mud is spread over the bottom, slowly add saltwater to it in order to cause it to become damp. Be careful not to breathe any dust emitted into the air as it becomes wetted. Do not pour so much water over it that it becomes completely submerged. If you add too much water, scoop some of the excess water out and then add the remaining third of the mud to soak in the water. Once the mud is uniformly just damp, put a layer of plastic over it (such as a plastic trash bag or two, and hold the bag(s) in place with a few stone weights. The bags are used temporarily only, for preventing the mud from clouding the water you will add to the aquarium. With the bag(s) in place, slowly pour water in over them so that the water level rises without stirring up the mud. When the aquarium is full, carefully remove the stone weights and the bags.

Thickness of the bed

A mud bottom tank can be set up with a deep layer or a thin layer of mud. A layer about two inches deep is sufficient for most set ups, but deeper layers could be used to duplicate special habitats for creatures that form tubes or burrows in deep mud.

The Smithsonian Institution's facility in Ft Pierce Florida has this mangrove exhibit managed by Bill Hoffman that features a mud bottom and a tidal change system shown in chapter 7. J. Sprung

Closeup photo of the viewing window offering a cross section of the stratified layers of different oxygen concentration in a mudbed. Note the pink and green photosynthetic bacteria typical of a high nutrient low oxygen environment. J. Sprung

Plumbing and Electric

When we visit many hobbyists and professionals and review the systems used in their aquariums, we often encounter serious flaws in the system design that do not relate to the application of the usual biological, physical, and chemical considerations that form the basis of what we call *techniques*. Such flaws can be so serious that they risk the success of the display, the life of the aquarists, or the safety of the building. In addition, design considerations also relate to the aesthetics of the display, and its *intrusion* in our space, including such things as the generation of heat and noise. Finally, the design of the system can make a big difference on the home electric bill. Using energy efficient designs can keep the cost of running the system low. In this chapter, we discuss how to design the aquarium plumbing and electrical systems. We also review some of the common errors we have seen and offer suggestions for how to avoid such mistakes.

Joe Biesterfeld's plumbing system is well designed. The pipes and filter components are labelled, which facilitates maintenance as well as long-distance communication with anyone caring for the aquarium. J. Sprung

This *Montipora* spp. dominated reef aquarium at *Vivarium Karlsrhue*, in Karlsrhue, Germany depends on a well-engineered plumbing and electrical system behind the scenes. J. Sprung

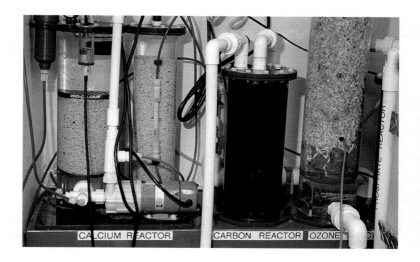

CALCIUM REACTOR   CARBON REACTOR OZONE

Plumbing

Proper plumbing for aquariums is an art as well as a science. It can be done in a way that looks clean and very organized, but at the same time it can also be flawed because of loss of flow or for other reasons. Before we can begin a discussion about plumbing design, we will first discuss the materials and parts available. These can be divided into three main areas: piping/hoses, fittings and valves. In this chapter, we use primarily North American units due to our familiarity with them. Different standard sizes exist around the world, but we leave it to the reader to the make the proper conversions and extrapolations to the standards used in other countries.

Piping and tubing

PVC (polyvinyl chloride) **pipe**

PVC pipe is available in several wall thicknesses, but the most commonly used in aquarium plumbing in North America are referred to as schedule 40 and schedule 80. Schedule 40 is the most commonly used thickness, while schedule 80 is mostly used in high pressure (>60 psi) systems or for use with compressed gasses. Schedule 80 has a thicker wall, resulting in a smaller internal

PVC pipe comes in a variety of diameters and wall thickness. J.C. Delbeek

diameter but the same outer diameter as schedule 40 pipe. The narrower internal diameter also results in higher backpressure and hence greater head pressure for a pump to overcome. Schedule 80 pipe is often also used when excessive heat gain is a problem or when cool liquids are being moved through humid areas, cutting down on condensation on the pipes. However, using schedule 40 in conjunction with foam pipe insulation will achieve the same effect without the increase in backpressure associated with using schedule 80. In our opinion, schedule 40 is more than adequate for aquarium plumbing systems, and is much less expensive than schedule 80. There is a third type of PVC pipe, schedule 20, which is thinner walled than schedule 40, but we recommend it only be used in low pressure situations e.g. as a standpipe in an overflow.

PVC pipe comes in various sizes from 1/2 inch internal diameter (ID) to more than 8 inches. One of its greatest advantages is its strength; PVC pipe does not kink, cannot be easily crushed and it resists negative pressure. The downside of using PVC is that, unless you use threaded pipe, you will have to prime and cement the pipe, something that is very easy to do but can get very messy and frustrating if you make a mistake!

There are various other materials that can be used in aquarium plumbing but these are much more expensive than PVC (e.g. CPVC, PVDF, polypropylene) and are not necessary for aquarium applications. Some aquarists might be tempted to use cheaper ABS (acrylonitrile-butadiene-styrene) piping, but cheaper versions of this material are primarily used in drains, waste and vent applications, and may contain anti-bacterial/fungal agents that could be harmful in reef aquaria.

Flexible PVC

Flexible PVC hose (aka spa-flex) is available in various diameters from 1/2 to 3 inches ID. Since it is flexible, it facilitates making connections at any angle, creating small bends, and connecting equipment in a non-linear fashion. It is also forgiving of errors in measurement. It offers all of the same benefits of schedule 40 PVC and will withstand negative pressure, but compared to rigid PVC, it is easier to cut, and install. Like rigid PVC, it must be primed and cemented to other plumbing fittings. Flexible PVC is slightly more expensive than rigid PVC, and many stores sell it only in long lengths, however, some hardware stores and on-line vendors sell it in cut-to-order lengths. Flexible PVC hose requires the use of special cement designed specifically to bond flexible PVC to rigid PVC, so be sure you purchase the appropriate type. These cements are designed to remain somewhat flexible when cured so that they can flex with the PVC hose. If you use normal PVC cement, it will be less able to flex and may crack and release over time. Short flexible PVC hose lengths have an obvious curve because the material is sold in coils. Don't fight this set shape; use the curve it already has to your advantage. In general, flexible PVC is more prone to releasing from fittings over time, and we do not recommend its use on the outlets of high-pressure pumps.

Tip: Never force flexible PVC hose over a barb fitting. It is not designed for this type of application; it should be cemented into fittings, not forced over them. Forcing it over a barb fitting may cause the hose to split over time and/or work loose.

Vinyl hose

Flexible clear vinyl hose is commonly used for plumbing connections in canister filters. Most new canister filters come pre-packaged with lengths of clear or green vinyl hose to connect them to the aquarium. Vinyl hose comes in various diameters, from 3/16" internal diameter (ID), commonly used for air supply connections, up to 1 1/4" ID. Vinyl hose is easy to work with, very flexible, cuts easily, and can be fitted over barbed hose fittings and secured with hose clamps. Vinyl tubing has some disadvantages, however. The flexible walls make it kink easily, it collapses under negative pressure, and it crushes easily. These features cause an obstruction of flow that reduces pump output or, if located on the suction side of the pump, destroys the pump altogether. For this reason, larger circulating pumps should not be connected with clear vinyl hose but canister filters and hobby pumps are designed for 1/2 inch or 3/4 inch diameter hose and work fine with it. It is possible to use reinforced vinyl hose, aka Tygon tubing for larger pumps. This type of hose has a weave of nylon threads imbedded in the plastic that affords greater resistance to negative pressure and kinking. However, over time, even this type of hose can collapse or kink.

Use of clear PVC pipe or clear flexible PVC hose

The use of clear PVC pipe is desirable under certain circumstances to be able to observe flow in the plumbing, but for most systems clear pipe is not needed. Any situation where the pipe will be illuminated for any part of the day will lead to the growth of algae in the pipe that will obstruct the view. In small diameter flexible hoses, such as the 1/2 inch translucent soft hose used with submersible hobby pumps or canister filters, the growth of algae can significantly impact the volume of water being pumped. This drop in water flow occurs slowly, and may lead to sudden problems with gas exchange in the aquarium. If such hose must be used, it should be assembled in joined short lengths that can be removed periodically and cleaned with a foxtail brush. However, aquarists often neglect this for extended periods, resulting in a significant drop in circulation. In addition, foxtail brushes are not able to reach beyond a couple of feet, so longer lengths of hose are very difficult to clear of algae growth. To counteract this effect, some companies have produced a vinyl hose for aquariums that is opaque black. While such hose prevents the growth of algae, it eliminates the ability to see obstructions, including detritus and biofilms that still accumulate. These can be cleared with a foxtail brush, or by periodically squeezing the hose along its length while the pump is running. The loosened coating of bio-film will break free and flow into the aquarium.

Use of pool hose with soft cuffs

When wet/dry filters had their surge in popularity in the late 1980's, the use of plastic flexible hoses from the swimming pool industry became popular for conducting the water from the overflow drain to the wet dry filter. These hoses are still used today on some popular commercial filters and by many hobbyists who build their own sumps or filters. While there is nothing wrong with the hoses, and from a design point of view their flexibility simplifies the plumbing, there is one flaw to consider: the soft cuffs that connect these hoses to standard pipe may suddenly split and leak. Leaks occur at stress points (such as where the cuff fits over a pipe) due to the formation of a crack in the cuff when the cuff becomes old and brittle due to the loss of softening agents. Leaks also occur where the cuffs are bonded to the hose. If the use of these flexible hoses is unavoidable, then we recommend replacing them at regular intervals to avoid the potential for a leak. Replacing the hose once per year is sufficient.

Attaching flexible vinyl hoses to hose barb fittings

Pushing a length of flexible hose onto a barbed hose fitting might seem like a simple procedure, and it is. However, to make it an *easy* procedure it is important to soften the end of the hose first by soaking it in hot water. Heat a coffee cup full of water in a microwave oven until it boils. Handling it with care to avoid scalding your skin, insert the end of the hose in the cup for about half a minute and then remove the hose and push it onto the barbed fitting. It is best to have the fitting already installed in place, as it can be difficult to turn with a hose attached! Using the steam released by a tea kettle or rice cooker also works to soften the tubing.

Hose clamps

Two types of clamping devices are commonly used for securing flexible hose on fittings, one made of stainless steel, the other of plastic. The stainless steel variety is best and safest for high-pressure applications (e.g. pump outlets), while the plastic variety is easy to use and suitable for most aquarium hose connections. Use stainless steel clamps that have a stainless steel set screw (not all of them do). Calculate the diameter clamp needed by including twice the wall thickness of the hose in addition to the inside diameter. Check all clamped connections at least twice a year for leaks, corrosion or cracking, and replace as needed.

Use of cemented fittings

Whenever long lengths of pipe or hose are used in a plumbing installation, there should always be places where the connections can be separated so that periodic cleaning of the insides of the pipes can be accomplished. The use of union and threaded fittings makes this task possible, as we explain in the next section. Nevertheless, the use of PVC cement to solvent-bond pipe fittings is common practice for most connections in a PVC plumbing installation since it can withstand higher pressure than threaded joints and it is the surest way to prevent leaks.

Fittings

Fittings are used in aquarium plumbing for a variety of reasons. Their main function is to join two or more pieces of pipe or hose together. They allow for tight turns (e.g. elbows); the joining of discordant sizes of pipe/hose together (e.g. reducers); they allow sections of pipe or hose to be easily disconnected and reconnected (e.g. unions); and they can split pipe/hose into different paths (e.g. tees). There are dozens of fittings available but we will discuss those that are commonly used in home aquaria where pipe sizes of 2" ID or less are normally used.

Pipe fitting styles

The ends of pipe fittings can be one of three types: slip (S), threaded (T) and spigot (SPIG). Slip fittings allow pipe or hose to be directly inserted into the ends and bonded in place with

Every aquarist's dream ... a well-stocked PVC fitting section. J.C. Delbeek

This display and parts department was a nice feature in the specialty aquarium store, *Biotop Aquaristik*, in Germany. J. Sprung

cement. Threaded connectors have male or female ends that, uh, screw together. Fittings that have a threaded outer end are known as male pipe thread fittings (MPT), while those fittings with internal threads are female pipe thread fittings (FPT). A catalog description of a fitting includes these codes to define the type of attachment. For example, a one inch 90 degree elbow may be designated as S x S, which means both ends of the elbow have slip openings. If the designation were, MPT x S, then one end has an external thread and the other is slip. If one end of a fitting is designed to slip inside another fitting then it is referred to as a spigot (SP) fitting; these are found mainly on reducing bushings and elbows. Elbows (90 degree fittings) are called *ell's* and the spigot version of a 90 degree fitting is called a *street ell.*

With threaded fittings, one must use Teflon tape on the male end to prevent leaks and limit salt creep. Threaded fittings used with threaded pipe (aka *nipples*) seems like the best choice because they don't require cement, curing time, and you can put them together and take them apart whenever you need to. However, assembly of threaded fittings requires the use of a pipe wrench to tightly join the fittings, and the fittings may still leak, producing at least some salt creep. Threaded fittings are primarily used to incorporate into a plumbing system equipment such as pumps, protein skimmers, canister filters, UV sterilizers, calcium reactors or anything else that you might periodically need to remove and service. They are also useful for making temporary plumbing connections to test a filtration or pumping system. Of course glued connections are much less expensive to install, and dismantling them is usually quite simple, involving a few cuts only or the use of unions.

It is our recommendation to use cemented fittings for most connections, with some threaded fittings or unions to allow the plumbing to be easily disassembled for cleaning or for moving the set up. Cemented fittings don't leak (when done properly of course!). Using cemented connections also simplifies the task of plumbing, because you only have to buy one type of fitting (slip x slip), not mixed types (slip x thread, bushings, reducers, etc.) that are hard to find and later time consuming to sort out. The goal should be to use as few fittings as possible, keeping in mind that the more fittings that are added, the greater the head pressure becomes in the system, the harder the main pump must work and the lower the flow rate becomes.

Loc-line™ fittings

Loc-line plumbing consists of interlocking plastic pipe segments and fittings that allow the aquarist to create articulated return lines within the aquarium. These can be used to direct outflows in any direction within the tank. There are also various outlet attachments designed to spray water in a wide pattern or to concentrate it in a tight stream. These systems are only for use in submerged situations since they are not leak proof. We discuss these in more detail in chapter 7.

How to apply Teflon tape to threaded fittings/pipe

There are several important rules regarding Teflon tape use. When installing Teflon tape hold the fitting in your left hand, wrapping the tape clockwise around the threads. This way the tape tightens when the parts are screwed together. For threaded fitting connections on the suction side of a pump, or when joining two types of different materials (e.g. PVC and plastic hose barbs) use excess tape (about 10-12 turns) to prevent air suction or water leaks. For other fittings about 6 turns is sufficient.

Loc-line™ fittings, available from pet dealers or from *modularhose.com*, offer many solutions to directing water flow inside the aquarium. Photo courtesy of *modularhose.com*

Wrap Teflon tape clockwise, with the fitting in your left hand. Hold the tape in place with your thumb to begin and pull the tape tightly as you wind it around the fitting. Note the orientation of the tape roller, this position allows you to maintain tension on the tape as you wind it over the threads. J.C. Delbeek

Continue wrapping, keeping the tape taught. J.C. Delbeek

Caution: A thick wad of Teflon tape can stress the walls of the fitting screwed over it. The stressed wall can crack and leak. DO NOT over-tighten fittings. This commonly occurs when fittings are screwed into pump intakes and outlets.

Quick disconnect

Several aquarium suppliers offer quick disconnect fittings that allow for the rapid assembly and disassembly of plumbing lines. These fittings are mainly designed for use with vinyl tubing and allow one to conveniently disconnect intake and return lines between pumps, filters and aquariums for cleaning. When combined with valves they allow for the easy isolation and removal of an external pump without draining a sump or tank in the process. Unfortunately, these fittings come in only a few sizes and are often proprietary designs for use on certain filtration systems. Many of these systems also rely on o-rings that can deteriorate over time or trap small particles, causing leaks to develop.

Bulkheads

A bulkhead converts a hole in your sump or tank into a plumbed fitting that you can use for your filtration system. They come in thread and slip configurations and in a wide array of sizes and styles. Bulkheads allow you to connect pumps to sumps, place returns in tank bottoms and walls, or to create overflows in tank walls.

The most important thing to remember when using bulkhead fittings is the massive size difference between the size of the hole and the size of PVC that you will be able to put into the bulkhead fitting. The size of the bulkhead given only refers to the interior size of the fitting, not it's outer diameter. For example, to install one inch PVC pipe/hose via a bulkhead fitting into your sump, you would first have

A selection of bulkheads reflects the wide range of diversity in design. J.C. Delbeek

This bulkhead was installed improperly, with the gasket on the outside. The salt-creep is a sign of a slow leak. J. Sprung

to drill a 1 3⁄4" hole in the sump and install a 1" bulkhead fitting. This piece of equipment should only be drilled and installed by someone with a fair bit of experience, because you can't *un-drill* a hole in your tank or sump. It is important to drill the hole so that the bulkhead fits in snugly with very little play available. If the hole is too large, the gasket will not sit properly and will be pulled into the hole and distorted as the bulkhead is tightened, causing a leak. Another important consideration when planning where to install the bulkhead is to make sure to allow enough room on either side of the bulkhead for the lip, gasket and locking ring. You must also have enough clearance on all sides to allow for the installation of elbows and to allow you to reach the locking ring easily to tighten it securely.

One common mistake in bulkhead installations is improper placement of the gasket on the fitting. The gasket should be installed between the fixed bulkhead lip and the inside wall of the aquarium, not between the lock nut and the outside aquarium wall. Otherwise, the lock nut can twist and distort the gasket, which could cause it to leak. In addition, putting the gasket on the inside prevents water from passing through the tank wall. If the gasket were on the outside, water would wick along the threads, pass into the hole in the tank wall and be in contact with the bare unsealed surface, which is not a good idea if the tank is made of fiberglass, wood or concrete. Finally, the inner lip of a bulkhead is often not flat; they sometimes have raised areas caused by the way they are made in molds. If you tighten this against the glass, you could crack it; the gasket helps to cushion this.

In some instances, you might want to place the female side (lip) of the bulkhead on the outside of the tank, in order to reduce the amount of space the bulkhead takes up between the tank and a wall. You should put the gasket on the outside in this case, but you would still have the problem mentioned above regarding the water entering the hole and making contact with the material the tank is made from. This is not a problem of course with typical glass or acrylic aquariums. There is also a slight increase in the risk of a leak with a gasket located on the outside, and it may be difficult or impossible to tighten a lock nut located on the inside. If you do such a reverse install of the bulkhead, we recommend using a gasket on both the inside and the outside, to reduce the risk of leaks.

TIP: Do not over tighten the locking ring of the bulkhead. This can distort the gasket, causing it to leak and could, in extreme cases, cause the glass/acrylic to crack.

Selecting the appropriate size bulkhead is often a lot of guesswork mixed with luck. The selection of the correct bulkhead size first requires completion of your tank system design. From this design, you can determine the flow rate required and the height of the water column above the bulkhead. Figure 3a shows how to measure the water column height, (h) for various bulkhead locations.

Based on your system design, calculate the gallons per minute of flow required and the value for h in inches. Using table 3.1, start with your h value, move across the row to the gallons per minute closest to your system flow rate. The bulkhead size will be the column heading I.D. Most overflows designs result in values of h equal to only 0.5 or 1 inches since this is how much the water will rise when it passes over the edge.

As in all systems, the configuration of the piping, including number of fittings, length and pipe size will cause variation in the flow rate

Figure 3a. Water column height (h) for various bulkhead locations.
Source: Steve Jackson, *Aquatic Eco-Systems*, Inc.

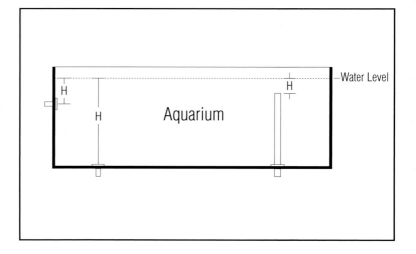

due to friction losses. In addition, the use of Durso standpipes and overflow weirs can alter how much water can pass, with some claiming higher throughputs than should be theoretically possible.

Table 3.1. Bulkhead flow in gallons per minute at constant water column height (h) in inches.

	Bulkhead I.D. in inches					
	0.5"	0.75"	1"	1.25"	1.5	2
h in inches	**Flow (gallons per minute)**					
0.5"	0.8	1.8	3.3	5.1	7.4	13.1
1"	1.2	2.6	4.6	7.2	10.4	18.6
2"	1.6	3.7	6.6	10.3	14.8	26.3
3"	2.0	4.5	8.0	12.6	18.1	32.2
6"	2.8	6.4	11.4	17.8	25.6	45.5
12"	4.0	9.0	16.1	25.1	36.2	64.4
18"	4.9	11.1	19.7	30.8	44.3	78.8
24"	5.7	12.8	22.8	35.6	51.2	91.0
30"	6.4	14.3	25.4	39.7	57.2	101.7
36"	7.0	15.7	27.8	43.5	62.7	111.5
42"		30.1	47.0	67.7	120.4	
48"		32.1	50.2	72.4	128.7	
54"		34.1	53.3	76.8	136.5	
60"		36.0	56.2	80.9	143.9	

* Source: Steve Jackson, Aquatic Eco-Systems, Inc.

Unions

A union allows you to take the plumbing apart, so that it is easy to remove a specific piece of equipment or section of plumbing and can be placed in between a ball valve and a piece of equipment, in between pieces of equipment, or in between all fittings either leading into or out of the tank. Unions have internal diameters of 1/2 inch to 3 inches and greater, and are available in either thread or slip configurations.

For sumps located within a stand or cabinet, it is wise to plan the plumbing to allow the sump to be removed without having to tear the stand or cabinet apart. The use of unions helps make this possible. Be sure to locate them where they are easy to secure, away from cabinet support braces. When you plan your plumbing project, plan the ball valves and unions together so that you can shut off flow to, and remove any piece of equipment from, your filtration system. Alternatively, many plumbing supply stores now offer combination ball valve/union coupling valves known as tru-unions. These combine the functionality of a ball valve with that of a union, they require less cementing and reduce the number of fittings and hence, resistance to water flow. They also shorten the distance between a bulkhead and a pump. Both unions and tru-union valves contain o-rings. These should be carefully checked for particles and cleaned to ensure a good seal. A light coating of silicon grease helps to maintain these o-rings.

Various sizes of slip and thread unions. Note the internal o-ring that must be seated properly when tightening the fitting. J.C. Delbeek

TIP: The orientation of the union can be important! Install unions so that they can easily be unscrewed in the standard counter clockwise fashion. Non-toxic plumber's silicone grease can be sparingly put on the outer threads to keep the fitting easy to unscrew.

TIP: Install the union such that when a pump or piece of equipment is removed, the part of union that holds the o-ring, remains in place. This way, it is less likely to lose the o-ring when moving the equipment or pump out of position for cleaning.

Elbows

Elbow fittings are used where changes are needed in the direction of plumbing such as when returning water over the edge of a tank or turning a corner. There are several types of elbows available of which the 90 degree is the most common. These come in a variety of configurations such as slip x slip, slip x thread or thread x thread. A special type of 90 degree elbow is called a street ell. This has either a slip or thread opening on one end while the other has either a spigot (SPIG) or male pipe thread (MPT). This allows the elbow to be slipped or screwed directly into another fitting reducing the amount of space needed to install it. Reducing elbows are also available.

TIP: Never ever place an elbow fitting directly on the inlet or outlet of a pump, doing so increases backpressure on the outlet and increases head pressure on the inlet, resulting in decreased output and an overworked pump (see *plumbing the pump* later in this chapter).

90 degree elbows come in a variety of sizes.
J.C. Delbeek

45 degree elbows. J.C. Delbeek

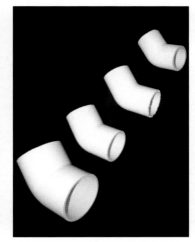

Street ells showing both spigot and male threaded
ends. J.C. Delbeek

PVC couplers. J.C. Delbeek

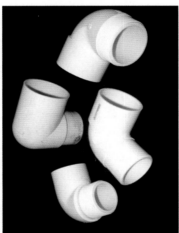

Elbows can also be found as 45 degree fittings and are usually slip x
slip. Forty-five degree elbows are used when only a slight change in
plumbing direction is needed and are useful for directing a
subsurface water return downwards. A common misconception is
that using two 45 degree elbows instead of a single 90 degree elbow
results in a more gentle curve and hence, less resistance. This is not
true at the pipe sizes usually used in hobbyist systems. For example,
one 90 degree 1 inch elbow has the equivalent friction loss of 2.6
feet of 1 inch pipe, while the two 45 degree elbows needed to make
the same turn would have a friction loss equivalent to 2.8 feet of 1
inch pipe i.e. slightly worse.

A third type of elbow is the long sweep. These offer a gentle curve
of 90 degrees and require more room than a normal 90 degree
elbow, but offer much less resistance. Our advice is to use long

sweeps whenever possible, however, long sweeps appear to be more commonly available for hobbyist use in countries outside of North America.

Couplings

Couplers are very simple fittings; they join two pieces of pipe or hose together and come in a variety of sizes. They can be either slip x slip or thread x thread and come in very handy when you discover an error in your plumbing and you need to either shorten or lengthen a section. Couplers allow you to remove the offending section and cement in a new one. Reducing couplings are used to permanently join two different sizes of pipe together. For example, you could join a 3/4" pipe to 1" or 1 1/2" to 3/4".

Adapters

Adapters are similar to couplings in that they allow you to join two pieces of pipe or hose together, but they also allow you to join them to pieces of equipment such as pumps, protein skimmers or filters. There are two types of adapters, male and female as we mentioned previously. The use of male and female adapters together allow for easy joining and dismantling of sections of pipe or hose.

Male adapters have a slip opening on one end and a male threaded one on the other. These are used on the outlets and inlets of pumps, filters and protein skimmers where the male end threads into the equipment and the pipe/hose is cemented into the slip portion. Male adapters also come as reducers where, for example, the male end may be 3/4" threaded and the slip end is 1". This allows you to run larger diameter plumbing directly into or out of equipment without the need for extra fittings. This type of adapter is particularly useful for running large diameter piping right up to the intake of a pump that may have a smaller diameter inlet.

Male adapters. J.C. Delbeek

A variety of female adapters. J.C. Delbeek

A wide variety of tees showing normal, reducing and threaded tees. J.C. Delbeek

An example of how NOT to install a tee fitting, with water entering from the branch instead of the run of the tee fitting on the left. J.C. Delbeek

Female adapters have one slip end and one internal (female) threaded end. These fittings also come as reducers. These are particularly useful on the outlets of pumps that have male threaded fittings and allow you to immediately upsize the plumbing when you exit the pump, reducing backpressure and increasing flow.

Tees

Tee fittings look just like their name. They allow side streams (branches) to be taken from the main plumbing line (run) and come in a variety of configurations. All three openings can be either slip or thread. The branch opening can also be thread while the other two are slip.

The branch opening can also be a reduced diameter than the other two allowing it to act as a reducer; this type of tee is called a reducing-tee.

These are useful when running a side out line to a piece of equipment that may have a smaller diameter inlet than the main line.

One common mistake we often see with the installation of tee fittings occurs when an aquarist wants to split a return line into two streams to feed water to returns at opposite ends of the tank. In this case, the incoming line is fed into the branch of the tee and the outlets are on either end. This causes a great deal of backpressure and results in reduced flow out both ends. The correct way to do this is to take one line from the branch to one outlet and the rest of the water continues through the run to the other outlet. Valves are then used after the tee to control the flow out of each outlet.

The correct orientation for a tee fitting is shown. Water enters from the bottom run and exits from the top run and side branch. Note: reducing bushings were used on the top of the run and the branch to reduce the outlets from 1 1/2 inch to 1 inch ID. J.C. Delbeek

Reducer bushings

Bushings are designed to slip or be screwed into a fitting and reduce its size. They can be male threaded or spigot on the end that fits into the other fitting and slip or female threaded on the other end, and any combination thereof. Reducer bushings are used to allow different sizes of pipes to be used and to allow large diameter fittings to be reduced down to very small openings with a single fitting. For example, a 2 inch fitting could be reduced down to 1/2 inch threaded fitting into which a barb could be screwed to allow a small stream to exit.

Caps and plugs

Cap fittings are just that, they are used to cap or seal an end of pipe. Slip caps simply slip over the end of a pipe and are cemented in place. Threaded caps can be screwed onto the end

Reducer bushings of various sizes and insertion types e.g. thread and spigot. J.C. Delbeek

A variety of caps and plugs. J.C. Delbeek

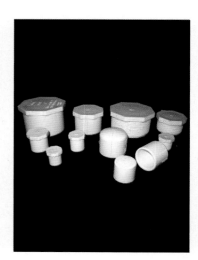

of a male adapter to seal a pipe with the option of removing it and adding something later.

Plugs are similar to caps in that they are used to seal plumbing but in this case, they slip or thread into a fitting. Spigot plugs are cemented in place and are a permanent closure of the fitting. Threaded plugs can be used to temporarily seal a female adapter or a threaded branch of a tee. As with threaded caps, this allows for the addition of equipment or more plumbing later.

Hose fittings

A male hose adaptor connected to a plastic faucet and gate valve assembly can be used to build a drain/fill mechanism that can be connected to a regular garden hose. Since the gate valve on these inexpensive hose faucets has a good chance of leaking some day, it is essential that the connection be made with a ball valve before the faucet fitting. This assembly only works on closed loop recirculating pumps that draw water from the bottom of the aquarium and return it to the aquarium. Put a tee in line before the pump followed by a ball valve on the branch, followed by the faucet fitting. This connection provides a way to quickly drain the tank with a garden hose, or a way to fill it up with a hose connected to a pump located in a remote water-mixing reservoir. A hose adaptor nipple fitting that converts from pipe thread to hose thread could also be used this way with a ball valve, thus eliminating the faucet fitting altogether. The main point here is to eliminate the chore of carrying five gallon buckets full of water!

Barb fittings

Barb fittings are intended for use with vinyl tubing. These fittings provide many of the functions of the fittings intended for PVC pipe/hose such as elbows, couplers, and male and female adapters mentioned above. These are the fitting type most often used by hobbyists. Hose clamps are necessary whenever barb fittings are used to ensure that the tubing does not come off the fitting.

A selection of barb fittings. J.C. Delbeek

There are a myriad of other connectors, adapters, elbows, and couplings available from the hardware store to fit any need you could possibly have. It takes careful planning to make an effective plumbing design and to avoid assembling and cementing parts in the wrong sequence. Time spent researching what will go where and what parts can best be used where will save time and money later on by not having to correct for poor planning. Obviously if you have a 90 degree corner to negotiate with PVC, then use a 90 degree elbow for the job, but there are times when you may need something a little more specific. You can reduce your 1" PVC pipe to a 3/4" fitting in order to put in a piece of equipment with 3/4" fittings, and then enlarge it again to 1" on the outflow side of the filter. You can enlarge your plumbing to fit a pump, etc., etc. … the possibilities are endless.

Valves

Ball valves

Ball valves provide the ability to control the flow through the piping system. Primarily they are used to turn the flow on or off for servicing equipment. They can also be used to control the flow rate by slightly closing them, although gate valves are a better alternative when fine control over the flow rate is desired. When used in conjunction with a separate union fitting, they allow for the easy removal of pumps, chillers, UV sterilizers, protein skimmers, chemical reactors, calcium reactors, etc. for servicing or replacement.

There are various styles and manufacturers of standard ball valves. J.C. Delbeek

A tru-union ball valve. The unions at the top and bottom allow the valve to be closed and the plumbing to be removed from either end. J.C. Delbeek

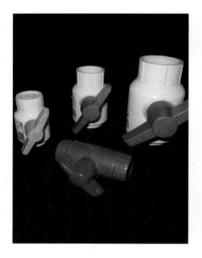

There are various types of ball valves available but not all are created equal in quality. Higher quality valves are more expensive but can make up for their cost in durability and lower replacement rates. Cheaper valves are more prone to developing leaks, especially around the handle shaft, or the ball itself may seize up over time,

making adjustments impossible. Valves that are more expensive usually have removable handles, which can be a nice feature if you want to insure that wandering hands can't easily change your valve settings. Three-way ball valves are also available. These allow the water path to be diverted from one pipe to another by rotating the handle through 360 degrees. These are usually used in conjunction with an actuator (either electric or pneumatic) that will turn the handle automatically, allowing alternating currents to be created in an aquarium by alternating between one of two returns. Such systems are usually used on larger aquariums and are costly. See chapter 7 for more details about them.

Ball valves that incorporate unions are the most effective design since they eliminate the need for separate unions on either side of the valve. Single union valves have a union on only one end of the valve. This allows you to turn off the valve, easily unscrew one end, and remove the piece of equipment attached to it from the system. Tru-union ball valves have a union on both ends of the valve and allow for greater flexibility in removing equipment from a system without having to cut pipes or hoses.

The use of ball valves is common for regulating flow on the pressure side of pumps. However, never control flow through a pump by restricting the pump inlet as this can cause significant damage to the

Gate valves are often used to control protein skimmers due to their fine range of adjustment. J.C. Delbeek

pump and impeller. You should never restrict the pump intake; this is the key to maximum performance for all centrifugal pump designs. Ball valves can be used on the suction side of pumps, but only if the sole purpose is to allow the pump to be separated from it's plumbing to an aquarium or sump. In order to separate sections of plumbing so that they can be easily dismantled and cleaned, ball valves must be positioned to close off water flow in the pipes before the union fitting. Again, tru-union ball valves are best used in these instances.

Gate valves

Gate valves are used primarily in flow control situations where fine adjustment is needed. Instead of a rotating ball inside, they use a sliding gate section that moves up or down depending on which way the valve handle is rotated. This allows for fine control over how much water is let through the valve. Gate valves should be used on the inflow or outflow of a protein skimmer where small changes in water flow can have a large effect on the water level in the skimmer. Ball valves simply do not allow for the fine range of adjustment that gate valves provide. In addition, gate valves do not become jammed by calcium carbonate deposits, while ball valves sometimes do.

Valves on drains

While it might seem like a good idea to have a ball valve on an overflow drain, in general this is not necessary (since the drain will empty anyway when the power is shut off). Furthermore, using a valve to restrict the flow in a drain sets up the potential for blockage of the drain. Snails, fish, anemones, algae, etc. may wander over the overflow and into the drain, resulting in a blockage, which could lead to the tank overflowing as the entire sump gets pumped up to the display aquarium.

Check valves

The use of check valves to prevent backflow in pipes with outflow below the water surface is unreliable for permanent operation of a reef aquarium display. The principal reason is that failure of such a check-valve system can result in a flood that would damage the aquarium stand, the floor, the carpet, anything on the floor, electrical appliances, the ceiling of the apartment below and its floor, and the ceiling of the apartment below that (depending on the size of the tank). This damage is aside from the loss of life to the aquarium inhabitants that may be left high and dry. The failure of check valve systems is inevitable since they rely on proper seating of a ball, flapper, or other device, and a perfect seating will eventually be prevented by the growth of biofilms, tube worms, sponges, etc. that occurs in the plumbing in reef aquariums. Another type of failure called *hammer* occurs when the fall of water due to gravity closes the check valve, and recoil of the falling water opens it up again. A cycle of closing and opening proceeds, releasing a little water with each cycle and producing a hammering sound. Bottom line: It is very easy to design plumbing systems without check valves, so this problem is best avoided by design.

Check valves are also sometimes used for keeping prime in pumps located above the water level from which they draw. In this situation, the failure of the check valve would eventually cause the pump to run dry.

When installing a check valve, be sure to orient it properly. On the outside of the valve there is an embossed arrow indicating the direction the water should be flowing through the valve. Always orient a check valve vertically. Otherwise, it may not seal completely when the flow stops. Finally, check valves should be located as close as possible to the outlet of a pump to lessen the chance of rattling

Check valves are used to prevent back flows. Shown here is a range of sizes of ball check valves. An internal PVC ball settles on the fitting inlet when the flow stops, sealing the opening and preventing backflow. J.C. Delbeek

noises caused by the ball or flap vibrating within the housing, to maximize static head pressure, and to ensure a good seal when the pump stops. Placing the check valve close to the pump outlet also prevents a large amount of water being released from the line when the pump is removed. Placing the check valve before the pump is also possible, but if the pump is removed, water can flow back out through the check valve. In addition, if the check valve breaks, fragments can be drawn into the pump, damaging the impeller or causing the pump to seize-up.

Pump selection

Of course, no plumbing job is complete without a pump. The pump is the heart of any plumbing system and supplies water to the aquarium as well as any additional equipment attached to the tank. A properly selected water pump can make or break the plumbing design and a poorly designed plumbing system can have a significant impact on how well a pump will function.

Types of pumps

There is two types of pump designs commonly used in marine aquariums: the direct drive and the magnetic drive. Direct drive pumps have a motor with a central drive shaft that has an impeller attached to the other end. The impeller sits in a watertight housing with a water inlet and outlet. A seal is required on the shaft between the housing and the motor to prevent leaks. Unfortunately, this is also the weak point in this design as the seal eventually wears and begins to leak, requiring it to be replaced. Good quality direct drive pumps require new seals every few years, while inferior pumps require replacement more frequently. Another drawback is that direct drive pumps transfer a lot of heat from the motor to the water via the drive shaft. Direct drive pumps are not commonly used by hobbyists but are commonly used on larger systems such as those found in public aquariums, aquaculture facilities or marinelife wholesale facilities. Direct drive pumps can range in size from 1/2 horsepower (HP) to over 30 HP! If you plan to purchase a direct drive pump, make sure that the shaft seal is designed to withstand exposure to saltwater.

Magnetic drive pumps are by far the most common design used in home aquariums. In this design, the motor shaft is attached to a large magnet with a hollow core. The pump housing is designed so that this magnet can fit around a depression in the housing. The impeller is then attached to a smaller magnet that slides over a small shaft inside the housing depression. As the outer magnet turns, the inner magnet is also forced to turn, spinning the impeller and pushing water through the outlet of the pump housing. In this design, water never encounters the outer magnet, and heat transfer from the motor

In a direct drive pump the impeller is connected to the motor by a drive shaft. J. Sprung

A magnetic drive pump has an impeller attached to a magnet that rotates around a fixed-position shaft. J. Sprung

to the water is effectively reduced. This does not mean that this design does not generate heat; it does, due to the friction of the moving magnet on the shaft in the housing.

Powerheads work by a similar principle. These have a coil imbedded in epoxy that effects a field around the impeller magnet that causes it to turn. This coil becomes hot however, so a submersible installation heats the water a lot- much more than a direct drive type pump or external magnetic drive pump. The coil heat of an externally mounted magnetic drive pumps also heats the water, but not as much since the heat is also dissipated to the air.

Pump installation

Location

Most pumps used in the hobby operate on the basis that they will be pushing water upwards, not pulling water upwards. What this means is that if the pump is located above the water source, it won't be able to pull water upwards to the intake when first started. Pumps that can do so are called self-priming, if you do not have a self-priming pump, then you must place the pump below the water level of the supplying water body i.e. the main tank or the sump. Although it is possible to start a non-self-priming pump by sucking on the discharge line, this often results in a mouth full of saltwater and a mess on the floor, walls and your clothes. In addition, if the power fails for any reason, the pump will loose prime, the impeller housing will fill with air and when the pump restarts it will run dry, damaging the impeller and housing. The use of a check valve can help to maintain prime in such an installation, but as we already explained, it will eventually fail. Therefore, it is important that the intake of the pump must be below the water of the supplying body of water.

Keep in mind access to electrical outlets when situating your main pump. Most pumps come with a fixed cord length and you need to insure that the cord can reach the outlet. It is also a good idea to leave enough cord to allow a drip loop to be formed. This means that the cord has a loop in it such that if any water were to run down the cord it would drip off the bottom of the loop instead of running directly down the cord into the pump motor housing or into the electrical outlet causing an electrical short. If the pump cord is too short, have an electrician add a longer cord.

In most installations, the main circulation pump is located below the tank, attached to a sump. However, some people do not like the noise of pumps, filters and falling water in the same room as the tank, and elect to move the entire filtration and pumping system into another room or even another floor of the home. This certainly has its benefits but the extra distance puts a greater burden on the pump and this must be taken into consideration when purchasing the right pump for the job. We discuss this in more detail in the next section.

Wherever the main circulation pump is situated, it needs to be properly supported. This usually consists of a small block of Styrofoam, neoprene rubber padding or similar material. This padding acts to cushion the pump, decreases vibrational noise, and protects the base of the pump from the occasional water spill. Remember to factor in this padding when determining the pump inlet height when situating any bulkheads that will supply it.

Tip: Old neoprene compruter mousepads are great sources of these cushions.

Plumbing the pump

The most common way to plumb a main pump to a system is to draw water from the sump via a bulkhead. In some cases smaller, submersible pumps are placed directly in the sump. These pumps work fine for smaller systems but have the drawback of adding heat directly from the motor to the water since it is submerged. For this reason, externally plumbed pumps should be used whenever possible.

When establishing where to place a bulkhead in the sump one must consider several things before drilling any holes. The bulkhead, whenever possible, should be situated such that the path from the bulkhead to the pump intake does not require any right angle turns. All too often, we have seen elbows located directly on the inlet or outlet of a pump. Installing elbows in these locations increases resistance, reduces flow rates and hinders the operation of the pump. If elbows cannot be avoided then you should use the largest size elbow you can fit into the space allowed, along with the largest bulkhead and piping.

This brings us to the next point, which is to never restrict the intake of a pump by using valves or by using pipe diameters smaller than the intake of the pump. In fact, you should always try to maximize the intake pipe size and not restrict it until the point at which it actually enters the pump via a reducing fitting. The reason for this is that the larger diameter allows for less resistance and hence a greater flow rate. For example, if we had a flow rate of 420 gallons per hour, then using 100 feet of 1/2" pipe would be like trying the push the water up a height of 43 feet, while 100 feet of 1" pipe would be the equivalent of raising the water only 3.2 feet, a substantial difference in resistance! Therefore, always maximize the intake line size so that you never restrict the intake of the pump, and thereby reduce its capacity. In extreme cases, if the pump intake is severely restricted air bubbles can form and collapse within the pump head, causing damage to the impeller and/or pump. This is called cavitation. Cavitation can also occur if the head pressure on the outlet of the pump is too low. Lastly, maintain as long and straight a distance as possible between the sump and the intake of the pump. This reduces the turbulence of the water at the intake of the pump caused by water entering the bulkhead in the sump; this again maximizes flow rates by reducing friction within the pipe.

The easiest and safest way to determine the location to drill a hole for a sump bulkhead is to first assemble the plumbing between the intake of the pump and the sump, and attach it to the pump. This includes all piping, fittings and valves. Next place the pump on its support padding, move it into the planned position and place the open end of the plumbing against the sump wall. Using a small carpenter's level, ensure it is level and then outline the pipe opening with a marker on the sump wall. This will give you a close approximation of where to drill the hole for the bulkhead. Small variations in height can be compensated for by adjusting the thickness of the support pad. The use of flexible PVC on the intake side of the pump also allows some flexibility in placing the pump and allows for some margin of error when drilling the bulkhead hole in the sump.

Valves and fittings

As we mentioned, a ball valve and union should always be used on the inlet and outlet of the pump, this allows for easy removal of the pump without losing water. The order should be: bulkhead - ball valve - union - pump intake. On the pump outlet, the order should be: pump outlet - union - ball valve. By closing, both ball valves and unscrewing the unions you can remove the pump without losing water from the sump or tank. As mentioned previously, the use of tru or single union ball valves allows for even greater flexibility and ease of use, and require fewer parts to be installed. These should be used whenever feasible.

Intake Strainers

Protecting the pump is a concern when pump intakes are located in areas where debris, tank inhabitants or algae can be sucked in and severely restrict the pump intake. Strainers are designed to prevent these objects from entering the intake and should not be confused with sponge filters that can rapidly clog and restrict flow; these should never be used on the intake end of a main pump. Intake strainers generally are not designed to be water filters (requiring frequent cleaning), but rather pump protectors and usually consist of large pore plastic mesh. The greater the surface area the strainer provides, the lower the flow rate across its entire surface and the less chance of trapping objects or organisms. When properly designed, intake strainers should not restrict flow but only prevent the entry of foreign matter into a pump. The general recommendation is that the strainer screen surface area be a minimum of one square foot for every ten gallons of water per minute pumped (Aquatic Ecosystems, Tech Talks).

A strainer can be easily constructed by using a section of PVC pipe 25 to 50% larger in diameter than the size of the bulkhead intake. Select a fitting type that will allow you to insert this pipe into the bulkhead and then cap the other end of the pipe. Using a circular hole saw, drill several holes in the pipe to achieve the necessary surface area. Then using large pore plastic mesh, wrap a piece around the pipe and fasten it with plastic cable ties. This gives you an easily removable strainer for your pump intake. Commercial strainers are also available in a variety of sizes. Avoid using the small plastic strainers that often come packaged with small bulkheads, these are inadequate for high flow rates and foul quickly. Regardless of the type of strainer you select, it must be kept free of fouling organisms and should be cleaned on a regular basis. Failure to do so will result in reduced pump efficiency, higher electrical costs and in severe cases, pump damage.

Choosing the right pump

Most hobbyists give very little thought to pump selection other than to look at how many gallons/liters per hour the pump can supply. Unfortunately, a pump's flow rating gives you very little information as to whether or not it is suitable for your application, it is a starting point at best. The flow rate given for pumps is the maximum rate they can produce when pumping water up a minimum distance, usually one foot. The distance a pump is required to send water vertically is known as the head pressure (see definition below). Some pumps are designed to give very high flow rates but only at very little head pressure, while other designs are designed to give medium to high flows at various head pressures. The flow rate you wish to have through the plumbing system [volume (gallons/liters) per hour or volume (gallons/liters) per minute] is the most important factor you need to determine for your system. This is followed in importance by the total head pressure. You need to know the flow rate through the system before you can determine the total head pressure. Once these two factors have been determined, then a pump can be selected that will best meet the demands of the system.

TIP: The pump(s) used to exchange water between the aquarium, sump and filtration components, should not be solely relied upon to create water motion in the main aquarium. Use powerheads or high-flow pumps plumbed on a closed recirculating loop to achieve more flow. This avoids wasting electricity to fight head. The exchange between aquarium and sump can be as low as 1 to 3 turnovers per hour.

TIP: Protein skimmers offer variable resistance to flow, so they often need periodic tweaking. It is best to use a dedicated pump for the protein skimmer instead of running it off your main circulation pump.

Calculating total dynamic head pressure

Head pressure refers not only to the vertical distance a pump must push the water, but also any resistance to flow created by pipes, fittings and valves. Therefore in order to calculate the *total* dynamic head (TDH) pressure you need to consider not only the vertical distance the water needs to be moved but also the pressure that results from the resistance of piping/hoses, fittings and valves to water flow.

TDH = vertical (static) head + friction loss head due to pipe + fittings + filters + valves + other restrictions to flow.

One common mistake made in determining vertical discharge head is to measure the vertical distance from the intake of the pump to the surface of the aquarium. This is not correct, it should be measured as the distance from the top of the water level of the sump to the top of the aquarium water surface. The height of water in the sump creates pressure on the intake of the pump, thereby helping it to move water upwards.

If you were drawing water directly from the tank, then the vertical discharge would be the distance from the surface of the water in the tank to the height of the return. In most cases where the returns are just below the surface, the total vertical head is 0, which means there is effectively no back pressure on the pump from water in the pipes. There is still, however, back pressure due to friction of the pipe/hose, fittings, valves and filtration equipment that needs to be accounted for.

If you are returning the water to the tank below the surface, you need to add this distance below the surface to the vertical head pressure since the pump has to work against this water height as well. As we just mentioned, in most hobbyists systems this is usually only a few inches, and is insignificant in the overall design and can be ignored. However, if the returns are a foot or more below the water line then this does need to be taken into account by adding that depth to the vertical head pressure.

Once you have determined the vertical height the pump must push the water, you need to decide what the flow rate will be through the system in order to calculate how much head pressure is added by the plumbing, valves and fittings. This is because the greater the velocity the more friction that is created. In looking at tables 3.2 and 3.3 it is clear that the larger the pipe diameter, the greater the flow it can handle. This is why it is important to use the largest pipe size possible from the main pump to the tank returns and/or other pieces of equipment. For most hobbyist applications, schedule 40 1 1/4 or 1 1/2 inch ID pipe would be the ideal choice, giving a wide range of maximum flows from 120 to 3600 gallons per hour and offering from four to almost ten times less resistance than 1 inch pipe.

Once you have determined the pipe size and flow rate you will have, measure the total length of piping in the system, in feet and round up to the nearest foot.

The next step is to add up all the fittings you will be using and then use table 3.4 to determine how many additional feet of pipe

Figure 3b. Sample system for total dynamic head calculation.

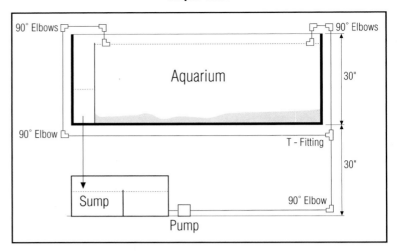

these would represent; add this to total length of piping. Ball valves will need to be treated somewhat differently. Generally, most commercial ball valves have schedule 80 internal diameters when fully opened, therefore simply measure the length of each ball valve used and add them together, then use table 3.4 to determine the effective head loss for that length of schedule 80 pipe for that ID ball valve

Once you have determined the total length of piping and the equivalent length of pipe represented by the fittings and valves, add them together. The next step is to determine how much friction head is created by this length of pipe. Using table 3.2, find your targeted flow rate in gallons per hour, or the next highest number. Follow the table to the right until you reach the column that represents your pipe ID. The value there is the friction head created by one foot of pipe of that ID. Multiply this number by the number of feet you calculated and this will give the total equivalent head for your system. Add this number to the vertical head and you have your total dynamic head.

If the diameter of the return line is reduced at any point, add a number of head-feet to your calculation equal to the percentage of reduction. If, for example, you've calculated a head pressure of ten feet in a 1 inch pipe and you then decrease the diameter of the pipe to 3/4 inch, add 25% or 2.5 feet to your head pressure (http://www.aquariumpros.com/articles/headpress.shtml).

Table 3.2. Friction head in feet per foot of schedule 40 PVC pipe of various internal diameters, at various flow rates in gallons per hour. * Modified from: Harrington Plastics Co.

Gallons per hour	1/2"	3/4"	1"	1 1/4"	1 1/2"	2"
60	0.02	0.005				
120	0.04	0.01	0.01	0.001	0.001	
300	0.23	0.06	0.02	0.004	0.002	0.001
420	0.43	0.11	0.03	0.01	0.005	0.001
600	0.82	0.20	0.06	0.02	0.007	0.002
900	0.42	0.13	0.03	0.02	0.005	
1200	0.72	0.22	0.06	0.03	0.008	
1500		0.33	0.08	0.04	0.01	
1800		0.46	0.12	0.06	0.02	
2100			0.16	0.07	0.02	
2400			0.20	0.09	0.03	
2700			0.25	0.12	0.03	
3000			0.31	0.14	0.04	
3600				0.20	0.06	
4200					0.08	

Table 3.3. Friction head in feet per foot of schedule 80 PVC pipe of various internal diameters, at various flow rates in gallons per hour.* Modified from: Harrington Plastics Co.

Gallons per hour	1/2"	3/4"	1"	1 1/4"	1 1/2"	2"
60	0.04	0.009				
120	0.08	0.017	0.009	0.002	0.001	
300	0.45	0.097	0.03	0.007	0.003	0.001
420	0.83	0.18	0.05	0.012	0.06	0.002
600		0.34	0.10	0.023	0.01	0.003
900		0.72	0.20	0.049	0.02	0.006
1200			0.35	0.083	0.04	0.011
1500			0.52	0.13	0.06	0.016
1800			0.73	0.18	0.08	0.025
2100				0.23	0.11	0.03
2400				0.30	0.14	0.04
2700				0.37	0.17	0.05
3000				0.45	0.20	0.06
3600					0.29	0.08
4200						0.11

Table 3.4. Equivalent length of various internal diameter thermoplastic pipe in feet. * Modified from: Harrington Plastics Co.

Fitting/Valve	1/2"	3/4"	1"	1 1/4"	1 1/2"	2"
Gate valve (fully open)	0.7	0.9	1.1	1.5	1.7	2.2
Ball valve (fully open)	Same as an equivalent of schedule 80 pipe					
90 degree elbow	1.6	2.1	2.6	3.5	4.0	5.5
45 degree elbow	0.8	1.1	1.4	1.8	2.1	2.8
90 degree sweep	1.0	1.4	1.7	2.3	2.7	4.3
90 street ell	2.6	3.4	4.4	5.8	6.7	8.6
45 street ell	1.3	1.8	2.3	3.0	3.5	4.5
Tee (flow through run)	1.0	1.4	1.7	2.3	2.7	4.3
Tee (flow through branch)	4.0	5.1	6.0	6.9	8.1	12

Example: We have setup up a 72 gallon aquarium with two 1 inch returns located at opposite ends of the tank. The tank is 48 inches long and 30 inches tall and the sump is located in a cabinet below the tank. We would like a flow rate of 350 gallons per hour through this system.

Using figure 3b, we will determine the total dynamic head for this system. This is a relatively simple system used to circulate water through the tank from the sump. The piping used to and from the pump is 1 1/2 inch ID schedule 40 PVC. There are five 1 1/2 inch schedule 40 PVC 90 degree elbows and one tee fitting. There are two 1 1/2 inch tru-union ball valves. The returns are reduced to 1 inch ID when they enter the water; therefore there are two 1" ID 90 degree schedule 40 elbows plus 2 x 6 inches of 1" ID schedule 40 PVC pipe, which represent the returns.

The vertical (static) head for this system is determined by measuring the distance from the operating water level in the sump to the surface of the water in the tank, a distance of 4.5 feet.

(1) SH = 4.5 feet

We measure a total plumbing length of 5 feet + 3 feet + 0.5 foot of 1 1/2 inch schedule 40 pipe = 8.5 feet. There is an additional 0.5 feet of 1"= inch schedule 40 PVC pipe. Using table 3.2, we find that 350 gallons per hour is not on the table so we round up to 420 gallons per hour. At 420 gallons per hour, there would be a friction head loss equivalent to 0.005 feet for every foot of pipe. Using our total pipe length of 8.5 feet we get:

(2) 1 1/2" pipe friction head loss = 0.005 x 8.5ft = 0.04 feet

We repeat the above steps for the 1 inch pipe and get:

(3) 1" pipe friction head loss = 0.03 x 0.5ft = 0.015 feet

Therefore the total friction head loss due to piping is:

(4)   (2) + (3) = 0.055 feet

We now need to add the fittings into our calculation. Using table 3.4, we see that one 1 1/2 inch schedule 40 PVC 90 degree elbow is equivalent to four feet of 1 1/2" schedule 40 PVC pipe. We have five such elbows therefore:

(5) Total equivalent length of 1 1/2 inch sch 40 pipe = 5 x 4ft = 20 feet

Using the frictional head loss of 1 1/2 inch pipe from (2) we find:

(6) Frictional head loss for five 1 1/2 inch elbows = 20 x 0.005 = 0.1 feet

Repeating the above steps for the two 1 inch elbows we get:

(7) Frictional head loss for two 1 inch 90 elbows= (2 x 2.6) x 0.3 = 1.56 feet

Therefore the total frictional head loss for the elbows is:

(8)   (6) + (7) = 1.66 feet

Now we need to calculate the frictional head loss caused by the two tru-union 1 1/2 inch ball valves at a flow rate of 420 gallons per hour. From table 3.4, we see that this head loss is equivalent to an equal length of schedule 80 PVC pipe. Each ball valve is 8 inches in length, therefore:

(9) Frictional head loss of two 1 1/2 inch ball valves = $\dfrac{(2 \times 8) \times 0.06}{12}$ = 0.08 feet

The last fitting is the tee fitting. From table 3.4 we see that the flow rate through the run causes less frictional head loss than the flow rate though the branch. Using tables 3.4 and 3.2 and repeating step 6 for each part of the tee we get:

(10) Frictional head loss through the run = 2.7 x 0.005 = 0.014 feet

and

(11) Frictional head loss through the branch = 8.1 x 0.005 = 0.044 feet

Therefore the total frictional head loss caused by the tee fitting is:

(12)   (10 + (11) = 0.058 feet

Add up all of the above to find the total dynamic head for the example system.

(13) Total Dynamic Head (TDH) = SH + (4) + (8) + (9) + (12)
                              = 4.5 + 0.055 + 1.66 + 0.08 + 0.058 = 6.35 feet

However, we are not quite done. Recall that the pipe size is reduced just before it enters the water from 1 1/2 inch to 1 inch ID. Therefore, we need to add 33% or 3.3 feet, which represents the head pressure incurred by the pipe reduction. Therefore the final TDH is:

(15) Final TDH = (13) + 3.3
              = 6.35 + 3.3
              = ~10 feet

If you plan to have the main pump run other equipment such as canister filters, UV sterilizers or any other piece of equipment that will offer additional resistance then you should add from 2 to 10 feet of additional head pressure depending on the type of equipment.

For a more detailed explanation of head pressure and calculations to determine head pressure due to frictional loss, we highly recommend Dr. Pablo Escobal's excellent book *Aquatic Systems Engineering: Devices and How They Function.*

Finally, the American website, www.reefs.org contains a Microsoft Excel spreadsheet that was developed by Dr. Sanjay Joshi, Nathan Paden and Shane Graber (Joshi *et al.* 2003). This spreadsheet allows you to enter the number, type and size of fittings and piping used and it will make all the necessary calculations to determine total dynamic head pressure for the system. Another American website, www.reefcentral.com contains an online head loss calculator that allows you to determine head loss by inputting details of your plumbing system and pump type: http://www.reefcentral.com/calc/hlc2.php. These resources greatly simplify the process of calculating the flow characteristics of a system, allowing for proper pump selection.

Pump curves

Now that we have done this tedious exercise, where is the payoff? It comes when you go to select a pump to run your system. In our example, we found that we need a pump that can deliver 420 gallons per hour (7 gallons per minute) at a head of 10 feet. This is where the pump curve provided by the pump manufacturer becomes of use. Reefs.org contains a useful table of pump types available to the American hobby along with all their specifications and pump curves at http://reefs.org/library/pumps/.

Each pump has its own relationship between head and flow rate, depending on the design of the pump, and this information can be gleaned from its pump curve. For any pump, the flow rate will reduce as the amount of head increases. A pump performance curve is a graph that shows you how much water a pump can push at any given head pressure. Figures 3c and 3d show typical pump curves for two common aquarium pumps. The aim is to find a pump whose curve meets the needs as outlined by the total dynamic head pressure calculations and the desired flow rate. From the example above, it can be seen that the Iwaki would come the closest to meeting the need for 420 gph at 10 feet of head pressure.

When choosing a pump it is acceptable to select one that is slightly more powerful than required. However, if the head pressure of the

Figure 3c. Pump pressure curve for a Little Giant 3 MDQX-SC water pump. Source: Aquatic Ecosystems

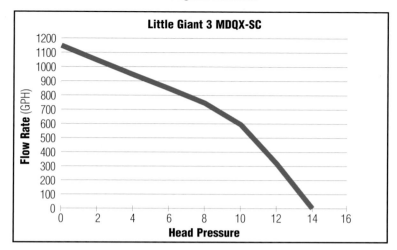

Figure 3d. Pump pressure curve for an Iwaki MD/WMD 30-RXT. Source: Aquatic Ecosystems

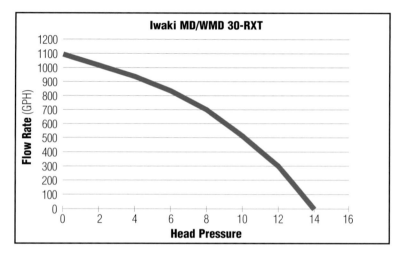

system is too low compared to the flow rate (i.e. the head pressure lies well below the curve at any given flow rate) then the pump will operate at a much higher flow rate and draw more electrical current than normal; a situation known as motor overload. This leads to an electrically inefficient situation and eventual damage to the pump. The answer, which may seem counterintuitive, is to increase the head pressure on the pump by throttling down the flow from the outlet using the outlet valve or another restriction. Pumps are rated for the electrical current (measured in amperes (A)) they should normally draw, and this is usually indicated on the pump or in the documentation accompanying it. Using an ammeter, you can check if your pump is drawing the correct amount of electrical current. If the amperage reads too high then you need to throttle down the pump to achieve the proper amperage and water flow rate.

Several companies handle water pumps in a wide range of sizes. Most of these have websites and/or catalogues that provide detailed pump curves for all the models they handle e.g. Aquatic EcoSystems Inc. in the United States. Such companies can also offer you advice as to which pump model they carry is best suited to your application.

Pump noise

Before settling on a pump, it is useful to check how much noise the pump produces. A certain pump model may meet your pumping needs but may prove too noisy to use in the living- or bedroom. Look for the same model already in operation on an aquarium and judge for yourself if the noise level is acceptable. Intrusive pump noise can be reduced by use of an insulated aquarium cabinet or by locating the pump away from the main aquarium.

Planning the design

Once you think you know where all the equipment will permanently sit, what size pipe you are going to use, as well as what fittings and valves you will need, you should sit down and draw up a plumbing design of exactly what it should look like. It seems like a simple step but we have found this is where most people tend to get careless and problems develop later on in the process due to poor sketches and an inadequate parts list. By drawing out what you want to do beforehand, you will get a feel for the overall layout and suitability, what parts you will need and how many of each type. Using this design, make a shopping list of all the needed parts and their quantity. Check that a couple of times against your design, and then head to the hardware/plumbing store to purchase everything.

A common misconception is that an effective plumbing design is one that uses all sorts of fittings and turns to snake plumbing around all kinds of obstacles while allowing for the maximum number of accessories to be added. While these feats of plumbing ingenuity may impress family and friends, nothing could be further from the truth. The more turns and fittings you use the greater the friction in the system and the greater backpressure that is created. This increases head pressure in the system and means your main water pump must work harder, reducing flow and efficiency. Truly effective plumbing designs use as few fittings as needed to allow for easy disassembly and avoids sharp turns whenever possible.

Once you are satisfied with the plan and purchased your supplies, the next step should be to layout the fittings in the pattern that you want to assemble them. At this point, you may discover any errors in your design or in your estimation of the number and types of parts you need. It is always better to find this out before you begin cutting and cementing. It is also at this time that you should plan in what order you will assemble the pipe and fittings. An error here can result in a lot of cursing and cutting and re-cementing. That's why it is always best to have a few coupler fittings of the appropriate diameter on hand. These allow you to cut and insert new sections or remove fittings that were put in the wrong place.

Cutting PVC pipe

Rough cuts in PVC can be made using a simple hacksaw but for the neatest cuts a set of PVC pipe cutters of the size appropriate for the pipe you are working on give the cleanest cuts. Once the pipe is cut, make sure it is square on the ends. If the cut is slightly off that is acceptable but sharp angles need to be redone. If you have never used PVC cutters before it's a good idea to practice on some scrap pipe until you can consistently produce a clean, square cut. After cutting pipe, it is a good idea to bevel the cut end using some sandpaper or a beveling tool designed specifically for this purpose. The reason for this is that when PVC pipe is cut with either a PVC cutter or a hacksaw, the cut end often has a raised edge or burr that makes insertion into a fitting difficult and can affect the seating of the pipe into the fitting. This burr can also wipe cement away when the pipe is inserted into the fitting. Use sandpaper to remove the burr.

Measure pipe lengths accurately, not only the distance between the fittings but also the distance inside the fitting that the pipe will extend. When cutting pipe it is sometimes better to cut the lengths slightly longer than you think you will need. This allows for some error in measurement. It's much easier to shorten a pipe that is too long than it is to make a short pipe longer! The final thing that should be done before cementing, which most people never seem to have the patience for is to pre-fit all the pipe and fittings before actually cementing anything together to check fitting placements and pipe lengths.

Cementing PVC pipe and fittings

Once you have cut and pre-assembled your plumbing and are happy with the layout its time to start cementing. Although many people give little thought to the actual act of cementing, several tricks can be employed to help make cementing a more pleasant and quicker task.

First, a word about PVC cements. There is a wide variety of cement on the market, some are designed for high-pressure applications, some are designed to dry quickly, some take several hours, and some can even be used in wet environments. Make sure you read the label of any cement very carefully and make sure it is safe to use with potable water. Such cements are intended for use in systems that handle drinking water and are therefore non-toxic once dried. There are also cements used for rigid pipe only and others that are intended for use with both rigid and flexible PVC tubing. Again, read the label carefully and check to see what materials the cement can be used on and what the recommended drying time is. If in doubt ask a sales clerk and explain that you plan to use the product in an aquarium. Light-bodied, clear cements (e.g. #710) can be used for schedule 40 pipe and fittings up to 5 cm (2 in.) in ID. Clear, medium-bodied cement (e.g. #705) is used for schedule 40 pipe up to 15 cm (6 in.) ID, while gray, heavy-bodied cement (e.g. #711) is used for schedule 80 pipe and fittings through 20 cm (8 in) ID and schedule 40 fittings and pipe from 15-20 cm (6 to 8 in.) ID. Finally, extra-heavy-bodied, gray cement (e.g. #719) is used for all schedule sizes over 20 cm (8 in) ID, however, it can be used for smaller sizes of schedule 40 and 80 as well, giving a very secure bond.

TIP: PVC cement has a shelf life of about two years. Always check the manufacture date before you purchase or use a can.

TIP: Never use thinner with PVC cement; it will make it less effective. If the consistency of the cement has changed from the condition it was in when you bought it, discard it.

A good selection of PVC glues and applicators can be seen here, be sure to select the proper glue for the job. J.C. Delbeek

Before cementing, make sure that the surfaces to be cemented are free of grit and grease. Wipe the pieces to be cemented with a clean dry cloth then apply the PVC primer. The primer acts to clean and soften the PVC making for a more secure bond with the cement. Once you have applied primer to both the outside end of the pipe and the inside of the fitting to be cemented avoid touching these surfaces again. Next apply liberal amounts of cement to both surfaces then quickly fit them together. As you insert the pipe give a slight quarter turn twist as you push the pipe in as far as it will go, then hold it for 30 seconds. The twisting action helps to seat the pipe cleanly into the fitting and spreads the cement evenly around the joint. As the cement sets, it may expand slightly, pushing the pipe out of the fitting; that is why you should hold it in place for 30 seconds or so until the cement can begin to set up. Wipe off any excess cement from the pipe, including the bead or ring of glue that will accumulate at the end of the joint. This bead does not strengthen the joint and may actually soften the pipe in that area. However, in our experience, leaving the bead in place has not resulted in any problems in standard hobbyist applications. Remember to apply enough cement to coat the entire surface of the fitting and the pipe, and let the cement cure on ALL of your plumbing parts before pressurizing.

Set and cure time
Set time is the amount of time required before you should handle or move the cemented portion, while cure time is the time required before the joint can be pressurized. This curing time allows the bond

to achieve its full strength and reduces the amount of volatile organic compounds that enter the water. Cure and set times vary with type of cement, temperature and operating pressure so always follow the PVC cement manufacturer's recommendations.

CAUTION: Cements and primers contain highly volatile solvents, make sure you avoid inhaling the fumes and always use them in well-ventilated areas or use fans to pass air over the work area. ALWAYS KEEP PVC CEMENT AND PRIMER OUT OF THE REACH OF CHILDREN.

Wear safety goggles to protect your eyes from splashes of primer and cement, and gloves to protect your hands. Finally, place newspaper or other disposable material under the work area to catch any drips or spills.

Securing the plumbing

Whenever you have long runs of pipe/hose vertically or horizontally, securing it becomes very important in order to avoid stress on fittings and equipment connections, to reduce vibrations and movement, and to prevent sagging of the plumbing. Several different clamping systems made of metal, plastic or fiberglass can be used to secure your plumbing.

Pipe clamps

Very simple pipe clamps can be used. These U-shaped clamps have a flange on one or both sides of the U with holes by which the clamp can be fastened using screws to the tank cabinet or a wall. They come in a wide variety of sizes to accommodate any size of plumbing. The drawbacks are that they must be unscrewed in order to remove the pipe and there must be room to use the screwdriver, but they do provide a very secure hold.

Click hangers

Click hangers are usually made of plastic and are mounted using a single screw through the center of the device. An adjustable ring that can be opened allows for easy insertion of the pipe after the hanger has been secured to the cabinet or wall. This allows for easy removal as well. These also come in a variety of sizes to accommodate various sizes of pipe or hose but are not as secure as the previous clamp type.

Channel lock and pipe straps

Fiberglass channel material that can be cut in any length can be used to secure large diameter pipes or run multiple lines parallel to each other. This material, called channel lock, requires some drilling and cutting to use but offers a very secure method for holding plumbing lines. Pipe straps are slid into the channel and then tightened around the pipe to hold it very securely in place.

U-shaped pipe clamps offer very secure fastening of PVC pipe. J.C. Delbeek

(right) Clik-hangers allow for the easy removal of pipe without the need for screwdrivers. J.C. Delbeek

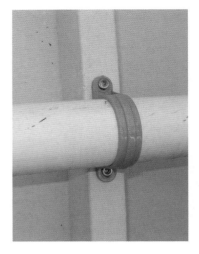

Using channel lock on the wall, several pipe straps can be used to fasten a wide variety of plumbing sizes at once. J.C. Delbeek

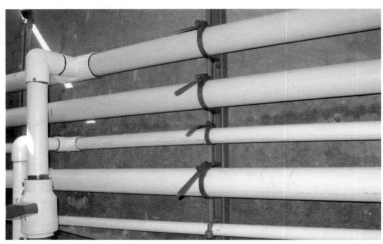

(above) A variety of pipe clamp styles and sizes are available. J.C. Delbeek

Subsurface returns

At this point, we need to briefly discuss the location of the pump return. If your pump return is located below the surface and you are using a sump, when the pump shuts off a siphon will start, passing water from the tank down to a sump, draining the tank and potentially overflowing the sump. If the return is just below the surface, and the sump is designed to handle the excess volume, then this is not a problem. However, if your return is low in the water column or your sump volume is small then you need to modify the return to prevent back siphoning. This is easily accomplished by drilling one or two small holes in the return line just below the surface. When the pump stops, water will be sucked through these holes until air begins to be sucked in and the siphon breaks. Of course, if the holes become plugged by filamentous algae, coralline algae, or salt creep they will not act as siphon breaks, so these holes need to be cleared as part of a monthly maintenance routine. Systems that use closed loop circulation filtration and water motion systems, and forego a sump, do not have the potential for back siphoning problems. As we described earlier in this chapter, we don't recommend the use of check valves to prevent back siphoning.

Testing the system

Once the whole system is plumbed and the cement is cured, make sure all the screw fittings, unions, pumps and valves are tightly secured. Next, fill the tank with tapwater and start the circulation pump(s) to check for leaks. Check every connection and fitting for a drop of water. Water gushing somewhere would be easy to spot, but it is more likely to flow out slowly, so let it run for several hours. There will be at least one or two leaks. If there are leaks, drain the water, and fix them. Do another leak check. Once ALL of the leaks are fixed, fill the tank with tap water again, and turn on all of the pumps and run the entire system for 24 hours. This last step helps to remove any volatile organics aka *fumes* from the PVC cement. In addition, you may find that the pumps produce many bubbles, drains produce slurping noises, or the sump might overflow when the power is shut off. These issues can be resolved before you set up the tank. Excessive bubble generation might be coming from the overflow drain, from the outflow of a protein skimmer, it might indicate pump cavitation, or it could simply be a low water level in the sump.

TIP: When a pump is running, leaks after the outlet drip, while leaks at or before the inlet connection suck air. Fine air bubbles from the pump return may indicate a leak before the intake of the pump.

It is normal for the water flow to be a little noisy at first. After saltwater is added to the system, within a week or so the pipes will accumulate a slimy biofilm inside that will reduce the sound. Your ears will also have become acclimated to the sound by that time as well. It is possible to reduce the sound further by installing pipe insulation over a noisy section.

Electrical do's, don'ts and considerations

Very often, little consideration is given to the design of the electrical supply for reef aquariums. The common trend is to just plug equipment into wall outlets, add a power strip or two when more outlets are needed, and hope for the best. Very little consideration is given to the actual electrical current, power and voltage that aquarium equipment requires and how these will affect the electrical circuits where the aquarium will be located, particularly in older homes. Not only does it make sense to first determine the electrical needs of your equipment, it is critical to ensure the safety of your family and home. Knowing the electrical usage of your aquarium also helps in determining the annual electrical operating costs.

Lights, pumps, filters, and monitoring/controlling equipment all require power. A poorly planned electrical system can compromise the most sophisticated aquarium set up and is a safety risk for the home. In the left photo, note that a powerfilter is positioned dangerously over an electrical outlet. In the photo on the right, a large number of electrical cables are plugged into numerous outlets on powerstrips located in an unsafe position behind and below the aquarium. J. Sprung

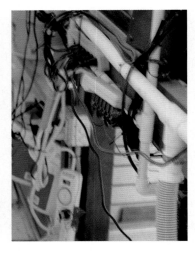

For any aquarium installation, but particularly large ones and/or ones that will employ a lot of lighting and pumps, consulting with a qualified electrician should be your first step. Only they can determine whether your electrical system can handle the load you plan to add, and whether the wiring and electrical outlets present in the location where the tank will be located is adequate. Although aquarium hobbyists love the do-it-yourself nature of the hobby, when it comes to electricity one should always consult with a qualified electrician to ensure what is planned meets the local electrical code and will not end up causing a fire!

It is common knowledge that electricity and salt water can be a deadly combination. However, we are often *shocked* to see the state of some electrical wiring or lamp installations. In the following sections, we will offer several tips on how to avoid some of the common mistakes made by hobbyists when it comes to the installation of electrical devices around saltwater.

Cable management systems

Just as there are systems for guiding and securing plumbing, there are similar methods that can be used to manage the electrical cables. The computer industry and hardware stores are sources for numerous handy devices that make the management of large numbers of electrical cords a snap. Without such aids, the aquarium cabinet becomes a scary, dangerous, and ugly tangle of wires.

Wiring

Electrical wiring is a crucial component of any electrical system. If you plan to construct your own lighting system be sure to consult with an electrician as to what type and thickness of wiring is required for your particular application. Even some commercial aquarium lighting

The effects of high heat, salt air and inadequate wiring are evident in these two pictures of a failed metal halide pendant fixture. J.C. Delbeek

systems we have seen have used inadequate wiring internally. The wires become brittle and their insulation crumbles within a short period due to the high heat and UV wavelengths inside the fixture, and the moisture content of the air found around aquariums corrodes the exposed wires. Proper wire gauge is necessary for high intensity metal halide fixtures. We have seen transformers catch fire when the wrong gauge of wire was used.

Location of power strips and outlets

We have seen reef aquariums set up and maintained with the utmost care and on a budget that would be the envy of some small countries but with electrical connections and power cords installed in a completely haphazard manner. The electrical supply (outlets or power strips) should never be located where water might drip or spray onto it. The use of a drip loop (see drawing) is common practice to prevent water from flowing along an electrical cord into the power outlet or into a piece of electrical equipment such as a pump.

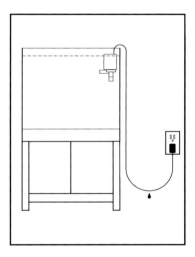

Figure 3e. A so-called *drip loop* prevents the possibility of water running along an electrical cord and into an outlet. Any water running along the cord will simply drop down at the bottom of the loop.

It is common practice to locate an aquarium next to a wall and to have the electrical outlet behind the aquarium stand. This is acceptable in many cases, but if the aquarium has a hang-on-the-back power filter or overflow, there is a significant risk that water will someday spill directly onto the outlet. It is therefore wise to locate the aquarium, overflow or power filter in such a way that this cannot happen. Ideally, electrical outlets could be placed much higher than the aquarium water surface, or the aquarium and the electrical outlets could be located a safe distance from each other such that there is no chance of aquarium water encountering the outlets.

Ground fault interrupter (GFI)

Although every home uses circuit breakers and fuses to protect against electrical fires, these devices are designed to protect equipment and are too slow to protect people from electrical shocks. This has lead to the development of the ground fault interrupter (GFI) outlet. The use of GFI outlets is required by electrical code under certain situations, particularly where water is near the electrical outlets. These outlets contain built-in electronic circuit breakers that are much faster (10 milliseconds) than mechanical circuit breakers, they trip immediately when there is a surge of electrical current, interrupting the flow of electricity. Thus, GFI's are commonly used around aquariums, where they have no doubt saved a few lives.

These devices are, however, very sensitive and even momentary power surges in the electrical mains can cause them to trip. This presents a serious problem for reef aquariums because the cessation of power can lead to suffocation of the aquarium inhabitants. Several options are available to avoid this scenario. One option is to locate power supplies far from the aquarium and high up where water cannot reach them. Another is to employ a battery back-up system to run essential water circulating devices for at least ten hours to prevent the depletion of oxygen during the night, when photosynthesis in the aquarium stops releasing oxygen.

Emergency power and disaster preparedness

The high density of life in reef aquariums rapidly consumes oxygen from the water in the event of a power failure, particularly in a dark room. Battery backup devices can offer hours of air or water pumping, depending on the system, and the batteries can be recharged when the power comes back on. In addition, long-term power outages necessitate preparations for maintaining temperature (heating or chilling), depending on location and time of year. Durso (2002) offers a wealth of useful suggestions for building an emergency backup power supply to keep your aquarium living when the electricity is out, as well as many helpful suggestions regarding temperature control. We summarize some of the information here, along with our own experience.

Battery operated pumps

Provided temperature is within the normal range, the least expensive and most practical emergency backup system that will by itself keep your aquarium's inhabitants alive for days, is a battery operated air pump. These are must-have items for every reef aquarist. Durso (2002) recommends the Penn-Plax *Silent Air* Model B11 that uses one or two D size batteries. With two D batteries it can operate continuously for nearly 5 days. It has another useful feature: it turns itself on when it detects the AC power has gone out. Similar battery-operated air pumps must be manually turned on when needed. These pumps are quite powerful but don't have the capacity to pump very deep, so they are best suited for average sized aquariums; large aquariums will need stronger pumps.

In a slightly more expensive but convenient option, Otto Aquarium Products makes two models of battery backup air pumps (SA 9500 and SA 11000) that are plugged into a normal wall AC outlet and automatically switch to DC (battery) power when the power is out. The battery recharges when the power comes back on, an advantage that justifies the higher cost. The larger unit also has a strong pumping capacity.

Battery backup systems

Inverters
An option for backup power is to use DC/AC power converters, a.k.a. *inverters* that are available from hardware and home electronics stores. They can be connected to a 12V car battery or, preferably, to higher capacity boat (a.k.a. marine) batteries. Inverters can be used to power one or more small water pumps and/or an aquarium heater. They can also be connected directly to a car cigarette lighter, providing power to an air pump for unlimited air while transporting animals over long distances, or, during extremely lengthy power outages (e.g. after a hurricane), they can be used to power the equipment in a home aquarium using a car parked in the driveway or garage. Another option during a long power outage is to periodically use a running car to charge a few batteries. This way, there is always a spare battery to connect with an inverter to power the aquarium equipment.

Caution: If you connect the inverter to a running car, or use the car to charge other batteries, don't leave the car running in a closed garage where carbon monoxide fumes would collect, and don't forget to put the parking break on. Also, keep an eye on the car to be sure no one steals it! Of course be mindful of children who might be tempted to drive it.

Uninterrupted power supply (UPS)
The use of uninterrupted power supply (UPS) *battery backup* systems is a common practice with computers, and the technology is easily adapted to the maintenance of life support systems in aquariums. However, most computer UPS systems are designed to keep the computer running for a few minutes only, to give the user enough time to save the work and shut down. Such a small capacity UPS will not help an aquarium. The UPS must have sufficient capacity to power a small pump for several hours. UPS batteries are typically rated for 3-5 years or 200 complete full-load discharge cycles if the batteries have been maintained within manufacturer

specifications. When the battery fails, it may be less expensive to purchase a new UPS instead of replacing the battery. Durso (2002) offers additional information regarding the utility of the different types of UPS units. In general, for most aquariums it is better to invest in battery operated air pumps, DC/AC power inverters, or a generator. One nice feature of a UPS is that it automatically switches on when the power is off, keeping a pump working continuously without the need to manually switch its power supply on. A UPS does this flawlessly of course until its battery fails.

Automatic switching using an inverter

One may produce a similar effect, though in this case for a backup pump that is otherwise off when the power is on, by using a relay switch connected to the home electrical outlet and to an inverter connected to a marine battery. The relay switch must be the type that is open (i.e. off) when the power supply is on, and closed (which completes the circuit) when the power supply is off. An emergency backup pump plugged into the inverter's outlet will thus be switched on automatically when the power supply to the house is off. This set-up will work flawlessly until either the relay fails (which won't happen for a long time) or the pump fails (which is possible if it becomes encrusted and resists starting).

A DC/AC power inverter can be a real life-saver! Used with a relay and battery it can automatically power an air pump or small magnetic drive pump for many hours or days. Photo courtesy of *Northern Tool and Equipment company.*

Peace of mind may be bought with a quiet, liquid propane powered generator connected to the electrical panel of your house. A switch automatically starts the generator when there is a power outage. Photo courtesy of *Northern Tool and Equipment company.*

Important notes: the wires between the battery, relay switch, and inverter must be heavy gauge, like automotive battery cables. The conversion of 12V to 120V means the inverters draw a lot of amps! In addition, keep the wire runs short, and oversized, to avoid voltage drop and even heavier compensating loads. To keep the battery charged, use an automotive trickle charger. Although the general concept is quite simple and the parts are readily available, one should consult a licensed electrician regarding the parts selection, design, installation and maintenance of such a battery backup system.

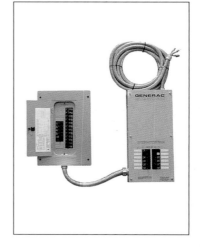

It is also possible to use a powerful 12V air pump with a large AC/DC wall transformer obtainable from a home electronics store. Connect an automatic trickle charger to a boat battery, with a relay in line with a parallel power run to the air pump (so that the AC/DC transformer doesn't charge the battery and the pump doesn't draw from it). This configuration could run for days, with capacity to pump air in one or several aquariums (with a gang valve to distribute the air).

Generator

Long-term power failure from hurricanes, earthquakes or other natural disasters requires the use of a generator to supply power to run the pumps and chiller (or heater, if necessary). Your investment in a reef tank probably justifies the purchase of a small, gasoline or natural gas-powered generator for emergencies. Durso (2002) compares the advantages and disadvantages of the different types of generators commonly available, as well as maintenance considerations. In general, a gasoline-powered generator is the best option. It is important to mention that a generator must not be run in an enclosed basement. All internal combustion engines produce carbon monoxide gas that would fill the basement area and enter the house, a very unsafe condition! A generator must therefore be located outside.

Temperature

As we discussed in chapter 2, temperature is critical to the survival of the aquarium's inhabitants. When the source of electricity is out, particularly in the middle of summer or winter, the temperature of the aquarium can quickly drift too high or too low. As long as the ambient air temperature is between 21 and 27 °C (70 and 80 °F), emergency temperature control measures need not be taken.

When the power is out in a warm climate, the ambient air temperature around the aquarium may exceed 32 °C (90 °F), and this presents a need for cooling. The application of evaporative cooling by means of a small electric fan powered by a UPS or inverter would work well for low humidity environments, but not so well in a very high humidity environment. An alternative is to place a block of ice in a plastic bag and float it in the aquarium, replacing it as often as needed.

In cold climates, if the ambient air temperature during a power outage is above 60 degrees, the use of typical aquarium heaters powered by a DC/AC power inverter will be sufficient to maintain the water temperature within the normal range for a reef aquarium. It may be necessary to insulate the aquarium during a power outage by surrounding all sides with Styrofoam sheets and blankets. If the top is covered, be sure that there is an air input into the aquarium to provide adequate exchange of oxygen and carbon dioxide. Heaters should be moved from the sump to the main display aquariums, to conserve the heating effect where it is needed.

Whatever your power backup system is, don't wait for disaster to strike to see if it works. Try a few test runs on a weekend or when you have the spare time to be sure your system will work. It is especially important in regions that experience extreme seasonal weather conditions such as hurricanes, typhoons and tornados, to test the system monthly during these seasons to confirm it is in perfect operating condition.

Power requirements for a typical reef aquarium

There is no disguising the fact that reef aquariums are power hogs. Lighting systems, pumps, heaters and chillers all require vast amounts of electricity and this results in high operating costs. More energy efficient pumps, chillers and lighting systems are beginning to appear on the market (e.g. power compact and T5 fluorescent lights, thermoelectric chillers, electronic ballasts and variable speed pumps), but the fact remains, reef aquariums are expensive to operate. In some regions, adding a reef aquarium can double or even triple the monthly electrical bill. Several online calculators allow you to estimate how much it will cost per month and per year to run your aquarium (e.g. http://www.reefcentral.com/calc/tank_elec_calc.php). By entering how many Watts each piece of equipment uses, how long you run each piece per day and what the hourly cost of electricity is in your area, you can determine the total cost of running your system per year.

Lighting

High intensity lighting systems can easily reach over 1000 Watts (W) in total. Depending on the wiring in the area you wish to place the tank, you may need to install a dedicated electrical circuit for just the lighting. Again, consulting with an electrician is advisable, especially when working with large systems that will require larger pumps and a chiller as well.

Unshielded bulbs

As part of the urge to build systems as economically as possible many hobbyists elect to install their own lighting fixtures into the hood above the aquarium. This usually consists of a couple of metal halide lamps screwed into a mogul base with a sheet of polished aluminium behind it along with a handful of fluorescent lamps, all screwed into the lid of the canopy. In some cases, even bare tombstone ends are used with the fluorescents instead of waterproof end-caps. While certainly cost effective, such arrangements are also very dangerous. We have seen setups where the bulbs and ballasts

A shard of glass is clearly seen lying on the glass shield of this 250 W metal halide fixture. The metal halide lamp was in service for only two weeks when the outer envelop broke and this shard was created. If the fixture had not had a shield, the shard would have fallen into the tank. Ultraviolet light measured under the unit increased by 20 % as measured by an *Apogee* UV meter. J.C. Delbeek

were heavily spotted with dried salt from previous spills and splashes. Saltwater splashes can easily drench such setups and cause electrical shortages, imploding lamps, and even fires in poorly designed systems. In situations where the lamps are of the double-ended variety and no protective shielding is used, large amounts of ultraviolet light emitted from the lamp can cause eye damage and will rapidly degrade any material exposed to it. It is not uncommon for metal halide lamps to shatter unexpectedly. Without a shielded fixture these shards will fall in the tank, and in an open topped system, fly into the room.

Lighting systems should always be shielded by the proper materials to prevent excessive ultraviolet light from reaching the aquarium or the aquarists eyes, and to block any splashed or spilled water from reaching the lights and electrical wiring. Failure to do so may even void any home insurance policies you have.

Ballast location
With lighting systems, it is also common for the associated electrical ballasts to be housed in the same canopy or inside the aquarium stand where they are susceptible to being wetted and exposed to salt-laden air. This is also a recipe for disaster. Ballasts are best located apart from the aquarium in a separate water-poof enclosure where they can be protected from water, and their heat can be easily dissipated without adding to the heat load of the aquarium. An electrician can specify the proper ballast enclosure for you.

Chiller installation and electrical requirements
Many hobbyists install chillers on their systems to help compensate for location (i.e. outdoor aquarium), the use of high intensity light and several pumps (or large pumps) that can add heat to the water. As we mention in chapter 4, placing a chiller in the same location as the sump and plumbing is counter-productive since the heat output of the chiller will heat this space and the water in it. Either place the chiller in a location away from the water path or install a strong ventilation system to remove the heat as quickly and efficiently as possible.

Chillers are tremendous power users and as such careful consideration should be given to the wiring and electrical system that supplies them. A dedicated electrical circuit may be required depending in your present wiring system. In some cases, a dedicated 220 Volt line may be needed so that you can use a 220V version chiller that draws a lower amperage (typically 40-50% lower than a 110V configured chiller).

It is a peculiar feature of some chillers that when given an electrical supply just slightly below their requirement, they may operate (i.e. you see the display illuminated and hear the fan motor turn on), but not chill the water. This can be remedied by giving the chiller a dedicated circuit with the proper capacity. Furthermore, chillers that are maintained properly (i.e. regularly cleaning the condenser grill, keeping the system properly charged with refrigerant) will run more efficiently and consume less electricity than poorly maintained ones that will actually draw more electricity.

Pump considerations

After the lighting and chilling systems, water pumps are the next major electrical users in a reef aquarium. Aside from making it more efficient in moving water in your system, properly sizing your main water pump can actually save you money on your electrical bill. A pump that is oversized or does not have enough back pressure on it will actually draw more electricity than normal, costing more in operating costs in the long run.

Table 3.5. Typical electrical requirements for metal halide lights and chillers.

Equipment	Current (Amps)	Voltage (Volts)	Wattage (Watts)
metal halide	1.5	120	175
metal halide	2.1	120	250
metal halide	3.4	120	400
metal halide	8.4	120	1000
1/4 HP chiller	5.4	115	621
1/3 HP chiller	7.2	115	828
1/2 HP chiller	9.5	115	1092.5
3/4 HP chiller	4.8	230	1104
3/4 HP chiller	13	115	1495
1 HP chiller	7.2	230	1656

Table 3.6. Electrical usage of the equipment on a typical 250 gallon reef aquarium setup.

Equipment	Current (Amps)	Voltage (Volts)	Wattage (Watts)
400 W metal halide	3.9	115	400
400 W metal halide	3.9	115	400
28 W power compact FL	0.24	115	28
28 W power compact FL	0.24	115	28
28 W power compact FL	0.24	115	28
28 W power compact FL	0.24	115	28
Iwaki 100 RLT pump	3.4	115	380
1/2 HP Chiller *	9.5	115	1092.5
Octopus controller	0.05	115	6
Gemini Powerhead	0.1-0.3	110	11-33
Powerhead for calcium reactor	0.04	115	5
Eheim 1060 for skimmer	0.43	115	50

Using the online calculator at ReefCentral.com, the maximum monthly electrical cost for running this system would be $226.22 at a rate of $0.16/KWH.
* Since it is difficult to know how often a chiller is active per day, a 24 hour/12 month a year maximum was assumed in calculating the monthly electrical cost.

Other electric considerations

Induced currents and grounding probes

Fluorescent bulbs produce induced voltage because of their relatively large surface area, the fact that the entire bulb length has an ionized gas within it radiating at 60 Hz, and it is close to the aquarium. Thus, we can measure induced voltages in our aquarium from them. The effect of metal halide lamps is different, owing to the distance of the lamp from the water surface and its smaller size. Electric pumps, power lines, heaters, and other electrical devices also produce induced voltage. A reference giving empirical data collected from a typical reef aquarium can be found on the Internet at the following URL: http://www.aquarium.net/1298/1298_3.shtml.

The use of *grounding probes* to draw the induced voltage out of the aquarium has been discussed in numerous articles in the aquarium literature and online. The design is quite simple, involving just an exposed tip of titanium wire sealed into a probe inserted in the water, with the titanium wire connected externally to copper wire that is connected to the grounding screw of an electrical outlet. The commercial introduction of this simple device was associated with numerous articles suggesting that poor appetite, erratic behavior, and head and lateral line disease in fish could be attributed to *stray voltage*. The use of grounding probes anecdotally was reported to cure these problems. An alternative view of the effects of grounding probes can be found online at the following URL: http://avdil.gtri.gatech.edu/RCM/RCM/Aquarium/GroundingProbes.html.

A good analogy is given at this site, which illustrates the different effects of voltage and current. We modify it slightly here to describe something actually witnessed (J. Sprung, pers obs.): Birds that sit on electrical power lines can be in direct contact with 10,000 volts, but are unharmed. If a bird sitting on an upper line is positioned directly over another bird sitting on another power line, and they contact each other, the moment they do a current will pass through the body of the lower bird, killing it instantly while doing extreme damage to the feet of the bird above it. After a loud *pop!* one observes two birds falling, one dead and smoking the other with contorted feet, but alive and breathing heavily. It is the current, the flow of electrons that does harm or kills, not the voltage, which is merely the potential energy. Adding a grounding probe to an aquarium provides a current path that did not already exist. A fish passing between the source of voltage and the probe will experience an electrical current, which can't be a good thing. Induced voltages and currents are usually small and therefore not an issue for the safety of the aquarist or the health of the aquarium's inhabitants. With a grounding probe, however, the situation for the aquarium inhabitants could be made worse, considering the creation of a current path.

Physical and Chemical Parameters of Reef Aquarium Water

The goal of achieving a successful reef aquarium is controlled by physical and chemical limits that characterize the reef environment. This chapter covers the important parameters and the technical devices, system design considerations, and maintenance routines employed to maintain these parameters within appropriate limits. When we discuss the most important parameters for a reef aquarium, often the focus of attention is the live stony corals. Therefore it is important to clarify this point and make a distinction between what's important for reef building corals compared to what is important for other creatures, such as fishes, shrimp, algae, or sponges. Fortunately, their physical and chemical needs often overlap.

Temperature
Temperature is the most critical physical parameter for captive reef systems. If all other parameters are ideal, but the temperature is not, the reef will not thrive. The temperature in reef aquariums should be maintained between 22-27 °C (72-80 °F) for the best results, and kept as stable as possible. In our experience, the center of this temperature range, 23-25 °C (74-78 °F), is ideal. If the temperature varies plus or minus one or two degrees Fahrenheit during the course of the day, this is not a problem. Wide fluctuations can be harmful though, especially to the fishes' health, since temperature fluctuations are commonly associated with the incidence of *Cryptocaryon irritans* (saltwater *ich*) in aquariums. Marshall and Clode (2004) show a maximum calcification rate at 25 °C (77°F) for the corals *Galaxea* and *Dendrophyllia*, but that is for specimens acclimated to a specific temperature range. Other research shows the temperature of maximum calcification rate varies depending on the local normal temperature.

Scleronephthya sp. on a deep reef slope in the Solomon Islands. J. Sprung

Our *high* temperature limit of 27 °C (80 °F) for reef aquariums might seem strange to anyone familiar with coral reefs in tropical seas. In the natural setting, the most diverse coral reefs have water temperatures between 28 and 32 °C (82 and 87 °F) for several months of the year. Following the logic that *Mother Nature knows best*, Shimek (1997, 2000) proposes that a temperature in this range is best for captive reefs. Our experience with aquariums has demonstrated that the temperature in a closed aquarium should not be maintained near the natural thermal tolerances of corals; on the contrary, it should be maintained significantly lower. The reason for this is due to more than one effect.

Our recommendation to maintain reef aquariums at cooler temperatures assumes that the goal is to maintain a diverse population of corals, other reef life and fish in a stable environment that promotes their long-term health with minimal risk of disease or accidental suffocation. Reproductive cycles in fish and corals involve cues that include temperature. High temperature in combination with longer day lengths and salinity changes trigger spawning in the natural environment and in aquariums. Fish spawning does not cause any problem in a closed aquarium. However, coral, anemone, tridacnid clam, sea cucumber, sea urchin and snail spawnings, in other words a mass reef orgy, which commonly occurs in the wild during the warmest months, can be a major problem for closed system aquariums. The release of gametes into the water rapidly consumes oxygen, poisons the tank, clogs the filters, or causes the protein skimmer foam to collapse, among other things. While sexual reproduction of delicate marinelife such as corals and tridacnid clams sounds like a wonderful event for the captive aquarist to pursue, it is not something that can be safely managed in a typical closed system aquarium. This is just one of the risks involved in maintaining high temperatures. Captive sexual reproduction of corals and other invertebrates is best pursued in a farming situation under controlled conditions and with large volumes of water or the ability to remove the animals from the spawning tank. However, we should add that keeping temperatures at a lower level and/or constant, does not guarantee that spawning will not occur. For example, bulb-tipped anemones, *Entacmaea quadricolor*, and giant clams, *Tridacna gigas*, have spawned in a display at the Waikiki Aquarium despite being kept at a constant temperature of 25 °C (77 °F). However, this display also receives natural sunlight and moonlight, and it may be that temperature is not as important a cue for these species as it may be for corals. While studying coral spawning events in the western Pacific, Penland *et al*. (2004), confirmed that corals living at essentially the same temperature year round spawned in response to solar insolation. Thus, maintaining a constant, lower temperature in aquariums cannot be considered the definitive means of preventing mass spawning. Furthermore, no study has been made to determine if there is a threshold temperature that inhibits spawning. It is nevertheless probably true that mass spawning can be limited by keeping the temperature cool and constant while at the same time maintaining a constant annual photoperiod and light intensity that is below typical maxima for these parameters.

The principle difference regarding temperature between the natural environment and the aquarium has to do with oxygen availability. As the water temperature increases, the amount of oxygen the water can hold decreases. The difference in oxygen saturation at 26 °C (78 °F) compared to 29 °C (84 °F) is not much, about 6%. However, the increase in water temperature causes a much more significant issue, the increase in metabolism, and consequently respiration, of the life (bacteria, algae, microorganisms, corals, fish, etc.) in the aquarium. The increase in respiration also rises sharply as the thermal tolerance of an

A section of the 20,900 L (5500 gal) Barrier Reef exhibit at the Waikiki Aquarium, Honoulu, Hawaii. J.C. Delbeek

The affect on water quality is evident in this photo of a spawning event. The tank had to be flushed with seawater for 24 hours to remove the gametes and clear the water. J.C. Delbeek

animal is approached. This increase in metabolism associated with increase in temperature happens in the natural environment as well, but there it is not as critical as in aquariums because of the ratio of water volume to mass of life. In a closed body of water (i.e. an aquarium), high temperature increases the demand for oxygen while at the same time the solubility of oxygen is decreasing. This effect is pronounced because the water from which the oxygen is being drawn is of a small volume. Furthermore, at night when there is no photosynthesis to replenish oxygen in the water, both plant and animal life consume and deplete dissolved oxygen. Theoretically, this problem can be remedied by exposing as much of the water surface to air or pure oxygen as possible in the shortest period. A pressurized contact chamber for rapidly increasing oxygen content in the water is another fix for a deficient oxygen level caused by high temperature (see Burleson, 1989). Such feats of engineering are not necessary if one simply avoids letting the temperature get too high. Modern *natural aquarium* designs employing reverse daylight photosynthesis (RDP) provide photosynthetically generated oxygen into the display at night, tending to prevent a major drop in oxygen levels. This simple design promotes a healthy aquarium environment across a broader range of temperature than systems that don't employ it.

Aside from the connection between temperature, oxygen, and respiration, there are other problems associated with high temperature. Research on coral bleaching has repeatedly shown that when temperatures exceed the natural temperature extremes by as little as 1 or 2 °C (2 to 3 °F) for relatively short periods of time (a few days only), bleaching and subsequent death in corals can occur. For example, summer temperatures in Fiji normally run up to 28 °C (82 °F) but stay there for only a few months of

An entire reef in Pacific Harbor, Fiji, contained mostly bleached corals in 2000. The bright pastel colours are due to the absence of zooxanthellae that normally mask these coral pigments. B. Carlson

the year then drop back down to the low 20's (70's) in the winter. In January 2000, water temperatures began to rise above 28 °C (82 °F) in Fiji, reaching as high as 29 °C (84 °F) and briefly 30 °C (86 °F) in some areas. These temperatures resulted in extensive coral bleaching and mass coral death throughout many of the rich coral reefs of Fiji beginning in March and extending into June of that year (E. Lovell, pers. comm.).

Fernando Nosratpour, assistant Aquarium curator at the Birch Aquarium at Scripps in San Diego, reports that the temperature in his Indo-Pacific reef tank ranges from 25-28 °C (77-83 °F) but is only at 28 °C (83 °F) for one week in the summer. However, if the temperature rises to 28.9/29.4 °C (84/85 °F) for ten days or more then signs of bleaching begin to appear in the corals (F. Nosratpour, pers. comm.).

In our experience, the incidence of rapid tissue necrosis (RTN) and other bacterial diseases that affect corals also increases with increasing temperature. Recent scientific research on coral disease supports our aquarium observations. A newly discovered non-virulent species of *Vibrio* bacteria, *Vibrio coralliilyticus*, becomes virulent at just 2 °C (3 °F) above normal water temperatures and causes complete tissue loss in *Pocillopora damicornis* (Ben-Haim and Rosenberg, 2002; Ben-Haim *et al.* 2003). Ben-Haim and Rosenberg (2002) showed that when corals were inoculated with the bacterium at 20 and 25 °C (68 and 77 °F), no disease appeared after 20 days, but that 100% of the tested fragments showed disease and died at 27 and 29 °C (80.6 and 84.2 °F) after just 16 days (the rate was slightly faster at 29 °C than 27 °C). The corals of Curacao, Netherlands Antilles, normally spawn at temperatures of 29 °C (84 °F) during the spawning season. To induce spawning in

A close-up view of bleached corals in Beqa, Fiji, 2000. B. Carlson

a closed system, Dirk Peterson of the Rotterdam Zoo, simulated the natural temperature cycle of the specific location where the corals were collected by slowly raising the tank temperature over several months. He found that when the temperature reached 28 °C (82.6 °F) an outbreak of Dark Spots Disease occurred, a disease that normally occurs in Curacao at temperatures well above 28 °C (82.6 °F) (Gil-Agudelo *et al.*, 2004). Peterson concluded that conditions within the aquarium might have contributed to this outbreak since the daily temperature fluctuated more than 4.5 °F (3 °C) and may have created a more stressful situation for the corals (D. Peterson, pers. comm.).

It is acceptable to allow a reef aquarium to become warmer temporarily during the warmer months of the year [e.g. a maximum of 28 °C (82 °F)], bearing in mind that this presents the risk (or benefit, depending on your goals) of stimulating reproduction in the corals or other marinelife. We caution against allowing rapid temperature increases, large increases and sustained high temperatures for more than a few weeks out of the year. If an aquarium is run close to the thermal tolerance of corals, then any equipment malfunction or other change resulting in a slight increase in temperature could lead to bleaching or disease outbreak.

We have also had the opportunity to observe the effects of high temperatures and wide temperature fluctuations on corals, other invertebrates, and fishes maintained in outdoor aquariums under natural sunlight (J. Sprung, pers. obs.). As the temperature exceeded 30 °C (86 °F) many corals bleached and died, even when shaded, but some bleached and recovered, surviving for up to two weeks even at daily maximums during the daylight period approaching 35 °C (95

A section of the outdoor Edge of the Reef exhibit at the Waikiki Aquarium. B. Carlson

°F), before they were removed from the aquarium. Most fishes tolerate this extreme heat as long as it occurs when algae are producing oxygen, keeping the water saturated. At night, when the aquariums are not blasted by the sun the oxygen level is compensated by a temperature drop to 27 °C (80 °F) or lower. This experience demonstrates tolerance levels for hermit crabs, serpent stars, snails, a few corals, and various fishes. It is not clear why these temperature fluctuations did not produce disease in the fishes. In any case, we mention this only to record our observation of what is possible, not what we recommend for long-term stability. These outdoor examples duplicate shallow tidepools, not reefs. At the Waikiki Aquarium, a 26,600 L (7000 gal) outdoor open system Hawaiian reef exhibit, the *Edge of the Reef,* has been maintained since 1986. This exhibit receives direct sunlight and in the summer months, water temperature can easily climb above 27 °C (80 °F). When this occurs, native Hawaiian corals unaccustomed to the high temperature, such as *Montipora capitata,* begin to lighten in colour and sections begin to bleach or suffer RTN. Hawaiian reef fishes are also less tolerant of temperatures over 27 °C (80 °F) than their south Pacific counterparts and begin to show signs of stress such as increased respiration rates and lower disease tolerance (J.C. Delbeek, pers. obs.).

The bottom line is that an aquarium environment is not the same as the ocean environment. Light fields, light intensity, water chemistry, volume, and water motion in aquariums are all significantly different from those in the ocean. All of these factors affect how a coral reacts to higher temperatures and ultraviolet light (see Brown *et al.*, 2002; Kuffner, 2002; and Nordemar *et al.* 2003). Couple this with the fact that most aquariums contain a mixture of corals from a wide variety of habitats (and sometimes different oceans!), and one can see that a temperature recommendation that is close to the thermal tolerance of many corals is not based on careful consideration of the ramifications for other corals or the captive ecosystem as a whole. While it is certainly possible to keep aquariums at temperatures higher than we recommend, we believe the risks involved far outweigh any advantages.

In summary, it is better to maintain a coral tank well below its thermal extreme to: 1) lessen the chance of coral bleaching and bacterial disease that could devastate the collection and 2), reduce the chance of a low oxygen level at night especially in systems with deep sand beds and no RDP system.

Temperature measurement

Measuring temperature accurately is critical to a successful reef aquarium. There are several options for measuring temperature but we recommend utilizing at least two thermometers and checking them frequently. For a quick glance, it is okay to use the inexpensive plastic strips that adhere to the glass and have a temperature scale with a coloured background that changes to highlight the temperature. Slightly more accurate are digital thermometers with a separate temperature probe that is located in the aquarium. Of course, the probe must remain submerged, away from any heat sources and in a location receiving sufficient water movement to register the true temperature of the water. There are several smaller digital temperature sensors sold for the aquarium market that use small metal probes at the end of a cord but few of these probes are meant for continuous immersion in saltwater. In these cases, it is a wise precaution to protect the probe from direct contact with seawater to prevent corrosion. Dipping the probe in clear epoxy, using heat shrink tubing, or encasing it in plastic tubing that is sealed at both ends with some silicone glue are effective means to water-proof the probe and prevent corrosion and subsequent probe failure.

Wireless temperature monitors allow sensors and displays to be located in various locations without the need for connecting wires. *American Marine* Inc.

A battery operated digital temperature monitor from *Pentair Aquatics* that measures the temperature in the aquarium and in the air surrounding it. J. Sprung

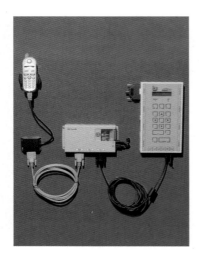

This *IKS* aquarium controller from Germany has a cell phone option that can send text messages to any number programmed in to it, allowing for instant alerts of any changes in tank temperature, pH or power status. D. Knop

There are now wireless temperature monitors available that allow for the monitoring of an aquarium from another location in the home. The temperature sensor is placed in the aquarium while the display can be placed in another location where it may be viewed more frequently, without the worry of wires being required. Wireless sensors are particularly useful in systems that have sumps placed in other locations; in addition, units that can receive input from two or more sensors can be used to monitor temperatures from several remote locations as well as the main aquarium.

Having a thermometer will not help much unless you check it on a regular basis. Make sure you place thermometers where they can easily be seen and check them at least twice a day, preferably first thing in the morning and before you go to bed. Digital temperature sensors with an audible alarm are highly recommended, as they will alert you when the aquarium temperature rises or falls above the set point. Having an alarm does not negate the need for daily temperature checks since these systems can and do fail. There are also integrated controller units on the market that can be linked directly to the Internet or to the telephone system (hard-wired, pager or cellular) that will call any number you program in to it whenever there is a system problem such as an electrical outage, pump failure or a change in temperature. Finally, most cooling systems have integrated temperature controllers with digital displays. However, it is still a good idea to have another temperature sensor in the main aquarium as well since many of these integrated sensors only measure the water in the chilling system itself, which can vary a few degrees from the actual temperature in the aquarium, or a lot if the pump stops sending water through the chiller.

Temperature controller probe placement

There are several temperature controllers on the market today designed to remotely control heaters/chillers. The heating/cooling unit is plugged into the controller and a probe from the controller is located in the aquarium. In this case is it wise to place the temperature probe in the same location where the heating or chilling device draws its water. If, for example, the temperature probe is placed in the aquarium, and the heater is placed in the sump, a sump pump failure will allow the tank temperature to drop and the heater will be activated, cooking the sump. Similarly, if the heater is placed in the tank and the probe is in the sump, a sump pump failure would have devastating results on the tank's inhabitants. In the case of a chiller, if the main sump pump fails, the temperature probe will call for cooling from the chiller and the chiller will run indefinitely, causing it to freeze up. Most chillers have built-in temperature controllers to prevent this, but if you decide to use an additional external controller, then set the built-in chiller controller to a point a couple of degrees below that of the external controller's. In this way, if the external controller fails or the circulating pump for the chiller fails, the internal controller will turn the chiller off and prevent it from freezing up or running continuously. When a chiller is directly connected to the aquarium, and its temperature probe fails, the chiller will run continuously, and the result demonstrates the devastating effect global cooling could have on coral reefs. This fault could be prevented by design, if for example the built-in chiller controller was plugged into a second temperature controller as we just described.

In our experience, electronic controllers rarely fail but their temperature probes do so frequently. To guard against probe failure, seal the probe against exposure to seawater by either dipping the probe in epoxy, sealing it inside airline tubing or covering it with heat shrink tubing as we mentioned previously. The use of a temperature sensor with an audio alarm is highly recommended.

Methods for temperature control

Reef aquariums make extensive use of high intensity lighting systems, high capacity pumps, motorized water flow controllers, and submersible powerheads, all of which generate heat that ends up being transferred to the aquarium. In addition, calcium reactors and protein skimmers often employ powerful pumps that can generate a significant amount of heat. Therefore, it should not be surprising that most reef tanks need to employ some sort of cooling system; either passive or active.

Passive cooling solutions

The first step in cooling the aquarium is to prevent overheating. The main filtration and pumps should be located in a cooler portion of the home such as a basement, in a small dry alcove outside the house, or in an unheated garage if possible. Using the natural cooling these locations provide will cool the water and will allow less heat to build-up in the cabinet and around the body of water in the system.

Most home aquarists do not have the luxury of an area where they can separate their filtration system from the main aquarium. The sump and all the pumps, filters and other equipment are wedged into the space under the aquarium, often hidden behind closed doors. This is a major area for overheating. To reduce heat build-up in this space use adequate ventilation holes along the sides and

This aquarium in a doctor's office in Japan has an open lighting system, preventing the accumulation of heat over the water surface. J.C. Delbeek

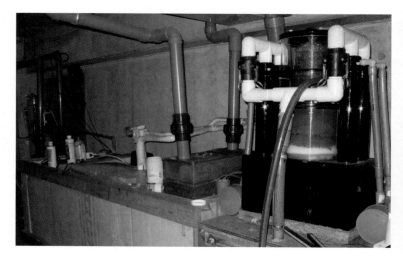

The filtration system for this reef tank is located in the parking garage below. Note the insulated sump. J.C. Delbeek

An outdoor chilling and filtration system adjacent to a fish room on the top of an apartment building in Osaka, Japan. J.C. Delbeek

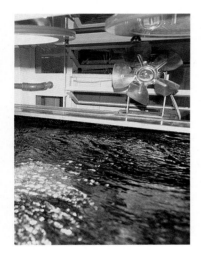

This reef aquarium created by Carlos Moreno in Sao Paulo Brazil has a special cooling system that employs fans connected to a thermostat. When the temperature rises, the fans switch on and cool the tank by increasing the evaporation rate. J. Sprung

back, or better yet, have no backing on the cabinet. If necessary you could add a few small muffin fans like those used in computers to blow air into the area and force the hot air out through the ventilation holes. You can also design your sump so that it is open on top, providing a larger surface area for evaporative cooling. A fan directed at the surface of the sump, would further increase the evaporation rate and cool the water a few degrees more. However, in areas or seasons with high humidity, the amount of evaporative cooling will be limited.

To prevent overheating caused by lighting, you should ensure that the top of the tank has adequate air ventilation, either by having a hanging light fixture over an open aquarium, or by having a well-ventilated (or fan-cooled) light hood. This will not only retard heat build-up in the hood but will also aid gas exchange and evaporative cooling. Evaporative cooling can also be enhanced by using a fan to blow air over the water surface, providing an extremely effective method to reduce the tank temperature a few degrees. In some climates or applications, this form of cooling might be all that is required, and may only be needed during certain times of the year. In addition, the use of a fan blowing across the surface of the water accomplishes some other benefits. It creates wavelets that increase the water surface area, and the rate of gas exchange. It also sets up circulation within the aquarium by pushing water toward the opposite wall, forcing surface water downward and bringing subsurface water to the top.

Active cooling solutions

The most expensive but effective solution to control a consistently high temperature is to purchase an aquarium chiller designed for saltwater use. Many styles and capacity ranges are available and both the price and quality of the units have improved in recent years.

There are a number of factors that are involved in determining what size chiller is required for a particular application. The system volume is of course a very important component, but it is only one part of the equation. One must also know the minimum temperature you want the system to run at and how much heat is being added to the system. Heat sources include pumps, lighting, friction caused by water flowing in the pipes, sunlight (if applicable), the air temperature over the tank water surface and in the sump area, and the room temperature the tank is in. The difference between the upper temperatures your tank would reach without cooling and the temperature you wish to maintain is known as the differential or pull-down temperature.

One way to determine the heat load is to run all the planned lighting, pumps and accessories when first testing and flushing the plumbing system with freshwater. Run everything for a day or two then measure the temperature of the system. This will represent the maximum temperature the system will attain without cooling. Subtract your minimum operating temperature from this value and you will have the differential. It is then a simple matter to use the provided chart to determine what size chiller is required for your system size and required pull-down temperature. For example, using table 4.1 as a guide, if you have a system of 684 L (180 gal.) and you need to pull down the temperature by 11 °C (20 °F) you would need at least a 1/3 HP chiller.

When sizing the chiller keep in mind that a unit that is slightly larger than required does not cost more to operate since it will only come on as needed. In contrast, a chiller that is undersized for the application will run all the time and cost more in electricity to operate. It is also wise to slightly oversize the chiller to allow for the future addition of more heat generating equipment or lighting; to allow for higher room temperatures in the warmer months of the year; and to allow you to drop the temperature a few degrees in case of a disease outbreak or coral bleaching event. Choosing a chiller that is significantly larger than required is not a good idea since it will frequently run for very short periods of time, a condition known as *short-cycling*, which is not good for the mechanics of the chiller and will shorten its life.

Table 4.1. Chiller sizing chart (in gallons) for non-insulated tanks. Source: Aquatic Ecosystems Inc., reprinted here with permission.

HP	Temperature Difference from Ambient (°F)			
	10^0	20^0	30^0	40^0
1/6	90	45	30	23
1/5	144	72	50	40
1/4	260	130	90	70
1/3	360	181	130	100
1/2	550	280	200	154
3/4	826	420	300	231
1	1,321	672	500	370
1 1/2	2,115	1.075	800	555
2	2,640	1,320	850	670
3	3,960	1,980	1,275	1,005
4	5,280	2,640	1,700	1,340
5	6,600	3,300	2,125	1,675
8	10,560	5,280	3,400	2,680
10	13,200	6,600	4,250	3,350

Some caveats about chillers

The maximum ambient temperature around the chiller is important since the heat exchange cannot take place if the ambient air temperature is too high. Most chillers must be located where the ambient air temperature does not exceed 35°C (95 °F). Therefore, when placing a chiller outside, summer temperature extremes may reduce its efficiency or stop it from working altogether. A shaded location can prevent this from happening. On that subject, most chillers cannot be left in the open where they are exposed to rain, high humidity, or direct sunlight. Therefore, some kind of enclosure must be used anyway. However, in order to work properly, a chiller must have adequate cross ventilation to vent off the heat removed from the aquarium so be careful not to restrict air flow through the enclosure.

In warm regions that can experience cool evenings, freezing of the chiller cooling chamber can occur in units that are mounted outside. This happens when the water flow through the chiller is not high enough and the coolant coils in the chiller develop ice on them. To prevent this from happening make sure you have adequate water flow through the chiller. A sure sign that too little of the tank's water volume is passing through the chiller is that the chiller will run constantly while barely maintaining the desired temperature. If the chilling chamber does develop ice, simply turn off the chiller while continuing to pass water through it and wait about 30 minutes then restart it. This should melt the ice that has developed in the contact chamber. Adjust your water flow or increase the size of the pump so that more water will flow through the chiller. Be sure to follow the recommendations in the chiller manufacturer's instruction manual for minimum and maximum flow rates.

A somewhat less expensive solution for keeping the aquarium cool is to purchase an air conditioner unit for the aquarium room. This has an added comfort benefit for the aquarist of course, which may help you convince your spouse of the extra expense! It may or may not be cheaper in the end than using a chiller, considering the cost of electricity to run an air conditioner constantly, set cold enough to keep the tank cool.

Location of the chiller

A chiller kept indoors does add considerable heat to a room, causing the room's air conditioner (if present) to work harder in a silly, wasteful battle. Therefore, it is best to locate the chiller in a garage, basement, attic, or other location where the added heat will not pose a problem. The room where the chiller is located must have adequate ventilation to vent the heat (the higher the temperature around the chiller, the longer it has to work to exhaust the heat removed from the tank). In addition, the water vapor produced by the chiller must be either evaporated or passed to a drain. Placing the chiller under the tank next to the sump is probably the worst location for it. The exhausted heat will raise the water temperature reducing the chiller's efficiency making it work harder and shortening the life of the unit.

Tip: The use of foam pipe insulation on water lines leading to and from the chiller reduces heat gain. Similarly, when used on heated systems in cold climates, the insulation will reduce heat loss.

In-line vs. drop-in chillers

Chillers come in two basic styles; in-line and drop-in. In-line chillers are attached directly in the plumbing path with water actively flowing through the chilling chamber and around the coils. Drop-in chillers have no cooling chamber; instead, the cooling coil is placed directly into the tank or sump. This allows drop-in chillers to be added quickly to an aquarium without any additional plumbing required, or moved to another aquarium if needed. This makes them ideal for use in systems that only require cooling during certain times of the year. Their drawbacks are that they come in a limited range of sizes, their coils must be able to fit into a sump space or a partitioned space in the aquarium, and the chilling capacity is limited by the amount of water you can pass around the coil or through the sump. In-line chillers are more difficult to install initially but they come in a wide range of sizes, and you can pump the required amount of water through them via an independent plumbing loop.

Small chilling probes can be used for smaller aquariums or several can be used together on larger ones. J. Sprung

Thermoelectric chillers

A recent introduction to the aquarium chiller arena is the thermoelectric chiller that cools via the Peltier effect. In these units, cooling and heating is done electrically, without compressors, gases (CFC's) and few, if any, moving parts. While their use is currently restricted to small volumes because of their limited capacity, they offer a practical means of both chilling and heating a small aquarium; they are silent and they consume less energy than traditional chillers. Smaller, thru-the-tank wall cooling probes are also available for use with *nano reefs*, where they can be installed through a wall of the aquarium or sump. With these, more than one unit can be used to allow greater cooling capacity, but there is a limit to how much their capacity can be scaled up for larger tanks or for tanks that need a larger degree of cooling. A point can also be reached where it is more cost effective to purchase a single conventional chiller.

Other cooling methods

Swamp coolers

The company *Deltec* GMBH is marketing a modified *swamp cooler* style chiller for use in aquariums. The basic design is quite like a trickle filter, but with a large volume of air blowing over the media on which the water passes. This effects rapid evaporation and a significant temperature drop IF the ambient humidity in the air is low enough. In high-humidity environments, the evaporative cooling effect doesn't work well. The double layer spiral of black Enkamat and white polyester may look familiar to *old reefers*. It is the same material used in early trickle filter designs. However, since the point of this media is to slow the flow of water as air is blown across it, the media should be maintained in an unclogged condition. Thus, it should periodically be removed and cleaned by

These *Deltec Eco-coolers* are modified evaporative *swamp coolers*. They can be used to chill an aquarium at low energy cost if the ambient humidity is low. The larger one, right, has a cooling capacity of 1800W, with a power consumption of only 88W! It is recommended for aquariums up to 2000 L (525 gal.) Photos courtesy of *Deltec* GMBH.

soaking it for a few days in a bucket containing nine parts water and one part chlorine bleach. Afterwards the DLS material can be rinsed with a stream of water from a garden hose and soaked in plain water with a liberal amount of dechlorinator added and then air-dried before re-installing it. A rotation can be done with two spiral rolls; one being used while the other is being cleaned. The periodic cleaning with bleach also prevents the system from becoming a biological filter. Although more labour intensive than a chiller, they are much less expensive and cheaper to run.

Small refrigerators

Small refrigerators or so-called bar fridges are often used by hobbyists seeking an inexpensive alternative to using a chiller. By placing several feet of coiled plastic hose within the fridge and running tank water through it, it is possible to get a small cooling effect. However, given the poor heat transfer rate of the plastic hose this method is not very efficient. The efficiency can be somewhat improved by placing a bucket of water in the fridge and placing the hose inside the water but this method is still not as efficient or reliable as a dedicated chiller. It does make a great place to store beer and wine though.

Ground cooling

In areas with low enough year round ground temperatures (< 18 °C (65 °F)), aquarists who live in homes with an adjacent yard can construct a system that uses ground cooling to lower tank temperatures. This consists of a large diameter PVC pipe (i.e. 5 cm (2 in.)) sunk into the ground to a depth of 3 m (10 ft.) or so. The bottom of the pipe is capped and the top has a 2" x 2" x 1" reducing T- fitting. A 1 inch PVC pipe is placed inside the 2 inch pipe to within a few inches of the bottom and extends out the top of the tee

Figure 4a. A ground cooling system developed by Mr. Deurloo in the Netherlands. * Modified from Lindenberg, 1987.

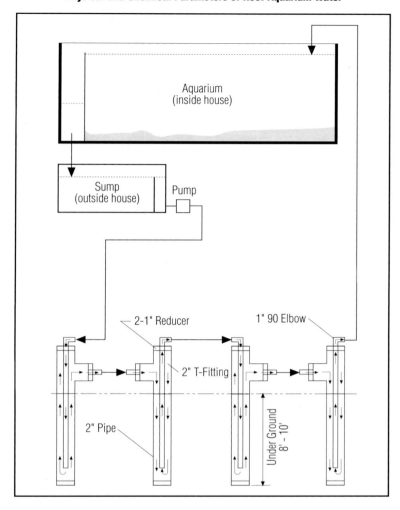

fitting. A 2 inch to 1 inch reducing fitting is then filed or sanded so that it can slip over the 1 inch pipe and can be glued in place so that a few inches extends above the top of the reducer. Trim the length of the 1 inch pipe so that when glued in to the reducer it still sits a few inches from the bottom of the 2 inch pipe, and then glue the reducer/pipe assembly into the top of the tee fitting. Water is pumped from the sump into the top of the tee, travels down the 1 inch pipe and exits out the bottom where it then rises back up the 2 inch pipe and exits out the branch of the tee. This basic design could be constructed with several pipes in parallel to achieve a stronger effect by cooling a larger volume of water (see figure 4a, above).

Heating

Under most circumstances, the temperature *problem* for reef aquariums is a need for cooling. This is because the pumps used to

The day after- this is what happened to the corals in a reef aquarium that got chilled down to about 18 °C (65 °F) for several hours during a cold front. Subsequently some of them died. J. Sprung

circulate water and the high intensity lighting required in a reef aquarium tend to raise the temperature. Despite this, in cold climates the need for heating can be very important as well. The lower critical temperature for a reef aquarium is about 21 °C (70 °F). Below this temperature, many reef corals will bleach or exhibit poor expansion (Saxby *et al.*, 2003). Ideally, the heating system will prevent the temperature from falling below 22 °C (72 °F).

Types of heaters

There are several heating systems available for reef aquariums, but most aquarists use commercially available glass or ceramic housing submersible heaters with a built-in thermostat. Hang on heaters that were once popular in fish-only aquariums, are less efficient because they are only partially submerged and should be avoided.

The *Theo* heater. Photo courtesy of *Hydor* ®.

Heating cable systems, popularized for freshwater plant displays where they are used to create convection currents in the substratum, may be possible to use in marine aquariums, but this must be confirmed with the manufacturer. With their use, the substratum becomes a heat source. A negative feature is that a failure of the cable means you would have to dig it out, and replacing it means removal of the substratum and at least some of the rock. Heating cable systems are also not suitable for aquariums that do not use a substratum.

Another option, the heating mat, could be employed most effectively in small *nano* reef aquariums. In this design, the heating element is located in a mat that is placed underneath the aquarium. The mat is in contact with the bottom of the aquarium and it is connected to a separate thermostat or temperature controller. Such a design must also incorporate a special kind of heating element that has a

relatively low maximum temperature (see *Hydor PTC heating system*), otherwise it risks overheating and shattering the bottom glass of the aquarium. The advantage is that it provides uniform heating at the bottom of the aquarium, which sets up convection through the substrate. In addition, it is not actually submerged in the water, so there is no risk of any chemical affect on the water (which is a risk with glass submersible heaters, if they should shatter in the aquarium). Of course in many cases, a mat type heater cannot easily be installed after the aquarium has been set up, nor can it easily be replaced if the heating element fails. These problems are practical to work around in small aquarium set ups that can easily be lifted when the water is drained out. Heating mats are not feasible at present for larger displays since the maximum temperature limit they must have to prevent overheating the bottom glass restricts their capacity to heat a large volume of water.

Above: The *ETH heater* has a PTC heating element enclosed in a convenient compact flow-through chamber. Photo courtesy of *Hydor*®.

The PTC polymer heating element. Photo courtesy of *Hydor*®.

Far right: this small heating pad could be used with a thermostat for nano reef aquariums of all sizes. Photo courtesy of *Hydor*®.

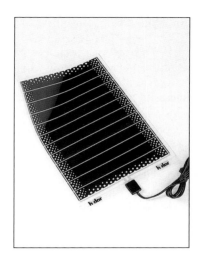

The *Visi-Therm*® *Stealth* Submersible Aquarium Heater from *Marineland Aquarium Products* has a tough outer casing that makes it much safer to use in aquariums with live rock. J. Sprung

The *Visi-Therm*® *Stealth Mini-Therm* Submersible Aquarium Heater from *Marineland Aquarium Products* is ideal for mid-sized nano reef aquariums. J. Sprung

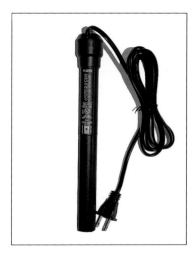

Hydor® PTC heating system

A new heating system recently introduced by the company *Hydor* has a patented heating element in which the traditional metal resistor coils have been replaced by a special polymer sheet, silk-screened with heating ink. The element operates with the exclusive positive temperature coefficient (PTC) system. In this system, in the case of an overcurrent situation, resistance rises within the PTC. This additional resistance in the circuit has the effect of reducing the overall current, so the heating is reduced. Once the overcurrent situation is removed, the PTC cools, its internal temperature drops, the resistance returns to a low state and heating begins again

The *Hydor* PTC heating system is available in the traditional glass tube style called THEO, except that the glass is a special shatterproof material. The PTC system is also available in a convenient flow through heater called ETH (External Thermal Heater) that has hose barb input and output ports. *Hydor* also makes a small pad-style heater with a set temperature, and it has application for extremely small aquariums of 12 L (3 gal.) or less.

Important caveats about submersible glass and ceramic heaters

Be sure to check the manufacturer's specifications to see that the heater you choose is saltwater safe. Always unplug a traditional glass submersible heater about 15 minutes before removing it from the aquarium. This will allow it to cool before you remove it. It takes time for the coiled heating element to cool to the point that it stops heating the glass envelope. Removing a hot heater from the tank is sure to cause it to crack, or to cause a burn where you touch it or where it rests. Conversely, never plug in a heater before you place it in the water because it may quickly heat up and crack the glass envelope before you have a chance to place it into the water, or cause it to shatter the moment it is submerged.

Unplug the heater whenever you work on your aquarium. It is easy to forget the heater is on when you do a water change, and exposing a plugged in heater to air can cause it to shatter when it overheats and is then re-immersed. Unplugging the heater also reduces the risk of electrical shock if the glass heater is broken or breaks while you are working with your hands in the aquarium. Of course, you must remember to plug it back in afterwards. In addition, for added safety any heater or chiller should be plugged into a GFI outlet (see chapter 3). The PTC heating system devised by *Hydor* does not overheat this way and can be left plugged in, even when exposed to air.

Tips: Many sumps are designed with weirs to direct water flow. As a result, the chamber from which the pump draws water can be drained without water being lost from other chambers. Place your heater(s) in one of these other chambers to lessen the risk of shattering a heater in case your pump drains the main sump chamber or you neglect adding water for evaporation. A heater in the display aquarium keeps the tank warm if the sump pump fails.

How to size a heater for a given size aquarium

Heaters come in different capacities that are measured in Watts (W). A general rule of thumb for calculating the capacity heater required for a given tank is to multiply the number of gallons in the aquarium by 5 to determine the wattage of the heater to use (e.g. a ten gallon aquarium needs a 10 x 5 = 50 W heater). A more precise method involves a consideration of the ambient air temperature and the desired aquarium temperature in addition to the size of the aquarium.

Table 4.2. Heater Size Guide. Source: *Aquarium Systems* Inc. Heater Selection Guide based on the *Visi-Therm®* heater.

| | **Heating Degrees Required** | | |
Gallons/Liters	5°C/9°F	10°C/18°F	15°C/27°F
5 gal/25 L	25 Watt	25 Watt	75 Watt
10 gal/50 L	50 Watt	50 Watt	100 Watt
20 gal/75 L	50 Watt	75 Watt	150 Watt
25 gal/100 L	75 Watt	100 Watt	200 Watt
40 gal/150 L	100 Watt	150 Watt	300 Watt
50 gal/200 L	150 Watt	200 Watt	two 200 Watt
65 gal/250 L	200 Watt	250 Watt	two 250 Watt
75 gal/300 L	250 Watt	300 Watt	two 300 Watt

Subtract the average ambient temperature in the room from the desired temperature to maintain in the aquarium. Using the above chart, match the size of the aquarium in the left column with the column that shows the number of heating degrees required. Choose the next larger wattage if the heating requirement is between levels. In larger tanks, or where the room temperature is significantly below the desired water temperature, two or more heaters should be used. Most reef aquariums use a sump below the aquarium where it is easy to locate heaters, and where the water turnover provides even distribution of the heat. For large aquariums without a sump or recirculating filter chamber, the heaters should be installed horizontally at opposite ends of the aquarium, near the bottom, to heat it more evenly.

An aquarium can be thought of as a single living organism. The exchange of oxygen and carbon dioxide between the air and water are critical for its health. This small closed reef aquarium depends both on the illumination to photosynthetically elevate the dissolved oxygen level, and aeration. Even with strong water circulation, in the dark the dissolved oxygen level in such a small system could fall dangerously low. Aeration that brings oxygen depleted water to the surface and replaces the atmosphere over the tank with new air helps to maintain dissolved gasses within safe levels.
J. Sprung

Oxygen meter from *American Marine* Inc.

Tip: It is a good idea to use more than one heater in an aquarium and to keep a spare heater handy as a back up, in case one stops working.

Size matters

Although the wattages may be the same, a submersible heater's tube length can vary with design. Because heat rises, short tube heaters oriented horizontally do not heat as efficiently as long ones mounted horizontally. The length of heater you choose also depends on the dimensions of the tank or sump where the heater will be located.

Gas exchange

An aquarium housing water and life can be thought of as a single living organism that consumes oxygen and respires carbon dioxide. These two gasses are not the only ones that dissolve into and out of the aquarium, but they are the most critical to the life housed within it. Understanding that an aquarium must interact with its environment dictates that certain design elements should be taken into consideration when designing your system. As we mentioned previously, designing the areas above and below the aquarium to maximize airflow away from the aquarium will also help to improve the exchange of oxygen and carbon dioxide between the water and the air, as well as help to cool the system. In chapter 1, we also recommended aquarium designs with a favourable surface to volume ratio, as this enhances gas exchange, and to avoid aquariums or sumps that are tall and narrow.

Oxygen (O_2)

The volume of oxygen contained in water is called dissolved oxygen (DO). Oxygen enters the water by transfer across the air-water interface and by photosynthesis by aquatic plants and algae. The amount of oxygen that water can hold (its saturation state) depends on the water temperature, salinity, and atmospheric pressure. The solubility of a gas increases with decreasing temperature; therefore, cool water holds more oxygen than warm water. The solubility of a gas also decreases with increasing salinity; so saltwater holds less oxygen than freshwater does. Finally, gas solubility decreases as atmospheric pressure decreases. Thus reef aquariums located at altitude, hold less oxygen in the water because of the decrease in relative pressure. Both the partial pressure and the saturation level of oxygen change with altitude.

For most reef aquariums at sea level within the normal specific gravity and temperature ranges given here, the oxygen level at saturation is approximately 5 mg/L. Coral reefs are often supersaturated with oxygen, so a value of 7 – 10 mg/L during the daylight hours is common (Adey and Loveland, 1991).

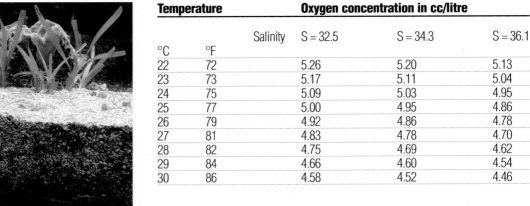

Temperature		Oxygen concentration in cc/litre		
	Salinity	S = 32.5	S = 34.3	S = 36.1
°C	°F			
22	72	5.26	5.20	5.13
23	73	5.17	5.11	5.04
24	75	5.09	5.03	4.95
25	77	5.00	4.95	4.86
26	79	4.92	4.86	4.78
27	81	4.83	4.78	4.70
28	82	4.75	4.69	4.62
29	84	4.66	4.60	4.54
30	86	4.58	4.52	4.46

Table 4.3. Oxygen concentration at saturation in seawater measured across a range of temperature and salinity. After deGraaf (1973).

Above: A thick layer of gravel or sand on the bottom becomes populated with a large amount of life and filled with organic matter that combined, deplete oxygen from the water rapidly. J. Sprung

Prolonged exposure to DO levels below saturation may not kill an organism, but is believed to reduce resistance to other environmental stresses. However, exposure to less than 30% saturation (less than 2 mg/L oxygen) for a prolonged period will kill many forms of aquatic life.

Low DO levels may result in fish mortality. A concentration of 5 mg/L DO (i.e. about saturation) is recommended for optimum fish health. Many species of reef fishes are sensitive to low DO levels, but this sensitivity to oxygen is species specific. Most reef fish are visibly distressed (rapid gill movements, gasping at the water surface) when the DO falls to about 3.5 mg/L. Mortality usually occurs at concentrations at or below 2 mg/L (Moe, 1989). The number of fish that die during a low oxygen event depends on how low the DO gets and how long it stays there. Usually larger fish are affected by low DO before smaller fish are. Fish may also develop a wider tolerance to lower DO levels in aquariums in time than they have when first harvested, so newer additions are more likely to be affected than older aquarium residents.

The DO level in an aquarium should be maintained close to saturation or a little higher. Supersaturation levels of oxygen are good to a point beyond which they are harmful. Harmfully high levels of oxygen can be reached within coral and anemone tissues because of photosynthesis (Dykens and Shick, 1984) but they are not obtainable in the water column in an aquarium unless pure oxygen is administered under pressure in a contact chamber. Pressurized cylinders used for ozone contact, known as oxygen reactors, should never be used with pure oxygen, since toxic supersaturated oxygen levels are easily reached with this kind of device (Burleson, 1989).

While photosynthesis during the day elevates the oxygen level in the water above saturation, at night, respiration tends to reduce it below saturation. Circulation is therefore especially important to keep the oxygen level from falling far below saturation at night. Good circulation prevents stratification of the water, and exposes the volume to the surface where

Oxygen bubbles on this live rock produced by photosynthesis elevate the DO level in the water during the day. J. Sprung

gas exchange occurs. In this way, oxygen-rich water at the surface is constantly being replaced from below by water containing less oxygen, creating a greater potential for exchange of oxygen and carbon dioxide across the air-water interface.

The oxygen transfer rate, defined as the time required for the DO concentration to achieve saturation (Spotte, 1992), refers to the transfer of oxygen across the air/water interface, and does not refer to the input of oxygen from photosynthesis. Flowing water is likely to have higher DO levels compared to stagnant water because the water movement at the air-water interface increases the surface area available to absorb the oxygen. The use of wave making devices capable of creating standing waves, or the use of fans blowing across the water surface creating wavelets has the ability to enhance the transfer of oxygen across the water surface because the actual water surface is increased by standing waves.

When the water surface is agitated with air currents or by water pumping devices, the surface area is increased and this increases the rate at which gasses pass across the interface between the air and the water. J. Sprung

Gas exchange occurs across the exposed water surface. If there is no surface-skimming and no agitation, films of organic substances and bacteria that reduce gas exchange soon develop on the water surface. Pushing water away from a surface-skimming weir also leads to the development of a surface film on the far end of the tank. J.C. Delbeek

In addition, the use of a surface-skimming weir (a.k.a. overflow) removes oxygen rich water from the surface and causes oxygen-depleted water to rise to the surface where it can pick up oxygen. It furthermore removes the surface film that prevents gas exchange across the water surface, and exposes the thin layer of skimmed water to air as it swirls down the drain to the reservoir below the aquarium. Rindels and Gulliver (1989) measured the effect of cascades on the oxygen transfer rate. *Going over the falls* is a trip that allows water to pick up oxygen to the point of supersaturation, much to the benefit of an aquatic system or aquarium. This action also balances the CO_2 content with the atmosphere and will expel excess nitrogen that may have been introduced by the main pump, as we shall discuss shortly.

Biological and chemical oxygen demand

The addition of organic matter depletes oxygen from an aquatic system. Microbes that break down the organic molecules consume oxygen, and oxygen combines with organic molecules as they decompose. If all oxygen is depleted, aerobic (oxygen-consuming) decomposition ceases and further organic breakdown is accomplished anaerobically. For their respiration, anaerobic microorganisms use oxygen bound to other molecules such as nitrates and sulfates. The oxygen-free conditions result in the mobilization of many otherwise insoluble compounds such as metal oxides. In addition, as sulfate (SO_4^{-2}) breaks down to hydrogen sulfide (H_2S), the water may smell like rotten eggs. In an aquarium with strong water agitation, the water column is aerobic. Therefore, anaerobic conditions are restricted to zones within rocks, sand, gravel, or filter media, and hydrogen sulfides as well as reduced metals are retained within a boundary layer capped by a layer of oxygen rich water. See the topic of advection, chapter 6, for a more detailed discussion.

Protein skimming removes organic compounds that would break down and consume oxygen. Protein skimming also creates more air/water interface surface by forming a large volume of tiny air bubbles. However, the latter feature does not do much to raise the oxygen transfer rate for the whole aquarium unless a significant portion of the volume of water in the aquarium is passed through the protein skimmer in a short period. For example, if the main circulating pump(s) for a reef aquarium are turned off, the water flow through a typical protein skimmer may not be sufficient to keep the DO level from falling too low at night in the display aquarium, and the fish could suffocate. Surprisingly, the use of an air bubbler in the display aquarium is all that would be required to prevent fish suffocation in the event of a circulating pump failure at night. Downdraft and Becket style protein skimmers have a higher capacity to elevate DO levels in aquariums due to their high flow-through rates and their use of a water cascade.

Protein skimming removes organic material, and by doing so helps to prevent oxygen depletion in the aquarium. J.C. Delbeek

Oxygen testing is not normally necessary in the general monitoring of the aquarium water quality, since the level tends to remain within the same daily range. It is lower at night when the plants aren't producing oxygen, and higher during the daylight period when they are. This also occurs in the natural setting on coral reefs, but the higher ratio of life to water volume in the confines of an aquarium means that DO levels can rapidly drop to much lower levels. In aquariums, the oxygen level changes appreciably only in the event of reduced circulation or pump failure, the putrefaction of a dead organism, or the fouling of the bottom substratum. Tanks with deep sand beds, however, do experience much lower oxygen levels at night due to high respiration rates by bacteria and other organisms living in the sand. Aquarists who maintain deep sand bed systems may want to monitor oxygen levels to determine how great a drop actually occurs at night and increase aeration or surface agitation at night to help offset any significant drop in oxygen. The use of reverse daylight photosynthesis (RDP) in an attached refugium is another option for preventing a large drop in the oxygen level at night (see the description of this method in chapters 6).

Aquariums that have no surface skimming but rely instead on submerged powerheads for circulation may have dangerously low oxygen levels at night, particularly if they have a deep sand bed, if the aquarium top is covered, or if the temperature is warm. The lack of a surface-skimming overflow necessitates some means of boosting the oxygen level at night, be it an airstone, a refugium with reverse daylight photosynthesis, or a high-flow powerfilter

Oxygen bubbles produced by photosynthesis become trapped in the tangle of filaments of the alga *Chaetomorpha* in an illuminated refugium aquarium. These remain for an extended period of time after the lights are off, slowly dissolving and helping to maintain oxygen concentration in the water. J. Sprung

By illuminating algae at night in a refugium attached to the display aquarium, the typical night-time drop in oxygen levels can be limited, to the benefit of the inhabitants in the display aquarium. J. Sprung

that has a cascade water return to the aquarium. Deep sand beds are an asset as long as the power is on and the water is flowing. In a power outage, they are a liability, since they rapidly deplete oxygen to the point that the fish and invertebrates may suffocate. It is important with any aquarium to have foolproof power backup systems or at least battery operated air pumps to circulate the water in the event of an extended power outage. This is especially true of systems employing a thick substratum. See chapter 3 for a discussion of emergency power systems.

Carbon dioxide (CO_2)

When atmospheric CO_2 dissolves in seawater it immediately becomes hydrated and forms carbonic acid, H_2CO_3. Carbonic acid is divalent, which means it can undergo two deprotonation reactions to form bicarbonate (HCO_3^-), and carbonate (CO_3^{-2}). The co-existence of carbonate and bicarbonate in seawater creates a chemical buffer system that regulates the pH and the partial pressure of CO_2 (pCO_2) of the oceans. The seawater buffering system (see *Alkalinity* later in this chapter) works because these compounds shift back and forth in equilibrium reactions when changes in the concentration of hydrogen ions occur, tending to maintain a pH of 8.2.

Most of the inorganic carbon in the ocean (about 88%) exists as bicarbonate. The concentration of carbonate ion in solution is approximately 11% while dissolved free CO_2 and carbonic acid make up only about 1% of the inorganic carbon dissolved in seawater (Stumm and Morgan, 1996). Proye and Gattuso (2003), offer a new program for calculating the parameters of the CO_2 system in seawater. It is available as an R package from the authors and runs on Mac OSX, Mac OS9, Unix, Linux and Windows operating systems.

The influence of photosynthesis by plants and respiration by animals and plants, is responsible for the daily variance in pH in aquatic systems, and is especially pronounced in closed systems where the ratio of water volume to living mass is closer to one. Because there is so little free CO_2 dissolved in seawater (about 0.18 to 0.44 mg/L), it is quickly exhausted by algae during photosynthesis, and so it is essentially not present when an aquarium is illuminated (deGraaf, 1968). When the algae use up available CO_2, they can use hydrocarbonates instead, and this can cause the pH to rise sharply if the water is not sufficiently aerated to supply additional atmospheric CO_2.

In reef aquariums with surface skimming overflows and protein skimmers, CO_2 is usually nearly at equilibrium with the atmosphere. Excesses can occur when CO_2 is purposely added to the system (e.g. using a calcium reactor, see chapter 5) or the environment where the tank is located has higher than normal CO_2 levels (e.g. a crowded room or a room that has very little air exchange with the outside). These can result in chronically low pH values (< 8.0) despite adequate alkalinity levels. Retention of excess CO_2 in the water because of poor circulation, or administration of CO_2 by means of a dosing system, causes the pH to decrease. As the CO_2 equilibrates with the atmosphere, the pH naturally returns to about 8.2 if the carbonate/bicarbonate buffer system is not depleted. We discuss this in detail in chapter 5.

Conversely, it is possible to have a high pH (>8.4) and a low or normal alkalinity level when administering calcium hydroxide (kalkwasser) solution during the day, since $Ca(OH)_2$ rapidly combines with available dissolved CO_2 and forms dissolved calcium bicarbonate. In the absence of the artificial addition of CO_2 to replenish what combines with kalkwasser, the pH can rise too high and alkalinity can be depleted. See *Calcium additions* in chapter 5 for detailed information on this topic. The affects of algae on CO_2 and pH can be balanced with the use of reverse daylight photosynthesis in a refugium(s) attached to the display (see chapters 5 and 6).

Nitrogen gas (N_2)

Nitrogen gas is not normally discussed by aquarists but it can be of concern if the water becomes supersaturated in nitrogen. This can occur when air and water are mixed under pressure such as when fine air bubbles are introduced into the intake of a large water pump. If this happens, nitrogen gas goes into solution and enters the bloodstream of the fish. The nitrogen then comes out of solution and fine nitrogen bubbles accumulate in the bloodstream resulting in problems when they enter extremely narrow blood vessels such as those in the gills, fin extremities, and the eyes. Symptoms include rapid breathing and/or bulging in both eyes as narrow blood vessels begin to rupture, and observable bubbles in the tips of fins, in gill filaments and in the eyes. Fortunately, this is a rare occurrence in reef aquaria with protein skimmers and surface overflows, since nitrogen is quickly expelled when the water is highly agitated at atmospheric pressure. Nitrogen gas supersaturation is more likely in systems that use large pumps of 1 HP or more.

Specific gravity (SG)

Specific gravity is used by aquarists to measure the salt content of seawater. Sometimes aquarists refer to specific gravity as *density*. This is not accurate since density is a value expressed as grams per cubic centimeter (g/cm^3), while specific gravity is a ratio of the density of a sample compared to the density of pure water at 4 °C. Pure (distilled) water at 4 °C has both a density and a specific gravity of 1. Substances with a specific gravity less than 1 are less dense than water, and float on it; substances with a specific gravity greater than 1 are more dense than water, and sink in pure water. Since specific gravity involves the ratio of one density value in g/cm3 to the density of another in g/cm3, the units cancel out and it is a dimensionless value. Specific gravity is symbolized as SG. Since it is a ratio of the density of one sample to another, and since density is dependent on temperature, an accurate measure of specific gravity requires that the sample and reference (distilled water) temperature are the same (Spotte, 1992). Aquarists who use a hydrometer to measure specific gravity actually are measuring observed, not true specific gravity, also referred to as a hydrometer reading, because the temperature of the sample and reference are not equal.

Moe (1989) has a conversion chart ranging from S=20 to S=40 and 20 °C (68 °F) to 30 °C (86 °F), based on a hydrometer calibrated at 15 °C (59 °F). We offer an abbreviated version here that covers the typical range of temperature and salinities in a reef aquarium.

Table 4.4. Conversion of observed SG to true SG and salinity, S, after Moe (1989).

Temperature of the Sample

°F		73.4	75.2	77.0	78.8	80.6	82.0	84.2
°C		23	24	25	26	27	28	29
S	True SG	Observed SG using a hydrometer calibrated at 15°C (59 °F)						
28	1.0206	1.0186	1.0184	1.0182	1.0179	1.0175	1.0172	1.0168
29	1.0214	1.0195	1.0192	1.0189	1.0186	1.0183	1.0180	1.0175
30	1.0222	1.0202	1.0199	1.0196	1.0193	1.0190	1.0187	1.0184
31	1.0229	1.0209	1.0207	1.0204	1.0201	1.0198	1.0195	1.0192
32	1.0237	1.0217	1.0214	1.0211	1.0208	1.0205	1.0202	1.0198
33	1.0245	1.0225	1.0221	1.0218	1.0215	1.0212	1.0209	1.0205
34	1.0252	1.0232	1.0229	1.0226	1.0223	1.0220	1.0217	1.0214
35	1.0260	1.0240	1.0237	1.0234	1.0231	1.0228	1.0225	1.0221

One of the features of specific gravity that is easily seen by reviewing table 4.4 is that the density of water decreases as temperature increases.

The specific gravity of seawater ranges from 1.022 to 1.030 in most regions (see table 4.5). The acceptable range for specific gravity in a marine aquarium is between 1.010 and 1.035. For a reef aquarium the range is a bit narrower, between 1.017 and 1.032. As we just explained, aquarists' measurements of specific gravity are only approximate. Estimates of salinity based on specific gravity may be much lower than the actual value (see Moe, 1989). An excellent discussion of specific gravity and the issues in measuring it can be found in Holmes-Farley (2002a).

Some aquarium industry hydrometers are calibrated at standard temperatures other than the often-cited 15 °C (59 °F), such as 25 °C (77 °F), a more typical tropical aquarium temperature (Holmes-Farley, 2002a).

It is important to note that there is no *correction* table for converting readings at temperatures other than the standard temperature 15°C (59 °F). If you don't know the standard temperature used for your hydrometer, using such a table may give highly inaccurate values (Holmes-Farley, 2002a).

Some marine aquarium hobby hydrometers claim to be accurate (i.e. no need for correction tables) over the range of typical aquarium temperatures; 20 – 29 °C (68 - 85 °F). For this to work, the hydrometer materials must change in density as a function of temperature at exactly the same proportion as seawater at all temperatures. Holmes-Farley (2002a) showed that some hobby hydrometers actually do this fairly well.

We have seen healthy marine fish, a few types of corals and other marinelife in nature at specific gravity values as low as 1.010. However, reefs do not usually occur at specific gravity values below 1.017. Reefs do grow at specific gravity levels up to 1.035 or a little higher, while some corals can tolerate up to 1.040 in areas such as the Persian Gulf. Full strength seawater is about halfway between the extremes of this range, about 1.025, and this is a common value on many open ocean reefs around the world. These reefs are typically not influenced by run-off from rains, and are not greatly influenced by evaporation, due to the high rate of exchange of water from the open sea.

Table 4.5. Coastal seawater salinity ranges for specific coral reef regions. After deGraaf, (1973)

	Salinity	**Specific Gravity** (true)
Red Sea	S = 40	1.0299
East Coast Africa	S = 32-35	1.0237-1.0260
Sri Lanka	S = 30-34	1.0222-1.0252
Singapore	S = 30-32	1.0222-1.0237
Caribbean Sea	S = 35	1.0260
Florida	S = 34-35	1.0252-1.0260
Philippines	S = 30-34	1.0222-1.0252
Sea of Java	S = 32	1.0237

Many reef aquarists maintain their aquariums at a slightly low specific gravity, approximately 1.022. This is fine. The most important aspect of specific gravity for a reef aquarium is stability at whatever value you choose. Constant fluctuation of specific gravity is stressful to invertebrates, plants, and microorganisms including bacteria. Stability is the key to making them thrive. Owing to the slightly higher specific gravity typically found on coral reefs, 1.025-1.026, some aquarium authors have suggested that it is best to maintain the same level in a reef aquarium. There is little to support this recommendation other than a *feeling* that it offers an environment closer to nature. One caveat with maintaining the specific gravity at 1.025 or higher: be sure to acclimate all new arrivals carefully to your system or quarantine system, since many pet dealers and wholesalers maintain their systems at a specific gravity of 1.018-1.022. In any case, it is always wise to check the specific gravity of the water with any new purchase. You may be very surprised!

A simple swing-arm hydrometer. J. Sprung

A glass float style hydrometer. J. Sprung

Table 4.6. How to use hydrometers. modified after Holmes-farley, 2002a, 2004b

How to Use a Standard Hydrometer

1. Make sure that the hydrometer is clean (no salt or calcium deposits). If any deposits won't easily dissolve, wash in dilute acid (such as vinegar). Rinse with freshwater after use to reduce deposits.

2. Gently insert the hydrometer into the aquarium or sample cylinder, being careful to prevent it from completely submerging. The part of the hydrometer above the water line should be dry because water, salt or mineral deposits on the exposed part will weigh down the hydrometer and give falsely low specific gravity readings.

3. Make sure that there are no air bubbles attached to the hydrometer. These buoy the hydrometer and yield a falsely high specific gravity reading.

4. Make sure that the hydrometer is at the same temperature as the water (and preferably the air).

5. Read the hydrometer at the plane of the water surface, not along the meniscus.

6. Do not leave the hydrometer floating around the tank between uses. If you do, difficult to remove deposits may form over time.

How to Use a Swing Arm Hydrometer

1. Make sure that the hydrometer is clean and free of salt deposits. Rinse with freshwater after use to reduce deposits.

2. Fill with sample to the indicated fill line.

3. Make sure that there are no air bubbles attached to the swing arm. Bubbles will buoy the swing arm and yield a falsely high specific gravity reading. Bubbles trapped at the pivot point also can alter the reading.

4. Make sure that the hydrometer is level. A slight tilt changes the reading.

Swing arm hydrometers should not be subjected to any temperature corrections in the normal range of use for a reef aquarium. Consistent accuracy may be improved, however, by checking the calibration with a standard solution.

Manipulation of specific gravity for disease control

Reduction of the specific gravity is occasionally used to control disease outbreaks in the fish, and is particularly effective against ciliates such as *Cryptocaryon irritans*, saltwater *ich*. Causing the specific gravity to drop from about 1.022 to 1.017 over the course of a few days by the addition of freshwater will not harm the reef aquarium (though it may kill certain algae, such as *Caulerpa* and coralline algae, and it may stress giant clams). The drop in specific gravity can effectively control the disease by slowing its reproductive cycle (Noga, 2000). After a few weeks with low specific gravity, when the fish have recovered from the disease, the specific gravity can be gradually increased back to its normal value and maintained there.

Specific gravity and ionic strength

Something else worth noting with respect to specific gravity is its affect on the concentration of calcium ions and alkalinity. Full strength seawater has a calcium level of about 400 to 450 mg/L, and an alkalinity of about 7 to 8 dKH. Specific gravity less than 1.025 is diluted from full strength seawater. Therefore, when one measures a calcium level of 380 mg/L at a specific gravity of 1.022 it is actually closer to natural levels than one may realize. Conversely, when full strength seawater calcium and alkalinity values are achieved at diluted specific gravity, they are really of higher concentration compared to the other ions. This is fine.

It is acceptable to maintain the calcium ion concentration a little shy of full strength values when the specific gravity is less than full strength. Alkalinity, however, should always be maintained at or above 7 dKH, to prevent harmful, large pH drops at night. This is especially important to correct when the specific gravity is lowered for the purpose of disease treatment, as we just described. The simplest way to manage the alkalinity when the specific gravity is dropped is to add some buffer to the water or to add a two-part alkalinity and calcium supplement to raise the values.

Salinity (S)

Salinity is a measure of the quantity of dissolved salts in seawater. It is common to find discussions of salinity using the units parts per thousand (ppt) by weight, or, in older texts, grams per liter (g/L), or grams per kilogram (g/kg) of water. However, the salinity of seawater is now defined as a dimensionless unit, S, that is the ratio of seawater conductivity to the conductivity of a defined solution of potassium chloride (Holmes-Farley, 2002a; Millero, 1996). Simpler solutions of salts are not defined the way seawater is, and are still reported as ppt.

Measuring salinity

Salinity can be calculated via measurements taken with a conductivity meter, or more simply by using a device called a refractometer that measures how light is bent by a thin film of water. Refractometers are generally easier to use than hydrometers and models that offer automatic temperature compensation do not suffer from the need to compensate for different temperatures. Refractometers are, however, more expensive than hydrometers. They are also not foolproof. It is wise to have a standard solution made up to check the accuracy of the refractometer (Holmes Farley, 2004b).

How to use a refractometer

A refractometer is a device that makes use of the fact that the greater the salinity of a solution the more light is refracted (bent) as it passes from the air into that solution. A few drops of solution are placed on the glass prism of the refractometer and by looking through the attached eyepiece a line appears on a calibrated scale and the salinity value is simply read off this scale. Both handheld and desktop refractometers are available and either can include automatic temperature compensation. Digital refractometers are also available and include automatic temperature correction, but they are much more expensive than mechanical units. There are also handheld digital refractometers that rely on fiber optics to measure salinity and provide a reading on an LCD screen. Such units are presently much more expensive than the simpler prism models, but they do look cool!

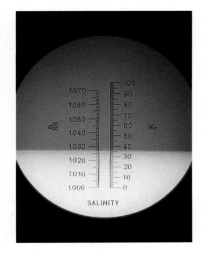

Looking through the eyepiece of a refractometer, the demarcation line between the dark blue and white area is where the scale needs to be read, in this case, the salinity is 36 0/00. A. Trevor-Jones

TIP: When using a refractometer take the reading as quickly as possible. The very thin film of water trapped between the prism and the cap will quickly evaporate and the salinity reading will rapidly climb as a result. It is also important to avoid trapping air bubbles between the prism and cap. If you do, the reading will not be accurate.

Salinity monitors

American Marine, Inc. produces a monitor for continuous salinity measurement. It is a conductivity monitor but is fully temperature compensated and the conversion chart will precisely show the corresponding density (specific gravity) or 0/00 salt (refractometer) values.

Maintaining specific gravity/salinity

The specific gravity/salinity of the aquarium water increases when water evaporates. Pure freshwater is used to replenish what evaporates. This replenishment can be done manually by adding the lost water daily with a jug, via a manually set drip feed, or automatically by using a dosing system attached to a freshwater reservoir. Level switches can also be used, such as simple mechanical float valve assemblies that open a valve attached to a freshwater reservoir. Under no circumstance should the valve be attached to the main water supply to the house, as a toilet float valve is installed. In that arrangement it is a safe bet the tank will one day be *flushed* with freshwater, even if, as an added safety feature, the connection is controlled by a timer. Other types of level sensing switches include mercury switches, floating collar switches, and optical infrared sensors. The level sensing switches are located where the water level changes with evaporation, either in the sump, or directly in the aquarium if there is no external sump. Two switches may be used as a safety precaution. One switch turns the dosing pump on when the level in the sump or tank falls, and it shuts the pump off when the correct level (or higher) is reached. The other switch is located above the first, and turns the dosing pump off if the water level is too high, in the event of failure of the lower switch. Level switches are also useful when attached to the main circulating pump, for preventing it from running dry if the sump level is too low, and they can be installed with an alarm to notify the aquarist of high or low water.

Variable dose metering pumps can also be used for the automatic addition of top-off water, with or without level sensing switches. When used without a level switch a dosing pump can simply be connected to an appliance timer to switch it on at intervals that allow dosing to match the rate at which water is lost by evaporation. This type of setup can work wonderfully provided the evaporation rate does not change seasonally. In areas where humidity and temperatures vary seasonally, evaporation rates will too, and the amount of water added automatically needs to be adjusted accordingly.

All of the above devices can also be used to dose kalkwasser as top-off water. However, as we shall explain in chapter 5, it is best to add kalkwasser in the evening hours as a slow drip, rather than over a 24-hour period.

Replenishing salts

As we explained, top-off water is freshwater since water is what evaporates, not salt. This fact is apart from another reality of marine aquarium keeping: salts will also be lost due to several other processes. Salts are lost to the collection and removal of skimmate from a protein skimmer, salt spray released by splashing and/or the popping of bubbles at the water surfaces in the aquarium and sump, and salt creep that forms due to capillary action along the margins of the aquarium, or small plumbing leaks. Depending on the frequency of water exchange, these salts, particularly what is lost to the skimmer, may need to

A salinity monitor produced by *American Marine* Inc.

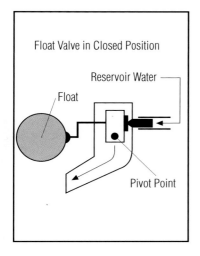

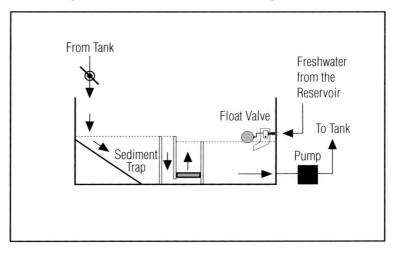

Figures 4b and 4c. A simple float valve assembly can be used to add top-off water to a sump. J.C. Delbeek

be replenished to maintain a stable SG. The use of a balanced ion two-part calcium and alkalinity supplement can achieve this salt replenishment quite well while boosting calcium and alkalinity levels, if the rate of supplement addition matches the rate of salt loss. Alternatively, a very small amount of artificial seawater mix could be added to the top-off water periodically, calculated based on the trend of salt loss for the particular aquarium. The simplest way to calculate this loss is to neglect the salt spray and simply measure the volume and specific gravity of saltwater removed per week by the protein skimmer. The drift in specific gravity due to skimmate water export in the average sized aquarium is slow in any case, so these measurements need not be so precise.

Electrical conductivity (EC)

Electrical conductivity estimates the amount of total dissolved salts (TDS), or the total amount of dissolved ions in the water. The sensor of a conductivity meter consists of two metal electrodes that are exactly 1.0 cm apart and protrude into the water. A constant voltage is applied across the electrodes. An electrical current flows through the water due to this voltage and it is proportional to the concentration of dissolved ions in the water - the more ions in the water, the more conductive it is and the higher the electrical current measured electronically. Distilled or deionized water has very few dissolved ions, so almost no current flow can be measured across the gap. The units for electrical conductivity are micro-Siemens per centimeter (µS/cm). Normal seawater has conductivity in the range of 50,000 - 60,000 µS/cm.

The ability of the water to conduct a current is very temperature dependent. In most instruments, EC values are automatically

corrected to a standard temperature of 25°C internally within the instrument. The temperature compensated conductivity probes usually have a temperature sensor such as a thermistor built in.

As we mentioned in the topic salinity, conductivity measurement can be used on a continuous basis to estimate salinity, but most aquarists find it practical to use a simple hydrometer to measure specific gravity, or a refractometer to measure salinity. A conductivity meter is also useful to measure the output water from a reverse osmosis water purifier to judge whether it is functioning at peak performance. The difference between raw tap water and reverse osmosis filtered water should be about 90% or greater.

pH

The pH of aquarium water is a measure of the concentration of hydrogen (H+) ions in solution. The concentration of hydroxide ions (OH-) is inversely proportional to the concentration of hydrogen ions. When the hydrogen ions are most abundant, the solution is acidic. If hydroxide ions are in greater abundance in a solution, the solution is alkaline or basic. Values of pH range from 0 to 14, or at least that is what we are always told. Actually, it is possible to have a negative pH, (hydrogen ion activity greater than 1 molar), or a pH greater than 14 (hydroxide ion activity greater than 1 molar). It has only become customary to use the scale between 0 and 14. The scale is logarithmic. Therefore, each gradation represents a factor of ten. For example, a pH of 8 is ten times more basic than a pH of 7 (i.e. a solution with a pH of 8 has 1/10 the H+ ions of a solution with a pH of 7). A pH of 9 is 100 times more basic than 7. If the pH is less than 7 the solution is acidic, if it is greater than 7 it is basic, and if it equals 7 it is neutral.

Small conductivity meters are now available in the hobby. *American Marine* Inc.

An inexpensive pH meter and pH controller from *American Marine*, Inc..

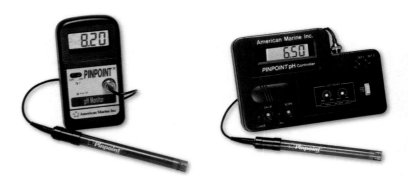

The pH can be measured with reagents and pH sensitive dye, or more accurately with an electrode and pH meter. A pH meter measures the voltage produced by hydrogen ions diffusing through the proton-permeable glass of an electrode immersed in the solution. A pH meter is a most valuable aid for the reef aquarist, but it must be calibrated often (once a month) to maintain accuracy. Generally, a pH probe lasts two to three years and then needs to be replaced. However, as soon as you find you can no longer calibrate the probe, it is time to replace it.

Table 4.7. Relative concentration of hydrogen and hydroxide ions at various pH levels.

pH	$[H^+]$ concentration in mol/L	$[OH^-]$ concentration in mol/L
0	10^0	10^{-14}
1	10^{-1}	10^{-13}
2	10^{-2}	10^{-12}
3	10^{-3}	10^{-11}
4	10^{-4}	10^{-10}
5	10^{-5}	10^{-9}
6	10^{-6}	10^{-8}
7	10^{-7}	10^{-7}
8	10^{-8}	10^{-6}
9	10^{-9}	10^{-5}
10	10^{-10}	10^{-4}
11	10^{-11}	10^{-3}
12	10^{-12}	10^{-2}
13	10^{-13}	10^{-1}
14	10^{-14}	10^0

*Important note: Oceanographers use three different pH scales: called *total*, *free* and *seawater* pH (Millero, 1996.) Aquarium pH measurement uses the NIST (formerly NBS) pH scale, and the pH buffers used for calibrating aquarium pH electrodes are NIST buffers. Since an electrode calibrated in NIST buffers reads approximately 0.2 pH units higher than an electrode calibrated on one of the pH scales commonly used by oceanographers, one has to keep in mind that ocean pH values reported by oceanographers are approximately 0.2 pH units lower than what one would observe testing the same water with an aquarium pH probe.

Seawater is a basic solution with a pH ranging from 8.0 to 8.25 typically*, but near high rates of photosynthesis and respiration, as on coral reefs, the pH may fall below 8.0 at night and rise above 8.4 during the day. In reef aquariums, the ideal pH does not fall below 8.1, nor climb above 8.5. A daily variance within these limits best promotes calcification. The range of acceptable tolerance is between about 7.6 and 9.0, but at the extremes, calcification is impeded, and some organisms may not be healthy.

The ideal pH range for calcification falls between about pH 8.2 and 8.5. At a fixed alkalinity, it becomes harder for organisms to calcify as the pH is lowered from about 8.2 downward. Likewise, it becomes harder to maintain a fixed alkalinity at higher pH, due to increased abiotic precipitation of calcium and magnesium carbonate that occurs at high pH levels (Holmes-Farley, pers comm.; see also chapter 5).

Low pH inhibits precipitation of calcium carbonate by calcifying organisms, and high pH tends to lower the calcium ion concentration. Some tanks will show wide fluctuations of pH from day to night, while others will remain stable. High carbonate hardness and alkalinity promote pH stability. As mentioned under the topic of carbon dioxide, respiration (which adds dissolved carbonic acid to the water) and photosynthesis (which removes dissolved CO_2) are important determining factors in the pH of aquariums. These processes are used to advantage in systems that incorporate *reverse daylight* illumination of an algal filter.

Organic acids and phosphates that tend to accumulate in closed systems, and the formation of nitric acid from biological filtration (nitrification), deplete the buffer capacity or alkalinity of the water (see *Alkalinity*). The acids deplete bicarbonate and calcium carbonate from the water, while phosphate lowers alkalinity by precipitating out of solution in compounds with calcium and magnesium carbonates. This is the cause of the long-term decline in pH characteristic of many closed system aquariums. Denitrification helps reverse the loss of alkalinity, as the bacteria involved liberate carbonates and bicarbonates from the breakdown of organic matter (see description of the Jaubert system in chapter 6).

Tip: If tank pH runs at the lower range of 7.6-8.0, then try to maintain the alkalinity at 3.0 meq/L (8.4 dKH) or higher. Increased alkalinity helps corals to calcify at low pH.

Alkalinity

This term confuses both novice and advanced hobbyists. Stated simply, the alkalinity of a solution refers to its capacity to buffer against drops in pH. Higher alkalinity affords greater ability to prevent rapid pH swings. Once the alkalinity is exhausted, the pH can fall rapidly. Alkalinity is provided in the aquarium by various negatively charged ionic compounds (anions) such as carbonates, bicarbonates, borates and hydroxides. The alkalinity of a sample of water can be measured by pH titration (Stumm and Morgan, 1996), and is defined as the amount of acid required to neutralize all of the weak bases in the solution (primarily bicarbonate and carbonate ion). The titration process uses the chelating agent EDTA (ethylenadiaminetetracetic acid) and an indicator dye such as Eriochrome black T (EBT). The values gained from the EDTA titration after some calculations are moles of Ca^{2+} and Mg^{2+}, which can be converted into parts per million (ppm) hardness of $CaCO_3$. The rather confusing term *carbonate hardness* has also been used to describe alkalinity, but this refers only to the carbonate and bicarbonate portions of alkalinity and does not take into consideration the other compounds involved. Therefore, *total* alkalinity is generally slightly higher than carbonate hardness (Spotte, 1979).

To further add to the confusion, there are several scales used to measure alkalinity. Two different units of measurement are commonly used by aquarists, milliequivalents per litre (meq/L), and degrees of carbonate (German = karbonat) hardness (dKH). A third scale, ppm $CaCO_3$, is used most often by marine scientists. There are numerous test kits available and they are all simple to use. Some test kits for alkalinity use the metric unit (meq/L), while others use the German unit, (dKH). To convert meq/L to dKH, multiply by 2.8. Natural seawater has an alkalinity of 2.1 to 2.5 (6-7 dKH). Alkalinity values in the aquarium should be maintained between 2.5 and 3.5 meq/L (7-10 dKH). Note: most alkalinity or dKH test kits use exactly the same titration. We discuss in detail the relationship between pH and alkalinity, how to maintain them and how to correct imbalances in both in chapter 5.

Table 4.8. Conversions for various alkalinity scales e.g. to convert dKH to meq/L divide by 2.8.

Units	dKH	meq/L	ppm $CaCO_3$
dKH		divide by 2.8	multiply by 17.9
milli equivalents (meq/L)	multiply by 2.8		multiply by 50
ppm $CaCO_3$	multiply by 0.05	divide by 17.9	

As we explained earlier in this chapter under the topic carbon dioxide, when atmospheric CO_2 dissolves in seawater it is hydrated to form carbonic acid, H_2CO_3. This hydration reaction is described by the following equilibrium system:

$$CO_2 + H_2O \rightarrow H_2CO_3 + H^+ \rightarrow HCO^-_3 + H^+ \rightarrow CO_3^{2-} + 2H^+$$

Natural variations in seawater pH due to biological activity cause the relative concentrations of CO_2 and CO_3^{2-} to vary inversely with each other, while changes in the concentration of HCO^-_3 are relatively much smaller.

The carbon cycle in the sea

The interaction between the carbonate species in seawater leads to a counter-intuitive inverse behaviour between CO_2 and CO_3^{2-}. When carbonate ions are removed from solution by the precipitation of solid $CaCO_3$, the bicarbonate ions undergo a disproportionation reaction until the equilibrium expressions are satisfied. The net result is an increase in the pCO_2 (partial pressure of carbon dioxide) of the water, despite the intuitive expectation that removal of a carbon species (CO_3^{2-}) should reduce the concentrations of all other carbon species. While formation of calcium carbonate increases the pCO_2, biological production near the sea surface results in the formation of organic particles that sink into deep water. This process, called the *biological pump* lowers the concentration of carbon, as well as other nutrients in open ocean surface waters. In deep waters, the nutrients, including carbon, are recycled.

Figure 4d. The carbon cycle as influenced by photosynthesis and respiration, as it occurs in the sea. In aquariums, the supply of bicarbonate ions can be depleted rapidly, altering this cycle. Modified, after Spotte (1992)

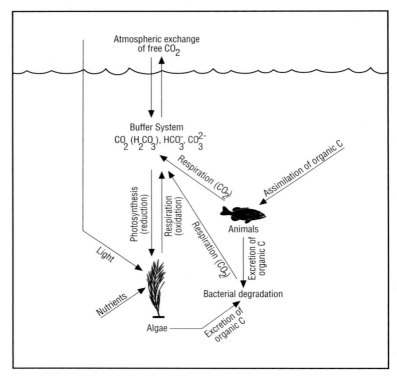

Figure 4e. The cycle of formation, deposition and dissolution of calcium carbonate also strongly influences the carbon cycle. After Barnes (1980)

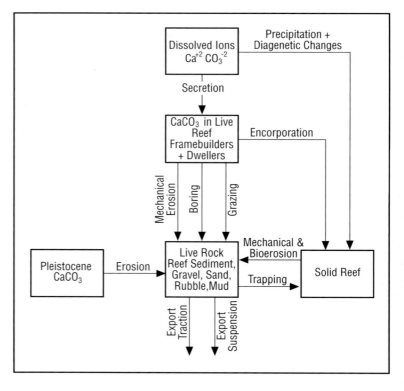

Carbon cycle in aquariums

In aquariums with rapidly growing corals, there is a high rate of calcification (precipitation of solid $CaCO_3$) relative to the volume of water. Given an unlimited supply of bicarbonate ions, this calcification theoretically would boost the pCO_2 in the water, but since it occurs during the illuminated period, the uptake of CO_2 by photosynthesis simultaneously consumes the CO_2. Furthermore, unlike the situation in the open sea, the supply of bicarbonate ions in a closed system aquarium is limited. Therefore, the formation of calcium carbonate skeletons rapidly depletes the supply of bicarbonate ions from aquarium water, so that the potential release of CO_2 from calcification becomes proportionately smaller, and the rate of calcification slows. Aquarists employ various methods to mimic the natural condition of maintaining an *unlimited* supply of bicarbonate ions, such as the use of calcium reactors, the addition of two-part calcium and alkalinity supplements, or the addition of *kalkwasser* (see chapter 5).

Calcium (Ca)

Calcium is the primary building block of the corals, clams, calcareous algae and many other organisms that we grow in our aquariums. Without adequate supplies of calcium, these organisms will not flourish. Calcium levels are measured in milligrams per litre (= parts per million, ppm). Calcium levels in natural seawater range from 380 to 480 mg/L depending on location and salinity. In our aquariums, calcium levels should be maintained between 350 and 450 mg/L to ensure proper growth of the calcifying plants and animals. We describe the numerous methods of maintaining the calcium level in chapter 5.

Measuring the calcium level

Test kits used by aquarists measure calcium in parts per million or milligrams per litre. The procedure involves a titration with EDTA and is simple to do. *American Marine* Inc. also offers a calcium meter for direct, continuous measurement of calcium levels for hobbyists. See chapter 5, *Measuring Calcium*, for a discussion of the utility of this meter.

Magnesium (Mg)

Magnesium is the third most abundant ion and second most abundant cation (positively charged ion) in seawater. Like other major elements, it is constant worldwide in its proportion with respect to the other major ions in seawater. The magnesium concentration is about 1285 ppm in natural seawater at S = 35 [= about 1.025 specific gravity at 25 °C (77 °F)] (Spotte, 1992). The concentration is less when the specific gravity is lower.

Magnesium forms ion pairs with several major and minor anions (negatively charged ions) in seawater. About half of the carbonate ion in seawater is tied up in ion pairs with magnesium ions, as is about a quarter of the borate, and about an eighth of the bicarbonate ions. Since bicarbonate, carbonate, and borate ions dominate the buffer system of seawater, magnesium has a very important influence as well (Bingman, 1999; Holmes-Farley, 2003).

At a pH value equal to the pKa of a buffer component, half of that component is present in the acid and half as the conjugate base form. Therefore, a buffer component with a pKa of 8.2 would have equal buffering capacity toward acid and base at pH 8.2. Salt concentration and ion-pairing with magnesium shifts the bicarbonate pKa value downward to a pH value closer to that of natural seawater. This effect makes seawater a better buffer between pH 8.0 and 8.5 with respect to the addition of either acid or base than if magnesium were not present (Bingman 1999; Holmes-Farley, 2003). The ion pairing of magnesium with carbonate also influences the amount of *free* or chemically available carbonate ions in seawater that may be used to form calcium carbonate skeletons by corals, clams, and other calcifying organisms (Bingman, 1999). In addition, magnesium has a big influence on the rate of precipitation of calcium carbonate. Magnesium ions adhere to the growing surface of exposed calcium carbonate crystal, *poisoning* it for further precipitation of calcium carbonate. Since magnesium reduces the rate of calcium carbonate precipitation this way, it makes the maintenance of high levels of calcium and alkalinity easier (Holmes-Farley, 2003c).

Biological roles of magnesium

Magnesium is essential for many biological processes of life including (but not limited to) DNA and RNA replication and thus cell division; the synthesis of adenosine triphosphate (ATP); structural roles in the cells; and chlorophyll formation. Magnesium is also incorporated into calcite deposited as skeletal support structures by some sponges, soft corals, and echinoderms. Calcareous algae also deposit magnesium in their skeletons in proportion to its concentration in the water.

Measuring magnesium in seawater

Oceanographers measure magnesium by atomic emission or atomic absorption spectroscopy. Aquarium hobby test kits work by precipitation of calcium, strontium and barium ions with sulfate, and then measure the soluble magnesium with an EDTA titration. Another method is to measure the total magnesium plus calcium (total hardness), and then use a calcium test to measure just calcium. Subtracting the calcium measurement gives the magnesium concentration (Bingman, 1999).

Ammonium and nitrite

Normally, ammonium and nitrite levels in an established aquarium are near zero. If you can measure detectable ammonia or nitrite, your aquarium is new and has not yet cycled completely or there is something decaying in the aquarium. You should carefully inspect your aquarium for any decaying animals or food or decaying matter on a new piece of live rock, and remove it immediately. Decaying live rock is easily recognized by the sulfur smell and the white film (a type of bacteria called *Beggiatoa*) that usually accompanies it (see chapter 2). Ammonium and nitrite can also be produced in the substrates (sand/gravel/rock) from (assimilative) nitrate reduction, but this does not produce significant measurable values in the water column in well-established aquariums. Elevated nitrite levels in the water can be indicative of incomplete denitrification, especially in systems that use denitrification filters that are not operated properly or are newly started. In chapter 6, we discuss the nitrogen cycle and its affect on ammonium, nitrite, and nitrate.

Nitrate

Nitrate is the end-product of nitrification, the process mediated by bacteria that converts nitrogen rich organic matter into ammonium, then nitrite and nitrate. The direct input that contributes to nitrate accumulation is in this case protein rich foods added to the aquarium. Nitrate also enters the aquarium from other sources. Unfiltered tap water used for topping off evaporation may contain significant amounts of nitrate in some regions, and this daily addition can lead to a persistent nitrate level. A natural process called nitrogen fixation also contributes to nitrate accumulation in aquariums, to the astonishment of the aquarist because it occurs without any obvious additions to the aquarium. Nitrogen fixation is accomplished by cyanobacteria that *fix* (gather and incorporate in their cells) dissolved nitrogen gas. The nitrogen gas enters the aquarium through the water surface, as nitrogen makes up 78% of air. The cyanobacteria then release this nitrogen as ammonium directly when they decompose or indirectly when they are eaten and digested by herbivores, producing a rise in nitrate ultimately.

The nitrate level in reef aquariums should be less than 1 ppm as nitrate-nitrogen (NO_3-N) ideally, but need not be maintained so low. In fact, elevated nitrate levels as high as 10 ppm nitrate-nitrogen (approximately = 40 ppm nitrate ion) may encourage more rapid growth of both soft and stony corals (D. Stüber, pers. comm.). The principal disadvantage to higher nitrate levels is the affect nitrification has on alkalinity and pH. The formation of nitrate depletes the alkalinity in a closed system through the release of protons (H+) in the conversion of ammonium to nitrite. In addition, nitrate-stimulated growth in corals also causes greater usage (removal) of calcium from the water but can lead to a less dense calcium carbonate structure due to rapid growth (Heslinga, 1989).

We bring this up to emphasize that if high nitrate levels are maintained, it is especially important to observe the calcium and alkalinity levels in the aquarium. Use of calcium and alkalinity supplementation effectively counters the depletion of calcium and alkalinity. Another potential side effect of enhanced skeletal growth due to elevated nitrate levels is a less dense skeleton, resulting in brittle tridacnid clams (Heslinga, 1989). It has also been proposed that high nitrate levels might necessitate higher additions of iodine for corals or other creatures that utilize iodine. This hypothesis has not been tested. The simple explanation is that the mechanism of nitrate uptake inhibits iodine (iodate) uptake, so higher nitrate levels mean lower iodine (iodate) uptake (Marlin Atkinson, pers. comm., 2004).

Tip: When comparing nitrate values with other aquarists or to published values, always make sure you know whether the value your test kit provides is nitrate-nitrogen or nitrate ion. Otherwise, your readings may seem too high or too low compared to others. To convert nitrate-nitrogen values to nitrate ion multiply by 4.

Table 4.9. The nitrate and phosphate levels in the saltwater well source compared to oceanic seawater at the Waikiki Aquarium.

	Nitrate (NO_3—N) mg/L	Orthophosphate (PO_4^{-3}) mg/L
Natural Seawater off Waikiki Aquarium	0.008	0.003
Waikiki Aquarium Saltwater well	0.074	0.02

Phosphate

Phosphate accumulation can cause problems in reef aquaria if allowed to build to levels above 0.045 ppm as orthophosphate (PO_4^{3-}), which is equivalent to 0.015 ppm measured as phosphate-phosphorous (PO_4 -P). Elevated phosphate levels fuel unwanted algae growth and interfere with the calcification processes of corals and coralline algae. It is nevertheless possible and common to maintain healthy reef aquariums or coral culture aquariums with phosphate concentrations as high as 0.1 ppm as orthophosphate, and various corals may tolerate even higher levels. However, for the best coral growth and least trouble with algae blooms, one should maintain a level at or below 0.045 mg/L as orthophosphate.

Many hobby test kits don't measure low enough to distinguish PO_4 -P levels between 0.015 and 0.02 ppm, but this low range makes a big difference on the growth of algae, particularly filamentous greens

Figure 4f. Phosphorus cycle
After Wheaton 1977

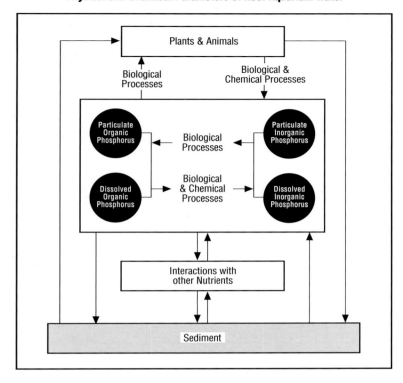

such as *Derbesia* and *Bryopsis*. Hobby test kits may suggest that the phosphate level is low when it is not, and this can be confusing to a hobbyist who is told that *high phosphate* causes algae to bloom. This can lead to the observation that although there is no measurable *phosphate* in the water, an aquarium still has microalgae growth.

In addition, phosphate is present in many forms in the aquarium, and not all of them can be easily measured. The majority of phosphate test kits used by aquarists measure only inorganic phosphate (orthophosphate) and ignore organic phosphates. In addition, algae, and the symbiotic bacteria that live on their surface, can secrete phosphatase enzymes that liberate usable orthophosphate from organically bound phosphate.

Sources of phosphate

Release of phosphate by denitrifiers

Barak *et al.* (2003) investigated the link between the phosphorus cycle and the nitrogen cycle. Phosphorus is commonly bound with organic matter in sediments. Under anoxic conditions, bacteria that reduce sulfate to sulfide, and nitrate to nitrite and nitrogen gas can liberate soluble orthophosphate from organic matter and release it into the water. This is observable in aquariums with a high organic load in the substratum (i.e. large detritus buildup). At times blooms of algae in these aquariums are associated with lower redox levels. In marine aquariums with a pH between 7.8 and 8.2, much of the phosphate liberated by bacteria in this manner binds to available calcium carbonate substrata or to calcium, strontium, iron or manganese in the water. It may also become bound with organic matter again, or be consumed and used by bacteria, algae, or other life. The amount of organic phosphate in the substratum and the amount of denitrification occurring there determine the amount of phosphate release. The pH, the available surfaces on solid calcium carbonate and presence of calcium and iron in the water all affect the amount of phosphate that remains available to algae. Solid surfaces of calcium carbonate become saturated with phosphate over time, and iron is typically limited in the water column. Some phosphate precipitates with calcium, but much remains available as orthophosphate or organic phosphate.

Top-off water

Top-off water can be a significant source of phosphate, as municipal and rural water supplies often contain phosphate in a variety of forms, both organic and inorganic. Use reverse osmosis or deionization to eliminate this potential source of phosphate. However, it is important to remember that reverse osmosis removes about 90-95% of a pollutant from the water. If the phosphate level is high in the source water, the 10% concentration remaining in the reverse osmosis product may still be significant. For example, a phosphate level of 1 ppm in the source water may give a level of 0.1 in the reverse osmosis product, which can produce chronic trouble with algae, depending on the evaporation top-off rate.

Other sources

Activated carbon is another potential source of phosphate. It is a simple matter to test it, as we describe in chapter 6. The main source of phosphate accumulation in aquariums is food. Although some aquarists advocate minimal feedings of the fish in a reef tank, this is not a wise practice; as we explain in chapter 10, feeding is beneficial to reef aquariums. Unless adequate food is available, some fish will slowly waste away. Moderate, but frequent feedings should be carried out at least several times a week but better daily. Active fish such as *Pseudanthias* spp. require small feedings several times a day to maintain their health. Tangs and surgeon fish may not get enough vegetable matter to eat in a reef tank, particularly smaller aquariums, and these fish should be provided with a constant supply of vegetables such as fresh seaweeds, leaf lettuce, bok choy, zucchini or (uncooked) seaweeds such as *nori*, or *Porphyra*. Other types of algae such as *Palmaria*, *Gracillaria*, and *Ulva*, are now widely available dry or fresh from your pet store.

The use of phosphate export and filter media that adsorb phosphate is now better understood and put to use than it was when we recommended in *The Reef Aquarium* volume one to *avoid adding excessive amounts of liquid food supplements, since they may contribute to phosphate accumulation* (Delbeek and Sprung, 1994). Because of the use of algae filters, granular iron based phosphate filter media, or biological phosphate reduction, it is now possible to realize the benefits of feeding heavily without the worry that it will pollute the water with phosphate. We further discuss phosphate control in chapter 6.

In larger aquariums with strong illumination and a deep substratum, the growth of algae and the development of populations of crustaceans and worms provide enough food for many fish to thrive with little or no feeding. Each aquarium differs in its food input requirement and ability to generate live food. Food additions, discussed in chapter 10, can also increase the biological productivity in systems with thick substrata.

Trace and minor elements

The subject of trace and minor elements in the marine environment and in closed system aquariums has been characterized in quite different ways by various authors of aquarium literature. The *old* idea was that *trace elements* were something that quickly became depleted in closed system aquariums. They were lost to a variety of factors, such as precipitation, uptake by plants and animals, adsorption by filter media or removed by the protein skimmer. While it is true that these processes do deplete trace elements, recent attention paid to the fate of individual elements based on analysis of the water from aquariums, suggest that some trace elements are not depleted but in fact accumulate in aquariums (Fosså and Nilsen, 1996; Shimek, 2001). However, one cannot generalize and say this is true for all trace elements. It certainly is not. In addition, even trace elements that accumulate in an aquarium may not necessarily be in the water, or at toxic levels, or even if they are in the water in high concentration, they may be strongly chelated and thus not biologically available at all (Sekha, 2003). What trace elements do in aquariums and why they are important is a complex subject sure to generate continued research and debate. The study of trace elements in the ocean and coastal ecosystems offers parallel perspectives.

What are trace and minor elements?

Although some elements found at trace levels are not metals, for example boron, iodine and nutrient elements such as phosphorus, trace elements are often considered synonymous with trace metals.

The preferred standard unit of measure used to describe trace element concentration is in moles (molar), which gives a measure of the actual *number* of ions present, as opposed to ppm (parts per million), which gives a measure of the *mass* of ions present. Morel and Price (2003) define trace elements as having a concentration less than 0.1 micromolar (μmol), while other authors use different definitions. Bruland and Lohan (2004) have concentrations of trace metals in seawater in the open sea falling within a range bounded by 10 mmol at the upper end and extending through fmol/kg seawater at the lower end [μ(micro)= 10^{-6}, n (nano)=10^{-9}, p (pico)=10^{-12}, and f (fempto)=10^{-15}]. A concentration of 10 mmol/kg (1 ppm by weight) is chosen arbitrarily as the concentration separating trace metals from the major and minor metals in seawater (Pilson, 1998).

Major elements are at a concentration of xmmol/kg and higher, while minor elements have a concentration in between trace and major (K. Bruland, pers. comm.). The mean concentration of a trace metal is strongly influenced by its deep-water value, particularly that found in the deep waters of the Pacific Ocean with its large volume. Table 4.10 presents the range of concentrations and their mean for some important elements in seawater along with an estimate of the major inorganic form or species found in seawater.

Trace elements in nature

A combination of processes controls the concentration and distribution of different trace elements in the sea. Inputs include rivers, windblown dust, and hydrothermal circulation at mid-ocean ridges. Removal of trace elements from the sea occurs mainly due to active removal by biological processes (incorporation into biomass), complexation, and passive attachment to living or nonliving particulate matter in the water column. The latter process leads to a sink for trace metals in sediments, but trace elements attached to

Table 4.10. The range of concentration in the sea of selected elements of special interest to aquarists. Modified after Bruland and Lohan (2004).

Element	Dom. inorg. species	Range in open sea	Mean concentration
Calcium	Ca^{2+}	10.1 - 10.3 mmol/kg	10.3 mmol/kg
Bromine	Br^-	–	0.84 mmol/kg
Boron	H_3BO^3	–	416 μmol/kg
Strontium	Sr^{2+}	–	90 μmol/kg
Silicate	H_4SiO_4	0.5 - 180 μmol/kg	100 μmol/kg
Phosphate	HPO_4^{2-}	0.001 - 3.5 μmol/kg	2.3 μmol/kg
Iodine	IO_3^-	400 - 460 nmol/kg	450 nmol/kg
Copper	$CuCO_3^0$	0.5 - 4.5 nmol/kg	3 nmol/kg
Iron	$Fe(OH)_2^+/Fe(OH)_3^0$	0.02 - 2 nmol/kg	0.5 nmol/kg
Manganese	Mn^{2+}	0.08 - 5 nmol/kg	0.3 nmol/kg

particles are also recycled in the water column and on sediment surfaces (Bruland and Lohan, 2004). Coastal regions have more dynamic distributions of trace elements than the open sea due to the higher potential for inputs (rivers and runoff) and uptake (shallow biologically productive marine habitats, and nutrient enriched, biologically more productive water columns). A great deal is now known about the concentrations and distributions of trace elements in the open sea [see for example the references in Bruland and Lohan (2004)], but there have not been similar peer reviewed studies conducted on coral reefs. Avid aquarist Richard Harker analyzed seawater samples from coral reefs and found surprisingly elevated levels compared to earlier published data for natural seawater (Harker, 2003, 2004a,b). Since trace metals are by definition in very small concentration, it is possible for the range of error in testing methods to give very imprecise results, and it is quite easy to contaminate samples before the test (Bruland and Lohan, 2004). More precise collection methods and testing procedures have yielded more reliable data for the open sea only recently (Bruland and Lohan, 2004). In the absence of new peer reviewed data for coral reef water from different regions, it is impossible to evaluate the accuracy of the data obtained by Harker (2003). We believe Harker's data is an intriguing impetus for more scientists to study trace element dynamics in coral reefs.

Why are trace elements important?

Trace elements are often called *micronutrients*. They are essential for many metabolic functions in plants, animals and microorganism, as we will explain shortly. It is almost a paradox that many of the elements in smallest concentration in the sea are so important to life.

Chelation and trace element availability

It is not the specific concentration of a trace element that is important; it can simply be the availability of it. The availability of trace elements to organisms living in aquatic systems is not only determined by the concentrations, but also by the chemical form of the elements. Naturally occurring chelating substances, organic ligands, form dissociable complexes with trace metal ions, keeping them in solution and maintaining the availability, or non-availability of their free ions. Humic substances in natural waters are believed to have this benefit. A similar capacity can be achieved with the synthetic chelator EDTA. Adding EDTA alone to water used to culture algae has been shown to enhance the growth of the algae (Darley, 1982). Its effect is probably both to increase the availability of trace metal ions already present in the water and to decrease the toxic levels of excess free metal ions. One may thus think of chelating substances as buffers that maintain metal ions at optimal levels. Excess EDTA (over chelating) can also be used to reduce the availability of free metal ions to levels that limit algal growth (Darley,

1982). In aquariums, the use of activated carbon to remove dissolved organic compounds from the water may also have an affect on trace element availability since it may strongly remove chelating substances. Conversely, allowing an aquarium to become very rich in dissolved organic matter may limit the availability of trace elements due to the *over-chelating* affect.

Marine algae and trace element availability

The practice of setting up *refugium* aquariums with *Caulerpa* spp. and other marine algae has become popular lately due to several benefits that result, in addition to the perception that using algae re-creates processes that occur in nature. One of the benefits of growing algae in an aquarium is that the algae release dissolved organic compounds that act as chelators, binding to elements and compounds in the water (see *Iron (Fe)*, later in this chapter). They excrete into the water nutritious organic substances called exudates that include polysaccharides, complex organic nitrogenous matter, vitamins, and phenolic compounds. Some of the dissolved organic matter contributes to the water staining in near-shore habitats and in recirculating aquariums. In the natural environment, some of the exudates aggregate to form large particles in the water column, part of the material known as *marine snow*. Soft corals and other filter feeders that feed on particulate organic matter (Fabricius and Dommisse, 2000) may obtain concentrated trace elements this way. Rates of exudation increase with photosynthesis during the light period and decrease in the dark (Ragan and Jensen, 1979) and, as is true for corals with symbiotic zooxanthellae, a significant amount of the carbon budget for seaweeds may be lost (exuded) as dissolved organic carbon (Hatcher *et al.*, 1977). In the natural setting, algal exudates probably help maintain availability of scarce free metal ions, and they may *save the day* in closed system aquariums by preventing potential harm should certain elements accumulate. This effect is in addition to the fact that algae take up trace elements as they grow, and export them when harvested from the aquarium.

Colloids and trace metals

Metal ions interact with inorganic ions such as chloride or sulfate, and they form complex molecules with organic compounds in the water. Some undissolved particles in the water also adsorb, or bind dissolved trace elements. By definition, dissolved elements pass through a 0.4 μm filter. Some tiny particles can also pass through such a filter with the metals attached. These particles are known as colloids. The association of trace elements with colloids affects their availability to aquatic organisms, and it affects the distribution, transport, and removal of trace elements in aquatic environments.

In the natural environment, physical and chemical interactions affect the rate at which trace elements are transferred from the dissolved to the particulate phase, and transported or exported. In one physical mechanism called *colloidal pumping*, an element attaches quickly to fine particles that in turn slowly aggregate into larger particles that become buried in the sediments thus removing the elements from the water column. This process no doubt also occurs in aquariums, but the affect of it must be different since we do not have an adjacent deep ocean nor a shoreline where thus-trapped elements can be deposited. However, we do have export mechanisms, as we will shortly explain. In chapter 6 we also show how, through *advection*, these buried trace elements can become available again.

Trace and minor elements in the aquarium

Boron (B)
Boron is found in seawater at a concentration of 4.4 mg/L (416 µmol/kg) and it occurs in two forms, boric acid, $B(OH)_3$ and borate, $B(OH)_4^-$. In its two forms, boron accounts for about 29% of the buffering system in natural seawater (Holmes-Farley, 2002d). As such, it also contributes to the buffering capacity in aquariums; however, maintaining a proper boron level is not entirely critical and most aquariums are only slightly deficient in boron anyway (Holmes-Farley, 2002d). However, boron deficiency may cause pigment loss in certain algae (Round, 1965).

Some commercial salts and buffers have highly elevated levels of borate in an attempt to stabilize pH swings in aquariums. These high borate levels can interfere with regular alkalinity test kits by giving a high total alkalinity value (measured as bicarbonate +carbonate + borate) without indicating whether the bicarbonate and carbonate levels are low, which are the components most critical to calcification. Boron test kits are available on the market as are boron supplements. Boron is determined by mannitol titration after removing carbon dioxide. For reef aquariums we recommend keeping boron at or near natural seawater concentrations. We further discuss the role of borate in water chemistry and alkalinity control in chapter 5.

Bromine (Br)
Bromine is similar to iodine and chlorine in its ability to act as an oxidizer and occurs at a concentration of about 65 ppm (840 µmol/kg) in natural seawater. However, these elements exist mainly as ions in seawater and as such are much less reactive e.g. bromide, iodide/iodate and chloride. Atkinson and Bingman (1999) showed some artificial seawater mixes were deficient in bromine though

formulations may have changed since that publication. However, suppliers of salts to public aquariums omit bromine primarily because of its affects with ozone. Ozonation of bromine results in the generation of highly oxidative by-products such as hypobromite, bromite and bromate ions (Bingman, 1997a). In addition, the organic brominated compounds produced by ozonation can theoretically cause serious problems as well (Bingman, 1997a). These compounds should be easily removed by activated carbon.

Although bromine is not depleted in fish-only aquariums, it may be depleted by macroalgae and other organisms in reef aquariums. Bromine has been found to be a component in a wide variety of marine organisms and many of the compounds it is a part of have cytotoxic or similarly aggressive properties that have made them the object of much attention in the search for antiviral, antimicrobial, anti-HIV, and anticancer agents (Bingman, 1997a). It is also known that red seaweeds incorporate it in their tissues, mainly because it is noxious, which inhibits herbivores from eating the algae. Some algae even exude organic substances containing bromine into the surrounding water as a means of competing with other algae and bacteria (Fenical, 1975). Such allelopathic interactions may be among the positive effects of growing red seaweeds in aquariums, when sufficient bromine is available to them.

Bingman (1997a) reported no adverse affects of adding bromide compounds to his aquarium at natural seawater values but did report perceivable improvement in coralline algae and sponge growth, though these observations were entirely subjective. Commercial supplements are available for adding bromides to a reef aquarium, but if you use them and ozone is used on the aquarium, then exercise caution by using activated carbon as well.

Bromide measurement in seawater is accomplished by oxidation to bromate and reaction with iodide to form iodine, which is titrated with thiosulfate. Inductively coupled plasma mass spectrometry (ICP mass spec) is an alternative. Hobbyists don't need to and generally don't bother testing for bromide. For those who are interested, Hach chemical company of Loveland, Colorado, USA (www.hach.com) sells a bromine test kit that does work in seawater but it can be interfered with by iodate and residual ozone.

Iodine (I)

Iodine is found in marine waters at a concentration of 0.06 ppm (460 nmol/kg). Iodine occurs in various forms in seawater, both inorganic and organic. The iodate ion (IO_3^-) is the stable form of iodine in seawater. However, in the euphotic zone, some of the IO_3^- is reduced to elemental iodine (I^-) by phytoplankton that reduce nitrate to nitrite (Bruland and Lohan, 2004). Given the large number of iodine species found in seawater, measuring iodine is fraught with problems. The addition of iodine to reef aquariums was first popularized by Peter Wilkens in his early books (Wilkens, 1989) but its benefits remain debated even today, though most reef aquarium hobbyists agree that at least occasional additions of iodine have positive effects. Some aquarium authors, however, propose that iodine additions should not be made (Shimek, 1999). The idea is that iodine can be adequately supplied with fish foods. In fact, iodine is supplied with fish foods, but its availability may not be consistent if foods are the only means of supplementing it. It is true that iodine must not be overdosed; it is toxic. Iodine kills bacteria, so positive effects observed may relate to curbing the growth of pathogenic bacteria strains. Nevertheless, iodine is incorporated in the tissues of red and brown seaweeds, and they need iodine supplements to grow. Some soft corals, including gorgonians, also incorporate iodine in their tissues.

Iodine supplements typically are made with potassium iodide, following the recipe of Wilkens (1990). Lugol's or strong iodine is a mixture of potassium iodide and iodine available from pharmacies, and some authors have proposed its use for supplementing iodine in aquariums. One must be especially careful about dosage with Lugol's since it is a concentrated source of iodine. Lugol's solution is also used in a diluted form as a prophylactic *dip* to sterilize corals, to prevent or treat bacterial infections. When we first wrote about iodine supplementation we provided formulae for making stock solutions (Delbeek and Sprung, 1994). However, given the widespread availability of iodine supplements today it is much more convenient to purchase them now than to make your own. Hobby test kits for measuring iodide/iodate exist, but we don't know how accurate they are.

Iron (Fe)

Holmes-Farley (2002b) gives a typical surface seawater value for iron of 0.000006 ppm. Bruland and Lohan, (2004) has the average concentration of iron in the sea at 540 pmol/kg, but in any case, its concentration is depleted in surface waters where it is scavenged by photosynthetic organisms (which are in turn preyed upon by other organisms). In surface waters, the mean concentration of dissolved iron is 70 pmol/kg (Bruland and Lohan, 2004). In coastal regions where deepwater upwelling occurs, iron rich deepwater mixing with surface water may elevate the iron concentration significantly (Johnson *et al.*, 1999). Iron may also enter coastal waters from river flows, and it settles as dust on the sea surface in some regions. Iron is stable as the +III oxidation state in oxygenated seawater as $Fe(OH)_2^-$. This form of iron is insoluble, and based on its chemistry, the concentration in seawater should be less than 200 pmol/kg (Millero, 1996). However, an organic ligand that binds iron very

The physical process known as *advection*, described in chapter 6, can draw water rich in reduced iron out of the sediments up into the water column, where it may combine with organic ligands. This process, driven by water motion, may help maintain iron availability around coral reefs.

strongly is present in open ocean seawater at concentrations near 0.6 nmol/L (Rue and Bruland, 1995). This ligand may prevent iron from being lost to the sediments and it certainly serves to keep the mean concentration of iron at a level much higher than it would be based on its solubility (Johnson *et al.*, 1997).

Organic compounds that tightly bind to other compounds are known as chelators. Chelators are produced naturally by a wide range of organisms that occur in our aquaria, particularly algae. Man-made chelators such as EDTA are often used in conjunction with iron and other additives to allow them to remain in solution longer and thus presumably, make them bio-available over a longer period to organisms in the tank. However, many of the chelators naturally produced may have the opposite effect regarding bioavailability. Therefore, when measuring iron levels most tests provide a total iron level but cannot determine how much of this is actually bio-available and how much is organically chelated and unavailable (Holmes-Farley, 2002c).

Iron is a component of the cytochrome molecule, and is thus a critical requirement for algae (including symbiotic zooxanthellae). Iron deficiency lowers the rate of photosynthesis. In alkaline waters (e.g. seawater), the amount of free iron in solution remains very low, but it can be available in colloidal form (Round, 1965). Iron is strongly limited in most marine aquariums due to the presence of chelators and/or precipitation. It can be supplied with unfiltered top-off water, trace element or iron supplements, and with some foods.

Studies of the affects of iron supplementation on corals have given mixed results. In some studies, the zooxanthellae in corals were shown to increase in number, darkening the coral *Stylophora pistillata* (Ferrier-Pages *et al.* 2001) whereas other studies have shown that corals (*Porites lutea*) actually lost zooxanthellae when exposed to elevated iron levels (Harland and Brown, 1989).

In our opinion, it is essential to add iron to aquariums for the health of zooxanthellate corals, anemones, and other marinelife, and it should be added as a supplement. When the growth of undesirable algae (particularly diatoms) is strong, iron supplementation can further promote this growth, even though it is not itself the cause. In addition, hydroxides of iron can be used to precipitate or adsorb phosphate, and thus can be used to limit algae growth (see *phosphate control* in chapter 6). There are several commercial test kits available to measure iron, but given the low levels of iron present in seawater, the utility of these kits is questionable.

Manganese (Mn)

The average concentration of manganese in seawater is 0.027 ppb (360 pmol/kg) (Johnson, 2000). Concentrations of dissolved manganese are high at the sea surface and they decrease with depth as dissolved Mn^{2+} is adsorbed onto sinking particles and removed to the sediment. Most of the Mn dissolved in seawater is Mn(II), present as the Mn^{2+} ion, which persists due to slow oxidation kinetics (Johnson, 2000). Manganese concentration is highest at the sea surface because sunlight causes photochemical reduction of Mn (IV) oxides to soluble Mn (II) (Morel and Price, 2003).

Manganese is a cofactor that is essential for chloroplast production and chlorophyll formation, and it participates and assists iron in energy release from energy transferring molecules during photosynthesis. Manganese is also involved in the uptake of

This *Goniopora* sp. responds to the addition of iron and manganese by expanding its polyps and developing intense coloration. These metals may be essential to its mechanism for coping with photosynthetically-produced oxygen free-radicals. J. Sprung

nitrogen, and its addition to algal cultures stimulates photosynthesis and growth. Manganese is required for growth in the light in some algae (Round, 1965) and it may similarly be required by other algae, including the zooxanthellae associated with corals and tridacnid clams. Manganese occurs in quite high concentration in common fish food ingredients. For example, we have these figures from Robert Brons (pers comm.): shrimp meal 30-50 mg/kg; fish meal 50-100 mg/kg; CyclopEeze 40 mg/kg; kelp meal 0.1% (1 g/kg) manganese! Despite the high inputs that could occur with food additions, manganese does not accumulate in aquariums. It is rapidly oxidized and precipitates out of solution. Since manganese is often limited in marine aquariums, it should be added via supplementation. Several commercial preparations containing chelated manganese exist. The dosage is not so critical, in our experience, mainly because

Trachyphyllia geoffroyi sometimes bleach after months of excellent health in aquariums. This condition can sometimes be reversed with the weekly addition of a supplement containing iron and manganese. Other causes for bleaching such as over-illumination or bacterial disease should also be investigated. J. Sprung

manganese does not persist very long in the water. Nevertheless, one should always follow instructions given with a product to avoid overdosing. Tom Frakes suggests caution with adding manganese, due to his own experience with unexplained fish mortalities at a fish hatchery when shipping fish in newly mixed artificial seawater that had a manganese level far above natural seawater (T. Frakes, pers. comm.).

Manganese also activates important enzymes, and is involved with superoxide dismutase, an enzyme that detoxifies oxygen free-radicals. This indicates a connection to the zooxanthellae and bleaching, which is often a response to the over-production of oxygen free radicals (Warner *et al.*, 1999; Downs *et al.*, 2002). Different forms of superoxide dismutase have iron or manganese. Other forms of superoxide dismutase have other metal ions associated with them, but only iron and manganese are likely to be limiting in closed aquariums (Shimek, 2002; Fosså and Nilsen, 1996).

The anecdotal observation that iron and manganese seem to help alleviate bleaching symptoms in *G. tenuidens*, (Sprung, 2003) and the literature concerning detoxification of oxygen free-radicals suggests these elements are useful to the coral, but does not necessarily suggest that *Goniopora* spp. have a special requirement for iron and manganese. More work on this subject is needed.

Molybdenum (Mo)
Dissolved molybdenum exists as the molybdate (MoO_4^{2-}) anion in seawater. The average concentration in natural seawater is 10 ppb (100 nmol/kg) (Johnson, 2000). Nitrogen fixation by blue-green algae requires adequate molybdenum and it is believed to also be involved in phosphatase activity (Round, 1965). There are anecdotal claims in aquarium literature that molybdenum supplementation stimulates the growth of cyanobacteria, but this has not been tested.

Molybdenum (along with iron) is utilized in both nitrogenase, the enzyme responsible for nitrogen fixation, and nitrate reductase, the enzyme required for denitrification (see the following url: http://www.princeton.edu/~cebic/N-cycle-detail.html). As such, Mo can become depleted in regions where denitrification is very active such as deep sand beds and within live rock. Unfortunately, testing for Mo requires sophisticated analytical equipment. Recent water analysis of closed aquariums (Shimek, 2002a,b) suggests that Mo is not limited, but accumulates due to food additions. However, as indicated in chapter 2, the methodologies of Shimek's studies have been called into question, and it may also be that natural seawater collected from reefs has elevated levels of some trace elements, similar to levels found in our aquariums (Harker, 2003, 2004a,b).

In the sea, Mo has an almost uniform distribution, with only a slight depletion at the surface. Although Mo is required as an essential metal co-factor in a number of enzymes such as nitrogenase, this requirement is small relative to the amount of Mo available and does not appreciably affect its distribution in the sea. In addition, negatively charged anions such as MoO_4^{2-} have a relatively low particle affinity at the slightly basic pH of seawater, so they do not adsorb readily onto them and are thus more stable in the water (Bruland and Lohan, 2004). It seems likely that Mo does not need to be supplemented in well-fed reef aquariums, but this has not been tested.

Silicon (Si)

Diatoms use silicate in the form of orthosilicic acid, $Si(OH)_4$, to form their siliceous skeletons, known as frustules. They also utilize silicate in DNA synthesis. Other Chrysophyta and Chlorophyta are also known to accumulate silicon or form siliceous scales. The concentration of silicate-silica in natural seawater ranges from a trace to as much as 4 mg/L. The average is 100 µmol/L. In natural freshwaters, the silicate concentration may also have this range, but in some localities, it may exceed 50 ppm. Concentrations of dissolved silicate are low at the ocean surface due to biological uptake by diatoms that can completely strip it from the water.

Aquarists try to limit the input of silicate into the aquarium because diatoms are viewed as a negative feature since they obstruct the view through the aquarium windows and will coat rock and sand surfaces. The method used for limiting silicate is purification (usually by reverse osmosis or deionization) of the freshwater used for top-off of evaporation. Since one might expect an R.O. filter to remove about 90-95% of a particular ion, if the source tap water has 50 ppm of silicate, there will still be 5 ppm left in the purified water. Therefore it is important to know the level of silicate in your tap water to be sure that the water filter can be effective at limiting silicate. Silicate is difficult to remove via reverse osmosis and in the above example, a secondary deionization filter placed after the R.O. filter would be needed to bring the silicate level below 0.5 ppm, an acceptable level for top-off water.

In closed system marine aquariums, the silicate level in the water can fall to levels that limit diatom growth due to a combination of infrequent water changes, use of purified top-off water, diatom grazing by herbivorous snails and fishes, and export (through siphoning or protein skimming) of the waste fecal pellets of the herbivores. There will always be some silicate available in glass aquariums because a small amount is supplied by dissolution of the glass itself, in addition to the small amount supplied with top-off water and food. Silica is only slightly soluble in seawater, and its cycle in nature is limited by the fact that diatoms that use it are insoluble except under very alkaline situations. For this reason, diatom growth slows with time as an aquarium ages. A large water change, which may significantly elevate the silicate level, normally produces a short-term bloom of diatom growth, usually appearing as a brown coat on the glass a day or so after the water change and lasting for only about a week.

Diatoms are important in food webs in marine ecosystems, and some authors of aquarium literature have pointed out that allowing them to grow (with sufficient herbivory) may be beneficial (Bingman, 2000). By promoting the growth of diatoms on surfaces within an aquarium, one may duplicate natural food webs that supply food to fishes and invertebrates. A close examination of surfaces with diatoms growing on them reveals a proliferation of copepods and other microorganisms. The same surfaces without diatoms feature far fewer creatures. Supplementation with silicate or with unfiltered tapwater has been suggested for supplying trace quantities to promote not only diatom but also sponge growth. Although it is true that many sponges use silicate to form spicules, the main limiting factor for growing some sponges in captivity is their food source (large quantities of dissolved organic matter), not silicate. We don't recommend adding silicate as a supplement for most display aquariums, though it is unavoidably added to some degree with top-off water or with water changes. The main reason not to add silicate is the increased maintenance chore of window cleaning that results from its addition. To some extent, this can be offset by having a large number of herbivorous snails cleaning the windows, but even these obstruct the view. The higher productivity associated with maintaining a natural seawater level of silicate may have some advantages in farming or fish culture and grow-out systems, where the excess production of micro-crustaceans that feed on diatoms can supplement the food requirements of the cultured animals. Free-floating diatoms may also provide a food source for corals, clams and other filter feeders.

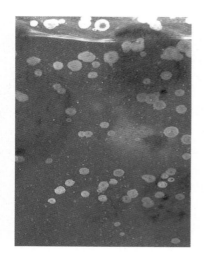

By promoting the growth of diatoms on surfaces within an aquarium, one may duplicate natural food webs that supply food to fishes and invertebrates. J. Sprung

Strontium (Sr)

Strontium occurs at a concentration of about 8 ppm (90 μM) in natural seawater at full strength salinity (S=35). It is chemically similar to calcium and is incorporated along with calcium in the skeletons and shells of marine invertebrates. Anecdotal reports by aquarists link strontium supplementation with rapid coral growth. One aquarium author proposes that these observations are meaningless and that strontium is a poison (Shimek, 1999). It is our opinion that no harm could possibly be done by attempting to maintain natural seawater values of strontium. We have also observed a positive influence on corals when making weekly additions of a strontium chloride solution to aquariums. In our opinion, strontium is an important supplement for reef aquariums with growing stony corals.

Clode and Marshall (2002), found that strontium occurred in high concentration in the mucous layers of *Galaxea fascicularis*, and proposed that the positively charged strontium neutralized negatively charged mucin glycoproteins. They further proposed a possible role that strontium could have in aiding calcification in corals by promoting the concentration of calcium ions near the ectodermal cell layer. By helping to form a stable mucin layer next to the ectodermis, strontium might help maintain an artificially high calcium concentration near the surface of the ectodermal cells. This would aid what is thought to be a limiting factor in calcification: the active transport of calcium. This hypothesis provides a plausible mechanism for aquarium corals to benefit from strontium additions (Holmes-Farley, 2003) but remains to be investigated.

Adding strontium

We once believed that the use of calcium reactors that dissolve aragonite gravel or coral skeletons as a means of maintaining calcium and alkalinity could preclude the need to add extra strontium, since the dissolving calcareous media would provide strontium ions as well. However, analyses of various calcium reactor substrates have shown that the Ca:Sr ratio in many popular brands is far below the normal ratios taken out by corals during calcification (Holmes-Farley, 2003). Therefore, it is likely that strontium supplementation is still required. On the other hand, artificial salt mixes often have higher than normal levels of strontium and if water changes are performed frequently enough, they could provide adequate levels of strontium. The use of two-part calcium and alkalinity supplements that contain strontium may also supply sufficient strontium if used regularly. Using calcium hydroxide to make kalkwasser for daily water top-off is another source of some strontium ions. Of course, the question of whether these sources are sufficient to maintain natural seawater levels depends on the rate at which strontium is consumed in aquaria by calcification and abiotic precipitation with calcium carbonate. Only periodic testing for strontium can determine if adequate levels are being maintained and, although hobby test kits exist, they are not simple to use. Using ICP analysis, Holmes-Farley (2003), found that samples of aquarium water often had strontium levels in the normal range or higher, and the lowest measurement was only 1/2 the natural seawater value. Based on its expected deposition with rapid calcification of corals, it was a surprise to find that the strontium level could be maintained so easily. This brings into question the accuracy of the testing method, or the accuracy of the analysis of calcium reactor media, or our understanding of the fate of strontium in reef aquariums or possibly all three. It is also possible that the use of strontium supplements explains the successful maintenance of strontium in the sampled aquariums (Holmes-Farley, 2003). In the *Reef Aquarium* volume one (Delbeek and Sprung, 1994), we gave instructions for making your own 10% strontium mix using strontium chloride hexahydrate. Several manufacturers now provide this element in a variety of forms, so it is more convenient to purchase these than to make your own.

Vitamins

A discussion of vitamins should focus primarily on their use in foods, not in the water. However, it is a fact that some vitamins are among the so-called *organic factors* in seawater (Round, 1965) that are required by algae (and presumably zooxanthellae as well). Cobalamin (B12), thiamin (B1), biotin, folic acid, pantothenic acid, and pyroxidine are known to be required by a large number of algae or at least to stimulate their growth (Round, 1965). Red and brown seaweeds uptake cobalamin, but some cyanobacteria are able to synthesize it, possibly being the principle source of this vitamin in natural waters (Round, 1965). It has also been suggested that oceanic blooms of dinoflagellates may be stimulated by influxes of cobalamin washed into the sea from soils during the rainy season (Round, 1965).

Some aquarium trace element supplements contain vitamins, and liquid vitamin supplements that can be added to the water exist. The addition of these *organic factors* to the water may produce improvements in the growth and health of seaweeds and corals, and liberal use may contribute to the growth of unwanted strains of algae. We suggest that their use as a water supplement be done conservatively. Having a fish population that receives daily feeding certainly supplies soluble vitamins to the water in any case. Many vitamins are quickly oxidized in seawater aquariums at normal temperature, light and pH levels. Therefore, vitamins intended for use in aquariums should be complexed with other compounds to retard oxidation.

Filtration and other affects on trace elements

Activated carbon and trace elements

Activated carbon is used for removing dissolved organic substances that lend a yellow cast to the water. The organic substances are adsorbed onto the carbon, which has an extremely high surface area because of its highly porous structure. In our aquariums, the use of activated carbon may thus have an affect on algae growth, since it may strongly reduce the availability of chelating substances, and therefore trace element availability (Sprung, 2002). Conversely, allowing a system to become very rich in dissolved organic matter may limit the growth of algae by the over-chelating effect. Although it is widely held that activated carbon will remove iodine from the water, this is not entirely correct. This belief can be traced to a confusing term, *iodine number*, used to indicate the total pore volume of carbon. This number refers to the uptake of iodine in the form I_2, which is not very soluble in water and is not present in seawater. The iodine number does not indicate that carbon will bind the forms of iodine that do occur in seawater [iodide (I^-) and iodate (IO_3^-)], but carbon may remove iodide after it is incorporated by organisms into organic molecules (R. Holmes-Farley, pers. comm.).

Calcium hydroxide and trace elements

The daily addition of calcium hydroxide aka kalkwasser (see chapter 5) for maintaining calcium and alkalinity has some additional side affects. It is known that calcium hydroxide affects phosphate levels (Wilkens, 1990; **Studt and Frakes, 1995;** Bingman, 1995), but it is not well studied how calcium hydroxide dosing might affect the concentration of dissolved trace elements. Hydroxides are known to precipitate trace metals and are used in industrial applications for that purpose (Holmes-Farley, 2003b). It stands to reason that the daily addition of kalkwasser may function as a way to lower the concentration of trace metals in solution. Prevention of heavy metal accumulation can be viewed as a positive attribute, but the loss of iron and manganese from the water might be expedited by kalkwasser additions too (Sprung, 2002). The addition of both iron and kalkwasser theoretically could result in a precipitation of phosphates with iron hydroxide, but this has not been tested in a marine aquarium. It would eventually also result in an accumulation of brownish mud, unless this was removed sufficiently by a protein skimmer or mechanical filter.

Protein skimming and trace elements

Protein skimmers, a.k.a. foam fractionators employ a column of tiny bubbles that scrub the water of organic substances that stick to the interface between air and water. These compounds form foam that gathers in the skimmer's collection cup and collapses into a thick brownish fluid. The dissolved material collected from the water includes organic compounds such as carbohydrates, amino acids, lipids, and a fair amount of phosphate bound organically. Protein skimming also removes inorganic compounds bound with organic compounds, resulting in a gradual removal of trace elements (Moe, 1989).

Protein skimming not only traps organic compounds, but also phytoplankton, bacteria, algae spores and filaments, and fine detritus. The export of detritus is a means of limiting phosphate accumulation in the aquarium, and the trapping of phytoplankton, bacteria, algal spores and algal filaments is a nutrient export mechanism that includes the export of trace micronutrients incorporated in the tissue mass of the algae and bacteria. As a side benefit, algal growth is slowed because the nutrients algae need to grow are limited by the protein skimmer. This effect is taken advantage of with the *vodka dosing* technique described in the topic *Biological filtration*, chapter 6.

Ozone use and trace elements

Ozone is sometimes used in protein skimmers or other contact chambers for water purification. It is produced by a spark (corona discharge) that converts the oxygen (O_2) in the air into ozone (O_3). It can also be produced by an ultraviolet light source. The O_3 molecule is unstable, and the extra oxygen atom readily combines with organic compounds, with an effect like chlorine bleach. Ozone is a powerful oxidizer, and its use in aquariums is best managed with a redox potential meter and an experienced aquarist. Ozone converts bromine to hypobromite, and oxidizes trace elements, chelators and may reduce their concentration in aquariums.

The oxidation of chelators may result in a sudden temporary increase in free ions of the elements the chelators were attached to e.g. iron, iodine. This depends, of course, on the rate at which the chelators would be oxidized by ozone, something that is not yet well known. In the case of iodine, if it were chelated in an organic form, excess ozone could make it suddenly available, but would not have the same effect on inorganic forms (iodide/iodate) (R. Holmes-Farley, pers. comm.).

Redox

Redox is an abbreviation for reduction/oxidation, referring to types of chemical reactions. Oxidation and reduction reactions occur by electron transfer and by atom transfer. Reducing compounds or agents are electron donors, and oxidizing compounds or agents are electron acceptors. The process of oxidation involves a loss of electrons to oxidizing compounds, and the process of reduction involves a gain of electrons from reducing compounds. The transfer of oxygen atoms may also occur in redox reactions. Oxidation occurs with the gain of an oxygen atom, and reduction occurs with the loss of an oxygen atom. The redox value provides information about which type of reaction is dominant in a system.

In aquariums, redox potential is useful to measure because it gives a relative measure of the water purity. The measurement is a potential based on the sum of redox reactions occurring in the water; the higher the redox value, the greater the potential for oxidation to occur, the lower the number, the greater the potential for reduction. Reduction occurs in deep substrata, where natural redox values are negative. Measurements of redox potential in the ocean vary from 350-400 millivolts (Moe, 1989) to as low as 160-190 millivolts (Wilkens and Birkholz, 1986). Caution is advised in any comparisons due to differences in measuring conditions, technique and equipment used. Recommended aquarium redox levels range from 350-450 millivolts but each aquarist must go by the appearance of his/her own aquarium. Differences in probe placement, frequency of cleaning the probe, bioload, fauna composition, etc. all affect redox readings. It is not so much the value that is important, but the appearance of your aquarium inhabitants and the trend in measured redox values. If you notice that the redox begins to decline rapidly, this is a sign that something is fouling in the aquarium and you should investigate the cause. It can be as simple as a burrowing fish burying and killing a sessile invertebrate located on or close to the sand bed.

An ORP monitor, left, and ORP controller, right, from *American Marine* Inc.

Aquarists should not forget that the appearance of the animals is the most important quality of the system. There is a common tendency for aquarists who have redox meters to become more concerned about the numbers on the digital display than the animals in the aquarium. It makes no sense to worry about redox numbers when the aquarium is fine. Don't ruin a good thing by striving for levels you hear are *best*. Far more important is the pH and alkalinity level. For example, a high redox level, which might please the aquarist, could occur with low pH and alkalinity, which does not please the corals. Of course, high redox can also occur with normal alkalinity and pH.

Control of redox is achieved naturally through sand bed and aquarium maintenance. Artificial manipulation of redox is achieved using ozone and a redox controller. While it is not essential equipment for a reef aquarium, an ozonizer and redox control equipment may have utility in the prevention of low redox events that sometimes precede sudden bacterial disease problems for corals and echinoderms in reef aquariums.

Ozone dosing is particularly useful for the removal of colored dissolved organic matter (CDOM) from the water. Very small amounts can keep the water crystal clear and lower the level of dissolved organic nitrogen (DON) in the water, without the need for activated carbon.

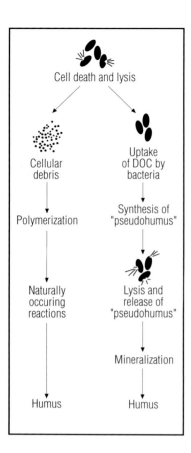

Cell death and lysis

Cellular debris

Polymerization

Naturally occuring reactions

Humus

Uptake of DOC by bacteria

Synthesis of "pseudohumus"

Lysis and release of "pseudohumus"

Mineralization

Humus

Proposed pathways for CDOM production in aquariums, after Spotte (1992).

Dissolved organic matter (DOM) production

Passive and active exudation by phytoplankton is a major source of DOM in seawater, including chromophoric or colored DOM (CDOM), a.k.a. *gelbstoff*, or *gilvin* (Rochelle-Newall *et al.* 2002). Bacteria in sediments and solid substrata also play an important role in the production of CDOM. In coastal areas, CDOM in the sea comes mainly from terrestrial freshwater runoff (Otis *et al.*, 2004). In tropical reef regions, seagrass beds and coral reef substrata are known to be primary CDOM sources (Boss and Zaneveld, 2003). Otis *et al.*, (2004) investigated the transport of CDOM between shallow banks and deep basins in the Bahamas. They found that CDOM was produced in the shallow banks where high rates of evaporation also elevated the salinity of the water compared to adjacent deep basin water that had a more stable salinity. The shallow bank water also was heated during the warm seasons and chilled during cold periods, and this set up density gradients that affected the exchange with deep basin water. The factors regulating production of DOM and CDOM (nutrient limitation, lability, and irradiance) are currently being investigated by Jean-Pierre Gattuso and his group of researchers in Monaco.

Importance of CDOM

Since CDOM is yellow, it strongly absorbs light wavelengths in the high-energy blue and UV range. It thus has an important role in protecting marine organisms from ultraviolet radiation (UVR), as well as roles in photochemical and photobiological processes (Nelson and Siegel, 2002). The protective benefit can be observed in aquariums, particularly when CDOM is allowed to accumulate and then is removed suddenly by the use of activated carbon or ozone. The change from yellow tinted water to colourless water allows a substantial increase in the penetration of blue and UV wavelengths, and may be accompanied by bleaching by corals and other photosynthetic organisms (Bingman, 1995b). We discuss UV dangers and the proper use of activated carbon in chapter 6.

Interaction DOM-POM-microorganisms

DOM can be transformed into particulate organic matter (POM) by both biotic (bacterial uptake) and abiotic processes such as coagulation of colloids into transparent exopolymeric particles (TEP). The production, size distribution and elemental composition (C and N) of TEP in the natural setting are also being investigated by Jean-Pierre Gattuso's group at the oceanographic laboratory in Villefranche-sur-mer, France (see http://www.obs-vlfr.fr/LOV/DBEM/objective3.htm for more information and a list of publications) in order to determine the role of these particles in the carbon cycle. We discuss biological pathways of dissolved and particulate organic matter and their control in chapter 6.

Turbidity and colour can become an issue when reef tanks reach large sizes such as this 378 m^3 (100,000 US gallon) reef tank at the Chiruami Aquarium, Okinawa, Japan and this 750 m^3 (198,000 US gallon) reef tank at the Burger's Zoo, Arnhem, The Netherlands. The Okinawa exhibit is an open system receiving filtered natural seawater whereas the Burger's exhibit is a closed system with minimal mechanical filtration. J.C. Delbeek

Turbidity

Turbidity refers to suspended matter in the water that obstructs the view. The matter can be air bubbles, particulate organic substances, dissolved organic substances, phytoplankton, zooplankton, and particulate inorganic matter such as clays or sand. For most small reef aquariums, turbidity is not an issue, since the distance of view through the water is short and most matter in the aquarium water is quickly removed by filtration methods or by filter feeding organisms. In much larger reef systems, turbidity can affect the view and ozone or mechanical filters such as rapid sand filters, are often used to improve visibility.

Calcium, Alkalinity and pH Maintenance

Calcifying organisms require calcium, a source of dissolved inorganic carbon (carbonates, bicarbonates, carbon dioxide) and the proper pH to allow calcification to occur. The mere presence of calcifying organisms in a closed system aquarium means that the water chemistry will quickly change unless these parameters are actively maintained by the aquarist. Before we elaborate on the numerous issues surrounding this topic, we want to give the reader a point of reference so that the magnitude of the problem is understood. It might seem like calcium and alkalinity maintenance is a long-term concern that can be managed periodically, but in fact the reactions involved in calcification, along with related photosynthesis and respiration, so profoundly dominate the water chemistry change in closed system aquaria that they often require some sort of management daily.

The small polyped stony coral dominated closed system reef aquarium of Jamie Cross is the kind of set up that demonstrates the highest demand for calcium and alkalinity supplementation. J.C. Delbeek

Bingman (1997) proposed a quantitative calcification model for reef aquariums, based on literature describing the rates of calcification on wild reefs at between 10 and 20 kg (22 and 44 lbs.) per square meter. In order to determine the potential calcium carbonate demand of a reef aquarium, multiply the area of the tank in meters by the figure for calcium carbonate formation on wild reefs. For example, given a brightly illuminated 684 L (180 gallon) aquarium (1.1 square meters projected area) with strong water-motion, live rock covering the projected area, and a large population of SPS corals, an aquarist would need to provide at least 11 kilograms (25 lbs.) of $CaCO_3$ equivalents per year (1.1 m^2 x 10 kg/m^2 = 11 kg). Assuming for the sake of the calculation that such an aquarium lacks coral predation and coral losses to disease, and since typical reef aquaria are maintained at higher alkalinity levels than natural seawater has, a reasonable engineering margin of double the expected rate should be delivered. Therefore, such a high-energy sps dominated aquarium should receive about 22 kg of $CaCO_3$ per year - that's nearly 50 lbs. of calcium carbonate equivalents, or about a pound per week! This is a substantial amount of calcium carbonate to deliver, and demonstrates the urgency of the problem involved in maintaining suitable growth conditions for corals confined to a finite body of water. Furthermore, as the corals grow, their demand increases.

Fortunately, the extreme example outlined by Bingman is the far end of the spectrum of reef aquaria. Reef aquaria with less illumination, lower water velocity, less live rock (i.e. more sand area, where net calcification is about 0 kg/square meter per year), and fewer calcifying corals require input of a lower amount of calcium carbonate equivalents. It should be evident that the dimensions of the aquarium, its composition of corals, rocks, and sand, and the rate of evaporation, relate to how successful one method or another of calcium and alkalinity supplementation will be at meeting the calcium carbonate demand.

Where else does all the calcium carbonate go?

While corals surely are the most important calcium carbonate depositors in an sps coral dominated reef aquarium, other creatures also play a significant role in the depletion of calcium and alkalinity from the water. Bingman (1998d) discusses the fate of calcium carbonate in typical reef aquaria, based on measurement data collected from a large number of established reef tanks, and concludes that biological calcification is the dominant factor, with inorganic deposition of calcium carbonate chalk accounting for less than 10 percent of the input. Coralline algae, which coat not only the rocks but also the walls (if allowed to do so), play a major role in the depletion, but have a lower influence compared to corals. Based on a survey of the literature concerning calcification on wild reefs, Bingman (1998d) assigned a calcification rate of 10 to 20 kg per square meter per year for reef aquarium surfaces dominated by sps stony corals, but only 4 kg per square meter per year for smooth coralline algae coated surfaces. Keeping the viewing windows and other walls free of them can significantly reduce the calcium and alkalinity demand of the system. It has been our experience, however, that coralline algae are out-competed by corals when the demand for calcium and alkalinity exceeds the inputs from the aquarist, in a coral dominated aquarium. The corals continue to grow when the coralline algae stop growing. Therefore, if the aquarium is maintained with calcium and alkalinity supplementation just shy of the demand, the result is an aquarium with corals that grow rapidly, and greenish rocks with few crustose coralline algae. If the aquarium has few corals, but coralline coated rock, the coralline algae grow in balance with the small population of corals when the calcium and alkalinity supply is just adequate to meet the demand. Supplying excess calcium and alkalinity in a balanced fashion promotes rapid growth in both.

This aquarium, which features an enormous concentration and diversity of stony corals for the water volume, has a high demand for calcium and carbonate alkalinity. The corals are obviously growing, but the rocks have almost no coralline algae. B. Mohr

Bacteria living within the sand bed can biologically deposit calcium carbonate and cause the solidification of portions of the bottom substrata. J. Sprung

Unlike the red crustose corallines, green calcareous *Halimeda* spp. appear to compete with corals, and continue growing even after the coralline algae *and* corals stop growing. *Halimeda* spp. are limited, however, by plant nutrients including iron, nitrogenous compounds and phosphorus. Calcifying molluscs and tube worms are another sink for calcium carbonate, as are soft corals and echinoderms, which have skeletal elements made of calcium carbonate.

When the calcium and alkalinity are at or above saturation, a certain amount of calcium carbonate spontaneously precipitates onto bare calcareous surfaces (such as sand or gravel), on aquarium heaters, and the impellers of magnetic drive pumps, but as we said, this is a minor loss compared to biological precipitation. Furthermore, some calcium ions are precipitated with phosphate, forming calcium phosphate solids that settle in the substrata. In addition, within sand beds and even in the water column there is bacteria mediated formation of calcium carbonate crystals (McCallum and Kishwar, 1970). The bacteria cause the formation of aragonite crystals, the same form of calcium carbonate deposited by corals. This sink to the bacteria fauna can be significant under certain circumstances, such as high levels of biological denitrification within the sand bed when the calcium and alkalinity are already far above saturation (Bingman, 1999d). The result is the formation of calcium carbonate deposits between sand grains that can produce a solidified mass or chunks in the sand bed (see further discussion of this under the topic biological filtration, in chapter 6). Under this biologically mediated special circumstance only, when the water is supersaturated with calcium carbonate, the net calcification in the sand bed exceeds the typical 0 kg/square meter per year cited by Bingman (1998d).

Coralline algae form calcareous crusts on the rocks, windows, and other surfaces in a reef aquarium, depleting calcium, magnesium, and alkalinity as they grow. J. Sprung

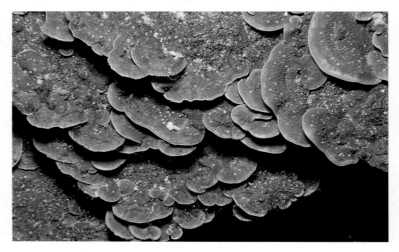

Small polyped stony corals require the saturation state of aragonite in the water to be above 1.0 to grow. Their growth rapidly pushes the saturation state downward, making the maintenance of ideal growth conditions a challenge. M. Resch

Calcium

The concentration of calcium in natural seawater at S=35 is about 400 mg/L. The level near coral reefs and in zones that are saltier than full strength seawater tends to be slightly elevated, at around 420 to as high as 480 mg/L (J. Sprung, pers. obs.). This simply means the aquarist should strive to maintain the calcium level in a reef aquarium near 400 mg/L at a specific gravity of about 1.025. Comparisons of measurements of the calcium ion concentration in seawater must include the salinity level (or specific gravity), since the calcium concentration increases when the salinity increases, and vice versa. In our experience, successful reef aquaria can be maintained with deficient calcium levels (less than 400 mg/L), but only when the carbonate hardness (alkalinity) is balanced or elevated. In experiments with the reef building coral *Stylophora pistillata*, calcification did not increase at dissolved calcium levels above

360 ppm (Tambutte *et al.*, 1996), though it decreased at concentrations below this level. Troubles with coral growth occur more because of low alkalinity than low calcium level. High alkalinity maintains a high pH, resulting in the ratio of calcium and bicarbonate ions in the water being closer to saturation, making calcification more likely. This is a key point to understand: it is the *saturation state* in the water of the aragonite form of calcium carbonate, not just the calcium concentration, which is the limiting parameter for coral growth and calcification by other calcifiers. We will revisit the topic of saturation later in this chapter.

The calcium level can be maintained above 400 mg/L, but it should not be much higher than 450 mg/L since such high calcium concentrations can cause a spontaneous loss of alkalinity as calcium carbonate may precipitate under certain conditions when the saturation point is exceeded. This is not a problem if the method of replenishment is *balanced*, as the loss of calcium and alkalinity will be replenished in the proper proportion. If the replenishment method is not balanced, the precipitation can produce a situation where the calcium level rises very high and the alkalinity plummets, or vice versa. We discuss the meaning of balanced replenishment, and correction of imbalances, later in this chapter.

The elevated dissolved calcium level around coral reefs seems a paradox; the place where calcium is being removed from the water most rapidly has a higher level of calcium in the water than the nearby open sea. The explanation for this phenomenon is both simple and complex, but the net effect is that the environment where coral reefs flourish is also a place where the calcium and alkalinity tend to be at or above the saturation state of aragonite in the open sea. Reef shallows exposed to intense illumination and ocean breezes lose water to evaporation, and the resulting slight elevation of specific gravity compared with the surrounding deep sea produces a slight increase in the concentration of all ions, including calcium (Cloud, 1962; Shinn *et al.*, 1989). Not only does the specific gravity of the water increase as it flows over the shallows, the temperature also increases, resulting in a lower solubility of carbon dioxide. Likewise, photosynthesis in the sunlit shallows removes carbon dioxide, elevates the pH of the water, further promoting a supersaturation condition for calcium and alkalinity, and thus the potential for calcification near coral reefs.

In addition, the amassed skeletons of the calcifying organisms (as rock, sand and gravel) are a reserve of calcium that is constantly being eroded mechanically and chemically, and dissolved through biological processes. Whether this reserve elevates the calcium level in the immediate environment has not been shown. It could have the opposite effect, as minute particles of calcium carbonate could

Whitings are spontaneous formations of calcium carbonate solids in the water column. They may be promoted by photosynthetically elevated pH in the already supersaturated seawater. This photo was taken over the Bahama bank. J. Sprung

The Bahama bank is a shallow platform that has reefs and great stretches of calcium carbonate sand precipitated from the seawater, forming spherical aragonite particles known as oolite. J. Sprung

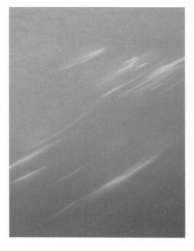

The formation of calcareous reef structures is supported by the physical effects of evaporation and erosion, which tend to elevate the saturation state of calcium carbonate in their vicinity. This photo was taken in Eilat, Israel. J. Sprung

act as seed sites for precipitation of calcium carbonate from the saturated seawater, or the net effect could be approximately neutral. In any case, the calcium and alkalinity levels in the sea are relatively constant, and most reefs receive calcium and alkalinity *replenishment* simply with the new water constantly flowing in from the open sea. By contrast, in a typical reef aquarium, when no calcium additions are made, the concentration of calcium in the water usually falls to a level between 250 and 350 mg/L in a short period. The rate of depletion is most pronounced in aquariums with coralline algae and sps corals.

Measuring calcium

Before considering how to increase the calcium level, it is best to invest in a good calcium test kit. Some of the commercially available calcium test kits are sold as calcium hardness kits. One must be sure that a conversion factor has been included with the kit's instructions since these kits measure calcium ion, but express it in terms of calcium carbonate in mg/L. The standard conversion is to multiply the calcium carbonate value by 0.4 (the calcium ion is 40% by mass of the calcium carbonate molecule). In addition, some kits are not designed to measure high calcium levels (this is indicated in the instructions). Measurement of water with over 400 mg/L may require that the test sample be diluted. A dilution using pure freshwater should be performed, usually by half, which will require a multiplication of the final value by two. Performing such dilutions additionally saves on the consumption of the titrant. Generally, calcium test kits are not precise and interference by other ions in seawater can lead to false high readings. Diluting the sample helps, but the variable concentration of magnesium, strontium, and other elements in the water makes precise readings impossible. However, calcium test kits don't need to be more precise than they are. A calcium value in excess of 550 mg/L when the alkalinity is at 7 dKH or higher, and the pH is above 8.2 is certainly a false reading, since this suggests highly supersaturated calcium carbonate, which should fall out of solution at the high pH. If the calcium level is really so high, the alkalinity must be lower. On the subject of test kits, it is also necessary to use a carbonate hardness (alkalinity) test kit to monitor that parameter, since calcium additions affect the alkalinity, as we will shortly explain.

For the techno-type reef keepers (if you are reading this book that probably means you) there is an alternative to calcium test kits. In January 2005, *American Marine* Inc. of Ridgefield Connecticut, USA introduced the PINPOINT ™ calcium monitor, an affordable and accurate digital calcium measurement instrument. Powered by a 9-volt battery or an AC adapter, it comes complete with calcium meter, calcium ion selective probe, and calibration and probe fluids. For more information, see www.americanmarineusa.com.

In a review of this monitor, Holmes-Farley (2005) concludes that it is reasonably accurate for aquarist use, and easy to calibrate. He also offers some caveats about operational parameters. The probe is not recommended for continuous immersion, and is used for spot testing only. It only works in saltwater, is very sensitive to temperature, sensitive to water movement, and takes time (minutes) to stabilize.

The PINPOINT™ calcium monitor.
American Marine Inc.

Alkalinity

Alkalinity is a generic term that encompasses a number of compounds that together, allow seawater to buffer the pH lowering effect of acid (hydrogen ions, H+). These compounds include bicarbonate, carbonate, borate, silicate, hydroxides and even phosphate. Collectively, these compounds represent the total alkalinity of seawater. Although other compounds contribute to the alkalinity of seawater, bicarbonate and carbonate are of the greatest importance since bicarbonate forms up to 90% and carbonate about 7% of the total alkalinity and, while they are not easily measured individually, total alkalinity is easily measured with a simple titration test kit. The titration determines how much acid is required to lower the pH of a water sample to the bicarbonate endpoint. This endpoint is achieved when all the bicarbonate in the sample has been converted to carbonic acid (see *alkalinity* in chapter 4.)

When just carbonate and bicarbonate are being measured, the correct term is carbonate alkalinity, which refers to the weighted sum of the concentrations of carbonate and bicarbonate ions in the water. Total alkalinity in natural seawater lies between 2.1 and 2.5 meq/L (6-7 dKH). In aquariums that have had little supplementation of alkalinity, values can be as low as 1.0 meq/L (2.8 dKH).

How to supplement calcium and alkalinity

When adding calcium and alkalinity it is important to do so in the same proportions as they are used in calcification to form calcium carbonate (Bingman, 1997d,b; Holmes-Farley, 2003b). The precipitation of calcium carbonate consumes its two components in an exact 1:1 ratio. This corresponds to one meq/L (2.8 dKH; 50 ppm $CaCO_3$ equivalents) for every 20 ppm of calcium (Bingman, 1997d,c; Holmes-Farley, 2004c). Calcium and alkalinity supplements that add them in these correct proportions are known as *balanced* supplements. The entire calcium and alkalinity contents of such balanced supplements can be combined to form calcium carbonate. Examples of balanced supplements include calcium hydroxide, calcium acetate, the product from a calcium reactor, and two-part calcium/alkalinity solutions. If you use a balanced supplementation scheme to maintain your calcium and alkalinity levels, in theory you should only encounter two possible problems; the levels are either too high for both or too low. There are, however, several ways that a system can become unbalanced despite using a balanced supplementation scheme. One example occurs when you use a salt mix (e.g. when starting an aquarium or for water changes) that is unbalanced in terms of calcium and alkalinity. In this case, the use of some balanced supplementation methods (e.g. kalkwasser or calcium acetate) will not correct the imbalance, while other methods (e.g. properly formulated two-part calcium and alkalinity supplements, calcium reactor using CO_2 and coral gravel) might or might not be able to do so (see methods of correcting imbalances at the end of this chapter). Another example occurs if, instead of using reverse osmosis water for water top-off, you use freshwater from a well that contains high levels of calcium and/or alkalinity. In addition, if you use a two-part calcium and alkalinity supplement, you can also create an unbalanced situation if they are not added at the same time and in the same proportions. Finally, it is well known that adding fresh calcareous gravel/sand (calcite or aragonite) to an aquarium can initially cause a drop in alkalinity due to the precipitation of magnesium carbonate onto the new exposed surfaces (Spotte, 1991). This can temporarily create an unbalanced situation until the surfaces develop a coating of biofilm (see discussion of biofilms in chapter 6). Additionally, other ionic imbalances affect the balance of calcium and alkalinity, such as the magnesium concentration. For example, using kalkwasser to maintain calcium and alkalinity promotes growth in organisms that deposit not only calcium but also magnesium in their skeletons. Since kalkwasser supplies only calcium, not magnesium, the long-term effect is a slow decline in magnesium levels (see chapter 4 for a discussion of magnesium's role in the seawater buffer system).

Table 5.1: The following alkalinity and corresponding calcium levels are what would be expected in a balanced situation in modified seawater.

meq/L	dKH	Calcium
0.50	1.4	350 ppm
0.75	2.1	375 ppm
2.0	5.6	400 ppm
3.25	9.1	425 ppm
4.5	12.6	450 ppm
5.75	16.1	475 ppm

Andy Hipkiss, a British aquarist, provides an online calculator that calculates the proper balanced amount of calcium or alkalinity for any corresponding alkalinity or calcium level (http://www.andy-hipkiss.co.uk/caalkcalc.htm). Jose Dieck provides a similar website, but his calculator also allows you to choose which method/product you want use and how much to add. Dieck's calculator provides this information for calcium and alkalinity as well as magnesium (http://home.comcast.net/~jdieck1/chem_calc3.html).

If you do not use balanced supplements, then it is possible to create an imbalance in the aquarium that can lead to problems in maintaining calcium, alkalinity and pH, as we will detail shortly. This is not to say that products designed to supplement only calcium or alkalinity do not have a purpose, they certainly do, but they should not be relied on exclusively to maintain calcium and alkalinity levels in a reef aquarium. These products give the aquarist the means to adjust grossly imbalanced water chemistry by boosting just calcium or just alkalinity, or to adjust the levels of a salt mix that may be low in calcium and/or alkalinity (Bingman, 1997a; Holmes-Farley, 2003b).

Methods used for raising the calcium and alkalinity levels in an aquarium

As we described in chapter 4, maintaining calcium, alkalinity and pH are closely linked and all three must be considered together when using any calcification maintenance system. Several methodologies can be used today for controlling calcium, alkalinity and pH levels; the method of choice for a particular aquarium depends on the rate of calcification in the aquarium. Whatever the method used, it should be easy to manage, not be prone to failure that could harm the aquariums inhabitants, not result in long-term changes in the water chemistry, and it should be economical to use and/or install. In fact, there is no supplementation method that perfectly matches all of these requirements, but some come close. Holmes-Farley (2003b) offers advice on the factors involved in choosing a method for a particular aquarium. The replenishment methods are not mutually exclusive and it is perfectly acceptable to use more than one method, as along as they are chemically balanced methods. We describe here the methods that have become widely utilized in reef aquarium husbandry, since they meet much of the aforementioned goals.

Dissolution of calcareous substrata

When calcification rates are low, simple dissolving of a calcareous substratum such as coral sand through bacterial respiration within the sand bed may be enough to maintain adequate calcium and alkalinity levels. This has been demonstrated with deep sand bed systems and Jaubert's plenum system that have a substantial mass of calcium carbonate substrata. Toonen and Wee (2005) performed a multifactor study of plenum versus non-plenum systems using deep (3.6 inch/9cm) and shallow (1 inch/2.5cm) sediment beds, and coarse (2 mm) and fine (0.2mm) sediments, over a 132 day period. They found that the highest mean alkalinity was 1.97 meq/L in aquariums with fine sediments and 1.69 meq/L in aquariums with coarse sediments. Calcium levels were significantly higher (340.4 mg/L) in fine than coarse sediment aquariums (327.9 mg/L). The pH level was also significantly higher in the tanks with fine sediments (8.22) than coarse sediments (8.10). These tanks had a small quantity of live rock and no coral so the calcium demand should have been low. This study emphasizes that dissolution of the sediments has only a very limited ability to maintain alkalinity and calcium necessary to support a system dominated by calcifying organisms. Since the authors used two different sources of calcareous media for coarse and fine substrata, the differences in chemical composition of the media may account for some of the differences observed. Percentage of calcite versus aragonite in the substrata, for example, affects its solubility, since these different forms of calcium carbonate have different solubility; aragonite is more soluble. It is respiration by microorganisms living in the water volume *within* the sand bed that dissolves the calcareous media when the calcium and alkalinity are at or above saturation for aragonite in the water above the substrata. If the calcium and alkalinity concentrations in the main body of water drop below the saturation level, then the calcareous substrata dissolves due to this effect, and calcification by calcifying creatures is inhibited.

Lang (1993) discusses the fate of calcium and strontium in coral reef mesocosm aquariums designed by Walter Adey of the Smithsonian Institution (see chapter 6 for a description of these systems). The coral reef mesocosms at the Pittsburgh Aqua-Zoo and the Smithsonian Institution were observed to lose approximately 30% of the initial calcium concentration within 2 years, and approximately half the strontium. The addition of the highly soluble dried segments of the calcareous green alga *Halimeda opuntia* as a supplement was able to bring the levels back upwards to natural seawater values for strontium and to slightly above natural seawater values for calcium. It is important to point out the comment that although the corals were healthy, *no major growth increases were observed* (Lang ,1993). By contrast, the growth of *Halimeda* was strong at times, and this alga and other calcifiers were the principle consumers in the system. It was further noted that the *coral reef mesocosm at the Pittsburgh Aqua-Zoo (had) been observed to lose approximately one to two inches of carbonate sediments per year*. This might be indicative of calcium carbonate in the water column above the substrate being below saturation, but not necessarily so. Some settling of sandy substrata is to be expected due to the bioturbation by infauna and the compacting effect of gravity. In addition, dissolution of aragonite is possible even at normal seawater equilibria (supersturation) for calcium carbonate (Walter and Burton, 1990). In addition, as we describe for Jaubert's system (see chapter 6), the biological activity of bacteria and microorganisms within the substrata can reduce the pH sufficiently there to cause the substrata to dissolve. The calcium carbonate saturation state in the water when this occurs has to be viewed in light of the other end of the spectrum, when the sand grains fuse due to biological precipitation of calcium carbonate by bacteria when the seawater is supersaturated with calcium carbonate (Bingman, 1999d). We suspect that dissolution surpasses precipitation up to a certain saturation state, after which precipitation dominates. See our discussion of saturation states at the end of this chapter.

Water changes

Water changes with a salt mix that produces water with a high calcium level are a practical means of raising the calcium level quickly. In fact, water changes alone can be used to maintain adequate calcium levels, but the calcium level alone is not the limiting factor for coral growth. The saturation state of calcium and carbonate alkalinity is. Periodic partial water change is therefore not a realistic means of keeping up with the demands of growing corals. Water change is of course a practical and inexpensive calcium and alkalinity maintenance system for open system aquariums that have a *continuous* feed of natural seawater. However, even in open system aquariums the saturation level of calcium carbonate is rapidly

The gravel bed in this aquarium has dropped by approximately 6mm (1/4 inch) in 6 months, a sign that the calcium and alkalinity are at times below NSW saturation levels; despite the fact it is an open system aquarium! J. Sprung

dropped by growing corals, such that the input of new seawater must be increased over time to meet the demand. Alternatively, another means of maintaining calcium and alkalinity can be employed to boost the saturation state (such as a calcium reactor or kalkwasser dosing).

Calcium hydroxide (kalkwasser)

Calcareous water, a.k.a. limewater, or *kalkwasser* in German, is a saturated solution of calcium hydroxide or calcium oxide in water. It was widely promoted by Peter Wilkens (1973) as a means of maintaining calcium and alkalinity levels. Before Wilkens promoted its application in the maintenance of reef aquariums, the use of limewater had been suggested by other aquarists for pH maintenance in fish displays at public aquariums (Brown, 1929; Atkins, 1931; Wilson, 1952, 1960). The idea was met with some bit of disagreement then as now, due mainly to misunderstandings regarding how to dose it and how it works.

Making kalkwasser

Either calcium hydroxide or calcium oxide may be used to make kalkwasser, and both barely dissolve at all. Only about 1.5 g (~1/2 teaspoon) will dissolve in a liter (one quart) of water, which means about 6 g (2/3 tablespoon) per 3.8 L (1 gallon), and even this requires vigorous stirring. Adding excess calcium hydroxide or oxide helps insure that a saturation state of calcium is maintained longer since the reaction of dissolved calcium hydroxide with carbon dioxide in the fresh water causes precipitation of calcium carbonate, lowering the amount of calcium ions dissolved in the water.

You can make the kalkwasser with water purified by reverse osmosis and/or deionization. This prevents the addition of plant nutrients with the make-up water, though some phosphate is precipitated with calcium in the alkaline solution. Some aquarists do not use or have access to purified water, while others do not need to use purified water because their tap water is not polluted.

Wilkens' original recommended procedure was to add excess calcium hydroxide or oxide, mix the solution vigorously and then allow it to settle for several hours until you see the clear, saturated kalkwasser solution above some undissolved white calcium hydroxide settled on the bottom (Wilkens, 1973). Siphon off the clear solution for use, and either discard the undissolved portion or add more water and calcium hydroxide or oxide, to make another batch. The calcium will react with carbon dioxide in the air to form a calcium carbonate crusty skin on the surface of the mixing container, and some calcium carbonate will fall out of solution and settle on the bottom along with the undissolved excess calcium hydroxide. The older the solution, the higher the concentration of insoluble calcium carbonate on the bottom of the container. This procedure works fine, but may be deficient for large aquariums that have low rates of evaporation. Other methods for dosing kalkwasser can supply more calcium and alkalinity, and we will discuss these shortly.

Characteristics of calcium hydroxide and calcium oxide

It makes no difference chemically whether one uses calcium oxide or calcium hydroxide. Calcium oxide is a little easier to handle because of its clumpy consistency, whereas calcium hydroxide is like talcum powder but worse, and the dust is very harmful to breathe. Calcium hydroxide dissolves more readily than calcium oxide, which simply means that calcium oxide requires a greater mixing effort. However, calcium oxide releases heat when dissolved in water, and significant amounts can be released if large amounts are added to water. Aquarists may also wonder if it matters what grade is used. Trace impurities (i.e. strontium, magnesium, iron, silicate) are beneficial but avoid grades with high levels of magnesium, phosphate, or heavy metals such as lead. Low quality calcium hydroxide may also have a high percentage of calcium carbonate, which will not dissolve. That means it is less potent (less calcium will dissolve by weight) compared to a purer product.

Storage of the dry powder

Dry calcium hydroxide and calcium oxide react with carbon dioxide in air to form calcium carbonate. For this reason, the storage container (jar, bag, etc.) must be sufficiently sealed to prevent contact with the air. Otherwise, the calcium hydroxide becomes less soluble as the percentage of calcium carbonate increases.

WHEN HANDLING CALCIUM HYDROXIDE OR CALCIUM OXIDE, A DUST MASK, GOGGLES AND GLOVES ARE NECESSARY PRECAUTIONS. THESE SUBSTANCES ARE CAUSTIC, THOUGH GETTING SOME ON YOUR HANDS IS QUICKLY REMEDIED BY RINSING WITH RUNNING WATER. INHALING OR INGESTING IT CAN CAUSE SERIOUS INJURY, AS CAN GETTING IT IN THE EYES. KEEP THESE CHEMICALS OUT OF THE REACH OF CHILDREN!

Mixing kalkwasser in a reservoir

Aquarists who try mixing the water in a calcium dosing reservoir by using a submersible powerhead soon discover that the pump becomes jammed with calcium deposits, or permanently damaged by sharp flakes of calcium carbonate from the surface skin that forms and sinks to the bottom. Using an air bubbler to mix the kalkwasser is an unsuitable practice because it continuously introduces CO_2, and causes most of the calcium to precipitate as calcium carbonate. The only ways to mix kalkwasser correctly by mechanical means are to employ a rotating armature attached to an overhead motor, or to use a magnetic stirring rod and spinner assembly (i.e. magnetic stirring plate).

Adding kalkwasser

Another precaution is most important to understand: don't add too much to the tank at once! Kalkwasser has a pH of nearly 12, and even a little bit will raise the pH in the aquarium temporarily ... a lot will raise the pH too high and could injure or kill the fish. If you have an automated pH controller with a CO_2 dosing system installed, this is less of a concern since the pH controller will cause the administering of CO_2 to counter the rise in pH from the kalkwasser addition to the aquarium. If you don't have a CO_2 system, then it is best to add kalkwasser slowly. The slow dosing of kalkwasser can be accomplished by using a small

The *Deltec* kalkwasser reactor uses an armature to slowly mix the calcium hydroxide solids at the bottom of the cylinder. J. Sprung

Kalkwasser is the most economical balanced calcium and alkalinity supplement. J. Sprung

siphon hose and clamp to drip it in; by using a dosing pump connected to an appliance timer; or by means of an automatic water make-up system using a level sensor switch to turn on a pump in a reservoir containing freshwater or kalkwasser. In the case of the latter, there is a risk of overdosing if the level sensing switch fails, or something other than evaporation causes the level in the sump to drop. Adding kalkwasser to the aquarium at night creates the least disruption of the pH, since there is more CO_2 in the water (which depresses the pH) after the lights have gone off, when the algae and zooxanthellae in the display stop photosynthesizing and respire CO_2 like all the rest of the life in the system. If the system includes an algal refugium or a turf scrubber operating on a reverse daylight cycle, the pH at night may not be depressed, so in this case there is no advantage to dosing kalkwasser at night.

Kalkwasser is the most economical method for maintaining calcium and alkalinity in a reef aquarium, especially for aquariums with low or moderate calcification rates. When calcium hydroxide is dissolved in water, the alkalinity supplied spontaneously converts into carbonate alkalinity in aquariums because hydroxide ions readily combine with carbon dioxide (which may originate from respired CO_2 or atmospheric CO_2 dissolved in the water) to form carbonates and bicarbonates. The alkalinity in the water is raised and the calcium supplied becomes useful for calcification.

This equation describes the making of kalkwasser.

$$Ca(OH)_2 + H_2O \rightarrow Ca^{2+} + 2\,OH^-$$

When carbon dioxide and hydroxide ions combine upon addition of kalkwasser to an aquarium, bicarbonate forms.

$$OH^- + CO_2 \rightarrow HCO_3^-$$

When hydroxide ions combine with bicarbonate ions upon addition of kalkwasser to an aquarium, carbonate ions and water are formed.

$$OH^- + HCO_3^- \rightarrow CO_3^{2-} + H_2O$$

This effect is dependant on the dosage, however. Klostermann (1991) shows the following reactions to demonstrate the effect of adding kalkwasser at different quantities. The equations are meant to be illustrative only, not to be interpreted literally with regard to the molar concentrations in the solutions.

1) $1/2Ca(OH)_2 + H_2CO_3 + HCO_3^- + CO_3^{2-} \rightarrow 1/2Ca^{2+} + 2HCO_3^- + CO_3^{2-} + H_2O$

2) $Ca(OH)_2 + H_2CO_3 + HCO_3^- + CO_3^{2-} \rightarrow Ca^{2+} + HCO_3^- + 2CO_3^{2-} + 2H_2O$

3) $3/2Ca(OH)_2 + H_2CO_3 + HCO_3^- + CO_3^{2-} \rightarrow 3/2Ca^{2+} + 3CO_3^{2-} + 3H_2O$

4) $2Ca(OH)_2 + H_2CO_3 + HCO_3^- + CO_3^{2-} \rightarrow 2Ca^{2+} + 3CO_3^{2-} + OH^- + 3H_2O$

Equation 1 shows a small dose of kalkwasser converting dissolved carbon dioxide into bicarbonate (HCO_3^-). In equation 2, the addition of more kalkwasser causes an increase in the amount of carbonate (CO_3^{2-}). In equation 3, an even larger dose of kalkwasser causes the loss of all bicarbonate alkalinity. In equation 4, with an even greater kalkwasser addition, we see that free hydroxide (caustic alkalinity) remains in solution, temporarily at least.

This illustration seems to suggest the notion that the hydroxide ions from dripping kalkwasser might drift around in the system for extended periods. In fact they don't. When kalkwasser is dosed into a reef aquarium, the primary reaction is hydroxide ions removing protons from bicarbonate ions, forming carbonate ions and water.

$$HCO_3^- + OH^- \rightarrow CO_3 + H_2O,$$

The interconversion of carbonic acid and bicarbonate ions, and the interconversion of bicarbonate and carbonate ions, involves the loss or uptake of a single proton. They reach equilibrium in the blink of an eye, and when the hydroxide ions deprotonate bicarbonate ions, the carbonate alkalinity of the system increases. The carbonate alkalinity isn't simply the sum of the molar concentrations of carbonate and bicarbonate ions in seawater; it is the weighted sum of these two concentrations, and carbonate ions have twice the weight of bicarbonate ions (Bingman, 2001). The increase in carbonate alkalinity raises the pH of the system. The amount of dissolved carbon dioxide goes down moments later, after the carbonic acid/dissolved carbon dioxide populations reach equilibrium values. Therefore, when we dose kalkwasser, the pH in the aquarium rises and the dissolved carbon dioxide concentration falls.

Though it raises carbonate alkalinity as we just described, kalkwasser doesn't add any inorganic carbon to the system to replace the inorganic carbon removed by calcification. This either comes from the atmosphere or occurs as the system gains additional carbon dioxide because it leaves the system at a lower rate when kalkwasser is added and the system pH is elevated. It is important to understand the dynamics of the way the dissolved carbon dioxide level is maintained. At the air/water interfaces in the system, there is a constant exchange of carbon dioxide from the water to the atmosphere and from the atmosphere into the water. At equilibrium, the loss equals the gain. When kalkwasser is added and the carbon dioxide concentration goes down in the water, *fewer carbon dioxide molecules leave the tank* to the atmosphere, but the rate at which they enter the water from the atmosphere is unchanged. Thus, the system gains inorganic carbon when kalkwasser is dosed.

It is common to notice a *drop* in alkalinity after kalkwasser dosing is initiated. This is not due to any harmful affect of kalkwasser, as is sometimes reported in aquarium literature. The loss of alkalinity simply results from kalkwasser's promotion of rapid calcification.

Aquarists can artificially raise the rate at which carbon dioxide molecules enter the water by administering pure carbon dioxide gas into the aquarium via a contact chamber, with the dosage rate managed by a pH controller. Such systems can be incorporated to boost the effectiveness of kalkwasser, as we explain shortly, or to prevent the pH from rising too high.

Kalkwasser is typically used daily as the sole source of make-up water for evaporation loss. Kalkwasser is most advantageous because it does not add anything to the water that accumulates, it precipitates phosphate from the water, thereby enhancing corals' ability to deposit calcium, and it maintains alkalinity (Bingman, 1995a). Furthermore, hydroxide ions added with kalkwasser can neutralize organic acids, and thus indirectly help to maintain the alkalinity and pH. They also combine with metal ions such as a copper, taking them out of solution (Holmes-Farley, 2003b). Peter Wilkens (pers. comm.) has observed that kalkwasser addition also enhances protein skimming, and he believes this results from the pH increase and reactions of calcium hydroxide with fatty acids and other organic compounds attracted to the air-water interface. Kalkwasser addition, especially combined with protein skimming, is a very effective means of helping to keep the dissolved inorganic phosphate level low, but in high fish load or high food input aquariums, this capacity is exceeded and the use of additional methods for inorganic phosphate management becomes a necessity (see our recommendations in chapters 4 and 6).

Limits of kalkwasser dosing

If you are adding a saturated solution of kalkwasser to an established reef tank that is deficient in calcium and has a low rate of evaporation, it may seem to take forever to get the calcium level up. This should not be too surprising since only a little over a gram per liter will be added with the make-up water, while at the same time the invertebrates are extracting the calcium from the water. Increasing the rate of evaporation (with fans blowing over the water surface, for example) can be a way to increase the rate of kalkwasser dosage to keep up with or exceed the demand for calcium and alkalinity.

When kalkwasser is used to replace evaporation, in the absence of a pH control system, the supply of calcium and alkalinity is often not sufficient to support calcification by a dense population of reef building corals in a large aquarium. This deficit is also enhanced in brightly illuminated aquariums in which algae deplete dissolved CO_2, elevate pH and promote calcification. Often both situations occur simultaneously since dense growth of reef building corals is encouraged by bright illumination. The deficit can be countered partially by using fans to increase the evaporation rate, or mixing stronger *milky* kalkwasser, but that comes with the risk of increasing the aquarium's pH to higher than natural seawater values, or worse, to toxic levels. Acetic acid (vinegar) can be used to boost the effectiveness of kalkwasser as we shall explain shortly, and this may be enough to allow kalkwasser dosing to meet the calcium and alkalinity demand. It is also common practice to use balanced two-part calcium and alkalinity supplements or a calcium reactor in conjunction with kalkwasser to achieve an adequate calcium and alkalinity level in an aquarium with a very high demand.

Overdosing

The possibility of an overdose exists with kalkwasser, but its affect is temporary, with the harm being caused by the high pH. If the pH goes too high, the fish die suddenly, an irreversible condition! At a high but sub-lethal level, the pH rise is enough to convert most of the bicarbonate ions in the water to carbonate (see our earlier demonstration of the reaction formulae for different dose amounts). When overdosed, the high pH combined with a high carbonate and calcium concentration, pushes the saturation state of calcium and carbonate is so high that it may cause the formation of a calcium (and magnesium) carbonate precipitation event that turns the water milky (a *snowstorm* or *white out*). In any case, within a short period the pH falls back down, though the buffering system needs to be restored.

In the absence of a pH control system that injects CO_2 into the aquarium, the addition of kalkwasser works fine for additions of less than 0.2 milliequivalents of alkalinity per liter of aquarium water. At higher additions, the pH rises too much (about 0.66 pH units on the addition of 0.5 meq/L of alkalinity via limewater, the equivalent of 1.2% of the aquarium volume in saturated limewater) (Holmes-Farley, 2002f). Holmes-Farley's figure leaves out the time element. In other words, aside from the effect of a single dose, how often can it be added? The answer is not so simple because it is different for each tank, depending on the production, retention and uptake of CO_2.

The system pH depends on the production and retention of CO_2 in the water, the CO_2 level in the air in the room where the aquarium is located, the depletion of CO_2 by algae growing in the aquarium, and the production of acids by biological processes within the aquarium. We have determined through trial and observation that one can safely add approximately 0.8 grams (1/4 teaspoon) of calcium hydroxide powder per 190 L (50 gallons) of aquarium per hour in aquariums that don't have a pH control system. At that rate of addition, the neutralization of CO_2 entering the average aquarium proceeds at a rate that will not cause the pH to rise too high for the life in the aquarium. Of course, the exact effect on the pH will vary in each aquarium, depending on the aforementioned factors. This figure provides two useful bits of information. First, two tablespoons (19.2 grams) of calcium hydroxide theoretically could be added to a 190 L (50 gallon) tank daily. This is a substantial amount, and meets the demand of the highest calcification rates one would expect for an aquarium of this size, especially if the aquarium is compact in dimension rather than long (a long aquarium of short height has a larger illuminated surface area than a tall box shaped aquarium). Unfortunately there is no existing simple means of dosing precisely this much kalkwasser hourly, but we can leave that as a challenge to the engineering folks. The second bit of information concerns risk. If the kalkwasser is added via an automatic top-off or dosing system, without a pH control system, exceeding a dosage of 0.8 grams (1/4 teaspoon) dry kalkwasser per hour per 190 L (50 gallons) has the potential to raise the pH unpredictably. It is common practice to mix kalkwasser and let it dose. Without even thinking about it, most aquarists routinely exceed 0.8 grams (1/4 teaspoon) dry kalkwasser per hour per 190 L (50 gallons), but for just short periods, since a top off system is usually restricted by a small level change in the sump, or a timer. The resulting rise in pH in the aquarium is brief and not harmful, but if the dosing equipment stays on for a little too long, the result can be disastrous. It is imperative to plan ahead for ways to prevent this from happening: for example limiting the size of the dosage reservoir, the amount of dry calcium hydroxide added to it, the rate of the dosing pump, or best of all, the time that the dosing pump can be on. This caution must be balanced by how often one wants to be involved with preparing kalkwasser.

Manual dosing

Following the guidelines we just gave, it is possible (though labor intensive) to manually add kalkwasser each day, adding no more than 0.8 grams (1/4 teaspoon) dry kalkwasser per 190 L (50 gallons) in any given dose. The calcium hydroxide can be added to a container and mixed with cool freshwater. This freshly mixed kalkwasser can then be slowly poured into a strong current stream to quickly mix it as it enters the aquarium. For a reef aquarium with a moderate amount of coral, the addition of 0.8 grams (1/4 teaspoon) dry kalkwasser per 190 L (50 gallons) two or three times per day (at least an hour apart) may be sufficient to meet the calcium and alkalinity demands of the system, until the corals grow sufficiently large!

Nilsen calcium doser a.k.a. Nilsen reactor

Nilsen (1990, 1991) describes a simple device that you can build for providing high-quality (fresh) kalkwasser as part of an automatic water make-up system. The design incorporates a magnetic spinner on a timer to repeatedly suspend the excess calcium hydroxide in the reactor tube, thus maintaining the saturation state. The dosing pump is not in the reaction tube, but in a separate, pure freshwater reservoir, which eliminates the possibility of the dosing pump getting jammed by calcium deposits. Connecting this dosing pump to a float switch in the sump will allow the system to automatically top-off the system in reaction to evaporation. You can forgo the dosing pump and simply connect the freshwater reservoir directly to the doser via a solenoid valve that is controlled by the float switch. When the water level in the sump drops, the float switch activates the solenoid valve to open and water flows into the

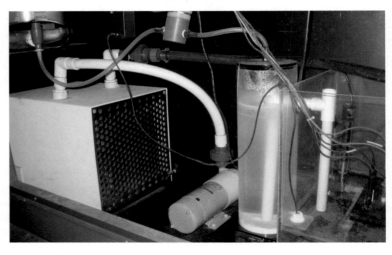

A *EuroReef* Nilsen kalkwasser doser in use at the Waikiki Aquarium. Note the solenoid (top center) connected to a float switch (bottom right) in the sump, controlling the flow from the freshwater reservoir in the upper left corner. J.C. Delbeek

This homemade calcium reactor in the Alsace region of France is based on the Nilsen design, using a simple Erlenmeyer flask. J. Sprung

doser by gravity. Of course, the container needs to be at a higher level than the doser is since the water flow relies on gravity.

The Nilsen design has been incorporated in some commercial products and some hobbyist homemade devices. We saw a small version utilized in the Alsace region of France, wherein the chamber was an Erlenmeyer flask sitting on top of a magnetic stirrer. The flask had a rubber stopper inserted in the top and the input and output lines passed through the stopper. As water was fed to the flask via the input line, it pressurized the flask and forced kalkwasser out of the output line.

This system works well but there is a caveat, which is true of any kalkwasser dosing system: as we mentioned previously, the amount of calcium hydroxide administered to an aquarium should not exceed 1/4 teaspoon (0.8 g) per 190 L (50 gallons) of aquarium per hour. When adding excess calcium hydroxide to the Nilsen reactor, it must be prevented from dosing more than the above-mentioned amount of calcium hydroxide. This potential for overdose can be managed by careful timing of the dosing, or it can be countered more directly by the use of a pH control system that opens a solenoid to supply CO_2 to the aquarium (thus acidifying the water) in the event that the pH exceeds the set point on the pH controller.

We have also seen good calcium reactor dosing systems that use a level sensing switch connected with an air pump and diaphragm to mix and or/dose the kalkwasser. The air driven diaphragm displaces the water and causes it to flow out of the reactor until the level in the sump causes the switch to shut off the air pump.

S-K doser

A very simple kalkwasser doser was developed by Mr. Matsumoto and Mr. Hamanoof of Tokyo, Japan in the mid-90's. This consists of a chamber in which freshwater is passed from a reservoir such that it enters into a lower section filled with calcium hydroxide, passes upwards and out the top of the unit and into the sump. This design prevents exposure of the calcium hydroxide to atmospheric CO_2 and allows for a controlled method of dosing kalkwasser when connected to a dosing pump and reservoir.

Enhanced methods for using kalkwasser

Fosså and Nilsen (1993, 1996) proposed a system that uses Nilsen's calcium doser (a vessel with a magnetic stirrer to suspend the kalkwasser, described earlier in this chapter) to produce milky supersaturated limewater in combination with carbon dioxide dosing regulated by a pH controller. The idea behind such a system is to provide metered amounts of carbon dioxide on demand to control the pH rise and allow a stronger effect for kalkwasser on calcium and alkalinity. By allowing a much greater amount of kalkwasser to be dosed, it can support rapid calcification rates.

The *S-K doser* is an elegant and simple way for dosing kalkwasser when used with a dosing pump. J.C. Delbeek

As with other *high-tech* options, aside from the investment involved in purchasing the technical equipment, a failure of the CO_2 metering apparatus in either the *on* or *off* positions would be disastrous for the aquarium. Such mechanical failures are extremely unlikely, but possible. Although mechanical devices such as automatic water make-up and pH controllers can maintain a more stable environment and make aquarium keeping simpler, the less complex your system is mechanically, the less prone it will be to equipment malfunction. Also, if you decide to use such automated equipment, be sure that it is well made, by a reliable manufacturer. Cheap is dear! Another problem with this method lies in the latency a.k.a *overshoot* of the dosing system. Although the controller will shut off the CO_2 supply, residual CO_2 in the contact chamber will continue to dissolve until exhausted, driving the pH lower by a few points. Likewise, when CO_2 is added in response to a rise in pH, it may take some time for the pH to drop, depending on the amount of kalkwasser added and the rate at which the CO_2 is added. These considerations have been addressed by some sophisticated programs in high-end computer based controllers.

A final word of caution about CO_2 dosing: the administering of CO_2 to saltwater aquariums can enhance algae growth. However, with control of other nutrients such as phosphate, nitrate, and silicate, and with sufficient herbivores, the growth of undesirable types of algae is limited.

A *batch* $CaCO_3/CO_2$ reactor

Another possibility is to employ CO_2 to dissolve kalkwasser in a batch fashion. This is essentially like a calcium reactor, but uses calcium carbonate powder or kalkwasser (which is quickly converted to calcium carbonate powder) instead of calcium carbonate gravel or chips as the media. This idea has not received much attention because there hasn't been a system created to make it something you can *set-and-forget* for an extended period

Giving kalkwasser a boost

Bingman (1999e) offers a *low-tech* way to add carbon dioxide along with kalkwasser. He proposes adding to the kalkwasser an organic source of carbon to provide the aquarium with excess CO_2 along with the kalkwasser. The organic carbon source stimulates biological activity that quickly digests it and releases excess CO_2. Bingman (1999e) tried acetic acid, glucose and calcium gluconate as sources of carbon, but suggested that acetic acid, otherwise known as white vinegar, was probably the easiest choice to obtain for most aquarists.

The concentration of saturated limewater at 25 °C (77 °F) is 0.0203 moles per liter. Each unit of calcium hydroxide would require two units of carbon dioxide to form calcium bicarbonate or one unit of carbon dioxide to form calcium carbonate. Bingman used one mole of carbon dioxide equivalents per one mole of calcium hydroxide as the maximum amount of dissolved organics to add in this way.

Table 5.2. Comparison of statistics for three compounds used to spike limewater with an organic source of carbon (After Bingman, 1999e).

Compound	Acetic acid	Glucose	Calcium gluconate
Number of Carbon atoms	2	6	12
Molar Mass grams per mole (g/M)	60.05	180.16	430.38
Mass per Mole-C (g/mole-C)	30.03	30.03	35.87
Maximum Concentration grams per liter (g/L)	0.61	0.61	0.73
Milliliters (mL) Vinegar per liter (L)	12.2	NA	NA

Oxidation of about 1/2 fl. oz. (12 mL) of vinegar per quart (liter) of limewater would provide enough carbon dioxide to balance the inorganic carbon removed from the aquarium when the calcium and alkalinity in a liter of saturated limewater is converted into calcium carbonate. This is the maximum concentration of acetic acid that one would add, and, in practice, Bingman (1999e) recommends adding no more than a quarter of this quantity (i.e. 1/10 fl. oz./3 mL vinegar per quart/liter of kalkwasser) to see how the aquarium tolerates it. The acetic acid is added to the top off water at the same time as the calcium hydroxide is added, and it should all be mixed together well. The acetic acid neutralizes some of the calcium hydroxide and forms calcium acetate, or actually largely dissociated calcium ions and acetate ions.

Substantially more calcium hydroxide than usual will dissolve in water when mixed with vinegar. Using the maximum concentration of acetic acid listed in table 5.2, about 36 percent more calcium hydroxide would dissolve compared to normal kalkwasser. Starting at one quarter the maximum dosage of acetic acid, as recommended by Bingman (1999e), the concentration of calcium is about 9 percent higher than in plain saturated kalkwasser. The pH of the mixture is also somewhat lower than a pure solution of calcium hydroxide in water.

White vinegar (made for human consumption) is ideal to use for this purpose. The acidity of vinegar varies, so start out with no more than a quarter of the maximum dose (no more than 1/10 fl. oz./3 mL per quart/liter) and make sure you make a saturated solution of limewater.

Spiking with acetic acid can allow one to substantially increase the amount of calcium and alkalinity that goes into the aquarium without adding a lot of extra carbon in the process. For some people who just can't quite make limewater work, adding small quantities of white vinegar might be enough to allow limewater to carry all of the calcification demand of your aquarium. Additionally, the dissolved carbon source may promote denitrification in the live rock and sand of the aquarium, thus lowering the nitrate level as a side benefit.

Dosing vinegar and kalkwasser with a pH controller
It is possible to use a pH controller to regulate a dosing system that adds kalkwasser and vinegar. Such a system would require two dosing pumps and a two channel pH controller with one channel to switch on a pump to dose vinegar if the pH is too high, and the other channel to dose kalkwasser if the pH is too low. The feed rate of the dosing pumps and volume of the vinegar and kalkwasser vessels could be designed to prevent a malfunction from causing tragic harm to the aquarium.

Calcium reactors (kalkreaktors)
Since the mid-90s, there has been an increasing development of the use of what used to be called a lime reactor. The new term for these reactors is kalkreaktor or calcium reactor. Not so long ago the term calcium reactor brought to mind Alf Nilsen's device for dosing saturated kalkwasser. Before the widespread recognition of that system, there was another device called a lime reactor. It employed carbon dioxide administered to a reactor chamber filled with chips of calcium carbonate. In the USA, the only commercially manufactured

system available in the 1980's was made by Tunze, though there was also a Dupla CO_2 reactor that could also be used this way. The increased popularity of this type of system can be traced to two individuals in Germany. First, in 1993 in the journal DATZ, Mr. Rolf Hebbinghaus of the Löbbecke Museum and Aquazoo in Düsseldorf wrote an article about a system he built using Eheim canister filters filled with coral gravel through which he administered CO_2 and passed a slow stream of water from the aquarium (Hebbinghaus, 1993). The effect of the CO_2 dissolving the calcareous gravel was a supply of calcium, alkalinity, and some CO_2 to the aquarium, in addition to various other elements contained in the coral gravel. Hebbinghaus' article demonstrated the success he was having with his large reef aquarium using this method to maintain calcium and alkalinity. In addition to the article from Hebbinghaus, Daniel Knop, an author and aquarium industry manufacturer, introduced a compact commercial calcium reactor system, and promoted its use widely. Now many manufacturers around the world have built many variations based on Hebbinghaus' system, and they have gained widespread acceptance in the industry and hobby.

The popularity of calcium reactors has boomed in particular since the trend of growing *Acropora*-dominated reef aquariums with other fast-growing small polyped corals necessitates a constant large supply of calcium and bicarbonate ions. Many aquarists continue to use kalkwasser supplementation and other methods, such as two-part calcium and alkalinity solutions, often combining methods. Nilsen and Brockmann (1995a,b), Stark (1995) and Bingman (1995c) review some of these methods and the advantages of kalkwasser vs. kalkreactors vs. the addition of calcium chloride and buffer.

Calcium reactor designs

Calcium reactors have not changed much since Hebbinghaus' original design. Models today vary in water flow direction, fluidizing the media or not, the method of CO_2 injection, the number of media chambers used and the way that excess CO_2 is dealt with.

Basic design and operation

A calcium reactor consists of a column made of acrylic or clear PVC that varies in length and width depending on the size of the system. This column is filled with a calcareous media such as coral gravel. Water is then circulated through the gravel by a dedicated pump. A small amount of CO_2 from a gas cylinder is injected into the column as well, acidifying the water to a pH of between 6.0 and 6.5. This causes the calcareous media to slowly dissolve, releasing calcium, carbonate and other minerals or elements that may be part of the media. Since 99% of most media is usually calcium carbonate, the addition of other elements is minor. However, inorganic phosphate release from some media can be enough to cause persistent algal problems and the aquarist should test for phosphate in the reactor effluent. Aquarium water is supplied to the reactor by a small pump and a small side stream is returned back to the aquarium. This side stream water is rich in calcium and carbonates but low in pH. Adjusting the flow rate out of the reactor and/or the amount of CO_2 injected into the reactor determines the pH in the reactor and the levels of calcium and alkalinity that are present in the effluent.

The proper CO_2 bubble rate and effluent flow is based on the need for calcium and alkalinity. Aquariums with low calcium and alkalinity levels require a more saturated effluent until appropriate levels are reached. Then the bubble rate and effluent flow can be adjusted to just maintain these parameters. Similarly, as the corals increase in size and number in a reef tank, calcium and alkalinity demand also increases and the calcium reactor will need to be adjusted.

We cannot give exact instructions on what flow rate is best since every tank is different in terms of size, and calcium and alkalinity demand. The aquarist needs to monitor the pH, calcium and alkalinity of the effluent to determine the best combination of CO_2 injection rate and water return rate to the aquarium. However, we do advise that when first setting up a calcium reactor on an aquarium, especially one that has a low alkalinity, it is wise to set it at a low CO_2 dosage rate to begin with. This accomplishes two things. It allows the alkalinity to rise slowly; rapid increases in alkalinity can cause coral bleaching to occur (J.C. Delbeek, pers. obs.). Secondly, the low alkalinity of the tank means that the addition of large amounts of CO_2 into the water could cause a significant drop in pH, which is also bad for the inhabitants of the tank. Once alkalinity levels have slowly climbed up into the acceptable range, the CO_2 injection rate can be increased if necessary.

Water flow direction

Several variations in the basic design have appeared on the market and each manufacturer touts features in their reactors they consider superior to others. In some models, the water flows through the reactor from top to bottom. This works for a while but the dissolution of the media results in the accumulation of fines in the lower portions of the media that causes a channeling of the flow initially and eventually the flow becomes severely restricted. The efficiency of the reactor is compromised since this prevents good contact of all the surfaces with water rich in CO_2. At this point, the reactor needs to be disassembled, the media rinsed clean of fines and new media is added to top-off the reactor.

In an attempt to alleviate this problem, newer reactors incorporate a reverse flow design where water rises upwards from the bottom of the chamber. This helps to suspend the fines but if the media is of a small size, the fines are merely transported to the bottom of the media by the pump and accumulate there. The result is that eventually the entire column of media is forced upwards due to water pressure and is pressed up against the top of cylinder. This can also happen when the media used is too fine and the pump too strong. While not necessarily a bad thing, if the pump intake is at the top of the chamber then media could be sucked into the pump damaging the impeller or, if the return to the tank is located at the top of the column, media could clog the outlet resulting in a build-up in pressure and eventually a very messy failure! For this reason, reverse flow designs usually have a screen located just below the top of the column to prevent media from moving into these areas. However, if the pump is inadvertently shut off or the power fails, the media collapses back down, releasing the fines resulting in a very milky reactor. When

An example of a compact calcium reactor design using small grain size media. J.C. Delbeek

For larger installations, more than one calcium reactor may be required to meet the demand for calcium and alkalinity. The columns are covered to prevent algae from growing in them in this sunlit location at the Waikiki Aquarium. J.C. Delbeek

power is restored or the pump is switched back on, this milky material is quickly passed into the aquarium.

For this reason, newer reverse flow reactor designs use larger media, which allows the fines to freely circulate and prevents the media from being forced upwards. In these designs, the outlet line must be large enough to allow for the passing of the fines. A valve on the outlet to control the flow back to the tank should be avoided to prevent clogging. In this case, the inlet line should be valved, leaving the outlet line to flow freely.

Fluidized design for a calcium reactor
As with granular filter media in upflow fluidized bed filters (see chapter 6), the use of uniformly sized calcareous particles in a

Top: In this design, a smaller chamber is filled with calcareous media and the effluent passes through this on its way to the aquarium. J.C. Delbeek

Above: On this *Korallin* calcium reactor, the bubble counter is integrated with the intake of the pump, the incoming tank water and the recirculation line, ensuring it remains filled with water at all times. The CO_2 line extends down into the counter where the released gas bubbles then rise upward and into the pump intake. J.C. Delbeek

fluidized bed has the potential to dramatically improve efficiency of the reactor. The side benefits of such an improvement might be a smaller scale reactor needed to achieve the desired supply of calcium and carbonate ions, and less adjustment needed to maintain the reactor in peak performance. A fluidized reactor employing special spherical calcium carbonate particles has been introduced by Deltec Aquarium Systems. Although we have not experimented with the idea, since fluidized sand biofilters use fine sand, it is possible that a calcium reactor could be designed to work with fluidized fine aragonite sand. An advantage is that the reactor media could be refilled via a dedicated plumbing supply line that is normally shut off, without the need to dismantle anything.

Two chamber designs

Since the pH of the reactor effluent tends to be rather low (6.2-6.7), some manufacturers have added a second chamber filled with calcareous media in series so that water passes from the first chamber to the second chamber before passing to the aquarium. This tends to dissolve the media in the second chamber, adding even more calcium and alkalinity to the water, and raises the pH of the effluent further as CO_2 is consumed, before it enters the aquarium. However, the pH is still lower than the tank and so some carbon dioxide is still added (Holmes-Farley, 2002g).

Carbon dioxide injection

A small amount of carbon dioxide is injected via a water filled bubble-counting chamber into the intake of the pump where it is thoroughly mixed. This CO_2 rich water is then recirculated within the column by the main pump. In most designs, the bubble counter chamber contains freshwater. The water eventually evaporates and requires frequent refilling. To counter this, a more viscous solution can be used such as glycerol. Other designs actually place the bubble counter upside down such that reactor water continuously passes through it on the way to the recirculation pump. The CO_2 is then released at the bottom of the chamber, via a tube passing through the top of the chamber, and rises up into the pump. This design ensures that the CO_2 injection chamber is always filled with water and the bubbles can always be seen rising within it on their way to the pump intake.

Usually CO_2 is supplied to the reactor on a continuous basis using a needle valve to adjust the rate of injection. Once the bubble rate is set, it maintains the rate of CO_2 input, but the bubble rate chosen nevertheless depends on frequent monitoring of the effluent pH to ensure that the proper level for media dissolution is maintained. In addition, as the media dissolves, less CO_2 will react with what is left. In systems that use a constant CO_2 injection, this means that less CO_2 is actually consumed in the reactor, so it passes instead into the aquarium, depressing the system pH. Excess carbon dioxide may also accumulate within the chamber forming a void at the top, which can cause the pump to lose suction in reverse flow designs, and stop water flow back to the tank.

An alternative is to use a pH probe and controller to dose CO_2 into the reactor as needed. In this case, the pH of the reactor water or effluent is constantly monitored. If the pH rises above the set point, a solenoid on the CO_2 supply line is opened; dosing CO_2 and lowering the pH back to the desired level, the solenoid is then closed. This helps to reduce CO_2 usage and ensures that a constant pH level is maintained within the reactor. As a safety precaution, be sure that the CO_2 solenoid is designed to be in the OFF state when no power is supplied to it. This will ensure that CO_2 is not sent to the reactor if there is a power interruption, otherwise, the reactor pH could be driven very low and this acidified water could severely affect the pH of the aquarium. Of course, the pH probe must be carefully cleaned and calibrated monthly so that it always reads the correct pH within the reactor.

Recycling carbon dioxide

One of the problems inherent in many calcium reactor designs is that the amount of CO_2 injected must be carefully balanced between not supplying enough with a resulting poor dissolution of the media, and adding too much resulting in gas accumulation at the top of the reactor. In a design developed in Germany by the aquarium equipment manufacturer *Schuran* (www.schuran.com), a small chamber is located at the top of the reactor: the gas/water separator. Here, excess CO_2 accumulates and is then passed back to the intake of the recirculation pump, where it is injected back into the bottom of the reactor. When used in combination with a pH probe and controller, this results in a very efficient use of CO_2. This design allows for high flow rates with high dKH values.

Media to use in a calcium reactor

The type of media to use in a calcium reactor has been the subject of some debate. The primary concern is cost, rate of dissolution and phosphate content. Some of the media that may be used, depending on the reactor design, include oolitic sand, foraminiferan tests, coral gravel, coralline algae marl, crushed coral, crushed limestone, marble chips, and merumized limestone beads. Some sources of media release phosphate when dissolved (Bingman 1997g; Hiller, 1999). This can result in significant amounts of phosphate being added to the aquarium over time. If you do not know the phosphate level of the reactor effluent, then it is a simple matter to test it using a phosphate test kit. If phosphate is found, the media can still be used if one simply passes the reactor effluent through some phosphate adsorbing media (i.e. granular iron based media) before it passes to

A small *Schuran* calcium reactor in use at the Rotterdam Zoo, The Netherlands. Note the gas/water separator at the top of the unit and the pH controller. J.C. Delbeek

A large *Schuran* calcium reactor for systems from 50,000 to 100,000 liters (13,000 and 26,000 gallons) in use at Burger's Zoo, Arnhem, The Netherlands. J.C. Delbeek

Large 2-4 cm (1 - 1 1/2 inch) coral gravel, consisting mainly of *Acropora* sp. branches, is an ideal medium to use in calcium reactors. This way your corals are not only tank grown, they're recycled. J. Sprung

the aquarium. It is also possible to pass the effluent through an algal turf filter or refugium first, where the macroalgae would absorb the phosphate and excess CO_2. In addition, the stimulation of growth by these nutrients would also help to scavenge nitrate from the water. Generally, calcium reactor media made of the aragonite form of calcium carbonate is preferable to the calcite form since the pH level required to dissolve it does not to need be as low as for calcite (Huntington, 2002).

Media size

In small reactors, fine media (2-4 mm diameter) can be used without too many problems. However, as the height of the reactor increases, the amount of resistance offered by fine media increases also and it is not uncommon for the reactor to clog easily with fines and/or in a reverse flow design, to be lifted upwards as a single mass by the recirculation pump. In this case, larger media (1-2 cm) should be used so that water can flow more easily through it.

Caveats of calcium reactor use

Aquarists using a calcium reactor for the first time sometimes report an increase in the growth of filamentous algae. This is to be expected since CO_2 is a fertilizer for the plants. Furthermore, the calcareous material used in the reactor, depending upon its composition, may supply a significant amount of phosphate to the water directly as it dissolves (Bingman, 1997g; Hiller, 1999, 2003a), thus increasing the phosphate level in the aquarium. While the use of kalkwasser keeps dissolved phosphate in the aquarium low by causing a precipitation of phosphate and enhancing phosphate export via the protein skimmer, the use of a calcium reactor does not offer these benefits. Therefore, dissolved phosphate tends to be slightly higher in systems using the reactor exclusively. This accumulation or supply of phosphate can be managed through various means such as protein skimming, the harvest of algae from an attached refugium, or by passing the effluent through granular ferric hydroxide (GFH) or granular ferric oxide hydroxide (GFO) filter materials that adsorb phosphate (see chapter 6). It has even been proposed that promoting the rapid growth of corals is a way to keep the dissolved phosphate level low (see for example, Stark, 1995). This is true since the process of calcification energetically *costs* a coral about 2 ATP (adensosine triphosphate) molecules per unit of $CaCO_3$ precipitated (McConnaughey, 2000). As the coral grows, more ATP is required to fuel the increase in calcification demand, aside from the need for phosphate to support the nutrient needs of the increasing coral tissue and zooxanthellae mass. McConnaughey and Whelan (1997) also point out that protons released during calcification could be used to gather nutrients, including phosphorus (see further discussion at the end of this chapter).

In closed system aquariums, the delicate balance of phosphate input and export can produce any of the following: 1) phosphate-limited coral growth (i.e. shortage of phosphate); 2) filamentous algae growth (slight excess phosphate) and 3) high phosphate cessation of calcification (Simkiss, 1964). To achieve a *balance*, the dissolved phosphate level should be kept between 0.010 and 0.020 ppm, but preferably below 0.015 ppm as PO_4 -P (see chapter 4).

There has been some speculation that older aquariums especially, which relied for years on kalkwasser additions to assist dissolved phosphate control, might see a sudden increase in dissolved phosphate (and increase in algae growth) when switching to the calcium reactor system. The reasoning proposed was that the extra CO_2 in the water and resulting suppression of pH would tend to allow phosphate precipitated on the gravel to come back into solution. Although it seems intuitive that it might, a slight decrease in pH does not cause a release of phosphate from the gravel or other substrates. The pH would have to fall well below 7.0 for this to occur.

Low system pH

Systems that run solely on calcium reactors tend to run at a lower pH, with a pH level typically 7.7 to 8.1 (Holmes-Farley, 2003b). This should not be surprising given the excess CO_2 and bicarbonate administered to the aquarium by the reactor. It is perfectly acceptable to run a reef aquarium at these levels of pH provided the alkalinity and calcium levels are maintained at or above natural seawater concentrations and/or calcium carbonate is at saturation.

As we mentioned, excess CO_2 exiting the reactor can be somewhat reduced by a two chamber design where the second chamber of media neutralizes excess CO_2, or when downdraft skimmers are employed, since the excess can be blown off to the atmosphere. However, two chamber designs do not typically raise the pH of the effluent to tank levels so the effluent is still somewhat acidic. If the effluent is heavily aerated before entering the tank or if it is injected into a downdraft skimmer for example, the sudden increase in pH could cause the calcium and carbonates to precipitate out of solution as calcium carbonate (Holmes-Farley, 2002g). The best solution is to combine a calcium reactor with the use of kalkwasser as the sole form of top-off for evaporation. The calcium hydroxide will combine with the CO_2 to form carbonates and bicarbonates, further boosting calcium and alkalinity levels in the process. The use of both a calcium reactor and kalkwasser doser has therefore become a very popular combination. Using a kalkwasser doser, linked to a pH controller, is also an effective combination for dealing with chronic low pH.

Other calcium and alkalinity sources

Natural water sources rich in calcium and alkalinity

Some aquarists are fortunate to live in an area where the tapwater or well water is extremely hard, rich in calcium and magnesium, as well as bicarbonate and carbonate, and not polluted. It is possible to maintain adequate or high levels of calcium in an aquarium by using this water, but the effect is limited to low rates of calcification. Maintaining proper calcium and alkalinity levels for rapidly growing corals requires a more concentrated source of calcium and alkalinity. In addition, these sources may not be balanced in terms of calcium and alkalinity and this would result in an imbalance over time.

Calcium acetate

Calcium acetate acts like a balanced calcium/alkalinity supplement, so it isn't useful for raising calcium concentration without also increasing alkalinity. Calcium acetate has four moles of carbon per mole of calcium. Calcification nominally needs only one mole of inorganic carbon per mole of calcium, so calcium acetate is carbon rich, and may suppress the pH of the system, more even than a calcium carbonate/CO_2 reactor. However, calcium acetate used in conjunction with kalkwasser is a nice combination, essentially like the combined use of kalkwasser and vinegar proposed by Bingman (1999e).

When dissolved in water, calcium acetate dissociates into calcium ions and acetate ions. The acetate is then rapidly converted into carbon dioxide, bicarbonate and water by bacteria in the tank according to the following proposed reaction:

$$CH_3COO^- \text{ (acetate)} + 2\ O_2 \rightarrow HCO_3^- + CO_2 + H_2O$$
(Holmes-Farley, 2003b).

Since calcium acetate is organic in nature and contains carbon, it is possible that the addition of this organic carbon could also aid denitrification in sand beds and live rock, thus lowering nitrate levels by the following reaction mediated by bacteria:

$$5\ CH_3COO^- \text{ (acetate)} + 8\ NO_3^- \rightarrow 10\ CO_2 + 4\ N_2 + 13\ OH^- + H_2O$$
(Holmes-Farley, 2003b).

Calcium chloride

Calcium chloride can be used to make a *quick-fix* solution to raising the calcium level, and some hobbyists use it alone to maintain the level (for specific dosing recommendations, see the online calculators we mentioned earlier in this chapter). The chief advantages of calcium chloride are that it dissolves quickly in water, a lot of it will dissolve in the water, and the addition of calcium chloride solution will not raise the pH. There are two disadvantages to using calcium chloride. One is that such additions raise the chlorinity of the aquarium's water, meaning that in time the balance of sodium and chloride ions in the aquarium water is off. The severity of this imbalance depends on the frequency of water changes. The other disadvantage is that rapid elevation of the calcium ion level often causes the alkalinity and pH to fall, requiring the subsequent addition of an alkalinity buffer. This leaves the aquarist baffled because the calcium level rises only a little, much less than it should have based on the weight of calcium chloride added, and the alkalinity falls. If a lot is added at once, the influx of calcium ions combines with free carbonate ions in the water, resulting in both falling out of solution as calcium carbonate (it could look like it is snowing in your tank!). When the calcium level reaches 550 mg/L or higher at a pH of 8.2 or higher, supersaturation has been reached and calcium carbonate precipitation will occur.

Kalkwasser additions also can cause this kind of alkalinity drop phenomenon. If a large dose is added to the aquarium at once, and no CO_2 system is used, the resulting rise in pH will cause precipitation of both calcium carbonate and magnesium carbonate. If the additions are made slowly, as with an automatic water make-up system or drip system, this is not a problem. To sum up: go slow. While no toxic effect results from adding calcium chloride solution all at once to the aquarium, if the same quantity is administered slowly over a period of days, the alkalinity will be more stable.

Alkalinity supplements

There may be times when alkalinity needs to be given a boost while leaving the calcium level the same. There are several alkalinity supplements on the market, commonly called *buffers*, which contain a mixture of carbonates, bicarbonates and borates in various proportions. We caution against the use of buffers with large proportions of borate though. While these do act to raise alkalinity as well as pH and maintain it at a higher level, they play havoc with standard alkalinity test kits and require the use of a specialized kit that takes into consideration the higher borate level in the water. The same applies to salt mixes that have elevated borate levels. We discuss how and when to add sodium carbonate and sodium bicarbonate later on in this chapter under the topic of correcting imbalances.

Calcium chloride and sodium bicarbonate/carbonate solutions

Simply adding solutions made from calcium chloride, sodium bicarbonate, and sodium carbonate in the correct proportions should suffice to replenish calcium and alkalinity. This is the concept behind the use of two-part balanced calcium and alkalinity solutions, but only in the most simplistic sense since the use of these three ingredients alone does not produce an ionic residual of the same composition as natural seawater. To do that one would also need to add magnesium, strontium, sulfate, potassium, borate, and other ions all in the proper ratio. The addition of calcium chloride and sodium bicarbonate to an aquarium, after the deposition of calcium carbonate, leaves excess sodium and chloride ions, which raises the specific gravity. To dilute this excess, a portion of the seawater is removed and replaced with freshwater. Depending on the rate of addition and the size of the aquarium, this correction may be necessary bimonthly or monthly, and the specific gravity should be checked at least every two weeks. The correction dilutes not only the excess sodium and chloride, but also the other ions, including calcium and alkalinity. With dilution but no water change, the long-term effect is that the water composition evolves in the direction of a brine of sodium chloride, with trace quantities of calcium and carbonate alkalinity. Bingman (1998b, 1999e) projected and discussed the long-term effects of this method, combined with water change and/or dilutions with freshwater to counter the rise in salinity. He also examined the effects of different rates of addition of calcium chloride and sodium bicarbonate. A combination of monthly dilutions and no water change with daily addition of calcium chloride and sodium bicarbonate in stoichiometric ratios reduced the concentrations of the ions other than sodium, chloride, calcium, and carbonate alkalinity, by about 65% in one year. Additionally, the dilutions without water change reduced the calcium ion concentration disproportionally with respect to carbonate alkalinity (Bingman, 1998b). Although the additions were made at stoichiometric ratios of calcium and alkalinity for the deposition of calcium carbonate skeletons, dilution with freshwater removed only a fraction of what remained of both in solution. Since seawater has a calcium:alkalinity ratio of about 10:1, the use of dilution to maintain specific gravity tends to drop the calcium level over time. However, properly formulated two-part calcium alkalinity solutions (see next section) factor this effect, so that dilutions do not result in such a disproportionate reduction of the calcium level.

Balanced-ion calcium/alkalinity supplements

It is possible to create solutions that achieve a balanced ionic residual, while supplying a much higher concentration of calcium ions and alkalinity. This is the concept behind the two-part solutions that have become popular for maintaining calcium and alkalinity. One part has calcium ions and associated ions such as magnesium and strontium, while the other part has alkalinity in the form of carbonate, bicarbonate, sulfate, and borate. Other ions may be included to make the recipe as close as possible to natural seawater ionic ratios. The dosing is simple and does not require any dosing apparatus. The aquarist adds one part to an area of strong water current and then an equal amount of the other part. The parts cannot be mixed together in a small container of water, since they react immediately to form calcium carbonate. They can safely be added in the aquarium of course because they are then diluted in a large volume of water.

After an increase in alkalinity and calcium ions, the net effect of these additions is a slow increase in the salinity, essentially like adding concentrated seawater to the aquarium. In principle, the ionic balance of the water is maintained. The increase in salinity from addition of balanced-ion calcium supplements is not necessarily problematic. In fact, in some systems this slow increase counters the loss of salt due to the export of aquarium water with skimmate from the protein skimmer. The method is safer than kalkwasser and does not require any kind of dosing system, although using an automated dosing system with two channels that dose in equal amounts makes it a very simple way to keep the calcium and alkalinity levels up. For systems with low evaporation rates that cannot seem to maintain high calcium levels with kalkwasser use alone, such supplements

C-Balance® from *Two Little Fishies* is formulated to maintain calcium, magnesium, strontium and alkalinity in reef aquariums, leaving a residual with the ionic composition of seawater. J. Sprung

can be especially helpful. However, the two-part balanced supplements are more expensive to use than kalkwasser, and can be cost prohibitive to use exclusively for large systems with a high calcium and alkalinity demand. Such systems benefit most from the installation of a calcium reactor, which can easily maintain their calcium and alkalinity demands.

Each aquarium is unique with respect to the use of two-part balanced ion calcium/alkalinity supplements, so it is not possible to give a precise dosage, only a range. The use of alkalinity and calcium test kits helps to give you an idea how to dose the tank. One may use a conservative starting dose added daily, but it may not be necessary to add it daily, or it may be necessary to add more than this. It is important not to add too much at once because doing so runs the risk of temporarily raising the pH too high and precipitating out calcium and alkalinity as calcium carbonate. As with the calcium chloride and sodium bicarbonate method described earlier, it is important to monitor the salinity with two part balanced supplements, and correct it as needed with partial water change and freshwater dilutions.

Balling method

Named after Hans Balling, this method consists of making your own two part balanced additive. In this case, a sodium chloride-free salt mix is used (*Tropic Marin* markets such a salt). The aquarist adds sodium carbonate, sodium bicarbonate and calcium chloride to the aquarium in the correct ratio such that the sodium and chloride added is in the same ratio as in natural seawater, and the calcium and bicarbonate ions are added in the correct proportion but at a much higher concentration. Using the sodium chloride free salt mix for water changes reduces the excess sodium and chloride ions added by the sodium carbonate, sodium bicarbonate, and calcium chloride. The problem with this method is that it is not ionically balanced, and can produce ionic imbalances over time. Magnesium chloride could also be added instead of some of the calcium chloride, as could strontium chloride. This is of course more work than using a prepackaged ionically balanced two-part solution but it is potentially cheaper since the chemicals can be ordered in bulk and can be mixed with water at home rather than having to purchase and/or ship liquid two part mixtures.

Solving calcium, alkalinity and pH problems

Due to any of a variety of reasons, all too often one or all three of these parameters fall out of their normal range and the task then becomes to fix the imbalance and bring the aquarium to some sort of equilibrium. If for example, the brand of salt used to start the aquarium or for water changes is unbalanced with respect to the amount of calcium or alkalinity, then the aquarium begins with an immediate problem. Starting up an aquarium with sterile aragonite or other calcium carbonate gravel or sand can also severely affect the alkalinity, as we described earlier in this chapter (see also chapter 6, under the topic biofilms). Furthermore, if individual calcium and alkalinity additives are used to maintain calcium and alkalinity levels, imbalances can occur if they are not added in the proper proportions. If such additives are used to correct problems with these two parameters, a seesaw effect can also occur. For example, if a calcium additive is added to boost the calcium level of the water, alkalinity may drop if too much is added and carbonates precipitate out with the excess calcium. An alkalinity additive is then used to raise the alkalinity but might precipitate out the excess calcium if too much is added at once, so more calcium is added, and so on, leading to a very perturbed system and a frustrated aquarist. This is why we recommended previously that a balanced supplementation scheme should be used to maintain calcium and alkalinity in reef aquariums. At the end of this chapter, we describe the corrective action to take in each of the possible imbalance situations.

Correcting pH problems

Before discussing pH problems, we need to remind aquarists that it is very important to double-check that the pH level you are measuring is indeed correct. If you use a pH test kit, have you tested the pH of a standard solution to check the accuracy of your test? How old are the reagents in your test kit? If you use a pH probe, when was it last calibrated? Have you compared the pH meter value to a test kit? Once you are sure that the pH level you are reading is accurate, and the pH is not where you want it, then and only then should you proceed to correct it.

One of the most common complaints we hear about someone's reef aquarium chemistry is that they cannot maintain a high pH level. The question that needs to be asked in such a situation is: what pH level is high enough? Most aquarists are under the assumption that the aquarium pH must be close to natural seawater at all times (8.2-8.5). While it is true that calcification rates decrease as pH falls below this range, as long as calcium and alkalinity values are maintained at or slightly above natural values (calcium = 400-480 ppm, alkalinity = 2.3 – 3.5 meq/L), calcification will still occur at acceptable rates at a pH as low as 7.8 (Holmes-Farley, 2002g). In fact, it is normal for the pH values on reefs to rise and fall in a 24-hour cycle in response to photosynthesis and respiration, especially in the case of isolated lagoons and tide pools.

Low pH

If the pH of the system is chronically below 7.8 then calcification begins to become restricted even if calcium and alkalinity are kept higher than normal. Such low levels of pH are most likely due to excess CO_2 in the water. The two most common reasons for excess CO_2 is excess CO_2 in the air surrounding the aquarium or the aggressive use of a calcium reactor or a CO_2 dosing system.

In homes that are airtight or have poor exchange with the exterior, CO_2 produced by respiration by people and pets, and CO_2 produced by gas burning appliances can lead to CO_2 levels up to twice that of exterior air (Holmes-Farley, 2002g) (see chapter 1 and 4). The solution is to either lower the CO_2 level of air entering the water or neutralize/consume the CO_2 once it is in the water. Opening windows (when possible) or locating skimmer and air pump air intakes outside the home via tubing can result in improved pH levels in some cases. Adding supplements that give a high pH to the water are very useful but must be used daily to combat low pH. Kalkwasser and sodium carbonate (washing soda) are the two most effective supplements that can be used in this manner (Holmes-Farley, 2002g). A calcium hydroxide dosing system (e.g. Nilsen reactor) could be linked to a pH controller to dose kalkwasser whenever pH falls below the set point. Finally, algae in a refugium can be used to consume the excess CO_2 and increase pH by linking the pH controller to the lights over the filter. When the pH drops below the set point, lights over the algae are switched on by the controller and CO_2 is consumed via photosynthesis, raising pH, with a side benefit of enhancing the uptake of nutrients such as ammonium, nitrate and phosphate.

The methods just described can also be used to deal with excess CO_2 from a calcium reactor, but the first step is to check the reactor for correct operation. Make sure that the CO_2 bubbling rate is where it should be and that calcium and alkalinity values in the effluent are where they should be. The use of kalkwasser dosing in combination with a calcium reactor also helps to reduce CO_2 accumulation.

Finally, low alkalinity can also result in low system pH, and occurs when calcification rates exceed the addition of alkalinity. This most commonly occurs when methods used to raise alkalinity do not themselves raise pH e.g. calcium reactors or sodium bicarbonate (Holmes-Farley, 2002g). This is best corrected by increasing alkalinity supplementation. A depleted alkalinity can also be caused by acidification of the water as when nitrification proceeds without denitrification.

Tip: If alkalinity is within the acceptable range, do NOT add more buffer in an attempt to raise a low pH. This will only exacerbate the problem by increasing alkalinity and it may cause a decrease in calcium.

Figure 5a illustrates the relationship between pH, alkalinity and CO_2 concentration in seawater. The blue line shows how alkalinity increases with pH at a normal concentration of CO_2, that is, the aquarium CO_2 level is in equilibrium with the atmosphere. In tanks that use a calcium reactor or are located in a room or home with higher than normal CO_2 levels, the pH level will be lower but the alkalinity can still be the same as at a normal CO_2 level (red line). One also can see that removing excess CO_2 from the water will increase pH while maintaining alkalinity (green line).

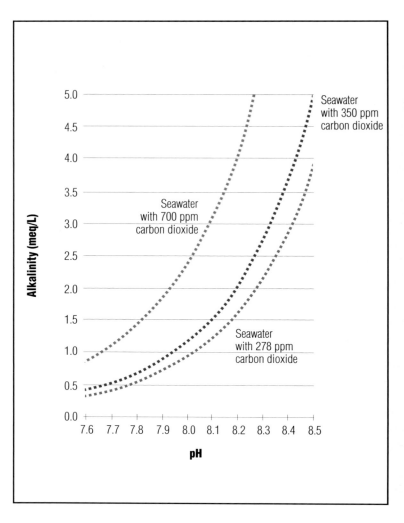

High pH problems

In tanks that use kalkwasser, the pH can sometimes run higher than 8.4. Similarly, aquariums that have abundant algal growth can also have a high pH. In both cases, the reason is the same and can be deduced from figure 5a; there is a shortage of CO_2. Adding too much kalkwasser results in CO_2 levels being lowered by conversion into carbonate and bicarbonate by the hydroxide ions in the calcium hydroxide. In the case of the algae, CO_2 is consumed during the day by photosynthesis.

The correction of either situation is the same; CO_2 needs to be added to the water, either by increasing gas exchange with the atmosphere (increased water agitation, protein skimmers, etc.) or by direct injection of CO_2 via a pH controller and CO_2 regulator. Another method to increase CO_2 is to add an organic acid such as vinegar, which breaks down into CO_2, by adding it directly to the aquarium or to the kalkwasser before using it (Holmes-Farley, 2002g).

Correcting calcium and alkalinity problems

One of the first steps in correcting calcium and alkalinity problems is to be sure you really do have a problem. There seems to be an obsession amongst hobbyists for their aquariums to exhibit elevated levels for both calcium and alkalinity, and to have a high pH. Unfortunately, this is not possible for a variety of reasons, the most compelling of which is that as pH rises, calcium carbonate solubility drops. This means that as pH increases, the chances of calcium and alkalinity combining to form insoluble calcium carbonate increases, and if the pH rises too quickly or too high, calcium and alkalinity levels will decrease as calcium carbonate forms and falls out of solution. In addition, to maintain the appropriate balance between calcium and alkalinity, a calcium level of 480 mg/L would require a dKH of 16! Therefore, unless your alkalinity and calcium levels are outside of the recommended ranges (calcium = 380-480 mg/L, alkalinity = 2.3-4.0 meq/L) you don't really have a problem (Holmes-Farley, 2002e). Of course, the only way to know what your levels are is to use test kits. Be sure your test kits contain reagents that have not passed their shelf life and if you are in doubt about a reading, try another test kit of a different brand to compare against the other. Since test kits are not 100% accurate, you would be wise to keep calcium and alkalinity levels in the middle of the acceptable ranges since they may actually be slightly higher or lower than what you measure (Holmes-Farley, 2002e).

Figures 5b, c and d are reproduced here, with permission, from Randy Holmes-Farley's 2002 *Advanced Aquarist Online* article dealing with solving calcium and alkalinity problems (Holmes-Farley, 2002e). In this diagram, the red square represents the target range for both calcium and alkalinity, and the blue dot represents natural seawater values. Each numbered zone outside of the target area has a specific set of directions to get back to the target.

If the tank's alkalinity and calcium levels are both elevated above normal values and fall within zone 1, the simple solution is to do nothing. In time, calcification will lower both levels in proportion and you will end up in the red box at which time you can resume supplementation of calcium and alkalinity, at a lower rate.

If your values fall within zone 2, then your balanced calcium supplement is not keeping up with the rate of calcification in your aquarium. In this case, you need to increase the amount you are adding. You can also use individual calcium and alkalinity supplements but these will require you to add them in the proper proportions and to measure calcium and alkalinity frequently to ensure you are doing so. If you cannot raise the levels easily, you may want to check the magnesium level. It should be around 1300 ppm. Magnesium inhibits the abiotic precipitation of calcium carbonate, and if it is low, you may be losing much of the alkalinity and calcium that you add, in this manner (Holmes-Farley, 2002e).

Tip: When correcting calcium and alkalinity imbalances, you may have to add more of a supplement than is normally recommended by the manufacturer. Be sure to check the maximum daily dosage listed on the label.

When calcium and alkalinity levels fall within zone 3 (figure 5c), it is usually the result of overdosing alkalinity relative to calcium (Holmes-Farley, 2002e). In this case, the proper course of action is to first increase the calcium level only so that you move back into the proper range for calcium. If you use a balanced supplement such as kalkwasser or a calcium reactor, you will only move further up in zone 3 since both calcium and alkalinity will be added. Therefore, the easiest way is to just use a calcium chloride supplement or any supplement that only adds calcium. Once you move within the parallel lines you can begin to use a balanced supplement again to move up into the target zone (figure 5c).

Values that fall within zone 4 (figure 5d) are the result of overdosing calcium relative to alkalinity. In this case, the solution is to add an alkalinity supplement to raise the alkalinity back into the desired range. If the alkalinity is below 4.0 meq/L then simply add enough supplement to raise it into the red zone. If the alkalinity is above 4.0 meq/L you can either do nothing and wait for it to drop and then take the same steps as we just mentioned, or you can add alkalinity,

Figure 5b. Possible values for calcium and alkalinity in marine aquaria. The blue dot represents natural seawater. Source: Holmes-Farley (2002e).

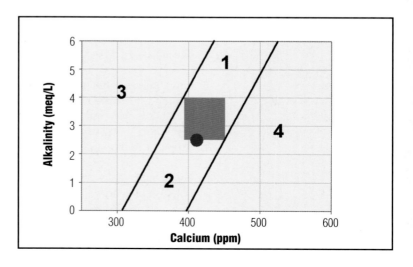

Figure 5c. To correct a low calcium level in zone 3, adding a calcium additive such as calcium chloride, will move the level into the proper range (the blue arrow). Source: Holmes-Farley (2002e).

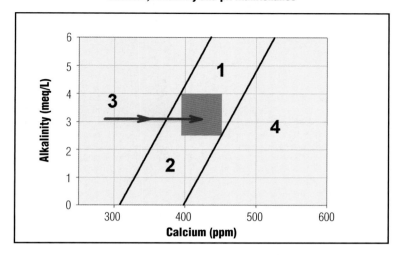

move the level into zone 1 then just let calcium and alkalinity fall on their own into the red zone (Holmes-Farley, 2002e). Of course, if you also have a pH over 8.2 you may experience a rapid loss of calcium carbonate as it precipitates out when you add the alkalinity supplement. In this case, measure the values and begin anew assessing how to bring them back in line.

Again, as with the previous situation, you do not want to use a balanced supplementation scheme otherwise you would end up raising calcium as well. Once you have increased alkalinity to the proper level, you should switch to using a balanced supplementation method.

What to use to boost the alkalinity depends on the aquarium pH. If the pH lies below 8.3, sodium carbonate (washing soda) is the best choice and if it is over 8.3, sodium bicarbonate (baking soda) is better to use since it will not raise pH dramatically (Holmes-Farley, 2002e). To raise 50 gallons (13 L) 1 meq/L (2.8 dKH) requires 16 grams of baking soda or 10 grams of washing soda (Holmes-Farley, 2002e). When using washing soda, make sure it does not contain any surfactants (added to aid in the formation of suds when washing clothes) or perfumes. Bingman (1997f) also described methods for correcting calcium and alkalinity imbalances using a single figure that we reproduce here. In figure 5e, the central diagonal line follows the slope of values of calcium and alkalinity that can be reached based on a starting point of 400 ppm calcium and a total alkalinity of 2.5 meq/L. Bingman included 10 and 20% tolerance bands around this line. The region between these lines and between 2.5 and 5.0 meq/L is marked by a dashed outline. The calcium and alkalinity values within this outlined area are ideal for a reef

Figure 5d. Correcting zone 4 imbalances by adding an alkalinity additive, such as baking soda, drives the alkalinity upwards (the blue arrow). Source: Holmes-Farley (2002e).

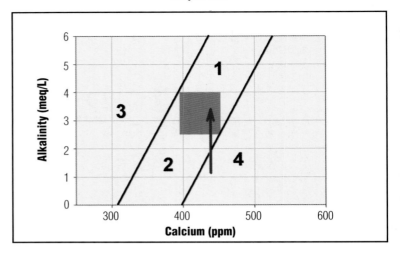

Figure 5e Corrective actions for calcium and alkalinity imbalances. After Bingman, 1997f.

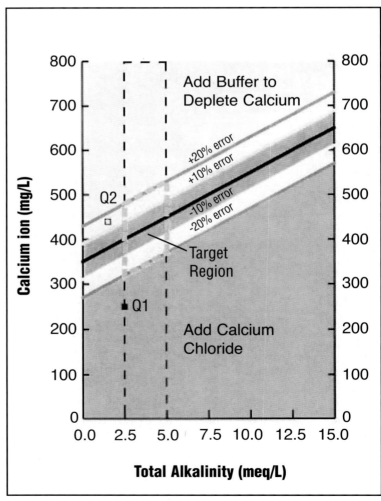

aquarium. If the values are above the upper 20 percent tolerance line, adding buffer (sodium bicarbonate) will deplete calcium and bring the values back within the bands. If the values are below the lower 20 percent tolerance line, adding calcium chloride will deplete alkalinity and bring the values back within the bands. When the values are within the 20 percent tolerance bands, adding more or less of a balanced calcium and alkalinity supplement will cause a balanced increase or decrease along the slope shown.

Calcium, alkalinity and pH are critical components in reef aquarium water chemistry. Understanding how they are interrelated and how to maintain the correct balance, or to correct imbalances in all three, will go a long way to making you successful in the maintenance of calcifying organisms.

Alkalinity and calcium carbonate saturation state

We have already described the popular supplementation methods, but wanted to finish the chapter with some additional background information that may interest some readers with a background in chemistry. Other readers may wish to avoid this section! At the beginning of the chapter, we mentioned the term saturation, and how combinations of calcium, alkalinity and pH may promote precipitation of calcium carbonate. Certain combinations of these parameters can produce a saturation or supersaturation state, described with the symbol Ω. A saturation state describes the condition of a given chemical equilibrium. Since we are discussing the saturation state of dissolved calcium and alkalinity with respect to precipitation of solid calcium carbonate, the reaction is:

$$Ca^{2+} \text{ (aqueous)} + CO_3^{2-} \text{ (aqueous)} \longleftrightarrow CaCO_3 \text{ (solid)}$$

An equilibrium reaction like this with aqueous components has a solubility product, symbolized as K_{sp}, which is the product of the thermodynamic activity of the components. The *activity* represents the apparent concentration. While the *activity* of the ions in solution is not the same as their concentration, they are often numerically very close. *Activity* is denoted by braces (e.g. $\{Ca^{2+}\}$), whereas concentrations are indicated by brackets (e.g. $[CO_3^{2-}]$).

K_{sp} = activity of component 1 x activity of component 2.

In this case it is represented:

$$K_{sp} = \{Ca^{2+}\} \times \{CO_3^{2-}\}$$

To describe the saturation state, Ω, we use the following formula:

$$\Omega = \frac{\{Ca^{2+}\} \times \{CO_3^{2-}\}}{K_{sp}}$$

When $\Omega = 1$, the solution is saturated, and precipitation can occur. When Ω is greater than 1, it is supersaturated, and when Ω is less than 1, the solution is undersaturated, which will cause dissolution of solid calcium carbonate in the solution. This simple description does not consider other effects that inhibit the precipitation of calcium carbonate from a solution. While a supersaturated condition of calcium carbonate in freshwater will produce spontaneous precipitation, it may or may not do so in seawater, due to the effects of other ions, such as magnesium and phosphorus, in the solution. Furthermore, the pH, temperature, pressure, and salinity also have roles in whether calcium carbonate will spontaneously fall out of solution. In any case, the formation of calcium carbonate skeletons by corals depends on the saturation condition being above 1.

Table 5.3 The saturation condition for aragonite at different calcium, alkalinity and pH values. After Holmes-Farley (2002h).

meq/L	Calcium	pH	Ω
2.5	410 ppm	7.7	1
1.0	340 ppm	8.2	1
2.5	410 ppm	8.2	3
4.0	410 ppm	8.0	3
2.5	260 ppm	8.4	3
5.0	410 ppm	8.2	6
8.0	410 ppm	8.0	6
4.2	410 ppm	8.45	6
2.5	820 ppm	8.2	6
2.5	410 ppm	8.7	6

We discuss this background information about saturation states because it is the saturation state of the crystal form of calcium carbonate known as aragonite, not the calcium level, which is the most limiting factor over the production of calcareous skeletons by corals. In natural seawater at a pH of 8.2, Ω = approximately 3 for aragonite, which means the concentration of calcium and alkalinity are supersaturated, and calcification by corals proceeds normally. At lower values for Ω, calcification by corals slows. If the value of Ω is increased above 3 in an aquarium, calcification can proceed more rapidly than it does in the sea. However, a higher supersaturation condition increases the likelihood of spontaneous precipitation of calcium carbonate in the water column. Given a supersaturation condition, precipitation can occur when the pH rises, or with the addition of a little more calcium or alkalinity. It is also promoted by a temperature increase, as evidenced by the precipitation of calcium carbonate on aquarium heaters. Another stimulus for the precipitation of calcium carbonate from solution is the presence of an electrical current. The electrical field causes minerals to precipitate from seawater, resulting in an accumulation of mainly calcium carbonate crusts on the electrified surface. Research into the enhanced formation of reef structures by applying weak electrical currents to iron mesh placed on the seafloor has been given the acronym ERCON (Electrochemical Reef Construction). In addition to encouraging spontaneous precipitation of calcium carbonate onto the electrified surface, the effect may also promote more rapid calcification in corals settled or transplanted onto the surface (Schuhmacher *et al.*, 2000). See www.globalcoral.org for an interesting time-series demonstration of this system in the Maldives.

Online saturation state calculators

Bingman (1998b) discusses the MS-DOS and Windows based co2sys program developed by Lewis and Wallace (1998), and related topics concerning the calculation of the saturation state of calcium carbonate in a reef aquarium. Other programs of this kind describing the seawater carbonate system are now available on the web, including the recent R-based version from Proye and Gatusso (2003), which can be run on Macintosh and Linux systems.

Coral calcification models

Corals promote the precipitation of calcium carbonate by artificially raising the level of Ω near their skeletons. How they do this is explained by an hypothesis proposed by McConnaughey and Whelan (1997), though the mechanisms of calcification by corals are not exclusively explained by this hypothesis. Furla *et al.* (2000) provide another perspective regarding the source of inorganic carbon for calcification. Using *Stylophora pistillata* microcolonies, they found that the major source (70-75%) of dissolved inorganic carbon (DIC) used in calcification was the coral's metabolic CO_2, and that only 25-30% of the DIC used in calcification originated from the external seawater. The metabolic source also explains a beneficial connection between photosynthesis and calcification, in that the symbiotic algae promote enhanced respiration by corals to the extent that metabolic CO_2 production by corals in the light is at least six times greater than what is required for calcification. Holmes-Farley (2002h) compares the calcification model proposed by Furla *et al.* (2000) with that of McConnaughey and Whelan (1997), and discusses other aspects of coral skeletogenesis and the implications for reef aquarium keepers.

243

The McConnaughey and Whelan hypothesis

McConnaughey and Whelan (1997) posit that when calcification runs in parallel with photosynthesis, the protons calcification provides convert bicarbonate ions into carbon dioxide that is then used for photosynthesis. This explains another beneficial connection of calcification and photosynthesis in reef building corals. While one can delve into the subject to greater levels of complexity, for our purposes we will explain the basic principles.

Calcification is represented traditionally with the following formula:

$$Ca^{2+} + 2\,HCO_3^- \rightarrow CaCO_3 + H_2CO_3$$

The H_2CO_3 is carbonic acid, which is another way of saying CO_2 dissolved in water. It is thus common to read that calcification produces CO_2, and that calcification cannot be a sink for excess global atmospheric CO_2. In alkaline seawater, the H_2CO_3 immediately converts to bicarbonate ions, HCO_3^-. This transition produces free H^+ (protons). Therefore, according to the McConnaughey and Whelan hypothesis, calcification is the process by which calcium ions (Ca^{2+}) combine with bicarbonate ions (HCO_3^-) to produce the mineral calcium carbonate ($CaCO_3$) and protons (hydrogen ions, H^+):

$$Ca^{2+} + HCO_3^- \rightarrow CaCO_3 + H^+$$

Since dissolved CO_2 rapidly converts to the bicarbonate ion, HCO_3^-, in alkaline water, there is essentially no free carbon dioxide available to plants (and zooxanthellate corals) to use for photosynthesis. They must somehow utilize bicarbonate ions as the principle source of inorganic carbon. The hydrogen ions produced by calcification and released into the boundary layer of water around calcareous plants or corals provides the needed access to a source of carbon for photosynthesis, as shown in the following bicarbonate conversion reaction:

$$2\,H^+ + 2\,HCO_3^- \rightarrow 2\,CO_2 + 2\,H_2O$$

Photosynthesis is described in the simplest sense by the following reaction:

$$CO_2 + H_2O \rightarrow CH_2O + O_2$$

Adding the calcification reaction and the photosynthesis reaction, we see that the ratio of calcification to photosynthesis can be one to one:

$$Ca^{2+} + 2\,HCO_3^- \rightarrow CaCO_3 + CH_2O + O_2$$

In a coral polyp, the symbionts and their photosynthesis occur in cells lining the internal gastrovascular system (coelenteron), mainly on the illuminated topside, while calcification is concentrated *far away*, in the basal epithelial tissues. Branching coral colonies such as *Acropora* and *Seriatopora* spp. concentrate the calcification at the apical branch tips, while foliose corals such as *Agaricia* and *Pavona* similarly calcify most rapidly at the pale outward edges, and the zooxanthellae colonize the area subsequently. McConnaughey and Whelan, (1997) explain the pale tips and edges this way. Calcification at the branch tips and edges generates protons that create CO_2 rich water within the coelenteron. This CO_2 rich water is directed by ciliary currents toward endodermal cells, so that zooxanthellae living within them have easy access to the CO_2 produced by calcification. The pale edges and branch tips, which are free of zooxanthellae, have high levels of energy rich ATP. Since there is essentially no photosynthesis occurring in the pale regions, the high concentration of ATP there is presumably made with organic compounds produced by zooxanthellae populating lower regions, and it is transported to the tips, either by a concentration gradient or ciliary currents (Fang *et al.*, 1983).

While it is outside of the scope of this chapter, we want to mention that McConnaughey and Whelan (1997) furthermore posit that the protons generated by calcification assist in nutrient assimilation by zooxanthellae, paralleling the way terrestrial plants use acid generated by calcification at the roots to leach nutrients (P, N, K, Mg, Fe, and Mn, among others) from soil. Since reef corals calcify faster when nutrients are low, the posited enhanced uptake of nutrients promoted by calcification promotes better calcification rates. The beneficial effect of algal filters on coral growth, and coral calcification on photosynthesis by adjacent algae, are supported by these ideas (see our discussion of algal filters in chapter 6).

In the sea, where the supply of bicarbonate ions is unlimited, symbiotic corals can utilize calcification to maintain or even elevate CO_2 concentrations in their boundary layers despite the photosynthetic uptake of CO_2 by the zooxanthellae. In closed system aquariums, the supply of bicarbonate ions is depleted by growing corals and calcareous algae, while calcium ions are also deposited with the skeletons and lost from the system. A depletion of alkalinity affects how much CO_2 can be produced by calcification. Thus, calcification and photosynthesis can be individually or simultaneously limited, especially in brightly illuminated aquaria with strong water motion, unless the supplies of calcium and alkalinity are maintained *unlimited* and balanced by an appropriate supplementation scheme.

Filtration

Maintaining life of any kind within the confines of an enclosed aquatic system requires control of the physical and chemical parameters of the water within the narrow range necessary for life. We commonly think that various filters or external apparatus should be used for maintaining water quality parameters. In fact, as the diversity of life and substrates increases in a living reef aquarium so that it more closely models a whole ecosystem, the maintenance of water quality is largely achieved by the animals, plants, and bacteria living throughout the system, rather than by artificial means of filtration. The balance of using both natural processes and artificial ones to the benefit of a stable closed system aquarium is a goal of reef aquarium keeping, and it is something that can easily be accomplished.

Mechanical filtration

The main function of a mechanical filter is to trap large particles from the water column in much the same way a vacuum cleaner traps dust and dirt, or an air filter catches air-borne dust. Trapping particulate matter from the water column reduces turbidity, especially noticeable in large reef displays and, when the particles are removed from the aquarium, it helps to reduce the amount of organic *stuff* available for mineralizing bacteria to convert into ammonia and other substances. The mechanical filter's function could be considered equivalent to the currents and tidal flushing on a natural reef, as both help to relocate and remove particulate matter. Mechanical filters typically remove particulate matter from the water column and concentrate it in one place in the aquarium. Tidal flushing in the natural environment moves suspended particulate matter from one place to another place. In nature, the particulate matter is broken up into smaller particles by water motion and detritivores, removed by filter feeders, or it settles in quiet areas, is deposited along shorelines, or in deep water, where it may be utilized by deposit feeders. The particulate matter is known to adsorb various substances, including ammonia, and it becomes populated by bacteria and other microorganisms, so it is nutritious (Wotton, 1988; Mills *et al.*, 2004). In a traditional forced flow mechanical trapping filter, water continues to pass through the

Protopalythoa vestitus photographed in the Solomon Islands. J. Sprung

trapped particles. This promotes the rapid digestion of the trapped particles by bacteria and microorganisms, adding nutrients to the water. This is one reason why a mechanical filter should be cleaned daily or not used at all on a reef aquarium.

Mechanical filters come in a variety of designs, though not all of them are suited to reef aquarium husbandry. Common materials for reef aquarium mechanical filters include sponge pads, fibrous mats, or polyester floss. Rapid sand, pleated cartridge, and diatomaceous earth filters are best suited to fish systems, or only for temporary use on reef aquariums. The key to proper mechanical filter design, if one is used at all, lies in regular cleaning. The easier a mechanical filter is to clean, the more likely you are to clean it on a regular basis. However, mechanical filtration is not necessary on a continuous basis for most reef aquariums, as we will shortly explain

Surface skimming

Surface skimming is the process wherein water is drawn off the surface of the aquarium by an overflow weir design that may or may not incorporate some form of mechanical filtration (see chapter 1). With this design one can efficiently remove floating particulate matter and dust that settles on the surface, and even some amino acids and fatty acids that collect at the surface because of their polar nature. The skimming keeps the water surface clean, and enhances gas exchange and light penetration.

Early overflow designs only allowed the mechanical filter material to be installed directly in the corner overflow where it was difficult to service. Additionally, if the mechanical filter became clogged, the design had the unappealing risk of impeding the flow through the drain sufficiently to cause the water to back up and overflow onto the floor. Subsequent designs had the mechanical filter placed in a

An easy to service filter sock designed to fit in the sump. J. Sprung

A simple design for permanent or temporary use of mechanical filtration. The drain from the overflow is plumbed to feed through the tee fitting into a filter sock that is held in place by a collar. The filter sock is easily removed for cleaning. J. Sprung

separate chamber that was more accessible or in the top of the trickle filter. A simpler design that we have often used is to locate a mechanical filter basket with polyester floss just where the water enters the sump. This design simplifies filter changing and inspection compared to location in the overflow chamber. An even better alternative recently popularized in aquarium keeping is the use of filter *socks* located in the sump. These are easier to install and clean than the simple floss or pad methods.

Mechanical filtration alternatives

Mechanical filtration can be accomplished more passively, by settlement in the sump or a connected *refugium* aquarium. If the sump has a sloped bottom or incorporates a series of slanted baffles, then particulate matter will settle at the lower ends where it can be removed by siphon or by means of a purge spigot installed there. When combined with surface skimming and a good foam fractionator, this design avoids the need to bother with cleaning and replacing mechanical filter media. However, the flow rate through the sump needs to be low enough or the sump large enough to allow the material to settle to the bottom before it can be pumped back to the aquarium. We have seen *settling filters* incorporating this design used in line with the sump, but the technique remains uncommon.

In a reef aquarium, it is not always necessary to use mechanical filter media. The advantages to avoiding mechanical filters are that more particulate matter is available for filter feeders, and more surface active material remains in the water, which enhances the performance of the protein skimmer. The particulate material left in the water also supplies a source of organic food for the heterotrophic denitrifying bacteria living in the substrates (rock, sand, gravel) and filter feeders such as polychaetes, sponges and clams, and detritivores such as sea cucumbers, seastars, amphipods, etc. However, without good circulation and populations of bottom stirring creatures, the particulate detritus can accumulate and promote algae blooms. As a general maintenance procedure, occasional *blasting* of the rocks with a powerhead or baster will prevent the formation of heavy deposits of detritus. This simulates an effect of storm surge on the reef. A mechanical filter can be installed just for this maintenance procedure, to be performed about every six months. In systems that incorporate a substratum such as sand or gravel, periodic siphoning of the upper layers may be needed to remove excess settled detritus too. See the topic sandbed filtration later in this chapter for exceptions to this.

Large public aquarium reef displays, however, need to use mechanical filtration to maintain *crystal clarity* through long viewing distances. It is common for such systems to incorporate mechanical filtration in the form of rapid sand filters and/or filter socks. An alternative is to use vortex filtration. Vortex filters are commonly used in aquaculture to

Walter Adey's Smithsonian microcosm had this refugium with a v-shaped bottom, used as a settling filter. Detritus is exported by purging the valve at the base. J.C. Delbeek

Figure 6a Vortex filter schematics. Top design with central overflow. Bottom design with filter sponge.

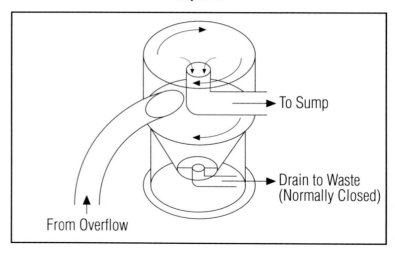

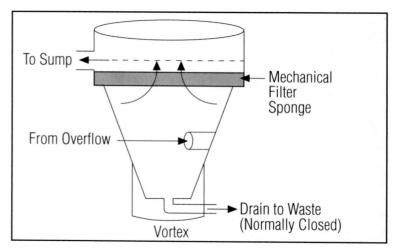

remove large particles. They work by injecting a stream of unfiltered water into a cone-shaped vessel where the particles are separated from the water by centrifugal force. The drawback to vortex filters is that they need to have a sufficiently large diameter to slow the flow down and allow particles to settle to the bottom.

UV sterilizers

Ultraviolet light of germicidal wavelength housed in a flow through device has long been used as a means to reduce the number of bacteria and pathogens in water. The application of UV sterilizers to aquariums has many benefits and really no downside other than heat addition to the water. Opponents of the idea point to the destruction of plankton as a downside, but this argument falls apart when one considers that plankton in a reef tank are both destroyed and produced by the aquarium's inhabitants.

Ultraviolet light acts by damaging the DNA within a living organism, such that it can no longer reproduce. However, bacteria have repair enzymes that can repair the damage caused by UV light. This is one of the reasons why UV units are not 100% effective in eliminating bacteria. In general, a UV sterilizer offers some valuable help in the control of water-borne pathogens, but it cannot be relied on to guarantee that disease problems won't occur (Spotte and Adams, 1981). The reason for this is simple: the pathogens continue to reproduce within the aquarium. Even if the UV sterilizer achieves a 100% kill rate, it is limited by the rate of flow through the UV sterilizer.

Spotte and Adams (1981) used differential equations to set a theoretical upper limit for the efficacy of UV radiation and demonstrated that, in a conventional closed system, the mass of pathogens never reaches zero even if the UV sterilizer has a 100% kill rate. Since a UV sterilizer cannot prevent the spread of water-borne pathogens in systems that are recirculated, then depending on the number of pathogens required to cause disease, the UV sterilizer may or may not be capable of preventing disease outbreak. The use of UV radiation in aquaculture is most effective in sterilization of raw water supplies and discharges into receiving waters, both of which are single-pass applications.

Types of UV technologies

There are two main technologies of UV lamps, low pressure and medium pressure. Both types come in low and high output wattages. Low pressure systems use monochromatic lamps while medium pressure systems use polychromatic lamps (Kalisvaart, 2004). Monochromatic lamps have one strong peak at 254 nm while polychromatic lamps have several peaks in intensity between 200 and 400 nm.

Table 6.1. UV lamp characteristics

Lamp Technology	Output	Wattage (W)
Low pressure	Low output	40-100
Low pressure	High output	16-280
Medium pressure	Low output	1000-4000
Medium pressure	High output	400-8000

Source: Kalisvaart, 2004

This is an important distinction; while both lamps will damage DNA, polychromatic lamps will damage a wider range of biomolecules including repair enzymes. This means that when the DNA of a bacterium is damaged it cannot be repaired and the organism dies. For this reason, medium pressure, polychromatic, high intensity UV systems give the best results when it comes to lowering and maintaining bacterial levels (Kalisvaart, 2004). Low pressure, monochromatic systems should be avoided where the water is exposed to light, since light stimulates the DNA repair process (Kalisvaart, 2004). Most hobbyist UV systems are low pressure and low output; however, higher intensity systems have recently appeared on the market but are still costly.

UV dosage

The common rule of thumb of wattage to gallons given by most hobbyist publications is really a meaningless recommendation since a variety of other factors such as flow rate, turbidity, temperature (UV lamps work best at 43.3 $^{\circ}$C/110 $^{\circ}$F), the nature of the target organism, as well as system volume all affect how strong the UV dosage should be. The wattage is just a starting point in selecting the proper size sterilizer for your system.

Ultraviolet intensity is measured in units of $\mu W/cm^2$ and the UV dosage is calculated as:

UV dosage = UV ($\mu W/cm^2$) intensity X time (seconds) = $\mu Ws/cm^2$

As can be seen from the equation, the effective UV dosage can be improved by either increasing the intensity of the lamp or decreasing the flow (Kalisvaart, 2004). For example, a unit that delivers 10,000 $\mu Ws/cm^2$ can be made to deliver a dosage of 20,000 $\mu Ws/cm^2$ simply by decreasing the flow by 50%. These two factors also have an influence on determining the correct sizing of a UV sterilizer for a particular system.

Using UV sterilizers

As we mentioned, the correct use of a UV sterilizer should take into account not only the wattage of the lamp but also the flow rate, turbidity and temperature of the water, as well as the target organism e.g. bacteria, viruses, ciliates. Fortunately, UV sterilizer manufacturers can advise you on which unit is best suited for your system using flow rate and UV lamp intensity to calculate the required UV dosage. One can also decrease the flow rate to achieve an even higher dosage if so desired, but then less water per hour will pass through the sterilizer, as we just mentioned.

When installing a UV sterilizer it is best to place the unit at the very end of the filtration system so that it receives the cleanest and clearest water possible, before it returns to the aquarium. Install the unit using true union valves or unions and ball valves, so that it can be isolated from the plumbing and easily removed for servicing. The unit should also be oriented so that the inlets and outlets are situated such that no air can be entrained in the unit. A drain line is a useful option since it allows the unit to be

Ultraviolet sterilizers are effective only when properly sized and installed. Note that in this installation at the Monterey Bay Aquarium, the inlet and outlet lines are on the upper side of the unit; this prevents the formation of air pockets. Unions are used on both lines to allow for easy disassembly while a drain line on the underside allows the unit to be easily drained for lamp replacement. There is also a flow meter on the inlet, which allows for the accurate determination of flow rate through the unit.
J.C. Delbeek

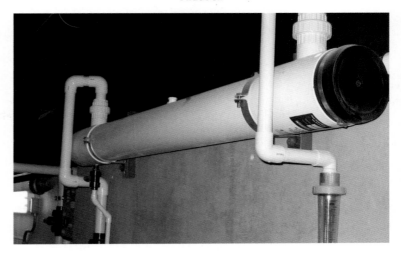

drained and opened for lamp replacement without having to remove the unit from the system. Finally, some form of flow meter should be installed on the inlet so that actual flow through the unit can be measured. In smaller systems where all the tank water enters the aquarium via the UV sterilizer, flow can be measured by collecting the return water in a container of known volume and timing how long it takes to fill; of course this is more time consuming and tedious than reading a flow meter!

Other operational factors

Ultraviolet lamps will lose their intensity rather quickly, dropping output by as much as 40% within six months (Aquatic Ecosystems, Tech Talks). One can therefore either oversize the unit by 40% to get a longer useful dosage life or replace the lamp every six months. Some designs incorporate a quartz sleeve over the bulb that prevents contact with the water, which would cool the bulb and thus alter the output intensity. These sleeves need to be kept clean of growths and other coatings (e.g. calcium carbonate may precipitate out of solution due to the high temperature of the sleeve), adding to their maintenance requirements. However, some designs include a sliding cleaning device to prevent buildup of detritus or slime on the sleeve, helping to maintain the kill efficiency and lowering maintenance time. Different designs also have different water thickness passing over the bulb. The thinner the volume of water the higher the effectiveness of the UV light in killing pathogens. Dr. Pablo Escobal's excellent book *Aquatic Systems Engineering: Devices and How They Function*, offers an in depth discussion of operational parameters of ultraviolet sterilizers and their proper use, and we recommend this reference for those wishing more information.

Table 6.2. Exposures Needed to Kill Microorganisms. Note the extremely high UV levels required to kill protozoans, similarly high dosages would be needed for *Cryptocaryon*.
Source: Aquatic Ecosystems, Tech Talks

Microorganism	µWs/cm^2
Staphylococcus aureus	6,600
E. coli	6,600
Mycobacterium tuberculosis	10,000
Salmonella sp.	10,000
Chlorella vugaris	22,000
Nematode (eggs)	92,000
Trichodina nigra (protozoan)	159,000
Paramecium (protozoan)	200,000
Ichthyophthirius sp. (ich) tomite (protozoan)	336,000

Alternative uses for UV light

In nature, UV light continuously bombards the oceans surface, breaking down larger organic molecules into smaller ones. In closed systems with a high animal load, dissolved organic nitrogen and dissolved organic carbon levels are often several times that of the ocean. Ishi and McGlathery (2003) found that calculated dissolved organic carbon levels dropped by 17% after 36 hours exposure to UV light mimicking the natural solar spectrum.

It has also recently been shown that in some reef aquaria, bacteria levels can also be several times higher than on a coral reef (Harker, 2001b). Preliminary results have also shown that waterborne bacterial levels will increase in a reef aquarium as the temperature rises as high as 30 °C (86 °F) (R. Harker, pers. comm.). Again, UV light may prove useful in lowering these levels. Activated carbon is often used in aquaria for removing DOC but it is also possible to reduce the level of DOC using ultraviolet light. The combined use of UV and carbon may prolong the useful life of activated carbon or other products that remove DOC.

Biological filtration

The use of biological filtration for water purification is universal in closed recirculating aquariums. The decomposition of organic and inorganic waste in the aquarium is accomplished by several types of bacteria, in addition to the activity of numerous worms, microscopic crustaceans, and protists. Bacteria proliferate in the sand, gravel and rock, and on all other substrata. Heterotrophic (chemoorganotrophic) bacteria convert amino acids to ammonium, a process called mineralization, and autotrophic (chemolithotrophic) nitrifying bacteria then convert ammonium to nitrite and nitrate, a process called nitrification. The biological oxidation of ammonia and nitrite prevents these substances from reaching toxic concentrations that would kill the inhabitants of an aquarium. Facultative anaerobic bacteria also known as denitrifying bacteria, if present, then break down the nitrate produced by the activity of nitrifying bacteria, and liberate free nitrogen gas. Other biological pathways exist for removal of nitrogenous compounds from the water in closed system aquariums, such as assimilation by algae and bacteria, and harvesting of their biomass.

Nitrification

Nitrification involves the bacterial oxidation of ammonium to nitrite and then nitrate. It proceeds as follows:

Step 1: NH_4^- (ammonium) $+ 3/2\ O_2 \rightarrow NO_2^-$ (nitrite) $+ H_2O + 2H^+$

Step 2: $NO_2^- + 1/2\ O_2 \rightarrow NO_3^-$ (nitrate) $+ 2H^+$.

Note that as nitrification proceeds, hydrogen ions (H^+) are released, which causes the pH to fall and depletes alkalinity.

The process mediated by autotrophic bacteria was first described by Winogradsky (1890), and the nitrification cycle has been described in

Figure 6b. Nitrification cycle and nitrogen transformations in the sea and in reef aquariums. Modified after Spotte, 1992.

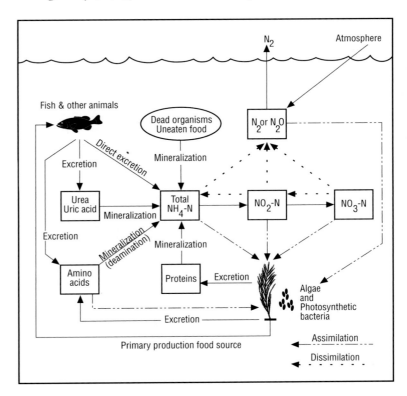

many books and articles about how to establish an aquarium. Texts describing biological filtration in the aquarium hobby have long held that there are two bacteria genera (and typically just two species) responsible for nitrification. The first, called *Nitrosomonas europaea*, oxidizes ammonia to nitrite, while the second, *Nitrobacter winogradskyi*, oxidizes nitrite to nitrate. These organisms are called nitrifiers and have been classified as belonging to the same family of bacteria. However, recent work on the phylogenetics of these organisms and their close relatives has shown that this classification is wrong and needs to be revised (Hovanec, 1998a).

Furthermore, Hovanec and DeLong (1996), and Hovanec *et al.* (1998), did not detect *Nitrobacter* in aquarium filters, but did detect *Nitrospira*-like bacteria. Even when *Nitrobacter* cultures are added to the system, they fail to become established. *Nitrobacter winogradskyi* and its close relatives are apparently *not* the nitrite-oxidizing bacteria in aquaria. Rather, the job is done by the *Nitrospira*-like bacteria.

This research suggests that *Nitrospira*-like bacteria are probably widespread in aquatic environments in which nitrite is available for oxidation. Hovanec found that *Nitrospira*-like bacteria are active nitrite oxidizers in aquaria and that *Nitrobacter* spp. are not present in significant numbers in wastewater facilities, as they are commonly presumed to be. However, his findings do not mean that *Nitrobacter* spp. don't exist or that *Nitrobacter* spp. do not oxidize nitrite. *Nitrobacter* exists and does oxidize nitrite in soils, but does not seem to play as important a role in aquatic environments as *Nitrospira*, as previously believed.

The fact that nitrifiers normally obtain cellular carbon by fixing dissolved CO_2 suggests that the limited availability of this gas during the day in an illuminated reef aquarium may influence their efficiency or capacity to convert ammonium to nitrate. However, nitrifying bacteria are considered facultative autotrophs, since they can also assimilate organic compounds as a source of cellular carbon and as an energy source during respiration (Spotte, 1992). In addition, nitrifiers grown in a wet/dry trickle filter have an unlimited supply of CO_2 from contact with air in the filter.

Nitrobacter is not really an obligate aerobe (such organisms must be in an environment that contains oxygen), and it can be grown heterotrophically (wherein it gets the carbon it needs from organic chemicals instead of just from CO_2, unlike autotrophic growth that relies on CO_2 as the carbon source). By contrast, it appears that *Nitrospira* spp. can only be grown autotrophically and aerobically, which makes sense considering their presence in aerobic biological filters. Schramm *et al.* (1999) offer a slightly different view of the reason for the scarcity of *Nitrobacter* in aquariums. They hypothesize that members of the *Nitrosomonas europaea* lineage and *Nitrobacter* sp. can out-compete *Nitrosospira* sp. and *Nitrospira* sp. in aquatic habitats with high nitrite concentrations because of their higher maximum growth rates. However, *Nitrosospira* sp. and *Nitrospira* sp. were better competitors in low nitrite environments (Schramm *et al.*, 1999).

Schramm *et al.* (2000) investigated the distribution of nitrifying bacteria of the genera *Nitrosomonas*, *Nitrosospira*, *Nitrobacter* and *Nitrospira* in a membrane-bound biofilm system with opposed supply of oxygen and ammonium. Gradients of oxygen, pH, nitrite and nitrate were determined by means of microsensors while the nitrifying populations along these gradients were identified and quantified using Fluorescence In Situ Hybridization (how appropriate, *FISH*) in combination with confocal laser scanning microscopy. The oxic part of the biofilm, which was subjected to high ammonium and nitrite concentrations, was dominated by *Nitrosomonas europaea*-like ammonia oxidizers and by members of the genus *Nitrobacter*. Cell numbers of *Nitrosospira* sp. were 1-2 orders of magnitude lower than *N. europaea*. *Nitrospira* sp. were virtually absent in this part of the biofilm, whereas they were most abundant at the oxic-anoxic interface. In the anoxic part of the biofilm, cell numbers of all nitrifiers were relatively low. These observations support the hypothesis that *N. europaea* and *Nitrobacter* sp. can out-compete *Nitrosospira* and *Nitrospira* spp. at high ammonia/nitrite and oxygen concentrations. Additionally, they suggest microaerophilic behaviour of a yet uncultured *Nitrospira* sp. as a factor of its environmental competitiveness in aquatic environments. Microaerophilic organisms require oxygen, but at a level lower than that typically found in Earth's normal sea-level atmosphere. *Nitrosospira* sp. and *Nitrospira* sp. were better competitors in low nitrite environments because of their lower Km values.

The Km value (aka Michaelis constant) describes the substrate binding power of an enzyme or, the *enzyme-substrate affinity*. In this definition, *substrate* refers to a chemical compound, such as nitrite, or ammonia. The Km value describes a reciprocal relationship. A *high* Km indicates a *low* affinity, and *vice versa*. The use of the term also applies to substrate affinity of bacteria. Since *Nitrospira* and *Nitrosospira* have low Km values, this means they have a high affinity for substrate (nitrite molecules), meaning they are better able to scavenge them at low nitrite concentrations. It is interesting to ponder whether in aquariums during the *break-in period Nitrobacter* might bloom briefly at a high nitrite concentration, then crash or quickly be replaced by *Nitrospira* and *Nitrosospira* as the concentration of nitrite decreases. Since the traditional *break-in* of a reef aquarium differs from that of a fish aquarium, in that there is not a prolonged high concentration of nitrite in the former, there may be a different series of events in the establishment of biological filtration in a reef aquarium. Live rock also probably harbours additional varieties of bacteria compared to a fish-only aquarium, not to mention a diverse assemblage of algae that consume nitrogenous waste.

Analysis of the bacteria found on live rock and in live sand needs to be done with reef aquariums in which live rock and live sand provide the bulk of biological filtration. In their submerged position, live rock and live sand differ substantially from the highly aerobic environment around the media in a wet/dry biological filter that is merely wetted by a thin water layer. In addition, there is another substantial difference between aquarium biological filter substrata and live substrata on reefs. The former are typically housed in dark boxes below or behind the aquarium while the former are brightly illuminated and associated with photosynthesizing algae. Furthermore, on the reef there is a close coupling between illuminated nitrogen fixing organisms (such as cyanobacteria) and nitrifying ones. In contrast to the findings of Hovanec and DeLong (1996) and Hovanec *et al.* (1998) for aquarium filters, Webb and Wiebe (1975) found *Nitrobacter agilis* on glass slides placed on a wild coral reef for 4 weeks. Of course, the diversity of life on reefs may provide some surprises, many more bacteria and other microorganisms may be involved with nitrification in *live* sand, gravel, or rock substrates on reefs than in simpler ecosystems such as lakes or average fish aquariums. It has yet to be shown whether this diversity is maintained in reef aquariums.

New tank syndrome

If sterile substrate (rock and sand) is used when an aquarium is first set up, the lack of populations of bacteria that accomplish biological filtration results in an inability to regulate the accumulation of nitrogenous waste produced by fishes or additions of food. This results in a rapid accumulation of ammonium that is toxic to fishes, otherwise known as *new tank syndrome*. This was a common problem in aquariums until the importance of the nitrogen cycle became known, and filters were designed to accommodate the necessary bacteria. In reef aquariums with live rock and their populations of associated bacteria, this *syndrome* rarely occurs.

The break-in or conditioning period

As we just mentioned, reef aquariums differ from fish-only aquariums in the initial period when the biological filtration is being established. Fish tanks are commonly *run-in, conditioned* or *cycled* with hardy animals first, to provide a source of ammonium (in addition to bacteria) to get the nitrification cycle going. The hardy animals survive the period of weeks or months when the ammonium and nitrite concentration in the water rises to levels that would stress more delicate marinelife. An alternative to using hardy animals is to use inorganic additions such as ammonium chloride to cycle an aquarium by adding a predetermined amount to achieve a target ammonium concentration. Reef tanks, by contrast, commonly start with the addition of live rock that already contains a significant population of nitrifying bacteria. The live rock is typically damaged a bit during shipping and handling, so that some plants and sponges may initially decompose, sending the ammonium and nitrite levels in the aquarium up, and thus promoting the *cycling* of the aquarium. In addition, it is now common practice to use live sand, which contains nitrifying bacteria as well as denitrifying bacteria.

We feel that the practice of using *disposable* fish or invertebrates to cycle an aquarium is neither necessary nor ethical. The use of living substrates (sand, gravel, rock) really simplifies the break-in period, and dramatically shortens the time it takes an aquarium to be able to support a *bioload*.

While it is possible to set up a new reef aquarium with fresh, newly imported live rock that is fouling, it is better to simply hold such rock in an aquarium or large vat(s) for a few weeks with temperature control and strong water circulation. This will give the rock a chance to become *cured* as we described in chapter 2. During this process, a great deal of detritus will be generated. Curing the rock in the display aquarium is less desirable because it presents the need to vacuum the excess detritus produced during this initial phase. In a vat, the accumulated detritus at the bottom is easy to discard. It can also be saved and used to seed a refugium with microfauna.

Since a deep gravel or sand bed provides sufficient area for the biological filtration of a typical aquarium, it is also possible to establish a new reef aquarium using excess old live sand or gravel from other reef aquariums. If one has many aquariums and/or refugia and lots of live sand in them, it is a simple matter to scoop out and replace some here and there, gathering together a sufficient quantity for use in establishing a new aquarium. Pet stores could easily offer this service, if they maintained large systems with excess live sand or gravel. A customer who sets up a new aquarium would have the option of purchasing sufficient live substrate to establish the biological filtration for the aquarium immediately. Extra pieces of live rock from the refugia can also be used. Starting a reef aquarium in this way completely eliminates the *break-in* period.

Denitrification

The nitrate that is produced by nitrification has a variety of fates. In addition to algae and higher plants, a variety of other organisms can absorb nitrate directly, using it to synthesize nitrogen-containing organic molecules, such as proteins and DNA (Holmes-Farley, 2001). There are two basic pathways by which nitrate is removed from the water. One is called denitrification, or dissimilatory nitrate reduction. In this process, nitrate is used in the biochemical pathway of respiration by either obligate or facultative anaerobic bacteria that consume organic substances as food. The other pathway is called assimilatory nitrate reduction, and it involves direct uptake of nitrogenous waste into tissue mass (such as algae or bacteria), often with intermediate steps, such as the conversion of nitrate to ammonium by bacteria. We discuss this process later in the chapter.

In dissimilatory nitrate reduction, what we traditionally think of when we discuss denitrification, bacteria reduce nitrate to nitrite, and eventually to di-nitrogen and nitrous oxide gases. These gases are then released into the water and are usually either lost to the atmosphere or absorbed by cyanobacteria. Since denitrification occurs mainly in the absence of oxygen, it is limited to sediments (bottom substrata) and anaerobic microhabitats such as occur in live rock or inside coral heads.

In this example that uses methanol as organic food, after Spotte (1992), the process of denitrification via dissimilatory nitrate reduction proceeds as follows:

$$NO_3^- + 5/6CH_3OH \rightarrow 1/2\ N_2 + 5/6\ CO_2 + 7/6\ H_2O + OH^-$$

Note that denitrification, which liberates OH^-, raises alkalinity, an effect opposite of nitrification, which releases H^+.

It has been shown that nitrification and denitrification occur in aerobic layers, where they are termed *coupled* since the processes occur simultaneously, mediated by bacteria in close proximity. Here anoxic microsites provide a habitat for anaerobic bacteria, while being surrounded by aerobic pore waters (Jenkins and Kemp, 1984). This is in contrast with the mental concept that the processes occur in separate aerobic and anaerobic zones. The importance of denitrification in coral reef nutrient budgets is not often discussed, but it has been shown to occur (Webb and Wiebe, 1975; Webb *et al.*, 1975; D'Elia, 1988).

Aquarists simply let denitrification proceed naturally within the live rocks and bottom substrata most modern reef aquariums use today. In most reef aquaria, these sites provide adequate denitrification to maintain levels below 0.5 ppm NO_3^- (Holmes-Farley, 2003b).

Filtration

Various strains of heterotrophic bacteria are known to function as denitrifiers under certain conditions. Spotte (1992) lists the following genera: *Alcaligenes* (=*Achromobacter*), *Azospirillum*, *Bacillus*, *Chromobacterium*, *Corneobacterium*, *Flavobacterium*, *Halobacterium*, *Kingella*, *Neissera*, *Paracoccus*, *Propionibacterium*, *Pseudomonas*, *Spirillum*, *Thiobacillus*, *Vibrio* and *Xanthomonas*.

Sources of nitrate

In recent years, there has been a trend to increase the amount of planktonic food added for corals and to add more fish, and hence more food for them. In systems that have a limited capacity for denitrification, nitrate levels will rise because of an increase in food additions. In some areas of the world, the tapwater supplied to homes may also be a source of nitrate. Without reverse osmosis or deionization systems, this nitrate can end up in the aquarium when the tapwater is used for evaporation replacement.

As we discuss in chapter 4, nitrate levels can rise to several times what is found on natural reefs without apparent negative effects on corals, but lower levels are preferred. In fish-only systems, nitrate levels can run much higher than in typical reef aquariums, also with no apparent negative effects.

As we discuss later in this chapter, *natural system approaches* help to maintain low nutrient levels with a minimum of ancillary filtration technology. Alternative methods of nitrate removal have also been developed such as carbon-based denitrators, sulfur filters, and various resins, zeolites, and enzyme compounds.

Fluid mechanics and biological filtration

We have discussed the basic chemistry and biology regarding the topic of biological filtration, but ignored the very important detail of physics. The way aquarium substrata *work* as biological filters involves physical processes rarely described adequately in aquarium literature. The flow of water through sand, gravel, and rock is an easy concept to understand. The mechanics of biological filtration in living substrates involves advection and diffusion processes that are a little more complicated to explain.

In contrast with undergravel filters, which utilize airlifts or pumps to draw or push water through the gravel, sand bed systems rely on a physical process known as advective transport that carries water, particles and dissolved matter through a porous medium such as a sand or gravel bed (Crank, 1983; Huettel *et al.*, 1998). Because the surface of the sediment is not smooth, water flowing over it generates some small turbulence.

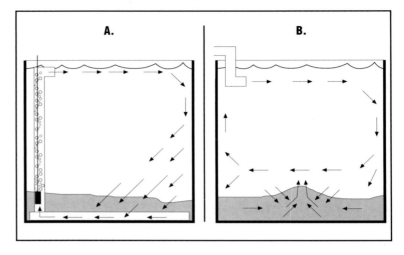

Figure 6c. A subgravel filter (left) forces water to pass through the gravel by actively drawing out water from beneath the substrate via a lift tube connected to the undergravel filter plate. The motion of water within an aquarium, right, causes a forced entry of water into the gravel by a process called advection.

Viewed at the scale of individual grains of sand, water pressure builds up on the side that faces the flow, and drops on the backside. The pressure difference causes water in the pore space below the surface grains to move, setting up a gradual flow through the sediment (Huettel and Gust, 1992). Water flow through the sediment decreases with sediment depth. The depth into which water flows in sediments is determined by the water's velocity above the sediment and the sediment's grain size. Higher water velocity and larger grain size promotes deeper effect of advective transport. Figures 6c-g illustrate this process. Additionally, any formation of a mound in the substrate, depressions in the substrate, or objects resting on the substrate (such as rocks) have dramatic effects on advective transport, as shown in figure 6f. In aquariums, the development of biofilms and accumulation of detritus also affect the depth of water movement

Figure 6d. The drawing A. represents a cross sectional view of a sediment bed in a relatively low velocity surge or tidal flow habitat. The lighter coloured cap of sediment is oxygented. Below it the darker sediment is anoxic. The u-shaped path represents the effect of infaunal organisms, whose burrows promote oxygen penetration deeper into the sediment, and the release of some anoxic pore water.

The drawing B. represents a cross sectional view of a sediment bed under a stronger surge flow, where ripples form on the bed surface. Under this flow regime, advection brings anoxic pore water upward through the sediment bed and out through the ridges of the ripples. In the natural environment, this effect is an important means of recycling nutrients such as reduced iron and other metals, nitrate, ammonia, silicate and phosphate.
Modified after Precht *et al.* (2004).

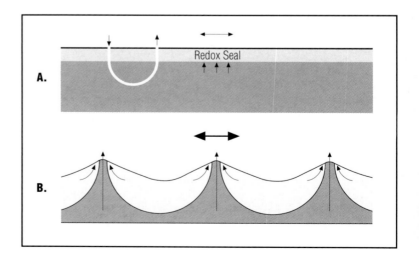

Figure 6e. In the drawing C, a strong to-and-fro surge causes the ripples on the sand surface to migrate slowly, altering the position of advective flow of water in the sand bed. In the drawing D. the surge is so strong that it causes the ripples on the sand surface to migrate quickly. This results in highly oxygenated water penetrating deeply into the sand bed, leaving a much deeper redox seal than in figure 6d, drawing A. Modified after Precht *et al.* (2004).

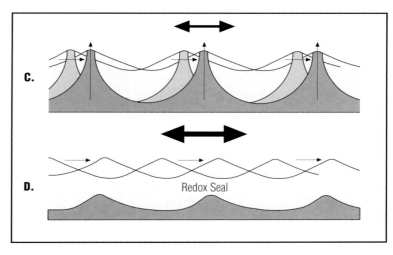

C.

D.

Redox Seal

The rhizomes of *Caulerpa* spp. sink into mud where they have a plentiful supply of ammonium. J. Sprung

in the sediment. Furthermore, bioturbation organisms that consume detritus and move within the sand bed, forming burrows, play a role in renewing the sediment's *porosity* (Aller, 1988). We have considered the effect of advective transport in sediments exposed to laminar current flows. The affect of surge alters the depth of influence on sediments by setting up pressure waves and forming ripples, the effects of which are shown in Figures 6d-e.

Grain size effects on advection

Capone *et al.* (1992) found ammonium concentrations vary among sediment types on coral reefs. Low concentrations occur in coarse and medium-grained carbonate sediments, fine-grained sediments had a steeper gradient and higher concentration at depth, while muddy sediments had the highest gradient and concentrations. It should be no wonder then that *Caulerpa* spp. grow so well in a mud-bottomed refugium. Their root-like rhizome is situated where it can uptake a plentiful supply of ammonium. Fine sediments also adsorb dissolved organic matter (DOC) (Tombascz *et al.*, 2000), thus promoting the growth of cyanobacteria that fix nitrogen, and ultimately promoting the growth of higher algae.

Rock effects on advection

A rock placed on a sand bottom in the presence of flowing water promotes advection that directs water from deep layers directly into the space occupied by the rock (see figure 6f). This effect transports ammonium rich water up into the rock, which stimulates the growth of algae, and stimulates nitrification and denitrification within the rock. The promotion of algae growth versus nitrification and denitrification depends on flow rate, oxygen concentration, herbivory, and other factors.

Figure 6f. A rock on the surface promotes advective
flow into the sand.
Modified after Huettel and Rusch (2000).

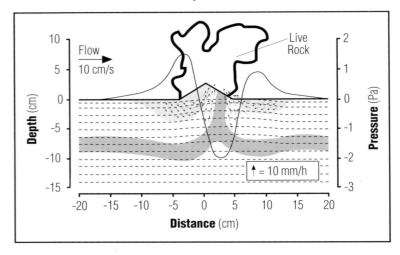

The iron deposited on the underside of this live rock
is evidence of pore water being advected upward into
the rock. The iron is soluble in the pore water deep
within the sand, but becomes oxidized and
precipitates as it moves upward. J. Sprung

The same model, viewed at a larger scale has a coral reef in the
open sea benefiting from internal upwelling (endo-upwelling)
caused by advection set up by prevailing ocean currents. This
idea, in addition to geothermal convection, was discussed by
Rougerie and Wauthy (1993).

Other advection effects

The flow of water into the substratum by advection also results in
the transport of particles and dissolved substances from the water
column into the substratum. Detritus, phytoplankton, zooplankton,
and dissolved and particulate organic matter all enter sand, gravel,
or rocks by this process. Deposit feeders (i.e. holothuroid sea
cucumbers, lugworms) are in effect *filter feeders* that utilize the
effect of advective transport that traps in the sand their food source:
phytoplankton and particulate organic carbon.

Advective removal of plankton by sediments essentially negates
any concerns about *plankton friendliness* of pumps with regard to
phytoplankton and small zooplankton. In addition, sand filtering
of particulate matter by advection disproves the notion, so often
repeated, that fine sand prevents detritus accumulation because
the detritus *merely settles on top.* If you have water movement, the
detritus moves into the sand.

Rocks are also porous, so advection makes them filter water
particles, including plankton. The capacity to do so is dependent
on the porosity of the rock and the velocity of the water flow.
Rocks placed on the sand also promote the advective deposition
of detritus in the sand beneath them.

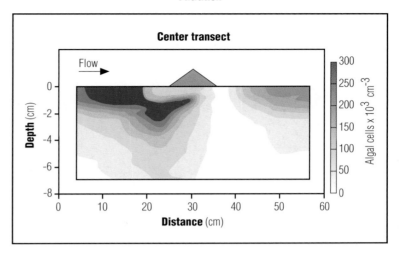

Figure 6g. Advection generated by laminar water flow over a sandbed forces phytoplankton into the sand where it decomposes or feeds deposit feeders. The shading represents measured concentrations of algal cells, indicated quantitatively in the scale on the right. Modified; after Huettel and Rusch (2000).

Diffusion and flow in the sand

When there is very slow water flow above the sand, movement of water and diffusion of the solutes it contains still occurs in the sand, albeit slowly. Early descriptions of Jaubert's method suggested that biological filtration in these systems occurred with movement of water and diffusion of solutes through the bottom substratum, and that for this reason one should leave as much of the bottom substratum exposed instead of covered by rock. With strong water motion, the movement of water and solutes into the substratum occurs by advection, not diffusion. Diffusion occurs deeper in the sand bed, moving solutes between it and the plenum. Furthermore, rocks placed on the substratum enhance the advective flow of water. However, rocks also promote advective upflow of deep pore water, which is not supposed to be promoted in Jaubert's method. In addition, since the advective flow of water into the substratum around rocks promotes deposition of detritus there, having rocks on the bottom reduces the porosity of the substratum. Reduced porosity means reduced flow, reduced oxygen content and thus reduced biological filtration, ultimately. The use of sand sifters and burrowing creatures, described in chapter 11, helps maintain substrate porosity.

Biofilms

The growth of bacteria on surfaces occurs not as one might imagine, as clusters of grape-like, spiraled or rod-like cells scattered here and there. It occurs as layers of gelatinous films with the cells imbedded. These layered films are called biofilms, and they develop with time into a thick complex mat of microbial species. The biofilm is initiated by one species of microbe producing a sticky polysaccharide attached to the surface. The growth of bacteria at the surface is enhanced by the nutrient concentration effect at surfaces in soil and water. Photosynthetic microbes (in light conditions) and aerobic

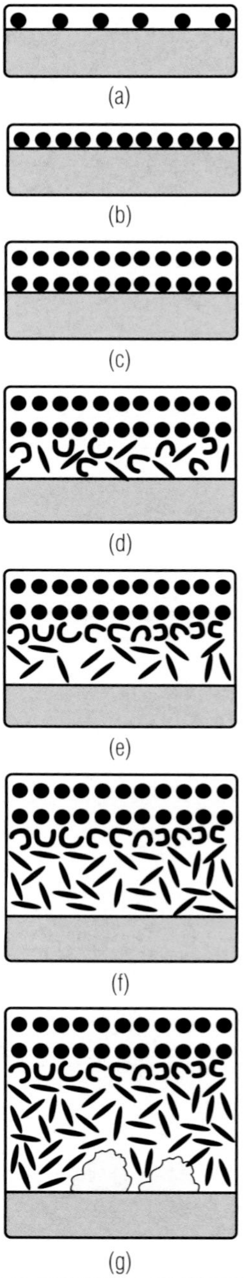

Figure 6h The proposed development of a biofilm follows a predictable buildup aerobes, (a), (b), (c), anaerobes, (d), (e), (f), and subsequent shedding as nutrient supplies become depleted near the base, (g). Modified after Spotte (1992).

microbes colonize the outer layers of the biofilm, while facultative heterotrophs occupy the middle regions. Chemolithotrophs may be abundant in the lower layers near an inorganic surface. Channels develop throughout the film, formed by amoebo-flagellate protozoa grazing on the bacteria (Spotte, 1992). The channels increase the porosity of the mat, allowing diffusion of nutrients, oxygen and carbon dioxide (see for example the same effect described for sediments, in Ray and Aller, 1985, and Rhoads and Boyer, 1982).

The previous discussion of advective and diffusive water flows through porous substrata applies to biofilms as well and relates to the efficiency of biological filtration. However, one difference is that high flow rates produce a shearing of the biofilm, tending to maintain it in a growth phase, while low flow rates allow the films to develop into thick mats that ultimately may suffocate, lose efficiency, die, and shed off from the substratum.

Positive effects of biofilms

Forming a barrier between bare limestone and seawater
Addition of fresh (dry or sterilized) aragonite to artificial seawater drops pH by 0.2 units and alkalinity by almost 50% (Adams and Spotte, 1985; Spotte, 1992). Biofilms formed by bacteria within a few days effectively coat sand or gravel grains and isolate the exposed aragonite surface, so that it no longer has this effect on alkalinity. This is another example of how bacteria stabilize the water quality in a closed system aquarium. *Live sand* already has this benefit, and it is possible to *seed* sterile sand by first placing it in a bucket of circulating saltwater from an aquarium for a week or so before introducing it to a display aquarium.

Sound reduction in plumbing
When the aquarium is first set up, the water passing through drain tubes often makes a distinctive gurgling sound (see chapter 3 for methods of reducing this effect). Within a month, the sound is noticeably reduced, not because the aquarist is accustomed to it, but because the inside surfaces of the pipes develop a biofilm that alters the way the water slides through. As we mentioned in chapter 3, if allowed to accumulate unchecked, biofilm development in narrow tubes can significantly reduce water flow.

Other biofilm effects
Development of biofilms on live rock can accomplish some unexpected results. One effect is that live rock surfaces may become *sticky*, making them an *absorption site* for phytoplankton and bacteria (hypothesis, Sprung 2004), or the bacteria and plankton may be trapped by advective water flow

forcing them into the biofilm. This could promote the development of other life forms on the rock that feed on the trapped material as well as on the biofilms. Because of this effect in closed system aquariums, water turbidity can be *cleared* by biofilms that trap particulate matter.

Yahel *et al.* (2003) showed that *bare* coralline algae coated live rock had the ability to clear phytoplankton from the water while identical but bleached (dead) control rocks lacked this ability. They proposed that the controls demonstrated that the depletion of phytoplankton occurred not by advection into the rock structure but instead was due to filter-feeding fauna living on the rock surface. They did not rule out the possibility that advection of phytoplankton into a biofilm could produce the phytoplankton clearing effect, since bleaching of the rocks would also destroy biofilms. However, they did demonstrate that live rock had a higher concentration of filter-feeding fauna than gravel collected in the same area, and that it had a higher ability to clear phytoplankton. That comparison supports the notion that the filter-feeding fauna (not the biofilms) are the principal means by which the phytoplankton is cleared from the water.

Sand clumping

The formation of biofilms has been associated with clumping of sand grains under certain conditions (Bingman, 1999). Bingman (1999) discusses the effects of acetic acid (vinegar) additions to boost the capacity of kalkwasser for calcium maintenance. One of the apparent side effects is that the excess dissolved organic additions could cause a proliferation of bacteria that produce sticky exopolymeric films within the sand bed. This is associated with loose clumping of sand grains. Shimek describes similar clumping, and points out that it can be distinguished from the calcium carbonate binding the sand because the clumps can be caused to fall apart by placing them in a solution containing bleach, which decomposes the bacterial films. Bacteria are known to have a role in the precipitation of calcium carbonate (aragonite) crystals from seawater in the marine environment (May and Guhathakurta, 1970), so it is not a simple matter to separate the concept of purely chemical versus biological binding of sand grains.

Note: Advective flow into the sand promotes the clumping by supplying organic food to the bacteria. The sand clumps where the water is forced downward into the sand.

Advective flow and old tank syndrome

The loss of porosity in the substrata due to the gradual deposition of detritus there by advective flow leads to a gradual reduction of the efficiency of biological nitrification and denitrification. This is largely the effect known as *old tank syndrome*. Old tank syndrome also involves other factors that tend to happen with time in a marine aquarium, such as decline in alkalinity and calcium levels, and increase in phosphate levels. We discuss remedies in Chapter 11.

Nitrifying filters

There are various biological filters designed to allow nitrification to occur. From undergravel filters, canister filters, external *biowheel* filters and trickle filters to fluidized bed filters they all share the same function: to convert ammonia to nitrate as efficiently and quickly as possible.

Trickle filters and fluidized bed filters are among the most efficient means of biological nitrification available to aquarists, but one does not need these, or external biological filter of any kind, in order to maintain a reef aquarium. The trend of relying on protein skimming combined with natural biological processes within the aquarium for the maintenance of water quality has achieved wide acceptance, but there will always be a spectrum of opinion about what pieces of equipment are really useful. Therefore, for the sake of completeness, we will discuss two nitrifying filter designs that are still used with some regularity in reef aquariums today.

Trickle filters

The concept of the trickle filter is not new to the aquarium hobby. Early designs were outlined in the popular aquarium literature in the late 1960's and 1970's (deGraaf, 1968; Siddall, 1977). However, it was not until articles by Dutch hobbyist George Smit were published in *Freshwater and Marine Aquarium* magazine in January 1986, that they became widely used in North America. Similar filters had already proved their efficiency in Europe 10 years earlier. They had also been widely used in aquaculture and public aquariums.

The main advantage of a trickle filter is its ability to fully oxygenate water in the biological filter chamber, which makes nitrification proceed very rapidly. A trickle filter consists of a chamber through which water is allowed to fall over some type of medium. The medium causes the water to spread out and cascade slowly downwards. It finally collects in another chamber (the sump) below the trickle filter. From there, it is pumped back to the aquarium. The medium of the trickle filter is not submerged in water. The water is merely allowed to fall through it. The term *dry* filter has also been used to describe this chamber, mainly to highlight the fact that the media is not submerged. As the water flows through the trickle filter, a thin film of water covers the media, resulting in a very thin barrier across which oxygen can easily diffuse. This allows a more thorough gas exchange for the oxygen hungry nitrifying bacteria living on the surfaces of the media. The result of this gas exchange is a very large population of aerobic nitrifying bacteria with no possibility of the formation of anaerobic areas. As long as the prefilter is performing its function, a properly designed trickle filter should never have to be cleaned.

Water is delivered to the trickle filter by a rotating spray bar or through a plate, in which numerous small holes have been drilled, commonly known as a drip plate. Another kind of wet/dry filter uses a rotating bio contactor (RBC) mounted over the sump. In this system, bacteria grow on a wheel of biological filter media (also called a *bio wheel*). The stream of water fed over the contactor makes it rotate like a mill or paddlewheel. As the wheel turns, the media is immersed in the sump and lifted out, allowing the water, mixed with air, to drain back through the media. Smaller versions of *bio wheel* filters are available that hang on the side of the aquarium.

There seems to be some debate about the merits of each type of trickle filter, but they all work fine biologically. Spray bars spread the water more thoroughly over the media, but are prone to clogging, and are more maintenance intensive. *Bio wheels* may stop turning, but that does not prevent them from functioning since the water will still trickle through the media before falling into the sump. Since there are no mechanical parts to stop, drip plates are less trouble to maintain, but they do require periodic cleaning to keep the perforations clear so that the water drips evenly over the media.

The media used in trickle filters has undergone an amazing explosion of variety. When they first appeared on the North American market in 1986, shallow trays with gravel were used. Then commercial units appeared that utilized a double-layered spiral coil of floss and plastic wire matting material (DLS). Although DLS is still available (and is now also used in *swamp cooler* style chillers, see chapter 4), there are also various balls, rings, blocks and other media previously used only in the water treatment industry. The plastic media known as biobale developed by CPR has the distinction of being chosen by NASA for research in closed circuit biofiltration. It seems that almost every month a new media appears along with various claims about its efficiency and superiority over existing media. There are only two factors that are important: usable surface area and void space (Moe, 1989).

The amount of surface area available to bacteria can sometimes be much less than that claimed by advertisements. Obviously the greater the available surface area, the more bacteria that can be grown, and the greater the nitrifying ability of the filter. Designs that decrease the size of the media or increase the number of protrusions such as ridges, bars, rods and bumps, provide greater surface area for growing bacteria.

Void space is the amount of empty space available in the dry chamber of a trickle filter after the media has been added. It is important for gas exchange, and to prevent clogging of the media by detritus or bacterial slime. If the media is too densely packed, then there will be a low void space and a large surface area. This impedes gas exchange, and clogging of the media can become a problem. If the media is too loosely packed, you will have a large void space and a low surface area. Although this may be ideal for gas exchange, it does not offer the most surface for nitrifying bacteria. The best media offers the greatest amount of surface area without significantly decreasing the amount of available void space.

In reef tanks using sufficient live rock, the issue of whose media has the greatest surface area is unimportant since these aquariums run quite successfully without a trickle filter. They rely instead on the bacterial population in the rock and other substrates, and the associated algal growth and photosynthetic organisms that consume nitrogenous wastes. With regard to gas exchange, surface water skimming over an overflow picks up oxygen and gives off carbon dioxide as it tumbles down to the sump below, and water brought to the surface by strong circulation promotes gas exchange too. A protein skimmer further assists with gas exchange, and removes compounds that contribute to biological and chemical oxygen demand (BOD and COD) See our discussion of oxygen in chapter 4.

Wilkens and Birkholz (1986) described the disadvantages of wet/dry biological filtration for reef aquariums. Our experience has shown that trickle filters are not only unnecessary for coral reef aquariums with adequate amounts of live rock, in fact, they can be detrimental in hard coral aquariums (Delbeek and Sprung, 1994). Hovanec (2003) compared water parameters for aquariums using different types of biological filtration, including a bio wheel trickle filter, a plenum (Jaubert's system) and a *Berlin system*. The preliminary data, based on only a six month duration, suggests that our observations and those of Wilkens and Birkholz are in error. This may be explained by the duration of the study, the low bioload of the systems or it may be an effect of the ratio of the quantity of substrate within the tank versus the trickle filter capacity. If there is sufficient submerged substrate for biological filtration within the aquarium, it may negate any nitrate producing effect of a wet/dry filter. We see several areas for followup in the study, and propose that a longer-term study should be done to observe the effects of the different filtration methods compared.

Wet/dry biological filtration efficiently converts ammonia to nitrate. Its affect on the stability of water quality in a reef aquarium using live rock and live sand depends on the relative size of these submerged sites for biological filtration, the flow rate through the filter, water velocity in the tank, food inputs, and light-driven photosynthesis, among other factors. Given sufficient submerged substrata (sand, gravel, live rock) there is no need for wet/dry filtration in reef aquariums. J. Sprung

Fluidized sand filters

Fluidized sand filters are biological filters that suspend sand in a column of water. They work well as biological filters, and they have the distinct advantage of never clogging with particulate matter. One disadvantage we can see is that if they are designed to hold water when the water flow is stopped, extended power failures could produce a situation where hydrogen sulfide would build up in the water filled column. Settled-sand coated by active, oxygen-consuming strains of bacteria will quickly deplete the water of oxygen causing the sand bed to become anaerobic. One could then have hydrogen sulfide flowing into the tank upon starting the filter up after an extended (more than 12 hour) power outage. If the column mostly drains in the event of power outages, the sand should naturally remain damp in the closed cylinder for several days, and oxygen would not be in short supply, so there would be no chance of hydrogen sulfide formation and the bacteria would remain damp enough to survive. Our comments here are not based on first hand experience with fluidized beds but on theory and experience with shutting off canister filters, which do differ significantly from fluidized beds. Canister filters typically have accumulated organic detritus that greatly assists in the rapid oxygen depletion by bacteria in the small water volume during a power outage. Fluidized beds lack the excess organic accumulation, since the fluidization prevents any detritus trapping and keeps biofilms in a thin active growth state.

A hobby aquarium sized fluidized sand filter from Schuran. J. Sprung

Closeup of the fluidized sand in a commercial sized system manufactured by RK2 Systems. J. Sprung

Nevertheless, fluidized beds do have the bacteria population capable of depleting the oxygen in the water within the filter during an extended power outage.

Since fluidized sand filters work very well as biological filters, they are popular now in large fish holding systems. When we are asked about them with respect to using them in reef aquaria, we must reiterate the point that there is no need for external nitrifying filters in reef aquaria when there is sufficient live rock and live sand in the aquarium. Therefore, although they do no harm, in our opinion one does not need to add such a filter to a reef aquarium. Fluidized sand filters are best employed on fish systems that need extra biological filtration. They are also useful for importers' or dealers' invertebrate or coral systems that receive large shipments with heavy biological demands.

Other use for the fluidized filter design

The principal of fluidizing the filter medium in a contact chamber does have some important advantages, and it has been employed in several new types of equipment for a variety of functions including biological and chemical filtration, and calcium reactor designs. We describe these applications later in this chapter.

Denitrifying filters

External carbon-driven denitrification filters

These filters use heterotrophic bacteria to convert nitrate into nitrogen gas in the absence of oxygen and in the presence of an organic carbon source. In many cases, the carbon source is methanol. The methanol is mixed with aquarium water in a controlled situation (such as fluid pumped through a coil) and the methanol is consumed by bacteria that use nitrate as an electron acceptor instead of oxygen as shown in the following reaction:

$$12 \, NO_3^- + 10 \, CH_3OH + 12 \, H^+ \rightarrow 10 \, CO_2 + 6 \, N_2 + 26 \, H_2O \text{ (Holmes-Farley, 2003b)}.$$

The result is that nitrate is removed from the aquarium. Initially these bacteria use oxygen, but once the oxygen level drops below a certain level, they switch to using nitrate. The water must move very slowly through these devices to ensure that the oxygen is quickly removed and nitrate is then consumed. During the start-up phase, nitrate and nitrite levels need to be measured frequently and the alcohol and water feed rates need to be adjusted accordingly. The demand for carbon will increase as the bacterial population increases, so the alcohol rate needs to be adjusted as time goes on. If there is too much carbon source added to the water flowing through the filter, all nitrate will be used up before the carbon source is depleted and hydrogen sulfide will form. Hydrogen sulfide is toxic and has the added feature of smelling like rotten eggs. If there is too much water flowing through the filter or too little alcohol is added, then nitrate will still be present or incomplete denitrification will occur and nitrite will be released into the aquarium. However, if the outflow of the external denitrification filter is directed into an aerated chamber, wet/dry, or other biological filter then the nitrite can be rapidly oxidized to nitrate. In any case, the outflow should always be directed into an aerated chamber where any hydrogen sulfide can quickly be oxidized. As one can imagine, this type of system needs to be monitored closely and careful control must be exerted over its operation.

Since we are dealing with bacteria being fed an endless supply of nutrients, these systems require regular removal of bacterial biomass (a fancy term for slime) to keep them working efficiently. Depending on the design of the reactor, this can be done either manually or by periodically increasing the flow through the system to dislodge this slime. A continuously operating powerful external pump plumbed on a closed loop through the denitrifying filter with a fixed media could be used to keep the biofilms from building up too heavily by shearing off the films with strong water flow, as long as the strong flow does not result in elevated dissolved oxygen levels.

An untested method that could also facilitate the removal of excess biofilm would be the installation of a wave-making device on the chamber that houses the support structure on which the bacteria are grown. If the wavemaker functioned periodically, it would shear off the excess biomass. Yet another solution to the buildup of biomass is the creation of a closed-loop fluidized reactor with plastic media. The feed through the reactor would be slow while the pump on a

A large-scale methanol reactor in use at the Burger's Ocean aquarium, Arnhem, The Netherlands. J.C. Delbeek

The accumulation of a brown bacterial film on the grids is evident in this close-up of Burger's methanol denitrifying filter. J.C. Delbeek

closed loop provides the force that keeps the media suspended and tumbling. The tumbling of the media would shear off excess biofilms. This is essentially the concept behind so-called moving bed bioreactors (MBBs) that are used in wastewater treatment and aquaculture, mainly for aerobic biological filtration. Tal *et al.* (2003) studied the microbial consortium growing on bead media in an MBB connected to a marine recirculating aquaculture system. Both ammonia and nitrite oxidizers, *Nitrosomonas cryotolerans* and *Nitrospira marina*, respectively, were found, as well as a number of heterotrophic bacteria, including *Pseudomonas* sp. and *Sphingomonas* sp. In addition, two *Planctomycetes* sp. were detected in the system suggesting the capability for anaerobic ammonia oxidation (anammox). The potential for carrying out different nitrogen transformation processes, nitrification, denitrification and anammox, by the bead consortium in both low and high organic loads was measured. Beads with a high organic load exhibited a lower nitrification rate (25 mg NH_3–$N/m_2/h$) than low organic load beads (31.5 mg NH_3–$N/m_2/h$) as well as the ability to carry out denitrification and anammox processes.

Whatever design is used, the sheared biofilm could be trapped by a mechanical filter and/or removed by protein skimming. A side benefit of this method might be that the sheared biofilms are a potential food source for filter feeders. Despite the benefits, given the complexity of their operation and the need for constant attention we do not recommend external carbon-based denitrators for typical home reef aquariums. There are far simpler ways to address excess nitrate levels, as we shall explain.

Assimilatory reduction of nitrate and phosphate with addition of carbon source: aka the *vodka* method

All living creatures need phosphate to survive, so the growth of any form of life within an aquarium can be a way to strip phosphate from the water. The death and decomposition of this biomass returns phosphate to the system, so a complete removal of phosphate requires harvest of the living organisms. This is the principle behind algal filters, and it is the principle behind a novel approach to phosphate and nitrate management in aquaria: promoting the rapid growth in the water column of bacteria that assimilate phosphate and nitrate, and harvesting their biomass with a protein skimmer.

The *Redfield ratio* or *Redfield stoichiometry* refers to the molar ratio of carbon (C), nitrogen (N) and phosphorus (P) in phytoplankton (principally diatoms). When nutrients are not limiting, most phytoplankton have the following molar ratio of elements: C:N:P = 106:16:1. It has been proposed that in aquariums with a high load of nitrate and phosphate, a source of carbon may be limiting growth of bacteria. It is common knowledge that organic substances accumulate in aquariums, but much of the organic accumulation is refractory, and thus not very available for use as food. Although there is still a high concentration of biologically usable organic matter in aquarium water, if we are dealing with high levels of nitrate and phosphate in aquariums, the supply of carbon to approach the Redfield ratio of about 100:1 for C:P may be limiting.

To stimulate the growth of bacteria, a source of carbon is used. One possible source is ethanol, which is easily supplied with vodka. The mechanism proposed differs from an external carbon-based denitrification filter. In the so-called *vodka* method the addition of ethanol directly to the aquarium stimulates the growth of heterotrophic bacteria in the water column that assimilate nitrogen and phosphorus in their living biomass, thus lowering the levels of dissolved nitrogen and phosphorous in the water. A protein skimmer

Figure 6i. The reduction of nitrate concentration (blue line) and phosphate concentration (green line) plotted with the dosage rate of ethanol (vodka). After- Mrutzek and Kokott (2004).

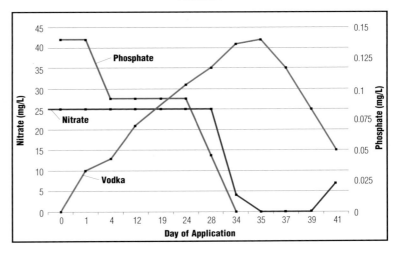

is the means of collecting and exporting this bacterial biomass. Trial and error has yielded a dosage rate of between 5 and 10 mL per day of vodka per 1000 L (260 gallons) of aquarium volume. This simple system affords a novel approach to maintaining low nutrient levels. It is reported to stimulate polyp expansion in soft corals (Mrutzek and Kokott, 2004), which may be a result of the bacterial biomass production that the corals can feed on, or it may be simply due to increased availability of the dissolved organic matter (ethanol), which soft corals may feed on as well. The increased polyp expansion observed parallels the observation in the Ecosystem Aquarium® system (described later in this chapter), suggesting that algae leachates (DOC) may play a similar role in stimulating bacteria biomass and feeding the corals. It is also intriguing to consider that forced biomass production might have a probiotic effect that could prevent the incidence of RTN and other bacterial diseases of corals. Ethanol is but one possible source of DOC to use. For example, the positive effects of vinegar (acetic acid) used to boost kalkwasser effectiveness (see chapter 5) may have a side benefit of promoting the assimilatory reduction of phosphate and nitrate by bacteria.

Caveats

The alcohol additions have to be made regularly and in the beginning, the amount has to be increased in very small steps. Overdosing can be associated with algal blooms. Once vodka dosing is initiated, the protein skimmer will remove a larger volume of organic matter from the water. At the same time, any mechanical filters will become clogged much more rapidly due to the rapid growth of bacteria biofilms. Mrutzek and Kokott (2004) report that aquariums with deep sand beds react differently to the addition of ethanol compared with aquariums with a shallow sand bed. Borneman (2004) questions whether cloudiness in the water indicates a bacterial bloom and posits it may simply be: *carbonate precipitation brought about by additional carbon addition and possibly microbial mediation.* Although it does not appear that Mrutzek and Kokott (2004) made any attempt to identify that the cloudiness was bacteria, the clogging of the mechanical filters and excessive protein skimming do suggest that it is bacteria, not precipitation of calcium carbonate.

Assimilatory reduction of nitrate and phosphate is also accomplished by other biological means. The first one to come to mind when discussing assimilation of nutrients is the incorporation of nitrate or phosphate into the tissues of algae. Thus the concept of algal filtration was born. The excess growth of algae is harvested and the nitrate and phosphate are removed from the system. Other creatures also are effective at assimilating nutrients. Fast growing corals are often overlooked as assimilators, but they are. *Xenia* spp. in particular can be very good assimilators of phosphate, and a refugium with them in mass culture could function to help maintain low levels of phosphate and nitrate.

Nitrate removal by the *AZNO₃* (Absolute Zero – Nitrates™) method

Donowitz (1998) described his experience with the product *AZ-NO3* produced by the company *Monolith Marine Monsters*. While Donowitz (1998) posits that it is composed of a carbohydrate that promotes the growth of bacteria and an enzyme that helps the bacteria assimilate nitrate, the manufacturer says the active ingredient is Cozymase (NADH, biologically known as coenzyme 1, which is the reduced form of nicotinamide adenine dinucleotide, NAD). A protein skimmer harvests the bacteria bloom and thus removes the assimilated nitrate. The product causes slight cloudiness in the water, consistent with a bacterial bloom, and a temporary drop in ORP (redox) levels (Donowitz, 1998). It is important to be sure that aeration is adequate, since bacterial blooms will deplete oxygen from the water.

The denitrifying dosage rate is 7 mL (0.25 ounces), daily, for each 182 to 227 L (50 to 60 gallons) of water volume in the aquarium. According to the manufacturer, the initial maintenance dosage should be 1/2 of the denitrifying dosage, and it should be steadily decreased until the point that nitrates can still be maintained at an undetectable level. The intent is to slowly wean the aquarium off the *AZ-NO3* product entirely, allowing the natural denitrification properties of the live rock and sand bed to come into full functioning.

According to the manufacturer, *AZ-NO3* may not work to its full effectiveness under the following conditions:

UV Sterilizer running near or above 50,000 microwatts - sec/cm^2.
Ozone saturation above 40% in the protein skimmer.
The aquarist not changing pre-filter pads and/or filter sponges in mechanical filters.

Assimilation of nitrate and phosphate can be accomplished by bacteria, algae, and even by fast growing corals such as *Xenia*. J. Sprung

Autotrophic: not needing any external energy or nutrient addition.

Heterotrophic: needing external energy or nutrient addition.

The sulfur reactor a.k.a. autotrophic sulfur denitrification (ASD)

The elimination of nitrate using a sulfur-based medium and autotrophic bacteria has gained popularity in Europe, but has been slow to catch on elsewhere. Large fish systems in public aquaria have benefited the most from these filters. For example, nitrate levels dropped from 220 mg/L to between 4 and 20 mg/L within a month in a 60,000 L (~ 16,000 gallons) fish system (Delaporte and Hignette, 2000). In most reef systems, nitrates rarely climb to these levels. However, as we have mentioned, recent trends of heavily feeding aquaria and the husbandry requirements of non-photosynthetic corals may require the addition of a denitrifying filter to offset nitrate accumulations due to massive food additions.

The attraction of this is method is that the sulfur acts as *food* (i.e. it supplies the energy) for the bacteria and since it is not soluble in water, it also allows the bacteria to colonize the substrate. Therefore, the bacteria have a more or less permanent source of energy without the need for the addition of any other energy source (e.g. methanol). The sulfur is consumed slowly but over the course of many years so it never needs to be completely replaced, only replenished every few years (Langouet, 2001).

Origin

Professor Guy Martin, a specialist in water treatment at the Engineer National School of Chemistry in Rennes, France, is credited with originating the idea of using elemental sulfur and autotrophic bacteria to eliminate nitrate, but he only applied it to fresh water treatment for drinking water. Beginning in 1991, Marc Langouet, a past student of Dr. Martin's, tested the method with seawater on his home reef aquariums, which was new, especially since no one knew if it would have toxic effects. By the end of 1994, after three years of experiments without apparent toxicity in numerous aquariums and species present at home, Langouet proposed this method to Michel Hignette, curator of the Musée des Arts Africains et Océaniens (MAAO) aquarium in Paris. There a pilot project was launched under his care. Since then, experiments were done on a much bigger scale, at the MAAO, as well as at the Grand Aquarium in Saint-Malo, where Langouet was technical and scientific director from June, 1st 1996 to mid-December 1997 (see Delaparte and Hignette (2000) for details about this aquarium). This resulted in the presentation of a paper by Michel Hignette, Benoît Lamort, Marc Langouet, Sebastian Leroy and Guy Martin in 1996 at the annual convention of the European Union of Aquarium Curators (EUAC) titled: *Elimination des nitrates par filtration biologique autotrophe sur soufre en aquariologie marine.*

Theory

Sulfur-based denitrification in freshwater is based upon autotrophic denitrification by sulfur oxidizing bacteria such as *Thiobacillus denitrificans* and *Thiomicrospira denitrificans*. Under aerobic conditions, these bacteria use oxygen as an electron acceptor, but under anoxic conditions, they oxidize reduced sulfur (S^{2-}, $S_2O_3^{2-}$, S0) to sulfate while reducing nitrate. In addition to nitrate, *T. denitrificans* can also use nitrite, NO or N_2O as an electron acceptor. Autotrophic denitrifiers utilize inorganic carbon compounds (e.g. CO_2, HCO_3^-) as their carbon source. Therefore, compared with heterotrophic denitrification such as is used in methanol denitrators, autotrophic denitrification has the advantage of not needing an external organic carbon source such as methanol or ethanol, making it a much less labour intensive process.

The chemical reaction is as follows:

Eq. 1) $55\,S + 20\,CO_2 + 50\,NO_3^- + 38\,H_2O + 4\,NH_4^+ \rightarrow 4\,C_5H_7O_2N + 25\,N_2 + 55\,SO_4^{2-} + 64\,H^+$

though this can be simplified to:

Eq. 2) $2\,H_2O + 5\,S + 6\,NO_3^- \rightarrow 3\,N_2 + 5\,SO_4^{2-} + 4\,H^+$ (Holmes-Farley, 2003b).

The mechanism by which sulfur is oxidized in seawater has not been thoroughly explored but Langouet's research has shown that it does work. What Langouet found, however, was that while the reaction does indeed result in the elimination of nitrate from the incoming aquarium water, it emerges with a low pH. Presumably, this is due to the excess hydrogen ions released by the reaction, but it could also be that these hydrogen ions combine with bicarbonate in the water to form carbon dioxide, and this causes the low pH (Langouet, 2001). To counter the pH drop, a second chamber (or even a third), containing calcareous gravel can be placed after the sulfur chamber such that the effluent from the

Figure 6j. Summary of the function of a sulfur reactor used to eliminate nitrate from aquarium water.

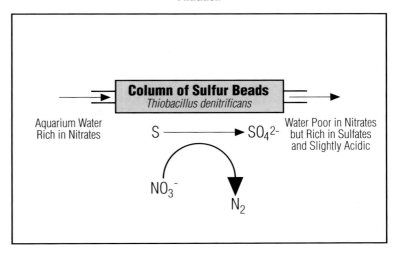

sulfur reactor passes through the gravel, dissolving some of it and raising the pH. If the acidity is due to only the hydrogen ions then the amount of calcium released is not significant (Holmes-Farley, 2003b) but if the low pH is due to CO_2 then this second chamber could act as a calcium reactor as well. Nevertheless, the production of calcium and bicarbonate ions from a calcareous reactor fed water from the sulfur reactor will not be very great. This system is meant for removal of nitrate, not for maintenance of calcium and alkalinity.

Langouet (2001) found that aerating the effluent increases the pH, indicating that the acidity is, at least in part, due to CO_2. Therefore, the chambers filled with calcareous gravel can act as calcium reactors. There are of course other ways to remove the excess CO_2, such as aeration, illuminated algae scrubbers or refugiums, or kalkwasser additions, but there is another compelling reason to use a calcareous reactor after the sulfur one: sulfate removal.

From equation #2 on page 34 it is obvious that sulfate is a major product of this process and one would expect a rise in sulfate in the aquarium. However, in seven years of experiments Langouet never observed any consequence of this sulfate addition, even in aquariums that had no water changes for years. Others also reported no increase in sulfate when using sulfur denitrators (Delaporte and Hignette, 2000). There are two explanations for this. The first is that the sulfur level in natural seawater is near 900 mg/L, in the form of 2.65 g/L sulfate (SO_4^{2-}). This is a significant quantity; therefore, the addition of sulfate by a sulfur reactor is miniscule (about 1.1 sulfate ions per nitrate ion) in comparison and can be easily managed through regular partial water changes of 20% per month. The second explanation is that when a sulfur reactor is used in combination with a calcareous reactor, the sulfate is actually precipitated onto the calcareous media (Delaporte and Hignette, 2000).

Affect on alkalinity

Due to the production of H+ ions one would expect the alkalinity of the effluent of the sulfur reactor to be lowered. However, when the flow through the reactor remains slow the alkalinity actually remains steady. It is thought that this is because the lower part of the reactor where the tank water enters is working as a heterotrophic area producing OH⁻ ions (with the help of DOC coming from the aquarium). These compensate for the production of H+ ions in the upper, autotrophic area of the reactor (when all the DOC has been involved in heterotrophic reaction) (M. Langouet, hypothesis) and are likely the reason why there is no decrease in alkalinity. This hypothesis has recently been confirmed by tests done by a colleague of Langouet's who added glucose to the sulfur reactor (and in doing so, increased the rate of the heterotrophic reaction) and observed an overall increase in alkalinity (M. Langouet, pers. comm.).

Reactor design

Sulfur reactors employ a relatively simple design. They consist of a chamber filled with 3.5 mm merumized beads of elemental sulfur normally used in the winemaking industry. Previously, Langouet (2001) had used bars of sulfur that had to be broken using a hammer. The beads make for a much better water flow with reduced clogging. Water from the tank is passed through the chamber in a reverse flow direction. The reverse flow design is important for a couple of reasons; it helps to prevent clogging caused by degraded sulfur beads and it allows for the release of nitrogen gas, which is a by-product of the reaction. Naturally, the reactor must not be airtight, so the nitrogen gas can escape. If the reactor is made from a vertical column, the water circulation should be from bottom to top since the natural tendency is for the gas to go up, and the flow rate adjustment valve should be located at the water input, not the output, to avoid pressurizing the cylinder. The output can be open to the air to facilitate the escape of the nitrogen gas produced.

As with heterotrophic bacteria, autotrophic bacteria preferentially use oxygen before they use nitrate. Therefore, in the first stages of the reactor, the oxygen in the incoming water is consumed; the nitrate will only be used further in the reactor once most of the oxygen is gone. Therefore, contact time and reactor height are important. To allow for sufficient contact time and adequate flow through, the column should be five times as tall as it is wide (Langouet, 2001).

Since the natural flow should be from bottom to top, and the sulfur is supplied as uniformly sized beads, it stands to reason that such a reactor could be installed in a columnar fluidized filter. However, since the sulfur beads are friable, fluidizing them would produce a powder.

Filtration

When the low nitrate water exits out the top of the reactor it should then pass through a second chamber filled with calcareous material to raise the pH and retain sulfate. The sulfur and the calcareous media should be in separate columns because sulfur doesn't deteriorate rapidly while the calcareous media does. The dimensions of the chambers, the amount of sulfur to use and the flow of the tank water through the reactor are all variables that need to be determined in order for the reactor to operate properly. Other designs are more like typical denitrification filters with chambers containing the sulfur, in combination with calcium carbonate powder, or in combination with calcium carbonate gravel in a modified Jaubert system (Langouet, 2001).

Operation of the sulfur filter

Sulfur amount

The volume of sulfur beads should be about 1% of the water volume of the aquarium if the initial nitrate level in the aquarium is below 50 mg/L (NO_3^-). It is possible to use a value of 2% of the water volume if the nitrate level is above 50 mg/L, but this requires a much larger reactor. An alternative would be to first reduce the nitrate level to 50 mg/L via water changes. You can run the 1% volume amount on systems with nitrate levels greater than 50 mg/L but it will take a very long time to lower the nitrates and if nitrate generation in the system is constant, the nitrate level may never lower (Langouet, 2001). You may encounter a situation where the nitrite level will never go to zero after start-up because of an inability to reduce the flow rate enough (a constant very low flow rate is very hard to regulate and maintain). The only way to solve the issue is to increase the sulfur percentage or to first reduce the nitrate level by at least 50% via water changes (M. Langouet, pers. comm., 2004).

Flow rate

When first starting the reactor it is best to use extremely low flow rates to speed the development of an anaerobic region in as much of the reactor as possible and to limit the amount of nitrite released into the aquarium. Langouet (2001) suggests a flow rate of one drop per second per two liters of sulfur. Once the nitrites disappear from the effluent, the flow can be increased to approximately 1 liter per hour per liter sulfur, but this depends on the nitrate level of the aquarium: the higher the nitrate level the lower the flow should be. If the flow is too fast, the nitrate will not be completely reduced, and the water exiting the reactor will still contain nitrate, and some nitrite. If the flow rate is too slow, the water exiting the reactor will have a hydrogen sulfide (rotten eggs) smell. If the flow is just right, the water exiting the reactor will have a nitrate reading of zero. According to Langouet (2001) the system tolerates flow rates up to 5 liters per hour per liter of sulfur used in the reactor.

A 300 L (79 gallon) sulfur reactor system used on a 600,000 L (157,895 gallon) fish only system at the Burger's Ocean aquarium, Arnhem, The Netherlands. Not seen in this picture are the two identically sized coral gravel chambers on the left that receive the effluent of these two reactors. J.C. Delbeek

The beaded nature of the sulfur is evident in this photo. This form is commonly sold in winemaking stores and sells for about $2 US/kg. J.C. Delbeek

Start-up

When one starts to use a sulfur reactor, there is initially a production of nitrite. The higher the nitrate concentration in the tank at start up, the more nitrite will be produced during the first days, before enough bacteria colonies have settled and developed in the reactor. To avoid risking potential harm from a rise in nitrite levels in the aquarium, if there is a high nitrate level in your tank, discard the water from the exit of the reactor during the first days, until the nitrite level in this water is low. In aquariums that already have efficient nitrification, this nitrite will simply be converted to nitrate without any perceptible increase in nitrite levels in the aquarium. Once the bacteria population in the sulfur reactor has increased enough, nitrite will also be consumed by the autotrophic bacteria; this usually occurs within three to five days of start-up and the drop in nitrite is rapid. Once the nitrite level drops, you can begin to increase the flow rate through the reactor until the desired flow rate of 1 liter per hour per liter of sulfur in the column (Langouet, 2001).

Maintenance

There are a few points that need to be remembered when working with these systems. Over time, the accumulation of sediments in the sulfur chamber can restrict flow in some regions of the reactor, resulting in the production of hydrogen sulfide. The autotrophic bacteria can use this as an energy source also but the rotten egg smell really tends to spoil the ambience of the living room. To prevent this, one should occasionally purge the system by dramatically increasing the flow through the reactor while directing the effluent into a waste bucket to flush out the sediments.

The calcareous reaction chamber will also tend to clog since this material will be quickly dissolved by the acidic effluent. Use of large size calcareous media will help prevent clogging. Since this is also the site of sulfate precipitation, the calcareous media needs to be replenished on a frequent basis and it must not be allowed to clog. Monitoring the breakdown of the calcareous gravel in the second stage of the system is also necessary to maintain adequate pH as the calcium concentration increases. An increase in calcium level without an equal increase in alkalinity may be pronounced in fish-only systems or systems without rapidly calcifying creatures. In systems with fast-growing corals and coralline algae, the balance of calcium and alkalinity may be naturally maintained. However, in large fish-only systems there are also reports of calcium levels not rising (presumably due to precipitation of calcium phosphate in the tank) and alkalinity rising (M. Janse, pers. comm.).

Several factors contribute to the maintenance of calcium and alkalinity levels in fish-only systems with sulphur reactors. The biomass in the system, the size of sulphur reactor, flow rate through the reactor, pH at the reactor exit and the size of the material in the calcareous part of the reactor, to name just a few, can all affect how calcium and alkalinity will respond (M. Langouet, pers. comm.). For example, one possibility is that a large biomass (plus the food added) could cause a large portion of the sulphur reactor to act as an heterotrophic system, producing significant amounts of OH^- and thereby increasing alkalinity (M. Langouet, pers. comm.). It should be clear that there is still much to be learned about the operation of sulphur reactors on marine aquariums.

Jaubert's method boosted by sulfur

Jaubert's method (see *Jaubert's Monaco system* later in this chapter) has nitrate reduction to nitrogen gas, and to some extent calcium dissolution, occurring directly inside the aquarium or in an attached refugium. The reduction is done in the lower part of a thick calcareous gravel layer (8 to 10 cm/3 to 4 inches). While this method works very well, it may be limited to aquariums with low or normal fish (feeding) loads. The method also seems to work best in brightly illuminated aquariums. This may be due to the evolution of oxygen in the water from photosynthesis by algae on the substratum, which may cause a greater movement of water through the gravel due to concentration gradients, or perhaps due to enhanced production of carbon-rich exudates by algae that consequently stimulate the activity of denitrifying bacteria. Brightly illuminated aquariums also may contain algae and photosynthetic cnidarians or tridacnid clams that also take nitrogenous waste from the water. Sometimes, particularly in low-illumination set ups or high feeding loads, nitrates are persistently present in the water in a Jaubert system. It is possible to make them disappear by accelerating the bacterial process through the introduction of organic compounds (glucose, for example) into the lower layer of sand through a tube that penetrates under the layer (Langouet, 1999).

Langouet (1999) proposed a hybrid internal sulfur reactor and Jaubert plenum system to push Jaubert's method beyond its limits, i.e. in a heavily fed or under-lit aquarium, *without* adding glucose under the sand bed, while still conserving its advantages i.e. its extreme simplicity, no external reactors, no flow rate to set, no clogging to worry about. To get rid of the limiting factor of the quantity of organic compounds present in the lower layer of sand, Langouet installed a thin layer (1/2 cm thick) of sulfur in the form of beads in the lower level of the sand bed sandwiched between two layers of plastic screen above the plenum. This allows the system to work in an autotrophic way instead of a carbon-heterotrophic-only way. Depending on the amount of nutrients added, the sulfur layer could be thinner or placed in selected areas and not over the entire bottom (Langouet, pers. comm., 2004).

In a system of this type, the reduction of nitrate could be slower than in systems using sulfur in flow-through reactors. However, the difference depends on the water velocity in the aquarium and the resulting advective flow through the substratum.

Langouet's 65 L (17 gallon) test aquarium received a $1cm^3$ cube of frozen *Artemia* every day, and the system maintained the nitrate level below the detection limits of a low range hobby test kit. The *Tubastraea aurea* in this aquarium remained open all day long, liking the strong water flow in the tank and the daily addition of food. The same was true for some *Actinia equina* anemones and two *Carotalcyon sagamianum* specimens. The pH was around 7.7, because of carbon dioxide present but this didn't appear to bother the invertebrates. The alkalinity remained between 6 and 7 dKH, the same as the alkalinity of the English Channel water (natural seawater) that Langouet used to fill the tank.

This very interesting method could also be easily established in the sump of an existing aquarium so that the whole setup wouldn't have to be rebuilt. The area covered by sulfur may not need to match the tank's entire footprint as it did in Langouet's test aquarium. The low pH is a consideration, but it should be noted that with Pr. Jaubert's method, the pH and alkalinity are generally lower than those found using the Berlin method (at least in the morning concerning the pH), and this is without noticeable consequence for the animals.

Degassing through aeration, which Langouet did not use, could have been used to raise the pH. Additionally, Langouet's test aquarium was not illuminated. The illumination would have raised the pH in the aquarium during the light period due to photosynthesis by algae. Alternatively an algae filter located in a refugium and set up on a reverse daylight cycle could be employed to strip carbon dioxide, raise pH as well as oxygen levels, and remove some phosphate.

Another solution to the low pH would be the addition of kalkwasser. If controlled by a pH controller that causes a dosing pump to administer kalkwasser when the pH falls below 7.9, the use of kalkwasser could take advantage of the presence of excess carbon dioxide in the water and promote rapid coral growth while maintaining the pH and precipitating phosphate.

Kalkreactor modification

Christophe Soler has suggested modifying the calcium reactor side of the sulfur system. Instead of setting up a conventional calcium reactor after the sulfur denitrator, Soler proposes using a kalkreactor filled, not with coral gravel, but with calcium carbonate powder. The acidic water flowing slowly [5 L (1.3 gallons)/h for a 500-liter (132 gallon) tank] will easily dissolve this powder, which has a much greater surface area than gravel, and thus a higher rate of dissolution. The produced calcium level should be equally greater. The internal mixing of the reactor would prevent the formation of mud.

Additional uses for the sulfur reactor.

Bromate (BrO_3^-), which is an ozonation byproduct, can be reduced to Br^- ion in denitrification filters (Rittmann and McCarty, 2001). The use of sulfur filters on aquarium systems that utilize ozone may be an effective way to insure that bromate levels don't get too high. Similarly, the formation of iodate may be limited by the use of a sulfur filter system. No one has studied the effect of such a filter system on phosphate levels. It is possible that phosphate-accumulating organisms would proliferate in such a system, giving it the added benefit of lowering phosphate. Conversely, organic phosphorus could be broken down by organisms living in a sulfur filter, so the net effect might be an increase in dissolved phosphate in the water (see chapter 4 for a description of the phosphorus cycle), which could be removed by adsorption or assimilation. The net effect would be to prevent the typical increase in phosphate that occurs within sediments.

It is interesting to ponder the effect of having a layer of sulfur in the sand bed over a plenum, combined with DOC dosing. Langouet suggests that DOC already in the tank does the trick, but in a heavily skimmed, activated carbon filtered tank, some simple DOC (e.g. methanol, ethanol, or vinegar) input could push the alkalinity up while at the same time promoting low nitrate and low phosphate (when combined with biomass removal by a protein skimmer).

While sulfur denitrification can be accomplished in reactors, it appears that the whole process can also be accomplished more simply *in-tank* or better *in-refugium*, without the need for external filter columns and flow adjustments, as Langouet (1999) has shown.

Direct addition of elemental sulfur to the aquarium

Sonnenschein (2004) proposes that one need not set up a reactor system to derive the benefits of sulfur based denitrification. In experimental aquaria, he demonstrated that small incremental doses of elemental sulfur accompanied by periodic additions of buffers (to counter the production of sulfuric acid) could achieve the same effect. The method was tested extensively at the St. Louis Children's Aquarium, and the following protocol was developed as a result. Treatments consisted of between 1.0 and 6.25 grams of sulfur per 380 L (100 gallons) added either weekly or monthly. The sulfur is oxidized to sulfate, and nitrate is reduced to nitrogen gas as a result. Sonnenschein (2004) notes that a side effect of this method is release of hydrogen sulfide gas from the substratum, which he postulated, *may have been an equilibrium adjustment to sulfate buildup.* Sonnenschein further noted that: *in traditional salt mixes… sulfur is at significantly lower levels than found in natural seawater.* Atkinson and Bingman (1997) showed this is true for some but not all commercially prepared artificial seawater mixes. Sulfur is supposed to make up 8 percent of the ion content of seawater, regardless of the salinity. It is intriguing to consider, as with the *Balling method* for calcium and alkalinity maintenance (see chapter 5), that a specially prepared artificial seawater mix could be used for water changes to offset long term ionic imbalances from sulfur addition. In this case, a recipe deficient in sulfate could be used for water changes to reduce the sulfate content in marine systems where doses of elemental sulfur are added for control of nitrate levels.

Substrate filtration principles

The use of bottom substrates to filter aquarium water has a long history. It is a part of all aquariums using sand or gravel on the bottom, whether or not the aquarist realizes its effect. Undergravel filters, popular during the 1960's to 1980's combined biological and mechanical filtration. *Natural system* aquarium methods (e.g. deep sand bed, Jaubert plenum system, Miracle Mud®, etc.), which we describe in detail later in this chapter, utilize live sand, mud, or gravel of varying thickness for biological filtration. These substrates also stimulate biological productivity, as they promote development of zooplankton, the offspring from populations of creatures, infauna, that live in the sand bed and feed on detritus. Such substrate filters can be installed either directly on the aquarium bottom or in a separate, attached tank.

In the substrate bed, there are bacteria that break down the available organic matter. At the substrate bed surface, they will use oxygen, as it is available and continuously supplied through advection. Deeper in the substrate bed, advection becomes slower and therefore the oxygen availability decreases and eventually stops completely. In the anoxic parts of the substrate bed, denitrification will take place. In cases where very deep substrate beds are used or there is a large amount of organic matter in the substrate bed, the amount of nitrate will not be sufficient for the bacteria to break down the organic matter completely. In such a case, sulfate will be used instead of nitrate and hydrogen sulfide will be produced. Since the introduction of organic denitrification filters, hydrogen sulfide has been a point of concern because quite a few people have lost fishes or even whole aquaria due to hydrogen sulfide poisoning. As it is quite easy to produce hydrogen sulfide in a denitrification filter, one might presume that hydrogen sulfide could be a major danger with substrate bed filters too. Some authors think it isn't, because of the following reason: hydrogen sulfide is a substance that contains sulfur in its most reduced redox state (-2). The main form of sulfur in seawater is sulfate (SO_4^{2-}), which contains sulfur in its most oxidized redox state (+6). Many chemoautotrophic bacteria gain energy by oxidizing sulfide, even better, some use not oxygen but nitrate for sulfide oxidation. The reaction is the same as occurs in sulfur-based denitrification filters with hydrogen sulfide used instead of elemental sulfur. If hydrogen sulfide is actually produced in the sediment, it will be in the lowermost part, or around a rotting thing buried somewhere in the substrate, even near the surface. To have a toxic effect it has to get out of the substrate. Shimek (1998) states with confidence that H_2S: *will NOT migrate up through the sediments to poison a tank,* and adds: *There is no real evidence to indicate that it may reach toxic levels in a deep sand bed.* The process of migration for H_2S is slow, at least where it is not affected by advection (there is practically no advective flow affecting the lower part of a very deep substrate bed, otherwise oxygen would be available and no sulfide would form). On the way up from the bottom of the tank through the fine sand into the water column, H_2S would be used as an energy source by sulfide oxidizing bacteria.

The reader who has followed the argument to this point will no doubt realize that there are some ifs and maybes about substrate depth and water flow affecting whether H_2S can present a problem or not, which does not lead the authors of this book to be as confident as Shimek that it cannot present a problem. Furthermore, the authors have had personal experience demonstrating that it can present a problem, particularly when a pump fails or slows over time, or during extended power outages. Disturbances to the integrity of the bottom substrata, as when a powerhead falls and digs out a depression in the sand, present another avenue for H_2S to make its toxicity known.

Despite the armchair theory and assurances that suggest a minimal risk, there are real risks associated with H_2S in a substrate bed. A big mistake one can make when observing the formation of a black layer of sulfide in a deep substrate bed is stirring. Stirring, may release hydrogen sulfide from the substrate into the water where it may kill the fishes. Mechanical stirring of a deep substrate bed can help to maintain its porosity. It is recommended in other methods such as the Berlin method, but it is shunned in the deep sand bed (DSB) approach, which even avoids the use of large sand sifting animals that could decimate populations of meiofauna that work the sand on a smaller scale, and slower timetable. Simply increasing the water motion above the substrate bed can be enough to cause any visible graying in the sand layers to recede due to an increase in the advective forcing of dissolved oxygen into the sand. We discuss substrate bed systems in more detail later in this chapter.

Refugia

Dr. Walter Adey of the Smithsonian Institution first used the term *refugia* to describe bodies of water separate from the main display but connected with it where populations of organisms (plants or animals) can develop freely without being preyed upon by fishes (Adey, 1983). The term also applies to places within the tank where these organisms may develop without being consumed directly by the fishes, such as within a stack of rocks or in the sand substrate. This concept is typically employed within other natural system aquariums, but Adey's use of connected aquariums is an ingenious way to accomplish numerous tasks. For example, such refugia can be used to settle out detritus, thereby eliminating the need for a mechanical filter. Refugia can also be used for supplemental biological filtration or for filtration by algae. One can also use these refugia to cultivate various micro-crustaceans that can serve as food for the system. Grass shrimp, mysids, peppermint shrimp and others, can be maintained in refugia where the fish won't eat them, and their offspring will drift back into the main display where they are eaten by fish and invertebrates. Even the culture of phytoplankton and zooplankton in so-called plankton reactors can be accomplished with a refugium type design. A refugium thus has important benefits to the maintenance of a diverse population of organisms in a natural aquarium. For the specialist who prefers to run live rock only aquariums with delicate butterfly- and angelfish species, a refugium can also be an area where *Aiptasia* anemones can be cultivated. Left unchecked, however, *Aiptasia* can easily overrun a refugium and deplete it of microcrustaceans so caution must be exercised. *Aiptasia* can be a useful *starter* food source for some species of butterflyfish that might otherwise prove difficult to keep in an aquarium since their diet is primarily composed of cnidarian polyps.

Refugium design

Aquarists can create a refugium quite easily by constructing a second, smaller aquarium plumbed with the main aquarium. The refugium may be plumbed to the system as an attachment to the sump below the aquarium; it can be located above the aquarium and plumbed so that water is fed to it and drained from it back to the display; or it can be plumbed to be located next to (on the same level as) the display tank. A refugium is not only a useful addition that filters and enhances the biological productivity of an aquarium, it is also one of the best inventions for an aquarist who wants to have another aquarium, but needs to be able to justify it to a spouse. You can just imagine the conversation: *Dear, it's not really another aquarium, it's a filter… and it's called a refugium…look it says so here in this book.*

Biological filtration in refugia

Biological filtration occurs within the display aquarium, but the incorporation of additional biological filtration capacity can be accomplished by attaching a refugium aquarium containing a large quantity of sand or gravel. A refugium may be set up for the use of a deep substrate bed with or without a plenum, leaving more room in the display tank.

As you can see, refugiums can take many forms, not necessarily aquariums. For example, a v -shaped bottom or baffle design (Delbeek and Sprung 1994) allows the refugium to be a settling trap that concentrates detritus and makes it easy to export from the system.

Algal turf scrubbers (ATS) as refugia

The use of algal turfs to filter the water in recirculating aquariums has been promoted by Dr. Adey (see Adey and Loveland, 1991). The algae are grown on screens in shallow, illuminated refugia attached to the display aquarium. The screens are scraped regularly (weekly) to harvest and remove the algae from the system, thus removing with the algal mass all the assimilated nutrients, as well as excess trace elements. Therefore, the algae accomplish filtration that compliments the biological filtration (nitrification/denitrification) that bacteria accomplish.

The illumination of an ATS is on an opposite timing cycle with the display aquarium, a technique called reverse daylight photosynthesis, or RDP. This technique serves to balance the concentration of dissolved carbon dioxide and thus stabilizes pH, and it ensures that the nighttime oxygen level does not fall sharply, which it often does in systems not employing RDP.

An additional benefit of algal filters is that the algae cultivated on the screens filter out dissolved inorganic nitrogen and phosphorus so efficiently that they limit certain types of algal growth in the display aquarium. However, ATSs may leach some dissolved organic exudates, so that some algae that utilize organic nutrients will continue to thrive despite the turf filter's competition for inorganic nutrients. These algal exudates may additionally enhance denitrification by heterotrophic bacteria living within the rock and sand/gravel substrata, a further connection between the biological filtration mediated by bacteria and the assimilation of nutrients by algae.

One more benefit of using algae as a filter is their ability to accumulate trace elements. Some believe that trace elements may accumulate to levels well above natural seawater values in closed aquarium systems. Growth of algae can slow this process by accumulating the excess trace elements. Harvesting the algae removes the excess elements from the system. Algae exudates are also natural chelating substances. These may keep any high levels of metals in the water biologically isolated and thus non-toxic (Sekha, 2003).

A turf filter is a refugium containing a diverse population of algae and animals that live within the turf. J. Sprung.

Algal turf scrubbers can also be considered refugia. The screens develop nice diversity of algae species in nutrient poor systems seeded with live rock from coral reefs. Tiny herbivorous amphipods and copepods also develop on algal turf screens and reduce their efficiency slightly by grazing the algae. Scraping the screen controls the population of amphipods on it, and is a disturbance that promotes diversity of algae species (Adey, 1983; Adey and Loveland, 1991). During the growth phase, the algae in properly maintained scrubbers are not heavily grazed, allowing them the opportunity to grow and release reproductive spores that flow back into the aquarium, simulating phytoplankton input (Adey and Loveland, 1991). This food source and the refugium habitat also promote the development of zooplankton populations, further benefiting filter-feeding invertebrates. If screens from an established reef microcosm are installed on a new system with bare limestone, the algal spores rapidly colonize the bare rock. Therefore, a potential use of ATSs is in the mariculture of live *plant rocks*. We discuss algal turf scrubbers in more detail later in this chapter.

Caulerpa and other higher algae in a refugium

The use of algal filters employing green algae of the genus *Caulerpa* as well as other algae has come into fashion lately, though it has been practiced in the aquarium hobby for at least 40 years. The popularity of refugium filters and the Ecosystem Aquarium® method of Leng Sy has stimulated renewed enthusiasm for this method, and generated interest in the effect not only of the plants but also of the substrates they grow in.

The *mud filter* borrows from both Dr. Adey's ATS design and his use of refugiums, but with one main difference: the algae are illuminated continuously. This means they are on a reverse light cycle with respect to the display aquarium at night, affording similar advantages. The algae in Leng Sy's EcoSystem Aquarium® are also grown on a Miracle Mud® substrate rather than on screens or live rock. In Dr. Adey's ATS, microalgae are used more effectively for nutrient export since they grow faster and are harvested regularly. The *Caulerpa* filters, including Leng Sy's mud system, achieve nutrient export when the *Caulerpa* is harvested, and via denitrification, which certainly occurs in the substrate. See our more detailed description of the *Ecosystem Aquarium® method* later in this chapter.

A mud filter with *Caulerpa* spp. D. Ong

Aquarists who grow algae in refugia note positive effects on the aquarium that can be attributed to several factors, including the effects on nutrient availability and water chemistry already mentioned. One possible additional effect relates to the fact that red seaweeds accumulate halogen-containing metabolites in their tissues. These metabolites released into the water may impede the growth of pathogenic bacteria as well as other algae. When red seaweeds are cultured in aquariums, their metabolites give the water that distinctive fresh aroma of the sea. Another positive effect of growing algae in refugia is an increased live food supply to the aquarium and the formation of so-called *food webs*. The algae themselves release spores in the water that are eaten by filter feeders, and these spores also stimulate the development of zooplankton that feed on them, which are in turn fed upon by other invertebrates. Algae do require some supplementation to thrive in algae filtered aquariums. The addition of iron and manganese is important for all plants. The red and brown seaweeds additionally need iodine and bromine. These elements are supplied to some extent with seafood added to the aquarium, but can be reliably added with commercially available supplements. The mud substrate in Leng Sy's mud system is important to the *Caulerpa* that root in it, as it supplies iron and other minerals in a way similar to the use of laterite in freshwater-planted aquariums.

Of course, algal filtration is already employed within the aquarium. With strong illumination and enough herbivores such as tangs and the small herbivorous snails (*Turbo* and *Astraea* spp.), the algae growing on the rocks and glass can be maintained at the highly productive state where it is almost not perceptible because it is being consumed as quickly as it grows. If the system employs strong water motion, then the herbivores' lightweight fecal pellets can easily be trapped in a mechanical or settling filter, or protein skimmer, and removed from the system. However, this use of algal filtration does not take advantage of the reverse-daylight benefits.

An outdoor mangrove refugium with red and black mangroves, set up by Jose Mendez in Miami Florida. J. Sprung

An indoor mangrove refugium set up by Julian Sprung, featuring the red mangrove, seagrass, lagoon corals, and zoanthids. J. Sprung

Mangrove refugia

Like the rise in popularity of algae filters, the incorporation of red mangroves (*Rhizophora* spp.) in marine aquariums has become popular, just as the interest in refugium aquariums and natural ecosystem models has grown. Published photographs of beautiful systems featuring the trees growing out of the water helped to further this direction (Sprung and Delbeek, 1997). Discussions on the Internet about mangroves have promoted the idea that they might be used to filter the water in much the same way algae are used in refugia to filter the water. In fact, algae are by far more efficient at removing nutrients from the water than mangroves are. The effect on water quality from one or several mangroves is negligible. Older, larger mangrove trees develop extensive root systems in the substrate and may ultimately have the ability to remove significant amounts of plant nutrients.

However, in most cases the positive effects attributed to mangrove seedlings planted in refugia are more likely due to the substratum they may be planted in since it is a site where significant biological activity can take place (see *Deep sand beds* and *Miracle Mud® filters*, later in this chapter). Mangroves add another interesting component to the aquarium and increase the diversity of habitats than can be recreated in the home, but should not be counted to on to offer up much in the way of filtration capability.

Seagrass refugia

Some aquarists who have been lucky enough to obtain live seagrass have incorporated them in refugium aquariums set up to model a distinct habitat, the seagrass zone (e.g. *Thalassia, Enhales, Ruppia, Halophila* and *Syringodium* spp.).

The beautiful seagrass display at the Waikiki Aquarium. Such a display could be connected to a reef aquarium as a refugium J. Sprung

Like mangroves, seagrasses are not as fast growing as algae, and are therefore not as effective in controlling nutrients in recirculating aquariums. They have ornamental value and, as with mangroves and *Caulerpa* filters, the substratum they grow in provides strong nitrification and denitrification capacity, which has the ability to limit algal growth. A densely planted seagrass display or refugium is still likely to need herbivores (fishes, snails) to control the growth of epiphytic algae on the blades, and may need predatory fishes to control populations of amphipods that might graze the seagrass blades. Caution should be exercised when choosing the herbivorous fish since several enjoy eating the tender growing tips of the seagrass. As with *Caulerpa* filters, the addition of iron and manganese is also important for seagrass health.

Lagoon refugia

These days reef aquarium enthusiasts have a great interest in so-called (small polyped stony (SPS) corals. The mere sound of SPS conveys a notion of super charged, high intensity, turbo, fuel-injected *power more power baby!!!* aquariums. The testosterone rush of a high-energy reef tank may bring satisfaction to many a reef aquarist, but the high-energy reef crest is not the same habitat where some other beautiful large polyped stony (LPS) corals exist. This discrepancy is a perfect excuse to set up a lagoon aquarium to house the LPS corals that don't require strong light or strong water motion. The low energy reef is beautiful and easily attached to a high-energy reef aquarium by adding a low energy refugium.

Fish incompatibility

It may seem like a stretch (in which case it probably is a stretch) to consider separating incompatible fishes in the same aquarium system by using refugium aquariums. In the purest sense, this is just a way to have two aquariums with just one body of water to maintain with the filtration, heating/cooling, and water top-off systems. In the creative sense, it can be used to supply inorganic nutrients to a reef aquarium. Dick Perrin of *Tropicorium*, a coral farm in Romulus, Michigan, USA, has set up a system with sharks connected to systems for growing corals. The excess nitrogen from the food inputs to the shark system fertilizes the coral system and promotes growth in the corals and tridacnid clams. However, it should be pointed out that the original live coral exhibit at the Steinhart Aquarium in San Francisco, also had a large shark exhibit connected to it and the corals in this system did poorly until the sharks were removed from the system. Such a design naturally requires careful planning with regard to the exchange of water between systems to avoid excess nutrients from harming the corals.

Plankton reactors

While refugiums containing various algae are known to produce both algal spores (a kind of phytoplankton) and populations of microcrustaceans and protozoans that feed on detritus and algal spores (a kind of zooplankton), the use of plankton reactors affords an ability to concentrate on the cultivation of phytoplankton and or zooplankton to feed the display aquarium. See chapter 10 for descriptions of these. Some commercial products exist for this purpose.

It is possible to culture phytoplankton in an illuminated refugium that receives a very slow feed of sterilized water from the aquarium. The water would overflow back to the aquarium, bringing with it a constant supply of food. The set up would have to be controlled so that it does not flush out the phytoplankton faster than they grow, and the input water would have to be treated, for example by

Note: See chapter 10 for additional discussion of plankton refugia, as well as the use of small refugia connected to a larger display to cultivate corals and other marinelife with high volume food requirements. The small refugium volume allows concentrated feeding while the large display dilutes the pollution.

running it through a UV sterilizer, to kill all life in it that would eat or compete with the phytoplankton. Bingman (2002) described a system for sterilizing tank water using hydrogen peroxide and UV light. However, the slow flow rates used resulted in the water becoming very warm. Bingman calculated this to be 60 $^{\circ}$C/140 $^{\circ}$F when used with the slowest flow rate of 25 L/min, assuming 100% conversion of UV light to heat. This necessitated adding CO_2 to the water to lower the pH and prevent scaling of the UV lamp sleeve due to $CaCO_3$ precipitation. The use of hydrogen peroxide and UV light results in the generation of free hydroxyl radicals, which convert organics into their inorganic constituents, presumably resulting in the production of inorganic nutrients (Bingman, 2002). Therefore, as the effluent from the UV contactor enters the phytoplankton reactors, CO_2 and inorganic nutrients are carried to the phytoplankton providing for their growth. However, how the system deals with the high temperature is not mentioned in Bingman's article. A thermoelectric chilling system could be employed here.

Since this recirculating system utilizes water from the display aquarium, the inorganic plant nutrients should naturally be present. Supplementing with trace elements (especially iron and manganese) and perhaps some vitamins may be necessary to maintain the cultures. We have also seen a simple version of such a system that co-cultures zooplankton (rotifers) in an adjacent refugium, utilizing water fed to it from the phytoplankton reactor (see chapter 10). When phytoplankton are normally grown in closed culture vessels, the population can quickly increase resulting in a depletion of nutrients. This causes the culture to *crash* i.e. the phytoplankton all die. To prevent this, cultures are periodically harvested and then restarted with fresh inoculations of phytoplankton. In a plankton reactor that has a continuous input and output of water, a careful balancing act must be achieved between phytoplankton population growth, nutrient input and the removal rate for feeding in order to avoid crashing the culture or diluting it.

As you can see, the concept of refugium designs encompasses many subjects, from filtration to feeding, and the creation of aquarium systems that closely duplicate processes that occur in natural ecosystems. Including a refugium in your aquarium system also affords the opportunity to build a unique aquarium design or it *might* just be another excuse to have just one more tank.

Reef aquariums today use both nitrification and denitrification to maintain water quality. Ancillary forms of biological filtration such as algal filters, Jaubert's system, Miracle Mud® filters, deep sand beds, methanol filters, vodka dosing, and sulfur reactors provide alternatives to the reliance on live rock and live sand to handle the accumulation of nitrates. When these ancillary filtration techniques are combined with phosphate removing techniques and adsorption media, displays with large fish loads and heavy feedings can be achieved without sacrificing the low nutrient requirements of delicate stony corals.

Chemical filtration

The topic of chemical filtration is described in just about every textbook written on marine aquarium keeping, yet few aquarists really seem to understand its capabilities, limitations and applications. There are numerous forms of filtration that fall under the category of chemical filtration, depending on their mode of operation. We will limit our discussion to the common forms of chemical filtration used in reef systems today as well as some newly introduced ones.

Due to the various biological processes that occur in an aquarium, a build-up of organic substances takes place. They are referred to as organic because they all contain the element carbon in their chemical composition. The list of these things is quite lengthy, and includes such goodies as amino acids, proteins, phenols, creosols, terpenoids, fats, carbohydrates, hydrocarbons, plant hormones, vitamins, carotenoids and various organic acids such as fatty, acetic, lactic, glycolic, malic and citric (deGraaf, 1968; Moe, 1989). Fortunately for us, we generally lump all these things together under the all-encompassing term, dissolved organic carbon (DOC). It is believed that these organic substances can have various deleterious effects on the aquarium inhabitants including reduced growth, reduced disease resistance, and metabolic stress.

When DOC compounds contain nitrogen, they are mineralized by bacteria present in the tank, into ammonia. The ammonia is utilized by plants, leading to excessive growth, or oxidized by nitrifying bacteria to the final product, nitrate, which may accumulate in the aquarium. Unfortunately, many DOCs are not mineralized and tend to build-up in the aquarium. That is why water changes are usually advocated. Many people think that water changes are designed to lower the nitrate concentration. While this may occur to some extent, the real reason is to lower the DOC content of the water. Since nitrate and DOC concentrations are sometimes directly related, and nitrate is easy to measure, it is often used as a yardstick to determine when to make a water change on a standard saltwater fish aquarium. In reef aquariums, DOC may accumulate while nitrate does not, because of denitrification and utilization of ammonia by algae, corals and clams. If we could remove much of the DOC before it accumulates or becomes converted into ammonia, we could reduce the need for water changes, lower the load on our filter, lower nitrate levels, and improve the growth and health of our organisms. These are the primary reasons behind the use of chemical filtration.

At this point we would just like to clarify that we are not saying that if you use chemical filtration, water changes will no longer be necessary. That is, of course, not true. No method of chemical filtration is 100% efficient and many substances are difficult to remove by chemical filtration. Water changes provide other benefits including the removal and dilution of DOC not removed by chemical filters, replenishment of trace elements that are lost to chemical filtration or biological processes, and diluting nitrate or phosphate accumulation. Even in the best-maintained aquariums, the affects of a water change on the inhabitants can be quite stunning. What chemical filtration does is help maintain a much lower concentration of DOC in the tank. This becomes extremely important when maintaining invertebrates such as stony corals. Corals, algae, and other marinelife leach many types of DOC into the water. The density of these organisms in a closed system reef aquarium results in heavy accumulation of DOC unless the filtration is there to remove it, and/or water changes are performed.

The other result of DOC accumulation is a gradual yellowing of the water. This yellowing is so gradual that most aquarists fail to notice it since they usually observe their aquarium several times a day. Combined with the use of high Kelvin lighting, which can mask the yellow colour due to the high blue output, the yellowing often goes unnoticed (likewise, low Kelvin lighting can make the water look more yellow than it is). This yellowing can reduce the amount of light that reaches corals and will reduce UV light penetration through the water. Therefore, one must be cautious when using chemical filtration methods to prevent them from removing this yellow colour too rapidly on systems where no chemical filtration has been used previously, since the sudden increase in light and UV levels can shock the corals and may cause them to bleach or otherwise react negatively (Bingman, 1995).

Granular activated carbon (GAC)
Granular activated carbon has been subjected to extremely high pressures and temperatures to drive out all impurities and gases leaving behind extremely porous and pure grains of carbon. Particle size, type of gas used, activation temperature and, in some instances, inorganic salts of zinc, copper, phosphate, silicate and sulfate added before activation, provide carbon with specific adsorption characteristics (Moe, 1989). Therefore, activated carbon can be tailored to the specific type of impurities that one wishes to remove. By creating such extremely porous structures within the carbon grains in effect, we have created a gigantic sponge that can absorb many impurities from the

passing water. Several substances can be used to produce activated carbon such as hardwoods, bituminous coal, lignite coal, coconut shells and pecan shells. Harker (1998a) found that carbons based on lignite coal removed colour from saltwater most effectively.

Activated carbon will remove a wide variety of organic molecules by simply trapping them in the carbon pores (absorption) or by chemically bonding them (adsorption). Adsorption relies on the fact that many organic molecules are polar in nature. This means that the two ends of a molecule differ in their affinity for water. One side is repelled by water and is termed hydrophobic (*water hating*) while the other end is attracted to water and is called hydrophilic (*water loving*). When a polar molecule comes close to a polar surface such as GAC, it becomes attached, effectively removing the molecule from solution.

To maintain colourless water like this, an aquarist may either adsorb DOC on activated carbon or oxidize it with ozone. M. Haaga

Aside from arguments regarding whether or not to use activated carbon, a common point of disagreement about GAC use concerns its placement in the system. Naturally, there are several options available. Some aquarists have a sump design that includes a chamber for activated carbon, with all or some of the water flowing through the chamber. Alternatively, one may hook up a canister filter to the sump, filled with GAC. Another option is to build an in-line contact chamber also known as a chemical reactor. This consists of a section of PVC pipe of approximately 5 - 7.5 cm (2 to 3 inches) in diameter with hose fittings and screens to hold the carbon in place. The pipe is filled with GAC and water is pumped through it, usually via a dedicated pump or a line tapped off the main circulating pump. The flow rate through the activated carbon can be adjusted with a ball valve, without restricting the circulation in the aquarium. The flow velocity through a chemical reactor presents another issue since granular and pelleted activated carbons are soft and friable. If the flow is too strong, it may cause the carbon granules or pellets to grind into powder, creating a black cloudy mess in the aquarium. In addition, it has been shown that moving water too quickly through the carbon actually results in reduced efficiency. Evidence suggests that adsorption rates decline when water moves past the carbon faster than 65 milliliters per minute, roughly one gallon per hour (Harker, 1998b).

Use of media bags and GAC placement

The GAC in a contact chamber or canister filter may be located in mesh media bags or sandwiched between layers of polyester floss to hold it in place. The drawback to this method is that unless the water is prefiltered, the GAC will trap detritus and flow will quickly become reduced as the polyester floss used to hold loose GAC in place in a contact filter clogs. Bags containing

GAC also tend to become clogged by particulate matter on the surface because the fine mesh necessary to keep carbon particles inside acts as a mechanical filter. This effectively isolates much of the GAC, puts backpressure on the line, and slows the water flow. Much of the water then ends up channeling between the bags. This problem can be solved by avoiding the use of bags, and installing the carbon in an upflow chemical reactor, as we shall describe shortly.

Alternatively, one may simply place bags of GAC in the sump. In sumps that do not have chambers for media, plastic baskets, eggcrate light diffuser material, or plastic panels can be used to create a media chamber. This method of carbon use is termed *passive*, since the water is not forced by a pump through the media, but generally flows around it. In natural system aquaria using no external filters, one or more bags of carbon can be placed behind the rockwork in a location where they may easily be retrieved, near the water movement generated by the rising air from the bubbler(s). This passive flow technique can keep the water from becoming noticeably yellow for several months.

Tip: When using media bags in a sump, make sure that the bags cannot slide around in the sump and become drawn up against the suction intake of the pump(s).

The removal of yellowing compounds should be done gradually to avoid shocking the corals with a sudden increase in visible light and UV wavelengths (Bingman, 1995). The passive method of activated carbon use (Delbeek and Sprung, 1994) does not remove colour as thoroughly as using a flow-through contact chamber, so it is inefficient in that respect (Harker, 1998). An alternative *go-slow* method is to place the carbon in a flow-through chemical reactor with a ball valve on the water feed to reduce the flow rate. In this way, the aquarist can control the rate of colour removal from the water. This is by far the best way to install activated carbon. In addition, such a slow flow arrangement can lead to the GAC filter becoming a denitrifying filter (Wilkens and Birkholz, 1986).

Usage of GAC

One of the most common questions concerning the use of GAC is how much to use and how often it should be replaced. These questions are very difficult to quantify simply because no two systems are identical and due to differences in carbon type and mass. Differences in bioload and the type of organisms being kept greatly influence the type and amount of DOC produced. For example, aquariums filled with macroalgae will produce a greater variety of DOCs than systems with very little algal growth. Thiel (1988) recommends using 36 ounces (1020 g) of GAC per 50 gallons (189 L), while Wilkens and Birkholz (1986) recommend 500 grams (17.6 ounces) per 100 litres (26.4 gallons), which is roughly equivalent. This recommendation is excessive! (see Harker, 1998b). Thiel later revised his recommendation to 3 tablespoons per gallon, while Spotte (1992) recommends even less, 1 g per liter (Harker, 1998b). Since it is unclear what type of carbon these recommendations are referring to, they are at best estimates. The true test of carbon usage is how effective it is at preventing the accumulation of colouring compounds as well as DON in the water. Harker (1998b) demonstrated that from a standpoint of efficiency, it is prudent to use the least amount of carbon required.

It is difficult to recommend a specific period after which the GAC should be replaced because of the differences in carbons, and the population composition in different aquariums. However, various authors state that GAC remains active for 5-7 months before needing replacement (Moe, 1989; Wilkens and Birkholz, 1986). Generally, the presence of yellowing substances in the water can be used as a guide to determine if your GAC needs replacing, since these compounds are easily removed by GAC, and start to accumulate when the GAC begins to lose its activity. Moe (1989) describes the following method. Obtain a strip of white plastic and colour one half a faint yellow with a non-water soluble marker. Place the strip in the water at one end of the tank and observe from the opposite end. When there is no longer a great contrast between the yellow half and the white half, your water contains yellowing substances and you should replace your GAC. Bingman (1995) offers another simple approach: Siphon out some aquarium water into a white 5 gallon pail or other white container. In an identical white container put the same volume of reverse osmosis water. If the aquarium water is yellow, you will see the difference when looking down at the water in the two containers.

GAC as a biological filter

Since GAC is a very porous substrate, and it adsorbs potentially nutritious organic substances, nitrifying and denitrifying bacteria will quickly colonize it. They may also be attracted to it by having an opposite surface charge. In a short period, activated carbon granules thus become biologically active. If you use large amounts of GAC, replacing all of it every six months or so could affect the denitrification potential of the aquarium when little substratum is used. It might be wiser to replace 30% with new carbon and rinse the remaining 70% with seawater (Wilkens and Birkholz, 1986). Put the new carbon in a separate bag and place it in front of the old carbon. This will preserve a large amount of the bacteria that have colonized the GAC. Of course, in reef aquariums that use a lot of live rock, sand beds, and/or refugia, the loss of denitrification potential when changing out activated carbon is of no concern because it is small compared to the other substrata. In addition, the use of a denitrification filter would also lessen the impact of replacing all the carbon at once. The biggest concern about replacing activated carbon in a reef tank is that adding a large amount of new GAC at once could result in a rapid clearing of the water and possible light shock to the corals as we have already mentioned. Wilkens and Birkholz (1986) recommend that if GAC is to be added to an established aquarium, it should be done gradually, say 20 grams (0.7 ounces) per 100 litres (26.4 gallons) monthly, until their recommendation of 500 grams (17.6 ounces) per 100 liters (26.4 gallons) is attained. Their recommendation is based on the same concern about preventing the rapid clearing of the water that could cause light shock. The use of a chemical reactor with flow rate controlled by a ball valve offers the most practical way to control the rate of clearing. We are not aware of anyone attempting to control the feed through such a reactor with an optical sensor, but the possibility exists!

Testing GAC for phosphate and silicate

There are several brands of GAC available in the marine trade today and all of them work well. What sets them apart is their ease of use, grain size and what they may leach into the water. It has long been know that some forms of GAC will leach phosphate into the aquarium water as we first reported in volume one (Delbeek and Sprung, 1994). The concern over the release of phosphate by granular activated carbons continues, with some authors dismissing its importance, others highlighting it. We still consider phosphate release by activated carbon an important consideration, though the inputs of phosphate with food added to the tank surely exceed the amount of phosphate released by some of the low phosphate activated carbons.

In some cases, GAC leach phosphate because the raw material they are made from (wood or coal) has a high phosphate content. Such carbons are intended for the purpose of air purification, not water purification. Manufacturers of such carbon will tell you that a few rinses in freshwater will eliminate most of the phosphate, and that the amount leached is not significant. This advice contradicts our experience. We could not rinse such carbon sufficiently to affect its ability to leach phosphate, and the amount leached can be significant (based on the test procedure described below).

The best way to determine if a GAC releases phosphate is to use a phosphate test kit. Add the reagent to purified freshwater and then add a few grains of GAC to the test vial. If you see blue trails coming off the pieces, you know it releases phosphate. Be sure to let the carbon sit in the test vial for at least 30 minutes. Some carbons will turn the solution blue immediately, while others obviously release much less phosphate, and take time to show that a trace of phosphate is released (Delbeek and Sprung, 1994).

It has also been shown that some forms of activated carbon leach silicates (M. Atkinson, pers. comm.). Silicate is a major nutrient for diatoms and excessive levels can lead to diatom blooms that will cover the glass and gravel with a golden brown layer (see chapter 4). Although the amount of silicate released by the activated carbon can be significant, use of such activated carbon tends to suppress diatom growth rather than promote it. This contradiction may relate to the adsorption of other plant nutrients (nitrate, phosphate) by fresh activated carbon (M. Atkinson, pers comm.). We have not witnessed any harm from this input of silicate. The source of the silicate is the raw material (coal) from which the carbon is manufactured.

Concerns of GAC usage

A potential problem with activated carbon is that as it ages, some of the substances it has adsorbed can be released back into the water (Spotte, 1979). However, if you change your GAC on a regular basis, you should be able to avoid this. Another caveat concerning GAC is that along with the other forms of chemical filtration mentioned here, it uncontrollably removes substances from the water, including some useful ones like trace elements. Therefore, water change and trace element additions take on added importance when chemical filtration is present. Some aquarists use activated carbon only a few days per month for these reasons; others use it continuously with no ill effects.

Two Little Fishies HydroCarbon®2 is a lignite based activated carbon that does not leach phosphate.
J. Sprung

Not all aquarists use activated carbon. In fact, some aquarists are vehemently opposed to its use, citing trace element depletion and the occurrence of mysterious ailments in corals or fishes as reasons to avoid using it. Most vehement opponents of activated carbon use have limited experience with it, and base their opinions on rumor and fear of the unknown more than first hand observation. We have pointed out the problem of trace element depletion. That is easily solved by supplemental replenishment or water changes. Further, we have pointed out that not all GAC is created equal (see Hovanec, 1993), and that some carbons can leach phosphate and silicate, while others do not. Therefore testing and choosing the right carbon is important. Mysterious ailments in fishes, such as the stimulation of head and lateral line erosion sometimes linked with activated carbon use (T. Frakes, pers. comm.), may be the result of substances leached by particular types of activated carbon, and not a feature of all types (Sprung, 1993). It has also been proposed that microscopic activated carbon particles may somehow irritate the lateral line of fish resulting in HLLE, but this hypothesis doesn't explain why some fish genera are more susceptible than others, nor why some activated carbons are associated with this condition while others are not. Of course HLLE is a symptom that can be produced by numerous causes, especially poor diet, but also various types of chemical irritants.

Aquarists follow a spectrum of activated carbon use. Some never use it, some use it periodically, only a few hours per week or a few days per month, and some use it continuously. Ultimately you will decide what works best for your aquarium based on the health of the inhabitants, and the aquarium's aesthetic appearance. In our opinion, GAC should be used continuously or nearly so, or not at all. Intermittent use of activated carbon can lead to light shocking corals if yellowing compounds are allowed to accumulate and then removed too quickly.

Phosphate adsorption media

Later in this chapter we discuss biological assimilation of phosphate as part of a natural filtration system, and control of phosphate via protein skimming. The control of phosphate levels with chemical filter media is another alternative. A number of products have appeared on the market in the last few years designed to remove inorganic phosphate (orthophosphate) from saltwater. The development of these products has allowed for the creation of marine aquarium systems with many more fish and invertebrates that need to be fed large volumes of food, than was previously possible.

Aluminium based phosphate adsorption media
Phosphate adsorption products based on aluminium oxide or hydroxide, usually consisting of small beads, are placed in media bags in contact chambers or simply placed in the sump as we described for GAC. Although these types of media are effective, it has been documented that they can cause problems with soft corals, particularly *Sarcophyton* spp., when used in amounts greater than what is recommended by the manufacturers. Although the reason has never been identified, it is speculated that an increase in dissolved aluminium is the cause (Holmes-Farley, 2003).

Phosphate pads
Sponges or pads coated with ferric hydroxide or aluminium oxides have also been on the market for some years and have proven quite effective. These pads are simply placed in the sump so that water can pass through them, or placed into special contact chambers where the pads can be stacked one on the other like pancakes, and replaced when exhausted.

Granular iron based phosphate adsorption media

The chemical filter media with the highest capacity for adsorbing phosphate are made from oxides and hydroxides of ferric iron. These media are manufactured as solid granules that have a high surface area for adsorption. Once the phosphate is adsorbed, it is tightly bound to the surface and will not be released. These media have the capacity to keep phosphate levels at or below 0.015 ppm, and are thus a useful tool in the management of algae, especially in heavily fed aquaria.

The capacity of iron-based media is ideal under normal reef aquarium circumstances, where the goal is to reduce a phosphate level from 0.5 ppm or less to 0.02 ppm or lower. Under these circumstances, depending on the quantity used and volume of the aquarium, the useful life of the media may be a few weeks to a few months. For aquariums with a higher phosphate level, the media will become saturated so quickly (hours or days instead of weeks or months) that it becomes too expensive or time consuming to replace the media. For aquariums with chronically high phosphate levels (above 0.5 ppm), one must rule out sources of phosphate besides food, top-off water, calcium reactor media and activated carbon, and include other methods of lowering the phosphate concentration, such as protein skimming, algal filtration, bacterial bloom and biomass harvesting, and kalkwasser dosing.

Caveats about granular iron based media

Harker (2004) demonstrated that two granular iron based media he tested had as a side effect the reduction of alkalinity and pH. Therefore, when using such media, it is important to monitor the alkalinity and boost it as needed to maintain proper levels (see chapter 5). Related to this problem, it is common for granular iron media to clump together, or become solid, presumably due to binding with calcium carbonate. For this reason the use of upflow filters has become the preferred method of installation since, among other advantages, it diminishes the occurrence of clumping.

Granular iron based media also remove DOC and therefore can influence the transparency of the water. When using these media, one should take the same precautions regarding light shock as we recommend for activated carbon use.

Upflow chemical filters or reactors

One of the drawbacks to using granular filter material such as GAC and granular ferric oxide/hydroxide media is the clogging with detritus and channeling of water flow that occurs with time. The use of the upflow principle in a bed of granular filter media has the advantage of not accumulating detritus and reducing the incidence of water channelling through the media. Thus, the water can be

The use of high capacity iron based phosphate adsorption media in an upflow filter has allowed for an increased fish density and increased rates of feeding. J. Sprung

filtered in a consistent fashion until the media is exhausted. Many granular filter media are composed of soft materials that are friable (easily broken by rubbing), so the tumbling of such media in a typical fluidized sand filter would produce fines in the water. This does not prevent the use of such media in an upflow filter. If the base of the upflow filter has a perforated plate that disperses the flow and the flow rate is adjusted to lift the media without causing tumbling, the desired effect can be achieved. This method is an effective means of utilizing GAC or granular ferric oxide/hydroxide media. These filter columns must have a mechanical filter sponge pads at the base and top, to retain the media within the reactor column, as well as perforated discs supporting the sponge pads. These retaining layers do trap detritus and must be cleaned every couple of months to maintain peak operating efficiency. Since the media must be changed every few months anyway, the pads can be cleaned at the same time. The flow to the reactor should be regulated by a valve on the feed line. One should never put a valve on the output since restricting the flow there would cause pressure to build up in the reactor, possibly causing a leak.

Lanthanum chloride heptahydrate ($LaCl_3 \cdot 7H_2O$)

The use of chemicals aside from kalkwasser (including iron) to precipitate orthophosphate (PO_4^{-3}) from the water column within the display is something not well studied, but possible. For example, the use of lanthanum chloride heptahydrate for the removal of orthophosphate was first introduced in the pool and spa industry. Since then, zoos and public aquariums have successfully used it to lower excessive phosphate from large fish and mammal exhibits, both marine and freshwater. When mixed with water, $LaCl_3 \cdot 7H_2O$ dissociates and the free La^{+3} ions combine with phosphate in a 1:1 ratio to form lanthanum phosphate, which is a precipitate, as shown in the following equation:

$$La^{+3} + PO_4^{-3} \rightarrow LaPO_4 \text{ (solid)}$$

Simply stated, it takes 1 ppm of lanthanum chloride heptahydrate to remove 1 ppm of orthophosphate. This reaction takes place within seconds and the bond is stable over a pH range of 5 to 11 (Orlebeke, unknown year). Therefore, once bound, it is unlikely that free lanthanum will enter solution again in the typical reef aquarium. The resulting precipitate is then removed by mechanical filtration and discarded. Since lanthanum has an ionic bonding level comparable to sodium it will also bond to and precipitate carbonate, arsenic, selenium and chromium (Orlebeke, unknown year). Therefore, aquarists should monitor alkalinity and pH levels closely when dosing lanthanum chloride heptahydrate and make adjustments as necessary.

Lanthanum chloride heptahydrate should be added to the sump or overflow such that the precipitate formed is quickly passed to the filtration system where it can be removed via mechanical filtration. It should be added slowly via the drip method and only in amounts that will partially remove the phosphate from the system. It is best to do this in stages over several weeks to avoid shocking the system by the sudden removal of orthophosphate and, potentially, the sudden lowering alkalinity and pH. Orthophosphate levels should be monitored closely until the desired level is reached. Adding it slowly also reduces the possibility of excessive cloudiness developing in the aquarium.

Lanthanum chloride heptahydrate is used in commercial products for swimming pools, such as *Zero-Phos*™ by *Vanson*, and *La35/Starver* by *Lo-Chlor* (Cover, 2004). These products are added in the surface skimmer so that they can mix with the water and then sent straight to the mechanical filters where the precipitated lanthanum phosphate can be quickly removed without passing back to the pool/aquarium.

Although lanthanum chloride has been employed successfully for phosphate control in fish systems (Ray Davis, pers. comm.), its potential to harm invertebrates is significant. Lanthanum is a calcium mimic with no known positive role, and it can easily play havoc with metabolic pathways in cells (C. Bingman, pers. comm.). While lanthanum chloride has been used in systems with corals with no apparent ill effects (T. Moore, Aquarium Curator, *Mirage/MGM Grand Hotel*, pers. comm.), we recommend extreme caution when using this potentially hazardous chemical in a reef aquarium.

Zeolites

Zeolites are naturally occurring minerals or industrially manufactured synthetic minerals that consist mostly of silica and aluminium plus other elements such as sodium, potassium, calcium, iron, and manganese. The special feature of zeolites is their crystal structure, which is porous and organized, like a sponge, giving zeolites their ability to absorb specific compounds. However, zeolites aren't just absorbers. They are actually ion-exchangers. The holes into which ammonium ions become bound are not empty but filled with sodium or potassium. Sodium and potassium are given off as ammonium is absorbed. Zeolites have been used in freshwater aquaria for a long time to rapidly reduce nutrient (ammonium) concentrations. In seawater, the high concentration of sodium, potassium, and calcium makes zeolites much less effective for ammonium absorption. However, in the last few years, a zeolite filter system, called *ZEOvit*, which was specifically designed for seawater, has been introduced. The main selling point is that it is reported to promote the maintenance of colours in SPS corals by limiting the dissolved nutrient levels (Kallmeyer, 2004). *ZEOvit* preferentially absorbs ammonium, but since the porous structure creates a large

The *ZEOvit* method is promoted as a means of maintaining low nutrient levels that promote the bright colours of SPS corals. This is what the special media looks like. J. Sprung

surface area for bacteria to settle on, it quickly becomes a biological filter. A dissolved carbon source added to the aquarium enhances the development of such biofilms, leading to a depletion of oxygen on the zeolite surfaces. The zeolite thus becomes an effective denitrification filter.. The *ZEOvit system* consists of the media, which is placed in a canister filter, and the addition of a carbon source. Some bacterial biomass is also shed from the zeolite and removed by protein skimming (Kallmeyer, 2004), but the zeolite pores ultimately become clogged by biofilms and adsorbed ions, necessitating periodic replacement of the media.

Caveats

The rapid removal of ammonium may shock corals, particularly in old tanks with higher nutrient concentrations where the corals and their zooxanthellae have adapted to the conditions. The sudden drop in dissolved nitrogenous compounds has reportedly caused massive die-off of colonies that had been growing well over decades (Kallmeyer, 2004). By contrast, new aquariums started with zeolite filtration don't exhibit this problem. We should point out that we have no firsthand experience with this method.

Molecular adsorption filters

The product *Poly-Filter*® from *Poly-Bio-Marine*, Inc® (www.poly-bio-marine.com) consists of pads made from a patented material bonded to a synthetic matrix of polymers that selectively adsorbs polar organics and nitrogen containing compounds onto their surface (Moe, 1989). According to the manufacturer, they also adsorb phosphate, copper, and numerous other compounds. The pad darkens as it become exhausted. The manufacturer also claims that its *Poly-Filter* pad is pre-treated with trace elements at concentrations normally found in synthetic seawater, and that it will adsorb only *excess* metals over this background level. *Poly-Bio-Marine,* Inc. also manufactures molecular adsorption discs for use in its filtration systems for purifying tapwater or well water. This system is an alternative to reverse osmosis and ion exchange filters.

Note: Amine based polymers used for protecting fish slime coats will bond to any organic scavenging resin as well as any ion exchange resin. When you regenerate the resin using bleach, they will then bond with the chlorine, forming toxic chloramine.

Purigen™ from *Seachem* (www.seachem.com) is a macroporous synthetic adsorbent polymer particle that can remove impurities from water, including various organic compounds, ammonia, nitrites and nitrates. According to the manufacturer, Purigen's impact on trace elements is minimal, it raises redox, and like activated carbon, it removes yellowing substances. Purigen darkens as it exhausts, and it is easily renewed by treating with bleach. The use of activated carbon with Purigen extends the useful life of Purigen.

Molecular adsorption media should be situated so that water is forced through the medium, not around it, with adequate prefiltration to prevent clogging of the media.

Protein skimming

If you've ever visited a beach on a windy day, you may recall seeing foam washing up on shore. This foam is produced by the churning action of the waves, combining air, the water, and certain polar organic compounds dissolved in it to form stable foam. The wind blows the foam to shore, and thus helps to purify the water. Protein skimming, or foam fractionation in aquacultural engineering terms, works in a similar manner, mixing fine air bubbles with water. By collecting the foam that forms, proteins, organic and inorganic compounds are removed from the aquarium water. This is very beneficial to the health of marine invertebrates and fish. Of the various chemical filtration methods available, only protein skimming physically removes most organics from the aquarium before they begin to break down (Moe, 1989). This reduces the load on the biological filter and raises the redox potential of the water. Protein skimmers primarily extract dissolved substances from solution, though electrostatic attraction to the bubble surfaces and physical trapping by the thick foam do also draw some particulate matter, bacteria, and phytoplankton out of the solution. The list of substances removed by skimming includes amino acids, proteins, fats, carbohydrates, phosphate, fatty acids, phenols, iodide, metals such as copper, iron, and zinc complexed with the proteins, detritus, and leachates of plant and animal origin. A skimmer thus lowers biological oxygen demand, chemical oxygen demand, and nitrate build-up (Dwivedy, 1973; Lomax, 1976). The removal of organic acids also helps to maintain the pH of the system (Dwivedy, 1973). Furthermore, since skimming removes toxic organic substances released into the water by the invertebrates (e.g. terpenes from soft corals), it makes it possible to keep a variety of coral species in a confined space. In addition to organic and inorganic compounds, protein skimmers also remove suspended solids, improving visibility and light penetration. In addition, protein skimmers also remove bacteria, and have been shown to be able to maintain very low levels of fecal coliform bacteria in marine mammal exhibits (Aiken, 2004).

Wind generated waves cause surface films of organics to collect on bubbles and produce foam that blows to shore, much the same way that a protein skimmer removes organic substances from aquarium water. J. Sprung

However, protein skimmers also serve another very useful task. The injection of air into the skimmer helps to bring the seawater into equilibrium with carbon dioxide in the atmosphere by expelling excess carbon dioxide from the water; resulting in a more stable pH in the tank. This air injection may also help to maintain oxygen levels near saturation in some protein skimmer designs. Gas exchange is also improved in the aquarium since the skimmer removes surfactants from the water, which would otherwise coat the aquarium water surface and slow gas exchange.

Disadvantages of skimming

There are mainly great advantages to the use of protein skimming, but the effectiveness of this filtration method comes with some disadvantages that should be mentioned. First, much of the organic matter removed by a protein skimmer could be utilized as food by filter feeding invertebrates. Generally, there is so much dissolved organic matter available in an aquarium that this is little reason to consider avoiding protein skimming. Similarly, however, the protein skimmer is effective at removing bacteria, phytoplankton and zooplankton, and thus it does lower the availability of food to the filter feeders.

There is still a great deal of debate about whether protein skimming removes a significant amount of trace elements, compared to the metabolic actions of the animals, plants, microorganisms and bacteria growing in the aquarium (Achterkamp, 1986; Keith, 1980). However, there is no doubt that some elements such as iodide and iron are removed both by skimmers and natural biological processes, and that they must be replenished.

A study by Japanese hobbyists on skimmate removed from a reef aquarium showed that this material can also contain calcium and magnesium (Mizuno, 2000). One gram of thick sludge-like skimmer effluent was air-dried, then dissolved in nitric acid and hydrogen peroxide and measured using an atomic absorption/flame emission spectrometer. Mizuno found approximately 202 mg/g of calcium, 21.2 mg/g of magnesium, 5.63 mg/g of phosphate and 30.3 micrograms/g of iron. Mizuno felt that since magnesium is normally bound to sulfate, that sulfate was also probably removed by the skimmer though this was not tested. It was also assumed that ionized iron in seawater becomes oxidized quickly in the skimmer and is removed as Fe_2O_3 (Mizuno, 2000).

Protein skimming theory

While the mechanics of protein skimming are simple to explain, the subject of protein skimming gets a little more complicated when we examine the chemical processes that make it effective. Certain molecules in the aquarium are attracted to the surface of air bubbles. They are referred to as surface-active molecules or surfactants. These organic molecules are polar (charged) at one end and non-polar (uncharged) at the other end. The polar end is attracted to water molecules (hydrophilic) and the non-polar end is repelled by water (hydrophobic). These surface-active molecules are attracted to a surface where the hydrophobic end of the molecule can be away from water and the hydrophilic end can remain in contact with water. Conveniently, air bubbles provide an excellent air-water interface for the surfactants to adhere. By mixing seawater rich in surfactants with a high concentration of fine air bubbles a stable

Note: Since protein skimmers effeciently remove bacteria and phytoplankton from the water, the iron these microorganisms assimilate is likely the main source of iron present in skimmate. Phosphate assimilated by bacteria and microalgae is also gathered by the skimmer this way. Bingman (1996) found that skimmate can be enriched in phosphate by a factor of nearly 100 relative to the concentration in the aquarium water. He proposed that kalkwasser may enhance this through the formation of calcium phosphate, which may have an affinity for air/water interfaces. This hypothesis is supported by the calcium found in Mizuno's study.

foam will result that will then rise to the top where it can be collected and removed. There are of course, several factors that determine how well a given skimmer design will perform its task; we will discuss these shortly.

Protein skimmer designs

No piece of marine aquarium filtration equipment has undergone more of a transformation over the last ten years than the protein skimmer. Once considered an odd looking add-on that was used only by European hobbyists, the explosion in reef aquarium popularity and technology in North America in the late 1980's brought the protein skimmer to the forefront of marine aquarium keeping. Today, the protein skimmer is a mainstay of most marine aquarium filtration systems.

Figure 6k. Because of their polar, non-polar nature, surfactants will orient themselves along the surface of an air bubble. Modified from Aiken, 2004.

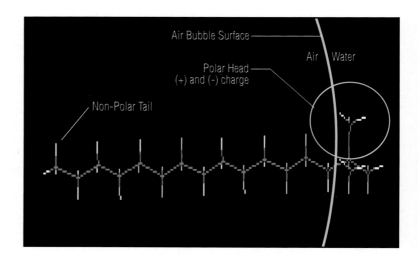

Figure 6l. When enough surfactants cover the surface of the bubble, stable foam begins to form. Modified from Aiken, 2004.

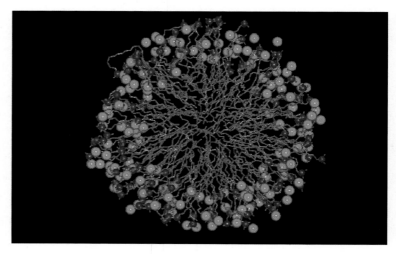

Early designs

Early protein skimmers were primarily manufactured in Europe in the 1970's and 80's. These used a design known as counter-current flow where water entered the upper portion of the water column of the skimmer and exited from the bottom. Air was injected at the bottom via a wooden air block and as the air bubbles rose upwards while the water moved downwards, surfactants were removed. This counter-current design increased the contact time between the air bubbles and water since the downward flowing water would slow the rise of the bubbles, increasing efficiency. For several years, skimmer columns became larger and larger, and 1.2 m (4 ft.) or higher skimmers were a common sight on reef aquariums. The basis for this increase in height was again, to increase the contact time and the amount of water that the skimmer could process per hour. Although wooden air blocks produced very fine bubbles, they only did so for a short period before they became clogged and swollen, reducing the amount of bubbles produced and increasing their size. Today, all but the smallest skimmers use alternative methods for creating air bubbles in the skimmer, though many still use a counter-current design or some variation of it.

Venturi skimmers

In the early 1990's, an alternative method of injecting air into the skimmer came into prominence. The Venturi skimmer, named after the principle of air injection used, began to appear on the market. A Venturi valve consists of a small device that directs the stream of water in a pipe through a very small opening or constriction in the pipe. There is a pressure differential between the two sides of this small opening; high pressure before it, and lower pressure after it. One or more small ports in the Venturi lead to the outside. The pressure drop after the constriction causes air to be sucked in through these openings, forming a very fine mixture of air and water, which is introduced into the bottom of the protein skimmer. In freestanding external skimmers with a Venturi located at the bottom, the air input port must have a hose attached to it that extends above the height of the skimmer to prevent water from back-flowing out of the Venturi when the power is off. A check valve system could also be employed to prevent back-flow of water, but we don't recommend check valves because they are not 100% reliable.

A Venturi rarely needs to be replaced, and circumvents many of the problems inherent in wooden air blocks, but it is not completely trouble-free either. To make the valve work properly, the water must enter under pressure. This requires that the water be pumped to the Venturi by a strong water pump. Some Venturi skimmers have the pump that powers the Venturi on a closed loop, taking water from the skimmer and sending it back to the skimmer, for the purpose of packing it with a dense column of air bubbles. The Venturi reduces the volume of the pump output, so it makes sense to use a separate pump to generate the bubbles, while gravity feed or another pump sends as much water through the skimmer as possible. The Venturi design is commonly used in large commercial skimmers, such as those found in public aquariums and aquaculture facilities.

Venturi skimmers tend to be extremely sensitive to changes in their immediate environment. For example, aerosol sprays, paint fumes, or wood dust in the same room as a Venturi operated skimmer may lead to a marked decrease in foam production for a few hours. These things also affect skimming with other types of protein skimmers, but less rapidly. Placing one's hands in the aquarium, or feeding the fish, can also cause a sudden temporary reduction in foam production due to fats and oils introduced to the water that lower the surface tension, hindering the formation of bubbles.

Figure 6m. External Venturi Skimmer Installation

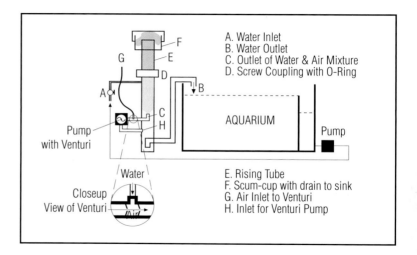

A. Water Inlet
B. Water Outlet
C. Outlet of Water & Air Mixture
D. Screw Coupling with O-Ring

E. Rising Tube
F. Scum-cup with drain to sink
G. Air Inlet to Venturi
H. Inlet for Venturi Pump

Using Venturi skimmers

As we mention above, we recommend that Venturi skimmers be run by a dedicated pump, do not use a feed line from a pump that is running another piece of equipment or returning to the main tank. The reason for this is that if there is any change in head pressure in the system, the pressure on the Venturi valve will change and this will affect bubble production. Venturi designs that use a dedicated pump for the Venturi in a closed loop with the skimmer, do not have this problem, and allows you to supply the skimmer with water in whatever manner you want.

Some Venturi skimmers have a valve attached that can be adjusted to give the optimum air volume to generate proper bubble size and abundance. This valve needs to be checked and adjusted during periodic cleaning of the skimmer.

In some designs, the opening for the air to enter the Venturi is placed very close to the water path. The inrushing of air through this small opening can cause evaporation to occur causing salt to crystallize or calcium carbonate to accumulate. The deposits formed will eventually result in restriction of the opening so that less air is drawn in and fewer air bubbles are generated. Therefore, this opening needs to be periodically checked for such deposits and, if necessary, the valve must be removed and cleaned with a weak acid solution such as vinegar. Another method that works is to periodically add a small amount of vinegar or freshwater to the air intake line so that it dissolves the blockage as it is sucked into the Venturi valve. If done on a weekly basis, this is often enough to keep the air opening from becoming clogged without having to periodically shut down the skimmer or remove the Venturi valve. One must remember to do this as part of a weekly maintenance schedule. A simpler alternative to manually adding a solution to the Venturi air feed line is to connect the pump driving the Venturi valve to a multi-event timer. Set the timer to turn the pump off for a minute or two, several times a day. This results in tank water flooding the Venturi, dissolving any deposits and maintaining maximum efficiency.

Aspirator skimmers

Another popular skimmer design uses a special aspirator system made from a high rpm pump and an impeller with pegs on it. Air is drawn in on the suction side of this pump, and the line is not constricted, in contrast with Venturi design. The advantages of this design are many. The pump does not need to be as large as it does with the Venturi design in order to develop sufficient pressure behind the constriction of the Venturi. The volume of air drawn into the stream of water is also much greater than by Venturi. The pegs on the impeller chop the air into fine bubbles, so this design packs the skimmer with a high density of fine bubbles making it very efficient for mixing a large amount of air with water. In early aspirator skimmers, the aspirator pump merely generated air on a closed loop, drawing water from the skimmer and sending it back to the skimmer. The air water mixture was injected at the bottom of the skimmer at the center, from a pipe directed straight up (i.e. no tangential flow). This afforded the same characteristics as a typical counter-current flow skimmer using an air stone at the bottom, except that the aspirator filled the column more thoroughly with bubbles. Water entered the skimmer at the top or side by gravity feed, or was injected by a separate pump.

Today's aspirator designs typically employ small submersible pumps that draw water from the sump, mix it with air then inject it directly into the skimmer. Small plastic pins on the impeller, much like the bristles on a hairbrush, mix the incoming air with the water creating very fine bubbles that are then injected into the bottom of the skimmer. These *pin wheel* skimmers have gained in popularity due to their smaller size and quiet operation, and the extremely fine bubbles they consistently create. The drawback of this design is that not as much water can be processed per unit time as in some other designs.

Using aspirator skimmers

Since water and air are mixed together by the impeller in this skimmer design, the condition of the impeller can affect the performance of the skimmer. Make sure that large particles such as snail shells, calcareous tubeworms or gravel cannot be sucked into the intake. These will lodge in the impeller pegs, reducing efficiency or worse cause some pegs to deform or break off. An intake screen should be placed over the pump opening to prevent this. Care should be exercised whenever cleaning the impeller since any damage to the pegs can adversely affect its performance and it is expensive to replace.

As with Venturi skimmers, the point where air is drawn into the impeller on an aspirator skimmer is prone to salt and calcium carbonate deposits forming and reducing air intake. Make sure to check this opening regularly and clean it as we mentioned previously for Venturi valves.

Downdraft skimmers

Just when we thought we'd seen all the ways to skin a cat, err, skim a tank, along comes an unlikely looking contraption utilizing a principle called downdraft to generate fine bubbles with high volume of air driven by a high pressure water stream. The result is a very strong capacity for foaming and therefore protein skimming the

The impeller of an aspirator skimmer consists of several dozen pegs that effectively chop the air into fine bubbles and mix them with the incoming water. *Euro-Reef* Inc.

A typical aspirator skimmer design. *Euro-Reef* Inc.

water. The first commercially marketed design for aquariums that used this principle was called the *ETS* skimmer patented by Gary Loehr of Beacon, New York and produced by *A. E. Tech*, Inc. http://www.superskimmer.com/

The *ETS* or *ETSS™* skimmer injects water through a narrow nozzle under pressure into the top of a column filled with bioballs. The downward rushing of water draws air in through holes in the top of this column. The resulting mixture of air and water creates fine bubbles that generate foam, which collects in a separate compartment and rises out the top while clean water exits from the bottom.

A big advantage of this design is that huge amounts of water and air can be pumped through the skimmer per hour. This results in very good gas exchange for the entire aquarium, with some input of CO_2 during the day, and off-gassing of CO_2 at night based on ambient CO_2 in the air where the skimmer is located. It also results in a more stable pH and high oxygenation of the water. The high air volume also means high water-air contact and great efficiency of skimming.

One *disadvantage* of this design is that it may be too efficient, stripping an aquarium of nutrients very quickly. As a result, early adopters of this design found that corals, particularly soft corals, in their reef tanks began to pale in colour and shrink in size. This was remedied by increased feeding of fishes in the system. Therefore, the by-product of this design was that it allowed for a higher bioload of fishes and heavier feedings of the tank than previously possible. Other disadvantages include a potentially high electrical consumption due to the large water pump used to send the water into the downdraft, the noise generated by the downdraft column(s) and the large size based on the height of the downdraft column(s).

Figure 6n. Schematic of a basic downdraft skimmer design.

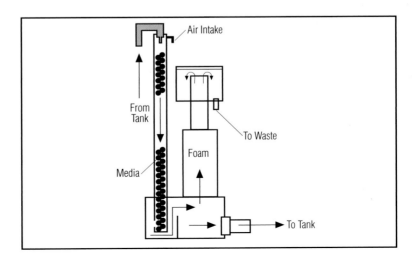

Using downdraft skimmers

As we mentioned with Venturi skimmers, downdraft skimmers are very sensitive to changes in water quality and air quality. Oils from foods or hands can cause a downdraft skimmer to stop producing foam for several hours afterwards. Similarly, smoke, cooking fumes, sawdust etc. sucked into the air intakes will cause a cessation in foam production for a period. When this occurs it is important to resist the temptation to adjust the flow rate in the skimmer. If you adjust the water flow at this time, when the skimmer begins to function properly again, it will quickly overflow the collection cup.

When first installing a downdraft skimmer on an aquarium, let the skimmer run for a few days with very little flow restriction on the outlet. Fresh acrylic inhibits the formation of foam and it will take a few days for the skimmer to begin to function properly. If you adjust the water column height to where the air-water interface is close to the top of the skimmer foam column, when the skimmer begins to produce foam it will overflow the skimmer cup and flood the area.

An *ETS* Downdraft skimmer in use at the Waikiki Aquarium. Note the ball valves on the air intake fittings at the top of the downdraft columns. J.C. Delbeek

The area where air is drawn into the top of the downdraft column(s) can become clogged over time with salt deposits. It is important to keep these areas clean of such salt deposits so that airflow is not reduced. If you notice over time that the foam does not reach as high as it used to, then the first thing to check are the air intakes. In some cases, downdraft skimmers pass so much water and draw in so much air, that the result is a very turbulent air-water mixture in the foam column. This turbulence causes wet foam to be ejected out into the skimmer cup and results in a very dilute foam and significant water loss from the aquarium in a short period. To solve this problem most aquarists reduce the water flow from the pump, believing this to be the problem. A better solution is to place valves on the air intakes. Reducing the amount of air injected reduces turbulence and produces more stable foam. The flow out of the skimmer may need to be reduced somewhat so that the foam can rise high enough to be ejected, but this has the added benefit of increasing contact time in the skimmer.

Beckett skimmers

Beckett skimmers are similar to downdraft skimmers in design and size; however, they use a different method of air injection. Instead of relying on the force of water hitting bioballs in a column to create air bubbles, they use a special nozzle called a *Beckett*, which is actually the name of the pond company that supplies nozzles of various types for use in water fountains. Beckett skimmers can be as tall as downdraft designs but lack the external mixing columns. In many respects they are similar to downdraft skimmers, and have many of the same advantages and disadvantages, but do not require as large a pump to operate and are not as tall.

This *MTC HSA1000* skimmer in use at the Waikiki Aquarium uses a Beckett fitting in the uppermost chamber to generate air bubbles. J.C. Delbeek

Spray Injection™ skimmers

In the late 1990's, an American hobbyist in San Diego, Jason Kim, developed another skimmer design that relied on a spray injector to direct a fine stream of water under pressure into a mixing chamber. This is not unlike the effect of using a garden hose with a spray nozzle on the end to create foaming water in a bucket. This patented design became known as the *AquaC* Spray Injection™ skimmer.

There are several advantages to this design but the most intriguing is the fact that this technology allows for a much smaller overall format without compromising performance. This allows for the placement of a very powerful skimmer into a small space such as a sump located in a cabinet with low clearance. The other big advantage of this design is that it operates with a much smaller pump than a comparable downdraft or Beckett skimmer. A disadvantage of earlier models was that the outlet valve was placed so low that fluctuations in sump level affected the level of water in the skimmer, affecting consistency. This necessitated raising the skimmer off the bottom of the sump. Newer models have the outlet higher on the unit so that water now exits freely above the water level in most sumps. The smaller pump means less water can be processed per hour versus a downdraft or Beckett design. However, this is more of an issue with larger systems or heavily stocked ones. Noise may also be an issue for some aquarists (Pro, 2004). The high cost of this skimmer is offset by the lower cost of the smaller pump required and the electrical savings this brings over time.

Centrifugal skimmers

The swirling of water in a skimmer column can be used to increase efficiency in a compact space by increasing air/water contact. Normally, turbulence at the top of the skimmer prevents the proper separation of dry from wet foam. However, lower in the

The *AquaC* model EV240 Spray Injection™ skimmer. J. Kim

The patented molded injector used in the *AquaC* Spray Injection™ skimmer. J. Kim

column high speed swirling of the air-water mixture causes a centrifuge effect, which can be employed to advantage. In *centrifugal skimmers*, the centrifugal action can also be used to separate water and foam, the water migrating outwards because it is heavier, and the air bubbles collecting in the center of the contact column. A physical barrier installed to prevent the swirling from extending to the top of the contact column allows smooth, uniform rising of the bubbles, and proper foam formation. Centrifugal action has one minor drawback. Some refractory organic compounds remain in the water and are cast outwards in the contact chamber, coating the inner surface. The accumulation of this yellowish carbohydrate sludge must be cleaned periodically to maintain peak operation of the skimmer.

Horizontal skimmers

One of the criticisms of large skimmer designs has been the amount of vertical space required for their operation. While hobbyists have seen the advent of more compact and efficient skimmer designs in the form of aspirator and downdraft designs, large systems still require large, tall skimmers to operate. In early 2000, Kevin Curlee at the Mote Marine Laboratory in Sarasota, Florida, developed a horizontal skimmer design that allows very large skimmers to be installed on systems over several thousand gallons, requiring less vertical space than skimmers of this capacity normally require. At the moment, this design really only works well for large systems with high flow rates, but it is possible that as refinements are made to the design, it will become applicable to smaller, home systems (K. Curlee, pers. comm. 2004).

Variables that affect skimming efficiency

Many variables can affect the operation of a protein skimmer including airflow rate, water flow rate, contact time, turbulence,

Tunze centrifugal skimmers offer a compact design that fits neatly in the sump without any plumbing. J. Sprung

temperature, pH, surface tension, specific gravity, column height and width, and mode of operation. The air injection method and bubble properties including size, distribution, and abundance are also factors. For more in-depth discussion of these and other factors that affect skimming, see Wheaton (1977).

Two major factors that aquarists can regulate are bubble size and contact time. Smaller bubbles provide more surface area per cubic cm for the surfactants, and rise through the water at a slower rate, providing more contact time. In order for the skimmer to work effectively, the air bubbles should be quite small, preferably between 0.5 mm and 0.8 mm in diameter (Achterkamp, 1986; Spotte, 1979; N. Tunze, pers. comm.). If the bubbles are too small, they no longer rise because they aren't buoyant, and they tend to dissolve rather than collect surfactants (Moe, 1989). As the surfactants coat the bubble

A small horizontal skimmer design with an eductor air injector designed by Chris Maupin at the Mote Marine Laboratory, Sarasota, FL. J.C. Delbeek

A 100 gpm horizontal skimmer on a 10526 L (40,000 gallon) tank at the Mote Marine Laboratory, Sarasota, FL. K. Curlee

A 300 gpm horizontal skimmer on a 505,400 L (133,000 gallon) tank at the Mote Marine Laboratory, Sarasota, FL. After installation, the DO rose by 8%. K. Curlee

surfaces, they form a *skin* (Moe, 1989), which gives the bubbles stability of form and maintains their size. This is caused by the effect surfactants have on the surface tension of air bubbles. The more surfactants in the water, the smaller the bubbles will be (Spotte, 1979), until a supersaturation point is reached; then the surface tension that maintained the bubble size is broken, and the bubbles group together and become larger. If supersaturation occurs throughout the column, all the bubbles become large, the foam collapses, and skimming ceases. Surface tension is also broken by fats or oils introduced into the water, as from the aquarist's hand.

At the top of the foam riser tube, the heavy concentration of surfactants collecting there causes the bubbles to group together and become larger. As this top layer rises and collapses, excess water drains back downwards, allowing the formation of a thick, stable, dry foam on top of a wetter foam layer. Wilkens (1973) discusses two basic types of foam that develop in effective skimmers. The first layer of wet foam is referred to as *standard* scum and the second as *protein* scum. It is the second layer, the *protein* scum, which concentrates harmful organic substances from solution. The standard scum is the layer of foam that develops because of protein molecules uniting with fine air bubbles. Protein scum is formed by organic substances, metals, etc. attaching themselves to the protein molecules in the standard scum. Protein scum is therefore found floating on top, where it gathers more organic compounds from the standard scum beneath it. Protein scum also leaves a solid deposit on the inside surface of the uppermost part of the skimmer column. The constant supply of air pushes the dry foam up and out of the contact column into a collection cup, or into a pipe, that directs the foam to a waste vessel.

The most common method for making fine bubbles used to be an air stone, usually a wooden air block. However, there are a number of problems with using air driven stones or wooden blocks. An air pump does not supply a constant air pressure over time, so the rate of bubble formation varies considerably. Secondly, wooden air blocks are very susceptible to rotting, which blocks many of the air pores. This results in a varying bubble size and rate of production, which ultimately results in a poorly functioning skimmer. An alternative to the wooden air block and air pump combination is the use of a Venturi valve. The Venturi can consistently produce fine bubbles as long as the water feeding it is of a constant pressure and the air intake is kept free of deposits. With the advent of aspirator and downdraft skimmer designs, most skimmers today can consistently produce fine bubbles without any intervention by the aquarist, and process much more water volume than early wooden airstone models could.

It is important that the air bubbles have as much contact time with the water in the column as possible, and contact time is enhanced by tall columns. We have seen skimmers for large systems that were over 2.6 m (8 ft.) tall! Of course, this is not practical for most home aquaria, but the contact tube should be as long as possible. Long columns also allow more time for drainage to occur, producing dryer foam, especially with high volumes of air input (Wheaton, 1977). Newer skimmer designs allow for shorter columns but with increased contact time due to the path the water follows, increasing efficiency, or by processing more tank water per hour, thereby allowing the water to be processed more frequently, negating the shorter contact time.

The pH of the water has an impact on foam formation. The pH of aquarium water is not constant, but follows a typical range over the course of a day. The operation of the skimmer, therefore, varies with the change in pH. The higher the pH, the greater the affinity of organic molecules to the surfaces of the bubbles because of enhanced electrostatic attraction. The structure of many proteins is also sensitive to pH, and extraction of a type of protein is greatest at its particular isoelectric pH. Since proteins have different isoelectric pH values, some may be skimmed better than others in the aquarium's range of pH (Wheaton, 1977).

Specific gravity affects skimming because the dissolved salts and other compounds in the water increase the stability of the tiny bubbles by increasing the viscosity of the water. Specific gravity also affects electrical charge attractions of compounds to the bubbles, and the surface tension of the water. Surface tension increases with increasing specific gravity. Although skimmers aren't supposed to function well in freshwater, they can be made to work when there are sufficient organics (i.e. crud) in the water that enhance the stability of the tiny bubbles, heavily stocked koi ponds, for instance, benefit from the application of protein skimming. There are now several protein skimmers designs available for use in freshwater systems.

Temperature affects protein skimming as well. As temperature increases, surface tension decreases. At high temperatures the foam breaks more readily, so the formation of stable, dry foam is impeded. However, in the range of ideal temperature for reef aquariums, between 21-27 °C (70-80 °F), the temperature affects on protein skimming efficiency are subtle. Nevertheless, certain surface-active substances foam only within certain temperature ranges. Therefore, not all surface-active materials will be removed from solution by the skimmer, and some will be removed more slowly than others will because the temperature is not in the ideal range for them to foam (Wheaton, 1977).

Effect of skimmer design on efficiency

The volume of air, water flow rate, and the design of the *neck* (foam riser tube) and water exit pipe of the protein skimmer all affect its capacity to filter an aquarium. Increasing the volume of air increases the surfaces for attachment of organic compounds. This increases foam formation and the efficiency of stripping organics from a given volume of water. Increasing the flow of water through a protein skimmer increases the rate at which the aquarium water is being purified. Combining these two parameters, one can see that for a given size skimmer there is a maximum flow rate of water and maximum volume of air that can be injected to achieve the best skimming for its size and construction.

A *Sanders* freshwater skimmer in use on a koi quarantine facility. J.C. Delbeek

The design of the neck and exit pipe of the skimmer are limiting aspects of its construction with respect to the ability to pump a high volume of air or water through. When high volumes of air are injected into a skimmer with a short, constricted neck, wet foam rapidly flows out the top and floods the floor. Likewise, increasing the volume of water flowing through the skimmer increases the water level in it, and thus pushes the foam level higher, with a similar flood-prone result. When the neck is not constricted, is very tall, or both, these increases in air and water flow do not cause a flood so easily, the skimmer can be packed full of tiny air bubbles, and it can process a good turnover of water. We have observed many protein skimmers operating well below the capacity possible for the size of the contact column. If the column is made of clear pipe, and you can see through the bubbles, then the skimmer is not being used efficiently. It should look like dense *whitewater*. Higher airflow rates increase the available bubble surfaces until bubble coalescence occurs in the column at a rate faster than the generation of new surfaces (Wheaton, 1977). That limit of air input is never reached in typical protein skimmers because water and foam spew out the top long before. If increasing the volume of air slightly tends to cause the foam to flood out of the top of the neck, the design of the skimmer needs to be changed. Build a taller, wider neck to solve this problem, allowing the skimmer to be packed with high density of fine bubbles. Similarly, the size of the water exit pipe should be larger in diameter than the water input, so that increases in water flow readily drain out, and do not cause much increase in the water level in the skimmer. Most skimmers today use a wide neck design with large outlets because they process much more water and air than earlier designs did. The wider necks prevent overflowing of the skimmer, particularly for downdraft designs that rapidly process huge amounts of water and air.

Size of the skimmer

As a rule of thumb, we recommend that the entire volume of the aquarium be passed through the skimmer(s) at least once per hour, preferably more. Use this figure as a guide to determine the size and number of protein skimmers you will need.

With an external protein skimmer, the size of the skimmer is not restricted by the size of the aquarium. This is a very important consideration because the larger the skimmer is the greater the volume of water that can be pumped through it. In addition, the greater the length of the skimmer, the greater the contact time between the water and the rising column of air bubbles, which is a limiting factor in the efficiency of any skimmer. While this is true for many skimmer designs, the beauty of the downdraft design is that much more water and air can be processed than normally possible with a typical columnar skimmer filled with water. As a result, these skimmers do not need to be as tall and those designed for smaller tanks can now fit under the tank whereas a comparable capacity columnar skimmer would have to stand outside of the cabinet. Giant commercial skimmers still typically employ a type of Venturi or aspirator to supply the enormous amounts of air required.

The column diameter influences the operation of the skimmer as well. If airflow is constant, increasing a protein skimmer's diameter decreases the available bubble surface area per volume of water (i.e. if the pipe diameter is bigger, you have more water and the same amount of bubbles). If the air volume is also increased, a skimmer with a wide diameter can process more water efficiently.

Purchasing a skimmer

When purchasing a protein skimmer, there are a few points to look for. First, can the skimmer be easily and completely disassembled for cleaning? Can the skimmer cup and foam riser tube be easily removed for frequent emptying and cleaning? Check the length of the foam riser tube or *neck*. If it is too short and narrow, the foam will not dry out and concentrate properly (see earlier discussion of the *neck*). If the skimmer is plumbed in line, make sure the inlet and outlet tubes are of sufficient dimensions to handle adequate flow. Finally, look at the types of valves included with the skimmer. While ball valves are fine for on/off operations, they are clumsy for fine adjustments of water flow. Much better are gate valves, which can be used to make very fine adjustments in flow rate (see chapter 3). In-sump or in-tank skimmers such as Tunze centrifugal skimmers, should have a wide neck and sufficiently large collection cup. Hang-on the back skimmers should also have a properly proportioned cup, and should process at least 2x the tank volume per hour.

Tip: Never purchase a protein skimmer whose maximum capacity is the same size as your aquarium. These aquarium size recommendations for skimmers are generalizations at best. Purchase a skimmer whose maximum capacity is greater than the size of your aquarium.

Installing the skimmer

Because there are so many different types of protein skimmers, it follows that there are numerous ways to install them on an aquarium. Protein skimmers will foam no matter where they are located on a system, but some methods do produce better results.

Inside the tank and hang-on designs

Protein skimmers designed to be mounted inside the tank or hung on the back, can be very efficient, and eliminate the need for plumbing because the reef aquarium can be operated with no external sump. Hang-on skimmer designs allow for easy retrofitting of existing aquariums, without the need to tear down a system or install a sump or overflow.

Larger aquariums using internal protein or hang-on skimmers may require multiple skimmer units, because the size of the skimmers limits their capacity. The main drawback to internal skimmers is aesthetics, though they can be hidden from view quite easily. When multiple units are required, it may be preferable to locate the skimmers in a sump behind or below the aquarium, fed by surface skimmed water. Some internal skimmers are designed to draw water off the surface of the aquarium or sump where they are located, which enhances their efficiency.

The Remora™ is a spray injection skimmer designed to hang on the side of the aquarium or sump. J. Kim

External skimmers

External skimmers can be located far from the exhibit to avoid detracting from the appearance of the living-room decor, and they can be made big, though efficiency is more important than monstrous size. The ideal way to install an external protein skimmer is to feed it all of the surface skimmed water from the overflow, without any form of mechanical or chemical pre-filtration. Protein skimmers do collect and remove some particulate matter from the water. When mechanical filters trap particulate matter, the water circulates over it until it decays. Also, as mechanical filters become coated with particulate matter they become better at trapping really fine matter, including carbohydrates and amino acids; so they trap and decay material that the skimmer could remove from the water. Chemical filters located before the skimmer would also trap and retain compounds that the skimmer could remove completely from the system. Chemical filter media (i.e. activated carbon) should be located after the skimmer. Since the skimmer is taking water from the overflow, be sure to install a strainer there to prevent fish from entering the skimmer after an accidental trip over the falls. A standpipe will retain some water in the overflow, so a fish that finds its way there can have room to swim around until you retrieve it. Of course, the skimmer must have large enough diameter input and exit pipes, so that it can handle the water volume coming from the overflow.

When a skimmer is installed so that it receives water from the overflow drain, it cannot feed water directly back to the tank unless the return is fed by a pump or airlift. Generally, the water from a protein skimmer installed this way drains to a sump. From there, it is pumped back to the aquarium. The upper level of the exit pipe returning water from the skimmer is critical for the proper level of water inside the skimmer. If the pipe level is too low, the water level in the skimmer will be too low unless a valve on the exit pipe restricts the flow, causing the water level to rise. A design requiring such restriction of flow is a poor design because it limits the volume of water that the skimmer can process, and it is tricky to adjust. It is best to have a wide exit pipe with no restriction, with a fixed water level that is elevated only by the volume of air pumped into the column.

External protein skimmers can also be installed in such a way that they receive water directly from the pump that sends water back to the aquarium from the sump, with a gate valve on the feed to regulate the volume the skimmer receives. Be aware that when the power goes off, some water will drain back to the sump from the skimmer. Be sure that the sump is of sufficient size to handle this back flow. The water exiting the skimmer may be directed to the aquarium or back to the sump, depending on the location of the skimmer and its height.

Alternatively, a dedicated pump can be used that draws water from the overflow chamber, sending it to the skimmer, which drains back to the aquarium. In order for this design to work, a second hole or a siphon can be installed in the overflow chamber to feed the dedicated pump. The main drain of the overflow is separate, and simply drains water to the sump. A standpipe on the main drain maintains a static water level in the overflow chamber. With this design, it is possible to achieve two advantages. One is that the dedicated pump can be of greater capacity than the pump that returns water from the sump, allowing the tank volume to be processed more quickly through the skimmer. The second advantage is that the surface skimming action will be enhanced by the increased volume of water flowing over the overflow. This will also raise the water level in the aquarium slightly. Don't forget to have a strainer on the suction for this pump to prevent mincing fish or invertebrates that wander over the overflow.

Sump mounted skimmers

Many skimmers today are placed directly in the sump. This allows the unit to be hidden from view and exposes it directly to water coming from the surface overflow. As with external skimmers, it is best to place any chemical filtration after the skimmer so that the skimmer can remove as much of the organics as possible, prolonging the useful life of the chemical media.

In some designs, the skimmer is fed by water coming from the main pump line while in others a dedicated pump, often a submersible one, is used. The submersible pumps work fine but as we mentioned in chapter 4, they do impart significant heat to the aquarium and this must be taken into consideration when designing the tank cooling system.

Sump mounted skimmers can release water filled with fine air bubbles that must be prevented from entering the return pump to the tank. Fine bubbles sucked into the intake of a pump can result in supersaturation of the water, leading to gas bubble disease in the fish (see chapter 4). Bubbles released into the display are also aesthetically displeasing. The use of foam sleeves over skimmer outlets, foam pads, or baffles in the sump help reduce the carry over of small bubbles into the sump and/or into the main system pump.

The skimmer in operation

You will have to watch your skimmer closely at first to make sure that the flow is just right. Too great a flow will result in a full foam tube and collection cup, a wet floor and an empty aquarium! To guard against a mess on the floor, drill a hole near the top edge of the collection cup, and install a drainage tube of at least 1/2 inch diameter that leads to a large waste container. Do not allow the skimmed off material to flow back into the aquarium; it is toxic when so concentrated.

You should notice a dark brown fluid and sludge accumulating in the collection cup after only a few days. Initially you might have to empty the collection cup twice a day, but the output will soon slow down appreciably. The skimmer is still working, there just isn't as much left to remove, that's all. You'll notice that the skimmer will begin to work furiously after feedings, water changes, addition of trace elements, or the addition of fresh live rock (boy will it ever foam after you put in live rock!). A reduction in output from the skimmer is not always caused by the lack of substances to remove from the water. In time, the skimmer becomes dirty, and this impedes its performance.

In order for your skimmer to keep working at peak efficiency, it must be kept clean. Every few days or about once a week, depending on how quickly scum accumulates, the foam collection

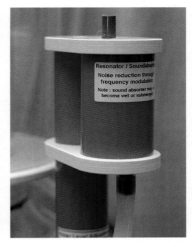

This sump mounted skimmer designed and manufactured by Klaus Jansen in Germany uses his custom Red Dragon pump with aspirator to generate the bubbles, and a foam cartridge on the exit to eliminate bubbles from this stream. J. Sprung

Klaus Jansen's protein skimmer also features a special noise reduction system, far right, to eliminate the sound produced by the air intake hose. J. Sprung

tube should be scrubbed clean. Every three to four months the main body tube may require some scrubbing. A bottlebrush works fine for the main and foam collection tubes while a coffee percolator brush works great on smaller tubes. The inside of the skimmer must be kept clear of algae and any build-up of organic material on the sides. For transparent skimmers, algae growth can be impeded by covering the main body with some opaque material.

There are a few things to keep an eye on when using a protein skimmer. First, the continuous removal of small amounts of seawater by the skimmer, along with replenishment of evaporated water with freshwater, can lead to a gradual lowering of salinity. Therefore, the periodic addition of seawater to the make-up reservoir may be necessary to maintain the desired level of salinity. Secondly, efficient skimmers can remove some trace elements as we mentioned already. The regular addition of trace elements may be especially necessary when protein skimming is used (see chapter 4). Finally, the addition of certain buffers, vitamins and molecular adsorption filter pads can cause the skimmer to foam excessively. Rinse prefilter material and molecular absorption pads in pure freshwater before using them, and add buffers or vitamins very slowly, in small amounts.

The use of ozone with protein skimming
Ozone can be used to improve the efficiency of a protein skimmer in the removal of dissolved organic matter (DOM). Ozone can also be used to disinfect the water within a protein skimmer but a germicidal level of ozone greatly hinders the performance of the skimmer, as we will explain shortly; these levels are normally used in systems with a high bacterial load such as marine mammal systems.

Small organic and inorganic particles often have a similar electrostatic charge. Since like charges repel, these particles remain in the water and are not removed by skimming. However, by using small amounts of ozone, the charges of some of these particles can be changed causing them to clump together with unlike charged particles in a process known as microflocculation (Aiken, 2004). These larger particles are then more susceptible to removal by protein skimming, however, if too much ozone is added then all the particles are altered, no unlike charges remain, and microflocculation does not occur. At higher levels, the ozone will also be begin to break apart the carbon bonds of the long-chain polar molecules attached to the air bubbles within the skimmer, causing them to break apart and go back into solution. This is why a protein skimmer stops producing foam when too much ozone is added. For these reasons, if ozone is used in a protein skimmer the applied ozone dose should be between 0.01 and 0.03 mg O_3/L of water flow through a protein skimmer per minute (Aiken, 2004). When using ozone in this manner, it is best used in conjunction with a redox/ORP controller, which can control the level of ozone added. Levels of 0.10-1.0 mg/L are typically used in contact chambers for germicidal oxidation/disinfection (Aiken, 2004).

Controlling ozone dosage

As we mentioned in chapter 4, ozone is a powerful oxidant and should be used with care. Using too much ozone can lead to formation of residual oxidants such as bromite, bromate and hypobromous acid. Collectively these are referred to as total residual oxidants (TRO). For coral systems, a maximum TRO level of 0.02 mg/L has been suggested (Aiken and Smith, 2004). The level of TRO may be measured using a DPD (N,N-diethyl-p-phenylenediamine) total chlorine colourimetric test (APHA) or an indigo trisulfonate Accu Vac analysis available from Hach (www.hach.com) (Aiken and Smith, 2004). The aquarist should note that ORP alone is not a measurement of the level of TRO and a high ORP level is not always indicative of high TRO levels (Aiken and Smith, 2004). For this reason, if you are using ozone, a test for TRO should be conducted if you suspect high levels of TRO as indicated by the appearance of your animals or unusually high ORP values. Overdosing of ozone can produce excessive levels of TRO but can also result in the direct release of unreacted ozone into the aquarium. It is very important to match ozone dosing rate to biological demand! If oxidizing agents are not consumed by reducing compounds, or excessive ozone is used, persistent and dangerous oxidants may result and ultimately enter an exhibit (Aiken and Smith, 2004)! In the event of an ozone overdose, 2.81 grams of sodium thiosulfate may be used to neutralize 1.00 gram of TRO. The amount needed can be calculated using the following formula:

$$\text{Grams of sodium thiosulphate required} = \frac{\text{Volume (liters) x TRO (mg/L)}}{1000} \text{ X } 2.81$$

From: Aiken and Smith, 2004.

The best way to dose ozone into a skimmer is in conjunction with a redox controller that can be set at high and low ORP set points. Aiken and Smith (2004) recommend a value of between 300 and 380 mV, which is quite conservative seeing that coral reefs can have ORP values of 380 mV or even higher. In chapter 4, we recommended a target of 350-450 mV and this has proven to be acceptable in most instances. As we also mentioned in chapter 4, ORP meters are notoriously unreliable and tend to drift out of calibration easily, therefore if you choose to use one, frequent calibration will be necessary.

One problem with using an ORP controller to regulate the dosage of ozone is that if the amount of ozone being added is too high, the ozone will be constantly switched on and off, meaning there is not a continuous delivery of ozone. This was the problem with the early use of ozone in reef aquariums. The ozone generator was set to its maximum value and the ORP controller simply turned it on or off in response to the ORP level in the aquarium. This was a very inefficient method of using ozone since it meant that no ozone was being added for a good part of the day, and the extremely high levels of ozone added when the unit was on, most likely oxidized the organics so fully, that protein skimming was essentially halted. On the other hand, if not enough ozone is added, ozone will be continuously added but the ORP value will not rise high enough. In either of the above cases, the amount of ozone added needs to be adjusted. The ideal situation is where the ORP value naturally fluctuates around the ideal ORP value without hitting the low or high set point of the controller. Unfortunately, the ozone settings of hobbyist ozone units do not offer a good indication of the amount of ozone actually being delivered to the aquarium. There are various factors that affect the amount of ozone generated such as air pressure, humidity and airflow rate through the unit. The amount of ozone actually added to the aquarium is a factor of the flow rate through the protein skimmer or contact chamber. The best that hobbyists can do is to assure that the ozone unit output is set as we just described, so that the ORP naturally fluctuates within the ideal range and the controller is used to prevent excessive amounts of ozone from being added. The majority of hobbyist reef systems do not employ ozone, and we do not feel that the complications of its use offer significant benefits that can not be realized through alternative, less complicated means, as evidenced by the levels of ORP that are naturally attained in these system. However, the scale of the system affects the significance of the benefit. Large public aquarium systems can employ ozone for water clarification and the reduction of organics, and this application is more cost effective than the use of activated carbon.

For those that wish to apply the type of system employed by public aquariums we offer the following. The applied ozone dose (AOD) can be calculated using values provided by several monitoring devices: 1) a flow meter on the water inlet of the protein skimmer to measure liters of water per minute entering the skimmer, 2) an air flow meter to measure the amount of air pumped into the protein skimmer in liters/minute and 3) a high concentration ozone gas monitor to measure the concentration (mg/L) of ozone in the air supplied to the protein skimmer. Using values from this equipment and the following formula, the AOD can be calculated:

$$\text{Applied Ozone Dose} = \frac{\text{Liters of air/minute} \quad X \quad \text{mg of ozone/liter of air}}{\text{Liters of water/minute}}$$

The AOD should be used as the starting point for an ozone dosing strategy, while measuring TRO should be used as the final control for ozone dosing. Only through the monitoring of AOD, TRO, ORP and taking into account the effects of husbandry (i.e. water changes, adding or removing animals, feeding, cleaning filters, etc.) can an appropriate ozone dosing strategy be employed (Aiken and Smith, 2004).

One aspect of Aiken and Smith's presentation that we feel was not adequately considered was that for reef systems, the biological actions of the inhabitants and their effect on ORP values has to be taken into account. Through biological processes within the aquarium, ORP levels tend to fall during the day as biological activity increases and rise again during the evening. This natural fall and rise needs to be taken into consideration when setting ORP controllers. High or low ORP values may be part of the natural cycle of the aquarium and be entirely independent of the dosing of ozone.

The final word

At the introduction of the topic of protein skimming, we described the natural process of wind and waves generating foam that washes up on shorelines. The foam that collects around coral reefs, best observed at low tide on exposed reef flats, plays a role in nutrient exchange of carbon, nitrogen, and phosphorous. Some of the foam may be broken down by intense solar UV wavelengths that are capable of breaking chemical bonds (much as ozone does). Some of the foam is washed by tides and wind to inner areas of the reef and associated seagrass and mangrove ecosystems. Proteins, carbohydrates, trace elements, bacteria, and other *stuff* attached to bubbles is a significant source of food to filter feeding or particulate feeding organisms in these areas. Mixing of surface waters in the open sea by wind and waves also sets up circulation cells known as Langmuir circulation, and causes any skimmed substances to get mixed back into the water as particulate matter. The particulate matter formed is known to be an important food source (Wotton, 1988). By demonstrating its obvious occurrence in the natural setting, we wish to emphasize that protein skimming is a natural process, and that it is easily duplicated in the care of aquarium systems.

Protein skimming is one of the simplest and most efficient means of water purification for the maintenance of live corals and for the creation of model ecosystems. So much benefit to the aquarium is provided by a device that simply mixes the water with fine bubbles of air.

Reef aquariums without protein skimmers?

Some schools of thought about reef aquarium management shun the use of protein skimming, while others brand it as unnecessary. Indeed, one can establish and maintain reef aquariums without protein skimming. This is easy to demonstrate by including sufficient substratum (sand or gravel) for biological filtration to effect the rapid mineralization of compounds that would otherwise be removed by the protein skimmer. Adding a large sand bed to an existing system filtered with a protein skimmer will reduce the output of the protein skimmer.

Filter-feeding invertebrates such as this feather duster worm get their nutrition from many of the particles and dissolved material that a protein skimmer removes from the water. J. Sprung

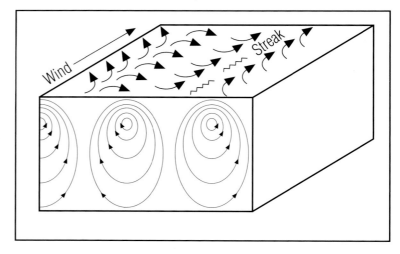

Figure 6o. Langmuir circulation in the sea viewed from the water surface and in cross section. The wind generates circulation that causes organic substances to aggregate along the lines on the surface called windrows. The aggregated material forms both foam that is driven to shore, and particles that are remixed in the water along the circulation lines shown. This circulation in shallow water promotes advection of the particulate mater into the substrata. After Lebedev et al., 1989.

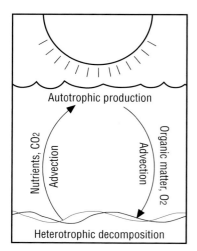

The cultivation of algae in turf filters or refugia also provides an export mechanism that can be a partial substitute for protein skimming, and a compliment to the activity of bacteria living on the substrates. Protein skimmers, in contrast, cannot be thought of as a substitute for the biological filtration that occurs on substrates within an aquarium system. An aquarium can be managed without a protein skimmer, but not without biological filtration. Protein skimmers will nevertheless always be a useful filtration device for enhancing gas exchange, and removing certain types of dissolved organic compounds, bacteria and especially phosphate.

Figure 6p.1. (above) Coral reef nutrient dynamics involve the recycling of coral mucus in the sand bed. Biological decomposition of this source of DOC and POC liberates other nutrients. This recycling is especially promoted in skimmerless aquariums. Example, Heron Island reef ecosystem, Figure 6p.2. (right).

1) Insoluble mucus release: C: 27.7, N: 1.9, P: 0.3 kmol/day

2) Soluble mucus release: C: 90.9, N: 7.6, P: 1.3 kmol/day. Contribution to oxygen consumption in water 0.1 to 2.5%. About 15% of lagoon water is filtered per day through the sand bed. Carbon turnover $\geq$ 7%/hour.

3) Mucus with trapped particles (marine snow): C: 181.8, N: 17.0, P: 0.2 kmol/day

4) Rapid entry by advection into sand bed, consumption by benthic fauna and bacteria, causing 10-20% of the oxygen consumption in the sandbed.

5) Potential nutrient realease: N: 18.2, P: 0.4 kmol/day

Modified, after Huettel, 2004.

www.ocean.fsu.edu/faculty/huettel/coral.html

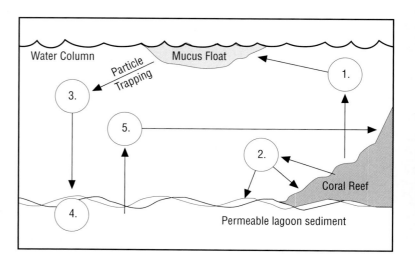

Far be it from me to be skeptical of Mr. Lee; I believe him implicitly; but here's the hitch: Where is an aquarist who wants to set up a tank like this going to get live coral (rock)?...There is an alternative: Move to the Island of Bali. Lots of palm trees, beautiful native girls, beautiful marine fishes, and live coral by the tons. Coming anyone?

— editorial comment following the article by Lee Chin Eng
published in Tropical Fish Hobbyist Magazine, February, 1961

Several methods or *disciplines* exist regarding the proper way to establish a living reef aquarium. While some feature the use of technology to purify the water with an assortment of external filter devices and fancy electronic gadgets, other *natural* approaches rely mostly on biological filtration occurring within the aquarium's rock, sand and gravel decor. *Natural systems* of many kinds have been gaining in popularity over the last two decades. As a result, the reef aquarium hobby has grown internationally, with systems that are successful, affordable and manageable for the average aquarist. Who would have imagined, in 1961, that live rock and corals from the tropical seas would be distributed by air cargo to be utilized in aquariums all over the world? Then who would have imagined that farming live rock and corals would become another industry?

The Lee Chin Eng natural system

Long before the reef-keeping craze took hold of the aquarium hobby, Lee Chin Eng of the Prinsen Park Aquarium, Jakarta, Indonesia wrote an article published in *Tropical Fish Hobbyist Magazine* (Eng, 1961), describing a system, if you can call it that, which he called *Nature's system of Keeping Marine Fishes*. The method was developed in 1955 by Mr. Tan Soen Hway of Banguwangi, East Java, but it is attributed to Lee Chin Eng since he wrote about it.

In his 1961 article, Lee Chin Eng wrote: *Here is Nature's system: Follow Nature as closely as possible; all can be done except wave and current in the aquarium, but this could be duplicated with an airstone. Set up a non-toxic aquarium, collect and pour in real sea water of a density of approximately 1.022. Don't filter the water but keep the aerator running in order to keep the plankton living. Select nicely shaped corals from the sea that contain microscopic plants and sea-weeds, arrange the corals all over the bottom and with many hiding-places in the back. Never boil or bleach the corals; if you do, you kill all the necessary plants, worms and other marine animals which live among these corals and which are the very important things that help balance the aquarium. If you put in the right corals, within a day or two the water will become crystal clear, after which you may put in anemones for your Clownfishes.*

The brief article also discussed the success Mr. Lee had with numerous delicate fishes, and the spawning and rearing of clownfish. It is clear from the description that he used the word *coral* to describe both live corals and live coral rock. Riseley (1971) gives more detail regarding Lee's use of live sand and live rock. If you thought that natural systems began with Lee Chin Eng, you would be mistaken. The earliest marine aquariums were essentially natural system aquariums, being duplications of tidepool habitats. One of the earliest publications featuring a reef aquarium, from the 1920's in Indonesia, also employed the natural system method (Verwey, 1930).

As one can tell from Lee's description, there really isn't much to explain about the set up, at least on the surface. Of course, what happens in these aquariums biologically, chemically and physically is another story. The basic set up includes a layer of *live* sand or gravel, live rock, seawater and an air bubbler. It is apparent from photos of Mr. Lee's aquariums that he at least sometimes moved the water with large bubbles escaping from beneath flat stones instead of relying on the finer bubbles produced by an airstone. A modern Lee Chin Eng-style installation might include powerheads for moving the water in addition to the air bubbler, and would likely have some form of high intensity lighting. Lee's aquariums utilized some artificial and some natural daylight. Modern reef keepers would also pay attention to the calcium and alkalinity levels to promote the growth of corals. Mr. Lee did not focus his attention on growing corals. His was a natural system for maintaining fishes.

In our experience, these systems are easy to create and maintain. However, there are a couple of caveats: 1. As with any saltwater system employing air bubbles to move the water, one must be careful about salt creep developing and falling back into the tank and; 2. Since no surface skimming is employed, the nighttime oxygen level can fall quite low, which limits the capacity to house a large fish population. 3. The live rock used must be cured first (see chapter 2), as this is the key to developing the bacteria needed to biologically filter the water, and decomposing any sponges or other marinelife that died in transport. This key point about biological filtration was not well understood when Robert P.L. Straughan wrote in the June 1961 issue of *Tropical Fish Hobbyist* magazine:

No doubt many hobbyists will be interested in starting a natural aquarium after reading Mr. Lee Chin Eng's article about Nature's system of keeping marine fishes...if they do start one, they will need two things: live coral and a plentiful supply of pinch type clothespins. The coral is for the aquarium and the clothespins are for your nose when the coral dies, for the odor will be devastating...

In the same article, he added the following caveat:

one little overlooked piece of information may cause plenty of trouble for you.

Starting the aquarium with fresh uncured rock was possible for Lee Chin Eng because there was little transport involved, and so nothing on the rock died and fouled. This was the *little overlooked piece of information* that prevented many aquarists from realizing Eng's success. All that was needed was to wait a few weeks for the rock to cure, but this was never done since the natural response to the problem would be to *GET THE STINK OUT*, as Straughan recounts:

I was plagued by the smell of dead coral in one of my New England aquarium shops, back in 1948. I had set up a tank, using live coral, and I must admit that it looked beautifully natural. Upon opening the store on the very next morning, however, it seemed that the door was actually straining under the odor of the pungent gas that had been generated by the decaying organisms in the tank. The smell nearly made my hair stand on end.

Faced with such a mess, no one would just let the tank sit. The next step was to throw everything out and develop a strong conviction backed by such a memorable odiferous lesson that this natural system stuff was a hoax. Had the live rock been properly maintained with strong water circulation and aeration, the smell generated during the few weeks of curing would have been minimal, and the bad experience would have been avoided. It took another 20 years for this to be widely realized, and then the reef-keeping hobby could grow. By that time, however, the simplicity of Lee's system was lost and technical gadgets and external biological filters were promoted as the basis for the filtration. Nearly another 20 years later, the deconstruction of technology brings us back to appreciating numerous simple natural systems, all basically variations on what Lee Chin Eng wrote about. The inclusion of a surface skimmer in the design, for example, would essentially convert Lee's system to a *Berlin* system, but without a protein skimmer.

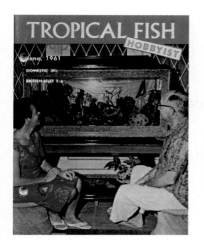

The aquarium of Mr. and Mrs. Saunders setup by Lee Chin Eng in 1960. Originally published on the cover of *Tropical Fish Hobbyist* magazine, in June, 1961.

Figure 6q. Lee Chin Eng's System

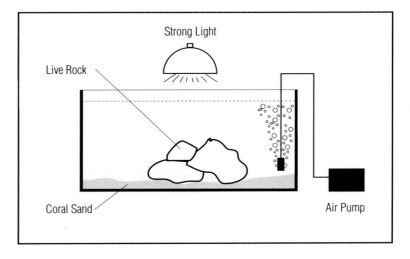

A close-up photo of the Saunders' Lee Chin Eng natural system aquarium. Originally published in *Tropical Fish Hobbyist* magazine, June, 1961.

One of the earliest published photos of a reef aquarium, taken in April 1930 at the Onrust Aquarium in Indonesia (Verwey, 1930).

Dr. Bruce Carlson, photographed at the Waikiki Aquarium in 1978 with the first exhibit of live south Pacific corals at a US aquarium. The system employed for maintaining it was similar to Eng's, but included an undergravel filter. The sideburns were in style then but had no influence on the functioning of the system. Waikiki Aquarium

Jaubert's Monaco system

The public aquarium displays and the coral reef research facilities located in the Oceanographic Museum of Monaco utilize a system developed by Dr. Jean Jaubert of the University of Nice, France, which uses a very simple system for biological filtration. The system employs a unique form of biological filtration (French patent number 03 28474) within the aquarium utilizing the calcareous substratum (coral sand and gravel) and the various micro- and meiofaunal organisms contained within (Jaubert, 1989). The tank contains a perforated false bottom, similar to an undergravel filter plate, under which a body of confined water exists in a *void space* known as the plenum. A thick layer of calcareous gravel is placed on top of this plate. The oxygen content of the water above the gravel is high while that of the water below the plate is low. This allows aerobic

One of the largest Jaubert Monaco style exhibits in the world, this 500,000 L (132,086 gallon) exhibit can be seen at the National Museum of Marine Biology and Aquarium in Taiwan (http://www.nmmba.gov.tw/). Dr. A-Y. Fan

nitrifying bacteria to colonize the upper layer and heterotrophic denitrifying bacteria to exist in the lower layer (Jaubert, 1989). Jaubert (1989) theorized that movement of substances such as oxygen, nitrate, ammonium, nitrite, nitrogen and carbon dioxide through the substratum, occurred solely by the process of diffusion.

Large organic debris is broken down by small burrowing animals in the upper layer and their wastes, in turn are mineralized by aerobic bacteria. Nitrification then occurs in the upper layer and the subsequent nitrate produced, diffuses downwards where denitrifying bacteria convert the nitrate to atmospheric nitrogen (Jaubert, 1989). Yellowing compounds are supposedly eliminated or neutralized by undetermined processes (Jaubert, 1989). Jaubert claimed that acidic secretions by bacteria are neutralized by the calcareous sand and the resulting input of calcium ions was adequate to keep calcium levels high enough to allow for growth of the hard corals in the system. In our experience, the calcium and alkalinity demands of today's SPS dominated reef aquaria cannot be met by the use of a plenum system located within the aquarium alone and Jaubert also later changed his opinion on this, as we shall discuss shortly.

Since Jaubert's system was first featured there, it has come to be called the *Monaco System* by some aquarists. Others call it simply *Jaubert's method* or *Natural Nitrate Reduction* (NNR), the latter name coined by American aquarist/author Bob Goemans, who has written extensively about his own experiences with modified Jaubert systems. Jaubert's system was first introduced to North American aquarists by Tom Frakes, who visited Jaubert and reported what he saw in Monaco in his talk at the first Marine Aquarium Conference of North America, MACNA I, held in Toronto Canada in 1989, and subsequently in his article in SeaScope (Frakes, 1993). In 1990, we also published a detailed account of Jaubert's system as well as the Berlin system (Delbeek and Sprung, 1990).

The museum in Monaco is located on the shore of the Mediterranean, and has a limitless supply of natural seawater on tap. The aquarium systems can be managed as open system aquariums, and many of the displays there are maintained via water exchange of 5% per day with Mediterranean seawater. Some are closed systems. A feature of most of the aquariums is prolific growth of corals, particularly of *Stylophora pistillata*, *Pavona* spp., *Montipora* spp., *Galaxea fascicularis* and *Acropora* spp., but also many other species of stony and soft corals. Most of the corals there are from the Red Sea, but there are also some Caribbean gorgonians and some corals from Indonesia. Many of the exhibits are created entirely with corals grown *in house* at the Museum, not harvested from the wild. The aquariums also feature large populations of colourful reef fishes, including many butterfly and angelfish species not commonly maintained together with live corals in aquaria.

The plenum

The plenum space should be at least 1 cm (3/8 inch) in height but can be quite a bit taller. For most home aquariums, a plenum space of about 2 to 3 cm (about 3/4 to 1.6 inches) is sufficient. A support structure must be utilized to hold the weight of the gravel and any rocks placed over the plenum. It must also be stable in seawater. Since it is installed in the gravel bed at the bottom of the aquarium, any repair would require emptying the tank completely. The support can be as simple and inexpensive as the plastic plate from an undergravel filter, or it can be constructed by attaching plastic screening to a sheet of the inexpensive grid-like plastic light diffuser material *eggcrate*, supported by cut lengths of PVC pipe. Jaubert uses thin rigid PVC sheets perforated with a grid of thousands of small holes, and cut lengths of PVC pipe for supports attached underneath. It is important to use an open structured material (i.e. with many holes) that allows dissolved compounds to diffuse between the gravel layer and the plenum space, but does not allow the gravel to fall through the holes into the plenum.

It is important here to define diffusive flow because it is something often misunderstood by aquarists. The diffusion that takes place from the body of water above the sand into the sand bed and into the plenum space does not, in the strictest definition, involve movement of water. In the strict definition of diffusion, things dissolved in the water (the solutes), not the water itself, are exchanged or transported between the above-mentioned different water bodies. The process is driven by concentration gradients and biologically mediated reactions. In the real world (including aquariums), the process is assisted by the movement of the water above the sand bed caused by currents and wave action, and within the sand bed due to the activity of burrowing infauna. Such water movement enhances advective movement of both water and solutes from the water above into the sand bed, continuously bringing more of the latter deeper in the sand bed where it then diffuses downward into the plenum. Biologically mediated reactions tend to produce redox zones in the sand bed that prevent, inhibit or slow down the outward diffusion of certain solutes (H_2S for example). These processes occur within any sand bed, whether a plenum is placed there or not.

The function of the plenum, the distinguishing feature of Jaubert's system, appears at first to be shrouded by mystery. Many aquarists believe the plenum serves no function. Our experience contradicts their opinion. In our experience, Jaubert's system does work differently for biological filtration than just putting gravel on the aquarium bottom without a plenum. However, according to Toonan and Wee (2004), the difference in efficiency of nitrification and denitrification rates measurable in the body of water above the sand bed may be insignificant. In our experience, the gravel placed over a plenum is not as badly filled with detritus over time. If our observation regarding detritus accumulation is correct, and the difference is significant, the long-term efficiency of the sand bed for both nitrification and denitrification may be more stable when a plenum is used, even if the difference is not significant within the first year or two. However, the placement of rock on the sand bed, which is minimized in Jaubert's system, may be the main reason for the reduced detritus load (see earlier discussion of advection).

The plenum provides a layer of water below the gravel bed that maintains a level of dissolved oxygen above zero. Therefore, the gravel in Jaubert's system is sandwiched between the highly

A tight fitting plenum and screen flush with the walls of the aquarium prevents the passage of gravel below and provides a view of the plenum space. A. Correa

A newly set up plenum system exhibits layering of water in the plenum space. The yellow colour may be a bacteria bloom or concentrated dissolved organic matter. In either case, the concentrating effect of diffusive flow is illustrated. J. Sprung

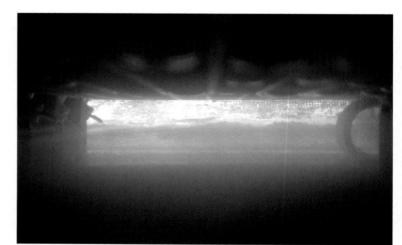

The plenum can be constructed with PVC pipe, plastic light diffuser eggcrate, cable ties, and plastic screen. J. Sprung

The dimensions of the plenum support can be smaller than the bottom of the tank so that gravel can fill the space between it and the glass. The support must prevent gravel from sliding into the plenum space of course. J. Sprung

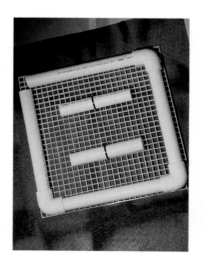

oxygenated aquarium water circulating above it, and the plenum water, which maintains a low but generally stable level of dissolved oxygen. Hydrogen sulfide can form in any thick sand bed, but since the gravel is sandwiched between oxygenated zones in Jaubert's system, it tends to prevent the formation of hydrogen sulfide, a common occurrence in deep sand beds without a plenum. Since hydrogen sulfide inhibits biological filtration (Spotte, 1992), the prevention of its formation has the opposite effect. Within the gravel bed above the plenum, there are regions where the oxygen level approaches zero. That is where denitrification occurs. One might wonder what maintains the oxygen in the plenum space. It is likely produced by partial breakdown of nitrate, but it may be a byproduct of other reactions within the deeper layers of the gravel. These reactions involve the breakdown of organic matter, both dissolved and particulate, a

(Above) A simple aquarium created by Julian Sprung using Jaubert's system, dominated by a single Leather coral. J. Sprung

This Jaubert system set up with live sand finer than the recommended 3-6mm size exhibited hydrogen sulfide formation extending from the plenum upwards into the gravel bed for the first two weeks. Afterwards it did not have this problem and invertebrates could be seen living in the plenum space. J. Sprung

This aquarium, using a deep layer of fine sand without a plenum, shows an example of hydrogen sulfide development, the dark spot against the glass. Development of H2S pockets are more common in finer substrata, but can occur in any deep sand or gravel layer. The plenum seems to reduce their occurrence, however. J. Sprung

food source for some of the bacteria that convert nitrate to nitrogen gas. The gravel does not become extremely dirty with accumulated detritus apparently because the denitrifying bacteria utilize the detritus, or possibly, because there is less rock placed on the bottom so there is less advective forcing of detritus into the substratum. Of course, in any sand bed, worms, protozoans, copepods, amphipods, and other creatures also help to maintain a healthy environment by feeding on detritus while gradually turning over the sand and gravel. There is a lot of life in the bottom substratum.

Differences between Jaubert's system and other sand bed filtration methods aside from the plenum, can account for biological filtration capacity differences. The size of gravel used affects the pore water (water within substrata) oxygen levels, organic levels, and ammonia levels (Capone *et al.*, 1992). The volume of sand or gravel used is another difference that can account for a differing biological filtration capacity. For example, Berlin systems have 2.5 cm (1 inch) to 7.5 cm (3 inches) of bottom substrata, compared to 10 cm (4 inches) in Jaubert's system. The quantity of rock is also different. Berlin systems generally use much more rock than Jaubert systems, which would compensate for the lower quantity of bottom substrata. The preliminary study by Toonen and Wee (2004) needs to be followed up with further comparisons that consider the non-equal aspects of these systems when established according to their strict definitions.

The substratum

The gravel in Jaubert's systems has been termed *live* sand, as it has in other natural systems such as Eng's (Riseley, 1971) and Dr. Adey's (Adey and Loveland, 1991). The use of this term in connection with Jaubert's systems is misleading because the size of the grains used is much coarser than sand. Other authors describing the installation of a plenum and sand bed have suggested layering different size grains of gravel and sand, starting with coarse on the bottom and becoming fine on the top. Since the sand bed is not intended to function as a mechanical filter, and because it must allow good diffusion of solutes in order to function properly, the idea about layering makes no sense, since it could inhibit diffusion. Jaubert does not make layers of different size sands in his aquaria. He uses one type of coarse gravel only (grains mostly between 2 and 5 mm), not sand. Jaubert uses a screen midway in the gravel between the plenum and the top of the gravel, to prevent burrowing creatures from disturbing the lower layer and exposing the plenum. It is possible to set up aquariums without any such screen by just leaving out the diggers (i.e. gobies, pistol shrimps). If you want to have burrowing creatures, you must use a screen, approximately 5 cm (2 inches) above the plenum. A better alternative to placing a screen there was devised by Todd Schwarz. He covers the screen with a couple of layers of the black plastic geotextile material called Enkamat®. It has a structure that is tight enough to prevent diggers from disturbing the lower gravel layers and open enough to allow gravel to seep through it.

This modified plenum support structure built by Todd Schwarz uses the geotextile material Enkamat® to prevent burrowers from exposing the water of the plenum space. The gravel simply slides into the void spaces of the Enkamat®. J. Sprung

The gravel bed should be approximately 8-10 cm (3.2 - 4 inches) thick. The Jaubert system does not work well with a layer of gravel less than 8 cm (3.2 inches) thick over a plenum. If the gravel layer is too thin, denitrification is incomplete. As a result, the nitrate level remains high in the aquarium, and there may be a chronic problem with nitrite as well. The same problem occurs if burrowing fish or invertebrates are allowed to excavate and reduce the amount of gravel covering the plenum or if water currents push sand to create thinner areas over sections of the plenum. In a Jaubert system installation at the Enoshima Aquarium in Japan, strong water currents aimed directly downward onto the bottom gravel resulted in elevated nitrate levels as oxygen enriched water was forced deeply into the gravel bed, hindering denitrification (J.C. Delbeek, pers. obs.). Many aquarists believe the thick layer of gravel is a negative feature to the Jaubert system, from an aesthetic point of view. In addition, a thick layer of gravel along with a plenum can greatly reduce the space available in the aquarium for live rock, corals and fish. These aesthetic and functional concerns can be resolved by utilizing the Jaubert system with the thick gravel bed in an attached refugium aquarium. In this way, the display aquarium can contain as much or as little gravel as is deemed aesthetically pleasing.

Aquariums with no plenum can achieve denitrification in a thinner layer of fine sand, but in our opinion, it is not as effective as a thicker layer of coarse gravel over a plenum. The fine sand method also has a higher risk of developing hydrogen sulfide gas

This display aquarium at *The Fish Store and More* in Atlanta, Georgia uses Jaubert's method. Note the amount of space given to the gravel bed. J. Sprung.

(which can kill fish rapidly if it escapes suddenly), though this risk can be reduced to nothing by the use of strong water currents. Author Dr. Ron Shimek is a proponent of the use of thick beds [25 cm (10 inches) or more] of fine sand without a plenum. He claims that such thick beds do not have a problem with hydrogen sulfide, and they function well for denitrification. The method works as good as any other natural system, with some caveats, and we describe it in more detail separately.

Another distinguishing feature of Jaubert's aquariums is the paucity of live rock. Aquarists familiar with the *Berlin method* are accustomed to live rock filling 1/3 or more of the aquarium volume. In a properly established Jaubert system aquarium there is much less rock, leaving wide expanses of the bottom uncovered. The reason for this is twofold. First, since the biological filtration occurs within the gravel bed, the live rock is not needed for biological filtration. One can set up a Jaubert system with no rock at all. Its purpose is just for decoration and the introduction of biodiversity. The second reason for the paucity of rock is that the surface of the gravel bed should be left uncovered as much as possible. This allows unrestricted exchange of oxygen and other dissolved substances, and minimizes advection of detritus into the substrata.

Having less mass of rock in the aquarium offers some other advantages. It offers more freedom of design for beautiful, natural-looking aquascapes. In fact, some of the aquascapes at the Oceanographic Museum in Monaco are the nicest we have ever seen in a public aquarium. Having less rock also means that there is less demand for calcium carbonate because calcium depositing coralline algae normally cover the surface of live rock.

An exhibit at the Oceanographic Museum in Monaco featuring a Red Sea regal angelfish, lionfish, a large bubble coral, and the soft coral *Sinularia*. J. Sprung

Another display at the Oceanographic Museum in Monaco. Note that the live rock is suspended from the rear wall of the aquarium, leaving the substrata below it uncovered. J. Sprung.

Filtration

With the introduction of Jaubert's method to the aquarium industry, there has been a proliferation of erroneous claims and recommendations, some made by Jaubert himself, but most by other people who had little experience with the system. We address these issues here, along with some observations of our own, now that we've had many years to test the system.

Protein skimming

Since the denitrifying bacteria need an organic food source, one might suppose that using a protein skimmer could result in a removal of too much of this food, to the detriment of the performance of the system for denitrification. It seems like a reasonable assumption, but in practice, the use of protein skimming does not have any noticeable effect on the denitrifying ability of a Jaubert system. Conversely, it is our experience that the installation

This Jaubert system set up by Carlos Moreno (far left) in Brazil features a reef crest environment with high flow. It also is skimmed with *Tunze* protein skimmers and uses a Knop calcium reactor. J. Sprung.

of a large surface area gravel bed over a plenum does in fact reduce the output of the protein skimmer! Therefore, one can say that the gravel bed can biologically process much of what the protein skimmer removes, and it does so in competition with the skimmer. Nevertheless, protein skimmers are effective at removing phosphate from the water, an advantage that must be addressed in systems running without skimmers.

Algae

As in any strongly illuminated aquarium, the management of algae creates a need for herbivores, so Jaubert's system is no exception in this regard. However, one noticeable difference in these systems is that a properly functioning gravel bed of sufficient size will dramatically reduce the growth of algae on the windows of the aquarium. The bacteria in a healthy gravel bed are capable of breaking down nitrogenous waste so quickly as to be able to limit the growth of algae (and corals- we'll say more about that in a moment). Starting from scratch with a sterile system, however, Jaubert systems show a prolific growth of macroalgae lasting approximately six months. Thereafter the algae growth slows down or stops completely unless the aquarium is fed heavily enough to increase its growth.

Yellow water

Yellowing of the water in closed system aquariums is an inevitable effect due to the accumulation of dissolved large organic compounds. While it is true that some dissolved organic compounds are broken down by the processes in the gravel bed in Jaubert's system, this does not mean that the processes prevent the water from turning yellow. Jaubert's systems may not become yellow as quickly or as severely as other aquariums, but they do become yellow. Activated carbon or ozone can be used to manage water-tinting dissolved organic matter.

Aeration

Many of the closed system aquariums in Monaco utilize aeration for water motion. The benefits include the removal of phosphate (Spotte, 1992), no heat transfer to the water, low electrical power consumption, and plankton-friendliness. The disadvantage of aeration is salt spray formation, which produces salt creep and corrosion of materials near the aquarium. A potential problem with Jaubert systems is solved by aeration. If the aquarium does not employ a surface-skimming overflow, the nighttime oxygen level may fall to extremely low levels (J. Sprung, pers. obs.), which is stressful or even fatal to fishes. It is likely that a low oxygen level at night could also promote the release of hydrogen sulfide from the gravel, which would suffocate the fishes. A surface-skimming overflow insures sufficient gas exchange to keep the oxygen from falling too low, and rapidly causes an off gassing of any hydrogen sulfide. In the absence of a surface-skimming overflow, it is necessary to include an airstone or bubbler to keep the oxygen level up at night and quickly dissipate any hydrogen sulfide that might be released into the water.

Calcium and trace element maintenance

Jaubert originally promoted the idea that the aragonite gravel in his systems dissolves, and that this dissolution supplies the calcium and alkalinity needed for coral growth. Deep within the gravel bed the pH is low, and this effect, along with the production of organic acids may dissolve the gravel, liberating some calcium and carbonate to the water.

Filtration

Jaubert's explanation of the dissolution of calcareous sand is tied to the denitrification process. Denitrifying heterotrophic bacteria in the sand bed oxidize the organic carbon (equation 1) they feed on by reducing nitrates. This organic carbon is mainly produced as the waste of the small organisms that live in the sand bed. The most effective of these are worms, which collect their food by sweeping the surface of the sand with their tentacles. When the organic food used by the bacteria is broken down, it results in the production of carbonic acid (dissolved carbon dioxide) within the sand bed, which hydrates and slowly dissolves the sand grains (equations 2 & 3).

$$1.\ CH_2O + O_2 \rightarrow CO_2 + H_2O$$
$$2.\ CO_2 + H_2O \rightarrow H_2CO_3$$
$$3.\ H_2CO_3 + CaCO_3 \rightarrow 2HCO_3^- + Ca^{2+}$$

Jaubert (1989) reported calcium levels of 460 - 520 mg/L measured in one of his experimental aquariums, but this aquarium had a much lower number of SPS corals than some modern reef aquariums. In aquariums with strong illumination and strong coral growth, the quantity of calcium and carbonates released is not sufficient to keep up with the demand as we mentioned in chapter 5. Jaubert later observed (J. Jaubert, pers. comm.) that the addition of kalkwasser or other means of calcium and alkalinity maintenance must be employed to maintain the calcium and alkalinity demands for his closed system aquariums when they have large coral populations.

Some authors have suggested that the dissolving substratum provides an ample supply of all necessary trace elements. This is simply not true. It is true that dissolving gravel supplies some strontium, magnesium, and other minerals such as iron, but not

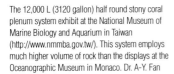

The 12,000 L (3120 gallon) half round stony coral plenum system exhibit at the National Museum of Marine Biology and Aquarium in Taiwan (http://www.nmmba.gov.tw/). This system employs much higher volume of rock than the displays at the Oceanographic Museum in Monaco. Dr. A-Y. Fan

sufficiently to meet the requirements of the growing corals, and there are other elements such as iodine that are not supplied by dissolving of the gravel. One must remember that the food added to the aquarium is an important source of trace elements, and water changes may bring in a supply of a few trace elements in excess of natural seawater values. See chapter 4 for a detailed discussion of this topic.

Light

Illumination of a Jaubert system aquarium is not different from what is used for any other reef aquarium system. The effect of the light is important as it relates to the effect photosynthesis has on the oxygen and pH of the body of water above the gravel. Jaubert's patent refers to this effect, comparing the high dissolved oxygen and high pH in the aquarium water with the low dissolved oxygen and low pH of the water in the gravel and plenum. This potential difference caused by the effect of the light assists the diffusion of dissolved substances through the gravel.

Gravel turning into rock

Some aquarists have reported a problem with gravel fusing into a solid mass of rock. This occurrence of course can prevent the proper functioning of the gravel bed as a biological filter, though if the mass is still porous it might not be so problematic. We believe this problem is caused by a combination of very high alkalinity and pH levels, combined with certain types of aragonite gravel, oolitic sand in particular. The problem is not common, and until the exact environmental causes are described, we cannot offer definitive advice on how to prevent it. It may be related to spontaneous precipitation of calcium carbonate fusing the grains together, but an alternative hypothesis proposed by Shimek (2001) is that it is not caused by calcium carbonate at all, but by bacterial exopolymers, polysaccharide compounds outside the bacterial cell walls and secreted by the bacteria. It is possible that more than one process can cause sand or gravel to fuse into a solid mass. For example, we have witnessed sponges growing within the gravel bed that caused localized solid masses as the gravel became incorporated within the tissue mass of the sponge.

Plenum water

Some authors have suggested that the plenum water accumulates nutrients and therefore needs to be changed periodically. Jaubert never made this claim. Through a tube extending up from the plenum, or a bulkhead fitting with a drain and valve underneath the aquarium, it is possible to take water samples from the plenum for testing.

Delbeek (unpubl. data; 2000 MACNA XIII presentation) studied the levels of various water quality parameters in the plenum of a 1900 L (500 gallon) reef aquarium at the Waikiki Aquarium over a three year period. The aquarium was set up using water from the Waikiki Aquarium's saltwater well, a source that is high in inorganic nutrients (Atkinson *et al.*, 1995). Water changes (~10 %) were made infrequently using this water and therefore represented periodic inputs of ammonia, phosphate and silicate. The plenum was constructed with fly screen over Vexar screening laid on a platform of fiberglass grating. Two inch, PVC couplings were attached to the bottom of the grating to create the plenum space. Fine live sand collected from off of Waikiki by SCUBA was mixed with coarse calcareous gravel to create a bed of approximately 10 cm (4 inches) in thickness. Lighting consisted of two 400 W Radium 20,000 K metal halides and

The Waikiki Aquarium's surge coral exhibit constructed with a plenum. Photo taken in December 1997, 1.5 years after set up. B. Carlson

natural sunlight. Filtration was composed of an ETS 1800 protein skimmer and a small amount of activated carbon. There was no mechanical filtration of any kind used. Water motion consisted of two Carlson surge devices (see CSD, chapter 7) of 55 and 35 gallons capacity, powerheads and a single return line from the pump feeding water to the CSDs. An MKR II calcium reactor was used and 10 mL of a 1% solution of potassium iodide was added weekly. The pH ranged from 8.1-8.4 over 24 hours and the alkalinity was maintained between 2.0 and 3.0 meq/L. Water samples were taken every three months from the aquarium and, via a bulkhead and valve, from below the plenum. Testing was performed by filtering the tank and plenum water samples through a sediment filter and then refrigerating them before sending them to the University of Hawaii for analysis.

Graph A. Ammonia levels in plenum and tank water, contrasted with natural seawater and Waikiki Aquarium saltwater well-water values. Day 0 on all graphs represents 20 days after initial tank setup.

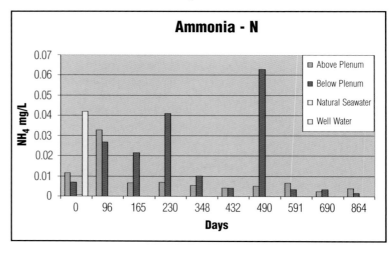

Ammonia (NH$_4$)

After a period of about four months, the ammonia levels within the aquarium fell to a level ranging between 0.002 and 0.005 mg/L, values approximately five times that of natural seawater levels. Ammonia levels in the plenum sometimes showed much higher levels and at other times lower levels. A fluctuation in ammonia levels in both the aquarium and plenum can be seen over the course of the study.

Nitrite/Nitrate (NO$_2$/NO$_3$)

Nitrite/nitrate levels in the aquarium took almost a year to drop to close to natural seawater values; at times, it even dropped below nsw levels. The plenum levels were always higher but never exceeded 0.1 mg/L after the first year. Fluctuations in nitrite/nitrate levels can be seen in both the plenum and the aquarium water.

Graph B. Nitrite/Nitrate levels in plenum and tank water, contrasted with natural seawater and Waikiki Aquarium saltwater well-water values.

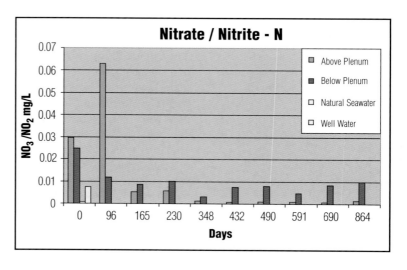

Graph C. Organic nitrogen levels in plenum and tank water, contrasted with natural seawater and Waikiki Aquarium saltwater well-water values.

Graph D. Inorganic phosphate levels in plenum and tank water, contrasted with natural seawater values and Waikiki Aquarium saltwater well-water values.

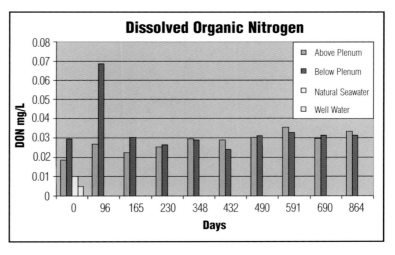

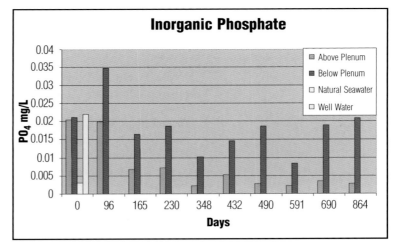

Dissolved organic nitrogen (DON)

Dissolved organic nitrogen levels varied little between the plenum and the aquarium. Values were two to three times higher than natural seawater values over the course of the study. There were slight fluctuations in DON levels over the three years of the study accompanied by a gradual yet steady increase over time in both the aquarium and plenum. The elevated DON levels were most likely due to inadequate activated carbon usage. The use of ozone or ultraviolet light may have lowered DON levels to that of nsw.

Inorganic phosphate (PO_4)

In graph D, it can be seen that phosphate levels fluctuated throughout the study with plenum levels three to five times that of aquarium water levels. Inorganic phosphate levels in the water column took over a year to reach natural seawater levels and could

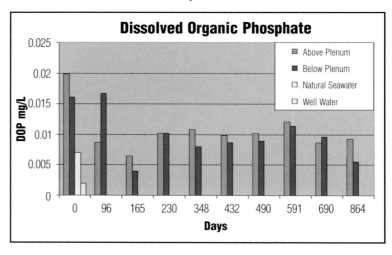

Graph E. Dissolved organic phosphate levels in plenum and tank water, contrasted with natural seawater values and Waikiki Aquarium saltwater well-water values.

sometimes be lower than natural seawater levels. It is interesting to note that the plenum levels never rose much above 0.02 mg/L, the value that is often cited as the maximum value to be tolerated in a reef aquarium. It is also interesting to note that the phosphate levels in the plenum lag behind the levels in the aquarium, that is, the aquarium levels drop, and then the plenum levels drop.

Dissolved organic phosphate (DOP)

As with DON, DOP levels between the plenum and water column did not differ that greatly. Levels remained constant and are close to or 0.5-1.0X that of natural seawater values but fluctuation in levels in both water bodies can be seen over the course of the year.

Silicate

Silicate levels dropped below natural seawater levels in the aquarium water, but remained slightly elevated in the plenum. As with the other parameters tested, silicate levels fluctuated over the course of the study.

Our practical experience with this system, including measurement of nitrate and phosphate levels from plenum water samples, convinces us that the system is dynamic, and so the plenum water is not a nutrient sink. At times nutrient levels rise, but they also fall again, so they do not accumulate. It is true that nitrate and nitrite may be found in the plenum water at levels much higher than in the water above the gravel. Sometimes phosphate and silicate levels are elevated in the plenum as well. However, the levels do not stay high, and the plenum water does not cause sudden fluctuations in the water quality of the aquarium, as has been suggested by some authors. An exception can occur when a burrowing fish or shrimp moves away enough

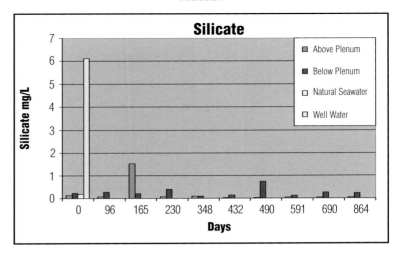

Graph F. Silicate levels in plenum and tank water, contrasted with natural seawater values and Waikiki Aquarium saltwater well-water values.

gravel to expose the plenum water. That could cause a sudden nutrient influx into the tank and a resulting strong growth of algae. The second screen layer or use of Enkamat[®] described earlier prevents such burrowing from exposing the plenum.

One of the interesting results of the Waikiki Aquarium plenum study was the periodic rise and fall in all of the parameters studied. One possible explanation was offered by Dr. Marlin Atkinson of the University of Hawaii. In nutrient analyses of the Biosphere 2 ocean system, Dr. Atkinson found similar fluctuations in nutrient levels. He attributed these to changes in productivity of the ocean due to seasonal changes in light levels. When light levels and photoperiod was greatest in the summer months, productivity increased and nutrient levels dropped. In the winter months, productivity dropped and nutrient levels rose. The same may have occurred with the Waikiki Aquarium plenum system since the system was exposed to natural light and photoperiod. However, similar fluctuations in nutrient levels were found in a plenum system operated at the Great Barrier Reef Marine Park Aquarium (aka ReefHQ) in Townsville, Australia, but this system was not exposed to natural sunlight (P. Hough, unpubl. data). In addition, Pecorelli *et al.* (2004) also reported no seasonal fluctuations in water quality in the 2.5 million liter (~660,000 gallons) tank at the Great Barrier Reef Marine Park Authority Aquarium (ReefHQ), which is open to natural sunlight, though it should be pointed out that this system does not have a plenum. However, it does bring to mind the question of what role the ATS filters (or the algae in the system) had on mitigating increases in nutrients during periods of lower productivity in the winter.

The Australian plenum system also exhibited a similar lag time between plenum and surface water nutrient levels as seen in the Waikiki Aquarium study. It should be clear that a plenum system is a dynamic one, with nutrients exhibiting periodic fluctuations. Paul Hough, former curator of the GBRMPA, related to us that he found that any changes to the aquarium such as new animal additions, water changes, loss of organisms etc., caused subsequent changes in the plenum with nutrient levels fluctuating more widely. Eventually the fluctuations reduced. In general, a plenum system can take anywhere from three to six months before inorganic nutrient levels begin to approach natural seawater levels. There was a gradual increase in DON and DOP, but it cannot be determined whether this is a signature of plenum systems in general. Given that DON levels also increased over time in the large ATS reef system at ReefHQ (K. Michalek-Wagner, pers. comm.), it's likely that this is a function of closed systems in general.

It has been suggested that one can maintain a Jaubert system with a drain or other means of drawing water out of the plenum. In case the redox level drops too low (i.e. the system is about to produce sulfide) a small amount of water is slowly withdrawn from the plenum and fresh water penetrates deeper into the sediment. It has also been proposed to withdraw nutrient laden water from below the plenum in this manner to remove it from the system. In practice this idea and construction is not necessary. However, placing a valved outlet such that water can be removed from the plenum does allow for nutrient, pH and redox testing and evaluation of the plenums operation as was done in the Waikiki Aquarium study.

Set up techniques

Standard Jaubert Monaco system

The *standard* Monaco system aquarium is very easy and inexpensive to install. All one needs are the aquarium, cover, lights, the plenum, screen, gravel, an air pump, air tubing, heating/chilling (if needed), and air diffusers. The water motion is accomplished by means of the air diffusers. Additional water flow can be accomplished with submersible water pumps or by plumbing in line water circulation pumps. In any case, when using the *standard* Monaco system there should be at least one air diffuser that can be operated at night by means of a timer or run continuously. As explained previously, in systems that don't have a surface-skimming overflow, the nighttime aeration is essential to prevent sudden losses of fish due to a sharp drop in the oxygen level at night (see chapter 4). During the day, photosynthesis by plants elevates the level of dissolved oxygen in the water above saturation. At night, the lack of oxygen production by plants (because there is no light) and the uptake of oxygen by plants, fishes and other creatures, causes a large drop in dissolved oxygen. This is especially pronounced in a standard Monaco system because the enormous population of bacteria and microorganisms in the live sand bottom within the aquarium will further deplete oxygen (see chapter 4). During the day, the elevated oxygen concentration in the water circulating above the gravel bed penetrates the gravel and thus keeps the low oxygen layer (and any hydrogen sulfide, if present) within the interstitial water of the gravel bed deep below its surface. At night because of the drop in oxygen level in the water above the gravel, the lowest dissolved oxygen level within the interstitial water in the gravel bed approaches the top of the bed. If there is hydrogen sulfide gas within the gravel bed, it may be released at night, which is the worst possible time for the sake of the fish. Hydrogen sulfide is a poison that rapidly depletes oxygen from the water and suffocates fish. Release of hydrogen sulfide from the gravel at night may occur occasionally. It only becomes problematic for the fish if there is not sufficient agitation of the water surface and aeration, which *blow* the hydrogen sulfide gas from the water and elevate dissolved oxygen. Normally there is little if any hydrogen sulfide production in a Monaco system and low oxygen concentration alone is the nighttime threat, the same as it is in any reef aquarium system that has a high density of life in a small volume of water (see chapter 4 for a discussion of normal dissolved oxygen levels).

The oxygen depletion at night is not corrected by simply increasing horizontal water circulation with water pumps. The addition of a protein skimmer does not solve the problem either, though those that operate on the downdraft, Beckett and injection methods may provide some additional aeration (see *Protein skimmers*, this chapter), due to the air/water interface agitation caused in these designs and due to the large amount of water they can process per hour. However, one should not depend on the skimmer alone to keep the oxygen levels up at night. The surface breaking affect of aeration supplied by an air pump and air stone or bubbler in the tank, or the use of a surface skimming overflow drain is needed to correct the problem. An appropriately sized submersible water pump placed on the bottom of the aquarium to send water directly upward to the surface, creating a *boiling* effect like a natural spring can also solve the oxygen problem. However, as the pump becomes clogged over time, and the output is reduced, the surface agitation subsequently becomes reduced, which increases the risk of a lethal low oxygen level at night. As an alternative, one could plumb a pump in-line with a removable mechanical filter on the intake to achieve the same effect. However, a backup switch and battery-powered air pump are needed to be secure. Finer sand tends to produce lower oxygen levels at night compared to coarse gravel. This is one of the reasons for using coarse gravel instead of sand.

Jaubert system with surface skimming overflow

The use of a surface-skimming overflow in the design of a Jaubert system eliminates the problem with low nighttime oxygen level. The constant renewal of the water surface plus the cascading of water over the overflow and down the drainpipe effectively oxygenates the water. In our opinion, this is the best way to set up a Jaubert system for most reef aquarium applications. The only problem with surface skimming overflow designs is that anemones, nudibranchs, shrimps, sea cucumbers, or other delicate creatures might wander over the overflow or become damaged by being drawn into the overflow's strainer grid (see chapter 1 for suggestions on how to prevent this).

Jaubert system as an attached refugium

The use of Jaubert's method in an attached *refugium* is a simple way to *upgrade* any existing aquarium to make use of the nitrate lowering ability of a plenum system. A separate aquarium is set up with a surface skimming overflow and plenum. Water from the main display is pumped to the refugium and it drains from the refugium back to the display aquarium or back to the sump from the display aquarium. It is also possible to make the refugium work as part of the sump, having water drain to it from the display tank. In this case, the refugium should drain to a second sump from which a pump sends water back to the display tank (see diagram). When the Jaubert system is employed in an attached refugium aquarium, the photoperiod can be set to be opposite that of the main display aquarium. Such *reverse daylight* systems offer advantages in the balance of oxygen and carbon dioxide production in the system, and thus help to balance the swings in dissolved oxygen and pH from day to night (Adey and Loveland, 1991).

Jaubert system plenum installation

Fill the aquarium with properly mixed and aerated saltwater to a height of about 8 cm (3 inches). Then put the plenum support structure down, making sure to shake out any trapped air bubbles. If this support structure is an undergravel filter plate, put the plate directly on the bottom. The space underneath it is sufficient as a plenum. Be sure to cap off the lift tube holes. After rinsing the gravel a few times in a bucket with tap water, put the first layer down on top of the plate. Add the gravel until you have made a layer approximately 5 cm (2 inches) thick. Next put a layer of plastic window screen, cut to fit the inside dimension of the aquarium, on top of the gravel. This will prevent burrowing organisms from disturbing the lower gravel layer. An alternative would be to install layers of Enkamat® in this position for the same purpose as we described earlier. If that material is used, it is to be placed directly on the plenum support in layers to a thickness of approximately 5 cm (2 inches). The first layer of gravel is added on top of the Enkamat®, and the gravel simply sorts through it to fill the spaces between the Enkamat® filaments (see photo). Next, add another 5 cm (2 inches) of gravel on top. It is also possible to add live gravel from another aquarium at this time on top instead. Then put a dinner plate on top in the middle of the tank and pour the rest of the saltwater in over the plate (which prevents the water from stirring up the gravel as you pour). Once the water is added the circulation pumps should be started. Lighting should be provided as usual for a photoperiod of approximately 12 hours.

In discussing the set up procedure, it is important to point out that what many aquarists do with plenums is not what is done in the traditional Jaubert method in Monaco or in systems set up by the established marketing firm, Sea Promotion. They use much coarser gravel than typical aquarium hobbyists use, they condition the gravel in separate systems with microorganisms before placing it in the tank, and they add ammonia and nitrate to ensure the nitrification AND denitrification cycles are complete BEFORE they even add live rock. They also culture a specific range of microorganisms in separate gravel beds, which they use to seed their beds (this concept is similar to the *detritivore kit* discussed with DSB systems later in this chapter). These differences may account for the range of experience encountered by hobbyists trying this system.

Adding rock to a Jaubert system

Jaubert systems do not need, and should not have, a large amount of live rock in them. The biological filtration is accomplished by the gravel, so the rock is used for aesthetic purposes and for introducing biodiversity (mainly species of algae, microorganisms, and invertebrates).

Building an aquascape that does not touch the bottom substratum offers some aesthetically pleasing possibilities and physical challenges that we describe in chapter 9. J. Sprung

In the simplest approach, one may add one or two rocks to the aquarium, placing them on top of the gravel. The corals and other invertebrates can be placed on or attached to these rocks. The less one covers the gravel the better because the system operates by advection and diffusion of water and dissolved gasses across the gravel surface. Recalling our description earlier in this chapter of how a rock placed on a sand or gravel bottom enhances advection of water into the substrata below the rock and the upwelling of pore water into the rock, one can see the benefit of suspending the rocks so that they do not connect with the substrata in Jaubert's system. A large rock placed deeply in the substratum in Jaubert's system may promote upwelling of plenum water into the space just below the rock. One can altogether forego adding rocks to the aquarium, using just live corals attached to the walls for the decoration. This type of aquascape is employed in some of the displays in Monaco, with an aesthetically pleasing result.

If the aquarium is large it is wise to plan the aquascape, and it is possible to begin constructing it when the aquarium is dry. The rocks used can be dry porous limestone, coral skeletons, or artificial rock. Lightweight pieces may be cemented to the walls of the aquarium while still dry using a suitable non-toxic epoxy. A large open-design rock structure can also be constructed dry within the aquarium using hydraulic cement to hold the rocks together. Jaubert and his team have designed and built some of the most magnificent displays this way. After the aquarium is filled with water, one may add a few pieces of live rock to *seed* the system with coralline algae, and live corals can be attached to the dead rock and walls of the aquarium with underwater epoxy. See chapter 9 for more detailed instructions on using underwater cements.

Maintaining a Jaubert system aquarium

Harvesting algae

Jaubert systems often exhibit strong algae growth in the first six months. This needs to be harvested once a week initially, then less afterwards. When a protein skimmer is employed on a Monaco system the growth of algae is much reduced. In addition, the use of herbivores such as *Diadema setosum* is effective in limiting the growth of various algae, but they can only be employed in large aquariums. Small hermit crabs are effective for tiny aquariums.

Water changes

During the first three or four months, it is not necessary to change water. One may rely on the harvest of algae to remove excess nutrients. Once the algae growth begins to slow down, start water changes of five or ten percent per month. We have set up some Jaubert aquariums with no water change at all (for several years). If no water changes are done, it is especially crucial to monitor salinity, calcium and alkalinity, as well as supplement calcium, trace elements and alkalinity. Salinity drift can be managed with automatic water top-off to replenish evaporation and the occasional addition of some saltwater to replace salts lost due to spray and protein skimming (if one is used). Our recommendation is to perform water changes following the advice we give in chapter 11.

Capacity

Initially the biological filtration in a newly set up Jaubert system does not have the capacity to process large food inputs, even when some live sand is added. It takes several months for the system to mature. The decrease in algae growth is an indicator of maturation. Measuring the decline of nitrate is another means of checking the system's capacity. In testing and comparing the tank water and plenum water, we have found that the system takes approximately three months to begin to consistently maintain low nitrate levels (J.C. Delbeek, unpubl. data).

Cleaning the gravel

It is not necessary to stir and clean the gravel in Jaubert system aquariums. In our experience, the gravel in these systems does not become overly clogged with detritus. It seems that the denitrification process helps to break down some of the detritus, so that heavy accumulations are rare. Various worms and other creatures in the gravel also process the detritus. One can employ some animals that help keep the gravel surface clean, and other animals that keep the glass adjacent to the gravel clean. For cleaning the gravel surface, sea cucumbers are particularly effective, as are small conchs (*Strombus* spp.), small hermit crabs, and serpent starfish. Small snails of the genus *Stomatella* (see Delbeek and Sprung, 1994) often reproduce on the rocks and in the gravel, and they are good herbivores. One should not utilize sand sifters that actively dig deeply, such as various sifting gobies, unless a screen is installed to prevent them from digging too deeply. Several species of chiton that commonly live on the undersides of live rock are particularly effective at cleaning the glass adjacent to the gravel. They actually burrow through the gravel while attached to the glass, feeding on algae growing there.

Airstone maintenance

If airstones are used for water circulation, they must be cleaned or replaced periodically to insure the adequate flow of air. Sometimes salt or minerals build up inside the airline tube, and this must be cleared periodically. When aeration is used, it may lead to accumulation of salt deposits around the aquarium perimeter. This *salt creep* must never be allowed to accumulate on electrical apparatus and it must not be allowed to fall back into the aquarium where it could land on and injure sessile invertebrates.

Deep sand bed (DSB) filtration

The DSB filtration method incorporates a very thick layer of fine aragonite oolitic sand placed on the aquarium bottom. This is a variation of Eng's natural system, but with sand used for biological filtration to a greater extent than live rock. In the DSB filtration method, the sand really becomes the focus of the display since it is typically 15 cm (6 inches) or more deep, which means it occupies a significant amount of the viewing space in the aquarium. As with other *natural* filtration methods, installation of this system is easy and inexpensive, and it requires a minimum of care or expense to maintain. The sand bed serves the function not only of biological filter but also of provider of food for many suspension feeders (Shimek, 1998). Lowrie & Borneman (1998) conclude that deep sand bed filtration alone equals or even exceeds the results achieved with more *traditional* reef filtration methods employing strong protein skimming, and that it offers the basis for removing skimmers from well-established reef aquariums. There have been numerous such publications exuberantly promoting the benefits of deep sand beds. It is not a simple matter to make side-by-side comparisons to measure the *results* of different systems on a quantitative basis. The differences come from more than one variable. However, it can be observed and stated that various methods, including DSB in the absence of protein skimming, give qualitatively good results with reef aquariums.

The battle of the plenum vs. no-plenum camps

Toonen (1998) and Cohen (1998) propose that plenums (as used in Jaubert's system) are not needed, and that a deep sand bed accomplishes the same filtration capacity. Toonen and Wee (2005) found no significant difference between nitrogenous waste levels in tanks with and without a plenum, regardless of depth, sediment size or animal load (no animals vs. animal treatments). However, they did find a significant difference in final nitrate concentrations where deep (3.6 inch/9 cm) coarse and shallow (1 inch/2.5 cm) fine sediments had higher levels than shallow coarse and deep fine sediments. They also found that phosphate was significantly higher in aquaria with coarse than fine sediments, and in beds that were deep, whether or not a plenum was present.

However, the plenum is not the only distinguishing feature between the DSB method and Jaubert's system. The size of the sand grains and the oxygen level within the substrata are distinctly different. The affect of these different methods on the water chemistry within the tank may be less distinguishable, however, as supported by Toonen's later examinations (Toonen, 2004 MACNA presentation; Toonen and Wee, 2005). Toonen's (1998) description of plenums as a *complication* seems hard to support given that it is a simple device to build and requires no maintenance. The whole argument seems pointless since both methods work, are easy to establish and maintain, and take up about the same amount of space from the display tank or a refugium. One real distinguishing aspect, however, is that while Jaubert's system is defined as a way to biologically purify the water, the DSB method is defined to do both that and promote food webs through the cultivation of a dense infaunal population. Jaubert also incorporates infauna in his sand beds, but their function is mainly for maintaining the porosity of the sediment, which promotes it biological filtering capacity. This is not to say that Jaubert systems do not also promote food webs, just that this has not been promoted as a benefit, though logically, it should occur. The difference seems to be mainly one of philosophy, but it is nevertheless true that finer sediments support higher numbers of infauna.

Deep sand beds in other systems

It is an interesting fact that Adey (Adey and Loveland, 1991), whose system focuses on algae for filtration of the water, also is a proponent of placing a deep layer of fine aragonite sand on the bottom of a reef aquarium, except he incorporates it as a part of the habitat creation and establishment of food webs. Its function as a biological filter of the water is completely ignored.

Sand size

According to Shimek (1998), who is one of the most vocal proponents of this method, the *sand* used should be very fine. This contrasts with other methods that use coarse gravel (for example Jaubert's method). The term *sugar fine* has been adopted by DSB proponents to describe the sand grain size of choice. While the functioning of the sand bed as a biological filter is not affected

This deep sand bed is part of a culture system set up by Morgan Lidster employing algal turf filtration, located at Inland Aquatics, Terre Haute, Indiana. T. Siegel

A reef aquarium display with a deep sand bed featuring several types of anemones with clownfish. J. Sprung

whether the sand is silicate based or calcium carbonate based, the majority of DSB proponents use aragonite *sugar fine* oolitic sand from the Bahamas. According to Shimek, the size choice matters because sediment particle size determines the acceptability of the sediment to the organisms living in it. He suggests a grain size range averaging about 0.125 mm, and adds that with an average size finer than this, sediments can pack too tightly together. Toonen and Wee (2005) found that sediment size affected nutrient levels and might affect buffering ability. Coarse sediments (2.0 mm mean diameter) exhibited lower buffering capacity (calcium, alkalinity and pH) and much higher final phosphate concentrations than fine sediments (0.2 mm particle diameter). However, differences in chemical composition of the substrata used in the deep and fine sediments cannot be ruled out as the cause for the differences that Toonen and Wee observed.

Detritus accumulation

Some aquarists believe there is less accumulation of detritus in fine sand than in tanks with coarser gravel. The idea behind this assumption is that the pore space between the grains of the fine sand is much smaller than in coarser material, tending to keep detritus on the sediment surface where it may be eaten by the tank inhabitants or carried away into a mechanical or settling filter. The idea is wrong since advective forcing of water through the substratum, promoted by strong water circulation, guarantees that detritus will enter the sand, whatever its grain size. Shimek considers the buildup of detritus not a problem, since a thriving sediment meiofauna is capable of processing it. The meiofauna in fine marine sediments in nature include rotifers, gastrotrichs, kinorhynchs, nematodes, tardigrades, copepods, ostracods, turbellarians, oligochaetes, polychaetes, and a few specialized hydrozoans, nemerteans, bryozoans, gastropods, aplacophorans, holothurians and tunicates, and micro-crustaceans (such as isopods, copepods and amphipods) (Toonen, 2000a). In our aquaria, the diversity is much reduced, but it can be initiated, enhanced, or maintained by the introduction of fresh harvested or cultured live sand or detritivore kits (Shimek, 1998; Toonen, 2000a).

The DSB approach avoids the use of large sand sifting animals that could decimate populations of meiofauna that work the sand on a smaller scale, and slower timetable. In addition, manual cleaning of the sediments by siphoning or stirring results in significant removal or mortality of sediment dwelling organisms, and may severely damage the functional aspect of a deep sand bed (Shimek, 1998). Strong water motion that could dig out the sand and shift it around would have the same damaging effect. The approach is exactly opposite of other systems that employ strong currents, siphoning, stirring, or various large sifting organisms such as gobies, sand-sifting starfish to keep the sand bed turned over and thus maintain its porosity. Despite the contradiction, it works. Here is an example where mixing methods would sacrifice the effectiveness of the system. One other reason why large sand sifting creatures or strong water currents should not be used in the DSB method is that corals placed on the sand could easily become buried by excavating creatures or water currents shifting the sand.

During the initial set up phase of a DSB system using fresh live rock, there can be a significant amount of detritus expelled from the rock. An immature DSB will have trouble processing such a deluge of sediment and the aquarist may have to intervene by gently siphoning the upper few cm's of the sand to remove these initial pulses of sediment. A better alternative is to first cure the rock in a separate container and then place it in the aquarium, as we suggest in chapter 2 and this chapter. In this manner, the initial release of detritus occurs outside of the system. We recommend against placing fresh live rock on top of any substrate until it has been sufficiently cured in a separate system.

Shimek (1998) found between 10,000 and 40,000 infaunal organisms (which live and burrow within sediments) per square meter in his aquariums, and noted that a single organism burrowing and feeding in benthic sediments may disturb between 100 and 10,000,000 mm^3 per day. Naturally, the larger figure relates to larger organisms, such as burrowing worms. In any case, the activity of 10,000 or 40,000 organisms can move a lot of sediment! The infaunal organisms doing all of this moving about are actively consuming diatoms, phytoplankton trapped by advection, bacteria, bacterial films and detritus. Their activity not only moves the sand grains, it maintains the porosity of the oxic layer and promotes oxygen penetration that enables them to live there. They also maintain the active growth of bacteria within the sediment.

Cleanup crew

In the absence of large sand sifting creatures, other types of cleanup organisms are preferred for a DSB system. Burrowing omnivorous snails such as *Nassarius* spp. and relatives such as *Hyalina* spp. are a popular choice. Serpent stars and sea cucumbers that *mop* the sand surface are also used (Toonen, 2000a). Online vendors and some specialty pet shops sell detritivore kits, which may contain various worms, amphipods, copepods, mysid shrimp, tiny brittle star species, snails such as certain small *Strombus* spp., *Nassarius* spp., *Hyalina* spp., and *Stomatella varia*, and sand dwelling clams such as *Tapes* spp. These kits are useful for initiating the sand bed diversity and maintaining it in a healthy state. See chapter 11 for more details.

Support for rocks

Since the typical reef aquarium employs live rock, the placement of rocks in a DSB system requires some consideration. Merely placing rocks on top of a 15 cm (6 inches) deep sand layer will result in some subsidence with time. If the rocks are stacked, the subsidence could cause a collapse of part of the reef structure. Shimek (2001) states: *There is no need for any sort of platform to support the rock. I embed the live rock a bit into the sediment to give it stability.* Without a physical contact with the bottom, it is inevitable that such stability will be compromised by shifts in the sand due to dissolution of the substratum or the movement of worms through it. Some proponents of this method place *base rocks* down on the bare bottom of the tank to provide structural support to the rocks placed above them. This concept or any other structural solution seems more appropriate than denying the possibility of eventual movement. The problem exists with any aquascape using sand on the bottom, but it is enhanced when the sand is very deep. As we describe in chapter 9, various means can be employed to secure the base of the reef, raise the rockwork above the bottom of the tank, or even suspend it above a sand bed.

Oxygen

Nighttime oxygen levels and oxygen depletion during a power failure is a concern for all systems employing a deep sediment layer within the display aquarium, and the DSB is no exception. For coral farming systems, an extended power failure in systems with corals over DSB filters is a recipe for disaster, as the corals will suffocate when the nighttime oxygen level plummets. The use of DSB refugia isolates the oxygen consuming sand bed from a display or farm aquarium, helping to reduce the risk. We discuss other ways of managing oxygen levels in chapter 4 and backup power options in chapter 3.

Deep sand beds and coral culture are a popular mix, but not without risk. Backup power supply to maintain water turnover and aeration is especially important for such systems since the sand bed consumes oxygen rapidly. J. Sprung

Toonen (2000b) points out another oxygen related issue for DSB systems. For DSB system aquariums, the diversity of life in the sand will be reduced at higher temperatures. In the tropics, peak meiofaunal abundances occur in winter months when temperatures are at their lowest and the annual fluctuations in the abundance of the meiofauna because of temperature swings can vary by a factor of 5 or more. This observation in nature supports our discussion in chapter 4 of the importance of temperature and oxygen levels for closed system aquariums.

Set up methods

After the aquarium is set up with circulating seawater, sand and cured live rock, live sand collected from the sea, as a source of bacteria and infauna should be added. Shimek (1998) recommends using live sand in a quantity of at least 10% of the total tank volume by weight. This recommendation is a bit confusing since it mixes volume and weight, and the weight is related to the density of the substratum, which varies for live sand not only by its composition but also by the quantity of water it contains. Shimek's recommendation was probably just 10% of the height of the sandbed, but his main point was the more the merrier. The addition of detritivore kits help to supplement the diversity as well. The aquarium should be allowed to stabilize biologically for at least two weeks without adding any fishes. This stabilization period allows the infaunal animals to establish populations. Feeding the aquarium promotes development of these populations as well. Within a week, the formation of bubbles in the sand next to the glass will be visible. While some authors suggest this is an indication of biological denitrification, only actual testing of the gas will determine its true nature. In our opinion, these bubbles next to the glass are not

Note the gas bubbles in the sand next to the glass. Aquarists often believe these bubble are nitrogen produced by denitrification, but bubbles against the glass are usually oxygen produced by illuminated algae living there. J. Sprung

An established deep sandbed supports a community of creatures, large and small. A large worm is visible against the glass. J. Sprung

nitrogen gas produced by denitrification, but oxygen produced by algae illuminated there. In any case, after a few weeks the population of infauna will have reproduced sufficiently to be forming observable tubes and tracks in the sand against the glass.

Maintenance - nutrient export

Sand beds recycle nutrients, but excesses must be exported via the harvest of algae or of animals grown in the system. It is also common to use protein skimming for nutrient export on heavily fed systems. Stark (1998) posited that accumulation of phosphate and other nutrients in sand beds increases over time and advocated the monthly siphoning of the upper layer of sand to remove accumulate detritus and phosphate rich interstitial water. Although there is some loss of infauna, Stark argued that recolonization by infauna from lower layers would quickly repopulate the cleaned layer. His recommendation, while applicable to the Berlin method, is contrary to the design and maintenance recommendations of the DSB method.

Change of sand?

Shimek (1998) notes that the diversity of infauna diminishes with time. He attributes it to volume of the sand bed or whole system being too small for some species to maintain their populations. The remedy is periodically (about every year or so) adding detritivore kits, to boost infauna populations. Shimek (2002d) also proposes to replace the sand bed (and rocks) periodically (every 4 to 5 years, or more frequently) to prevent potentially toxic accumulations of metals. His recommendations in this area have received wide criticism. We don't recommend replacing large portions of a sand bed, nor replacement of the main base of established live rock with new pieces. Over time it becomes necessary to add some sand as the sand bed dissolves, and remove some rock or coral to provide space as the corals grow (see chapter 11).

DSB refugia

If one has an objection to devoting 15 cm (6 inches) of the display aquarium to a deep sand bed, the use of a refugium or refugia can resolve the matter. The sand bed or sand beds can be incorporated in them. This also helps with respect to high water velocity systems for SPS corals, in which the water motion in the main display can disturb the sand bed and compromise its function. Sand beds in refugia can operate with gentler water flows, preserving their productivity.

Modified use of sand beds

In addition to the traditional horizontal arrangement, Jaubert's patent included designs with the sand bed positioned vertically between two bodies of water (Jaubert, 1991). Aquarists playing with deep sand beds have tried using fine sand over plenums, and even using a plenum space to create positive pressure below a sand bed placed in a refugium, in effect making it a reverse flow undergravel filter (Matthews, 2004). We have not experimented with the latter method. Dick Perrin of *Tropicorium* in Romulus Michigan uses a modified Jaubert method in his coral farming vats, wherein the sand bed is located in a chamber suspended in the middle of the aquarium. The corals are placed on top of shelves or trays located over the sand bed, and a rolling current created by airlift circulates water over them and beneath the sand bed. The *plenum* is thus not isolated from the main body of water. This arrangement accomplishes not only biological filtration; it also results in more than half of the water volume being shaded at any given moment. In a sunlit greenhouse coral farm like *Tropicorium*, the design reduces the heat gain by the vats.

A deep sand bed provides the right habitat for a living seagrass display with mixed varieties of *Caulerpa* spp., at the Smithsonian Institution's facility in Ft. Pierce, FL. J. Sprung

Berlin method

The Berlin method of aquarium keeping gets its name from the aquarium society in Berlin that developed the method, based on the earlier work of Peter Wilkens. It was the first closed system method to demonstrate dramatic success with *Acropora* spp. and other small polyped reef building corals. The method is essentially a natural system, relying on live rock and live sand/gravel for biological filtration, but has several additional features that improve its capacity to house a large number of animals and specifically to grow stony corals. One of these is surface skimming. Having a surface skimmer that drains water to a sump helps to insure that the oxygen level won't fall too low at night, and the passing of surface active compounds directly to the protein skimmer ensures their removal and a lower production of nitrate as a result. The

Dietrich Stüber with his famous aquarium. J. Sprung

second addition that distinguishes the Berlin method from Eng's is the use of protein skimming. The Berlin method also actively manages calcium and alkalinity with daily dosing of kalkwasser, and supplements the water weekly with strontium and iodine, based on Wilkens' original recommendations for the cultivation of corals. We detailed the basics of the Berlin method in an article in Freshwater and Marine Aquarium magazine (Delbeek and Sprung, 1990), where we also described how to remove trickle filters from reef aquariums and run them with live rock and protein skimming alone. Although there was initial skepticism in North America, the trend caught on eventually and the Berlin system is now as commonplace around the world as it is in Europe.

Dietrich Stüber was and still is an active driving force in the development of this method, and it was his special aquarium that

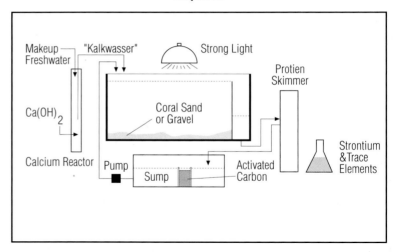

made it clear to the aquarium keeping world that the dream of growing reef-building corals had become a reality. Fragments of his *baby, Stüber's Acropora,* a domesticated form of *Acropora formosa,* have been passed from aquarium to aquarium all over Europe, and throughout north and south America for over twenty years now, having deposited tons of calcium carbonate along the way. Mr. Stüber was also the first to report regular planulae release from a colony and then later from new colonies of *Pocillopora damicornis* in his aquarium (Delbeek and Sprung, 1990). This coral too has been distributed widely as it easily fragments and grows quickly.

Use of live sand

The bottom substratum in typical Berlin method aquariums, in Berlin, is not sand but coarse coral gravel. The coral gravel preferred is in a size range of about 5 to 10 mm (1/4 to 1/2 inch), and the depth of the substratum is typically about 2.5 cm (1 inch). In a short period, the originally buff coloured gravel develops a coating of pink coralline algae and the green boring alga *Ostreobium.* Some Berlin aquaria utilize finer (1mm grain) coral sand, usually of a thickness not exceeding 7.5 cm (3 inches). When the *Berlin method* was introduced to the USA, it was a popular practice to manage reef aquariums with *bare bottoms,* so that it was at one time erroneously believed in the USA that a bare bottom was one of the features of the Berlin method. Typical Berlin systems utilizing coarse coral gravel employ periodic gravel vacuuming to remove accumulated detritus. An alternative is to include one or more *Pholidichthys leucotaenia* (Convict goby), which move the substratum and keep it from becoming clogged with detritus. This is essential for long term maintenance of Berlin system aquaria to prevent excessive detritus build-up that reduces the effectiveness of the substrate as a biological filter and leads to *old tank syndrome.*

In a tank with fine sand on the bottom, sand-sifting gobies (such as *Valenciennia* spp., and *Amblygobius* spp.) constantly work through and clean up the sediment surface. Their activity re-suspends any settled detritus into the water column. In coarser gravel, the detritus falls into the pores between the grains and cannot be re-suspended by gobies that only sift fine sand grains, but is easily managed by *Pholidichthys leucotaenia* that constantly digs burrows through sand or gravel, no matter what the grain size.

Bare-bottomed tanks employ strong water movement and switching currents in the display to prevent detritus buildup, and the detritus is caught in a mechanical filter, removed by protein skimming, or settled in the sump and periodically siphoned out. The *bare-bottomed* approach is not an aspect of the original Berlin system design, and it usually results in a higher accumulation of nitrate (when combined with a high bioload) unless sufficient denitrification is employed in attached refugia or filters.

Live rock

The use of live rock is a central feature of Berlin aquariums. They rely on it as the main site for biological filtration. To that end, they must utilize a minimum quantity to handle the biological nitrification. In addition to the live rock that is used as the aquascaping material, it is common for Berlin system aquariums to also have some live rock in the sump attached to the display. In that sense, there is some overlap with Tyree's E.G. filtration method, except that Berlin systems employ protein skimming. Some Berlin system aquaria use large sized coral gravel fragments in the sump instead of live rock. Other Berlin style aquaria utilize activated carbon in the sump for biological filtration. In each of these examples, the sump can be considered a large wet biological filter. Nevertheless, when there is sufficient rock and/or gravel in the display tank, no additional biological filter media is needed in the sump, so it is within the scope of Berlin system design to have a bare sump (from a biological point of view). The sump is utilized for surface skimming, water top-off, probe placement, or protein skimmer placement, among other sump conveniences.

Protein skimming

The Berlin method relies on protein skimming to compliment the ability of biological filtration to maintain water quality. The use of giant skimmers, however, was not in the original design. Berlin systems traditionally incorporated countercurrent style protein skimmers with wood airstones, or *Tunze* centrifugal skimmers. Ozone is generally not used in these systems although small amounts (i.e. < 5 mg/hr) can be used to increase the efficiency of the skimmer, to oxidize yellowing compounds in the water or in case of emergencies such as disease or microalgae outbreaks

(Delbeek and Sprung, 1990). Modern variations of protein skimmer design can be utilized of course, without compromising the system in any way.

Activated carbon

Berlin system aquariums typically incorporate a section for activated carbon in the sump. The carbon is used continuously, and only a portion of it is changed periodically. The remaining portion serves as additional biological filtration, with some capacity for denitrification.

Kalkwasser

The addition of a saturated solution of calcium hydroxide, kalkwasser, as top-off water was first proposed by Peter Wilkens for maintaining calcium and alkalinity and promoting the growth of corals. It is a central feature of the Berlin method. See our description of this method in chapter 5.

Circulation

Circulation of the water in Berlin system aquariums is typically accomplished with *Tunze* Turbelle® pumps controlled by a *Tunze* power timer. This affords strong water movement with random switching of current directions, and pulsed water flow. The recommended total flow rate for these powerheads is approximately 10 times the aquarium volume per hour, within the aquarium (Fosså and Nilsen, 1996). The flow rate through the sump does not have to be so fast due to the high velocity of water within the display itself. The typical turnover rate through the sump is two to five times the aquarium volume per hour.

Lighting

The Berlin system was the first whole system to specifically feature the use of the HQI daylight type (double-ended) metal halide lamp, now a popular choice for reef aquariums of all kinds. The daylight metal halides were supplemented by blue actinic fluorescent lamps. Typically, the blue lighting was used for the longest photoperiod approximately 12 to 13 hours, so that dawn and dusk could be simulated, while the metal halide lights were on for a shorter period, about 8 to 10 hours. Then, as now, the metal halide lamps were replaced at least every 12 months.

Element additions

The original Berlin system proponents regularly added two solutions of elements their experience had shown were vital to the success of their systems, strontium in the form of a 10% solution of strontium chloride and iodine in the form of a 1% solution of potassium iodide. These elements (Sr and I) are still added by most aquarium hobbyists today and their dosing has not changed much since the 1980s.

Algal turf scrubbers (ATS) and microcosm management

Dr. Walter Adey of the Smithsonian Institution's Natural History Museum in Washington D.C. began his development of a coral reef aquarium system in 1974 (Miller, 1980). These systems were characterized by the use of a patented *algal turf scrubber*. Algal scrubbers are shallow troughs with a plastic mesh screen illuminated by intense lighting. Water pumped to the troughs enters them by means of a dump bucket, generating a surge that helps the algae exchange gases and take up metabolites, while preventing over-illumination or over-shading. Various turf-forming algae are grown on these screens, and they remove ammonia, nitrate, phosphate and heavy metals from the water (Adey and Loveland, 1991). The screens are periodically *harvested* by removing them and scraping off the excess growth with a plastic wedge. The harvested algal mass is thus

A view of one end of the magnificent algal turf filtered Caribbean reef system created by Bill Hoffman at the Smithsonian Institution's facility in Ft. Pierce Florida. J. Sprung

removed from the system. It may be discarded, analyzed for nutrient content, or returned to the aquarium as food for the fishes and other creatures to stimulate higher productivity when nutrient levels are very low. The harvested screens are reinstalled with the still living cropped algae adhering to them.

These aquaria differ not only by their use of algae to filter the water, but also by the philosophy of their design and operation. They are designed specifically to model whole ecosystems, by setting up complex food webs and encouraging high productivity. They incorporate refugia (Adey and Loveland, 1991) to achieve these goals. The emphasis is not on the husbandry of individual specimens, but on the whole ecosystem. They are truly different from typical aquarium systems, in their use of algal turfs, the means of water movement and even in the aquascape design, as we

Algal turf filter showing the shallow layer of water over the turf algae cultivated on a screen. J. Sprung

A view of the screen in an Algal turf filter. J. Sprung

Harvesting the screen is easily accomplished with a plastic scraper. B. Hoffman

Bill Hoffman shows a mat of turf algae that has been dried in a de-humidifier. It can be weighed and analyzed to measure the export of nutrients. J. Sprung

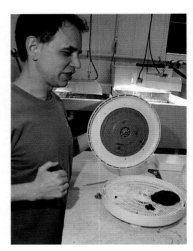

demonstrate in chapter 9. Adey's reef ecosystems have a lagoon section, a backreef, a reef crest and a forereef, but the *open ocean* is technically replaced by the algal turf filter that exports nutrients, imports some phytoplankton and zooplankton, and, by incorporating reverse-daylight photosynthesis, balances the day to night oxygen levels and pH. Adey's system uses live rock and live sand in deep sand beds, and refugia that, like algal turf filters, are operated with reverse daylight photosynthesis.

Other systems (Leng Sy's Ecosystem Aquarium® method for example) may employ algae on reverse daylight or 24 hour daylight schemes, but these *algal filters* using higher algae differ from turf scrubbers on several accounts. The algal filaments in an algal turf filter are simple strands, not differentiated into specialized forms or functions, so most cells in the plant mass are photosynthetic, which

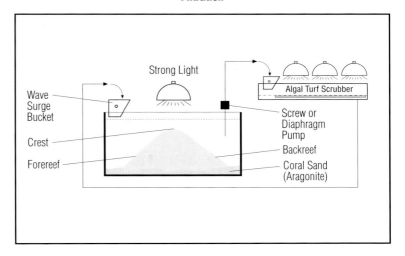

makes them more efficient at removing nutrients from the water. In contrast, higher algae like *Caulerpa*, with larger more complex bodies (thalli) have various non-photosynthetic cells for structural support, reproduction, and protection.

For the turf scrubber, wave action is crucial. Without surge there is a radical drop in turf photosynthesis because waves boosts the efficiency of the photosynthetic mechanism by serving as a light flasher (since the filaments sway back and forth and are thus illuminated then shaded). In addition, waves facilitates the exchange of metabolites needed or excreted by algae. Algal turf tissue production is 5-20 g dry weight per square meter per day. Algal turfs can absorb 0.3-1.2 g of nitrogen per day per square meter of screen (Adey and Loveland, 1991). We believe this is a higher figure than can be achieved by *Caulerpa*, but it is not known how much higher.

A closeup of live rock on a coral reef reveals a high diversity of algae so heavily grazed that only short turfs remain. J. Sprung

A view through the eyepiece of a dissecting microscope reveals the beauty of a mixed bed of turf algae.
J. Sprung

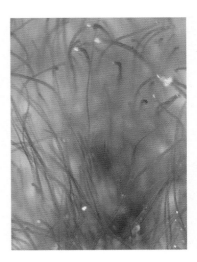

The role of bacteria in ATS systems

Adey and proponents of his system sometimes downplay the importance of biological filtration mediated by bacteria in their aquarium systems and on the natural reef, suggesting that the algae are the principal means for the removal of nitrogenous wastes (ammonia, nitrate). In fact, the presence of a deep sand substratum and thick structure of live rock within their systems as well as on wild reefs guarantees the importance of bacteria. We feel that the *bacterial biofilter versus algal filter* argument falls apart when one realizes that any natural system aquarium relies on the metabolism of both algae and bacteria, and the two compliment each other. To get a perspective on Adey's reasoning with regard to the function and origin of his system, it is helpful to see his comments in Adey and Loveland (1991) regarding bacteria abundance in sediments:

Bacteria, while extremely abundant in numbers, typically are a minor biomass element on most active and fully viable soft bottoms.

and

In noneutropic wild ecosystems, 10-30% of primary production is cycled through bacteria. Even in rich sediments, the wild equivalent of the biological filter, bacterial biomass is typically two orders of magnitude lower than infaunal (clams, worm, and crustacean) biomass (Rheinheimer, 1984). If a biological filter is used, a much larger proportion of production (or feed) is cycled through bacteria. Thus more oxygen is required from the water column and oxygen concentrations are lower- inevitably much below saturation no matter what aeration method is employed, short of bubbling oxygen.

Combine this with Adey and Loveland's (1991) comments regarding bacteria in biofilters:

In traditional aquarium technology, fish and a few larger accompanying invertebrates are living in a hotel. The only significant food available is provided by the aquarist. It is hoped that detritus produced by the fish will be minimal, but what does become available is captured by the bacterial filter and, along with ammonia, urea, and unused food, is broken down in the filter. The filter is thus the sewage or septic system for the aquarium. Unfortunately, in this case the water from the septic system is constantly recycled to the aquarium. The bacteriological filter, in exchange for the removal of ammonia and some particulates, returns to the aquarium water depleted in oxygen and plankton and high in dissolved nitrates and carbon dioxide. By contrast, the algal turf scrubber keeps oxygen near or above the saturation point and effectively removes all classes of dissolved animal wastes.

and

Extensive bacterial cultures in a filtering situation place bacteria in competition with algae and other plants for organic nutrients, particularly in the form of ammonia and urea.

The bias toward algae for water filtration is clearly present in these words. The points made are valid, except that the argument to use one for filtration versus the other is pointless since both forms are inevitably and inescapably present in closed system aquariums, whether or not the effect of one or the other is more important in the natural environment.

These two photos show six months of growth of *Acropora cervicornis* in the algal turf filtered Caribbean reef display managed by Bill Hoffman at the Smithsonian Institution's facility in Ft. Pierce, Florida. B. Hoffman

In Delbeek and Sprung (1994), we expressed that in our opinion: *Although algal turf scrubbers work quite well for mangrove and estuarine microcosms, producing model ecosystems that really look exactly like the natural environment, the results in the coral reef microcosms we have seen that rely exclusively on this type of filtration with little or no water change, are less spectacular.* This opinion, which we are revising with this book, was based on our personal observations at the time of several algal turf filtered public aquarium exhibits. As we explained in 1994: *The stony corals did not appear to grow much, and in some instances we saw what we believed was unacceptable mortality.* We have since seen a number of successful systems employing algal turf scrubbing in operation over a long period, and have spoken with quite a few marine scientists, coral reef biologists, and aquarium hobbyists who have used them, maintained them, or observed them. It is clear that algal turf filtration can be utilized successfully for growing corals, contrary to our earlier opinion, **provided certain operational conditions are met**, as we shall detail shortly.

Small and Adey (2001), demonstrated a positive effect of algae on coral growth, supporting the McConnaughey and Whelan (1997) hypothesis of bicarbonate ion neutralization in coral calcification (see chapter 5). A mature, high-biodiversity coral reef microcosm and its chambered subsets at the Smithsonian Institution's Marine Systems Laboratory were used to examine the relationship between calcification and photosynthesis. Through analysis of the microcosm's daily carbonate system, the study demonstrated that bicarbonate ion, not carbonate ion is the principal component of total alkalinity reduction in the water column (thus, bicarbonate ion is the principal measured component of calcification as typically

A section of the Caribbean reef at the Smithsonian in Washington D.C. around 1990. The corals were surviving but not growing much. J. Sprung

A section of the Caribbean reef at the Smithsonian facility in Ft. Pierce in 2005 shows obvious coral growth and very healthy corals. J. Sprung

measured on reef transects). While chamber-isolated free-living algae remove carbon dioxide, and raise pH and carbonate ion equivalent to that in the microcosm as a whole, no total alkalinity reduction due to calcification occurs. On the other hand, chamber isolated stony corals remove considerable bicarbonate, with very little pH or carbonate ion elevation. Combining the non-calcifying free-living macroalgae *Chondria* with stony corals in chamber subsets, the study showed it is possible to remove more carbon dioxide (elevating pH) and thereby increase coral calcification rates by 60 to 120% above zooxanthellae-mediated rates, to 20.6 kg (206 mol) and 185 kg (185 mol) $CaCO_3$ per meter per year for *Acropora* sp. and *Montipora* sp., respectively. McConnaughey and Whelan (1997) also state that symbiotic corals can be made to calcify rapidly in the dark when the oxygen level is artificially increased. This supports the use of algal filters operated with a reverse daylight regimen, to boost nighttime oxygen levels.

Room for improvement?

We believe there were some husbandry issues that accounted for the lack of success we had witnessed in algal turf filtered systems previously, and some of these were based on the philosophy of the system design as it related to maintenance, rather than real technical flaws. Algal turf filtered systems were based on early research into coral reef nutrient dynamics that suggested nitrogen and phosphate are tightly cycled within the reef ecosystem. Subsequent work has shown that while nutrients are cycled within the reef ecosystem, coral reefs also export large quantities of these nutrients (D'Elia, 1988) and can have significant import of inorganic nutrients (Rougerie and Wauthy, 1993), as well as plankton (Borneman, 2002; Hamner *et al.*, 1988).

Compare, for example, Adey's remarks in (Adey and Loveland, 1991):

0.15 g (dry) of flake food is added to the system (a 130 gallon home reef aquarium) each day.... While this may seem an exceptionally small amount of feed to be adding to the system per square meter of surface area, really it is about the same as that fed to the Smithsonian exhibit reef.

With Shimek's (1999) calculation based on Hamner *et al.* (1988):

The water flow over a reef was calculated at: 6,000 cubic meters of water/1 linear m of reef crest in 12 hr. If we assume a depth of 1 m on the reef crest, and using U. S. gallons, this is a flow rate of 2201 gallons/min. Adjusted to the volume of a 100 gallon aquarium: This is 834 gallons/minute. Such water flow brings 416,142 food items to the reef crest in a 12 hour period. This is equivalent to 5 oz. wet weight of food per day.

While we do not know how Shimek calculated the weight of 416,142 food items of varying size, we believe his point is correct, that the high volume of new water brings a lot of food to a given surface on the reef. Based on his estimate of the wet weight, and if the wet weight is roughly 95% water, the dry weight of this food would be roughly 5 grams, or about 33 times the amount of food Adey was adding to his systems.

However, Adey and Loveland (1991) also gives a figure for plankton import of 2 g (dry weight)/m^2 of reef/day, more in line with Shimek's. Since the footprint of a 494 L (130 gallon) aquarium is about 1 m^2, we don't know what calculation Adey used to determine that he should only add 0.15 g of dry feed to the aquarium.

Related to this food input, algae in the turf scrubbers also compete with the zooxanthellae of corals for the same inorganic nutrients (especially ammonium, but also phosphorus and nitrate), and important trace elements (such as iron and manganese). ATSs can out-compete corals for nitrogen and phosphorous due to the rate at which turf algae can remove them, leading to the gradual decline of the corals due to starvation (W. Hoffman, pers. comm.). This would account for reduced growth in corals, and could partially explain the positive effect Dr. Adey noted when he fed corals that exhibited tissue recession (Delbeek and Sprung, 1994).

The need to keep the dissolved nitrate level in reef aquariums at the very nutrient poor range found on coral reefs is one area where Adey's philosophy, supported by the low nitrogen levels that could be achieved by algal turf filtration, differs from other coral culturing methods. Atkinson *et al.* (1995) showed the kinds of growth rates in corals that could be achieved using water from a seawater well rich in ammonia and nitrate compared to typical reef water. In addition, the discovery that corals harbor symbiotic extracellular bacteria (Rohwer *et al.*, 2001, 2002) and intracellular cyanobacteria (Lesser *et al.*, 2004) that provide a source of reduced nitrogen emphasizes the normally nitrogen-limited growth of corals in very low nitrogen environments such as coral reefs (Borneman, 2004).

Yellow water

The use of algal turf scrubbers exclusively to filter an aquarium results in a yellowing of the water by organic leachates from the algae and ruptured algal cells. We posited (Delbeek and Sprung, 1994) that some of the leachates may contain substances that are toxic to some corals, but our own experience and that of others using this system suggests the *armchair* concept we proposed does not apply to the success or lack of it in closed aquariums. The leachates don't seem to harm the corals directly. The colour imparted to the water does alter the light spectrum that the corals receive, however. If the water is yellow, much of the blue wavelengths are absorbed by it. The golden brown symbiotic zooxanthellae use blue light most efficiently for photosynthesis (Benson, 1984). Corals living in yellow water must adapt to the new light field, which is quite different from the light on most reefs. The installation of higher Kelvin bulbs also makes a very significant change in the apparent colour of the water, but does not directly affect the presence of yellowing compounds. The explanation that the early Smithsonian reef mesocosms were yellow due to low Kelvin lighting was partially true. However, the low Kelvin bulbs used merely accentuated the yellow water, they did not create it

We should also point out that these systems do not become yellow simply because of the turf scrubbers. Bacteria can be a source of high molecular weight DON (Zehr and Ward, 2002), so the yellowing and DON accumulation characteristic of all closed system aquariums is probably mostly a result of bacteria, not algae. Leachates from algae, bacteria, invertebrates, and fish in any type of reef aquarium system will turn the water yellow (or green in large aquaria), even when protein skimming is employed. The trend in closed systems is to convert inorganic nitrogen to organic nitrogen, as was shown in measurements at the Waikiki Aquarium (Atkinson *et al.*, 1995). Activated carbon or ozone can be used to eliminate the colour, producing the clear blue of truly nutrient poor water. For example, the staff at the Great Barrier Reef Marine Park Authority Aquarium (ReefHQ), in Townsville, Australia, eventually resorted to small doses of ozone to clear the chronically yellow water in their main ATS reef tank, among the largest in the world at 2.5 million liters (~660,000 gallons).

It is curious that Jaubert described a *mysterious process* that eliminated the yellow compounds from his systems (Jaubert, 1989, 1991) and likewise Leng Sy makes a similar claim about his mud system (see next filtration topic). It is tempting to believe that a more natural process than the use of activated carbon or ozone could achieve blue water. In the natural environment, there are processes that affect the concentration of water-staining organics. Ultraviolet wavelengths in solar radiation are supposed to break down some of the colouring substances, and planktonic bacteria and protists may consume them to some extent. It is also known that iron oxides and clays are able to adsorb humic substances, and that they are one of the ways these substances are removed from the water in the natural environment (Tombácz *et al.*, 2000). This property can also be demonstrated with the granular iron based phosphate adsorption media, which have some capacity to remove yellow colour from the water in aquariums. It is thus likely that Leng Sy's mud also has some capacity initially to remove yellowing substances. Denitrifying bacteria utilize organic substances as food, but it is not known whether this significantly affects the accumulation of refractory organics such as those that give the water a yellow colour. A reproducible and controllable biological method for eliminating the yellow colour in aquariums has yet to be demonstrated or explained, though it has been reported by numerous authors.

Minor and trace elements

Certain major, minor and trace elements are critical for certain invertebrates, and success with these species in our systems depends on periodic replenishment. With algal filtration, the algae used to purify the water also remove trace elements, and as they are harvested from the system, the elements are removed with them. They must be replenished. Trace element depletion is a feature of many forms of filtration, not just algal filtration. Protein skimming and activated carbon also remove trace elements, and so do the invertebrates, plants and microorganisms. In a closed system aquarium, it does not take long for certain trace elements to become depleted, though some actually accumulate with time. Chapter 4 includes a detailed discussion of the subject of trace elements in reef aquariums. The loss of trace elements is not entirely undesirable. In fact, it is an attractive feature of algal filtration because it can be employed to advantage in the removal of toxic heavy metals that can accumulate or enter the system with make-up water, or from tank construction materials (Adey and Loveland, 1991). The disadvantage of trace element removal with any form of filtration is realized only when the philosophy of the aquarium keeper is to avoid any form of trace element replenishment via supplemental additions of trace elements, food, or by water change.

Calcium and alkalinity

To grow stony corals in captivity, the culture water should maintain a calcium level of between 400 and 450 mg/L, a carbonate hardness of about 8 dKH or greater, and a strontium level of about 8 mg/L. See chapters 4 and 5 for a discussion of the options for maintaining these levels. Without additions of calcium and strontium, these levels usually fall in closed systems, and this deficit is detrimental to stony corals and coralline algae. There is documented evidence that the calcium and strontium values in some of Dr. Adey's systems are NOT depleted (Meyer, 1991). Some replenishment is possible with hard make-up water, and via the gradual dissolving of the aragonite (coral or oolitic) sand substratum, but the capacity is very limited. In his home aquarium, Dr. Adey adds several hundred milligrams of aragonite sand every few weeks. The calcium is apparently supplied by acid secretions dissolving the sand in the deep substratum, and alkalinity by denitrification. Jaubert (1991), reports the ability to manage the calcium level by the same process. However, this process alone is not sufficient to maintain rapid coral growth (see chapter 5 and Jaubert system this chapter). At the Great Barrier Reef Marine Park Authority Aquarium (ReefHQ), after 17 years of operation, calcium levels did not rise above 250 mg/L and strontium levels ranged from 3-6 mg/L, despite the presence of 700 metric tons of coral rock and 200 metric tons of coral sand (Michalek-Wagner, 2004a, 2004b). To keep up with the demand for calcium and carbonate alkalinity in closed systems with rapidly growing stony corals, tridacnid clams and coralline algae, a more effective form of calcium and alkalinity supplementation must be used (see chapter 5).

Water motion

The use of dump buckets to return the water to the main aquarium, and on algal turf scrubbers can be problematical. Some dump bucket designs require frequent maintenance to ensure that they continue to operate properly. The salt from splash gets into the pivoting parts, and wears the surfaces until they don't turn as easily. Furthermore, the fine salt spray or droplets, generated by these devices promote corrosion problems in the immediate vicinity of the aquarium. The surge provided by the dump bucket, however, is very beneficial, and a significant improvement over mere circulation. However, in our experience, the small size of some dump mechanisms in home aquaria is insufficient when it comes to water motion generation, and other forms of water circulation need to be employed as well. Some mesocosm (large-scale) exhibits employ a different surge device, using air displacement in a chamber attached to the aquarium e.g. Great Barrier Reef Marine Park Authority Aquarium (ReefHQ), BioSphere 2. The sole reliance on dump buckets does not address the significant body of evidence for the importance of strong laminar water motion in overcoming boundary layer effects on coral, and its effect on nutrient and gas exchange (see chapter 7).

Plankton preservation

Highlighting the importance of plankton preservation is another of Adey's philosophical differences from typical hobbyist mentality. The idea is romantic and easily accepted, since the importance of plankton to wild reef communities is undisputable, as a means of reproduction, larval dispersal, and source of food. Adey does not use protein skimming because of its capacity to remove plankton, and the centrifugal pumps that are the mainstay for aquarists are avoided wherever possible. Instead, *plankton friendly* pumps such as diaphragm pumps, bellows pumps, or Archimedes screw pumps are used. The value of this idea diminishes for smaller exhibits when one observes how rapidly zooplankton is consumed by corals and other filter feeders, regardless of the type of pumps used.

It is not necessary to use plankton friendly pumping systems such as this Archimedes screw pump made from a hose wrapped around a turning axle, but it sure makes for an interesting story. T. Siegel.

Furthermore, the advective flow of phytoplankton into the substratum is another unavoidable loss that happens whether or not *friendly* pumps are used. Plankton survivability in reef aquaria is the product of a variety of factors, not just the filtration and pumping system. Reef structure heterogeneity and scale are two important factors that have a great deal of impact on how much plankton can survive in a reef system. Areas of low water motion become natural areas for plankton accumulation. For example, we have observed sizable mysid populations develop in quiet areas of sumps, despite water being constantly removed by centrifugal pumps and protein skimmers. Large reef aquaria such as the 3.8 million liter (1,000,000 gallon) *ocean* at Biosphere 2 have had successful recruitment of fishes that have planktonic larval phases, owing to the fact that with such volume they can achieve and maintain quite high density of zooplankton.

Mechanical filtration

Considering the philosophy of plankton preservation, the use of mechanical filtration is not a part of Adey's system, but the system does incorporate export of nutrients through removal of detritus from settling chambers with cone-shaped bottoms. This means of export is useful for any reef aquarium system, since the production of lightweight detritus is quite high, especially in strongly illuminated and grazed systems. In a way it is like using the entire surface of the reef and walls of the aquarium as a turf filter, with the *harvesting* of primary production being accomplished by herbivores who incorporate some of it in their body mass. The waste they excrete is recycled or trapped in the settling chambers and removed periodically.

The ReefHQ coral reef mesocosm

The 2.5 million liter (~660,000 gallon) coral reef exhibit at ReefHQ, the education center of the Great Barrier Marine Park Authority, which opened in 1987 to provide an analogue to the *real thing* on land was built as a closed system, using large-scale algal turf scrubber (ATS) technology and sand filters as the sole means of water purification.

After 17 years of this complex *experiment in progress*, the curators undertook radical changes in the life support system to address several issues in water quality (Michalek-Wagner, 2004c). Massive water changes were begun in July 2002, the sand filters were gradually phased out over a 7 month period ending in October 2002 and the ATSs were switched off in July 2003. Since November 2003, hundreds of larger fish were added, thousands of *Acanthochromis* spp. recruits arrived, the feeding regime was changed, ozone, calcium and alkalinity levels were manipulated, and 14 large water circulators were added, so it is impossible to attribute any changes in the chemistry/turbidity in the tank to the absence of the ATSs (K. Michalek-Wagner, pers. comm.). As we mentioned, both calcium and strontium levels were well below natural seawater values. In addition, the level of dissolved organic nitrogen (20.5 µM) was 500% that of natural reef waters. It is interesting to note, that levels of DON were also found to be higher than natural seawater in the Waikiki Aquarium's plenum system, described previously in this chapter. This appears to be a characteristic of closed systems in general and it would be interesting to know what the levels of DON are in other closed systems that employ activated carbon, ultraviolet light and/or ozone as part of their regular filtration.

Using nuclear magnetic resonance spectroscopy, Michalek-Wagner (2004a) tested the water both before and after passing through the ATS. She found a high concentration of di(2-ethylhexy)phthalate, a plasticizer, in the water coming from the ATS (Pecorelli *et al.*, 2004). This plasticizer is toxic to marinelife and came, presumably, from breakdown of the ATS trays due to exposure to UV from sunlight. Interestingly, there was no significant difference in the levels of DON, indicating that the ATS were not their source. However, the level of nitrate was reduced by 33% after passing through the ATS (Pecorelli *et al.*, 2004). After removal of the ATS filters, it was found that there was no significant difference in DON, nitrate, nitrite or redox levels in the tank. However, inorganic phosphate levels showed a significant decrease, as did pH, while afternoon oxygen levels increased (presumably due to increased algal growth in the tank) (Pecorelli *et al.*, 2004; Pecorelli *et al.*, in press). These results appear to indicate that the ATS did not significantly affect the levels of organic carbon, or organic or inorganic nitrogen in the aquarium; the main source appears to be within the tank itself, presumably from the deep sand bed and the decomposition of grazed marinelife. In addition, the results demonstrate that the algae and biomass in the tank play a major role in handling the inorganic nitrogen load, without the need for the ATS. The rupture of algal cells during harvesting releases phosphate, so the removal of the ATS actually resulted in a drop in inorganic phosphate levels (Pecorelli *et al.*, 2004). Massive (700,000 L/184,210 gallons) weekly water changes from a nearby tidal creek (accompanied by an extensive chemical and bioassay testing program) have now been undertaken, which has resulted in normal seawater values of calcium and strontium being attained, but dissolved DON remains elevated (Michalek-Wagner, 2004a). In addition, they have added large-scale protein skimmers and ozonation and have ceased using continuous sand-filtration (they are still used occasionally, for example after cleaning the tanks or after a heavy rainfall). These changes have resulted in greatly improved coral survival and an increase in invertebrate diversity (Michalek-Wagner, pers. comm.).

It is intriguing to see how even on large-scale reef aquariums the aquarists sometimes make more than one change at the same time. As a result, it is impossible to define the effect of the separate changes. We reported in Delbeek and Sprung (1994) the lack of success with corals in this aquarium, and it was one of the reasons for our criticism at that time of the ATS system. We believe that the recent improvements in this aquarium are more strongly a result of the protein skimming (which removes a large quantity of dissolved organic matter), ozone (which oxidizes water-staining organics), and water changing (which facilitates the maintenance of calcium and alkalinity levels) rather than the removal of the turf scrubbers. However, the effects of the plasticizer released by the degradation of the plastic ATS trays in this system is cause for concern, and may have been a contributing factor to the lack of success in this system.

Dr. Kirsten Michalek-Wagner, curator of the Great Barrier Reef Marine Park Authority Aquarium (ReefHQ), in her 2.5 million liter (~660,000 gallon) reef tank. One can really get in over one's head in this hobby!
D. Wachenfeld

The bank of algal turf filters formerly used at the Great Barrier Reef Marine Park Authority Aquarium.
A.J. Nilsen

Their removal was nevertheless a good demonstration that the ATSs were not needed to *filter* the water. The system has an enormous sand bed and abundant live rock capable of that. It is a pity though that the pendulum swung so far, since the turf filters illuminated at night could offer an improvement on nighttime oxygen levels and pH maintenance, even in such a large system. The problem with the installation of turf filters on this system was that they were located outside under canopies, where they received indirect sunlight. They were therefore never truly operating on a reverse daylight regime, though they did have metal halide lamps over them to illuminate them at night. They also took up an enormous amount of space that could have been used for coral culture, and required a great deal of maintenance. It is our experience that when protein skimming is initiated on an ATS filtered aquarium, the growth of algae in the ATS filters is reduced substantially. This means that when the two methods are combined, the size of the ATS could be scaled down. The minimum scaling required for an ATS to manage nighttime oxygen maintenance and pH balancing of the display aquarium has yet to be determined.

When sufficient food, calcium and trace element supplements are added, corals thrive in systems using algal turf scrubbers. The philosophy of creating complex food webs and whole ecosystem models also is good, and we wish to promote it. At one time, it was our opinion that the use of algae as a filter harms a reef aquarium. After more than 10 years of experimentation and observation of systems using algae in refugia and turf filters, it is now clear that our opinion was in error. The poor results with coral growth we reported in *The Reef Aquarium* volume one could be attributed to various factors, but especially several key husbandry issues that had been neglected such as alkalinity and calcium maintenance, food inputs, supplementation of trace elements such as iron and manganese, assimilation/removal of organics, lighting spectrum and predation.

The Ecosystem Aquarium® method a.k.a. the Miracle Mud® filter

In 1997, Leng Sy commercially introduced a unique *hybrid* filtration concept that featured a highly modified version of Adey's use of algae filtration and refugia, with numerous differences with respect to the aquarium design and system management. The original information published about this system came from several articles such as Paletta and Hildreth (1997), Paletta (1998) and Frakes (2000).

Paletta (1998) calls the Ecosystem Aquarium® method *a hybrid Jaubert system/algae filter.* In fact that is not really an accurate description since the key feature of Jaubert's method is a thick gravel bed sandwiched between the bulk water of the tank and a plenum space, none of which is used in Leng Sy's system. Paletta's reference

A well established Ecosystem Aquarium® filtered aquarium at *Underworld Products* in the UK. D. Ong.

A well established Ecosystem Aquarium® filtered aquarium at *Underworld Products* in the UK. D. Ong.

to Jaubert probably had more to do with the simplicity of the system rather than the mechanism of its functioning. The mud in the Ecosystem Aquarium® surely accomplishes some denitrification, but the process differs from the design of Jaubert. Paletta (2001) later describes the Ecosystem Aquarium® method as the *natural mud-filter method.*

The Ecosystem Aquarium® method uses surface skimming to draw water off the top of the tank into an overflow box from where it flows into the sump. The first chamber of the sump holds submersed bioballs intended primarily to break up any large pieces of detritus and to dissipate any large air bubbles that occur from the water draining down (Paletta, 2001). Paletta (2001) erroneously claims that the balls help oxygenate the water. The bacteria that colonize them in a short time would have the opposite effect, of course. In fact, the design of this first chamber could be modified to include a mechanical filter or, if space was not a concern, it could be a sediment trap. The water then flows through outlet slots near the bottom of a partition separating the first chamber from the main filtration chamber. The slots spread the water flow across a wider space so that it does not forcefully enter the main filter chamber, where the mud substratum is located. Also in this chamber, above the mud layer, is a large bed of *Caulerpa* spp. algae. The *Caulerpa* is illuminated 24 hours a day by a bank of fluorescent tubes. This algal bed performs several functions. It removes waste material from the tank, it helps to maintain a constant pH, and, by rooting in the mud, it helps to keep the mud from going anoxic since oxygen diffuses out of the rhizomes. A special feature of the system, as well as other natural filtration methods that use reverse daylight photosynthesis, is that it keeps the water well

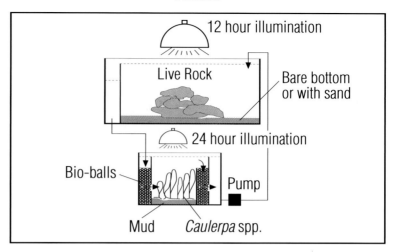

Figure 6t. Leng Sy's Ecosystem Aquarium® method. . Modified from: Pecorelli et al. 2004.

oxygenated both day and night. This method eliminates the need for air pumps PROVIDED THE POWER REMAINS ON AND/OR THE CIRCULATION PUMP CONTINUES TO FUNCTION. Paletta (2001) noted that wild pH fluctuations did not occur in his system. The pH bottomed out at 8.2 one hour prior to the lights being turned on in the main tank, and it rose to a maximum of 8.4 one hour prior to the light in the main tank going off at night.

Once the water passes through the mud/*Caulerpa*/algae chamber, it flows over a partition, through the slots near the bottom of a second partition and into a chamber that contains bioballs. A pump is located in the last chamber after the bioballs. The bioballs prevent algae from being drawn into the pump and fed into the main tank. The amount of water flowing through the filter should be at least three times the tank's volume per hour, with five times per hour being the optimum (Paletta, 2001).

The mud that Leng uses seems to have unique properties. It is described as 80% harvested oceanic mud blended with minerals and trace elements that are time released into the water column. It may simply aid in maintaining the *Caulerpa*. However, Leng Sy claims that his Miracle Mud® slowly gives off all necessary trace elements, and furthermore that because it becomes depleted of trace elements with time, it has to be partially exchanged periodically. His recommendation is to replace 1/2 of the mud after the first two years, and then 1/2 of the mud once per year thereafter. A simple mud replacement process is explained on the Ecosystem website, www.ecosystemaquarium.com.

Whatever its effect, it is claimed that this system would not work without the presence of the *mud*. Our own observations contradict this claim, since we have seen numerous refugium filters successfully using various fine-grained substrata with *Caulerpa*. We have nevertheless not done a long-term controlled comparison of these substrata and their affect on the algae cultivated in the refugium.

In 1995, after observing successful systems set up by Leng Sy using the Ecosystem Aquarium® method, Frakes set up a system using crushed coral as a substratum, but could not duplicate the results he had seen in Leng's tanks. He then passed the filter unit on to Mike Paletta who had become interested in this method. Mike's success and subsequent SeaScope articles in 1997 and 1998 inspired Frakes to take a second look at the EcoSystem Aquarium®, this time using the recommended mud substratum in the filter sump. Frakes (2000) made a 15 month comparison of a small EcoSystem Aquarium® and a Berlin style reef. He chose to set up two *identical reef aquariums* and equip one with an EcoSystem Aquarium® filter. The other aquarium was set up as a Berlin style reef tank, with a protein skimmer and using kalkwasser for evaporation replacement.

No sand was placed in the tanks, in order to facilitate detritus removal. This attempt to make the two tanks equivalent in fact changed the experiment: Although some aquarists set up reef aquariums without a sand or gravel bottom substratum, Berlin system tanks do normally have a bottom substratum and it provides supplemental biological filtration. The mud in the Ecosystem Aquarium® thus gave that aquarium a biological advantage over the Berlin system used in the comparison. Although we believe Frakes' attempt to make the aquariums identical gave a biological advantage to the system using more substratum, that is beside the main point that the Ecosystem Aquarium® method is an easy to establish and easy to maintain workable reef aquarium system.

Although it is claimed that mud is required for the Ecosystem Aquarium® method to work, we have seen numerous successful exhibits set up with modified versions of Leng Sy's system, using fine sand instead of mud. However, the use of the specially prepared mud in the Ecosystem Aquarium® method supports the long term growth of *Caulerpa* by supplying iron and other minerals. J. Sprung

Miracle Mud® looks like reddish brown sludge, feels like extremely fine silt and seems to be slightly buoyant as it does not pack down (Paletta and Hildreth, 1997). An analysis of the chemical composition of the mud (Sebralla and Kallmyer, 2001) shows that it contains a high concentration of iron and manganese, as well as silicate and other minerals. It does not contain coral gravel or other carbonates.

Although the mud is shipped dry (i.e. not live), within three months it is teeming with life such as worms, burrowing mollusks, copepods, mysids and amphipods (Paletta, 1998). Seeding the mud with a culture of mud-based organisms or *live mud* is possible (Paletta, 2000), and numerous vendors now sell such cultures. While it is not necessary to intervene this way to speed up the process, Paletta (2000) found it took approximately nine months for the mud to be fully colonized by burrowing worms, mysid shrimp and amphipods.

An overhead mud filter with *Caulerpa* and *Halimeda* filtering one of the coral systems at Exotic Aquariums in Miami Florida. J. Sprung

Small quantities of plankton are constantly flowing from the refugium back into the display tank. This probably accounts for the continuous polyp extension in virtually all corals kept in this system. The refugium certainly adds something to the water that stimulates polyps to open. It is possible that the *Caulerpa* and other algae leach dissolved organic substances that have this effect directly as a food source, or as an organic food that promotes bacteria to bloom in the water. Other algae growing in the refugium release spores or gametes that are essentially phytoplankton, and the production of zooplankton (protozoans) in the mud and algae in the refugium may contribute to the polyp response. In sump-style systems, the water that leaves the filter is pumped back up to the tank. Although it is commonly believed that animals rarely survive a ride through a pump, practical experience shows that larval fishes, zooplankton and phytoplankton can survive being passed through pumps. The manufacturer of the Ecosystem Aquarium® method filter also produces smaller hang-on systems that can be installed on the side or behind a tank. In these the water is pumped into the filter and goes back to the tank through an overflow in the filter, so the small animals from the filter pass to the aquarium without going through a pump.

The creatures that reproduce in the mud refugium certainly contribute food to the system, so it is indeed a special feature of the fine mud substratum that it promotes a high level of productivity. Sponges started from small cuttings grow without invertebrate food additions, as does the Chili coral, *Nephthyigorgia* sp. (Paletta, 1998), *Scleronephthya* sp. and gorgonians (Paletta, 2000). The combined productivity and lack of protein skimming is believed to be responsible for such success. Paletta (1998) also observed that Banggai cardinalfish offspring placed in the sump grew from one centimeter in length to adult size without ever having been fed directly. The only available food was whatever they could catch in the sump. It is hard to assign any significance to such observations since we have seen other systems also produce large numbers of Banggai cardinals in a similar manner that did not have mud or *Caulerpa* in them (J.C. Delbeek, pers. obs.).

The EcoSystem Aquarium® method, like other systems that use algae for filtration, fixes the end products of fish metabolism into plant tissue, thereby reducing the accumulation of harmful ammonia, nitrites and nitrates, and keeping the pH more stable. Paletta (1998) reported a phosphate level of 0.78 mg/L, and a nitrate-nitrogen level of 2.5 mg/L for an Ecosystem Aquarium® with a heavy load of fish. Leng Sy also claims that the EcoSystem Aquarium® method keeps fish healthier than other systems, and that his filtration system helps prevent and even cure lateral line disease. The latter claim is difficult to explain, but the general improvement of fish health can be attributed to the stability of oxygen levels and possibly the pH stability, features shared with other systems that use reverse daylight photosynthesis. Smit (1986) made similar claims about the early *minireef* systems, which interestingly featured large amounts of *Caulerpa* as a main component of the display. As a result, the late 80's and early 90's saw reef tanks dominated with *Caulerpa*, soft corals and LPS corals, and aquarists were as concerned about keeping *Caulerpa* as they were about keeping corals.

The Ecosystem Aquarium® system uses no protein skimmer or chemical filtration, and requires very little in the way of maintenance. The only recommended routine maintenance is a weekly or bimonthly 5% water exchange, removing detritus weekly, and calcium and buffer supplements, or the use of a calcium reactor. As in other reef aquarium systems, the light bulbs need to be replaced periodically (about once per year), in this case both on the display and on the refugium. As mentioned previously, a portion of the mud must be replaced periodically. The low set up cost and low maintenance are features it shares with Jaubert's system and the simplest natural systems of Eng (1961).

This beautiful Ecosystem Aquarium® filtered reef tank belongs to Des Ong, of Underworld Products in the UK. D. Ong

Growth of *Caulerpa* and other algae

While Paletta (2001) states: *after several years of growth in each system, the* Caulerpa *in the filters has never crashed and gone into sexual reproduction*. Frakes (2000) observes: *The* Caulerpa *in the EcoSystem Aquarium® went through several cycles. The feather bladed variety died back and gave way to the grape like C.* racemosa. It seems possible that the *Caulerpa* can produce gametes or spores that could settle and grow in the aquarium. Our personal experience with the system suggests that it rarely happens, however, so we agree with Paletta that the *Caulerpa* does remain in the filter, and does not spread to the aquarium, though the reason may not be that the gametes aren't shed. It is more likely that the cause has to do with availability of nutrients and herbivory in the display, as we will shortly explain. Furthermore, a mass die-off or reproduction event (release of gametes) of the *Caulerpa* would not cause the collapse of the aquarium, as opponents of the system sometimes suggest. The only harm such a bloom might cause is a lower oxygen level at night, which would not be a problem as long as the water circulation continues to operate to prevent oxygen levels from falling too low. In any case, maintaining a mixed bed (several species) of algae eliminates the chance of losing the entire bed of algae. In addition, the use of other algae that *go sexual;* the way *Caulerpa* does is an option that some aquarists take.

Paletta (2000) marvels over the fact that virtually no microalgae grows in the display tank using the EcoSystem Aquarium® filter, while the filter itself has a significant amount of algae, and leaves it as an unexplained mystery. This phenomenon is easy to explain. It occurs for two reasons. First, the display tank has herbivores that crop algae as they begin to grow. Second, the refugium is a small space that sees the entire volume of the water from the aquarium 3 to 5 times per hour, and thus all the nutrients it contains. That promotes the growth of algae there, compared to most parts of the display. The rate at which the entire nutrient content of the aquarium water passes over a given point in the tank is less than the rate at which the entire nutrient content of the aquarium water passes through the refugium. The same effect can be seen within most reef aquariums. It is the reason why hair algae and *Bryopsis* commonly grow on the screens in front of surface skimming overflows without spreading to the rest of the aquarium. In this position, they receive the most nutrients and light, and they escape herbivory.

While Paletta (2000) states: *For reasons still unclear to me, the* Caulerpa *has never out-grown the filter and needed to be harvested or removed. So, even after two years there is little maintenance involved in running this system.* Frakes (2000) observes: *The* Caulerpa *growth in the small chamber was amazing. It grew very densely into a brick-like mass with amphipods, snails, and mysid shrimp crawling about on it and in the chamber before it. About every 4 months nearly half the* Caulerpa *was harvested by ripping out over a pound at a time from the brick-like mass.* Paletta's comment refers to the issue of low maintenance, and it appears that these systems can be run without harvesting the *Caulerpa*. However, such a maintenance method means that nutrients are not being exported with the algae but instead with the detritus removal. In other systems, the harvest of algae or emptying of skimmate from a protein skimmer achieves nutrient export in between water changes. A static bed of *Caulerpa* can absorb nutrients up to a point, but unless it is actively growing, its affect on nutrient levels will be small, and it won't actively grow unless it is harvested periodically. A lack of *Caulerpa* growth can also occur due to an insufficient amount of CO_2 to nourish the *Caulerpa*. A cover over the refugium helps keep the CO_2 in the system, and can stimulate growth in the *Caulerpa* (Paletta, 2000).

Other *Caulerpa* issues

Though a proponent of the use of refugium filters, Borneman (2003) warns aquarists that the use of *Caulerpa* in filters is risky since *Caulerpa* spp. are known to contain potent toxins that could poison an aquarium simply by the release of these toxins into the water. We believe that Borneman's concerns about potential risks, though based on theoretically sound reasoning, are completely without merit. The success of a rather large number of public and private aquariums utilizing *Caulerpa* as filtration is evidence of the safety. By sharp contrast, that *Caulerpa* spp. can harm corals and other sessile invertebrates if allowed to overgrow them is well known to aquarists and scientists (Delbeek and Sprung, 1994). The toxins they contain can harm or kill coral tissue if the *Caulerpa* contacts the coral directly, and it is a simple fact that the growth rate of *Caulerpa* spp. exceeds most corals such that the *Caulerpa* can easily smother them. For this reason, including certain species of *Caulerpa* within a display aquarium housing stony corals is in fact risky, as it eventually becomes impossible to trim back the *Caulerpa* from the corals, and most corals lose the battle (Sprung, 2002). This problem does not occur when the Ecosystem Aquarium® method is used, as the *Caulerpa* spp. do not spread to the display tank. In addition, certain species of *Caulerpa* are quite easily managed even in a reef aquarium display, for example *Caulerpa taxifolia* and *Caulerpa prolifera*, so they pose no risk whatsoever. *Caulerpa lentillifera* and the dwarf form of *C. nummularia* are particularly unmanageable in reef aquariums (Sprung, 2002), so they should be avoided. Despite the toxins they contain, *Caulerpa* spp. grown in the filter can also be harvested and used as fresh, natural food for fish.

The discovery of *Caulerpa taxifolia* in the northern Mediterranean Sea in the 1980's and the recent discovery of it in a marina in southern California have caused much news media hysteria and enough concern to cause legislation to be passed regulating its import, sale and possession (see the *Introduction* for additional information about it and other *invasive species*). As a result of legislation concerning this species and similar looking relatives, the use of *Caulerpa* in aquarium filters seemed to be threatened right at the time it was becoming a popular trend in the aquarium hobby, offering a simple way to maintain aquariums that did not involve purchasing replacement plastic cartridges and other artificial filtration aids. In any event, the use of *Caulerpa taxifolia* in such filters in some regions is regulated by laws that prohibit the possession and transport of this species. This does not present a problem for most

This dwarf variety of *Caulerpa* cf. *nummularia* is potentially problematic in reef aquariums since it can smother corals and is impossible to remove. J. Sprung

Caulerpa taxifolia is beautiful and easy to manage in a refugium or in a display aquarium.
J. Sprung

The small grape *Caulerpa*, *Caulerpa lentillifera* is potentially harmful to corals and difficult to remove. J. Sprung

While easy to manage, *Caulerpa racemosa* has a boom and bust life cycle. J. Sprung

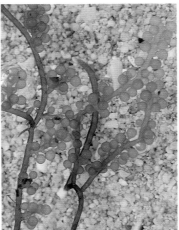

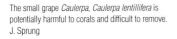

regions, where such laws don't exist, and of course, there are alternative species that can be used.

Use of *Chaetomorpha*

In the late 1980's, Doug Allen showed us an algal filter he used to filter the reef aquarium at the National Aquarium in Baltimore. In this algal filter he cultivated a single species of alga in the genus *Chaetomorpha*. This *spaghetti alga* is extremely easy to grow and harvest, making it an ideal choice for use in refugium filters. It has recently seen a surge in popularity in the aquarium trade as a species to be used in Ecosystem Aquarium® method filters. It and some other species of *Chaetomorpha* are now regularly cultivated and traded. In addition, red seaweeds such as *Halymenia, Botryocladia, Gracillaria,* and others, which are beautiful to look at, are also well suited to cultivation in refugia.

Chaetomorpha spiralis is an ideal species for refugiums.
J. Sprung

Halymenia from the Solomon Islands is one of many ornamental red seaweeds that can be cultivated in a refugium. J. Sprung

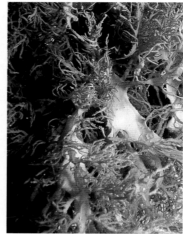

Hypnea pannosa is another ornamental red alga suitable for refugia. It has bright blue irridescent pigments and grows quickly. J. Sprung

Vince Rado of ORA shows their cultivated *Gracillaria*, which can be incorporated in a refugium. J. Sprung

Seagrass and mangroves

Interest in other marine aquatic plants for refugiums has resulted in the inclusion of seagrass and mangroves among the species housed in an Ecosystem Aquarium® filter. These do not grow as quickly as *Caulerpa* or other algae, but they offer a nice aesthetic dimension to the exhibit. The availability of seagrass to aquarists is currently in its infancy- sporadic collections made with permits. The future will involve mass clonal production of micro propagules and vegetative growth (see for example Bird and Jewett-Smith, 1994, and Woodhead and Bird, 1998). Mangrove availability is currently restricted to one or two species of Red mangrove (*Rhizophora mangle*) and the similar looking *Brugueria* spp.

Caveats

Paletta (2000) notes a shortcoming regarding the initial biological capacity of the Ecosystem Aquarium® filter. Before it has achieved a biological *equilibrium* or stable state, this system has a great deal of difficulty handling the large quantities of decomposing waste materials from fresh live rock. This inability to handle a large amount of waste is true of any reef aquarium system, of course, but Paletta sees the missing protein skimmer as contributing to this initial shortcoming. After the live rock is cured and the filter is established, there is no such weakness.

Another problem noted by Paletta (1998) is that the *Caulerpa* initially placed in the refugium may grow or float to the surface and die. Starting out with *Caulerpa* attached to gravel or initially weighing it down by placing small live rocks on it will reduce

This Ecosystem Aquarium® system belongs to Paul Endtricht, in Texas, and exhibits a nice diversity of zoanthids, tridacnid clams, and stony and soft corals. P.R. Endtricht

The Miracle Mud® filter situated under the aquarium. Note the growth of *Caulerpa taxifolia* initially added to the filter attached to rocks that weigh it down. P.R. Endtricht

this problem, as the *Caulerpa* readily roots in the mud. When harvesting the *Caulerpa* it is best to use a scissors to thin out the thick growth at the water surface rather than pulling on it, which would tend to separate the roots from the mud bed.

Paletta (2000) also notes that if the flow is too slow through the refugium, cyanobacteria may start to grow there, but when the flow rate is too great, it may result in tiny air bubbles passing through the sump and being pumped into the main tank. Additionally, too strong a flow can push the mud into uneven piles, which can cause the *Caulerpa* not to grow.

How much mud

A 12" by 4" by 6" middle chamber of the filter holds 3 pounds of EcoSystem mud in a layer about 1" deep.

How much light on the refugium

A 12" by 4" by 6" refugium is illuminated by an 18 watt, 4000K compact fluorescent bulb 24 hours a day.

Size of refugium compared to tank

Borneman (2003) refers to the biological filtration effect of a refugium compared to the main display, but ignores the other aspect of oxygen production and pH stabilization at night. Sizing the refugium must take into consideration all three issues, though the former issue may be disregarded for the very reason Borneman points out, namely that the biological filtration is managed by the substratum in the display aquarium (especially if it has sand or gravel).

Table 6.3: Ecosystem filter size recommendations, according to the manufacturer

Model	Ecosystem Aquarium® Filter Box	Tank Size (Gallons)	*Flow (Gallons Per Hour)	Miracle Mud® qty.
2410	24 x 10 x 12	40 to 65	600-800 GPH	10 lbs
3012	30 x 12 x 16	75 to 95	800-1000 GPH	20 lbs
3612	36 x 12 x 18	100 to 135	1000-1200 GPH	30 lbs
3616	36 x 16 x 18	150 to 240	1200-1500 GPH	40 lbs

Paletta (2001) wonders about the crystal clarity of the water in these systems, and says: *it may be a result of the 24-hour light cycle, because not having a dark cycle may prevent the production of gelvin (yellowing compounds), which are thought to be a product of algae's chloroplasts breaking down at night and being released into the water.* Paletta later noted that the yellow water eventually did occur. Leng Sy recommends that activated carbon use be restricted to just 12 hours once per week to prevent the yellow substances from accumulating.

The wonderful reef aquarium of Markus Resch is filtered by the Ecosystem Aquarium® system. M. Resch

Leng Sy maintains his tanks without a bottom substratum to allow for removal of the detritus that settles out during the week (Paletta, 2000). Once a week he siphons out ten gallons of water to remove detritus that has accumulated. In addition, the current in his tanks is quite high to keep detritus in suspension so that it can find its way to the filter. Such a mode of operation would supply a continuous source of nutrients to the *Caulerpa*, with the detritus that settled there. Paletta notes that adding a thin layer of substratum to his own tank, along with appropriate sand-sifting organisms produced no deleterious effects. Leng Sy says the purpose of a bottom substratum in a display aquarium is for decoration only. The substratum does not contribute to the filtration of the system. He maintains some systems without any sand or gravel on the bottom and recommends the substratum in the main tank be limited to 9 mm (3/8 inch) or less. He also recommends siphoning the substratum to remove detritus along with regular water changes.

Natural Environmental Gradient (EG) zonal filtration

Aquarist Steve Tyree wowed the reef aquarium keeping community in 1994 with a photo in *The Reef Aquarium* volume one of one of his SPS aquariums dominated by colourful *Acropora* spp. This photo precipitated a craze for colourful SPS corals that is still going strong ten years later. Tyree subsequently began researching a new angle on water filtration using refugia for reproducing the cryptic habitat that exists within the live rock structure of reefs. In these refugia, he cultivates sponges, tunicates and other forms of life that live by filter feeding, removing bacteria, microscopic animals, and dissolved organic substances from the water. He calls this method the Environmental Gradient (EG) Zonal Approach, or natural EG filtration. His idea is based upon recent research such as Richter and Wunsch (1999) and Bak, *et al.* (1998) that studies the roles of reef cavity dwelling suspension feeding. It is furthermore supported

Figure 6u. Top view schematic of Tyree's natural EG filtration system set up in an aquarium without plumbing. See the photo of this system on the next page. The aquarium is divided into three zones, with a perforated barrier separating the illuminated section from the cryptic zone where sponges, clams, tunicates, and other cryptic fauna are cultivated.

Figure 6v. Top view schematic of Tyree's natural EG filtration system set up in an aquarium without plumbing. The aquarium is divided into two zones, with a perforated barrier separating the illuminated section from the cryptic zone where sponges, clams, tunicates, and other cryptic fauna are cultivated.

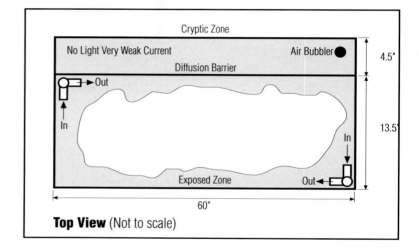

by research, such as Diaz and Ward (1997) and Corredor *et al.* (1988) that shows sponges can mediate nitrification, or that they may harbor a uniform microbial community (Diaz, 1997; Hentschel *et al.*, 2002). It is a feature of Tyree's system and other *natural systems* that dissolved organic matter and particulate organic matter from primary production on the reef surface is transported through the reef structure and utilized by consumers such as bacteria and cryptic animals living within the internal structure of the reef. Tyree's tri-zonal reef structure is reminiscent of the typical aquascape approach in Walter Adey's systems.

According to Tyree, his filtration method: *utilizes the cryptofauna located within the cryptic zones of the tropical reef platform. These animals are naturally suited to consume dissolved organics and bacteria. Berlin style reef aquaria utilize a protein skimmer to remove dissolved organics, but lack any natural method to control pelagic bacterial densities. The use of living sponges and sea squirts presents a much more natural method to maintain captive reef aquaria. Additional advantages of this new method are its low operational costs combined with the inherent ability to maintain a more diverse assemblage of macro organisms.*

Tyree's filtration angle offers a new perspective to natural system filtration, but it is hard to avoid noting that any aquarium with a substantial amount of live rock is already going to have substantial cryptic zones where these filter feeders will grow. What Tyree proposes that distinguishes his system from others is to set up attached refugiums or large sumps with cryptic zone habitats. The belief that a protein skimmer does not remove bacteria is not completely correct. However, the concept that sponges and other filter feeders in the dark recesses of the reef are capable of filtering

An EG refugium. Normally kept in the dark, this section was temporarily illuminated for photographic purposes S. Tyree

One of Tyree's reef aquarium systems. S. Tyree

out organic substances and bacteria is true. Since the system is skimmerless, organic matter that accumulates stimulates the production of bacterial biomass. This in turn is fed upon by sponges. Thus, phosphorus is removed from the water in a two-step process, but remains in the system as it is not harvested, except by siphoning detritus or with water change. What is unclear about Tyree's EG system is how one determines the capacity of the system. At what point can you add animals and what amounts of cryptic fauna are needed to handle a certain bioload? This is easy enough to judge from prior experience with Berlin system aquariums that rely on live rock for biological filtration. Since Tyree's system also employs live rock, it provides the foundation for the biological filtration, supplemented by the filtration effects of the cryptic fauna in refugia. Using Berlin system guidelines is a starting place for judging the bioload capacity of the system. The fact that sponges harbor nitrifying bacteria (Diaz and Ward 1997) means they provide additional potential for nitrification above the capacity provided by bacteria located in an on live rock. Theoretically, without sufficient denitrification in the aquarium substrata, the net effect of sponge-mediated nitrification would be an increase in nitrate.

Additionally, recent research (Yahel, 2003), demonstrates that organisms living on the surface of bare-looking live rock have amazing ability to remove phytoplankton and bacteria from the water. Additionally, as we discussed earlier in this chapter, film-forming bacteria that form slime (biofilm) on the surface of live rocks may have the ability to physically trap planktonic bacteria and phytoplankton. Subsequently other creatures living on the rock surface could consume the trapped cells, or the film-forming bacteria might be able to digest and consume them directly. This could in effect be a symbiotic relationship between the film forming bacteria and other creatures living on the rocks, or a variation on primary production where the primary producers, phytoplankton, are concentrated by adhesion or advective forcing to be consumed by bacteria, which in turn are fed upon. Shedding of the biofilm (by physical forcing- waves) could contribute to the POM in the water and thus represent additional nutrient cycling.

Calcium supplementation

Since Tyree's EG systems typically have only 1/2 or 1/4 of their volume populated by rapidly growing calcifying organisms, the daily calcium and alkalinity requirements can usually be managed with kalkwasser used to top off evaporation (see chapter 5). Large EG systems with a large exposed zone (the illuminated portion of the reef) may require a calcium reactor for maintaining calcium and alkalinity.

Natural systems – final thoughts

Reef aquaria can be maintained by a variety of methods, as long as the critical physical parameters of temperature, light, and water movement are within certain limits, and the accumulation of nutrients is kept in check. Not only are there many ways to maintain a reef aquarium, there are also many types of *reef aquaria*. Some aquaria emphasize mostly soft corals, some mostly stony corals. Some are full of upright algae such as *Caulerpa* and *Halimeda*, or smaller turf forming species, while others are dominated by pink and purple coralline algae. Different methods of filtration and water motion affect the ability to create these different types of closed ecosystems. Our discussion of aquascaping techniques (chapter 9) and the discussions of water movement (chapter 7) and lighting effects (chapter 8) all relate to how a natural system aquarium becomes what the aquarist intends to create.

Choosing the *best* system or the simplest one really depends on the type of environment you wish to create. Even differences in the type of make-up water used can have a dramatic impact on the resulting environment. In this regard, Dr. Adey's philosophical distinction between creating a whole living ecosystem versus a display for numerous chosen species applies. Most aquarists attempt the latter, while Adey is a proponent of the former. In our opinion, the best philosophy for the average aquarist combines the two, recognizing that the constraint of size (i.e. the captive environment) limits the ability to support all types of plants and animals found on the reef. It is the aquarist who places the creatures within the tank, so it is his/her responsibility to plan for the proper long-term maintenance of each specimen.

Reef *guruism*

We don't know why, but sometimes aquarists treat the various methods as if they were religions and their proponents prophets. We present them here as methods and proponents, explaining the reasoning behind the designs and operation, the intent of their proponents and how the systems could be improved, where that is possible. Our critical points are not meant to discredit any of the systems or their proponents, but to highlight features of the *original philosophy* that may need reconsideration, in our opinion. We present all of these systems here because each one teaches something valuable about the creation of a captive ecosystem, and each offers a reproducible technique for successfully establishing a coral reef community in a closed aquarium. As an aquarist, you will develop your own successful technique that may incorporate elements of one or several of these systems.

In our fast-growing salt water hobby the aquarist has the opportunity to learn and discover many new and interesting things. This is what makes the keeping of marine aquaria so fascinating. But, before you try anything new, stop for a second to evaluate the new idea or the new product. Examine it from the practical angle. Be a little skeptical. The new idea or product may be the best thing in the world and may have worked to perfection for the person advocating its use, but one little overlooked piece of information may cause plenty of trouble for you. Consider all the details before you take action: light, circulation, cleanliness, water composition, marine life etc. When all of these factors have been weighed, judge everything in the light of that old trustworthy ally, your own experience. Let you own experience provide the acid test for any new gimmick.

— Robert P.L. Straughan in Tropical Fish Hobbyist Magazine, June 1961

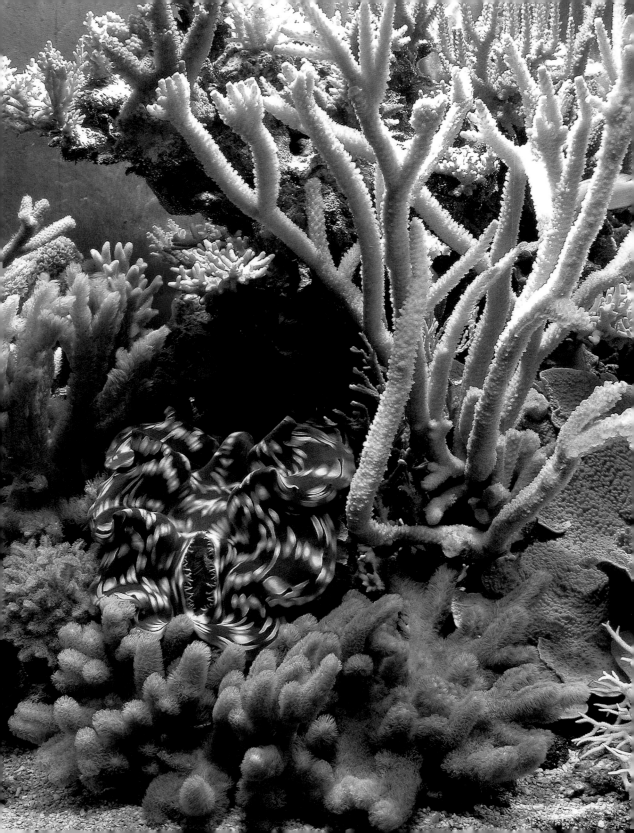

Water Motion

Water motion is something that aquarists often overlook, but it is one of the most critical physical parameters that determine the health of the aquarium as an environment and the inhabitants as individuals. When we first started keeping these reef tanks we were so concerned about filtration, and the *buzzword* was *turnover. How many times do I turn over the volume of water through a filter?* was the primary question about water movement. More important is the water motion within the tank, both its velocity and variability. Several studies in the hobbyist literature have looked at water flow in home aquaria, and they determined that many of the tanks examined had water flows that more closely matched lagoon environments than outer reef areas (see Riddle, 1996; Harker, 1998). However, the recent advances in water motion technology that we detail in this chapter afford more opportunity to achieve higher energy flows in aquariums. In addition, as we discussed in the topic of biological filtration in chapter 6, the flow is important because it promotes advective movement of water through the substrata and the maintenance of substrata porosity. A new round of evaluations of water motion in home aquaria using the new types of water moving technology should examine not only the physical parameters but also the effects on biological filtration and water chemistry.

Types of water motion

The aquarium of Alexander Girz, Nuremberg, Germany. M. Belosevic.

Three main types of water movement characterize the reef environment: surge, turbulence and laminar flow. Surge is the back and forth movement caused by ocean swells and wind-driven waves. As the waves move into shallow water, their circular motion components become compressed and flattened, causing the water to move back and forth. This is best demonstrated by the back and forth motion of large sea fans in shallow reef areas. Surge is an important factor in the biology of many reef organisms, especially flexible ones. The back and forth movement exposes more of the surface area to light, increases the feeding efficiency of polyps and greatly helps in the exchange of metabolites and gases with the water. Turbulence is a random swirling of water in all directions, often caused by opposite currents clashing or water swirling around objects. Laminar flow is water movement in one direction and is the type of flow commonly generated by aquarium pumps. It is typically encountered on deeper portions of the reef. Although small-scale turbulence can be generated in aquariums by laminar flow, the effect is usually isolated, not tank wide (Sprung, 1988).

The role of water motion

What's important about the flow of water is what it achieves. Water motion brings food, facilitates the exchange of oxygen and carbon dioxide with the environment, and enhances the uptake and release of nutrients and wastes. It does this by disturbing the boundary layer around a coral head/branch or any other creature.

The mass transfer (the diffusion of substances across a boundary layer, in this case the cell membrane) of gases and metabolites is required for organisms to survive, and this is especially so for submerged organisms. This mass transfer must occur across a boundary layer made up of still water that surrounds every surface underwater. If there isn't sufficient flow, an organism becomes isolated from the environment because of dampening of the water flow adjacent to it. This creates a thin film of motionless water surrounding the organism, hindering photosynthesis and respiration (Dennison and Barnes, 1988). Without sufficient water flow, the organism can consume all of the oxygen from this layer of water, and literally suffocate in its own waste. Water flowing across marine organisms causes forces to act upon this boundary layer. As a result, organisms in low-flow environments tend to have thicker boundary layers than organisms in high-flow environments. The thinner the boundary layer, the easier it is for diffusion to take place.

Water motion is also essential for calcification to proceed at optimum rates. Reduced water flow can lower dark calcification rates by up to 60% and light calcification by 25% (Dennison and Barnes, 1988). Strong water velocity not only strips away the thin layer of motionless water surrounding an organism, it also moves soft-bodied or flexible species back and forth, achieving the same end. Furthermore, strong water motion serves the same function that a heart does, in that it helps circulate the gelatinous internal fluids in corals through its impact on the coral's surface, aiding the exchange of respiratory gasses, dissolved food, and waste across their surface. The motion of the water literally pumps the organism. This is why pumping *Xenia* (pulse coral) pumps when the water is relatively still. The action circulates the internal fluid and allows *Xenia* to release CO_2 and uptake oxygen; during intense daylight, it promotes the release of excess photosynthetically generated oxygen too. Water motion achieves these functions for other corals that do not pulse, and the state of expansion of the coral tissue and polyps assists the exchange of respiratory gasses, food, and waste by increasing or decreasing surface area. The pumping action also serves a less obvious purpose: the pulsed illumination and shading of the organism. In many flexible species, surge water motion achieves this effect, preventing the organism from over-illumination or constant shade to either side because it moves back and forth.

On the reef, water motion and light are intimately related. The water motion alters the light. The ripples or waves on the water surface create so-called *glitter lines*, which pulse the light like a strobe, so that it is briefly brighter than ambient light and briefly less bright.

Water motion is also a factor in coral feeding. However, no one current flow is the best for all species. For example, Dai and Lin (1993) found that three Taiwanese asymbiotic gorgonians *Subergorgia suberosa*, *Acanthogorgia vegae* and *Melithaea ochracea* fed over a wide range of flow rates. The ability to keep polyps open was also related to flow rates and the size of their polyps. *Subergorgia suberosa* had the largest polyps, which were deformed by the lowest currents speeds (>10 cm/s), severely hindering prey capture. In contrast, *Melithaea ochracea*, which had the shortest and the least easily deformed polyps at high flow rates, could feed at the highest flow rates (40 cm/s). *Acanthogorgia vegae* had an intermediate polyp size and fed in flows of 0-24 cm/s. Although all three fed most effectively at flows of 8 cm/s, *S. suberosa* had the narrowest feeding range (5-10 cm/s) while *M. ochracea* had the widest range (4-40 cm/s) (Dai and Lin, 1993). This varying ability to feed in various current flows is a major factor in determining distribution on reefs. *Melithaea ochracea* is the most widely spread gorgonian on southern Taiwanese reefs, occurring on the upper part of reef fronts where currents are strong. *Subergorgia suberosa*, which feeds in a narrow range of flow velocities, has a restricted distribution pattern, being found on lower reef slopes or on sheltered boulders where currents are weaker. *Acanthogorgia vegae*, which can feed in relatively strong currents, is most commonly found on the semi-exposed reef fronts or the lateral side of boulders (Dai and Lin, 1993). Therefore, water flow and its interactions with polyps and colonies, appears to greatly influence distribution patterns of colonies, colony growth, size and morphology, and rates of gas exchange (in Fabricius *et al.*, 1995). Some aquarists have observed that some corals will open when food items are added to the aquarium. However, this is not always the case. For example, Mizrahi *et al.* (2001) found that if food were present at night, *Favia favus* would not open its polyps unless the correct water motion was present.

Recent evidence also points to a role for water motion in preventing coral bleaching. After the coral bleaching event in Palau in 1998, several observers noted that corals in high flow areas did not appear to have suffered as greatly as those in other areas did. As we mentioned previously, corals are surrounded by a boundary layer of motionless water. The stronger the water motion around the coral, the thinner this layer becomes. One of the theories of coral bleaching states that coral bleaching begins when the process of CO_2 fixation begins to break down under the influence of high temperature and/or irradiance, which leads to the accumulation of toxic oxygen radicals and their derivatives in the zooxanthellae. This leads to damaged pigments and proteins that results in the inactivation of photosynthesis and brings about bleaching. The removal of these derivatives by diffusion before they can cause damage could be the result of high water flows that compress the boundary layer, enhancing diffusion rates, and hence, mass transfer rates in the process (Nakamura and van Woesik, 2001). Increased water flow can also lead to a more rapid recovery from light induced bleaching, and most likely temperature induced bleaching as well (Nakamura *et al.*, 2003). It is also possible that the high flow rates assisted the corals simply by keeping them from suffocating at night. At high temperature, the dissolved oxygen is lower in concentration, and during a bleaching event, the biological oxygen demand, not to mention increased respiration rates of all creatures, leads to a rapid depletion of oxygen. Corals in shallow, high flow areas were in the best position to get as much oxygen as possible, given the high temperature.

Finally, water motion has also been shown to affect at the amount of microsporine-like amino acids (MAAs) present in *Porites compressa*. These are the chemicals responsible for blocking ultraviolet light. When comparing the levels of MAAs in corals from high and low water motion areas, those from the lower water motion areas had lower levels of MAAs, lower calcification rates and photosynthetic pigment production (Kuffner, 2002). Again, the role of the boundary layer in allowing the diffusion of chemical precursors of MAAs under different flow regimes may be the reason.

Tip: Given the role of water motion in coral bleaching the following measures should be considered by aquarists while recognizing the fact that some genera of corals do not tolerate high water flows e.g. *Cynarina, Alevopora, Plerogyra* etc.:

1) When changing lights or when moving to a much brighter lighting scheme, increase the water flow in the aquarium;
2) Increase the water flow when you expect temperature increases such as during the warmer months of the year or if you like to mimic nature and increase water temperatures during certain months;
3) Increase water flow if your cooling system fails and;
4) Increase water flow if introducing new specimens from dimmer aquaria or place these in areas with greater water flow.

Water motion and coral placement

When it comes to keeping reef organisms we must take into account the area from which they were collected, since this determines the forms of water movement to which they have adapted. The shape of the organism is often a clue, but it isn't always, and fortunately, most reef creatures have the ability to modify their orientation as they grow. However, portions of a colony may die off while others grow and give it a new shape.

Many organisms are adapted to zones where the water velocity is very slow most of the time, and they expand during these periods of calm, and retract in stormy or more turbulent times. These include mushroom anemones and some stony corals such as *Cynarina lacrymalis*, *Nemenzophyllia turbida*, and *Plerogyra sinuosa*. These should be placed somewhere in the tank where the currents are very slight.

The vast majority of reef organisms like a good turbulent flow, or surge, especially soft corals such as gorgonians, leather corals, *Anthelia*, and *Xenia*, and the branching and encrusting reef-building stony corals such as *Acropora*. Because they are sessile organisms, corals, sponges and other invertebrates orient their growth to the water flow, so that their ultimate shape is a product of the flow regime where they occur on the reef, in addition to their orientation toward or away from the light. As with lighting, if you can vary the energy, providing it in a pulsed fashion, so much the better, because that's what happens in the natural setting. Water motion does change. The tides change, waves come with storms, and the depth change associated with the tides alters the flow of currents. In an aquarium, you almost have to be some kind of engineer to figure out the best arrangement of currents to provide both turbulent and quiet zones to accommodate different organisms, based on the structure of the reef that you've built, where you have positioned the corals, and the means that you provide to vary the flow of water. Fortunately, there are more than a few water motion devices now available to hobbyists that offer several forms of water motion.

Options for Aquariums

With all of this background about water motion, it may seem like a complicated matter to provide a good circulatory system for a reef aquarium. Actually, it is quite a simple matter, but there are many options to choose from, and systems for circulating water in the reef tank can be made complex, if one so desires.

Main pump

The main pump in a system with an external sump refers to the one that returns water to the display tank from the sump. If one uses a powerful pump or more than one pump for this purpose, the need for accessory pumps or other means of water motion is diminished. It is not necessary to have additional pumps, but varying the flow is easier to accomplish when accessory pumps and devices are used. Many of the devices that we describe in this chapter to generate oscillating currents (e.g. rotating outlets, motorized ball valves) or increase flow (e.g. eductors) can also be used on the outlet(s) of the main pump.

Accessory pumps and other flow enhancing devices

Different types of accessory pumps may be used for additional circulation or variation of the flow within the aquarium. These include external dedicated recirculation pumps, powerheads and prop pumps. These devices may be used in conjunction with eductors, *wavemaker* switching devices, *pulse timer* switching devices, or with simple timers to create a variety of flow patterns and water motion.

Recirculation pumps

A dedicated recirculation pump offers a variety of options for water flow. J.C. Delbeek

External dedicated recirculation pumps have the advantage of not being an obstruction within the aquarium, and not contributing as much heat to the water as submersible powerheads or prop pumps. When using an external pump, the location of the intake is important. We have seen many aquariums equipped with recirculating pumps with the intake plumbed through the wall of the aquarium (either a side or the bottom), and outfitted with a strainer to prevent fish from being slurped into the motor. This technique works fine for fish-only aquariums, but is a disaster in the reef tank. Don't make this mistake! Wandering clownfish anemones, loose mushroom anemones, algae, sea cucumbers and other creatures end up against the strainer and often, through the pump. They become reef *puree*. The design of choice with this arrangement is simply to put the intake in the overflow. This arrangement can also be used for feeding the protein skimmer from the overflow. One caveat to this placement is that the intake must be placed low enough to prevent it from sucking in air. Since the overflow often has a cascade that produces air bubbles, the intake placed there will tend to pick up fine bubbles and send them into the aquarium. The use of a Durso standpipe, which maintains a high water level in the overflow, reduces the cascade air bubble generation (see chapter 1). Whether the intake is placed directly in the aquarium or in the overflow, an intake screen is necessary, since creatures do wander over the overflow. Be sure to situate the intake such that access to the screen for cleaning is not hindered.

Distributing flow

There are various fittings and piping systems available that can be used to extend the outlets of the main or recirculation pump. These work to direct water to various parts of the aquarium and in various

Locline fittings can be used to create a fan-like water return pattern. J.C. Delbeek

spray patterns. The most commonly available is the Loc-Line system, which uses a series of interlocking articulated fittings to create a flexible return pipe that can be oriented in almost any direction. Various outlet types can then be used on the end of the arm to create a variety of water return patterns ranging from a wide spray to a narrow stream. Such a system is useful for directing flow towards a specific region or spot in the tank, and allows the flow pattern to be easily changed by reorienting the piping. In this manner, you can blast the rockwork in one area of the tank to remove accumulated detritus one day and then select a different area the next day.

Variable speed pumps

Whether used as a main system pump or a dedicated recirculation pump, a variable speed pump can be used to create pulsing currents and to recreate tidal currents in large displays. These pumps have motors designed to receive variable electrical signals and rheostats are used to control their operation. There are only a few hobbyist-sized pumps designed to operate in this manner but they are readily available in larger sizes (5+ HP) and are commonly used in public aquarium installations.

Plankton friendliness

We do not agree with the assertion that centrifugal pumps should not be used because they harm plankton populations. We acknowledge that the point has some merit because pressure, shear, and turbulence inside some centrifugal pumps can kill a percentage of the phytoplankton and zooplankton that actually passes through the pump. One type of centrifugal pump was demonstrated to kill 90% of *Artemia salina* (brine shrimp) on a recirculating experimental set-up (Adey and Loveland, 1991). Brine shrimp are not a type of plankton found in reef aquariums, however, and reef aquariums are not exactly like small recirculating systems. Reef aquariums have a great deal of substrate heterogeneity, and much of the plankton generated in the system remains in the system around the substrates. It does not pass through the pumps. If you experiment with centrifugal pumps, you will discover that various sizes of plankton can be passed through them without causing any significant harm. Not all centrifugal pumps are alike, though. Impeller designs vary. In some pumps the volute (coiled impeller chamber) is large, and the blade is a small + shape in the middle, and some impellers are more disc-shaped, with internal blades or no blades at all. These kinds of designs have minimal impact on plankton. A more thorough examination of the affect on different types of plankton passing through different types of pumps would offer more valuable information than the demonstration that brine shrimp can be killed by a particular pump. It is true that additional experimentation is needed (Adey and Loveland, 1991), though we wish to emphasize that the concerns about pumps killing plankton are not so important for reef aquarium systems. Furthermore, alternative pumping systems such as diaphragm and screw pumps have four disadvantages: high cost, large size, noise, and frequent need for service or repair (Adey and Loveland, 1991). The difficulty keeping such organisms as sponges, bryozoans, hydroids, filter-feeding clams, or non-photosynthetic corals will not be solved by switching to these pumps. Difficulties with these organisms can be overcome by: the scale of the system (i.e. really big closed ecosystems can produce sufficient plankton to support filter-feeders); the use of refugia; or by the addition of cultured plankton for small systems.

On the subject of pumps, the failure of water circulating pumps or air pumps is an event that you can count on happening eventually. For this reason we recommend duplication of these items. If you have a natural system aquarium run by airstone only, use two air pumps, and replace the diaphragms periodically. For systems that use water circulating pumps, there should also be redundancy of pumps as a safeguard, and a bubbler in the tank provides still more safety. Even when water pumps are regularly cleaned and serviced, failure can occur. An additional spare pump kept packed in the closet may come in handy too, in the unlikely event that both pumps should fail, or for replacement parts.

Submersible pumps offer flexibility and freedom from plumbing, but some caution about their use is worth noting as we mentioned in chapter 4. Submersible pumps use the water to dissipate heat, so they tend to raise the temperature of the water. This effect is of most concern in small aquariums. In large aquariums, the temperature increase is slight. Some submersible pumps are filled with oil, and would pollute the tank if a leak in the pump casing developed. Likewise, a leak in the pump casing could result in electrical current in the aquarium. Saltwater and electricity are a deadly combination. This potentially very dangerous situation is made less dangerous by the use of a ground fault protection device, available from hardware stores (see chapter 3). Aside from the safety hazard from electrical current in the aquarium, such a failure of an electrical device (heater or pump for example) would introduce copper ions into the water by electrolysis, producing a toxic condition in a short period. It is important to inspect and maintain all submersible electric devices regularly.

Powerheads

The use of small water circulating pumps, aka powerheads helps to boost circulation in aquariums, over the circulation provided by the main circulating pump. Having more than one pump circulating water is also a kind of redundancy that prevents catastrophe should one of the pumps fail.

There are several kinds of powerheads available. The most typical is a submersible centrifugal pump that has its coil imbedded in an epoxy resin, which moves a cylindrical magnet attached to the impeller. Most models of this design are inexpensive. The downside of the design is that the coil gets hot as the pump operates and the cooling of the pump is accomplished by its contact with the water. Therefore, a large number of pumps can significantly raise the water temperature.

Powerheads also have intake strainers, and these can suck up and damage or kill delicate invertebrates such as anemones, snails, nudibranchs, sea cucumbers and starfish. They may also trap algae and other stuff, resulting in clogged intakes and reduced pump output unless frequently cleaned.

Another kind of powerhead is an overhead mounting type. In this design, the motor is not submersible, and only the impeller is inserted into the aquarium. The coil is air-cooled in this case, so it does not transfer heat to the aquarium. Overhead type motors are more expensive than the submersible types, and most require extra maintenance and expensive repair or part replacement, but they also are more powerful than most submersibles.

Powerheads are usually an obstruction to the decor in small aquariums less than 200 L (50 gallons), but are most useful for added circulation in large tanks. Manufacturers have been building smaller powerheads that are less noticeable, and these can be incorporated in smaller exhibits, concealed within the rockwork. One very significant disadvantage to powerheads is the risk of them sucking up small fish, wandering anemones, nudibranchs, sea cucumbers, or algae fragments. A mechanical filter cartridge attachment on the bottom of the powerhead prevents this possibility, but adds a potentially unsightly item that could detract from the décor and reduce flow as it clogs. Mechanical filter cartridges also need regular cleaning. Locating a powerhead strategically among rocks can effectively conceal its presence and prevent stray creatures or algae from getting sucked into the intake grid or port, but the powerheads themselves need to be serviced occasionally, and it is not desirable to have to pull apart a section of the reef to service them. We have seen aquarists who have simply left powerheads (unplugged) in place in the reef after they ceased working! In 2003, Tunze introduced a powerhead-concealing device that looks like a piece of rock on which you can encourage the growth of corals and coralline algae, in time concealing the true nature of the rock. Live rock can also be used to conceal a powerhead by drilling a hole through the rock and placing the powerhead behind it such that the outlet exits through the drilled hole. One can also encourage the growth of zoanthids or star polyps over the powerhead by affixing a few polyps using cyanoacrylate glue. These will grow and spread over the powerhead in time, totally concealing it. Of course, the powerhead intake and exit must be kept clear at all times, and if the powerhead fails, you have to either peel off the polyps or discard them. See chapter 9 for details on these methods.

One significant advantage to the use of powerheads is the ability to change flow direction or create pulse waves with timers or switching devices. With simple household utility timers, one can turn powerheads on or off for set intervals, simulating the change in water flow and direction associated with tidal change.

Powerhead motors come in two types: submersible synchronous motors and non-submersible non-synchronous motors. Both types work well, but the switching devices for them are different. The submersible types can be used with so-called *wave makers* that turn the pump on and off intermittently. Some submersible pumps do not tolerate these continuous hard starts and stops, and need to be restarted occasionally, or they stop working altogether, for example, when the magnet breaks loose from the impeller. Some wave-makers for these powerheads feature a softer start mechanism that is supposed to be kinder to powerhead operation. The submersible Turbelle® motors from Tunze have a breaking system that keeps the magnet from reversing direction. This design can be used with a special power timer to achieve more natural wave motion, but the breaks are subject to wear and eventually need to be replaced.

Non-synchronous motors can be used with a different kind of wave maker, the so-called *power* or interval timers that pulse the motor speed e.g. Tunze pulse timer. By accelerating and slowing the impeller, interval timers used with non-synchronous powerheads produce very natural wave-like currents, either with a pause or without one.

The Seio Super Flow pump is an energy efficient design that combines the basic magnetic drive powerhead with a propeller pump. It offers high flow across a broad front at low energy consumption, but is not designed to be used with interval timers. Photo Courtesy of TAAM.

Propeller pumps

An alternative to the standard centrifugal pump style powerhead is the prop pump design, short for propeller pump. The concept can be applied to direct drive pumps or to magnetic drive pumps, though the latter need to use a system that prevents reversing of the direction of rotation.

The advantage of using a propeller to move the water is that it creates a very large cross section pressure wave that moves a high volume without creating high velocity (shear). The motor used can also be of low power consumption, so the design is energy efficient. For example, a 35 watt direct drive motor can move approximately 38 m^3 (10,000 gallons) per hour. The first commercial prop-type pump

The Tunze Stream pump is another energy efficient magnetic drive propellor pump that moves a broad front of water at high volume with low shear. It has a special braking system on the impeller that insures the direction the impeller will turn, and it can be used with interval timers to simulate waves. Courtesy of Tunze GmbH.

Tunze makes a molded rock to conceal the stream pump. J. Sprung

A magnetic mount for the stream pump that holds it securely in any position. J. Sprung

available is the Tunze Turbelle® Stream pump. This unit comes in a variety of sizes and includes a mounting kit to attach the pump to the side of the aquarium. These pumps can be used in conjunction with a pulse timer to ramp the water flow up and down in a continuous cycle. Another option available is a piece of hollowed out stone that covers the pump to hide it from view (see chapter 9). The Turbelle® Stream pump is also incorporated in the Wave Box® system that is used to generate a surge in aquariums.

Hobby propeller pumps

There are also enterprising hobbyists who have been able to modify existing pumps into prop pumps. American hobbyists Jimmy Chen and Anthony Tse have modified several submersible pond pump models by affixing a propeller to the drive shaft. These pumps differ from powerheads in that they are direct drive pumps.

American hobbyist Jimmy Chen modified a submersible Little Giant pond pump to work as a prop pump by replacing the impeller and its housing with a propeller. The prototype design worked, but the pump shaft composition was not suitable for long-term immersion in saltwater. R. Harker

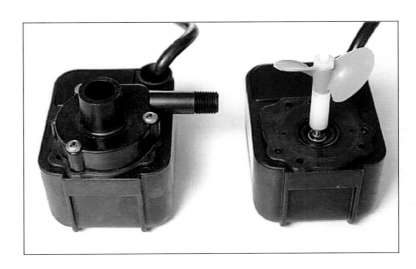

The VorTech™ Propeller Pump produced by EcoTech Marine® (www.ecotechmarine.com) places the motor outside the aquarium, and couples it magnetically with the impeller located within the aquarium. This design eliminates the need for a mounting bracket, and keeps the motor from transferring heat to the water. Unlike submersible powerheads, it keeps a source of AC electricity outside of the aquarium. The present design produces between 100 and 3000 gallons per hour. It is available with a microcontroller that can control the motor speed, and the controller has an automatic safety shut-off feature that senses a fault such as a propeller jam, bearing failure, or separation of the motor from the propeller. A wave controller accessory is available to control up to 10 Vortech pumps, and an available battery backup accessory produced by IceCap Inc. powers a Vortech propeller pump for up to 24 hours during a power outage.

At present, prop pumps tend to be rather bulky in appearance and are difficult if not impossible to totally conceal given the area of the water stream they produce. However, the combination of high flow and low power consumption make prop pumps especially attractive, and we feel that this technology can only improve as more manufacturers begin to produce such models.

Flow eductors

One option to increase water motion in an aquarium is to use pumps that are more powerful. This choice has the following disadvantages: larger pumps cost more to purchase; they generate more heat; they consume more electricity; and larger pumps typically make more noise than smaller pumps. An alternative to using larger pumps is to install a device originally developed for the chemical industry called an eductor (Harker, 2003). It increases water flow generated within the tank by a pump without the need to increase the pump size.

An eductor works somewhat like a Venturi, but instead of drawing air into a stream of water, the eductor, which is submerged, draws more water into the stream. Whereas a Venturi usually has just one port drawing air into a chamber where a pressure drop occurs, the eductor draws water into a series of openings in the narrow section of its nozzle, just ahead of a flared end where the water exits (see figure 7a).

Water from the pump enters the eductor through a narrow section, the reduced diameter causing an increase in the velocity and pressure of the water stream, much the same as a jet nozzle on a garden hose. The water exits the narrow portion of the eductor into a section with a much larger diameter, and this expansion

Figure 7a. A typical eductor compared to a venturi.

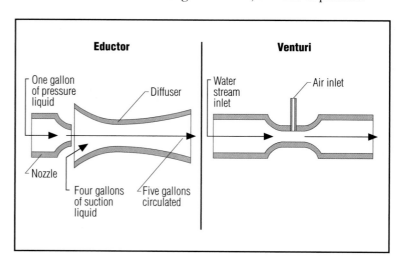

Just Joe Yaiullo of the Federation of Reef Aquarium Space travelers shows off a secret weapon he was testing: a large eductor. C. Paparo

A small eductor used on a circular reef aquarium display in the *Schuran* stand at the Interzoo Pet show in 2004. J. Sprung

creates a pressure drop that draws aquarium water through the surrounding slots into the stream, effectively increasing the flow generated by the pump in the aquarium.

The claimed output of an eductor varies with the design of the eductor and the pressure generated by the pump. To achieve high efficiencies from an eductor, the pump used must be pressure rated, as it has to be able to generate flow against the backpressure caused by the narrow section of the eductor. Some manufacturers claim that eductors can generate up to six times the flow of a pump, however, one can expect to achieve a water flow in the aquarium closer to three or four times the pumps rated output (Harker, 2003).

An eductor cannot be used to increase the volume of water pumped into the tank from a sump, but it does increase the volume of water within the aquarium that is circulated by the pump and it does so without significantly increasing the velocity of water at the outlet (the open end of the eductor). Harker (2003) showed a 245% increase in water volume circulated with only a 7% increase in water velocity. The flared end of the eductor creates a broad stream that is less traumatic for corals compared to the hard pressure stream generated by a larger pump generating the same volume of flow. Corals are thus able to grow within a few inches of the outlet of an eductor.

The eductors currently available are large. The smallest, a 3⁄4 inch i.d. model, is 15 cm (6 inches) long. However, a new style of eductor from Mazzei Injector Corporation is much shorter in length and would be a better choice for smaller aquariums or where hiding the eductor is of importance (http://www.mazzei.net). A word of caution: since a large volume of water is drawn through the radial slots, it is possible for snails, sea cucumbers, or other wandering marinelife to get sucked in and stuck on or in them.

The velocity of the water entering the slots is low because of the large number of them, but the possibility exists. Running the pump continuously helps prevent this problem to some extent. To maintain the eductor's output, one must periodically remove it to clean out algae, biofilms, and other gunk that may clog the slots or reduce their diameter.

The *Oloid®* agitator

With only 10-15% of the traditional pump power consumption usual for aquariums, the *Oloid® agitator* is a new and interesting choice for large aquariums that need to move large bodies of water, while cutting down on operating costs. Positioned just below the water surface, the pulse-type movement generates a strong current along the surface while bringing up deeper water from below. The fine oscillations created in the entire water body theoretically free up detritus, as well as prevent it from accumulating in the substratum. The shape of the agitator – the *Oloid®* – resembles an egg. It is driven by two axes and moves somewhat like a paddle or the tail fin of a fish. This generates a pulsing flow comparable to the repulsion created by fish.

This *Oloid®* 100 model was in use at the Monterey Bay Aquarium and provided a strong current in one of their larger exhibits. E. Seidel

Currently four type 400A *Oloid®* agitators (stainless steel versions) are used for the circulation and agitation of a 170 m^3 (45,000 US gallons) seawater aquarium at the Bochum Zoo in Bochum, Germany. The four installed units only use 800 W of power compared to the original bank of water circulating pumps that used 21 kW. The *Oloid®* agitators provide a water motion that is closer to nature, like those in a real reef, and according to the manufacturer, the sharks in this exhibit seem to feel more comfortable too. Drawbacks of the *Oloid®* include its high initial cost, corrosion issues in seawater and high rate of mechanical failure.

A similar *Oloid®* has been in use at the Burger's Ocean aquarium in The Netherlands since 2000. When working the device does produce a nice current effect, however, the original design was prone to frequent failure and several modifications had to be made by the manufacturer. This brings up the point that, as with any device with a large number of moving parts, mechanical failures can and do happen.

Given the ingenuity of hobbyists and aquarium manufacturers, it is probably only a matter of time until a device based on the *Oloid®* principle appears for the home aquarium market. For more information on the *Oloid®* as well as animation of its operation, go to: http://www.oloid.ch/index.html.

The 400A *Oloid*® agitators make waves in this shark exhibit at Bochum Zoo. Photo courtesy of Bochum Tierpark.

This demonstration aquarium in the *Schuran* stand at the 2004 Interzoo Pet show in Nuremberg, Germany showed the water moving effect of a small *Oloid*® model. Note the wave chops! J. Sprung

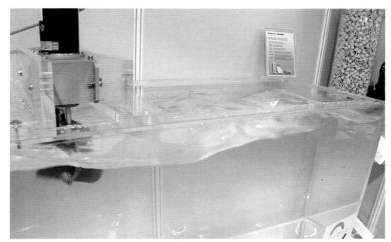

Wavemakers, rotating returns and current switchers

Various systems have been devised to effect water flow in the pulsed surge fashion typical of shallow reef environments. We present here a description of some of the systems that have been described in the aquarium literature, and used by aquarists.

Wavemakers

Several styles of *wavemakers* are based on switching devices that can operate several pumps or powerheads sequentially or randomly. By plugging the pumps/powerheads into the wavemaker, they can be operated in several different patterns creating tidal currents, alternating currents or random, chaotic currents within the aquarium. Some styles are simple power strips that contain timer controlled electrical outlets into which the pumps/powerheads are plugged.

Other designs are computerized and can be programmed to operate a number of pumps/powerheads in a variety of different ways. Wavemakers can be standalone units or they can be part of much more sophisticated monitors that operate lights, dosing systems and monitor water quality parameters.

A true wavemaker

The German aquarium equipment manufacturer *Tunze®* has developed a product called the *Wavebox*™. This consists of a *Tunze Turbelle®* Stream pump in a box housing that fits in the corner of an aquarium. The pump pushes water out of the box then stops, the water returns, fills the box and the pump starts again. This creates a pressure wave and eventually generates a standing wave in the tank using very little pump power, causing the water to rock back and forth in the aquarium very similar to the back and forth surge caused by passing waves as seen on

The *Tunze®* Wavebox creates a standing wave in the aquarium. J. Sprung

reefs in nature. Currently this device only works for tanks from 200 to 1,200 litres (52 to 317 US gallons). The type of water motion created is ideal for dislodging detritus and creating ripples in the sand. It also causes coral polyps to sway back and forth in a natural manner. However, the standing wave movement should be supplemented with circulation pumps and other water motion devices to effect good circulation.

Prerequisites for use of the Wavebox

It is necessary to maintain a water level several inches below the top of the aquarium. Otherwise, the wave created would crest over the wall and wet the floor. The display at the Tunze stand at the 2004 Interzoo trade show featured an aquarium with an overflow skimmer positioned in the center of the back wall of the aquarium, with a level sufficiently below the top of the tank to allow a nice wave. The central position was a fulcrum of sorts, located between the ends where the water rise and fall is greatest. The position of the water return from the sump should be low enough to keep it below the water surface when the wave passes. Otherwise, the returning water will create splash and noise when it is exposed by the drop in water. Having such a deeply positioned return necessitates the use of a siphon break to prevent back siphoning in the event of a power failure, or the use of a very large sump to catch the excess water volume that could siphon down in a power failure. The shifting of the mass of water also could stress the construction of an aquarium or the stand, so this must be considered when building an aquarium for this effect. It is clear that this device, while fantastic in its capability, is not something that can be popped into any tank. To use it one must have the right water height and proper construction.

Rotating returns

Several water flow direction-shifting products feature a means to rotate the water outlet from a pump or powerhead. The designs can be divided into two main categories; those powered by electric motors and those that rely on pump pressure to rotate. For example, there are now powerhead models with integrated rotating outlets that move in a horizontal plane from side to side e.g. ZooMed Power sweeps. There are also units on the market that use a small motor attached to the rim of the aquarium to physically rotate an entire powerhead e.g. the BM OSCI-Wave. As with any device with moving parts, failures will occur, so the aquarist should be prepared to replace such units eventually.

Sea Swirl™

The *Sea Swirl*™ is an electrically powered, tank rim mounted, non-submersible wave-maker that slowly rotates a submerged pump outlet through a 90 degree arc every 60 seconds. Similar devices that rely on water pressure instead of a motor to rotate the outlet lose more water pressure as it is sent through the unit and out the nozzle. At present, a 2.5 cm (1 inch) diameter pipe is the maximum size outlet available.

Hydor® Flo rotating deflector

This small, inexpensive deflector turns your existing powerhead into a wave-maker. When attached to the outlet of a powerhead, internal gears slowly rotate its down-turned outlet a full 360 degrees using the force of the incoming water from the powerhead; stronger pump outputs result in faster rotational rates.

Ocean Currents™ wave devices

Ocean Currents wave devices are a series of five compact, water driven devices that rely on water velocity to rotate an outlet nozzle. The units are attached in the aquarium via suction cups on the

The *Sea Swirl*™ attaches to the side of the aquarium and provides a motorized means to rotate the outlet of a circulation pump with very little loss in water pressure. J. Sprung

The *Hydor*® Flo attaches easily to powerheads using included adaptors. Photo used with permission of Drs. Foster and Smith.

Ocean Currents™ wave devices rely on water velocity to rotate the outlet nozzle. Photo used with permission of Ocean Currents.

bottom; optional mounting trays and outlet nozzles are also available. The five models vary in the degree of rotation and the type of water pattern they disperse. These devices require high volume, low-pressure pumps of at least 1893 lph (500 gph) to operate the rotational mechanism and there is a drop in pressure at the outlet because of backpressure generated by the unit. Nevertheless, they do offer a viable means to producing oscillating currents without the need for electricity. Be sure you prefilter any water entering these devices since grains of sand or other hard particles can jam the internal mechanism. The units can be disassembled for cleaning or repair if required, however. See http://www.ocean-currents.com for more information.

Current switching devices

Another method to alternate water currents and create chaotic flows in the aquarium is with current switching devices. These devices switch the water flow from a pump between two or more returns. Three forms of these devices exist, those that use motorized valves, those that use motorized rotational drums and those that rely on water pressure.

Motorized ball valves

Motorized ball valves located in the circulation plumbing create chaotic flow in a reef tank by turning ball valves on or off. An alternative to interval timing wavemakers that turn the pumps on and off, a motorized three-way ball valve opens and closes the flow in pipes, directing the water to the left and then to the right. This way the pumps are running continuously, which is better for them than being turned on and off at frequent intervals.

The three-way valve means that water enters the bottom, and goes out either to the right or the left, depending on the valve position.

Continuous flow means that the two channels are NOT mutually exclusive; that is, as the valve is turned, flow decreases in channel 1 at the same time it increases in channel 2, until you finally have flow from only one channel. This is beneficial because while the valve is changing, there is no large increase in backpressure on the pump and the flow is smoothly transitioned from one side to the other. A similar effect can be achieved by using two actuated ball valves one on each return, but if one of them fails as the other closes, the pump will have no where to send the water and the pump will either fail or a fitting or pipe may burst under the pressure.

The actuators have a rated 25% duty cycle, which means that for every 5 seconds they are *on* switching the valve, they must be off for 15 seconds. The actuators can burn out if they turn continuously or for intervals exceeding 25% duty. They are easy to set up by incorporating a wave timer to switch them on about every 2 minutes, or less frequently if you want to simulate tidal currents. Some units do not come prewired and require you to wire them to a repeat cycle timer.

There are a couple of drawbacks to motorized ball valves. First, they are expensive, but that alone hasn't stopped the average reef aquarist from experimenting! Smaller valves are cheaper, but 1.5 inch valves with actuators cost about $400 each. As we mentioned in chapter 3, you get what you pay for when it comes to valve quality, and the same holds true for actuated ball valves. Hayward and Asahi valves have outstanding reliability ratings, but are expensive. The second drawback to motorized ball valves is noise. They are only noisy when actuated, and the noise can be somewhat dampened by the cabinet or covered up by the other noises such as pumps or air-conditioning. The sound is something like an electric can opener. Those who can place the sump and pumps in another location (like a basement) can use actuated ball valves in this location without having to worry about any operation noise.

A 3-way motorized ball valve in use at Colorado's Ocean Journey. R. Brynda

Oceans Motions

Recently Paul Hayton formed a company in Toronto, Canada, Oceans Motions (www.oceansmotions.com), and developed a series of water motion devices that rely on a small motor turning a slotted drum, directing water flow to a series of outlets. As the motor rotates the drum, water is diverted from one pair of outlets to the next. All components in these devices are machined from solid PVC bar except for a Delrin drive shaft and polypropylene thrust seals that seal the unit, making it saltwater safe. There are units that have eight outlets (four on each side) and units that have four outlets arranged around a cylinder. PVC pipe can be threaded into the outlets and then positioned in various places within the aquarium.

The 8-way *Oceans Motions* using interchangeable rotating drums that can be used to create various alternating effects. Photos used with permission of Oceans Motions.

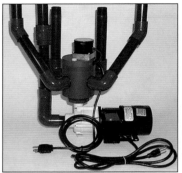

The 4-way Oceans Motions can be plumbed directly on the outlet of the pump or can be situated closer to the aquarium. Photos used with permission of Oceans Motions.

The *OM Squirt*, using magnets to form a connection between the motor and drum. Photos used with permission of Oceans Motions.

The *Revolution* comes in a variety of configurations. Photos used with permission of Oceans Motions.

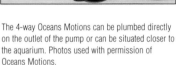

Oceans Motions, has also developed a unit called the OM Squirt, which uses sealed magnets to turn the drum, similar in concept to a magnetic drive pump, which eliminates the need for a direct drive shaft.

All of the above units rotate at 1 rpm, but a timer can be used to change this, as the motors can be easily turned on and off. Using a version 1 or 2 drum, the water would exit through an outlet once a minute, however due to the construction of version 3 drum (opposed outlets), each outlet would have water passing through it every 30 seconds.

Ocean Motions has also developed a rotating return that uses water pressure to rotate the outlets through 360, 180, 90 or 45 degrees. There are several configurations available but they are all designed to operate only with a flow that alternates on and off. Each time water is diverted to the unit it lowers itself downward into the tank by 1.25 cm (1/2 inch) and indexes 45 degrees, returning upwards when the water pressure is reduced. These are designed to work with the 8- and 4-way units mentioned previously but could also be used with 3-way ball valves or solenoids.

The *SCWD* Switching Current Water Director

The SCWD (pronounced *squid*), is a current switching device that provides alternating currents without the use of electricity. The SCWD mounts inline with 3/4" tubing, the two side ports alternate the output, while water enters the bottom port. The current SCWD

The *SCWD* unit in demonstration mode in the Champion Lighting Supply booth at MACNA. Water enters the bottom inlet and alternates out of either side outlet. The pickle jars were for display only! J.C. Delbeek

model runs on any pump with a minimum output of 190 L/h (50 gph) and a maximum output of 5320 L/h (1400 gph) at a maximum 5 psi. You can control the switching speed and current duration by modifying the volume of water flowing through the SCWD. For example, with a 2660 L/h (700 gph) Mag 7 pump the port rotation is at 10 second intervals. We do not recommend using a SCWD on your main pump unless you are happy with the frequency at which it will operate. You do not want to have to alter the main pump's output significantly in order to achieve the rotational frequency you want. It is better to use a dedicated recirculation pump with a SCWD so you can vary the rotation rate without affecting any other parameters in your plumbing system.

Make sure to prefilter the water entering the SCWD since particulates such as sand grains can jam the mechanism inside the unit. Since the unit cannot be dismantled, it cannot be easily cleaned or repaired. The manufacturer claims that unlike other water driven devices, the SCWD does not cause a significant increase in backpressure. At present only 3/4 inch SCWDs are available but the manufacturer has plans for larger models.

Surge generators

The generation of real surge within the aquarium is a challenge with numerous rewards, including improved health of the organisms, rapid growth, and the virtual elimination of dead spots and detritus accumulation. Pulsed water flow from powerheads achieves the same effects, but less dramatically than the techniques, we will describe here, yet they are not without their own disadvantages. The basic idea behind a surge device is the rapid release of a large volume of water into the aquarium. Smaller aquariums have less capacity to allow large volumes of water to be removed and then rapidly returned to the tank. As a result a smaller volume is used, and the resulting surge effect is less pronounced and of a shorter duration. Therefore, we feel that although they can be used on smaller systems, these devices are best suited to larger systems such as those commonly found in public aquariums. Surge devices should not be used as the sole means of water motion in a system, but more as an accessory to create added water motion that may be more realistic. Some coral species such as those *Acropora* and *Pocillopora* spp. found in areas with strong surge benefit the most from the use of a surge device in conjunction with other water motion devices. The creation of strong periodic surge also helps these species to maintain their morphology. If one wants to create a strong, long duration surge in a small system, then the way to do this is to use a larger sump than normal and provide a larger overflow than would normally be needed based on the size of the recirculation pump. In this way, the sump level will not drop too low as the surge device fills and the tank will not overflow when the surge occurs.

Surge device caveats

There are several factors in tank design that need to be taken into consideration when using any surge system that quickly releases a quantity of water into an aquarium. A surge device must be filled with water from the aquarium, which affects the water level in the aquarium if it doesn't have an overflow or sump, resulting in a drop in water level in the tank itself. Therefore, any returns or intakes must be below the lowest possible water level point. The same applies to any temperature probes and heating elements, or other equipment that needs to operate below the water line. Although aquariums that use sumps avoid the problem of a water level drop in the main aquarium, levels in the sump will drop instead each time the surge device is filled. Therefore, the sump should be designed such that any pump or other intakes are below the lowest possible water level. The volume of the sump should be designed so it can operate properly when the surge device is completely filled and it must be large enough to accommodate all the water from surge device without overflowing. For this reason, sumps that are long and wide are better than are ones that are tall and narrow, since the former will show less of a water level drop than the latter as the surge device fills.

Another problem that occurs with the drop in water level is that the water level sensing devices typically used to add top-off water automatically will not work if the sump level is constantly changing. One possible solution would be to install a float switch in the aquarium or sump and set it for the lowest "normal" water level. When the water level drops below that mark because of evaporation, the float switch will activate the inflow of new replacement water. Of course, this will be periodically interrupted when the surge device dumps water back into the aquarium but nonetheless it should work (Carlson, 1996). A solution to the top off problem can be accomplished by placing a float type hydrometer in an attached aquarium that has an overflow built in that maintains a constant water level. The specific gravity change causes a change in the height the hydrometer floats, and this can be utilized to activate a switch. Accuracy of this system also depends on maintenance of a constant temperature. Breder and Howley, (1931) describe such a device, which they call a salinostat.

The constant changing water level in the tank or sump will also cause flexing of the tank/sump walls. This constant flexing can, over time, cause joints or even entire panels to fail. Therefore, if the water level change in the sump or tank will be great, it would be wise to err on the side of caution and use thicker panels than you would normally use and make sure all bonds are reinforced.

Aquariums that use an overflow must have one designed to not only handle the normal recirculation flow rate, but also the periodic increase in water flow exiting the aquarium that accompanies the dumping of the surge device. Unless the overflow is designed with a drain size to handle this extra amount, the main tank could overflow before the overflow is able to compensate for the extra water.

All surge devices will add some air bubbles to the tank, either directly from the device itself or from the action of the water entering the tank under force. In either event, these bubbles will generate a fine mist in the air above the aquarium as they burst. This can lead to salt build-up on equipment above and around the tank, which needs to be removed periodically to avoid corrosion problems and the reduction in light as light fixtures get coated. Salt creep can also occur where the hood (if used) meets the tank rim. The loss of salt over time also means that the salinity of the water will gradually drop as a result, therefore periodic additions of salt would be required. There really is no way to avoid this problem other than avoiding the introduction of bubbles as much as possible. Some consider the extra maintenance a small price to pay for the benefits of the added water motion provided by a surge device.

All surge devices operate on gravity. Therefore, they must be placed above the aquarium or in a location that is higher than the top of the aquarium. The higher the device is above the aquarium the greater the surge effect and velocity of the water entering the aquarium. Because of this, these devices require space to be installed, and this must be taken into consideration when designing the system.

Finally, when water hits water, noise is created. Surge devices are noisy! Not only the water entering the aquarium but the devices themselves can make noise. The clanging and banging of a surge bucket as it dumps and rebounds, the loud slurping of a CSD as the surge cycle ends and sucks air, the escape of air in pneumatic pistons and wave machines, all create noise that you should try to minimize if you want to keep your sanity!

Wave/dump buckets

Surge motion in the aquarium can be generated by means of a simple device called a wave or "dump" bucket (see diagram). The bucket is designed such that its pivot point lies just above its center of gravity. Water is fed to the bucket from the aquarium and as it fills beyond the pivot point, it tips over and dumps water into the tank in one rush. The bucket pivot points can be made from plastic or nylon bearings or just PVC pipes of different diameter. Salt entering the bearings or rubbing parts will hinder the performance and may erode the plastic with time and the continuous turning of the pivot. A well-designed pivot avoids this problem. A poor design will necessitate constant re-

A dump bucket design by Rich Lerner, Colorado's Ocean Journey. The cross-sectional dimensions can be increased or decreased but the proportions should be kept the same to ensure the bucket dumps properly. However, the dump bucket can be any length. R. Lerner

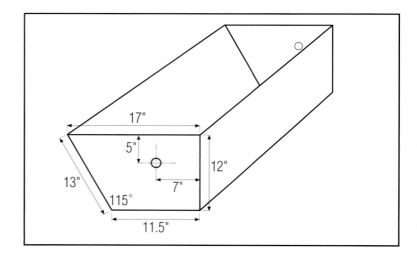

These twin dump buckets at Colorado's Ocean Journey aquarium, produced a sizable surge but also a great deal of splash. R. Brynda

The Surge exhibit at the Waikiki Aquarium before, during and after the surge bucket dumps. J.C. Delbeek

starting of the dumping action. Lubricants should be avoided since they can easily enter the aquarium from this location. Additionally, it is difficult to build a dump bucket that does not generate at least some splash, which is undesirable mainly because splash produces salt creep, corrosion problems and gradual loss of salt. Dump buckets are also noisy. Despite the disadvantages, the effect in the aquarium is wonderful, and really makes the animals and plants move back and forth in the same manner as waves in the sea. Large dump buckets are also used to great effect in large aquariums that simulate rocky coasts and shorelines.

Other dumping surge devices

There are several variations on the dump style surge device. One such variation is the use of an actuated valve at the base of a large reservoir. Such a device is used in the wave tank exhibit in the Kids

This variation on the dump bucket uses a pneumatically controlled gate system to release the contents of a reservoir. R. Brynda

Splash Zone area of the Monterey Bay Aquarium. Water is pumped to a reservoir located well above the exhibit. When the water level reaches the top it activates a float switch, signaling a 6 inch actuated butterfly valve at the bottom of the reservoir to open sending a large amount of water into the exhibit via a 6 inch PVC pipe, at once creating a very strong surge across the surface of the tank. When the water level drops, another float switch at the bottom of the reservoir is then activated to close the valve, and the reservoir refills.

A similar method can be used to pneumatically open gates, to allow the water to fall out of the side of the reservoir. This is similar to the method used in water parks to generate waves in wave-pools, and by Hollywood movie studios to simulate floods on sets.

Carlson surge device (CSD)

Dr. Bruce Carlson, former director of the Waikiki Aquarium, created another type of surge device for use with live corals. Based on a design known as a *bell and siphon* it can be installed on an aquarium to mimic the long duration surge found in channels on reef flats. The CSD consists of a stationary bucket above the aquarium into which water from the aquarium is fed (Carlson, 1996; Delbeek and Sprung, 1994). During the time this water is feeding into the bucket, the water level in the aquarium falls (except in tanks with sumps and overflows), simulating the water drawing back before a long wave. When the water in the bucket reaches a critical height, the large automatic siphon built into it rapidly empties the water back into the tank, generating lots of turbulence and powerful currents. Aside from the intrusive appearance and the noise, otherwise referred to as a *sucking sound*, they can create incredible water movement in the aquarium. In addition, the velocity of the surge will never change. The pump may age and pump water to the CSD at a lower rate,

The very first CSD was built in June 1988 and consisted of a 114 L (30 gallon) plastic barrel. B. Carlson

Two, 960 L (250 gallon) CSDs in use on a 20,900 L (5500 gallon) reef tank at the Waikiki Aquarium. J.C. Delbeek

Figure 7c. Schematic of a typical CSD.

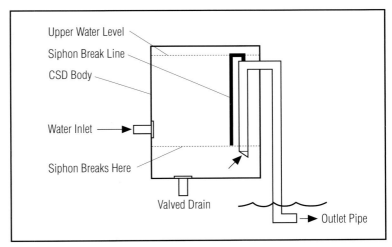

altering the periodicity, but the surge it creates will always have the same velocity. Once running, CSDs are extremely reliable. The Waikiki Aquarium has a 950 L (250 gallon) CSD operating on a 26,600 L (7000 gallon) outdoor Hawaiian coral exhibit since 1986, and a 760 L (200 gallon) CSD running on a outdoor 4560 L (1200 gallon) south Pacific coral farm since 1997, both have never failed to surge once started. The Aquarium has several more 950 L (250 gallon) surge towers running on various exhibits and coral propagation systems.

Several factors need to be taken into consideration when building a CSD. When pumping water into a CSD the flow rate must be set such that the CSD discharges and does so completely. If water is pumped in too quickly, the CSD will discharge but will not be able to break siphon at the end of the cycle. This causes the water level in the CSD to cycle up and down without completely filling or emptying. This actually can cause a very nice rhythmic pulsing in the tank not unlike the effect in a laboratory pipette washer, but does not usually run indefinitely. If water is pumped in too slowly, the level increases to the level of the upper elbow and simply runs out of the outlet pipe and into the aquarium. The water does not come in fast enough to rise above the inner elbow in order to develop sufficient head pressure to start a surge.

The diameter of the outlet pipe determines how quickly the CSD will drain, the greater the diameter, the greater the velocity of the surge but depending on the size of the CSD, the shorter the duration. For example, placing a 5 cm (2 inch) outlet on a 19 L (5 gallon) CSD will have shorter surge duration than a 2.5 cm (1 inch) outlet, but will have greater velocity.

The rate of filling of a CSD and the diameter of the outlet pipe are interrelated and the two must be matched in order to achieve a consistent and reliable surge. Luckily, there is a considerable amount of leeway between filling a CSD too slowly or too quickly, and it seems that the larger the diameter of outlet pipe, the larger the window of appropriate flow rate.

The height of the CSD above the aquarium influences the velocity of the water entering the aquarium and hence, the rate at which the CSD empties. The higher the CSD is above the aquarium, the greater the velocity and the faster it will empty. The increased velocity also makes it more difficult to break siphon at the end of the surge, depending on the filling rate of the CSD, and would require a larger diameter siphon break line or additional lines.

The shape and volume of a CSD also affects it ability to surge. If two CSDs have the same volume, but one is tall and narrow, while the other is short but wide, the water level in the tall one will rise faster. This means that given the same incoming rate of water flow, the tall one will start a surge more easily than the short one. In addition, a larger CSD will produce a longer duration surge than a smaller one, given the same outlet pipe diameter.

It should be clear that some experimenting is required with flow rates and CSD design before a reliable configuration is found. Volume and shape of the CSD, the height above the aquarium, the diameter of the outlet pipe, the diameter of the siphon break and the rate at which water is pumped into the CSD all affect its performance.

At least one manufacturer builds relatively small surge makers for home aquaria. It is also simple to construct one yourself and there are various design plans available online (search using the keywords: Carlson Surge Device).

Riddle (1996b) describes a 19 L (5 gallon) surge-generating device, but the size can be scaled according to your aquarium's needs. When scaling up be prepared to experiment. Small details that do not appear to be significant can profoundly affect performance. It may be necessary to build a prototype or two when changing the size of this device.

Modified CSDs

Since the publication of Dr. Carlson's article describing the construction and operation of the CSD (Carlson, 1996), there have been several modifications presented on this design. A search of the Internet will yield several variations on the design and how-to articles on building your own. The most commonly seen are those that use toilet flapper valves and floats. While these designs do offer the advantage of reduced bubble generation once the surge starts, we feel the majority of these designs are unnecessarily complicated in design and construction. The introduction of moving parts such as floats and flapper valves, both of which will show signs of wear over time and will need to be maintained or replaced periodically, negate the primary advantages of the CSD design: simple construction with little to no maintenance required. However, other modifications exhibit an extraordinary amount of ingenuity e.g. the reverse CSD.

Solving bubble generation

One of the problems with the early CSD design was the evacuation of air from the return line and the resulting introduction of large quantities of bubbles during the surge. The problem lay in the air evacuation line that was designed to allow the release of air from the downspout so that a siphon could begin. Once the water level in the CSD fell below the inlet to this line, air was sucked in much like a Venturi, and air bubbles were introduced to the tank. On smaller CSDs, this was not a big problem but when scaling up to 208 L (55 US gallon) and eventually 950 L (250 US gallon) CSDs that were located well above the aquarium, the velocity of the water exiting would create a significant Venturi effect! The solution was to extend the air evacuation line downwards so that it ended just above the inlet to the main siphon line. When the water level in the CSD fell low enough, air would enter the line and cause the siphon to begin to break. The drawback was that this usually resulted in a period of 10-15 seconds where air would be mixed with the effluent water, and air bubbles would be introduced at the end of the surge, before the main pipe would lose siphon.

To solve this problem, the air evacuation line was moved into the CSD and placed at the very top of the inside elbow instead of near the bottom of the outlet pipe in the tank (see photo). This is the point

This modification to the CSD by J.C. Delbeek results in a much faster siphon break, reducing noise and bubble discharge into the aquarium at the end of the cycle, and allowing for shorter operating cycles. A 1/2" hole is drilled and tapped at the elbow and a 3/4" siphon break is attached. J.C. Delbeek

The new coral farm surge towers at the Waikiki Aquarium operate with very little bubble formation and have a cleaner external appearance. J.C. Delbeek

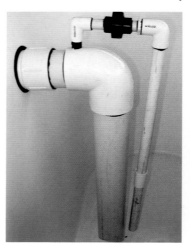

where suction should be the greatest and introducing air at this point, should cause the siphon to break very rapidly as the weight of the water causes it to fall out of both ends of the siphon pipe at the same time. In the example shown, a 3" PVC pipe was used as the siphon and a 1/2" hole was drilled and tapped into the top elbow. A 1/2" threaded nipple was inserted followed by a 1/2" 90 $^\circ$ S-T elbow, a 1/2" union, after which it was expanded to a 3/4" elbow, and a 3/4" PVC pipe which extended downwards and ended just above the inlet to the siphon pipe. The union allows the pipe to be dismantled for cleaning or modifications as needed. Another modification was to cut the end of the 3" siphon pipe with two 45° angles instead of the one used in the original CSD design, giving the end an arrowhead appearance. This helps to increase the surface area of the end of the pipe and, theoretically, cause it to break siphon faster. In operation, these modifications resulted in a very rapid loss of siphon with very little bubble introduction before, during and after the siphon. A side benefit has been a significant decrease in noise due to the elimination of air slurping at the end of the cycle.

Internal CSDs

A recent modification made by Dr. Bruce Carlson has been the development of a self-contained CSD. In this design, the siphon pipe exits through the bottom of the CSD and a larger pipe inside the CSD then sits over this pipe creating a gap between the two. The outer pipe is capped at the top and is slightly raised from the bottom creating a gap through which water can enter. As water fills the CSD, it enters through the bottom and rises up inside the gap between the two pipes. Once the water level rises above the cap of the outer pipe, enough head pressure is created to cause a siphon to begin and water exits the CSD via the smaller inner pipe. This design is extremely clean in appearance with no external pipes visible. It more closely matches the original *bell and siphon* concept.

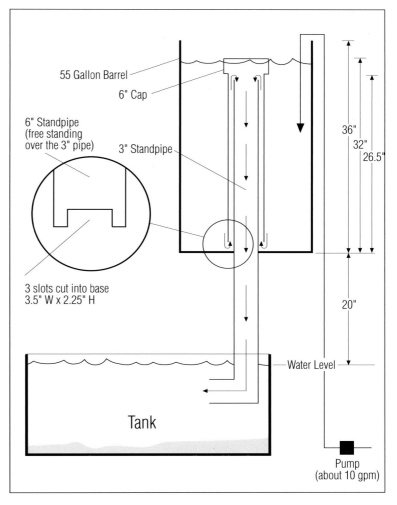

Figure 7d. A schematic representation of an internal CSD designed by Bruce Carlson. Note detail of the base of the internal standpipe.

55 Gallon Barrel

6" Cap

6" Standpipe (free standing over the 3" pipe)

3" Standpipe

36"
32"
26.5"

3 slots cut into base 3.5" W x 2.25" H

20"

Water Level

Tank

Pump (about 10 gpm)

An internal CSD in operation on a coral holding system. R. Davis

Forced CSD

When space is limited, CSDs are restricted in how large they can be. The size of the outlet pipe restricts how quickly a CSD can discharge its contents and how frequently it can surge. A method to increase the outlet pipe size and the frequency of the surge was developed by Jason Chriton at the National Aquarium in Baltimore (Jason is now at the South Carolina Aquarium). In this design, the top of the CSD is tightly sealed and an air vent is placed in the lid attached to an internal 1" check valve. As the CSD fills with water, air vents out via the check valve until the water level reaches the bottom of the valve. The flapper is modified by gluing a small piece of neoprene to its lower surface such that as the water rises, it floats upwards and blocks the vent. As water continues to be pumped into the CSD, pressure builds and forces the CSD to quickly discharge. Using this modification, the outlet pipe diameter can be increased to a much

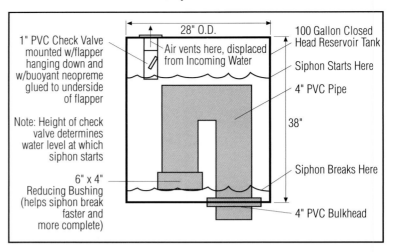

greater size causing the CSD to discharge more quickly. Obviously, the CSD must be made of material strong enough to withstand the increased pressure and any wall flexing that may occur as a result.

Reverse CSD

Carpenter (2000) describes the construction of a *push and release* surge device that has no moving parts beyond those required to provide low pressure air. The Reverse Carlson Surge Device (RCSD) was inspired by Dr. Carlson's device. It operates by using air to displace water in a submerged container, followed by the rapid release of the air, creating a bubble-free surge in an aquarium. Carpenter devised this device with Gary Dudley at the tenth annual Marine Aquarium Conference of North America and built a prototype at the end of 1998.

Their first unit was an inverted triangular box, open on the bottom, designed to fit into the back corner of Carpenter's 7600 L (2000 gallon) tank. The triangular box was 90 cm (36 inches) on the two right angle sides and 90 cm (36 inches) deep displacing about 380 L (100 gallons). A "U" shaped Air Vent Construct (AVC) built into the box had one arm of the U inside the box, reaching to within three inches of the top; the other arm, outside the box, extended above the tank water level. In theory, as the box fills with air the water is pushed out the open bottom of the box, and water in the AVC is pushed, again by air, through the tube and out the top. When air reaches the bottom of the U, some will continue up the other arm of the U. This escaping air will displace some water reducing the weight of the column of water in the outside arm of the U and reducing the back pressure this column exerts on the air in the box. Once the pressure is reduced, more air escapes, reducing the pressure more and causing more air to escape, etc. This creates a cascade that eventually drives all the water out of the AVC. Once that occurs, the

Figure 7f. Reverse csd cycle. After Carpenter, 2000.

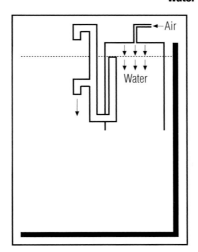 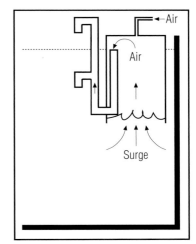

inside of the air-filled box is fully exposed to atmospheric pressure on the water, and the box vents all the air, resulting in tank water surging into the box. This incoming surge floods the box and the AVC and the cycle starts again. If you feel lost at this point, don't worry, so were we. Have a look at the diagram and try again.

While the theory made sense, the operation didn't quite work as Carpenter and Dudley expected. The pressure inside the box did not match the pressure outside it. Water pressure is variable on the box walls depending on the depth in the tank, resulting in a pressure imbalance. The prototype exploded several times. The design was modified in several aspects until a final version was worked out.Increasing the diameter in the AVC produced substantial improvements in vent times. The increase in pipe diameter also produced more vented water.

The surge created by this device is greatest near the device, and only lasts for a couple of seconds. Movement at the far end of the tank is only about 5 cm (2 inches), while polyps in the middle of the tank are flattened briefly and sway until the next surge (Carpenter, 2000). A valve on the air supply permits some control of surge timing.

Caveats

Some means of anchoring the device in the tank must be devised, because the upward pressure generated with each cycle is significant. The surge is also powerful enough to shake rocks or the whole reef structure apart. As we mentioned for other surge devices, the water level change of up to 7.5 cm (3 inches) that occurs during a cycle will interfere with water level sensing devices or overflows to sumps.

Figure 7g. Toilet flapper surge device.
After Borneman (2001)

Parts required:
5 L plastic cereal container
Fluidmaster 507 flush valve with bullseye flapper
Plastic float
50 mm PVC socket faucet
50 mm to 40 mm PVC reducing bushing
40 mm to 32 mm PVC reducing bushing
32 mm to 25 mm PVC reducing bushing
1m of 25 mm PVC piping
3 x 25 mm 90 degree elbows
1m 20 mm PVC piping
2 x 20 mm 90 degree elbows
PVC cement
Teflon tape
Cable tie
Maxi-Jet MJ1000 powerhead
Eheim 13/16 mm tubing
Eheim 13 mm 'J' tube

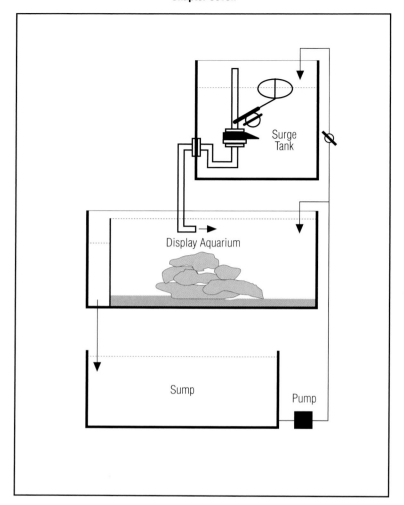

Flapper surge device

Borneman (2001) provides plans for a simple design like the Carlson device, but makes use of a flush device and float. The heart of the device is a Fluidmaster 507 Flush Valve with Bullseye Flapper that can be found in hardware stores or ordered from most plumbing suppliers. The device is reasonably quiet. Both starting and stopping the dump makes a small amount of noise. There are some bubbles entering the tank during the early parts of the dump, but these are not distracting. See Borneman (2001) for construction details.

Pistons and paddles

We have seen several other surge devices employed in aquariums in our travels to different public aquaria. The National Aquarium in Baltimore uses a paddle system controlled by an hydraulic arm to generate a beautiful back and forth surge in their living coral reef exhibit. The paddle is located behind the artificial rockwork. We have seen similar paddle systems moved by motor or air compressor at the Virginia Beach Science Museum, the Florida Aquarium in Tampa and the New York Aquarium. The drawback to this system is the mechanical wear and tear on the unit, which requires frequent maintenance to keep it functioning, and the need to construct support structures and rockwork to conceal the device. When it does work, it gives a wonderful to and fro motion to the water, which causes soft corals, and especially seafans, to sway back and forth in a very realistic manner.

The most magnificent surge device at a public aquarium is used on the giant kelp tank at the Monterey Bay Aquarium in Monterey, California. Thirty-foot growths of living kelp sway back and forth behind the tall windows in front of you, with natural sunlight streaming in as well. The device used to create the surge in this tall display was inspired by the actions of an oil derrick pumping jack. A metal plunger is pulled up and down in a cylinder filled with water connected to the main display. As it moves downwards, it forces water out and into the exhibit and as it moves upwards, it pulls water back into the chamber. Similar devices are now in use in large exhibits at other aquariums around the world such as the Florida Aquarium in Tampa. A commercially available system for home aquariums, the Wave2k moves a paddle up and down in a chamber to achieve essentially the same effect (www.wave2k.com).

At the Great Barrier Reef Aquarium in Townsville Australia, another kind of piston device is used, but no physical object is moved up and down or back and forth. A large chamber is situated above one end of their 2500 m^3 (660,430 US gallons) live coral exhibit, extending down toward the bottom of the tank where it opens to the water. Air is evacuated the chamber by a vacuum pump so that water is drawn into the chamber. When the suction is stopped, a valve opens, letting air rush back in and the water drops back down, propagating a tank-wide surge. A similar design is used in other aquariums exhibits such as those at the Long Beach Aquarium in Long Beach, CA. Water parks that have wave pools use similar technology. A variation on this design is to pump air into the chamber, forcing water out, and then opening a valve to release the air pressure, allowing water to move back in. The result of both these methods is the generation of a wave that moves through the tank. The drawback to this type of system is the noise generated as air rushes in or escapes; ideally, the air intake/release port is placed in an area where the noise is less intrusive and/or muffled in some manner.

This wave exhibit at the Long Beach Aquarium of the Pacific features tall waves generated by an air compressor system. J. Sprung

Water parks that need to create larger waves for surfing or body boarding use large reservoirs of water that can be quickly emptied by hydraulically controlled gates. When opened the reservoirs dump their contents at the deep end of a sloped pool, generating a large wave in the process. Again, these devices generate a great deal of noise.

The Wave ball

A rather ingenious device known as the Wave Ball was developed by a Belgian company back in the mid-90's. The system consists of a large plastic ball (the diameter used depends on the size of tank it is used in) that contains a series of pulleys and springs as well as sensors and a microcomputer. The pulleys and springs distort the shape of the ball causing it to bob up and down creating small wavelets. Sensors measure the amplitude, wavelength and frequency of the waves reflected back to the ball by the sides of the pool/aquarium and these then modify the action of the pulleys and springs to increase or decrease the size of the waves the ball will generate. This system can be added to any existing pool/aquarium to allow it to become a wave tank. The system is expensive and is only suited to very large aquariums at present. For more information on the Wave Ball, see http://www.wowcompany.com/indexnsuk.htm.

Tides

Some public aquarium exhibits and experimental research systems employ devices for simulating the rise and fall of tides. These systems allow for the duplication of intertidal zonation in marine aquaria, and make for stunning displays because the look of the exhibit changes every hour. Adey and Loveland (1991) describe methods for making tides in a closed aquarium. Tides are an important issue for intertidal habitats, but not a necessity for reef aquariums. However, the change in water height over coral reefs on daily, weekly, and longer time scales does play a role in modulating the rate of photosynthesis and calcification in corals (Cohen and Reves-Sohn, 2004), not to mention the importance of tides in stimulating reproductive cycles in all kinds of marinelife, including corals.

Tidal systems

To recreate the environment found along the shorelines of coral reefs and mangrove habitats, the recreation of tides can be both aesthetically pleasing and biologically beneficial. Tidal systems can also recreate tide pool habitats and allow for the keeping of organisms that can withstand short periods of exposure to air, or who like to venture out of the water to feed on algae covered rocks and sand beds e.g. mudskippers (*Periophthalmus*), the *leaping* blenny, *Alticus saliens*.

The leaping blenny, *Alticus saliens*, spends a great deal of time "leaping" amongst rocks above the waterline looking for food. This small, active fish makes for a fascinating and entertaining exhibit. J.C. Delbeek

This simple tidal system at the Smithsonian Institution's facility in Ft. Pierce uses a clock motor attached to an arm that lifts and lowers a hose connected to the overflow drain of the display aquarium. When the hose is lifted the water level in the tank rises, when it is lowered the water level falls. J. Sprung

There are several methods that can used to recreate tides with an aquarium, and we present here but just a few of them.

CSD tidal system

A similar tidal system can be constructed using a CSD. In this case, the goal is not to create a strong surge but a gentle, slow emptying of the CSD. This should be possible by adding tank water very slowly to the CSD to simulate a gradual falling tide in the main aquarium. To simulate a gradual rising tide, the return line from the CSD needs to be either very narrow or valved near the bottom. This would take some tweaking of incoming and exiting water rates but should be easy to accomplish.

Multiple pumps and overflows

Tides can be simulated by using two overflows and two or more water pumps. One pump is used to return water to the tank such the water returns to the sump via an overflow located at the lowest point of the tide. To simulate a rising tide, a second pump is turned on via a timer and more water is pumped back to the tank than the overflow can handle, this causes a gradual rise in the water level in the tank until it reaches the height of a second overflow, which then returns the water to sump also. Once the higher overflow level is reached, the second pump is switched off and the water level drops again.

Toilet flapper tide system

An apparatus for simulating a tide pool in an aquarium was patented by Jeff D. Boschert, US patent # 5,467,739. The device essentially follows the idea of the toilet flapper surge chamber described by Borneman, but instead of filling and draining with high frequency, it does so with low frequency. This lower

Figure 7h. Moe's toilet flapper tidal system aquarium.

frequency is achieved by having a second (or more) overflow drain(s) in the flapper chamber that controls the rate at which the flapper chamber fills. The amount of water displaced into the flapper chamber causes the water level to drop in the aquarium, simulating low tide. The tide drop occurs slowly as the flapper chamber fills and it rises a bit faster as the flapper chamber drains. The rate of flow coming out of the second overflow in the flapper chamber can be modified to alter the rate of tide change. As in the Borneman device (and a toilet tank), the emptying of the flapper tank causes the flapper to re-seat and start the fill cycle again. Connecting the fill pump to a timer or a level switch could allow for the maintenance of a longer high tide condition, and having multiple fill pumps could allow the tide rise to occur more slowly, by pumping more water back into the chamber during the time the flapper drain is draining. Of course the more complex the arrangement, the more likely it is to suffer a mechanical failure.

Marine multienvironment aquarium system

Martin Moe Jr. (in 1998 at the Florida Marine Aquarium Society), demonstrated a complete tidal aquarium system that he independently invented, which incorporates a sump and a fill and drain section with a toilet flapper, achieving a tide changing effect. This was an experimental prototype developed in an 84 L (30 gallon) tank just to work out the mechanics of the design, which has been accomplished. Moe included separate *pools* within the aquarium, where one could plant anemones, zoanthids, seaweeds, crabs, clams, and other tide pool creatures. An expansion on this concept to a larger scale, combining it with some of the aquascaping techniques we describe in chapter 9, with walls made from live rock or simulated rock, could make a really unique display! A complete description of the design, structure, operation, and maintenance of the system will be included in the second edition of Martin Moe's *The Marine Aquarium Reference*, now in preparation.

Marine Multi-Environment Aquarium System
The basic design of Moe's tide pool aquarium. M. Moe

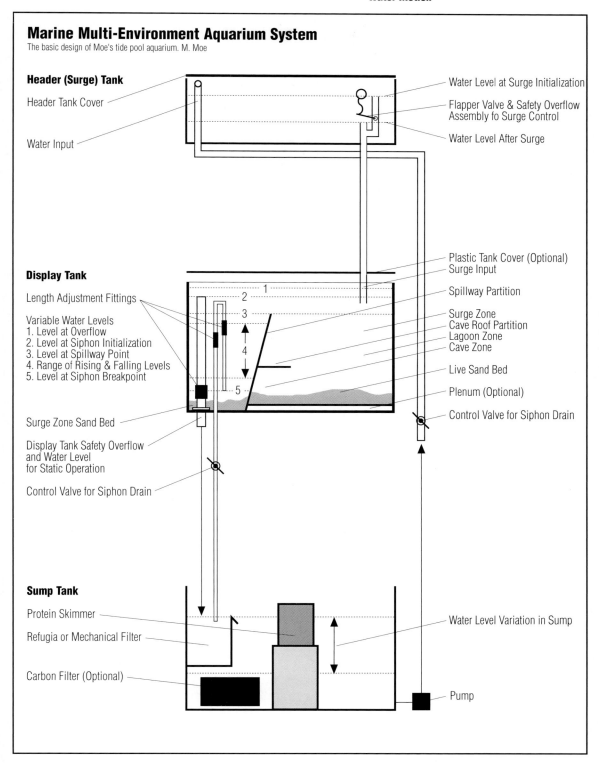

Header (Surge) Tank

Header Tank Cover

Water Input

Water Level at Surge Initialization

Flapper Valve & Safety Overflow Assembly fo Surge Control

Water Level After Surge

Display Tank

Length Adjustment Fittings

Variable Water Levels
1. Level at Overflow
2. Level at Siphon Initialization
3. Level at Spillway Point
4. Range of Rising & Falling Levels
5. Level at Siphon Breakpoint

Surge Zone Sand Bed

Display Tank Safety Overflow and Water Level for Static Operation

Control Valve for Siphon Drain

1
2
3
4
5

Plastic Tank Cover (Optional)
Surge Input

Spillway Partition

Surge Zone
Cave Roof Partition
Lagoon Zone
Cave Zone

Live Sand Bed

Plenum (Optional)

Control Valve for Siphon Drain

Sump Tank

Protein Skimmer

Refugia or Mechanical Filter

Carbon Filter (Optional)

Water Level Variation in Sump

Pump

Lighting

Reef aquariums rely on suitable artificial light sources to provide an aesthetically pleasing look and to provide a light field similar to what exists on an average reef. While there is no best type of lighting, there are considerations that determine what lights are best for a particular aquarium, depending on its dimensions and the types of creatures that will be maintained in it. There are also some important details concerning the usage of different types of lamps, reflector designs and orientation, ballast selection, and the proper orientation of marinelife in the aquarium. We discuss all of these issues in this chapter.

The importance of lighting isn't just a matter of aesthetics, though the look of a healthy tank has a lot to do with the lighting. Most of the things we keep in a reef tank depend on light for some or all of their nutrition; they are photosynthetic. The coral animal has within its tissues symbiotic plants called zooxanthellae that leak products of photosynthesis to their host. The zooxanthellae provide excess food and oxygen for the coral, and the coral's nitrogenous waste and carbon dioxide is food for the zooxanthellae. This association of plant and animal is a model of the whole reef, in a way, contained within the very organisms that build it. See chapters 1, 2, and 3 in *The Reef Aquarium* volume one for more information about the relationship between corals and zooxanthellae, and reef ecology.

A view of the lighting system over the reef display at Atlantis Marine World Aquarium, Long Island, NY. R. Harker

If you would like to keep invertebrates that rely on their symbiotic algae for nutrition, then the lighting takes on added importance. For invertebrates that lack zooxanthellae, such as *Dendronephthya* spp. soft corals, the orange sun coral, *Tubastraea* spp., and certain non-photosynthetic gorgonians, the lighting is not as important, except that some of these organisms actually prefer shade, and do not tolerate exposure to ultraviolet (UV) light.

For the aquarist it is important to know any characteristics about an organism that might offer a clue about the type of environment it came from. Our descriptions for the different species of coral and clams in chapters 12 and 13, and appendix A in *The Reef Aquarium* volume one are a guide regarding placement in the aquarium with respect to light. See also Sprung (1999, 2001a). We offer some additional generalities here.

Orientation of marinelife

Orientation of marinelife in the aquarium is a discipline of art more than science. You will learn how to place marinelife in such a way that it both thrives and looks beautiful. Although the light in our aquariums comes from above, and the specimens orient toward it in their growth and expansion, there is flexibility in the actual orientation of the specimens, in both position and angle of orientation.

Proper position in the aquarium depends on the physical aspects of: the aquarium's dimensions, its lighting system, and the structure of the reef it contains. Ledges in the aquarium create shady zones, as do the expanded tissues of corals that shade anything below them. The light is often less intense at either side of the aquarium, and more intense at the middle. Direct, unshaded lighting at the bottom of the aquarium is less intense than at the surface.

The angle of orientation of the specimen can have dramatic impact on its health and appearance. In the same location, a specimen such as a tridacnid clam can thrive if oriented facing straight up, but might not survive if oriented facing toward the viewing window. A coral in one location might expand beautifully and thrive when oriented more vertically, but remain closed and bleach when oriented facing directly upward under the light. These things we learn by trial and error.

Skylight versus sunlight

The illumination of the reef in nature is mainly from three sources: the sun, the sky, and reflection of light from the substrate upward (upwelling light). The distinction between sunlight and skylight is an important one. Skylight is quite like fluorescent lighting over an aquarium. It is uniformly diffused and without changing angles (though the colour temperature varies as the angle of the sun changes). Sunlight is a point source of light, more like a metal halide lamp, but one that changes direction over the course of a day as the sun moves across the sky. A point source of light such as a metal halide lamp is directional, but can be moved on a track to simulate change in sun orientation (see Calfo, 1993).

A metal halide and fluorescent lamp combination simulates the two light sources located above the reef, although the static position of lamps in a fixed position fixture does not reproduce the change in light angle that occurs with time of day and season. Such position changing is not necessary for a successful reef aquarium or for growing corals, which is fortunate, since the average aquarium does not have moving lights. However, duplicating the movement of the sun's position with rail systems does offer advantages in coral culture facilities, and alters the growth of corals (Calfo, 1993).

Total light received by the aquarium

Aquarists are often preoccupied with recreating the light intensity found on a natural coral reef. What most fail to realize is that the values often published in aquarium literature only represent a snapshot in time and do not include the effect of time, wherein the light value naturally increases and decreases over the course of the day as clouds briefly diffuse the light and the sun rises and sets. Maximum values in Hawaii can reach over 2200 μmol/m^2/s (J.C. Delbeek, pers. obs.), and some believe that such high values should be created over their aquarium too. However, providing such a high fixed value continuously over a reef aquarium should not be done since some corals can shut down their photosynthetic mechanisms at much lower values (e.g. 260 μmol/m^2/s for *Montipora patula*, see Riddle, 2004b).

A measure of the energy from the sun over a coral reef, over the course of a day, can offer a total quantity of photons for a given area. This is known as total integrated daylight (TIDLI). This measurement differs from the concept of intensity of the light, which changes from moment to moment and with changes in sun elevation. If we compare the sum of all photons for the day on the reef, in which the sun elevation changes, to an aquarium with a fixed source of light, we may find that a similar or even higher value is achieved. At the waters surface, equatorial sunlight over coral reefs typically generates over 50 mol/m^2 on a typical sunny day (Harker, 1999b). Reef tanks with artificial lighting have constant lighting, so it is a simple matter to multiply the total intensity of the lights by the length of time the lights are on. For example, if the lights over a reef tank are on 10 hours and generate 200 μmol/m^2/sec of light, the total integrated irradiance is 200 x 10 x 3600 (the number of seconds in an hour) or 7,200,000 μmol/m^2. This is normally converted to moles, so the final number is 7.2 mol/m^2. Some hobbyists design lighting systems as close as possible to 2000 μmol/m^2/s. However, this amount of light over a 12 hour light cycle would result in a TIDLI of 100 mol/m^2 at the surface, twice that of some natural reefs (R.Harker, pers. comm.). From this example, it should be obvious that increasing the amount of energy over an aquarium is not only a function of the light source but also, the photoperiod. Therefore, if one suspects the tank does not receive enough light, an increase in photoperiod could be applied instead of adding more lights. However, there are additional benefits from increasing light intensity, such as an increase in colour in some corals.

Aquascape effects

The structure of the aquascape is also critical with respect to the light field. Tall narrow aquariums almost beg aquarists to build rock walls upon which they can later place corals like trophies on shelves. This shape is not the shape of a coral reef. Reef walls in nature have few stony corals, located mainly on the upper parts of the wall where there is more light. Lower down the walls are mainly covered by coralline algae and sponges, and soft corals that feed on plankton drifting in the current.

Even in the shallows, the light intensity is far from constant. Light intensity gradually increases over the day, peaking between 1100 and 1400 hours, after which it gradually decreases again. Therefore, high intensity light is only present for a few hours per day. The affects of clouds and weather greatly reduce the amount of light that eventually reaches the water surface. Therefore, the number of hours and days when the reef actually receives the maximum amount of light available is quite small. Wilkens and Birkholz (1986) recorded the Lux readings at a depth of 1 m (3.3 ft.) on a reef in Indonesia. They found that values ranged from a low of 2,800 Lux in the morning to 14,000 Lux by 1100 hrs. and fluctuated after that point, due to intermittent sun and cloud, between values of 17,000 and 22,000 Lux, with peaks of 26,000 Lux from noon till 1400 hrs., falling quickly again in the late afternoon to values between 9,000 and 7,200 Lux.

These values are strongly attenuated with depth and suspended particles in the water caused by the turbulence from waves and tides, such that intensities drop off drastically within the first 5 to 10 metres (16 to 33 ft.) (Dustan, 1982). Jauch (1988) measured Lux levels in the northern Red Sea. At noon, he measured 120,000 Lux at the surface, 50,000-70,000 at the reef crest, 15,000 Lux at 15 m (50 ft.), and 2,000-4,000 Lux at 20 m (65 ft.). In the relatively particulate free, low DOC content water that exists in properly cared for aquariums, the amount of light filtering by the water may be negligible. However, even in relatively shallow aquariums, a huge drop-off in intensity occurs because the attenuation of the light with increasing distance from the lamps is far greater than the attenuation of sunlight in the sea. Light attenuation across a few centimeters or inches in an aquarium can be equivalent to the attenuation across several feet or meters in nature. This unnatural situation affects corals in a variety of ways. The most obvious is altering the growth and distribution of tissue on complexly shaped colonies (see Jaubert and Gattuso, 1989). Less obvious is the repositioning of pigments and zooxanthellae species within the coral. Corals can adapt to the unnatural attenuation of light in aquariums because they can adapt to the effects of fast growing neighbors and storm-caused shifts in their position or environment that can dramatically alter the light that they receive.

Figure 8a. Measurement of light intensity underwater at 4m and 18m depth at Lee Stocking Island in the Bahamas, on July 24 and July 25, respectively, in 1991. Courtesy of Dr. Phillip Dustan.

The spikes in these graphs represent periods of full sunshine and the valleys between them indicate the passage of clouds. Light intensity can vary by about 50% over very short time intervals, and it does so frequently over the course of the day. The second half of the day in the 4m depth graph shows a relatively clear sky condition, with little change in intensity for several hours.

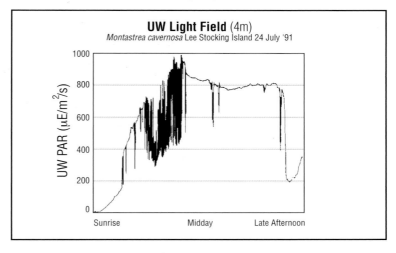

UW Light Field (4m)
Montastrea cavernosa Lee Stocking Island 24 July '91

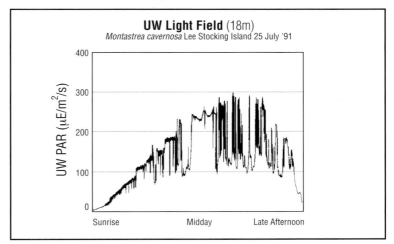

UW Light Field (18m)
Montastrea cavernosa Lee Stocking Island 25 July '91

This *Acropora* sp. demonstrates the effect of a fixed-position directional light source. The tops of the branches are bleached, due to excess light, a few millimeters away on the sides of the branches the tissue is normally pigmented, and just millimeters from that on the undersides there is tissue loss due to shading. J. Sprung

The odd shape of the colony of *Pocillopora* in this reef aquarium at Oceanopolis, Brest, France is a product of the fixed directional light it receives. D. Barthelemy

The 75 m^3 (20,000 gallon), 4.6 m (15 ft.) experimental reef tank at the transition site of the Steinhart Aquarium in San Francisco, utilizes ten Sill fixtures assembled by Selux Corp., each with a 2,000 W Osram HQI-TS 5500 K lamp, located 2.4 m (8 ft.) above the water. The maximum PAR recorded (3300 μmol/m^2/s) was a hotspot just below the surface. The other values represent PAR levels at the depth of various corals and giant clams in the tank. Note how the light intensity drops 85% at the center from just below the surface to the bottom.
B. Shepherd

Table 8.1. Using the Li-Cor LI-193 spherical 4π sensor, PAR measurements taken in the same tank above but using only a single 2000 W luminaire with a 10 degree reflector, at 30.5 cm (one foot) intervals under the centerline of the light. Values are an average of three trials where maximum PAR was recorded under the centerline of a single fixture with a new lamp. B Shepherd

Depth (ft)	**PAR** μmol/m^2/s
0.5	3692
1	3410
2	2770
3	2383
4	1958
5	1542
6	1365
7	1062
8	961
9	761
10	653
11	551
12	485
13	417
14	350
15	295

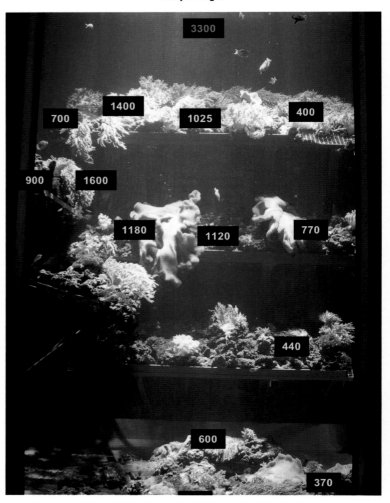

Figure 8b. Graphing the above data produces a characteristic exponential curve showing the drop-off in intensity with depth; only 8% of the light at the surface makes it to the bottom of the tank.
B. Shepherd

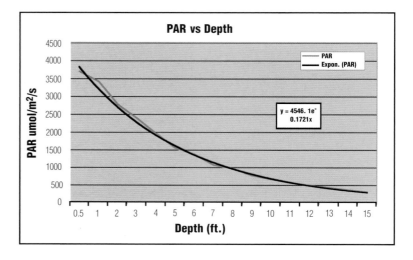

$$y = 4546.1e^{-0.1721x}$$

The greatest variety of coral growth occurs at depths between 10-15 m (33 and 50 ft.) where light intensities are lower than 20,000 Lux (Dustan, 1982) or 300 μmol/m^2/s (Harker, 1999b). Dustan (1982) found that specimens of the hard coral *Montastrea annularis*, which he transplanted from 30 m to 15 m, exhibited greatly reduced growth rates, algal bleaching, and suffered high mortality over a 2 year period. While other research has also shown that zooxanthellae maximize their function according to spectral conditions in their location (Kinzie *et al.*, 1984), Dustan concluded that there might be ecotypes of zooxanthellae such that those adapted to high light intensities function poorly in deeper habitats, and deep algae ecotypes are damaged by the higher light intensities of shallow water. If this is correct, then certain hard corals that are collected in shaded or deeper zones may not be able to adjust to the increased light intensities. This may account for some of the occasional reports of poor coral behaviour under intense lighting. Bleaching offers a possible means of adaptation for such corals (Buddemeier and Fautin, 1993; Ware, 1993; Baker, 2001). However, the importance of this effect is a subject of ongoing research (Hoegh-Guldberg, *et al.*, 2002; Coles and Brown, 2003). It is not so simple a situation that corals contain one ecotype of zooxanthellae or another. Many corals contain various types of zooxanthellae, distributed in different positions across their illuminated surfaces (tops versus sides versus undersides) (Rowan *et al.*, 1997; Rowan and Knowlton, 1995). What corals do in nature and what they do in aquariums are related matters, but they are not necessarily the same. It remains poorly studied how the composition of different zooxanthellae might change when a coral is placed in an aquarium that has a light field and nutrient content substantially different from its place of origin. Presumably (but not well studied), corals in captivity also exchange zooxanthellae, or experience changes in the composition of zooxanthellae across their surfaces. In this way, captive corals may be characterized by a different composition of zooxanthellae strains than they originally had. Furthermore, since captive corals may be mixed with other corals from different oceans, the zooxanthellae acquired in the aquarium may include strains that they would never have acquired in the natural setting.

The non-static nature of the light field

Marinelife depends on an environment whose physical parameters are in a state of non-static equilibrium. Consider for comparison the equilibriums maintained with respect to nutrient availability and water motion on the reef. It is known in the general sense that outer reef water is nutrient poor. Nevertheless, a passing school of herbivorous tangs, run-off from storms or a deep upwelling event, provides a concentrated pulse of nitrogenous waste and phosphorous to a given portion of reef. If this nutrient source was constant rather than a momentary or temporary pulse followed by assimilation and return to the nutrient poor state, the system would become saturated and the reef would suffocate under the growth of algae. Similarly, areas of the reef are exposed to high-energy pulses of water movement known as surge. If we could take the energy of a surge wave, and provide it constantly as a flowing stream current instead, many of the same organisms, which thrive in the pulsed water movement would be stripped off the substrate or peeled away from their skeleton. In the natural condition, there is a period of rest between the high-energy pulses, and there are days of calm and days of stormy destruction. Likewise, light comes in variable pulses in the natural setting (see figure 8a), but in our aquaria, the light source is relatively constant. To argue that a particular maximum intensity measured in the field is what we should duplicate over our aquaria lacks common sense when one considers the total period for which the light is at that intensity, and the periods of rest provided by the clouds, sedimentation, tides, seasonal changes in sun elevation, algae growth, etc. (see our discussion of total integrated daylight earlier in this chapter). The periods of rest provided by the passage of clouds can be measured in changes in the rate of photosynthesis, thus for the coral and zooxanthellae these clouds are akin to rhythmic breaths. Since the rest periods afford a reduction in the photosynthetic rate, they also provide a reduction in the formation of toxic oxygen free-radicals. At the same time, they may afford the coral or zooxanthellae time to use enzymes to detoxify oxygen free-radicals just produced. Without these pauses, the capacity to detoxify oxygen free-radicals may be close to its limit. The supply of iron and manganese (see chapter 4), which are used in the formation of free-radical detoxifying enzymes, may afford a higher capacity to deal with a continuous light intensity. Nevertheless, designing a lighting system that is non-static provides a way to keep the photosynthesis within its normal bounds.

Light and water movement are intimately related. We have mentioned the light alteration caused by sedimentation or depth of water associated with tides, but another affect that water motion has on the light is the formation of so-called *glitter lines*. These can be seen on the bottom of a swimming pool on a sunny day or in the aquarium when a point source of light, such as metal halide or an incandescent spotlight is used. Glitter lines are intensely magnified sunrays caused by the diffraction of the light by passing waves, chops, and ripples on the water surface. If one watches the passing bands closely, one notices that they are much brighter than the ambient light, while the areas in between the bands appear dimmer than the ambient light. Thus, the zooxanthellae receive a strobe-like effect as these bands trace across the coral. So again, we find the energy is being provided in pulses. Furthermore, just as when light is passed through a prism, the glitter lines are each separated into the different wavelengths composing the sunlight, and appear like

Wavelets on the water surface act like a lens and focus the light, causing *glitter lines*. These beams provide a strobe effect that increases the light intensity illuminating the bottom, briefly countering the attenuation of light with depth. They have been measured as having up to twice the intensity of light incident on the water surface (Falkowski et al., 1990). The effect requires a point source of light, such as the sun, metal halide, or halogen lamp. Reflected up off a white sandy bottom they also illuminate the undersides of reef ledges. J. Sprung

rainbow-hued stripes. One can only speculate about what physiological role, if any, such altered light might play.

In algae culture, high production yields are achieved with a system utilizing this principle of a pulsed light field. The commercially valuable alga *Gracillaria* is cultured in shallow troughs with strong aeration at the center. This keeps the plants tumbling so that they are exposed to the light as they cross the surface and are shaded as they pass back down to the bottom. There are important physiological reasons why the organisms require that their energy be provided in pulses. Scientists are becoming aware of details of physiology that allow the association between zooxanthellae and their hosts, and are studying the affects of light on this relationship.

Several studies have focused on the formation of toxic levels of oxygen within host tissues because of photosynthesis, and the physiological and behavioral adaptations by the host to counteract this problem (Dykens and Shick, 1982; Dykens and Shick, 1984; Lesser and Shick, 1989; Lesser *et al.*, 1990; Jones *et al.*, 2000, 2001). High concentrations of so-called superoxide or active singlet oxygen can easily poison both corals and anemones (Dykens and Shick, 1984). Often the coral quickly responds by expelling the symbiotic zooxanthellae. Shallow water anemones cope through various mechanisms including the use of enzymes such as superoxide dismutase to break down singlet oxygen, withdrawing their tentacles, covering the body column with gravel to protect it from the sun, and seasonally varying the amount and ratio of chlorophyll in their zooxanthellae to correspond with changes in light intensity (Dykens and Shick, 1984). Similar responses exist in corals. One can see why a constant light field might sometimes create a detrimental situation for a particular specimen. It is possible that it could tax the coral's ability to detoxify singlet oxygen produced by photosynthesis.

This deepwater *Cycloseris* sp. was placed in a shallow tray in full sunlight for photography. Within a few minutes excess oxygen bubbles could be seen in its tissues and it opened its mouth and contracted its tissues, clearly stressed by the affects of too much light. J. Sprung

This *Klyxum* sp (Colt coral) shows the symptoms of overillumination. The polyps on the upper portions of the branches are contracted. J. Sprung

The problem could be enhanced by very intense light, and if a certain trace element or compound required for this detoxification is in short supply.

The addition of an iodide supplement to the aquarium (usually potassium iodide or organic sources of iodine that break down in seawater and form iodide), greatly assists in preventing the loss of zooxanthellae and pigment or bleaching, and aids recovery after a bleaching event (Wilkens, 1986). The iodide might react with active oxygen and detoxify it, forming iodate (R. Buddemeier, pers. comm.). It is also possible that the effect of the iodine addition is against types of bacteria that may cause bleaching (Sprung, 2001b; Ben Haim *et al.*, 2003). In addition, studies of the calcification process note that iodide can be a calcification inhibitor (Furla *et al.*, 2000a,b). Since calcification and photosynthesis are intimately associated in zooxanthellate corals, it is possible that the calcification inhibiting effects could indirectly reduce photosynthesis, and thus limit the production of active oxygen. Whether or not this is related to the reason iodide seems to assist recovery from bleaching has not been demonstrated. The effect of the trace elements iron and manganese on coral pigmentation is more directly related to light: both are involved in the formation of light absorbing pigments and in the formation of enzymes that detoxify active oxygen (See chapter 4 and Sprung, 2002a).

Still another possible harmful effect from constant illumination is the duration of exposure to infrared (IR) light and its potential ability to literally heat up the animal itself, even when the water temperature is maintained constant. Sustained heat destroys photosynthetic capacity of zooxanthellae, and, through damage to photosystem II, resulting generation of oxygen radicals can result in irreversible damage, bleaching, or photosynthetic pigment loss Iglesias-Prieto (1997). Given the conditions of clear water and calm seas, IR can penetrate quite far. When diving one can feel its effect even at several meters depth: with the afternoon sun on one's back, a surf temperature of 29 °C (84 °F) is comfortably warm. If the sun is blocked by a passing cloud, one feels chilled suddenly. These temperature fluctuations undoubtedly play a role in the non-static equilibrium that characterizes the physical reef environment. In the aquarium, we have clear water, calm seas, and constant light from a source that may emit substantial amounts of IR. Without the periodic pauses offered in the natural environment by clouds, captive corals could be harmed by IR heating when they are placed too close to the lamp. Because of the rapid attenuation of light intensity in aquariums, harmful IR affects are only possible at the water surface, given the distance of the lamp from the water. Corals at the surface of the aquarium, if they are within about 20 cm (8 inches) of a high intensity metal halide lamp, may suffer from IR heating. High intensity fluorescents emit less IR, so it is less likely that they will harm corals, unless the corals are at the surface and within 5 cm (2 inches) of the lamp.

Infrared light could be important in the regulation of coral growth. Rapidly growing stony coral species such as *Acropora* often have no pigment or pale pigments in the zones of most rapid growth at the branch tips. There is a paradox evident in this situation. While the zooxanthellae provide the necessary energy for tissue growth, they may be nearly absent in the most rapidly calcifying tips. The paradox is at least partially explained by nutrient transport to the tips via an hypothesized mechanism driven by a concentration gradient (Fang *et al.*, 1989). Perhaps such a transport mechanism could be assisted by a temperature gradient. There could be a subtle temperature difference between the dark branches and paler tips. However, this pale tip can also be observed at the growing edge of the basal attachment of *Acropora* spp., which would not have a strong temperature gradient. Since far red light is associated with brown pigment loss, (Riddle, 2003), it stands to reason that infrared wavelengths could have a pigment regulating effect. At least the other causes for the pale tips could produce the benefit of protecting the coral tips from exposure to the most intense light. See our discussion of the McConnaughey and Whelan, (1997) hypothesis in chapter 5 for an additional explanation of the pale growing tips.

Ultraviolet (UV) light

In discussing possible damaging effects of light, one must not overlook ultraviolet (UV) light as a source for problems. Many marine organisms exist quite well in shallow waters, exposed to large amounts of UV light. These include hard and soft corals, anemones, giant clams, zoanthids, some sponges and algae (Chalker *et al.*, 1986). Many of these invertebrates contain zooxanthellae, which require light for photosynthesis. Therefore, the tissues of these organisms must be transparent to allow for the transmission of light. Jokiel and York (1984) showed that isolated zooxanthellae quickly die when exposed to UV-A and B at levels above 20% of incident surface radiation. It has been shown, however, that oxygen production does occur when zooxanthellae are exposed to UV-A, indicating that it can be used for photosynthesis (Halldal, 1968). Still, corals and clams are quite common in shallow waters, suggesting that they must have some mechanism for protection from UVR. In most cases, these organisms have developed UV absorbing compounds in the zooxanthellae and tissue cells. One class of compounds is called S-320, named after its absorption spectrum, which peaks at 320 nm. Currently S-320 is known to consist of three separate mycosporine-like amino acids; mycosporine-Gly, palythine and palythinol (Dunlap and Chalker, 1986). These compounds were originally isolated from the colonial anemone *Palythoa tuberculosa* and have since been found and studied in corals, sponges, algae, molluscs, echinoderms and tunicates (Dunlap and Chalker, 1986, Shick *et al.*, 1999; Shick and Dunlap, 2002; Shick, 2004).

While the effects of UV radiation (UVR) on reefs in the natural environment have been studied by numerous researchers (see for example Shick *et al.*, 1996), Riddle (2004c) discusses the effects of UVR from artificial light sources. Riddle (2004c) found that UVR caused photoinhibition in zooxanthellae after only one hour, though recovery did occur slowly once the UV lamp was removed. Riddle (2004c) goes on to point out that different species of corals have differing abilities to deal with UVR. Many of the lights used over aquariums, be they metal halide, fluorescents or power compact fluorescents produce UV light in varying degrees since they all

A handheld UV meter from Apogee Instruments, www.apogee-inst.com, combines UV-A and UV-B (most sensitive to UV-A), into one measurement in mol/m^2/s. The reading shown on this meter reflects outdoor UV intensity at 1:00 PM in February, at Honolulu, Hawaii. J.C. Delbeek

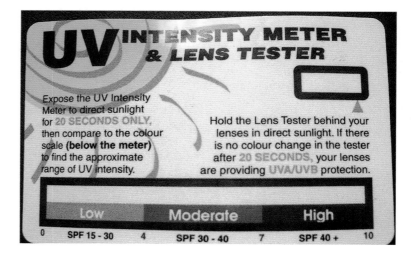

A simple reusable UVR sensitive card intended to gauge suntan lotion use and sunglass UVR protection, can also be used to gauge the level of UVR produced by aquarium lamps. These are widely available (e.g. www.scientificsonline.com) and being plasticized, should operate underwater as well as above. D. Riddle

contain mercury (Riddle, 2004c). The amount of UV produced varies from lamp to lamp; depending on design, phosphor and halide mix, and whether or not the fixture used has a shield of glass or acrylic. There are three types of UV light, A, B and C differentiated by their wavelengths. UV-C extends from 200-280 nanometers and is not considered a factor in marine aquariums since only germicidal lamps produce UV-C. However, UV-A (320-400 nm) and UV-B (280-320 nm) are produced by aquarium lighting. A UV meter can be used to measure the level of UV in an aquarium but only extremely expensive models can differentiate between UV-A and UV-B. Fortunately, most lamps and fixtures (but not all) prevent excessive UV from escaping into the aquarium. If a fixture comes with a shield, it should never be removed since they serve to not only prevent water from hitting the lamp, but also prevent excessive UV light from the lamp entering the aquarium (or harming the viewer!). This is especially true for double-ended metal halide lamps, which do not have the outer protective envelop found in mogul based metal halides, and thus produce excessive amounts of UV light. Such lamps require shields to reduce the amount of UV reaching the aquarium. Joshi and Marks (2002, 2004a) found that a glass shield reduced UV output markedly in 150 and 250W double-ended lamp fixtures.

Handheld UV sensors are available and are useful for determining the efficiency of UVR shielding in lamp fixtures and measuring UVR output from unshielded lamps (www.apogee-inst.com). These sensors must be recalibrated every three years in order to maintain their accuracy.

Many corals utilize light in the wavelengths between 360 and 380 nm, but too much intensity or too long a photoperiod for these wavelengths can harm them (Riddle, 2004c). The harm may be direct burning of the tissue, like sunburn, or it may result from the build-up of toxic singlet oxygen in the tissue, or damage to the actual photosynthetic mechanism within the zooxanthellae (Shick *et al.*, 1995; Dunlap *et al.*, 2000). While some species of zooxanthellae can produce UVR blocking pigments, not all types can (Riddle, 2004c). Signs of excessive UV light entering a reef aquarium may include bleaching of corals, zoanthids, corallimorpharians and anemones, excessive mucous production, shriveling of polyps, and the tissue may look like it is melting away. Usually the coral will be contracted in the most heavily illuminated areas, and the shaded or lower-down areas will be open. In soft corals, this gives the appearance of bald spots on the most heavily illuminated, top portions. In stony corals, the tips of the polyp tentacles may appear shriveled and may have a coating of excess mucus. High levels of UVR can also result in zooxanthellae expulsion and bleaching. See chapters 3, 6 and 10 in *The Reef Aquarium* volume one for a detailed description of UV light effects on corals and tridacnid clams, and how to deal with it.

Reasons to shield your lamps and/or check for UVR (after Riddle, 2004c):

1. Any number of environmental factors is greatly altered once a coral is collected and held in captivity before you purchase it. Therefore, UV-absorbing mycosporine-like amino acid (MAA) concentrations could change - likely drop - dramatically.

2. Some corals may never acquire appropriate MAAs or adapt to a high UVR environment.

3. Captive-grown corals could be grown in UVR-free conditions.

4. Since light and UVR production decrease with lamp age, coral MAA concentrations may decrease as well.

5. It is apparent from product testing that acrylic UVR shields lose effectiveness over time, and should be replaced periodically. Until we have a better understanding of the effects of environmental conditions on UVR-absorbing substances, it's probably not a bad idea to check your shielded lamps monthly.

6. Using the same lamp in a more efficient reflector could greatly increase the UVR dose.

7. The outer glass envelope could fail and expose the captive animals to significant increases of UVR, especially UV-C.

8. Lowering the fixture (luminaire) only a few inches can double the amount of UVR in the aquarium.

9. Introductory use of activated carbon, protein skimming (or upgrade) or drastic water change could increase the transmission of UVR (see chapter 6 and Bingman, 1995b).

Lighting Parameters

Three important qualities of light are of concern to the aquarium keeper: photoperiod, intensity and spectrum. All three of these can be manipulated to approximate conditions on any portion of a reef, on any reef in the world, and at any depth. However, natural sunlight intensity and attenuation with depth differs from artificial light sources in shallow aquariums, as do directional changes, and spectral characteristics, so that the light fields in aquaria do not exactly duplicate the light on a reef. Fortunately, the light fields we are able to create are more than adequate for the light loving creatures we keep in reef aquariums.

Note: When multiple lamp systems are used, the most intense lighting only needs to be on for about 4 to 5 hours during the middle of the photoperiod. This practice saves on electricity consumption. See page 464 for additional discussion.

Photoperiod

The photoperiod refers to the duration of illumination; how long the day is. In our experience, the best results are achieved when the day length is ten to twelve hours, not longer. Photosynthetic organisms need a dark period just as much as they need light. Since most reef aquaria are illuminated with more than one light source, it is convenient and desirable, though not absolutely necessary, to put the light fixtures on separate timing devices, so that the light gradually increases and decreases in intensity over the course of a day. If two or more different types of lamps are used, such timing of the lights also simulates the change in the spectral quality, or colour of the light, as the sun's elevation changes. After the lights have gone off, one can even use a low wattage blue incandescent or LED light to simulate moonlight, an important stimulus for reproduction in some corals and other marinelife (see chapters 3 and 13 in *The Reef Aquarium*, volume one).

Inventive aquarists have devised systems for simulating the passage of clouds. Such dimming of the light can be achieved through motorized blinds, a shade disc or cloud shape tracking across the light by means of an arm and motor or turntable assembly, and a rotating disc with clouds painted on it. Santiago Gutierrez (1991) describes a unique system he devised for cloud simulation. He incorporates a liquid crystal window between a metal halide pendant and his aquarium. When electric current is applied to the window it becomes clear, when no current is applied it becomes opaque. With this window and a timing device, it is possible to simulate cloudy periods and the passage of occasional clouds.

Recently, dimmable electronic ballasts have made it possible to very closely simulate cloud reduction of light intensity, as well as the gradual increase and decrease in light intensity that occurs with sunrise and sunset. The dimming of the lamps has an additional effect of providing not just a difference in intensity, but also a difference in spectrum, much like the change in the colour of sunlight as the sun rises and sets.

Measuring intensity

There is a variety of units used today in the measurement of light intensity, depending on the application i.e. commercial lighting, meteorology, agriculture, and terrestrial and aquatic biology. The lumen is the SI (International System) derived unit of luminous flux. A lumen is the amount of light that falls on a unit area at a unit distance from a source of one candela. Lumens are also referred to as foot-candles. Another measurement, which is sometimes confused with lumens, is Lux. One Lux is defined as one lumen falling perpendicularly on one square metre. One lumen equals 10.76 Lux.

A Lux meter is useful for measuring intensity over an aquarium to determine when lamps need to be replaced. Most units are NOT submersible so they can only be used above the surface. J.C. Delbeek

Measurements of Lux are most sensitive in the green portion of the spectrum and therefore, light that is high in green or yellow tends to have a higher Lux value than light that is high in blue. Lux is most often used in light intensity measurements since the human eye is most sensitive to green. Lux meters are useful for quick measurements of light intensity over an aquarium and are often used to judge how much the lamps in a lighting system have decreased in output over time. Therefore, Lux meters can be used to help guide the aquarist in deciding when to replace lamps. However, for organisms that photosynthesize and use light from the blue end of the spectrum all the way to the red end of the spectrum, Lux only provides information on a portion of the useable spectrum. Lux therefore is of limited meaning for use with photosynthetic organisms. For this reason, another measurement is used for this purpose, Photosynthetically Active Radiation (PAR).

Using the Lux meter pictured above, Harker (1998e) compared its readings to those from a high-end photographic Lux meter, and found that it did not have a photomic weighting factor. The photomic weighting factor allows the meter to give greater weight to light in the 500 to 600 nanometer wavelength range. This weighting produces higher Lux readings for lower colour temperature lighting. The fact that the pictured Lux meter does not do this actually works in the aquarist's favour since this means that the ratio between a PAR meter and this Lux meter is constant across all light sources; i.e. as PAR goes up, Lux, as measured by this meter, goes up at the same rate (Harker, 1998e). Harker (1998e) developed a formula that can be used to convert readings with this meter into PAR with 95% accuracy: PAR=1.53 + (0.0111) Lux. Simply multiply the Lux reading by 0.0111 and add 1.53 to get the PAR value.

The units for PAR can be specified in energy terms or in photon terms. In energy terms, PAR is expressed as PAR Irradiance, which is the total energy in the PAR range (400 nm to 700 nm). The unit of PAR Irradiance is Watt/m^2. When measured in photon terms, PAR is also called Photosynthetic Photon Flux Density (PPFD), which is a measure of the number of photons in the 400 nm to 700 nm waveband that are incident per unit time on a unit surface. When expressed in photon terms, all the photons across the visible spectrum are considered equal, independent of their energy. The quantity of photons is measured in moles of photons (1 mole of photons = 6.022 x 1023 photons). In practice, PPFD is measured in micromoles/m^2/second, or µmol/m^2/s (Joshi and Morgan, 1998).

There are now relatively inexpensive handheld PAR meters with submersible probes available (www.apogee-inst.com) but these models are not as accurate as professional models costing much more (e.g. the Li-Cor spherical 4π underwater sensor, LI-193, and the LI-1400 data logger combination, www.licor.com) as they are insensitive to wavelengths less than 440 nm (blue/violet) and above 650 nm (red) (Harker, 1999a). Therefore, aquarists should understand that in aquaria that have predominantly blue light, these meters tend to underestimate PAR for metal halides by 2 to 8% depending on their calibration (electronic light vs. sunlight). Still, these inexpensive models are a step up from a Lux meter when it comes to judging light levels in and over aquaria.

The *Li-Cor LI-1000* (replaced by the LI-1400) data logger connected to a LI-193 spherical 4π underwater sensor is the most common combination used for measuring PAR underwater. J.C. Delbeek

More expensive models offer a wider variety of light sensors, including spherical 4π underwater sensors (e.g. Li-Cor LI-193) that measure not only the light coming directly from above but also from the side and from below and are sensitive to a wider range of wavelengths. The Apogee meters use only 2π sensors, which means they only measure light coming directly from above and miss measuring light from the sides and below. This can be somewhat overcome by rotating the sensor to measure upwelling light and then adding this to the downwelling reading, but it is not as accurate as using a 4π sensor. The limitations of the Apogee instruments are discussed in detail on the Apogee website and anyone using their meter to conduct PAR studies in an aquarium should be aware of them.

The measurement of PAR, using a standard PAR meter, quantifies light intensity over the entire portion of the photosynthetic spectrum (400 nm - 700 nm) and integrates it into one reading. Therefore, while PAR is more useful than Lux, there is no way to determine which portion of the light spectrum is providing the most energy. Therefore, underwater, where the spectrum of available light varies with depth, or in aquariums that use lights offering a wide variety of spectra, PAR has its limitations. Naturally there is a piece of

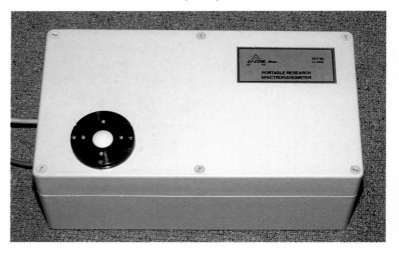

A small, portable spectroradiometer from *LiCor* Inc.; there are also submersible models available for oceanographic research. S. Joshi

equipment available that can go the next step and can actually separate the incoming light into its various components and assign a PAR value to each, the spectroradiophotometer. For example, the LiCor LI-1800/12 portable spectroradiometer is a relatively inexpensive meter, capable of measuring PAR from 300 nm to 850 nm at 2 nm intervals (www.licor.com).

At a cost of tens of thousands of US dollars, such equipment is not readily accessible to most hobbyists. Fortunately, some do have access to such equipment and have the expertise to use and interpret the results, to the benefit of us all. For example, American hobbyists Sanjay Joshi, Timothy Marks and David Morgan have produced an impressive body of work on the subject and their work has greatly increased our understanding of which lamps on the market produce what spectra and how these spectra vary with the type of ballast used and as the lamp ages. Sanjay Joshi has provided an extremely useful website that allows for the spectral comparison of various lamps on the market as well as copies of all of his articles on lighting: http://www.reeflightinginfo.arvixe.com. However, given the 2 nm interval of the Li-Cor unit, the ability of this spectrophotometer to resolve wavelengths is limited. Therefore, the interpretation of spectral results obtain from aquarium lamps using it should be treated with some skepticism as to their accuracy, especially when comparing them to spectral data on zooxanthellae absorption published in the scientific literature (R. Harker, pers. comm.). The data obtained with this instrument are approximations at best.

The sunlight over a tropical coral reef is very intense. Nevertheless, as we mentioned previously, so much intensity is not needed in our aquaria, which typically duplicate the environment from 5 to 20 m

(16 to 65 ft.) deep. The correct intensity of the light source(s) used on an aquarium depends on the animals kept, and the type of reef environment duplicated. Some corals will appear most colourful and expand best under fluorescent lighting. Others will grow and expand best under very intense metal halide light.

Spectrum

Visible light is a small portion of the electromagnetic spectrum of radiant energy that travels through space as electromagnetic waves, at a constant speed of 299,338 km (186,300 miles) per second. The colour of visible light is defined by wavelengths or spectra. The wavelength of light determines the colour perceived. Wavelengths between 400 nm and 420 nm appear violet, while those between 420 nm and 490 nm appear blue; the shorter wavelengths appearing more violet-blue, the longer ones more greenish blue. Green spectra fall between 490 nm and 560 nm, and yellow between 560 nm and 590 nm. From about 590 nm to 630 nm the light appears orange, and thereafter up to about 780 nm it is red. Red wavelengths are the longest visible waves. Beyond the visible red waves lies a region of energy called infrared. Below the violet wavelengths are ultraviolet waves. Neither ultraviolet nor infrared are visible to the human eye, but they have important physiological affects on coral reefs.

The colour of the light changes with increasing depth as it penetrates the water. This is one reason why the spectral properties of the light source are a concern. The other reason has to do with photosynthesis. The pigments involved with photosynthesis, both in seaweeds and in photosynthetic invertebrates, absorb certain wavelengths of light. Different organisms respond differently to light, even the same coral species from different places on the reef can be accustomed to different light fields. They adapt to their location by making modifications in their pigment densities and their shape, and there are different species of symbiotic zooxanthellae adapted to specific light regimes.

After only 3 m (10 feet) penetration into the water, most of the red wavelengths from the sunlight are gone, and ultraviolet wavelengths below 380 nanometers have been significantly reduced. The deeper the water, the more spectrally blue the light appears because most other wavelengths have been filtered out. Blue light penetrates water the deepest. It's no wonder, then, that the symbiotic zooxanthellae are yellow-brown in colour. This colour absorbs blue light best. While this is the colour of zooxanthellae, their host may have other photosynthetic pigments capable of absorbing light energy of different wavelengths, and transferring the energy to the zooxanthellae for photosynthesis.

Figure 8c. Transmission of visible light in water.
After Thurman & Webber (1984)

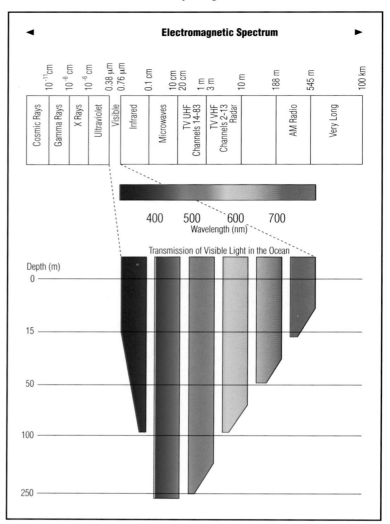

The colour of luminous bodies is defined by a system called colour temperature. Colour temperature describes the colour of a light source by comparison with a theoretical complete radiator or blackbody. Incandescent objects change colour as their temperature changes. First, they glow dull red, then as the temperature increases they glow bright red, orange, yellow, white, bluish white, and blue. Colour temperature is measured on the Kelvin temperature scale. On this scale, 0 Kelvin corresponds to –273 °C. A candle flame has a colour like a black body radiating at about 1800 Kelvin. It's colour temperature, therefore, is 1800 Kelvin. Of course, colour temperature is not a measure of the temperature of the light source. It is merely a definition of the colour, made by comparing it to the colour of a black body radiating at that temperature. Likewise, colour temperature can only be applied to light sources with colour that closely resembles the colour radiated by a black body. Metal halides are not true black bodies and neither are strongly coloured lamps, These lamps cannot be assigned an exact colour temperature, so as a matter of convenience they are given a correlated colour temperature (CCT) rating that is approximate. Therefore, the colour temperature ratings given to fluorescent and metal halide lamps are approximations at best. This is evident when spectral analysis is performed on various lamps and then compared to the Kelvin rating assigned by manufactures and/or distributors. For example, in testing of 250 W double-ended metal halide lamps Joshi (2004) found that spectral plots for several lamps were similar yet their Kelvin ratings were very different.

Choose lamps with a colour temperature roughly equivalent to daylight or higher. Lamps that emphasize red spectra nicely enhance the colours on some fish, and can be utilized sparingly for this purpose, but they may stimulate more rapid algae growth, which may or may not be desirable, depending on the kind of aquarium you wish to create.

It is also best to incorporate blue tubes with spectral peaks at 420 nanometers or 450 nanometers. These enhance the health of zooxanthellate corals, and duplicate the exquisite poster-like red and green fluorescence of the animals that can be seen on deep reefs. In our experience, it is better to use these blue tubes as a major portion of the lighting when all fluorescents are used, not merely a supplement. We recommend roughly a 1 to 1 ratio of blue light to daylight wattage on tanks using fluorescent lighting. This can be accomplished by using lamps of different colour temperatures or by using lamps that mix equal amounts of blue and white light emitting phosphors in one tube; these so-called 50/50 type lamps work well. It does not hurt to add one or more wide spectrum lamps to add a little red and yellow to the spectrum to enhance warm colours and counterbalance the cooler white/blue lamps, but they should not dominate the light field.

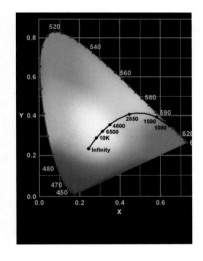

Figure 8d. Correlated colour temperature indicating the placement of several Kelvin lamp ratings. One can see that as the colour temperature increases, the colour shifts towards blue/white. Source: S. Joshi

Aquarists using metal halide lights often incorporate two or more blue fluorescent tubes, or choose from an array of high Kelvin metal halide lamps with blue spectra and eliminate the additional fluorescents. Having separate lamps does offer advantages, however. The fluorescents can be used for twilight time in the morning and evening when the metal halides are off, and to enhance the colours of the animals during the rest of the photoperiod when the metal halides are on. The shorter photoperiod for the metal halide translates into additional cost savings in several areas:

1) less electricity is used for running the metal halide lamps a shorter period of time;

2) less heat is generated when the metal halide photoperiod is shortened, so the air conditioning or chiller for the tank operates less, thus reducing electrical usage; and

3) a shorter photoperiod means the lamp's useful life will be extended from the point of view of how often new lamps are needed, which offers a savings in annual equipment expenditure.

These savings make up for the expense involved in buying and maintaining a separate fluorescent lighting system. As with fluorescent systems, the use of electronic ballasts with metal halides affords the opportunity to dim the lamps before shutting them off. This will also reduce electrical consumption and as metal halide lamps dim, they become bluer in colour, so twilight is simulated.

In order to maintain the useful colour temperature and intensity of fluorescent tubes, it is best to replace them at least once a year, but perhaps as often as every six months for V.H.O. lamps. You should judge this requirement by the appearance and health of the invertebrates or by measuring the light output of the lamps each month. Writing the replacement date on the fluorescent lamp with magic marker or placing a piece of tape with the replacement date written on it close to the lamp is helpful, as is keeping a logbook for this purpose. Metal halide lamps should also be replaced about once per year, since their colour temperature and intensity changes with use as well. The replacement schedule varies with the type of lamp and ballast combination used. For example, high Kelvin metal halides that have a large proportion of blue, need to be replaced more frequently since blue is the first colour to decrease in intensity with age. Newer compact, T5, and T8 fluorescents, when used with electronic ballasts will produce useful light for a longer period than standard T12 lamps on electromagnetic ballasts. See chapter 11 for more on when and how to replace lamps.

Types of Lighting Systems

Aquarists may now choose from an enormous range of workable lighting options. We cannot mention every lamp on the market, but we will describe the different formats available, and offer some guidelines to help in your choice.

The technology of lighting has undergone tremendous changes in the last 10 years. The advent of more efficient electronic ballast, fluorescent and metal halide technologies have resulted in significant increases in electrical savings and lumen per Watt efficiency, across all lighting types. As the push for more energy efficient lighting systems continues around the world, these technologies will also result in more efficient lighting systems for aquariums.

Though aquarists now have many options available for illuminating an aquarium, they fit conveniently into three categories: fluorescent, high intensity discharge (HID), and LED. Within these categories, there are a few different formats, and plenty of lamps from which to choose.

Forms of lighting that are not recommended for reef tanks include HID mercury vapour and sodium vapour lamps, as well as HQL and HQI-NDL lighting, which have colour temperatures (4300 K) and spectrums that aren't ideal. These lamps can be used successfully for reef aquariums, provided UV emissions are blocked and temperature is managed. With 4300 K light, the colours of the animals and appearance of the tank is not as good as with daylight spectrum, but most corals will still grow as long as they receive bright light. Quartz halogen lamps, which are inexpensive and readily available from hardware or department stores, are also unsuitable because of the tremendous amount of heat they produce. Quartz halogen fixtures get so hot that they are a fire hazard in any application. If the heat is not an issue (in cold or chilled rooms), the intensity of quartz halogen lamps is sufficient to grow corals, even though the spectrum is poor, at around 4000 K.

Efficiency/efficacy

One of the factors in choosing the correct lighting system for an aquarium concerns the efficiency of that light source in converting electrical energy into light. This parameter is known as luminous efficiency or efficacy. Efficacy is defined as the ratio of luminous flux to total radiated flux, and is measured in lumen per Watt (lm/W) or as a percentage of 680 lm/W, the efficiency of a monochromatic source of wavelength 556 nm (a yellow-green colour to which the human eye is most sensitive). Efficacy is a useful parameter for comparing the relative efficiencies of various light sources, and lamp and ballast combinations. A different measure, the overall efficacy, is defined as the ratio of luminous flux to total energy input. This is less than or equal to the luminous efficiency.

Lamp fixtures

There are several varieties of fixtures available for lighting aquariums. Some designs hold the lamps horizontally above the aquarium (e.g. metal halide, fluorescent, compact fluorescent) while others hold the lamps vertically (e.g. metal halide, compact fluorescent, LED). Fixtures can be very boxy in shape or look smooth and sleek, some are shaped like funnels or pots, while others can look like as appealing as trashcans or oil drums. Some fixtures incorporate baffles on the sides to control the spread of light as it leaves the fixture, much like the lights on a TV or movie set. Many fixtures hold a mix of lamps for different purposes: fluorescents for dawn and dusk periods and to enhance fluorescence in corals, metal halides for peak lighting periods, and LEDs to simulate moonlight.

The combination of a fixture, reflector and lens is called a luminaire. There are several companies that now provide luminaires tailored for specific lamps and ballasts such that hobbyists need no longer mix and match components to construct a lighting system. These complete luminaires take a lot of the guesswork out of determining the proper fixture, reflector design, lamp position, and ballast type to use with a certain lamp.

Fixtures should be designed so that they can be adequately cooled. Most commercially available fixtures are designed to work with certain types of lamps. For example, metal halide lamps are often housed in sealed commercial fixtures so that the internal temperature rises high enough for the lamp to operate at its peak. In this case, cooling is a function of the material the fixture is made of and the shape. In other designs, cooling is more active, using vents and fans to move air through a fixture. The critical aspect is the ideal working temperature of the lamp, which differs between types and wattages, which we will discuss shortly.

A fixture and the reflector it houses form an extremely important part of the lighting system. Unless the fixture and reflector are properly designed and matched with the proper lamp (position, shape and size), the amount of usable light produced in the aquarium can be affected drastically. Unfortunately, many of the early aquarium lighting systems sold in North America did not incorporate ideal reflector and fixture design, resulting in very inefficient light output. Fortunately, the fixtures in the hobby have dramatically improved in this regard. We will discuss reflector design in more detail shortly.

Fixture mounting options

There are a wide variety of fixture designs and mounting methods available today. There are some designs that sit directly on the aquarium, forming a hood over the tank with openings for power cords, ventilation and plumbing. Such fixtures form the canopy, which completely covers the aquarium. While aesthetically pleasing, they are difficult to service and unless protected, prone to the damaging effects of water splashes and salt spray. Since they are designed to fit exactly on the aquarium, they can only be used on that size of aquarium.

Hobbyists often simply add reflectors and lamps to existing aquarium hoods in an attempt to save money. While this is certainly feasible, we recommend caution whenever installing such a system unless you are familiar with proper wiring techniques, electrical codes in your area, and take precautions to prevent water from the aquarium coming into contact with electrical connections (see chapter 3 for more information on wiring aquariums).

There are now dozens of manufacturers producing ready built lighting fixtures for aquariums. These can feature any combination of fluorescent, metal halide and LED lamps. There are fixtures designed to sit directly on the edges of the tank using supports, while others can be hung or be mounted above the tank from the ceiling via wires or brackets attached to adjacent walls. We favour designs that offer the greatest flexibility when it comes to positioning the light over the tank. This means they can be used on a wide variety of tank shapes and can be easily moved laterally and/or up and down, for servicing the aquarium.

Open top aquarium designs using hanging fixtures allow for the greatest flexibility. The fixtures can be easily raised when old lamps are replaced with new ones, they can be moved out of the way when servicing the tank, and multiple fixtures can be set at different heights to light different depths of the tank. If the tank is behind a wall or inside an enclosure, aesthetics are not as important and it is easy to build a setup that allows for the hoisting of fixtures out of the way. Elegant commercial designs are also available that look more aesthetically pleasing for use in areas that will be directly viewed.

Here, bicycle hoists were modified to hold 400 W metal halide/compact fluorescent fixtures above an aquarium. This allows them to be set at different heights and easily moved out of the way during tank maintenance. J.C. Delbeek

These hanging fixtures use stainless steel wire hangers to suspend the lights over the tank. Note the wire grid above the tank, which allows the fixtures to be placed in any location. Note moveable baffles to direct stray light downward. J.C. Delbeek

A combination of hanging and wall-mounted fixtures is used over this open aquarium design in Japan. Note moveable baffles to direct stray light downward. J.C. Delbeek

This display at Aquamarine Fukushima aquarium in Onahama, Japan uses a suspended fiberglass rack system to support the lights above their freestanding Palau coral exhibit. J.C. Delbeek

A fluorescent light system. J. Sprung

A new metal halide light fixture produced by Energy Savers Unlimited. It is designed to clip on the wall of an aquarium. J. Sprung

No matter what type of design is used to suspend the lighting system above the aquarium, steps should be taken to prevent the fixture from dropping into the tank in case of failure. This can be anything from an extra support line tied to the fixture and ceiling, or a bracketing system on top of the tank that would prevent the fixture from falling into the water.

Fixture cooling

With the large variety of lighting solutions available and the trend to use several different ones over the same aquarium, it comes as no surprise that these are often combined into the same fixture. While these offer savings in space and cost, there are some caveats that need to be discussed. Most types of lamp have an ideal ambient temperature at which they perform to their peak efficiency, maximizing the amount of light per Watt of energy used, while also promoting maximum lamp life. There are some ballasts that tend to drive lamps slightly higher than their required wattage, thereby producing more light and heat at the expense of lamp life and spectrum stability. This is akin to overclocking a computer's CPU in order to increase its speed slightly. Doing this is fine, provided you are aware of and can accept the possible consequences.

As we mentioned, lamps usually have an ideal ambient operating temperature. For metal halides, ambient temperatures over 38 °C (100 °F) are common while the ideal ambient temperatures for fluorescent lamps tend to be much lower, at 25 °C (77 °F) for T12 and T8 lamps, and 35 °C (95 °F) for T5 lamps (Fetters, 2003). These values vary with wattage and lamp design, but generally metal halides are designed to operate at much higher temperatures than fluorescent lamps, both regular and compact fluorescent. Fin and Ouelette (1992) point out that a 1% loss in light output (for fluorescent lamps in general), as well as a

A new luminaire produced by *Energy Savers Unlimited*, with metal halide and power compact fluorescent lamps located in separate reflective channels, and blue led moonlights. J. Sprung

drop in efficacy, can be expected for every 1.1°C (2 °F) they operate above their optimum ambient temperature. For this reason it is essential that the ambient temperature within a fixture be maintained close to the ideal temperature for the type of lamp being used, either by active or passive cooling.

One can see how mixing lamp types within the same fixture can lead to compromises in cooling and lamp efficiency. In some fixture designs, metal halides and fluorescents are housed in separate compartments in an attempt to isolate and cool them separately, unfortunately most fixtures don't do this, placing both types next to each other, which is less efficient, shortening the life of the fluorescents and decreasing their lumen output. Likewise, metal halides that are not allowed to function in their ideal ambient temperature will also not be used to their utmost capability. For this reason, we feel that luminaires for metal halides and other lamp types should be thermally separated or housed in separate fixtures in order to maximize their efficiency. See chapter 4 for suggestions on cooling light fixtures.

Light fixture orientation

The angle of orientation of the light source can have a dramatic effect on the growth of photosynthetic organisms. Taking the natural setting as an example, as the Earth rotates on its axis; the sun's path across the sky casts light at a range of angles that illuminate a point on the reef differently at different times of the day. This effect, combined with the shadows cast by nearby structures and the light reflection from the sandy bottom, creates a constantly changing light field. Most aquariums do not accurately duplicate this effect, although some coral farms do achieve a simulation of it by using light rail set-ups for their lighting systems. Such light rails have the light fixtures moving on tracks. Calfo (2003) describes this type of system and its similarity to the illumination on wild reefs.

Figure 8e. A schematic of a track lighting system, showing how the angles of illumination entering the aquarium change as the luminaire is moved along the track. After Calfo, 2003

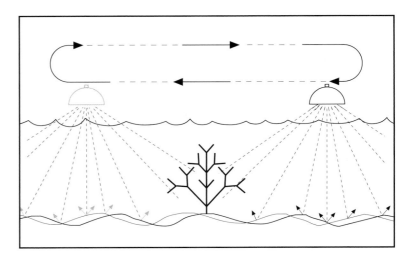

Reflectors

Fluorescent and metal halide lamps both produce light around their entire surface, though metal halides do not do so equally due to the design and supports of the internal glass tube. This means that light travels in all directions from the lamp. Depending on the height of the lamp over an aquarium, only about 25% of the light produced enters the tank directly (Harker, 1999c). For this reason, a method must be employed to redirect the remaining light downwards, into the aquarium: this is the role of a reflector in a light fixture. Reflectors also distribute light to as much of the tank as possible. This light spread can be configured to give uniform distribution of light or directed spot illumination, depending on the design of the reflector (Harker, 1999c). The better the design and materials used for the reflector, the more light that will be redirected into the aquarium. Choosing the correct reflector for a lamp involves a number of factors. The type of lamp you will be using (fluorescent, HID), the orientation of the lamp, the shape of the lamp (double-ended or mogul or linear), the shape of the aquarium, the height of reflector over the aquarium, the layout of rock work in the tank, and the type of effect you plan to create all come into play.

Reflector design and light intensity

Reflector designs have to balance two conflicting requirements; spread vs. intensity (Joshi and Marks, 2003a). A focused beam of light will provide greater intensity over a smaller area, while a diffused output will provide greater coverage but at a lower intensity. Depending on your objective, whether you want to provide a strong spot light effect on an area of the reef, or want to broadly light a wide area of the tank, different reflectors may be more suitable (Joshi and Marks, 2003a). Of course, the spread or intensity of light can also be changed by simply raising or lower the fixture.

Reflectors in early lighting fixtures consisted of the inside of the fixture painted white, or at best had a piece of aluminum fixed behind the lamp. Many hobbyists who retrofit systems used the same configurations. Some manufacturers added a few bends to the aluminum sheet, but the results still fell far short of a properly designed reflector. Aftermarket reflectors were also available but these again were little more than bent sheets of aluminum. One of the problems with these reflector designs, when used with metal halide lamps, was that light was reflected not only back into the tank but also onto the lamp. This resulted in the lamp inner envelope becoming much hotter than it was designed to, reducing the useable life of the lamp. Flat reflectors also tend to spread the light over a wide area (depending on the material used i.e. white paint, specular aluminum, hammertone, standard aluminum, etc.) thus reducing hot spots but also reducing intensity. This may be perfectly acceptable if

 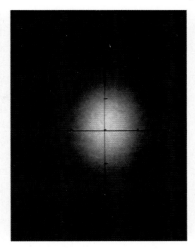 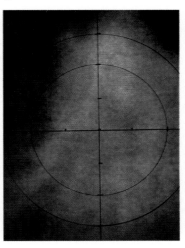

The effect of reflector material on light dispersion can be seen in these pictures of the reflection patterns produced by three reflective materials used behind a metal halide lamp. From left to right, specular aluminum, white paint and hammertone aluminum. R. Harker

the intent is to evenly spread the light from a point source of lighting to avoid creating hotspots when using metal halides. However, diffuse sources of light (e.g. fluorescents) would be better served by reflectors that concentrate the light instead of diffusing an already diffuse light source (Harker, 1999c). There are now much better reflector designs available for constructing new lighting systems or retrofitting old ones. Commercial luminaries are also now available with much better integrated reflectors.

Reflector types

The type of reflector used depends on the type of lamp used and its orientation. For fluorescent lamps, (regular or compact), which are normally mounted horizontally, 2-D parabolic reflectors are the best option. These consist of a piece of folded material, usually highly reflective specular aluminum, bent so as to form multiple reflecting surfaces, along with mounting clips to hold the lamp at the precise focal point of the parabola such that all reflected light rays exit the reflector in parallel. Better reflector designs have a ridge running down the centerline such that any light striking it is directed to the side and not directly back to the lamp. Good fluorescent lamp reflectors also use this technique to reflect light around the lamp, reducing the amount of light that might be blocked by the lamp. Some fluorescent lamps, in addition, are manufactured with an internal reflector as part of the lamp.

The use of a good reflector on fluorescent lamps may increase the light redirected into the aquarium by as much as 50%. A low profile aquarium using standard output tubes with reflectors could achieve results close to that of high output tubes without reflectors, for instance. High output (T12, Super T8 or T5HO) tubes are brighter still, and with a proper reflector, the intensity of light cast into the aquarium compares with metal halide light sources, although the spread of the light is different, since metal halides are a point source of light.

The 2-D parabolic reflectors are also used for metal halide lamps that are mounted horizontally. However, some designs, such as the Diamond LumenArc III reflector, use a 12-sided, optically engineered design to surround the lamp on all sides including the ends, and direct more light downwards. Joshi and Marks (2003b) found that this reflector offered the best overall coverage amongst those tested with a 400 W mogul base metal halide. An added bonus is that this design also features an adjustable socket assembly that allows the lamp to be precisely centered. Detracting from these benefits is the fact that it is large.

Double-ended metal halides are also mounted horizontally, but due to their small size and known geometry, the reflectors can be designed better and more light enters the tank as a result. Joshi and Marks (2003b) found that 250 W double-ended metal halides housed in manufactured luminaires, despite having 37% less power, produced just slightly less light than 400 W mogul based lamps and reflectors used in an earlier study (Joshi and Marks, 2003a). In a similar study, Harker (2002c,d) compared a 150 W double-ended luminaire to a 175 W mogul base lamp with a reflector. He found that while the efficiency of both lamps was virtually identical, when used with reflectors the double-ended luminaire produced 140% more light, had a much lower drop in intensity with distance, and produced more intense light over a larger area than the mogul base lamp and reflector combination (Harker, 2002d). The reason for this is that when designing a luminaire the engineer must know the exact geometry of the lamp in order to design the facets of the reflector. In contrast, the designer of a reflector designed for single ended lamps used over aquariums has to make certain assumptions about the geometry of the lamp used due to the wide variety of shapes and sizes available and how the reflector will be used (Harker, 2002d). In the 150 W luminaire, the lamp geometry was known, the reflector was situated very close to the lamp, therefore the reflector center ridge that reflects light away from the upper part of the lamp was just a fraction of an inch from the lamp. This means that reflected light rays have a much shorter distance to travel than in more open reflector designs such as those used with mogul base lamps, resulting in higher intensity (Harker, 2002d).

One other notable difference between mogul and double-ended lamps concerns the number and location of so-called hot spots. Generally, aquarists try to avoid placing a specimen directly under a metal halide in the belief that this represents the brightest spot. However, Harker (1999c) and Joshi and Marks (2003a,b) demonstrated that this might not be true for all reflectors. Many of the reflectors used with 400 W mogul based lamps (except those used in the Diamond Light LumenArc III fixture) showed two hotspots on either side of the center line as the fixture was raised, whereas double-ended lamps showed a single peak directly under the lamp (Joshi and Mark, 2003a,b). It is felt that this split in the light distribution pattern for mogul based lamps is due to the shadow cast by the bar that holds the inner envelop within the outer envelop; double-ended lamps do not have this bar (Joshi and Marks, 2003a,b).

The reflector format for aquariums has traditionally spread the light to fill the aquarium. The intensity of the light emitted by fluorescent or metal halide lamps thus drops off rapidly with increasing distance from the lamp. This feature of artificial light duplicates the light attenuation with increasing depth on a coral reef, but on a much smaller scale. This effect is quite unnatural on the scale it occurs in aquariums. For example, depending on the intensity of the light source, a 1 cm increase in distance from the lamp might equal a 1 m (3.3 ft.) depth increase in the sea. This intensity drop-off can be reduced if the lamp is paired with a properly design reflector.

The material from which the reflector in a luminaire is constructed can significantly increase the amount of light redirected into the aquarium, compensating for light intensity drop-off caused by increased spread (see Harker, 1999c). In 1996, Digital Oceans introduced the Spiderlight reflector. It used a highly polished specular, mirror-like aluminum reflective material made by Alcoa called Everbrite (Harker, 1999c). There are now several reflectors available using specular aluminum with various facets arranged such as to redirect as much light as possible downwards into the aquarium and away from the lamp. One of the advantages of increased reflector efficiency is that fixtures can be situated further from the aquarium yet still provide adequate intensity for most reef aquariums while reducing the amount of heat next to the water surface. However, not all reflectors are constructed to the same degree of precision and a poorly designed specular reflector can still create hotspots in an aquarium (R. Harker, pers. comm.).

Reflector design can also significantly modify the drop off of light intensity. The use of a parabolic reflector design (2-D or 3-D, see next section), as is done with floodlights (HID lamps) and inside of photocopiers (fluorescent lamps), has the ability to throw a narrow beam that maintains intensity better over long distances. In addition to the effect of the parabolic reflector, a lens placed in front of the lamp can also focus the light to achieve a narrow beam. This offers some distinct advantages over the traditional horizontal metal halide luminaire design. One advantage is that a lamp of lower wattage with a parabolic reflector will produce intensity in the aquarium comparable to a higher wattage lamp used with a spreading reflector. This means that less energy will be used to illuminate the

A 2-D parabolic reflector assembled with a mogul lamp base. Note the multifaceted specular aluminum and the ridge in the middle for deflecting light rays to the sides. R. Harker

Pendant luminaries can direct the majority of light into an aquarium and can outperfom just about any other luminaire design provided they use a well engineered parabolic reflector paired with the correct lamp shape and position. R. Harker

An interior view of the parabolic reflector inside the above pendant luminaires. Note the adjustable outer ring, which allows for removal and a much wider beam spread if desired. R. Harker

These 2000 Watt Sill parabolic fixtures use light baffles to reduce light spillage and direct as much light as possible downwards. B. Shepherd

aquarium. Another advantage is that the luminaire can be located far above the aquarium, so that it never obstructs the view into it. This allows open-top aquariums to be created, which may or may not be preferred, depending on the proclivity for objects or appendages to be inserted into the open top! Unfortunately, both designs also focus infrared and UVR, so a spot source of light will also concentrate these. The focusing of the heat is substantially reduced by locating the light at a safe distance from the aquarium and UVR can be greatly reduced by the use of UVR absorbing shields. The heat focusing does not cause a serious issue with respect to the water temperature, but it can cause a problem for corals or other marine life because it can literally heat up their tissues directly, despite the ambient water temperature. As with all intense light sources, one must be careful not to over-illuminate the corals.

Lamp positioning

Luminaires incorporate the reflector into the design of the fixture and the lamp is mounted such as to gain the maximum performance from the lamp/reflector combination. Correct positioning of the lamp can be critical in 3-D parabolic luminaires i.e. cone-shaped. These have a focal point at which the lamp must be positioned so that all the light rays leaving the luminaire are parallel. If the lamp is not in the correct position, the light rays will scatter and, as we mentioned previously, light may be directed back onto the lamp. For this reason, if you plan to change the shape or size of lamp used in a manufactured luminaire, check first with the manufacturer so that they can determine if the lamp will still be positioned correctly. In luminaires that use 2-D parabolic reflectors, i.e. a 2-D swept section of parabola created by bending sheet metal in to planar

Parabolic metal halide reflectors are designed with a narrow tolerance when it comes to lamp position.
J.C. Delbeek

segments (Joshi and Marks, 2003a) not all the light is utilized since some of it escapes from the ends; this is most notable with metal halide lamps. In these luminaires, lamp positioning is still important and clips or bases are designed so that the lamp filament is held in place at the focal point of the reflector.

Reflector analysis

Sanjay Joshi and Timothy Marks tested a variety of metal halide lamp/reflector/ballast combinations (Joshi and Marks, 2003a, 2003b, 2004b), as has Richard Harker (Harker, 1999c). For detailed analyses of available reflector designs, we urge the reader to consult these online resources. Due to the pace at which the marine aquarium industry introduces new equipment and designs, the Internet is the best source for the latest information and reviews.

Ballasts

The third part of any lighting system is the ballast. The ballast regulates the electrical flow to the lamp and determines how much energy it receives. The correct pairing of lights and ballasts is critical. One needs to know exactly what type of ballast is best suited to the lamps being used in order to gain maximum energy savings and to drive the lamp to its proper rating and longevity. Therefore, selecting the proper ballasts for a lighting system can be a bit confusing.

Fortunately, times have changed since we wrote volume one of *The Reef Aquarium*. In the early 1990s, it was common for reef aquarium hobbyists to build their own lighting systems from components (lamps, sockets, reflectors, ballasts) purchased from several places. Now most aquarists simply purchase a ready-made lighting system, whether fluorescent or metal halide while the do-it-yourselfers can still buy cheaper retrofit systems that contain all the parts but lack a fancy chassis. However, the aquarist may still need to do some research to know which ballast is best suited for which lamp in order to feel comfortable in their purchase.

Fluorescent ballasts

Up until the 1980s, there were few options when it came to fluorescent ballast technology. Ballasts consisted of heavy, brick-like, tar filled magnetic ballasts. Not only were these heavy, but they also generated a lot of heat and thus were not very efficient. While these ballasts are still available, most fluorescent systems now come standard with electronic ballasts. Introduced in the early 1980s and gaining wide acceptance by the 1990s in North America, electronic ballasts offer numerous advantages over magnetic ballasts, and anyone considering using fluorescent lamps should use the corresponding electronic ballast.

The benefits of electronic ballasts are many but one of the most often quoted is their greater efficacy. For example, using electronic ballasts, T8 lamps can have as much as 15-20% greater efficacy than when used with magnetic ballasts. They also produce much less heat, are smaller and lighter in size, and a single ballast can drive from one to four lamps without any need to change ballasts when the number of lamps change. These ballasts can also sense if regular output (R.O.), high output (H.O.) or very high output (V.H.O.) lamps are used, and will adjust their power output accordingly. Therefore, if lamp wattages are changed, the same ballast can be used. Previously, the aquarist had to select the proper ballast for not only the various wattages but also the various lengths and this often lead to some aquarists unknowingly underdriving H.O. and V.H.O. lamps by using the incorrect ballast; electronic ballasts eliminate this problem. Since the traditional varieties of H.O. and V.H.O. ballasts were like large, heavy, hot bricks, the new generation of small, cool and lightweight electronic ballasts is a welcome development!

Electronic ballasts are also available that provide continuous, flicker free dimming for most fluorescent lamps. Dimming ranges are typically 100% to 10%, 100% to 5% or 100% to 1% (we discuss dimmable ballasts later in this chapter). Claims are also made for increased light output and longer lumen maintenance (i.e. there is a smaller drop in light output over the life of the lamp), which would reduce the rate at which lamps need to be replaced. It remains to be seen how real these long term benefits are for lamps used over reef aquariums where maintaining intensity is critical. Finally, new models of electronic ballasts feature universal input voltage that will accept any line voltage between 120-277 V. This means the ballast can automatically use the applied voltage without special taps or switches (Fetters, 2003). This allows one to replace the ballast without having to worry about what the line voltage is.

Metal halide ballasts

Choosing the correct ballast for a metal halide lamp is more complicated than for fluorescent lamps, not only are there magnetic and electronic ballasts available, but also lamps used in North America can come from Europe, the United States or Asia, all of which have differing electrical standards. This means that choosing the correct ballast is especially critical. Improper ballasts may not power the lamp correctly, or may have problems starting the lamp when turned on. If the lamp is not powered correctly, it will use more power than required and will produce a different spectrum. Furthermore, mogul based lamps and double-ended lamps can behave differently depending on the ballasts used (Joshi, 2004). In addition, the magnetic ballast standard used in North America for mogul based lamps and double-ended lamps is different. Depending on lamp voltage, ANSI-M57, 58, or M59 ballasts are used for mogul based lamps, while ANSI-M80 or M81 ballasts are used for double-ended lamps.

In North America, the use of European lamps has resulted in ballasts appearing with the designation HQI. The term HQI is being used by the aquarium lighting companies to specify ballasts for the European (primarily German made lamps), the single ended 400 W and double ended 250W and 150W lamps. However, HQI® is a registered trademark of OSRAM GmbH in Germany. In some cases, the HQI ballasts sold within the aquarium hobby are standard ANSI ballasts recommended for the lamps by the manufacturers (e.g. ANSI-M80 and M81 ballasts for the doubled ended 150 W and 250 W double-ended lamps) (Joshi and Marks, 2002). In other cases, they are ballasts not specifically designed for these lamps, but sold as HQI because they are claimed to match the operating specifics of the

European lamps. This confusion is brought on in large part by the fact that the lamps are being made in Europe under European specifications and there may not be a direct match with the ANSI ballast specifications (Joshi and Marks, 2002). There is considerable trial and error required to find ballasts for these lamps, and the issue of whether these ballasts are in fact suitable for the lamps is open to debate (Joshi and Marks, 2002).

Metal halide ballasts can also be modified to produce higher voltages and some of the ballasts coming from Asia have been altered to do so. This results in a greater output of light, but at the cost of greater electrical consumption. The effect of overdriving a lamp on lamp life and spectrum stability is also not known.

Electronic metal halide ballasts are a relatively recent development in the marine aquarium hobby, but have been used in industry for several years. Metal halide lamps operate on the gaseous discharge principle; this requires a high enough energy level to ignite the gases within the lamp. Magnetic tar ballasts do this by stepping up the incoming voltage. A second means to ignite the gases is to increase the frequency of the incoming voltage rather than the voltage itself (Harker, 1998d). This is the principle behind an electronic ballast. By increasing the radio frequency of the voltage, the gases within the lamp will become excited. As we mentioned, this method has been used in fluorescent ballasts for quite some time, but only in the last few years has it been applied to metal halide ballasts.

A 150 watt Icecap electronic ballast. J. Sprung

Electronic ballasts offer several of the advantages we listed previously for electronic fluorescent ballasts, namely greater efficacy, lower heat generation, smaller size and lighter weight, and they produce less noise than magnetic ballasts. In addition, electronic metal halide ballasts have much lower tolerances for input line voltage variation and output power variations, resulting in better colour stability in the light produced by the lamp. Electronic metal halide ballasts also have the advantage of being a single unit, whereas the standard magnetic metal halide ballasts consist of a ballast, capacitor and igniter. Results of using electronic ballasts with metal halides have been mixed (Joshi and Marks, 2004c). The first ballasts to appear were for 150 W and 250 W metal halides, and these were fairly reliable. Unfortunately, the same could not be said for the 400 W ballasts. The reliability of electronic metal halide ballasts is much better now and many of the newer models can drive a wide range of lamps with little problem. There are still some differences in how these ballasts perform with various lamps, and differences in performance exist between models from different electronic ballast manufacturers. Some of these differences may be due to the frequencies the ballasts generate to ignite the arc within a lamp. Unless the frequency the ballast generates matches the frequency the lamp requires, the lamp may or may not ignite. If the lamp does ignite, the arc generated may be unstable because a resonance is created between the lamp plasma and the frequency of the electronic ballast, resulting in lamp flickering, which is sometimes not apparent even when an unstable arc is generated. An unstable arc produces lower intensity light, and may shorten usable lamp life (Harker, 1998d). For example, Harker (1998d) found that when running U.S. or Asian lamps with an electronic ballast designed to run European metal halide lamps, an unstable plasma arc was created. He also found that electronic ballasts generated a broad plasma arc, while standard magnetic ballasts generated a narrow one, which may result in longer lamp life. Harker's work underscores the importance of choosing the correct electronic ballast/metal halide lamp combination.

A stable plasma arc (left) is created when the electronic ballast and lamp radio frequency are correctly matched, if not, an unstable S-shaped plasma arc (right) is generated. R. Harker

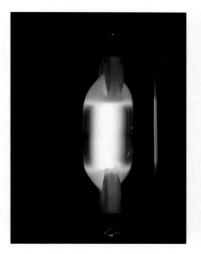 

American aquarist Sanjay Joshi has provided a website (www.reeflightinginfo.arvixe.com) where the specifications and properties of various metal halide lamps and ballasts are listed. Using pulldown menus and check boxes, one can compare the performance of a particular metal halide lamp over a range of ballasts, or one can check the performance of single ballasts with a wide range of currently available metal halide lamps. As we mentioned previously, all of Sanjay's articles are also listed on his site and together, they form an invaluable resource for the reef aquarist looking for information on the latest metal halide lamps and ballasts. In addition, Sanjay's articles published from 2002 onwards, demonstrate the rapid advancement in electronic ballast performance and the variations in performance between ballast brands.

Cost savings

As we mentioned previously in this chapter, electronic ballasts are supplanting magnetic ballasts throughout the lighting industry. One of the selling points for electronic ballasts is that they use less electricity and will therefore result in greater cost savings for power consumption, compared to magnetic ballasts. The real amount saved (or not) depends on several factors: the difference in cost of the ballast(s), the cost of electricity in your area, how long you run the ballasts for each day, and how frequently you change the lamps. Using such data one can compute the pay back period, or in other words, how long do you need to run an electronic ballast before you begin to save money versus running a magnetic ballast. One can compute the pay back period using the following formulae provide by Joshi and Morgan (2001) for use with electronic metal halide ballasts:

Running Cost Per Day = (Power Consumed in KWH) X Cost of Electricity per KWH

Where: Power consumed in KWH = (Power consumed by ballast X hours of use per day)/1000

Do this for each of the ballasts being compared. Then compute the:

Savings/Day = Running cost per day of using ballast 1 - Running cost per day of using Ballast 2

Pay back period = Difference in initial cost of ballasts/(Savings/Day)

These formulae will give you an idea of how much money you can save per year using electronic metal halide ballasts but does not take into account how much money may be saved by potentially reducing relamping rates. Further testing is required before it can be said with certainty that electronic metal halide ballasts reduce the need for lamp changes. On the other hand, the efficiency of electronic fluorescent ballasts is well documented in the lighting industry and costs are definitely reduced over time. However, the needs of a warehouse or office space are different from reef aquarium needs, where intensity fall-off is of much greater concern since even a slight drop in intensity will affect the organisms in the aquarium.

Finally, some electronic ballasts produce more intensity with certain lamps than other electronic ballasts do by overdriving the lamps to achieve higher intensities (Harker, 1998d, 2001a). In general, while magnetic ballasts draw more power (voltage and current) they also produce higher PAR values in most cases, though some recently introduced electronic ballasts are closing the gap in intensity while offering greater efficacy; it is only a matter of time before electronic ballasts outperform standard magnetic ballasts (see Harker, 1998d; Joshi, 2005a,b). In industrial applications, electrical cost savings are highly desirable; therefore, if an electronic ballast saves on electrical costs and produces somewhat less light, then this is acceptable. However, in reef aquariums, the focus is more on light intensity than on efficiency. If some electronic ballasts produce more lumens per Watt than a traditional magnetic tar ballast, but produce less total intensity, then the efficiency may be a moot point (Harker, 1998d). There are now electronic ballasts available with integrated microprocessors that monitor lamp burn hours, thermal output, energy efficiency and control dimming. These so-called intelligent electronic ballasts, can be linked to a computer for control and monitoring.

Lamp types

Fluorescent

In a fluorescent lamp, electrons produced by cathodes at both ends of the lamp excite argon and mercury vapour gasses within the lamp, which then emit UV light. The UV light reacts with a phosphor coating on the inside surface of the lamp, causing these phosphors to fluoresce and emit light. The coating consists of a blend of metallic and rare-earth phosphor salts. The blend used is specific to the lamp type and controls the colour (spectrum) of light it produces. This process is more efficient than conventional incandescent lamps because less of the energy used is converted to heat and more is converted to usable light. The lamp's glass prevents harmful UV light from escaping, but some UV A and B is still emitted. The germicidal fluorescent lamps used in UV sterilizers have no inner coating, so most of the UV produced inside the lamp exits through the glass tube. See http://www.goodmart.com/facts/light_bulbs/fluorescent_diagram.aspx for an animation of how a fluorescent lamp works.

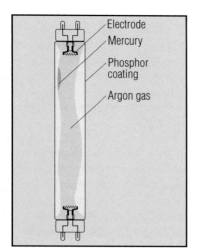

Figure 8f. Cutaway view of a fluorescent lamp showing the electrodes, mercury, gas and phosphor coating.

Fluorescent lamp designs

Fluorescent tubes have been used for many years to illuminate aquaria, and the interest in reef systems has stimulated the development of many new spectral options. When we published *The Reef Aquarium*, volume one in 1994, the majority of fluorescent lamps used in North America were the standard 3.75 cm (1.5 inch) diameter T12 lamp, while in Europe, the 2.5 cm (1 inch) T8 lamps were the norm. These were available in a range of lengths and wattages and were designated as R.O, H.O. or V.H.O. depending on their output. While it was possible to maintain a successful low profile (height) reef aquarium with standard output tubes, we felt at the time that it was better to incorporate some of the H.O. or V.H.O. lamps. These required special, expensive ballasts, but we felt that the benefit of the extra intensity was worth it. The situation today is rapidly shifting away from standard T12 lamps towards newer technologies in fluorescent lamp and ballast design, resulting in greater light output and lower electrical consumption. We will cover these newer designs in detail later in this chapter but will briefly mention them here.

Straight fluorescent lamps are the longtime standard for the aquarium industry, and are available in a few formats. The T12 format is the most common in usage both in homes and in aquariums, and offers the greatest range of spectral types allowing one to recreate a wide range of lighting effects. For home and industrial lighting, the newer and more energy efficient T8 lamps, in combination with electronic ballasts, are rapidly replacing T12 lamps and ballasts. This change is also occurring in the aquarium hobby as more T8 lamp types become available. There are now even slimmer and higher output T5 and T6 lamps available, which have been growing in popularity for aquarium use since 2000. These formats are also available in high output versions. It is now possible to rival the intensity of metal halide lamps with the newer format lamps since their increased efficacy and small size allow more light to be placed above the aquarium in the same amount of space that would formerly have been occupied by T12 lamps. The drawback to these formats is that they also generate more heat than standard T12 lamps.

Before the interest in T5 tubes, the new wave for fluorescent lights was power compact fluorescents (also known as compact fluorescent lamps CFL in the lighting industry). Compact fluorescent lamps operate in the same fashion as conventional fluorescent tubes. However, they did not become practical until the invention of rare-earth/aluminate phosphors in the late 1970s. Using a folded or spiral thin tube design, these lamps are able to double or even quadruple the light producing area in the same space used by a single fluorescent. Therefore the folded/spiral design allows for more light to be produced in a small space, making them ideal for use on smaller systems that previously could not get enough light for growing corals without overheating the tank. The thinness of the tubes allows very low profile fixtures to be used. When used in conjunction with electronic ballasts these lighting systems can use up to 40% less energy. Power compacts are available in several formats as well, including u-shaped tubes and spring shaped lamps with ends that screw into an incandescent lamp socket. The spring type lamps have been marketed as an energy efficient replacement for incandescent lamps. A 17-watt compact fluorescent spring lamp gives the same amount of light as a 75-watt incandescent lamp, with a longer burning life. This format is now readily available in 24 and 32 watt, which are quite bright considering the small amount of space they occupy and the low power consumption.

Multi-bar format CF.
J. Sprung

Mogul base CF spot lamp with built-in reflector.
J. Sprung

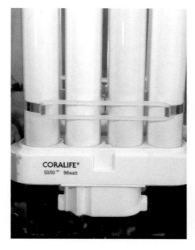

The thin nature of PC lamps allows for the use of slim fixtures, such as this CoraLife model, that allow lighting in tight spaces. J.C. Delbeek

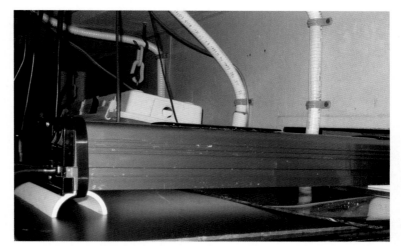

The small size and high output of CFLs have been a boon to aquarium lighting, especially in smaller systems that could not easily accommodate traditional straight fluorescents but still required high light levels. Their small size has also allowed them to be incorporated into luminaires with metal halides in more compact form factors.

In the aquarium trade, PCs range in power from 9 W to 96 W, come in lengths of 17.5 cm (7 inches) to 85 cm (34 inches), and can use either a bi-pin or square quad-pin connector. Common screw in mogul base lamps are also available and these can be used on smaller systems or as accent lights in larger systems. Some mogul based PC lamps use a single twin tube, double twin tube, or a spiral tube design. Power compacts work best with electronic ballasts, and real energy savings can be realized when compared to standard T12 fluorescent or incandescent lamps due to their lower power consumption and heat production.

T5, T6, and T8 fluorescent lamps

The drive for greater energy efficiency in lighting has lead the lighting industry to develop some new fluorescent lamp types, T8, T6 and T5. These lamps are designed to replace the standard T12 fluorescent lamps typically used in North America. In fact, some states (e.g. Hawaii) have mandated that T8 lamps and electronic ballasts must be installed in all state facilities whenever T12 systems are replaced or new buildings are constructed.

There are several advantages to these systems over the older T12 systems. They are slimmer (T8= 2.5 cm/1 inch, T6 and T5 = 1.5 cm/5/8 inch) than a T12 (3.75 cm/1.5 inches) lamp, which means that either more lamps can be placed in the same space or fewer lamps are needed to achieve the same intensity. The T5, T6 and T8 lamps run at a lower wattage but produce more lumens per Watt than T12 lamps, and are thus much more energy efficient. When combined with electronic ballasts, these newer lamps also exhibit much lower lumen fall-off over the first part of their rated lifespan and little to no shift in colour. There is also a significant decrease in electrical usage with T8 lamps saving up to 40% of the energy used in a T12 lamp, while T6 and T5 lamps are 12-18% more efficient than a T8 lamp.

When choosing at T8, T6, or T5 lighting system, it is critical that the ballast used is matched to the lamp. Unless the proper ballast is used, the lamp will not operate efficiently and will not provide the normal operating life of the lamp. Check with the lamp manufacturer as to which type of electronic ballast they recommend for use with their lamp e.g. rapid start or instant start; low, standard or high ballast factor, etc. Ready made fixtures include the correct equipment.

The slimmer design of the T8 lamp, allows more lamps to be installed over the aquarium as can be seen in this six lamp fixture. J.C. Delbeek

T5 lamps use a mini bipin, G5 base and are currently shorter than T8 and T12 lamps, so they are not interchangeable with them and require their own fixture. T6 fluorescent lamps are being touted as the next generation of T5 lamps because they are direct replacements for lamps used in standard T8 or T12 fixtures. Though the tube is the same narrow diameter as the T5, the T6 lamps have a standard bipin (G13 base) connection, and are standard lengths (24", 36", and 48"), so they fit into the older fixtures designed for T8 and T12 lamps, and can also use the same ballast as T5 and T8 lamps. However, T6 lamps have thicker glass, which makes them more durable, and they operate at slightly lower ambient temperatures than standard T5 lamps. The development of this replacement lamp in the lighting industry was quickly followed by a range of specialty lights for the aquarium industry based on the T6 format. These include bi-coloured white and actinic lamps and curved lamps designed to fit in the canopy used over a bow-front aquarium.

Both T8 and T5 lamps come in two forms; regular output (T5/T8) and high output (T5HO/T8HO). T6 lamps are available in regular output and V.H.O. The T5HO lamps put out almost twice as much light as a T8 lamp of the same length. Therefore, nearly half as many T5HO lamps are required over a given space compared with T8 lamps, and if you want to further increase the amount of light over the space, there is room for more T5HO lamps. T5HO lamps are slightly less energy efficient than

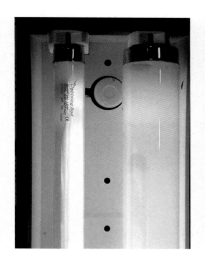

T6 lamps can be used in a standard light fixture, but offer much higher light output. Compare the intensity of the T6 lamp to the adjacent T12 tube. J. Sprung

A range of T6 specialty aquarium lamps, including a bi-coloured blue and daylight version and curved lamps for use with bow-front aquariums, was introduced by Quantum Aquatics at the Global Pet Expo show in Orlando, Florida, March 2005. J. Sprung

standard T5 lamps: standard T5s offer an efficacy of about 104 lumens per Watt, whereas T5 HOs and T8s offer approximately 90 lumens per Watt (http://www.nstaronline.com/your_business/energy_advisor/PA_48.html). Both standard T5 and T5HO lamps maintain superior light output over time, only losing 5% of their initial lumen rating in the first 40% of rated life due to their much lower mercury content (3 mg vs. 15 mg for T8 and T12 lamps) (Fetters, 2003; Knisley, 2003). T5HO lamps are available in 24 W, 39W, 54W and 80W in nominal linear lengths of two, three, four and five feet respectively, and in a 55W circular shape. The four-foot 54W lamp is most common (DiLouie, 2004). T5HO lamps require special ballasts that cannot be used with T8, T12 or T5 lamps.

T5 systems are especially suitable for the higher temperatures found in indirect, confined systems (where there is little or no air circulation), because they are designed to produce their peak light output at 35 °C (95 °F) vs. 25 °C (77 °F) for T12 and T8 lamps (Fetters, 2003). As we mentioned previously, using fluorescent lamps inside of fixtures with metal halides most likely hinders the performance of the lamp and shortens its useful life due to the high temperatures created by the metal halides. Given their different ideal operating temperatures, fluorescent and metal halide lamps should be housed separately whenever possible. However, given their higher ambient working temperatures, T5 lamps may perform better in combined fixtures with metal halides than T8 or T12 lamps.

Alternatives to T5HO lamps are Super T8 lamps. These lamps, when combined with special high-efficiency electronic ballasts,

The L-shaped reef aquarium of Berndt Mohr, featuring a high diversity of very colourful sps and lps corals, is illuminated by banks of T5 lamps. B. Mohr

can further reduce energy consumption by 15-20 percent energy savings versus conventional T8 lamps and electronic ballasts, while producing more light at the same wattage. They are, however, more expensive than standard T8 lamps.

Dimmable metal halide and fluorescent systems

As we mentioned earlier in this chapter, the introduction of electronic ballast systems that are capable of dimming metal halide and fluorescent lamps offer the ability to simulate twilight periods and sunrise/sunset without the need for supplemental lighting. This is potentially useful for fish or invertebrates (e.g. squid/cuttlefish) that are sensitive to the sudden extinguishing of all light in an aquarium. The gradual dimming, simulating the onset of sunset, also encourages spawning behaviour in fishes that broadcast spawn during this time such as angelfish, wrasses, anthias, tangs and surgeonfishes.

Dimmable fluorescent systems are now commonplace in both industrial, home and aquarium systems. The technology is now mature and offers numerous benefits for energy savings. When used with compatible lamps, dimmable fluorescent ballasts can run them between 100% and 1% of rated lumen output. Dimmable ballasts are now available for T12, T8, T6, T5HO and T5 lamps, as well as some compact fluorescent lamps. The latest dimming ballasts can now be used on AC line-phase controllers, which means they can be used with standard incandescent wall-box dimmer controllers.

The obvious choice for using dimmable fluorescent ballasts would be to simulate dawn and dusk periods in an aquarium. By using dimmable ballasts, a single control system can increase brightness in the morning and gradually decrease brightness in the evening. The advantage is that several timers are not needed and all lamps can be dimmed or increased at once instead of turning several lamps on or off.

Metal halide dimming systems are available but their reliability is not yet as good as fluorescent systems. There are several potential drawbacks to metal halide dimming systems. First, it is not recommended to run lamps at less than 50% of their normal output, as this severely affects the life of the lamp. As the metal halide dims, the colour spectrum shifts towards the blue end of the spectrum as the lamp cools and lamp flicker may increase. Another problem is that the efficacy of the lamp decreases as the light output decreases, in other words you get less light per Watt as the lamp dims. Despite the present state of the art, we do not doubt that better technology and electronic ballast designs may allow dimmable metal halide systems that are reliable, with fewer drawbacks.

Given the low cost of using low wattage fluorescents, it may be more cost effective to use these to simulate dawn and dusk periods than to invest in a dimmable metal halide setup. The metal halide can be turned on and off within the longer photoperiod of the fluorescents. Multiple fluorescents can be timed to come on and turn off in sequence to simulate the sunrise and sunset effect, or a dimmable fluorescent system could be used.

Using fluorescent lamps

Fluorescent lights are quite handy to use since they are easily installed and maintained by the average hobbyist, and they are substantially less expensive than metal halide lamps. However, more fluorescent lamps are required to match the intensity of a metal halide lamp, so the cost of replacing lamps may be similar. There are so many different types of lamps available that an aquarist can easily develop a combination that will duplicate the exact spectrum desired. Since light intensity attenuates with respect to distance from the lamp, and since fluorescent lamps are typically mounted closer to the water than metal halide lamps are, the upper regions of an aquarium lit by fluorescents can be quite bright. For shallow tanks, less than 45 cm (18 inches), four to six standard fluorescents with reflectors provides enough lighting for most corals, while fewer T8, T6 or T8 lamps would be required.

Using high output (H.O.) or very high output (V.H.O.) fluorescent lamps provides more intensity than standard output lamps. As we mentioned previously, electronic ballasts can handle a wide range of outputs of T12 lamps, but the newer SuperT8 and T5HO lamps may require special ballasts. When using H.O. and V.H.O. lamps you must be aware that some of these can also produce potentially harmful amounts of UV, and may need to be shielded appropriately.

The traditional recommendation for fluorescent lights over aquariums has been to use a combination of daylight spectrum and actinic (420 nm) type lamps, primarily to ensure a spectrum heavy in the end blue and low in the red (Delbeek and Sprung, 1994). However, there are now a great number of fluorescent lamps available from aquarium industry sources, and the choice of lamps may seem bewildering. Many of these lamps combine both daylight and actinic characteristics offering an all-in-one solution, while others offer specialty spectra. Not to worry, they all work. Any listing or recommendation of lamps we could make will eventually become obsolete as new lamps are constantly being introduced. We suggest that aquarists choose lamps based on the satisfactory (or magnificent) appearance of aquariums (and specimens) using particular types of lamps.

The manufacturers of lighting fixtures for aquariums now make canopies with four or six fluorescent lamps. These commercial units are easy to install. Many aquarists build their own custom canopies, and we feel that this is fine, but certainly more complicated for someone who isn't familiar with proper wiring techniques. Building your own fluorescent lighting system typically involves the use of waterproof end-caps and lamp-holding clips. These two items make it possible to fit the lamps right next to each other, so that six or more lamps can be mounted over a 30 cm (12 inch) wide aquarium. End-caps do not last forever, especially with V.H.O. tubes that quickly break down plastic with heat and ultraviolet wavelengths. Changing the lamps when end-caps are used can be a real chore, and they become brittle after a couple of years. Sometimes plastic clips become brittle and break, but there are strong, long-lasting types available. With the new T5 fixtures, one has the option to replace both lamp and end-caps as a single unit.

Salt on the bulbs

Because fluorescent bulbs are located so close to the water, splash results in the deposition of salt on the bulbs. While this doesn't harm fluorescent bulbs, it reduces the light entering the tank dramatically. A removable sheet of acrylic to protect the bulbs from splash will reduce some of the light intensity (by about 15%), but makes maintenance easier. Dust or salt creep/spray on bulbs or the cover lens can markedly reduce the amount of light that enters the aquarium. As we discuss in chapter 11, it is a simple matter to wipe the sheet down about once per week with a damp cloth. If you must wipe the bulbs down, turn them off first and let them cool down.

Salt on an exposed metal halide lamp will become etched into the glass by the intense heat of the lamp. A splash of water on a hot metal halide lamp can even shatter the glass envelope. Therefore, metal halide bulbs should have a cover glass to prevent splash or salt spray from reaching them.

Lamp temperature

Lamp temperature affects lamp life and colour. To cool the air in the canopy, fans are typically installed that push or pull air through the space. Be sure not to blow air directly onto the lamps, which could cool them too much. Calfo (2003) recommends exhausting air from canopies by sucking it out rather than blowing it in. In *The Reef Aquarium* volume one, we recommended exactly the opposite, because drawing air out of an aquarium hood mounted on top of an aquarium would pull humid air through the fan and cause it to corrode rapidly. A solution is to simply be sure not to blow the air directly over the lamps. If the canopy is not directly on top of the aquarium, the concern about moisture is eliminated and the recommendation to position the fans to draw air out of the canopy makes sense. One or more vent ports should be installed in the canopy to allow the air to flow out. The upper edge of the port(s) should be as close as possible to the top of the canopy to help vent out the hottest air. We discuss cooling in detail in chapter 4 and the importance of maintaining correct ambient temperatures for lamps, previously in this chapter.

Cost considerations

Fluorescent fixtures can be cheaper to install initially than metal halide systems, but the replacement of multiple lamps and, ultimately, end-caps, may make them slightly more expensive to maintain than metal halide. However, fluorescent systems may be more energy efficient when used with electronic ballasts and the newer lamp sizes discussed previously.

Metal halide lamps

Metal halide lamps belong to a family of lamps known as high intensity discharge (HID) lamps. These are differentiated by the metals contained in the arc tube: high-pressure sodium (sodium), mercury vapor (mercury) and metal halide (metallic halides). Of the three types of HID lighting, high-pressure sodium and metal halide are the most efficacious and offer the best colour. High-pressure sodium lamps offer greater efficiency at the expense of colour with an orangish light, while metal halides offer superior colour quality with a bright white light, and are the best HID solution for reef aquariums.

High intensity discharge lamps produce light by striking an electrical arc across tungsten electrodes housed inside a specially designed inner glass (quartz) tube (the arc tube). This arc tube is

Figure 8g. The construction of globe, near right, and double-ended, far right, metal halide lamps. The double-ended lamp is the 250W format. See photos on page 495 of other formats and lamp types.

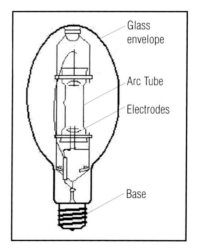
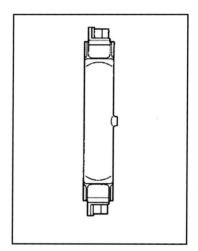

filled with both gas and metals. The gas aids in the starting of the lamp while the action of the electrons in the arc stream colliding with atoms of vapourized metals results in the emission of light energy. See http://www.goodmart.com/facts/light_bulbs/hid_diagram.aspx for an animation of how an HID lamp operates.

The mixture of metallic metals inside the inner glass tube of metal halides determines the spectrum of the light emitted, which allows for a great deal of variety in lamp spectra. This ability to adjust the light spectrum and change the Kelvin rating of a lamp is both a boon and a curse to the reefkeeping hobby. It has lead to endless debates as to which lamp provides the best spectrum, which lamp best recreates the light field found on a coral reef and which lamps result in the best colouration in corals. These debates are further fueled by claims made by manufacturers about lamp Kelvin ratings, which are sometimes more a product of fantasy than fact.

The ideal spectrum for a metal halide depends entirely on what region of a reef and what depth one is trying to recreate. Using spectra from several popular metal halide mogul based lamps (running on magnetic ballasts) used in North America, and normalizing them to account for decreasing intensity (i.e. simulating increasing depth), Sanjay Joshi showed that most of these lamps over-represent some portions of the spectrum compared to natural sunlight, while under representing others. Not surprisingly, lamps with higher Kelvin ratings showed the greatest discrepancies.

Figure 8h. This plot shows the spectrum and intensity for natural sunlight at various depths along with average PAR (PPFD) values for each depth. As can be seen, red, oranges and yellows drop off substantially with depth, while blues and greens also decrease. Source: S. Joshi

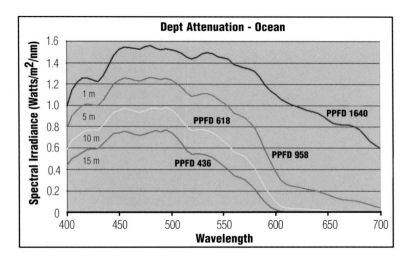

Figure 8i. The normalized spectrum of an Iwasaki 6500 K, 400 Watt lamp, compared to natural sunlight at various depths in the ocean. Note the peaks in blue, green and yellow. However, the overall spectrum matches natural sunlight well. S. Joshi

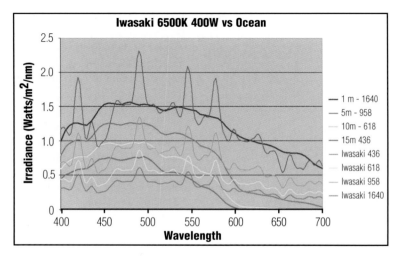

Figure 8j. The normalized spectrum of an Ushio 10,000 K, 400 Watt lamp, compared to natural sunlight at various depths in the ocean. Note the greater amount of green and blue. S. Joshi

Figure 8k. The normalized spectrum of a Radium 20,000 K, 400 Watt lamp, compared to natural sunlight at various depths in the ocean. S. Joshi

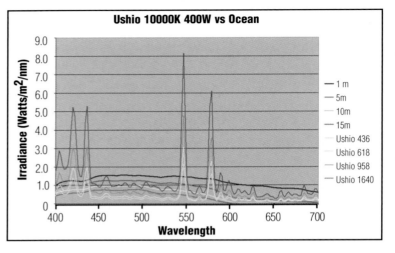

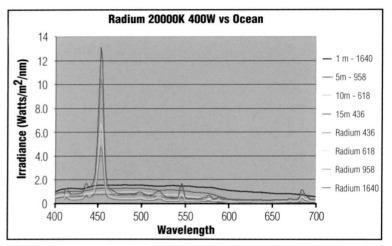

The lesson here is that different lamps can be used to create different regions of the reef. If one were trying to create shallow regions, then lamps with a wider spectrum would be best. If one were trying to recreate greater depths, than lamps with spectra heavy in the blue and violet end would be best. However, viewing deeply blue/violet aquaria does not always look as visually appealing as one with a broader colour spectrum. It is also clear that due to the nature of their construction, every metal halide lamp will only show peaks at wavelengths corresponding to the emission spectra of the metallic halides used in the lamp. It should therefore be clear that no metal halide provides a reasonably natural sunlight spectrum. However, the ability of photosynthetic animals to adapt to drastically different light fields enables them to survive in the very unnatural light created by artificial light sources.

Metal halide lamp design

There are two basic lamp designs available in metal halide lamps. In one design, the inner envelope is suspended via support wires inside a larger, glass outer envelope. The shape and size of this outer envelop is highly variable depending on wattage, base design and fixture size. This outer envelope helps to reduce the ultraviolet light generated by the reactions taking place within the inner envelope. Therefore, any lamp with a compromised outer envelope should be discarded.

Metal halide lamps with outer envelopes come in a variety of lamp shapes and sizes. These are designated using a letter and numbering system. The letters designate the shape of the lamp (e.g. BT = lamp shape where E = elliptical, T = tubular) and the number is a measure of the widest portion of the lamp, in 1/8's of an inch. For example, the two globe-shaped lamps in the top of the picture of mogul based metal halide lamps are both 1000 Watt, 6500 K lamps, but the one on the left is a BT37 design while the one on the right is a BT56. When choosing a fixture make sure the lamp you wish to use fits into the fixture and positions the inner element in the proper position relative to the reflector; this is especially critical with parabolic reflectors. Luminaire manufacturers should provide a listing of what lamp shapes and sizes are appropriate for their fixture.

Double-ended lamps have no outer envelope and the lamp is held at both ends within a fixture by ceramic tips. Since there is no outer envelope to reduce UV light output, these lamps are housed in fixtures with an UV absorbing glass shield. Some hobbyists remove this protective shielding in an attempt to maximize the light from a double-ended luminaire. Doing so provides a small increase in intensity (an average of 18% according to Joshi and Marks, 2004a) but a substantial increase in UV light also occurs. This will not only harm aquarium inhabitants, it will also degrade materials within and around the aquarium, and provide a serious health hazard to anyone who views the lamp.

CAUTION: DOUBLED-ENDED LAMPS SHOULD NEVER BE OPERATED WITHOUT AN ULTRAVIOLET BLOCKING SHIELD IN PLACE. THE ULTRAVIOLET LIGHT PRODUCED BY AN UNSHIELDED DOUBLE-ENDED LAMP CAN CAUSE SEVERE DAMAGE TO AQUATIC ORGANISMS, DEGRADE EXPOSED MATERIALS AND DAMAGE UNPROTECTED HUMAN EYES.

Since 1994, the availability and selection of metal halide lamps has increased substantially! There are now a bewildering array of wattages, Kelvin values, shapes and styles from which to choose.

Top: Double ended 150 watt metal halide lamp. J. Sprung

Above: Mogul based metal halide lamps come in a wide variety of shapes and sizes; shown here is but a small sample. J.C. Delbeek

The bottom line, fortunately, is that they all work and are suitable for use on reef aquariums. Using metal halide lighting has now come down to a matter of aesthetics as much as biology.

Using metal halides

Aquarium industry metal halide lamps range from 75 Watts to 400 Watts. Most aquarists are using either 175 or 150 Watt lamps, which are ideal for average aquariums of 280 L (100 gallons) or less, not taller than 76 cm (30 inches). For aquariums taller than 76 cm (30 inches), 250 Watt or 400 Watt lamps should be used. Some aquarists use 1000 Watt fixtures with great success, but we cannot comment on their electric bill. Large public aquariums commonly use fixtures of 1000 Watts or higher.

An important factor is the degree of heating that the light will cause in the tank. Metal halide lamps should be about 30 cm (1 ft.) above the water surface to prevent overheating of the water. They can be located closer to the water when a chiller is used to maintain the water temperature. High intensity metal halide light sources can damage photosynthetic corals if they are located too close to the lamp. High rates of photosynthesis can produce oxygen free radicals, discussed earlier. Infrared light emitted from the lamps also has the potential ability to elevate the temperature of coral tissue close to the water surface when there is not sufficient distance between the lamp and the specimen, and insufficient water circulation to effect cooling.

Metal halide lamps with Kelvin ratings over 5500 provide enough blue spectral intensity. Our experience also shows that supplemental blue lighting is not necessary for success, but the use of blue lamps for twilight periods at dawn and dusk also provides natural simulation of the start and end of daylight. Proper adjustment of these periods can stimulate spawning events in both fish and corals, and the glowing appearance of fluorescent corals under blue light is a breathtaking sight. Manufacturers of lighting fixtures for metal halide lamps have models that include blue fluorescent lamps in the fixtures, and this is what most aquarists prefer.

Metal halide lamps and nipples

When the inner envelope of a metal halide lamp is manufactured, gas is injected into it and the envelope is then sealed. The result is a small raised bump on the surface known as a nipple. Several aquarists have observed that when lamps are mounted horizontally and this nipple is situated below the mid-plane of the lamp, the colour spectrum is different (usually more yellow) than if the nipple is situated above the mid-plane. Harker (2002a; 2002b) investigated this apparent effect and found that there were too many variables in lamp type, design and age to be able to predict what effect, if any, nipple orientation would have on the generated light field. In some

The nipple on the inner envelope is clearly visible in this 10,000 Kelvin 400 W mogul based metal halide lamp. J.C. Delbeek

This fixture contains two new 175 W 10,000 Kelvin metal halide lamps of the same brand. The lamp on the left has the nipple pointing below the horizontal plane of the fixture; the one on the right has the nipple above the horizontal plane of the fixture. The difference in visible colour is substantial. We have also observed this effect in 400 W 10,000 Kelvin metal halides. J.C. Delbeek

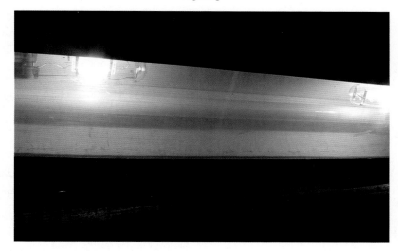

In this photo the lamp on the left, the same one as in the previous picture, was rotated so that the nipple was facing above the horizontal plane of the lamp. There is an obvious change in lamp colour from yellow/green to blue/violet, visible to both the eye and camera lens. J.C. Delbeek

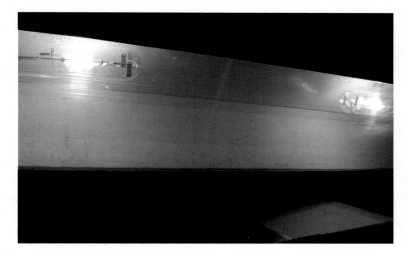

cases, the intensity of the light on the nipple side was higher in others it was lower. In some orientations, the spectrum was slightly higher and in others, it was lower (Harker, 2002b). Harker (2002b) concluded that given the type of lamp, the age of the lamp, the ballast, wiring, and the hostile environment of a reef tank, it is impossible to predict how any lamp will react. Harker's (2002b) measurement of lamp colour temperature showed slight differences related to nipple orientation but he felt that these differences would be difficult to discern. Harker (2002b) indicated that, in his opinion, the position of the support wire in the lamp was a better predictor of which orientation produced a greater light intensity than the position of the nipple.

In contrast with Harker's findings, we have frequently observed that some lamps do appear yellow/green to the eye if the nipple is oriented below the mid-plane. If two identical lamps in the same fixture exhibit differences in colour, we recommend that the nipple orientation be the first thing checked. In some cases, it is very difficult to reorient a mogul lamp in its socket and still achieve electrical contact. In this situation, one option is to remount the socket in the fixture so that a snugly fit lamp orients the nipple above the horizontal plane of the lamp. Whether the nipple or if something else within the lamp is responsible for this effect, it is a real phenomenon that deserves further investigation.

CAUTION: NEVER OVER TIGHTEN A MOGUL BASED LAMP! DOING SO CAN EASILY CRACK THE JOINT BETWEEN THE OUTER ENVELOP AND THE MOGUL BASE, OR WORSE, THE LAMP MAY SHATTER IN YOUR HAND.

Iwasaki metal halide flood and spot lamps

Recently (2004), a new hybrid metal halide lamp appeared on the market. Manufactured by Iwasaki, the Eye Color Arc PAR™ combines a 70 or 150 W double-ended metal halide lamp with a reflector in either a PAR36 (wide beam) or PAR38 (narrow beam) lamp shape (see http://www.eyelighting.com/colorarc_par.html). These lamps are available in colour temperatures of 3500, 4500, or 6500 K. However, only the 70 W 6500 K lamps have a CRI of 96, while all the 150 W lamps have a CRI of 96. There are also pink and blue versions available. These lamps have a standard mogul base and this can screw into almost any standard fixture. The use of an electronic ballast is recommend in order to achieve the most efficient combination of energy used and light produced (Schiemer, 2004). Scheimer (2004) found that the 150 W 6500 K PAR36 lamps gave the best results in terms of appearance and coral growth in his test system. A luminaire for this lamp is currently provided by IceCap Industries (http://www.icecapinc.com/lamp.htm). The low wattage

The PAR 36 (left) and PAR 38 (right) lamp shapes. Provided by EYE Lighting International of North America, Inc.

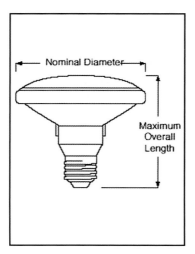

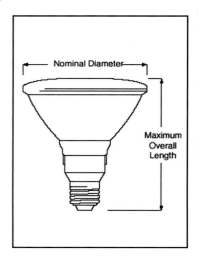

A 150 W PAR36 Eye Color Arc Lamp powered by an electronic ballast and mounted in a compact fixture manufactured by Icecap Inc. J. Sprung

but high intensity makes these lamps best suited for smaller aquariums or for use as accent lights on larger aquariums. The narrow beam lamp would also be useful for mounting lamps higher above the aquarium, allowing for unobstructed viewing of the aquarium from above.

New trends in aquarium lighting

There is a new lamp made every week for the aquarium hobby it seems. When we had the 6500K daylight metal halide lamps, it seemed nothing could be better. Then came the 10000 K lamps, then 20000 K. At the present rate of increase, our 50000 K lamps will be obsolete because the following week the 700000000000 K lamp will be introduced (for those keeping score, that's the 7 hundred billion Kelvin, surely the best yet). New hobbyists are confused by these numbers. What they refer to is the colour temperature, which really is a fancy way of qualifying the spectrum produced by the lamp. The high Kelvin lamps have a bluer spectrum. Whereas one could supplement daylight spectrum metal halides with blue fluorescent lights, the newer high Kelvin blue metal halides can be supplemented with daylight spectrum fluorescents or metal halides. Either solution works.

Of course, the exceedingly larger numbers we just depicted were done so in jest. As we described earlier, daylight has a colour temperature of approximately 6000 K. Lamps with 10000 K or 20000 K, which are popular currently, can have a strongly blue spectrum, and often produce more UVR than lower colour temperature lamps. While many aquarists like the effect that the high Kelvin lamps have on the fluorescent colours of the corals, one has to be very careful about UVR produced by high Kelvin lamps. Without a UVR absorbing lens these lamps may emit too much UVR for the corals to withstand. Double-ended metal halide lamps must always be employed with a glass lens to filter out harmful UVR . Mogul based lamps lamps have a protective glass envelope, but the high Kelvin versions may still emit too much UVR for certain corals. Since UVR can stimulate rapid photosynthesis and the production of active oxygen and superoxide radicals in the coral tissue, the coral may bleach in response. As we have mentioned several times in this chapter, we strongly encourage the use of protective shielding for all lamp types. In our opinion, the protection they offer the lamp, the organisms and the hobbyist far outweigh any possible advantages offered by not using them.

DALI (Digital Addressable Lighting Interface)
A new lighting protocol known as Digital Addressable Lighting Interface (DALI) is slowly becoming available in North America. This two-way communication protocol allows for the construction of a

digital lighting network where the electronic ballast can not only receive information from a central computer but also send information on its status. The protocol requires DALI compatible hardware such as ballasts, lamps, controls and wiring all networked to a central computer, which allows ballasts to be controlled separately. The control wiring is simplified by two polarity-free connections leading to and from the ballast, in other words there are no + or − terminals to worry about. Digital ballasts can soft start fluorescent lamps to maximize lamp life; cut lamps out at end of life; gradually dim lamps at the end of the day or gradually increase them at the start of the day over a continuous range; and start lamps at any point in their dimming range from 100% to 1% (DiLouie, 2002). Currently DALI has been implemented by manufacturers of select T8, T5 and compact fluorescent lamps and ballasts. Other lighting technologies may provide DALI support in the future.

The promise of DALI for aquarists lies in the degree of control that it offers over lighting. For public aquariums, it allows multiple lighting systems to be programmed and controlled from a central system and for items such as light switches to be reassigned from one lighting system to another. For the home aquarist, we can envision lighting systems that: 1. Can be programmed to simulate photoperiods from any point in the world; 2. Simulate the random passing of clouds over an aquarium; and 3. Link the lighting system to a light intensity sensor to adjust for increase in light levels such as sunlight entering for part of the day or a bright light being turned on or off in the room. We feel that this technology holds many interesting possibilities for the aquarium industry, especially public aquariums, fish hatcheries and aquaculture facilities.

Pulse-start metal halide lamps

Most metal halide lamps use a startup system known as probe-start, which uses three electrodes to ignite the gases within the lamp. Lower wattage metal halides have long used another method called pulse-start, which uses only two electrodes while a high-voltage igniter is added that provides 3-4 kV pulses to ionize the gas and produce the glow discharge (DiLouie, 2004). Pulse-start metal halides offer higher light output, higher lumen maintenance, greater energy efficiency (15% more efficient), a whiter light, and re-strike faster after a power outage (DuLouie, 2004). Today, pulse-start metal halides are available in wattages up to 1000 W but their colour temperatures are still somewhat low by reef aquarium standards (5000 K or less). This can be offset by the use of higher Kelvin fluorescent lamps or the use of coloured filters. Pulse-start lamps can only be used with pulse start ballasts. It is only a matter of time before pulse-start metal halide lamps improve their Kelvin and CRI ratings, and become attractive to reef keepers (e.g.

http://www.venturelighting.com/LampsHTMLDocuments/NaturalW
hite_lamps.html#375W).

Pulse-start ballasts can be used with higher Kelvin non-pulse start
metal halide lamps commonly used in the aquarium hobby, but it
remains to be seen if these ballasts offer the same benefits to non-
pulse start lamps as they do to pulse-start lamps (Joshi and Marks,
2002). Joshi and Marks (2002) did find, however, that two used 175
W mogul based metal halides (3200 hours total over a period of 11
months), which had been run using a pulse-start ballast, had PAR
values very close to new lamps. If this finding is accurate and
reproducible, then it demonstrates a significant advantage to using
pulse-start ballasts with non-pulse start lamps.

Ceramic metal halide (CMH) lamps

Metal halides are notorious for poor colour consistency where
colours can range all over the map from lamp to lamp within the
same batch. Metal halides also tend to lose their intensity rapidly.
Ceramic arc tube metal halide lamps, commonly designated CMH
or CDM, use a polycrystalline alumina (PCA) ceramic material (the
same as used in sodium pressure lamps) for the arc tube within
the lamp instead of quartz. Ceramic metal halide lamps were
introduced to reduce the problem of colour shift of standard metal
halide lamps. The PCA material reduces the sodium loss that
causes colour shift (Fetters, 2003).

Ceramic metal halide lamps have an average rated life of 6000-20,000
hours while their lumen maintenance values fall in the 70 –80%
range. While current colour temperatures are low (4000-5000 K)
compared to the metal halides commonly used in reef aquariums,
they have excellent colour rendering (CRI 85 and above) (Fetters,
2003). Pulse-start CMHs are also available, but again, these perform
best on electronic ballasts (DiLouie, 2004). The advantages of the
combination of CMHs and electronic ballasts include 10-20% greater
light output (which also results in a corresponding higher efficacy)
and limited colour shift (Fetters, 2003). Ceramic metal halides come
in a variety of lamp types, wattages and sizes, and are regularly used
in the hydroponics industry. It is entirely possible that as their colour
temperatures improve, or with the use of coloured filters, or if used
in combination with high Kelvin lamps, this type of metal halide may
be come popular for reef aquariums.

Programmable photoperiod timers

Aquarists interested in spawning corals and fish are interested in
stimulating natural spawning cycles. This is can be achieved by
seasonally altering temperature and photoperiod, and by installing a
moonlight to simulate the phases of the moon. There are commercial

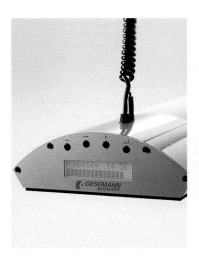

Giesemann Lichttechnik manufactures luminaires with built-in programmable timers. J. Sprung

This custom designed photoperiod timing system is installed on a coral holding system (visible through the window) at the Georgia Aquarium. B. Carlson

systems available in the aquarium trade for simulating the phases of the moon, but systems to control photoperiod over the course of the year are less common. Photoperiod timers are often used in commercial applications to control lighting on outdoor signage so that the sign lights come on at dusk, and go off at dawn, over the course of the year and automatically adjust their photoperiod based on the latitude of their location. Timers can be used for this task and 365-day programmable timers are readily available but expensive. Custom systems can be constructed, but are also expensive. We believe that a photoperiod timer will likely become a standard option in programmable lighting fixtures in the future. Although moon phases and rise in temperature are commonly known as the stimuli for coral spawning, corals also mass spawn in tropical regions where the temperature varies very little. Penland *et al.* (2004) showed that in these cases the rise toward and fall from solar insolation maxima, the maxima of electromagnetic energy incident on the surface of the earth, coincides with coral spawning. Their work suggests that simply manipulating the photoperiod and light intensity can achieve the stimulus, without temperature rise. Insolation maxima occur twice per year, at the vernal and autumnal equinoxes, when the geometric center of the sun crosses the equator. See our warnings in chapter 4 regarding the risks associated with coral spawning in closed system aquariums.

The Advanced Control Lighting System (ACLS)

A recent introduction to the aquarium market is the ACLS, a programmable dimming electronic ballast for metal halide aquarium lighting systems developed by the SFILIGOI Company of Italy (www.sfiligoi.it). The unit can operate a single 150 W, 250 W or 400 W lamp, or two 250 W lamps. According to the company's literature, this system has a number of intriguing capabilities. Aside from the

The ACLS unit produced by the SFILIGOI Company of Italy offers a wide range of lighting control options. Photo courtesy of SFILIGOI Company.

ability to slowly ramp up and ramp down metal halide lamps to simulate sunrise and sunset respectively (common to all models, only the 250 W and 400 W models offer additional capabilities), the unit also allows for the use of a moonlight and the simulation of cloudy days. While other controllers on the market have provided some of these functions, what sets the ACLS apart is the ability to enter latitude and longitude in order to mimic the photoperiod and its changes over the entire year. This allows the unit to simulate the photoperiod for any spot in the world, increasing photoperiod in the summer, and decreasing it in winter. In addition, the unit has an automatic setting that is used when a new lamp is installed. This setting reduces lamp output slightly then slowly increases it over a period of several weeks to full intensity, avoiding light shocking corals. Finally, the unit also contains standard timers that can be used for additional fluorescent or metal halide lamps. One intriguing application of this technology is to use two ACLS units to control two lamps, one at each end of the tank. Using this setup, one side ramps up first, then the other side. At the end of the day, the first side to come on then dims and then the other side dims. This mimics the movement of the sun across the sky, increasing light from one side as it rises, with maximum intensity from directly above, then a gradual shift to the other side as the sunsets. Finally, the unit has a RS485 port for connection to a computer, up to 654 ACLS units can be connected to a single computer.

Light emitting diode (LED) lighting

A light emitting diode or LED is a semiconductor diode that emits incoherent monochromatic light when an electric current passes through it, a form of electroluminescence. The colour depends on the semiconducting material used, and can be near ultraviolet, visible, and near infrared. LEDs offer benefits in terms of maintenance and safety. The typical working lifetime of a device, including the lamp, is ten years, which is much longer than the lifetimes of most other light sources. LEDs give off less heat than incandescent light lamps and are less fragile than fluorescent lamps. Since an individual device is smaller than a centimeter in length, LED-based light sources used for illumination and outdoor signals are built using clusters of tens of devices. LED lights can also be easily dimmed without affecting their life.

LED colour

Conventional LEDs are made of semiconducting inorganic minerals and the type of material used dictates the wavelength of light produced. Research into LED lighting is extensive due to the promise of low heat emission, low wattage, high light output and long life. The development of LEDs began with infrared and red devices, and technological advances have made possible the production of devices with ever-shorter wavelengths. Blue LEDs became available in the late 1990s. They can be added to existing red and green LEDs to produce white light. Zinc selenide (ZnSe) LEDs can produce white light by emitting blue light from the pn junction, which is then mixed with red-to-green light created by photoluminescence in the ZnSe.

The most recent innovation in LED technology is a device that can emit ultraviolet light. When ultraviolet light illuminates certain materials, these materials will fluoresce or give off visible light. White light LEDs have been produced by building ultraviolet elements inside material that fluoresces to produce white light. Ultraviolet and blue LEDs are relatively expensive compared to the more common reds, greens, yellows and infrareds and are thus less commonly used in commercial applications. Currently research on LEDs is centering on the production of a pure white LED.

LED function and efficiency

Unlike incandescent lamps, which can operate with either AC or DC, LEDs require a DC supply of the correct polarity. Typical LEDs are designed to operate with an electrical supply of not more than 30-60 milliWatts. LEDs with larger semiconductor die sizes capable of continuous use at one Watt of input power were introduced in 1999. The larger semiconductor dies were mounted to metal slugs that promote heat removal from the LED die. In 2002, 5 Watt LEDs became available with efficiencies of 18-22 lumens per Watt. By 2005 or sooner, 10 Watt LEDs will be available with efficiencies of 60 lumens per Watt. These will produce about as much light as a common 50 Watt incandescent lamp, and will make the use of LEDs for general illumination needs a practical reality. There are now lamps available that contain multiple LEDs and all the circuitry necessary together in a small lamp that can screw directly into any incandescent fixture without the need for separate power converters.

This LED lamp contains 25 blue LEDs and can screw directly into a standard 110 VAC incandescent mogul mount fixture. J.C. Delbeek

Organic LED (OLED)

In the last few years (up to 2003), there has also been much research into organic LEDs or OLEDs, which are made of semiconducting organic polymers. The best efficiency of an OLED so far is about 10%. These promise to be much cheaper to fabricate than inorganic LEDs, and large arrays of them can be deposited on a screen using simple printing methods to create a colour graphic display. As this book is being written, OLEDS are already being used in cell phones, MP3 players, digital cameras and other devices that use small displays. Manufacturers have demonstrated larger screens in laptop and computer display panels, and it is only a matter of time before even larger displays become available. How this technology will evolve is an exciting thing to ponder, and it may offer some new options for aquarium lighting, particularly in small aquariums. We can imagine a computer-controlled OLED light panel (like an LCD

TV panel) that simulates the sky, with clouds passing by and spectral changes that occur as the sun changes angle.

Uses

LED's are used in many applications now, including message displays and status indicator lights on electronic equipment; traffic signals and crosswalk signs; bicycle lighting; flashlights a.k.a. torches in the U.K.; backlights for LCD displays; signaling/emergency beacons and strobes; infrared remote controllers, sensors (e.g. mechanical and optical mice); and LED printers.

For aquariums, LED's became popular first as moonlight simulators and later for illuminating very small aquariums, and as spotlights to highlight specimens. Blue LEDs have the added benefit of enhancing fluorescence in corals and can be used to add additional excitation energy to the aquarium or in place of actinic lamps for small aquariums. The technologies for LED production are developing rapidly and more intense lighting systems will eventually appear on the market. LED light output degrades fairly rapidly if ambient heat builds up around the LED, therefore these lights should never be used inside of metal halide light fixtures.

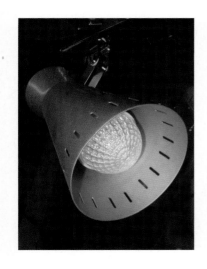

Lamps that can screw into standard incandescent fixtures can hold tens of LEDs in various colour combinations. Here 25 blue LEDs are in a single lamp. J.C. Delbeek

Thackry (in press) calculated the cost to replace the two 250 Watt 14,000 K double-ended metal halides and two 110 Watt VHO actinic fluorescent lamps on his 284 L (75 US gallon) aquarium, with white LEDs. Using a Li-Cor 192SA PAR sensor and his current lighting system, he measured 450 $\mu mol/m^2/s$ halfway down in the tank in the brightest spot. Thackry calculated that 600 white LEDs could achieve a PAR of 456 $\mu mol/m^2/s$ at the surface of the water. However, the cost of the power supply, circuit boards, reflectors, and the labour to assemble the LED array and associated parts, would amount to about $5000 US!

The efficiency, lumen output and cost per lumen of LEDs will only increase such that efficacy should reach over 160 lm/W over the next 5 to 10 years (DiLouie, 2003). Along with this increase in efficacy, a corresponding decrease in price should also occur as LED use becomes widespread and manufacturing costs decrease.

MR16 halogen lighting

Home track lighting systems use a special type of halogen lamp called the MR16. This small lamp has a built-in reflector that can be manufactured with a variety of different beam angles. The narrow beam angle lamps can throw a bright spot of light onto a small area from a considerable distance. Most MR16 halogen lamps have low colour temperature yellowish light, but there are newer lamps with filters that can produce a daylight colour temperature. While the MR16 format is not suitable for large aquariums, it is very useful in

An MR16 format lamp with narrow beam and daylight colour. J. Sprung.

An MR16 format LED lamp. J. Sprung.

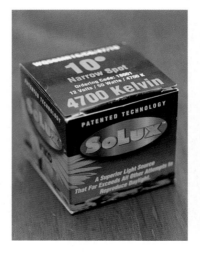

These 20 Watt HID lighting fixtures can be used to light small exhibits or highlight specimens in larger exhibits.

Here a combination of low wattage track lighting HID lamps, and blue and red LED lights are used to light a display of nanoreefs in Osaka, Japan. J.C. Delbeek

small aquariums (76 L / 20 gallons or less) or for spot accents in larger set-ups. The fixtures for mounting the lamps are limited at present, but the basic system could easily be custom fitted to work in an aquarium hood. The MR16 format has also been adapted for use with LED lighting systems.

Cold Cathode Fluorescent (CCF) lighting

Cold Cathode Fluorescent (CCF) lighting is another new lighting development that is sure to spark interest in aquarium applications. Commonly used as the backlights for LCD displays and *eye rings* in automobile headlights, this technology has features like LED such as low power consumption, long life, and high efficiency. Instead of a filament, the light is generated by a gas in the lamp. The luminosity is higher per Watt than fluorescent lamps, CCF's produce up to 80 lumens per Watt, but

A ccf desklamp. Courtesy of Brookstone

generate as much as 50% less heat, and use up to 75% less power. CCF's are available in many colours, including daylight and blue lamps.

Special lighting effects

Traditionally an illumination system is mounted above an aquarium. With some modification of the aquarium design, it is also possible to consider other angles of illumination for special effects that are both aesthetically pleasing and biologically beneficial.

Front lighting

Mounting a light source above and in front of the aquarium achieves a very pleasing effect in that the reflective pigments on fishes and tridacnid clams are highlighted. This makes them really glow, something that clever pet dealers have taken advantage of in the creation of show displays in their shops. Incandescent or halogen spotlights can be installed so that they aim at the front of the aquarium to achieve this effect. Even one fluorescent tube mounted so that it is in front of the viewing window will produce this effect.

Background lighting

Many public aquariums (for example, the Oceanographic Museum in Monaco and Monterey Bay Aquarium) have some displays that are backlit. Fluorescent tubes are mounted horizontally against the back panel, which is backed with one or more layers of blue and white translucent acrylic. This sends an even blue light into the aquarium and creates the illusion of deep blue water. See chapter 9 for a complete description of this technique.

Coral colour

In large polyped (LPS) hermatypic stony corals, the appearance of fluorescent red or orange pigment, usually a type of phycoerythrin, indicates that the coral utilizes green light. In some corals, the bright fluorescent colour does not appear under normal daylight, but is apparent only under green or blue-green light. The light field in turbid, near-shore waters is typically quite green. Red pigment is common in corals from this area, and in corals from deep water. Red morphs of *Cycloseris*, *Cynarina*, *Trachyphyllia*, *Lobophyllia*, *Symphyllia*, and *Blastomussa* are occasionally available. Aquarium lighting for them, therefore, can be bright but indirect (i.e. not directly under the lamp). Lighting with strong emphasis of green spectrum will enhance their colour, but make other specimens in the aquarium appear duller.

The appearance of purple, blue, or pink pigment in corals that have zooxanthellae is typical of the most shallow, highly illuminated condition, but not exclusively so. A few acroporid corals from deep water have blue or purple pigments. Most stony corals with these pigments should be placed in the brightest spot in the tank, with strong water flow for at least part of the day. Non-photosynthetic corals with these colours (i.e. *Dendronephthya* soft corals) generally prefer shade. Vivid fluorescent/reflective coral colouration, in many cases, is possible to promote without exposure to UVR (Riddle, 2004b). Small polyped stony corals (SPS) such as *Seriatopora, Stylophora* and a few *Acropora* species may have blue, pink, or red colour morphs from shallow water. The red or pink colour in these examples is only slightly fluorescent or not fluorescent at all, in contrast with the highly fluorescent reds found in deep water LPS corals, which are produced by a different kind of pigment. See Dove et al., (1995) for a discussion of the characteristics of the blue and pink pigments in shallow water sps corals.

Fluorescence in corals

Fluorescence in corals is a very popular topic of debate in not only hobbyist circles but also in the scientific community. Hobbyists are most interested in the colours of their corals and how best to make them more colourful. However, the scientific community is more concerned with the role that these pigments play in coral physiology, and how this fluorescence could be used for remote sensing applications of coral reefs. Recent studies are now beginning to show that the commonly believed functions of these pigments are not holding up under scrutiny (e.g. Mazel *et al.*, 2003; Mazel and Fuchs, 2003).

Green fluorescent protein (GFP)

One of the first fluorescent proteins identified was the green fluorescent protein (GFP) in the hydromedusa *Aequorea victoria*. Subsequent studies have shown that a large number of Caribbean and Indo-Pacific corals have fluorescent pigments that are closely related to GFP. Bingman (1995b, 1999) made this connection in the aquarium grey literature years in advance of the research later conducted and published by coral reef researchers in the scientific literature (see Dove *et al.*, 2001). The GFP in corals emits a spectrum that peaks at 500-518 nanometers resulting in a strong green colour. It has been suggested that fluorescence can have one or both of the following two roles: 1) provide photoprotection under highlight levels and/or 2) enhance photosynthesis in low- light conditions by providing additional photons. This fluorescence can be seen under normal light conditions or in some cases it only becomes visible when light with the appropriate wavelength is used.

Using molecular and biophysical approaches, Mazel *et al.* (2003) studied the ecological role of this pigment in the photobiology of nineteen Caribbean corals. They found no evidence of GFP photon absorption to either enhance or reduce photosynthetic activity. If GFP plays a role in photosynthesis by either adding or taking away photons, then one would expect to see a correlation with depth as one does with other protective compounds such as mycosporine-like amino acids (MAAs) that protect against ultraviolet light. However, there does not appear to be such a correlation in the corals examined (*Montastrea faveolata* and *M. cavernosa*). The authors concluded that photoprotection afforded by GFP is negligible in Caribbean corals, compared to other non-photochemical methods they use to reduce the effects of excess excitation energy.

A pet theory of aquarists is that ultraviolet light is involved in the production of fluorescent pigments. However, UV protection is likely not the role GFP plays. Mazel *et al.* (2003) could find no evidence of an excitation peak in the range of UV (200-400 nanometers), suggesting GFP plays no role in UV protection. The authors, however, are quick to point out that it is still possible that GFP may play a role in helping a coral deal with environmental stresses such as high light, UV or temperature levels by as yet, undiscovered mechanisms. There is preliminary evidence that GFP levels are inversely correlated with superoxide dismutase (SOD) protein levels in corals exposed to light and temperature levels that produce superoxide radicals (SOD is involved in their reduction). It seems possible that GFP plays a role in the production of SOD or at least that the production of SOD involves or occurs after loss of GFP concentration. The area of coral fluorescence is a very hot topic in the scientific community and more research will eventually reveal the roles of fluorescent pigments in coral biology.

Effect of light on coral fluorescence

Most early studies on coral colour focused on qualitative observations of the colour and quantitative measurements of its spectral characteristics. It was noticed decades ago that in many cases the bright, natural colours of corals were often augmented by or due mainly to fluorescent pigments found in the animal tissue. This effect is especially noticeable with corals that appear orange or red at depth, where those colours are already absent in the downwelling light due to the filtering characteristics of the water as light passes through it.

Many corals exhibit green fluorescent pigments. This *Bali green slimer* staghorn coral is a popular example. G. Schiemer

As most hobbyists know, corals can be colourful even without fluorescent pigments. Corals are predominantly brown because the zooxanthellae they contain are brown due to the fact they absorb most other colours. Other colours can also be found in the host tissues and are the result of non-fluorescent pigments. When corals bleach, the loss of zooxanthellae or zooxanthellae pigments reveals the pastel colours of the underlying animal tissue (see chapter 4). The density of the zooxanthellae brown pigment can serve as an enhancing background to the other pigments, or it can mask them entirely. In addition, the rapidly growing tips of branching corals (e.g. *Acropora*) or the edges of plate forming species (e.g. *Montipora capricornis*) lack zooxanthellae, so that the coral tissue colour is readily visible.

However, what many people may not realize is that fluorescent pigments are not always visible to us under natural daylight. For example, a coral that appears brown to our eyes under natural ambient light may glow green under ultraviolet or blue light. This can be explained by several factors such as the spectral distribution of the ambient light and the strength of the fluorescence. Mazel and Fuchs (2003) measured coral reflectance and fluorescence, and downwelling spectral irradiance to explore the contribution of fluorescence to the spectral signatures of several Caribbean and Pacific corals as a function of variations in depth, solar zenith angle and fluorescence efficiency. They used the spectra from several pigments from both Caribbean (p486, p515 and p 575) and Indo-Pacific corals (p538 and p583); the number refers to the wavelength emission peak of the fluorescence produced. Four of the emission spectra produced strongly saturated colours while the fifth p486, was relatively unsaturated. Both p515 and p538 produced a bright green fluorescence while p575 and p583 produced orange to red. It is important to note here that the emission spectrums of all of these pigments were independent of the excitation spectrum, the emission wavelengths are averages and there can be quite a bit of variation, and that the excitation spectrum can vary from specimen to specimen for any given pigment.

The degree of fluorescence observed varies due to the spectrum of the downwelling light, which varies with increasing depth, turbidity (e.g. inshore waters are often green in colour) and the amount of reflectance of the coral tissue in general. Mazel and Fuchs (2003) found that some of the fluorescent pigments they examined were more visible then others and it became obvious that the mere presence of a fluorescent pigment was not a guarantee that the coral would exhibit fluorescence under ambient light conditions. It is therefore appropriate to divide the fluorescent response between those pigments that exhibit overt fluorescence only under ambient light, and those that exhibit covert fluorescence only when illuminated with an appropriate light source in darkness. This last form is of course also emitted under natural light but is overwhelmed by the reflected light of the coral and therefore not visible to the naked eye.

In general, fluorescent pigments that absorb wavelengths that:

a) are transmitted well by water,
b) have high fluorescent efficiency,
c) emit fluorescent wavelengths that are only moderately attenuated by water and,
d) emit at wavelengths to which the human eye is most sensitive,

are able to produce the most striking fluorescent effects for human eyes. This is especially true for p575 and p583, which emit in the orange range of the spectrum, one that is attenuated enough by water to reduce any competing influence from downwelling light and coral reflectance, but not strong enough to reduce the emitted light. These corals absorb heavily in the green range of the spectrum, which is still easily transmitted through water. The greenish pigment, p515, is the most widespread in corals. It fluoresces in a region of the spectrum that is not heavily attenuated by seawater, which suggests that it would be overwhelmed by ambient light. However, the high efficiency of this pigment and the sensitivity of the human eye to green combine to give a high level of visible fluorescence. In contrast to the two previous pigments, the blue-green p486 is not readily observed in nature. This is due to several factors. Namely, this portion of the spectrum is readily transmitted by water so the degree of coral reflectance is high. Combined with the low efficiency and low percentage colour saturation of p486, the reflectance is great enough to overwhelm the fluorescence emitted by p486 under natural ambient lighting conditions. Due to the above factors, green and orange emissions are the ones most commonly seen by divers and are the ones most striking in reef aquariums dominated by high Kelvin lighting.

For aquarists these observations help to explain why corals may appear certain colours under certain lamps. Obviously lamps in the blue end of the spectrum such as actinic 0_3, provide light of such a narrow spectrum that corals illuminated by them exhibit intense fluorescence. It might also be interesting to add a little green to some lamp combinations to stimulate those corals that might contain red or orange fluorescent pigments such as *Trachyphyllia* and *Cynarina*.

A word of caution: the mere presence of fluorescent pigments or any colour for that matter should not be used as a sign that these pigments have a specific function related to the lighting or photosynthesis. There is certainly a reason for the colour, but there may be some biological or chemical function of the pigment that has nothing to do with its affect on light, and the colour may be merely a neutral by-product. No one knows yet what the functions are of the many pigments of corals, and some may merely be due to genetic variation.

What is still not clear is why some corals develop colour under some lamps as opposed to other lamps. Many of us have observed that corals will change colour when lights are changed from one Kelvin rating to another or from one wattage to another. If coral pigments offer no protection against ultraviolet light or high intensity as the papers of Mazel *et al.* (2003) and Mazel and Fuchs (2003) seem to suggest, then could it be that the pigments are merely a by-product of some other reaction that is being driven by light intensity or the presence of ultraviolet light? We think this is an area that aquarists should be working on with scientists ... the results would be very useful to both fields!

After acclimating pink *Pocillopora meandrina* to shaded natural sunlight levels below the threshold for formation of the fluorescent pink pigment, they soon become zooxanthellae brown. Riddle (2003) found that illuminating pre-acclimated brown *Pocillopora meandrina* with intense monochromatic blue light from an LED lighting system promoted pink pigment formation in the spot where it illuminated the coral. He found that monochromatic red lights produced by an LED lighting system caused bleaching in the same shade-adapted brown corals. Riddle's experiment shows that narrow bandwidths of essentially pure red or blue wavelengths have profoundly different effects on zooxanthellae health and host tissue pigmentation. Riddle speculated that the pink pigment formation stimulated by an increase in blue light intensity might be a response by the coral to protect itself (via reflection) from the photosynthetically more efficient long-wave red light, which it would normally also encounter with an increase of light intensity in shallow water. Monochromatic red light (680 nm) is about 36% more efficient in the promotion of photosynthesis than monochromatic blue light (460 nm) (Riddle, 2003; Hall and Rao, 1999).

Zooxanthellae contain pigments involved in photoprotective dynamic photoinhibition (i.e. xanthophylls diadinoxanthin and diatoxanthin), which in effect absorb excess light and keep it from stimulating photosynthesis. These pigments absorb blue wavelengths, not red wavelengths. Since the zooxanthellae don't have the ability to rapidly photoprotect against increases in red light, they might bleach when suddenly exposed to increased amounts of red radiation. Riddle's experiment with red light bears this out and suggests that red light might play a role in regulating zooxanthellae pigmentation and density.

Of course, this has implications for aquarists since red wavelengths in artificial light sources might play a role in regulating zooxanthellae pigmentation and density in captive corals. The right combination of red and blue spectra could produce a situation where fluorescent colour is stimulated by blue spectra while the background brown zooxanthellae pigment is reduced by red spectra. A reduction in the brown background colour allows the white skeleton to become more apparent as background, and often this makes fluorescent corals appear more brightly coloured.

Dove *et al.* (1995) isolated and characterized the pink and blue pigments of pocilloporid and acroporid corals. They found that the absorption spectrum of the pink pigment suggests it does not protect against photobleaching of the major photosynthetic pigments because its absorbance spectrum does not coincide with those of chlorophyll a and c, and is, if anything, curiously complementary to these compounds.

Notice that Dove *et al.* (1995) use absorbance as a measurement of ability to protect against harmful light. Riddle (2003) also notes that corals lack an ability to filter out red light. However, Dove, *et al.* (1995) did not discuss reflectance, which is Riddle's idea. According to Dove *et al.* (1995), the pink pigment absorbs lots of green light ... that is no surprise, since it is the complementary colour. They go on to suggest that the pink pigment might function in the coral's immunological and chemical defense systems because they note that pink coloured morphs have a competitive advantage over yellow or brown morphs. In aquariums, *Pocillopora damicornis* morphs that develop pink pigment are able to kill the brown morph on contact (J. Sprung, pers obs.). They also grow slower, producing denser skeletons. Could they be different species, or is the inherited ability to form this colour linked with other traits? Since not all forms of *Pocillopora meandrina* develop pink pigment, Riddle's generalization about the possible function of the pigment in protecting the coral should be revised to be specific only to forms that develop this pigment.

This *Seriatopora hystrix* photographed in the Solomon Islands exhibits the tissue damaging effect of intense illumination. The most exposed branch tips are bleached and have partially lost tissue. J. Sprung

We have been discussing fluorescent green, blue, pink, and orange pigments as if they occurred independently in corals. In fact, it is not unusual for corals to possess combinations of pigments aside from the brown colour of their resident zooxanthellae. When two pigments occur in the same tissue, an interesting effect occurs. The coral may look orange at depth, and green in daylight, as we demonstrate below in the photos of a fungid (probably *Cycloseris* sp.) at 90 feet deep in Indonesia. Zooxanthellae in corals living in shaded areas or deep water alter the ratios of their photopigments and become more efficient in absorption of red wavelengths (Titlyanov *et al.*, 1980). The ambient blue-green light at this depth produces reddish orange fluorescence that can be absorbed more efficiently by the zooxanthellae, amplifying the photosynthesis in the low light environment. The flash produced green fluorescence in the deep

This fungiid coral was photographed at 28 m (90 feet) in the Lembeh Strait region of Sulawesi, Indonesia. The coral was bright orange in appearance but when the picture was taken with flash, the coral appeared green. Corals can contain several fluorescent pigments at once. It appears the flash overwhelmed the orange fluorescence but the green was strong enough not to be washed out, or was reflective. With the aid of Adobe Photoshop™, the original appearance of the coral can be recreated. J.C. Delbeek

dwelling coral. That green pigment could absorb the red light from the flash, offering protection from a sudden blast of light that could damage the zooxanthellae. In a shallow water coral, such as a pink form of *Pocillopora*, the ambient high intensity solar blue light wavelengths make the coral develop a pink pigment that is more apparent than an underlying green pigment that could be observed using a blue flash. It is possible that the pink pigment can assist not only in the reflection of red wavelengths, but also in absorption of the green fluorescence stimulated by the intensity of blue light in shallow water. Thus, we can see a potential for two pigments to work together to protect the coral. However, would the underlying green pigment absorb the orange fluorescence in the example of the deepwater fungiid, reducing its hypothesized photosynthesis enhancing benefit?

The answer to this question is addressed by Salih *et al*., (1998, 2000). These papers demonstrate that pigment chromatophores with different functions aggregate in cell layers above and below the symbiotic zooxanthellae. The aggregation in layers above the zooxanthellae suggests a solar screening function. In the case of the fungiid, it is likely that the green pigment was above the zooxanthellae, and the orange pigment below. Salih *et al*., (1998) provide evidence that fluorescent granules of corals protect against high UVA and blue irradiance by absorbing these wavelengths, and protect against other photosynthetically active radiation by reflecting a large portion of visible light. In shade acclimated corals, they propose that the pigment granules located within or below the region of the zooxanthellae have a light enhancement function, in which they amplify the available light and thus enhance photosynthesis through fluorescent coupling, back scattering, and reflection.

Other sources of fluorescence

Newly settled colonies of the Caribbean coral *Montastrea cavernosa*, consisting of just a few polyps, are intensely fluorescent red or orange, with slightly visible underlying green pigment. The colonies look like spots of fluorescent orange paint on shipwrecks in south Florida. As they grow, the green becomes more prevalent, and the orange fades or is restricted to the more shaded periphery. Lesser *et al*., (2004) discovered that this fluorescence is not produced by the coral tissue nor by the zooxanthellae, but is a product of a symbiotic cyanobacteria within the host cells. We have also observed a red fluorescent pigment associated with the juvenile form of the coral *Fungia granulosa* (Sprung, 1999). Although it has not been proven, we suspect this colour in the juvenile is also related to a symbiotic cyanobacterium. The function of this fluorescence is likely to be enhancement of photosynthesis in low light environments. Newly settled corals are often shaded by adjacent rock, algae, corals, or other sessile life. The cyanobacterium may also benefit the host by

The juvenile of *Fungia granulosa* is a flashy fluorescent red with white bands. The adult form is a non-descript brown. J. Sprung

supplying fixed nitrogen. It is possible that symbiotic cyanobacteria are widespread in reef building corals, and that some of the pigments we have attributed to the coral tissue may be their products.

Response of coral to artificial lighting

Coral placement in the tank is a critical factor. New specimens should NOT be placed near the surface directly under a metal halide fixture! Many well-intentioned aquarists have reasoned that they are rejuvenating their corals after a period of mistreatment in a dealer's tanks. This is like running out on the first sunny day in the spring and lying in the sun for eight hours, hoping to make up for lost light and vitamin D synthesis deficiency acquired during the winter. You quickly damage your skin because it has not had a chance to build up the necessary protective pigments. The same can occur with corals. The chloroplasts in the zooxanthellae of corals behave in a similar manner to those found in plants (Benson, 1984). Under lower light levels, they produce more chlorophyll, and with increased light they reduce the level of chlorophyll. Plants growing under the canopy of a forest have broader, darker green leaves than the same species growing in the full sunshine. Corals are like these plants. If exposed to lower light levels they become darker in colour and their growth form becomes more elongated or tabular in an attempt to capture more light by increasing their surface area. They also have lower levels of UV filtering compounds such as MAAs. Corals from shallow water tend to be lighter in colour, and most have higher levels of UV absorbing compounds and accessory pigments that tint them with beautiful fluorescent blues and greens, which absorb and reflect different portions of the light. By placing corals that have become low-light adapted or temporarily light starved into a brightly lit location, you run the real risk of light-shock, which may damage the coral beyond its capacity to repair itself. Place newly acquired corals away from direct light. Gradually, over a period of a few weeks, they can be moved closer to the light. Falkowski and Dubinsky (1981) found that the Red Sea coral, *Stylophora pistillata*, required 4 weeks to adapt from shade to light conditions when transplanted. Many hard corals offered for sale in North America (e.g. *Catalaphyllia*, *Trachyphyllia* and *Euphyllia*) come from deeper water, from shaded areas, or from turbid shallow waters, and if they are placed in a brightly illuminated aquarium, they should be gradually acclimated to the intense light. Corals can adapt to a variety of light levels, but do so slowly. Quickly changing light intensity, either up or down, can bring about negative consequences.

Metal halide and fluorescent lighting produce UVR, which can be harmful to those corals that lack appropriate UV shielding compounds (Mohan, 1990; Riddle, 2004c). Corals collected from deeper water, or ones that have lost their protective compounds during shipment and captivity, are prone to injury from excess ultraviolet wavelengths. Fixtures with inadequate UV shielding can literally burn corals. As we mentioned previously, double-ended metal halide lamps must be used in fixtures with UV shielding. Lamps already encased in UV absorbing material such as the glass envelope in globe style and metal arc lamps, should still have some sort of UVR shielding since they can still produce UVR in significant quantities despite the envelope (Riddle, 2004c). Shields also protect the lamps from water splashes that could cause the hot glass envelope to shatter. Do not be concerned if small amounts of UVA spectra are still transmitted by a particular lamp, since the majority of zooxanthellae containing invertebrates can easily tolerate it. However, some creatures may not tolerate it, and the aquarist should be aware of this possibility when troubleshooting a problem with a particular specimen. Please refer to chapter 3 in volume one, and this chapter for additional information about the nature of ultraviolet light and its affect on corals.

Ultraviolet absorbing lenses, made from acrylic or special coated glass, while they may reduce the light intensity by only 10 to 20 percent, afford protection at least when it is needed. Because of the heat generated by metal halide lamps, only tempered glass should be used for the lens, while either glass or acrylic may be used with fluorescents, if such lenses are needed at all. In general, UV is a concern only with some H.O. and V.H.O. fluorescent lamps, with metal halide lamps that don't have a glass envelope, and with some high Kelvin metal halide lamps that do (Riddle, 2004c). When corals are placed in the aquarium, it is a good idea to gradually acclimate them to the light intensity by using short photoperiods or blocking the light for a portion of the day. If the water conditions are good, but the coral seems to contract in the most heavily illuminated portions, it may be necessary to move the coral down lower or incorporate a UV absorbing lens.

Light intensity and other parameters in concert
High light levels increase calcification rates. There are numerous studies that have demonstrated that calcification rates in hard corals are dependent on light energy and that light-enhanced calcification appears to be essential to the construction and maintenance of coral reefs (Dustan, 1982). Therefore, systems with a high light intensity remove calcium from the water at such a rate that they quickly deplete the level of calcium and carbonate alkalinity. For this reason, intensely lit systems must be used in conjunction with an appropriate calcium and alkalinity maintenance method. See chapter 5 for information on maintaining calcium and alkalinity. On a related topic, Riddle (2004a) showed that low water motion limits photosynthesis in zooxanthellae, even as light intensity increases. Therefore, one cannot view the effects of lighting separately from the physical effects of water flow. The limiting effect could relate to

boundary layer effects such as gas exchange, nutrient supply, metabolite exchange, polyp expansion (which alters the zooxanthellae's exposure to light) or some other factor. All of these factors, light intensity, water motion, nutrient levels, calcium and alkalinity levels, and temperature, affect how corals react to light. Any condition thought to be related to light intensity, should also be examined with respect to the other factors; one should not assume that light alone is the problem. See chapters 4 and 7 for more information on the effect of temperature and water motion on corals, respectively. See chapter 4 for a discussion of the effect of trace elements such as iron and manganese on photosynthesis. See chapter 5 for information about how corals calcify, and chapter 10 for information about how feeding affects calcification.

Acclimating corals to light

Acclimation to the new intensity is also important when increasing light intensity onto an existing aquarium. Initially, the lights should only be on for a few hours a day. This time period can gradually be increased as the animals adapt to the higher light levels. If you use more than one lamp, they should come on in stages with all the lights being on for only 2-4 hours and then sequentially turned off over a period of a few hours. This photoperiod can gradually be increased to an ideal maximum of 8-10 hours per day of metal halide light, with the balance of the 12 hour total photoperiod being just fluorescent or low intensity HID lights.

A word of advice about replacing high intensity lamps; it helps if your fixture can be raised. When putting in new lamps you will be increasing the intensity of the light and the corals may react negatively. By raising the fixture, you decrease the intensity and give the corals a chance to adapt. Over a period of a few weeks, you can slowly lower the fixture again. Using a light rail system (moving light fixture) can eliminate or reduce the need to photo-acclimate corals when changing the lamps. See chapter 11 for more information on replacing lamps and precautions to take.

Activated carbon and light penetration

Activated carbon is used mainly for removing water-staining organic compounds to keep the water crystal clear. Since the carbon removes yellowing organic substances from the water, it has a significant impact on the light spectrum and intensity that penetrates the water. Use of activated carbon can effectively double the intensity of visible wavelengths penetrating to the bottom of a deep tank (Bingman, 1995). More importantly, it can dramatically increase the penetration of UV wavelengths at all depths. Yellowing substances are efficient filters of UV light (that's why sunglasses have a yellow-brown tint). The reason the UV is of importance is that it stimulates rapid photosynthetic production of active oxygen or superoxides (peroxide for example) in the coral tissues by zooxanthellae. Therefore, when the water is very clear the coral must have efficient means of dealing with the toxic active oxygen or have good UV blocking pigments (Bingman, 1995a). We discuss this further in chapter 6.

Artificial lighting and environmental responsibility

The lighting systems employed on aquariums today contain toxic compounds such as mercury and phosphor coatings that should not be allowed to enter the environment. When disposing of used lamps and ballasts, check with local authorities on the recommended method for disposal. Because fluorescent lamps contain mercury, the federal government and most states consider these products hazardous waste, and regulate their disposal according to the EPA's Toxicity Characteristic Leaching Procedure (TCLP) test (McQuillen, 2001). Although these disposal regulations are in a constant state of flux due to constant debate over the danger of lamp mercury, as of 2001 thirty-four states are very strict about their requirements. In Florida and Minnesota, for instance, those who dispose more than ten lamps a month must use a recycling program (McQuillen, 2001). Many municipalities and manufacturers offer recycling programs for fluorescent lamps where the mercury is reused to make new lamps, the phosphor coatings are used in cement manufacture, and the glass and aluminum can be recycled and sold. Recycling lamps containing mercury is an effective way to prevent mercury from polluting the environment, and is an important part of any energy-efficient lighting strategy (McQuillen, 2001).

Some manufacturers (e.g. Philips, GE, Osram/Sylvania) are now producing low mercury fluorescent lamps that have 80% or less mercury than before (McQuillen, 2001). Whether or not this technology will be featured in lamps used for reef aquariums remains to be seen but the environmentally responsible aquarist should be aware that it does exist.

Those looking to upgrade their old lighting systems from magnetic to electronic ballasts should also check on the proper disposal of magnetic ballasts. Older models (1978 and earlier) contained oil tainted with PCBs, and must be incinerated in special 6,000 °F furnaces that break down PCBs. Hobbyists should keep in mind that being environmentally responsible does not end with how their specimens were acquired, but also how their systems are constructed, run and maintained.

Aquascaping

A reef aquarium provides many opportunities to learn about the natural environment and enjoy its beauty. Aquascaping combines beauty with laws of biology and physics, while the process of building a reef in an aquarium involves these things combined with ingenuity, planning and patience. Devising unique ways to carry out the construction, imagining how the corals will grow to achieve the aquascape you want to create, and knowing that an aquascape takes time to develop its potential, make the hobby of reefkeeping challenging and so enjoyable.

Design considerations

Many factors work together to deliver a system with visual *impact*. With the greater degree of success that many hobbyists are now enjoying in keeping reef aquariums, we believe it is time to focus more attention on the overall appearance of the system, not just the health of the inhabitants. Such an aesthetic approach to reef aquarium aquascape design where form, colour and arrangement of specimens are given greater consideration is akin to the freshwater-planted aquarium hobby where plant selection and layout, and aquascape design are the focus. This should be the main consideration, even if the aquarist has additional goals for the aquascape, such as the recreation of a specific habitat. It is true, nevertheless, that the random growth of corals, under proper conditions, will soon produce an aquascape so beautiful that it may appear to have been planned. To maintain the beauty achieved by this growth requires careful planning and pruning, as is the case with freshwater-planted aquariums, or landscaped gardens. Is this requirement at odds with the concept of maintaining a *wild* ecosystem (Adey and Loveland, 1991)? We don't think so. The scale of our systems eliminates the possibility of including natural pruners such as storms, coral nipping fishes, other predators and eroders that help to maintain a healthy natural reef. The aquarist's hand must be a substitute for these effects.

Rockwork is one of the most important considerations that, unfortunately, often receives the least amount of attention. Typically, rocks are simply piled up along the back wall with

Scale, form, colour, and motion are some of the elements that make the art of aquascaping a reef aquarium such a joy and a challenge. This is a small section of one of Julian Sprung's aquariums. J. Sprung

This scene is part of the reef display at Underworld Products in the UK. D. Ong

Bill Hoffman has really achieved the illusion of being on a Caribbean reef with the display at The Smithsonian's facility in Ft. Pierce, FL. J. Sprung

perhaps a few gaps here and there. As many corals as possible are then placed haphazardly along this *wall*. That was the style of most reef tanks in the 1980s when the axiom for live rock was *the more the better* and seems to still be the prevailing habit today. As more people become involved in this hobby, we are beginning to see some alternative thinking resulting in layouts that are more interesting. Live rock mounds separated by patches of live sand with overhangs, crevices, archways and caves are becoming more commonplace as hobbyists begin to realize that more is not always necessarily better when it comes to live rock. The use of new techniques to attach and support live rock, and the use of other rock-like materials allow for more creative aquascape design, as we will explain later in this chapter.

Aquarium design is not limited to the interior of the aquarium, but also involves the exterior and how it blends in with the décor of the room. Consideration should be given to the design of the cabinetry and hood of the aquarium, and how this fits in with the surroundings, while remaining functional. Effort should also be made to conceal wiring, plumbing and equipment so that they are not immediately visible when viewing the aquarium from the primary viewing angle. This effort is part of the considerations for planning an aquarium in which the aquarist manages to blend the life support science with artistry to achieve a total design that is well composed and achieves an illusion of being a slice of nature.

The world-famous aquarist Takashi Amano, whose books featuring *Nature Aquarium Worlds* have inspired new widespread interest in planted freshwater aquariums, is essentially a gifted photographer as well as an accomplished aquarist. In his books, one finds sections dedicated to his

This gorgonian-dominated soft coral display in a custom made aquarium in the *Elos* stand at Interzoo 2004 was beautiful inside and out. J. Sprung

Often the best view of a reef aquarium is from above. This can be the focus of a whole display, or portions of it, as we show in the pond aquariums, later in this chapter. This is a behind the scenes view of the Penn State Aquarium. S. Joshi

photographic studies of scenes in nature, juxtaposed with the scenes he creates in aquariums. This combination gives the sensitive aquarist an understanding that great aquascape design not only borrows from nature, but also is much the same as a well-composed photograph. The bottom line is creating a scene that is both believable and unbelievably beautiful. This goal applies whether the display is viewed from the front as a window, which is the typical public aquarium view; from two, three, or four sides; or from the top and one or more sides. Some of our suggestions apply to only one or the other of these arrangements.

Aquarists should strive to fully conceal all the life support system components (overflows, returns, plumbing, etc.) and create a truly considered vista. This means that the scene has to be well composed and balanced, just like an underwater photograph. For example, the main focal point should be to one side, not be in the direct center otherwise it looks contrived. Badly thought out and randomly shot underwater photographs don't work visually, and neither do ill-considered aquarium layout designs for the same reasons.

Effects of scale

When planning any aquarium the aquascape scale should be considered. Will the aquascape be a slice of nature at the same scale? Most aquariums are not slices, but instead are scaled down, with a higher diversity of species for the given space. Most aquariums also distort the scale of height, by their aquascape AND by the attenuation of light from artificial light sources with depth. It is possible to purposefully design an aquarium to be scaled correctly, or to be scaled at a predetermined fraction of reality. With truly miniature habitats in so-called *nano* reef aquariums, most novices make the mistake of decorating as if they were building a much larger reef aquarium. Using an old formula, they determine that a 38 L (10 gallon) reef tank should have 10 or 15 lbs of live rock. While it will hold this much live rock, and live rock is interesting to look at, this does not leave much room for an interesting aquascape. In these small exhibits, a more interesting approach is to build the aquascape with small pieces of live rock, or just with live corals, using no live rock at all. The choice of corals can be considered too, avoiding species that grow too large, and including ones that are easily pruned, so that a *bonsai* style reef garden can be achieved. Whatever the size of the aquarium, the species chosen and size of the reef should *fit* the space.

A proper scale is evident in this small 75 litre (20 gallon) reef aquarium, aquascaped with almost no live rock. Maintaining its beauty requires frequent pruning. The *Sarcophyton* sp. leather coral on the left side is about ready to be trimmed. J. Sprung

Zonation

Related to scaling of the aquascape is the zonation of reefs that can be duplicated in a closed aquarium. On a large view, one may think of zonation as the distinction between oceanic reef, lagoon, seagrass, and mangrove habitats. On a smaller view, one can look at what species occur on the reef slope, the reef flat, or the backreef/lagoon. It is a feature of most home and public reef aquariums that fishes from these different habitats are put in the same aquarium without any physical barriers, and they all school together at the water surface at feeding time in a very unnatural looking aggregation! Most reef aquarium aquascapes are not zoned to segregate the fishes, even if the corals are placed correctly. Building physical barriers that create a reef slope, reef flat, tidepool, and lagoon are possibilities that offer the chance to create a more realistic reef exhibit. In a public aquarium, this is often achieved in separate exhibits, even if they are connected through plumbing, but it can also be done in a single exhibit. For example, there is a wonderful exhibit at the Burger's Ocean aquarium in Arnhem, The Netherlands, which depicts a reef drop-off backed by the open ocean. By having a narrow, raised floor near the front window, covered with sand, gravel, artificial coral bommies and a shipwreck, a habitat for reef fish is created. The rest of the tank is dimly lit with walls and flooring painted dark blue. This results in all the small tropical fish staying in the brightly lit front near the window, while the larger, pelagic fish such as sharks swimming in and out from the dimly lit rear of the tank. When you see large fish approach out of the darkened gloom the effect is just like diving on the edge of coral reef drop-off. We must not forget, of course, that all reef aquariums are artificial habitats, and it is up to the aquarist to decide what aspect of reality will be duplicated, and what will be pure fantasy.

Viewed from the front, this exhibit at the Burger's Ocean aquarium gives the impression of diving along the edge of tropical reef drop-off. J.C. Delbeek

When viewed from above, it is clear how the drop-off effect is achieved. The small reef fish stay in the brightly lit front of the tank where the habitats are located, and the larger, pelagic fish swim throughout the exhibit. This could be achieved on a smaller scale for the home aquarium J.C. Delbeek

The shallow brightly illuminated colorful sps garden has become a popular aquascaping challenge. It requires frequent pruning to maintain separation of numerous species. This is the aquarium of Paolo Broggi, Milan, Italy. M. Belosevic

This deepwater reef habitat was created by Kyoshi Endoh. K. Endoh

Joe Biesterfeld has one display composed of three separate aquariums plumbed together in the same filtration system. Such an arrangement allows incompatible creatures to be housed in different zones. J. Sprung

Joe Biesterfeld's outdoor pond reef aquarium offers a different perspective on a reef aquarium, and a nice view for Joe Yaiullo and Sanjay Joshi. J. Sprung

Another outdoor pond reef aquarium, at Coral World, Eilat, Israel. A herd of *Diadema* urchins keeps the sand and rock spotlessly clean. J. Sprung

The edge of the reef exhibit at the Waikiki Aquarium can be viewed from side windows or from above. J.C. Delbeek

Use of aquarium backgrounds

While many aquarists take great pains to run wiring and plumbing behind their aquariums, these are often still in plain view through the rear window! We often see pictures of beautiful aquariums with healthy corals only to have the illusion of being in the natural environment shattered by wiring, plumbing and equipment clearly visible sitting behind the tank. With a clear rear window, you can also see the wall treatment behind the tank and any shadows created by the tank lighting and hood.

These problems can be solved in a number of ways. You can create the rockwork such that there are sections on the ends that hide the corners of the rear window of the tank and it is behind these areas where you could place the external wires, plumbing and/or equipment. However, the easiest way to hide external equipment behind the tank is to use a background. This can be as simple as a coloured piece of paper or acrylic attached to the back of the aquarium. Of course, acrylic aquariums can also be purchased with solid coloured rear panes and with these, hiding wiring, plumbing and equipment behind the aquarium, is not an issue.

Some hobbyists encourage the growth of coralline algae on the non-viewing panes of the aquarium and this can nicely serve as a background to the aquarium. However, coralline algae can sometimes die-off without warning, leaving behind a patchwork of live pink areas and dead white ones that become overgrown with algae. Tanks that have coralline algae splayed in haphazard patterns over the back wall tend to be very distracting and just plain messy looking. We therefore offer here some alternatives we feel are aesthetically much more pleasing.

Translucent panels

The use of backlighting in conjunction with coloured translucent acrylic panels on the back of the aquarium can achieve a wonderful 3-dimensional effect. This technique was popularized by David Powell at the Monterey Bay Aquarium where it was used to create an open ocean effect with their stunning sea jelly displays. The effect is achieved by placing blue panels, two or more depending on the colour and intensity of effect you wish to attain, against the outer rear wall of the tank with a diffuse light cast through them from behind the tank. The key is to place the lights far enough away from the rear window to cover it with an even, diffuse light. This requires that some space be left behind the tank to allow a light box containing one or more fluorescent lights to be installed. The last outer piece of acrylic facing the light box should be translucent white, the same type

The magnificent *Chrysaora fuscescens* exhibit at the Monterey Bay Aquarium, utilizes backlighting to great effect. The luminous fluorescence of the blue background has to be seen in person. The process of printing with CMYK cannot reproduce it accurately. K. Delbeek

Using two acrylic panels (one transparent blue and one translucent white) and back lighting; a 3-D like luminous blue background can be created as seen in this 950 L (250 gallon) reef exhibit at the Waikiki Aquarium, Honolulu, Hawaii. The number and colour of panels as well as the intensity of backlighting can be varied to achieve a variety of effects. J.C. Delbeek

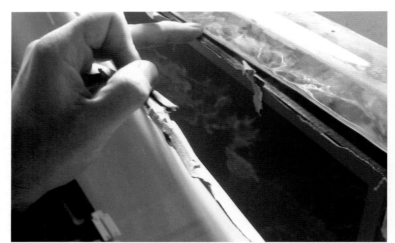

A fluorescent fixture can be used to back light a tank using coloured acrylic panels or stray light from the overhead metal halide lights used to illuminate the aquariumcan be reflected into the pannels from a white reflective surface located behind the aquarium. J.C. Delbeek

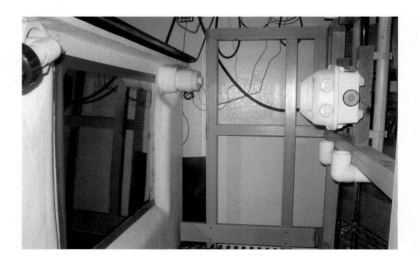

as used in a slide/negative viewing light box, in order to spread the light out into a more diffuse pattern. If the space behind the tank is limited, an alternative would be to place a white piece of material (e.g. paper, linen sheet) on the wall behind the tank, and a light is then shone down along the material by placing a fluorescent lamp at the top edge of the material. The diffuse glow of light creates a 3-dimensional background effect and makes the tank look deeper than it actually is.

This method does not work well if you have equipment hanging on the back of the tank, or any plumbing or wiring behind the tank that would cast an unacceptable shadow. Therefore, this method is better used to create the 3-D effect than for hiding equipment.

Use of removable backdrops

An alternative to an external backdrop is to use a removable insert that can be easily slipped *inside* the tank behind the rockwork to cover the visible portions of the back- or sidewalls. Coloured, flexible and inert wall-covering materials such as Korogard® (www.korogard.com), are available that can be easily cut to fit into an existing space. These can then be removed once a week or so for cleaning. You could also have two or three pieces that you could simply swap out and clean later. This allows you to have a backdrop in your aquarium that remains clean. Fiberglass sheeting can also be used to make a backdrop and can be painted any colour using marine epoxy paint or you can use a design or pattern of your own choosing. Backdrops are very useful for hiding equipment in corners such as in intake pipes or outlets, since the backdrop can curve in the corners, hiding the edge behind it.

The use of a backdrop would have been beneficial in this Jaubert system soft coral exhibit at the National Museum of Marine Biology and Aquarium in Taiwan (http://www.nmmba.gov.tw/). A backdrop hides plumbing and can be removed easily for cleaning to prevent the accumulation of coralline algae. Compare this aquarium's appearance with the pictures from the Waikiki Aquarium, Honolulu, Hawaii on the next page. A-Y. Fan

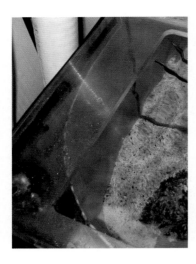

Backdrops can be used in small aquariums too, as seen above right in this 18.9 L (5 gallon) display designed by Norton Chan at the Waikiki Aquarium, Honolulu, Hawaii. The backdrop effectively hides the undergravel filter tubes and airlines, above, left. The point where the sand meets the background is nevertheless somewhat distracting if not hidden from the primary viewing angle. J.C. Delbeek

The natural curve of the backdrop eliminates corners

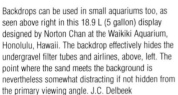

The use of an internal tank backdrop allows for a clean appearance and adds the illusion of depth as shown in this 4560 L (1200 gallon) exhibit designed by Kirk Murakami at the Waikiki Aquarium, Honolulu, Hawaii. There are no seams or plumbing visible, in contrast to the exhibit in Taiwan shown on the previous page. Judicious placement of live rock ensures that the backdrop-sand boundary is not visible when viewed from the front. J.C. Delbeek

Using backdrops effectively

The main drawback to using any external background is that you need to keep the rear-viewing window spotless in order to maintain the effect. Therefore, you need to arrange your rockwork and corals so that all windows can be easily accessed for cleaning or such that only small portions of the back- or sidewall are directly visible to lessen the surface area you need to keep clean. Also, keep in mind that corals will grow and will affect your ability to access the windows and keep them clean. Removable backdrops within the tank simplify the problem, but may not give the same three-dimensional lighting effect as a rear lit panel.

With coloured backgrounds or backdrops, the illusion can be ruined by the point where a sand bottom meets the blue background, forming an obvious line. Placing a sand dune or rocks a visually suitable distance in front of the back wall helps to remove from view the obvious hard line at the back of the display. In a small display, the line can only be hidden with a careful arrangement of live rock. A similar consideration is the water line at the rear of the aquarium. The point where the turbulent water surface meets the back wall against a smooth background is very apparent sometimes. Other times it isn't, due to lighting effects. When it is a problem, a solution can be achieved by hiding the edge with a visual baffle such as an overhang or arch of rock. The height of an acrylic aquarium designed for front viewing only can also be used to hide this effect, since the refractive distortion of the acrylic view panel leaves the surface out of sight. However, a view of the surface turbulence can be a nice effect that ADDS to the illusion of being in nature, so it should not always be avoided. It is particularly beautiful to observe in reef aquariums because of the reflection of the colourful corals seen when looking up into the turbulent surface.

For aquariums viewed from the front only, another consideration is the point where the forward edge of live rock meets the sidewalls of the aquarium close to the front viewing window. If the tank has return profiles at the front so that the view of the sidewalls bleeds off and out of the line of vision, the problem is avoided.

Finally, when a blue backlit panel is just visible between rocks, or at points that simulate a cave or groove between reef spurs, it is most effective at simulating the appearance of open water.

The look of endless blue of open water seen in this natural groove in the Solomon Islands can be achieved in an aquarium using a backlit blue background. Having Julian in the background is of course, optional. J.C. Delbeek

Hiding equipment

Equipment and plumbing visible within an aquarium can also be a big distraction that reduces the visual impact of a display. A lot of effort goes into acquiring beautiful corals and creating pleasing aquascapes to imitate nature yet most hobbyists think nothing of having the overflow box, a big return pipe, or a powerhead right in the middle of their creation. When planning the aquarium design and plumbing, every effort should be made to minimize the visibility of the equipment used to create the illusion of a living reef in your home. The use of a removable backdrop to hide equipment and plumbing in the corners is of course one method as we have just discussed but several other techniques can also be employed to help lessen the impact of in-tank equipment. For example, plumbing and powerheads can be hidden within rockwork or behind corals. Equipment colours that blend in with the rockwork can be used.

Above: This overflow box in Terry Siegel's aquarium has become encrusted by the coral *Pavona*. J. Sprung

Covering return pipes with zoanthids is easy to accomplish with cyanoacrylate gel used to tack a few polyps at a time onto the pipe. Within a few months the same pipe is hard to detect because it is covered with zoanthids and *Xenia*. J. Sprung

The use of bulkhead returns is less intrusive and should be used whenever possible. Arrange the rockwork so equipment behind it is out of the line of sight. Make use of the sump or refugium to hold equipment like heaters and thermometers. Finally, one can attach encrusting corals or algae to outlets and overflow boxes; zoanthids, star polyps and *Xenia* can all be used to conceal equipment as they will rapidly grow and reproduce, covering the equipment.

Model building

Whenever professional aquarists begin designing new exhibits, they will first make several sketches, exploring different aquascaping designs. Once a design is settled on, the next step is to construct a scale model of the tank. Then using modeling clay or just good old Plasticine or Playdo, they create the aquascape. This may seem like a

This model was built by Kirk Murakami of the Waikiki Aquarium and was used to plan the construction of a concrete aquascape in a new exhibit. J.C. Delbeek

Top view of the 3-D model of the tropical reef and lagoon exhibit at the Kattegatcentret Aquarium in Denmark, designed and built by David Lazenby. D. Lazenby

bit much but it really does help in visualizing what the rockwork will look like, much better than a sketch can. Visualizing in this way also helps to highlight any design flaws or problems before the actual rockwork is constructed and can save costly mistakes.

Live rock

A chapter about aquascaping for reef aquariums must include a discussion of live rock, the biological benefits of which we already discussed in chapter 2.

How much live rock?
When the reef-keeping hobby got its start in North America there was a rule of thumb about live rock that suggested it was critical to use so many pounds per gallon for the purpose of biological filtration. Actually, at first it was suggested that this figure offered some sort of *biological stability* since the biological filtration offered at that time was a wet/dry filter. When aquarists started to recognize that the wet/dry filter was not necessary, the importance of the volume of rock was realized, as live rock really provided the capacity to handle the decomposition of nitrogenous waste, including denitrification. While live rock has thus been considered the *backbone* of a successful reef aquarium, forming the visual and biological centerpiece of the ecosystem, in recent years the use of another *living* substratum, live sand, has reduced the importance of the live rock as a biological filter. In fact, when sufficient live substratum (sand or gravel) is present, the live rock is not needed at all for biological filtration. Thus, a reef aquarium employing live sand can employ live rock solely for the purpose of decoration and a source of high diversity of algae, small crustaceans, and microorganisms. It is clear that one need not use much live rock at all. The decoration can be constructed from porous limestone with

interesting shapes instead. The reef can be built and cemented together dry, allowing infinite possibilities for the creative aquarist to make a spectacular reef scene. Later on, a small amount of live rock can be added to seed the aquarium with species that will spread throughout the reef structure. As we will explain in this chapter, artificial rock-like substrates can also be employed to construct a unique aquascape.

The amount of sand, gravel or rock to use can be discussed from a theoretical perspective, concerning the minimum amount of each needed for the purpose of biological filtration. It is a secondary topic to consider the quantities to use for purely aesthetic reasons. It is also possible for the aquascaping choices to be functional, as it is in Jaubert's system, or for the aquascape to be representational, as it is in the microcosm and mesocosm systems (see Adey and Loveland,

This beautiful display in the *Elos* booth at the Zoomark trade show featured aquarium grown *Acropora* colonies on a sand bottom. Corals growing this way benefit from the upwelling light reflected from the white sand. J. Sprung

The left side of Richard Harker's reef aquarium allows space for corals to build an aquascape. Note aquarium spawned *Pocillopora damicornis* colonies on the back wall, which add dimension to the aquascape. Also note the natural horizonatal form of the reef, a product of corals growing upward to the downwelling light. R. Harker

Bill Hoffman and his Adey-style reef-section aquascape. J. Sprung

The corals in this Jaubert system display at the Oceanographic Museum in Monaco were mainly glued to the side walls and have grown inward, forming a grotto. The blue background suggests the open sea. J. Yaiullo

1991). In the latter case, the aquascape represents a cross section of a coral reef, as if the viewing window sliced right through it. Such an aquascape really puts a side view of the reef as the front view of the aquarium. The rock is positioned thickly in layers like shingles, and right up against the viewing window so that in some places you can see into the deep zones of the reef structure. For this style of aquascape, the associated surge bucket as a means of water movement (Adey and Loveland, 1991) provides a duplication of the effect of incoming sea swells breaking over the reef crest and washing through the reef. In the case of a Jaubert style display, the rock is noticeably almost absent, and large expanses of bare gravel are exposed. This is a functional aspect of the design, since diffusion of solutes through the substratum is a key element of the way Jaubert's system works (see chapter 6).

Base rock

The use of so-called *base rock*, which is lower quality live rock without much growing on it became popular as a result of recommendations to use a certain amount of live rock per gallon as biological filtration. The idea was that the lower rocks that support upper rocks did not need to be the best quality since they were going to be shaded and out of view. Instead of base rock, some aquarists used plastic supports (eggcrate, for example), cinder block, quarried limestone rock, or other materials. A very tall exhibit might need a support base to build up the reef structure, but please note our comments in this chapter and in chapter 6 regarding reef walls.

Future availability

Live rock availability to the aquarium industry is something that changes every year based on new legislation in the regions from which it is harvested. Live rock is no longer legal to collect in Hawaii and Florida, nor from the Gulf of Mexico and Atlantic coast up to the Carolinas. Since the time of the ban on live rock harvest in Florida there has been some aquacultured rock coming out of the state, primarily from bottom leases in the Gulf of Mexico and Florida Keys. Other sources of wild collected rock have become established over the years, including but not limited to the Marshall Islands, Fiji, Tonga, Western Samoa, Indonesia, and a few Caribbean localities. The success of live rock aquaculture from an economical standpoint and from the standpoint of consumer acceptance is likely to reduce the aquarium industry demand for natural live rock over time. Live rock will continue to be harvested for the construction of roads and for making concrete (see the *Introduction* chapter for an idea of the scale of this harvest). The concrete used to make artificial live rock may be produced in some instances from natural live rock, an ironic case of recycling!

Aquacultured artificial live rock

Two companies in the Pacific, Indo-Pacific Sea Farms (ISPF) and Walt Smith International (WSI), have entered the aquacultured rock arena with artificial substrates made from limestone, coral fragments and cement. Indo-Pacific Sea Farms seeds their rock with coralline algae and other life, and cultures them in a system that is fed natural seawater pumped from the ocean off Kona, Hawaii. Walt Smith International, operating in Fiji, plants their rocks in suitable locations where marinelife naturally settles on them, and the rocks are later harvested, as is done in Florida. It appears that enterprising companies are gearing up to be able to produce *artificial* live rock as an alternative to the wild harvest. Locating their operations in the places where wild harvest once existed is a positive feature. It offers the opportunity to employ local workers and keep economic benefits in the coastal communities where live rock industries developed. See chapter 1 for further information and photos of artificial live rock production at WSI.

Other options- alternatives to live rock

Aquarists can construct their reefs with substrates that later become live rock in the aquarium as it matures. Any attractively shaped porous limestone is the most natural choice, but there are other options as well, which we cover here.

Limestone and cement

It is possible to build the reef structure dry, with pieces of limestone fused together with pure Portland cement. Coral skeletons can also be incorporated in the structure. Once the cement dries and hardens, the structure must be soaked for a couple of weeks in a heavy brine solution to cure it and lower the pH. Once the structure has cured and the brine solution is drained and flushed out, the tank can be set up.

Aragacrete rocks

The technique for building rocks from a combination of aragonite gravel and Portland cement was described by LeRoy Headlee of the Geothermal Aquaculture Research Foundation (www.garf.org) in Boise, Idaho. The process is quite simple, but it takes skill, imagination and artistry to produce attractively shaped rocks.

Headlee uses Styrofoam shipping boxes for making the molds. This useful technique means the finished live rocks fit in the standard Styrofoam boxes used for shipping fish. (See the demonstration on page 544 where the rocks are made in an aquarium instead, so that they fit perfectly in it.) Styrofoam boxes also hold the heat generated as the concrete hardens. If they are kept at room temperature, the rocks will be hard enough to remove in 24 hours, but will be stronger still in 48 hours. When removing the rocks from the boxes some aragonite will fall off. It can be brushed off in a container of water and saved for later use. The freshly made rocks still need to be *cured* because the cement used is highly alkaline and raises the pH of the surrounding water. The rocks can be placed under water for a week to finish curing. It is also helpful to add an acid to the soaking water such as white vinegar, letting them soak in it for 12 hours and then rinsing them in freshwater to remove any excess acid. At this point, it is a wise precaution to place the rocks in a container of freshwater of a known pH then measure the pH again after 24 hours. The pH should not rise or fall more than one pH unit (e.g. 7.9 >8.0 < 8.1), this insures that the rock is fully cured before placing it in an aquarium.

Making *aragacrete* rock

To make aragacrete, mix 4 to 6 parts (by volume) of aragonite sand with 1 part #3 Portland cement. One can add many types of gravel, shells, coral fragments, or limestone pieces to the aragacrete mixture to achieve different shapes, density, and surface textures. We have also seen some examples where lightweight plastic turnings or beads were incorporated in the mixture to make the rocks weigh less. Mix the aragacrete with clean fresh water to a pasty consistency. When you are mixing the water and aragonite gravel try to get the mixture as dry as possible, while still getting it wet enough to hold together when you squeeze a hand full. The dryer you can make the mixture the stronger your final product will be.

Tip: Cement is very alkaline, so one should always use rubber gloves and protective eyewear when handling it.

Place a fair amount of pre-moistened damp aragonite sand into an appropriately sized container (e.g. Styrofoam fish box). Dig holes in the damp sand to form a mold of the shape of the rock you wish to make. Avoid exposing the bottom of the box to prevent forming an unnatural flat edge. Push the *aragacrete* mixture into the mold and form it with your hands. Rods or pipe can be pushed in to form holes. Additional damp sand can be used as filler, or poured into holes to create caves, and tunnels. A neat trick is to use coarse rock salt to make small pits and holes in the surface of the rock. This is achieved by pressing pieces of rock salt into the areas you wish to create texture and allow the aragacrete to dry. You can also create greater porosity inside the rock by mixing in sea salt, which is coarser than normal table salt, as you knead the aragacrete. As you later cure the rock in freshwater, the salt will dissolve, leaving behind small holes or pits on the surface or within the rock depending on where you put the salt. The rock salt method can be used with a variety of artificial rockwork techniques.

Three different grades of calcareous gravel were used in this demonstration to make *aragacrete* rock within an empty aquarium. The two largest sizes were mixed with concrete to form the shape of the rock. A. Correa

This initial rock/cement mixture was then placed and shaped inside an aquarium placed on its side and lined on the inside with plastic. While the cement is still wet, the fine gravel is added and the rock is buried. Once the rock hardens, the sand is removed, revealing the encrusted artificial rock. A. Correa

Alex Correa's made these rocks inside his home aquarium. This technique allows for the creation of rock with a smooth, flat surface to rest on. A. Correa

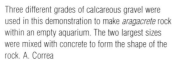

Polyurethane (insulation) foam rockwork

Some large public and private reef aquariums in Europe have very little limestone rock at all in them. What looks like rock in these tanks is actually polyurethane foam, which has been shaped to look like rock. Once cured, the material is rigid and can then be sculpted into any shape to create texture, depressions, shelves and overhangs. The surface is attractive to coralline algae, which rapidly colonize it, making it virtually indistinguishable from the real McCoy. The Aquaria-Vattenmuseet in Stockholm, Sweden, Hagenbeck's Tierpark in Hamburg, Germany and the Löbbecke Museum in Düsseldorf have large reef displays with such material used as a substrate. In *The Reef Aquarium* volume one, we cautioned aquarists about the use of such materials because of the possibility of toxic compounds leaching into the water. The success at the aquariums mentioned above, however, indicates that acceptable inert versions of these materials do exist. Generally, two types of polyurethane are used for aquariums: structural and cavity filling. The rockwork used in public aquariums is structural polyurethane. It is dense foam that is spray applied into a mold usually, and cures within minutes into a hard plastic surface. To cut it, one must use an electric saw. Colour tints can be added to the rock in a slightly complicated process. A carrier is sprayed into the mold before the polyurethane foam, so that it can be absorbed into the polyurethane surface. Then coloured pigments suspended in a solvent medium are painted onto the rocks by hand.

Cavity filling polyurethanes are used to attach rocks together or fill gaps between them. It is sometimes used by aquarium hobbyists to develop interesting backgrounds or aquascapes.

CAUTION: Polyurethane foam is extremely FLAMMABLE during dispensing. DO NOT SMOKE OR USE NEAR OPEN FLAME. Polyurethane of any sort requires the wearing of a respirator with suitable filters for organic vapors. The solvent medium for pigments may remove oxygen from the air, so it should not be used in confined spaces. All polyurethane foams off-gas noxious fumes for several days until they are completely cured. The rockwork created should be soaked in the aquarium for several days after an air cure time of at least several days, to remove residual volatile organic vapors.

Meier (2003), details his experience using (cavity filling) polyurethane insulation foam for building the aquascape of an aquarium. The basic premise is to spray/apply insulation foam to the back and/or sides of the tank, and while it is still workable, push pieces of live rock, crushed coral, shells, barnacles, etc. into the drying foam. The foam itself hardens somewhat, and creates a natural looking rock-like background. Additionally, it can be used to conceal the un-natural looking plumbing, overflows, etc. Meier used standard GREAT STUFF™ foam made by DOW chemical company (http://www.dow.com/greatstuff/), in its regular, low expansion format. Standard GREAT STUFF sealant is a cream colour but in time, it will become coated with coralline algae and other encrusting organisms. If the initial colour is objectionable, it can be painted with non-toxic marine epoxy paint. There are other types for windows, etc. that expand more, and there is a formula with latex. Latex foam is open cell, which means that it can absorb water, but it might break down over time submerged in an aquarium. In contrast, GREAT STUFF foam is closed cell, meaning that moisture cannot penetrate it. While great for home insulation, this means that the material is very buoyant and may stress tank walls or may eventually separate from tank walls due to its tendency to float. The buoyancy of the low expansion format is not so bad, and it can be countered by the weight of live rock pieces or gravel mixed into it. The toxicity to marine life, if any, for the DOW products is not known and the aquarist should proceed with caution when using new materials in marine aquaria.

TIP: GREAT STUFF™ is very sticky stuff! When pumped out of the can it has the consistency of a roasted marshmallow. Be careful not to get it on clothing and on your hands. Wearing gloves is always a wise precaution.

Polyurethane foam cannot be removed from clothing. Use acetone or fingernail polish remover (with acetone) to remove un-cured foam from skin. Cured foam will wear off the skin in a few days and is harmless, but it can be removed quickly with an abrasive sponge or pumice stone while rinsing with soapy water. A skin conditioner should be applied afterwards to sooth any skin abraded by the pumice.

The foam does not apply on to a vertical wall, so you have to lay the tank/surface horizontally and apply the foam to one horizontal side at a time. Expect about an inch or so for expansion of a layer of the foam. The use of the can is a one-time deal. Once you start using it, you have to finish within a few hours, as it will seal itself shut within two hours if you stop. It is possible to extend the usable life of a can to 30 days or longer by inserting a 16-penny nail into the end of the clear plastic straw tip of the dispenser, which must be left screwed onto the can. GREAT STUFF adhesive sealant polyurethane foam must be dispensed at temperatures above 4.5 °C (40 °F), and the contents of the can should be as close to room temperature (21 °C/70 °F) as possible when dispensed.

Methods

Remembering the caveat that once the can is open you have to use it all within a few hours, it is nevertheless a good idea to test the working characteristics of the media first on a sheet of acrylic, glass or cardboard. Spray the foam, let it sit for about two to five minutes so that it starts to expand a little, then insert small pieces of live rock, limestone rocks, coral, shells, etc. While the surface is still tacky, one can push in large pieces of crushed coral gravel on top to give the surface of the foam some texture. Coral sand and small gravel pieces don't stick very well to it. In any case, the natural surface of the foam is very rock-like.

Once you have a good handle on the working characteristics, you can begin work on the tank aquascape. Use masking tape to mask off any places you don't want the polyurethane to stick, such as the overflow slots. Since the foam is still workable once completely cured it is easy enough to cut through it with a knife to modify any errors. Caves can also be made by carefully cutting the cured foam, and the surface can be re-sealed with the application of another fresh layer. When applying multiple layers of foam, make sure that the first layer of foam is allowed to cure before applying the next layer. The foam will not cure properly if foam is applied all at once in large quantity. Since the foam uses moisture in the air to cure, light misting of water between layers will speed up foam curing time. It will take about an hour for each side to cure sufficiently that you can turn the tank to work on another side. A few hours after the aquascape is finished, you can rinse the tank with water. Since the foam is composed of a spongy network of polyurethane and air, it will slowly soak up water. Meier (2003) suggests soaking the aquarium for a few days to remove any residual chemical substances released by the foam. It is probably not necessary to do so, however.

Building removable aquascape panels

One does not have to foam the tank walls directly. If you want to make the foam wall detachable, you can simply spray the foam onto 1/4 inch thick panels of acrylic. These can be *tacked* onto the aquarium walls with a small amount of silicone sealant. Meier observed that cured GREAT STUFF could be peeled cleanly off acrylic if necessary.

How much does a can of GREAT STUFF yield?

The theoretical yield of one-component foams is measured in linear feet of a 3/8 – 1/2 inch diameter bead. The 350 mL (12 oz.) can of GREAT STUFF Minimal Expanding Foam Sealant has about 76.2 m (250 linear feet). The 591 mL (20-oz.) can has about 128 m (420 feet). This works out to 1 or 2 square feet per 350 mL (12 oz.) can, depending on how thick you want the foam rockwork to be.

Making individual rocks with polyurethane

Polyurethane foam can be used to create *rocks* for inland aquaculture or by aquarists for their aquariums. The central problem to the use of this material for making rocks is that purely polyurethane rocks are buoyant as we previously mentioned. To make them neutral or negatively buoyant, one must incorporate rocks or gravel in its structure.

Mined limestone rocks or fossil corals

Various types of limestone rocks are mined for use in aquariums. Often they are denser and thus heavier than live rock, but their shapes can be quite attractive, due to the erosive effects of water. They may have sand or soil in some of the holes, which can be blasted out with a high pressure water stream from a garden hose or pressure cleaner (wearing safety goggles to protect your eyes). In some regions in southeast Asia, there are deposits of fossil corals near the coast. The export of this material requires a CITES permit as the rocks are clearly identifiable as scleractinia. The majority of the rocks are composed of *Porites* spp., though other corals are also present. The shapes of the rocks are nice and they are lightweight. In essence, they are like dried pieces of live rock. As with other forms of dry rocks, they can be cemented with Portland cement to form a nice aquascape. The fossil coral rocks sometimes have mud in the spaces between branches. This should be rinsed out with a strong stream of water before the rocks are used in the aquarium.

Ceramic

Some ceramics may leach harmful substances into the water, but most are inert when fired, and are suitable for building reef structures. We have seen pet dealers and hobbyists who use ceramic pots in their aquariums for fish breeding sites, or to place corals up off the substrate. This is perfectly safe to do, but we caution that heavy rocks should not be supported by ceramic pots, because they may become brittle and break in the water. Rock forms built from fired ceramics have good potential for reef aquarium building, since they would be porous like limestone, and the shapes can be quite marvelous.

Mined limestone from Florida. J. Sprung

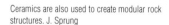

Ceramics are also used to create modular rock structures. J. Sprung

Resin based artificial rocks

The popularity of artificial corals made from resin has led naturally to the development of live rock pieces and panel inserts made by the same process. The result is an artificial live rock that cannot easily be distinguished from real live rock. This material has some very distinct advantages over all others. It is strong and rigid, and won't break or crumble as limestone rocks may. It is lightweight and can be manufactured with entrapped air to make it neutrally buoyant, so that otherwise impossible aquascapes could be realized. Delicate structures could be built that would remain suspended without support from below because they are weightless underwater. The resin-based material also has the advantage of being drillable so that cultured corals could simply be plugged into them. These features make them a dream for public aquariums, where they can be used to

Above: Another style of ceramic rock produced by *Aquaroche*, France. J. Sprung

Right: Is it real or is it resin? The shapes and colours achievable with resin can match live rock perfectly. These live rock replicas are produced by *Aneka Tirta Surya, PT* in Indonesia. J. Sprung

A very realistic resin based rock produced by *Oceans Reefs and Aquariums* (*ORA*), Ft. Pierce, FL. J. Sprung

Far right: Artificial rock manufactured by *Living Color* with holes for inserting either artificial corals or live coral fragments. J. Sprung

build a display that looks great instantly, and grows better looking with time. The panel inserts also afford a useful option for tall narrow public aquarium displays.

Shotcrete/gunite

In large reef exhibits, such as those usually found in public aquariums, it is not usually feasible to create rockwork from individual pieces of rock (live or man-made). In this case, other methods are employed to totally cover all the vertical surfaces with rockwork and to create large boulders. When you see large exhibits in public aquaria, this is usually the way that the rockwork is created within them.

Shotcrete/gunite is a specific type of concrete (Portland cement, lightweight aggregate, water, and admixtures) that are pneumatically

Shotcrete is applied during construction of this outdoor exhibit at the Waikiki Aquarium. With permission, Waikiki Aquarium

blown out the end of a pump hose onto the substrate, producing a rough, natural surface. The mixture consolidates at impact and develops a compressive strength similar to concrete. This form of concrete is commonly used to create naturalistic rock walls, boulders and to create in ground ponds and pools.

The difference between the two terms (gunite/shotcrete) has nothing to do with the materials they are made of but in the way they are mixed with water. Shotcrete is mixed with water first, and then delivered to the work site much the way premixed concrete is. It is then pumped down a hose to a nozzle and sprayed onto the substrate. When the mixture exits the nozzle, accelerators or other admixtures may be metered into the slurry along with air under pressure to increase the velocity of the material and improve control of the *shooting* process (Seegebrecht and Gebler, 2000). Gunite on the other hand, is a *dry* mix, in that it is blown down a hose and is then mixed with water and air from a separate hose at the nozzle. The advantage of the gunite application method is that the blend of concrete and water can be adjusted *on the fly* to create different effects to suit the changing conditions of the work area. For example, a dryer, firmer mix is best for recreating overhanging, steep or protruding features. The disadvantage of gunite is that the nozzleman's workmanship and experience are critical, since the nozzleman controls the critical water-to-mix ratio going into application equipment (Seegebrecht and Gebler, 2000), therefore it is important to have someone with experience in building aquascapes for aquariums. While shotcrete is easier to use for beginners, if a variety of rockwork areas need to be created, then different consistency batches need to be made for each and the rockwork needs to be constructed in stages over a greater period of time.

Once applied, the surface remains in a workable state for an hour or two during which time the concrete can be shaped and sculpted to create deep cracks and caves using a variety of hand tools or even compressed air. Texture can be added using wire brushes, sponges, shells, dead coral etc. Rock salt can also be pressed into the surface at this time to create a pockmarked texture when it later dissolves in the water during the curing process.

Both techniques require a support structure of plastic rods, cable ties and netting or even an under structure of lightweight concrete blocks. Sprayed concrete operators require suitable body and face protection from the concrete particles rebounding at speed from the working surface. Curing time depends on the thickness of the layers added, but usually takes about 7 days. After this time it should be cured in water as we described for artificial *aragacrete* rock.

Materials that facilitate reef construction

Cable ties

Solid plastic cable ties, commonly used by electricians and mechanics to secure bundles of wire, also have great use for securing rocks together when building the reef structure. These ties seem to have a million uses! Cable ties come in a variety of lengths and thickness, and in a variety of colours.

Caution: Be sure that the ties are solid plastic. Some ties are made with a metal core that can corrode and fail in an aquarium.

After planning the layout of the reef structure and selecting the rocks, a drill and masonry bit can be used to bore holes into the rocks to slip the cable ties through. Be careful when drilling holes, since

Cable ties are useful for attaching fiberglass grating and live rock when building an aquascape, as seen here at the Waikiki Aquarium, Honolulu, Hawaii. J.C. Delbeek

Coralline algae eventually covers submerged cable ties (center) as well as Thorite (above it), making them indistinguishable from live rock. J.C. Delbeek

limestone rock is brittle and easily crumbles from the vibration of the drill. Do not drill holes too close to the edges of rocks, since the leverage of the attached rock pulling on the hole near the edge of another rock can cause the cable to break through the hole, sending the rock(s) tumbling. Cinch up the cable ties tightly, and cut off the excess with a sharp scissors or wire cutter.

In an aquarium we saw in Norway, a wooden beam across the top was used to support large rocks, forming an otherwise impossible overhang/cave (see photos in Delbeek and Sprung, 1994). The rocks were tied to each other and to the beam with long, heavy duty, plastic cable ties. Cable ties may also be used to attach the uppermost rocks of a wall to plumbing along the back or sides of the tank, thereby affording greater support.

When using cable ties to secure large rocks, or rocks in large exhibits, heavy-duty types are more desirable. At the Burger's Zoo, the rockwork in their 750,000 L (198,000 gallon) reef tank was fastened to plastic mesh by cable ties. These cable ties eventually began to break, necessitating the reattachment of several tons of live rock using heavy-duty cable ties usually used on oil rigs in the North Sea! Plastic cable ties that can hold up to 250 pounds are available and should be used when strength is paramount (http://www.buycableties.com/index.html).

Any exposed cable ties will become encrusted with coralline algae with time, but their shape may still be distinguishable. You can use small amounts of epoxy or Thorite to cover the cable ties and hide their location. These materials will also become unrecognizable as coralline algae develop.

Monofilament line (a.k.a. *fishing line*, nylon wire)

Monofilament is one of the most versatile construction aids for building the aquascape. Its advantages include low cost, that it is inert, strong, and invisible. It is easy to work with if you have good manual dexterity, can tie knots, and use a scissors. In addition, its thin diameter allows you to use it in place of cable ties where the ties would be too broad. It is the ideal aid to attaching zoanthids, soft corals, or cuttings from corals to live rock, and when the specimen has made a strong attachment, the line may simply be cut with a scissors and removed, as if pulling out stitches after the wound has closed. The main disadvantage to monofilament line is that it can loosen up if the attached pieces are frequently disturbed, or if the knots aren't very tight.

Stainless steel wire

We have seen some hobbyists and public aquaria in Germany using a fine stainless steel wire instead of monofilament line. The wire is easy to cut, like monofilament, but does not need to be tied. It can be looped around and twisted to secure a specimen in place. We caution aquarists that stainless steel comes in different grades. Not all stainless steel can withstand the corrosive effect of saltwater. As with monofilament, the wire may be removed after the specimen has attached to the rock. Stainless steel wire should only be used as a temporary means to attach encrusting organisms until they can attach to the rock on their own and should not be used as a permanent attachment method.

Plastic toothpicks

When company comes over for dinner, your guests may smile knowingly as they eat hors d'oeuvres with their fingers and admire your reef. Your spouse will wonder why eventually everything in the house is used for the reef tank. Just as the plastic toothpicks are useful for spearing those little hot dogs, they work really well for soft corals since one end pierces and holds the coral while the other end can be inserted into the rockwork. Small, lightweight stony corals can also be positioned with toothpicks, as can small live rocks. It may be helpful to combine the use of toothpicks with cement, gum or epoxies, which are described later in this chapter. One of the best uses for plastic toothpicks is for the placement of sponges that were collected without a base. As with soft corals, the toothpick(s) can be inserted into the sponge, and the opposite end(s) pushed into the rock.

Eggcrate

Eggcrate is manufactured as a diffuser for overhead fluorescent lights. It is a grid-like plastic material with squares approximately 1 cm (0.5 inch) wide. The typical colour is white, but it is also available in black. Metallic-like eggcrate, manufactured to lend a high-tech look to overhead fluorescents, is probably unsuitable for use inside aquariums. When aquariums with bare bottoms were in vogue, some people used eggcrate to minimize the rocks' contact with the bottom and prevent the formation of detritus under the rock, by elevating them above the bottom with platforms constructed of eggcrate.

Eggcrate is rigid but easy to cut with wire cutters or a table saw, and pieces can be glued together with PVC cement or, preferably, secured with solid plastic cable ties. It is a versatile material for aquarists, for use in the fabrication of undergravel filters, plenums, mechanical or chemical filter chambers, as a strainer to block the flow of curious fish over the overflow and to provide elevation to the live rock in reef aquariums. Eggcrate can also be used to construct staircase-like structures for placing live rock on. In this manner, the illusion of a tank filled with live rock can be created while allowing excellent water circulation around the live rock.

For dealers, eggcrate *staircases* are ideal for live coral tanks, as they allow the corals to be sorted by species, prevent them from falling, and afford good circulation around the specimens, not to mention easy tank maintenance. Eggcrate is fine for dealer's holding tanks, but it is not the most flexible construction device for building a natural-looking display tank. Eggcrate limits the decorative potential of the aquarium. It is difficult to build a reef that doesn't look like a wall on eggcrate. There are better ways to achieve the same positive aspects of eggcrate, in our opinion without the limitations (see *Plastic screws, acrylic sheets or rods, PVC pipe* in this chapter).

Fibergrate® and Chemgrate® fiberglass grating

For large exhibits, stronger materials such as Fibergrate® and Chemgrate® fiberglass grating (http://www.fibergrate.com), are better suited for building rockwork supports. Chemgrate® resins, CP-84 and FS-25, are commonly used in the food industry, have full USDA acceptance, and come in a variety of depths, resins, colours and panel sizes. It is used primarily to make lightweight but strong walkways, but its USDA acceptance also makes them safe for use in aquariums, and therefore it has many applications to construction of the decor in large aquariums.

Working with fiberglass grating

Although fiberglass grating works wonderfully well as a live rock support structure, preparing it for use is very labour intensive. First, the grating needs to be cut into the appropriate shapes needed to construct the planned supports. Cutting fiberglass grating generates a great deal of hazardous dust, therefore protective equipment must be used and protective clothing worn. Specialized cutting

Cutting fiberglass grating requires protective equipment and tools. Note dust masks, gloves, disposable suit, goggles, and old dirty sneakers- oh, those are Charles'. N. Chan

tools are also required that are designed to cut through fiberglass. Once all the shapes have been cut out, all cut surfaces must be coated with resin in order to seal them against moisture. Unless sealed, the fiberglass will delaminate over time, causing the grating to eventually fail, not a good thing with several hundred or more pounds of rock sitting on top of it.

Installation

Once the pieces have been cut and sealed, the panels need to be assembled. The very grate-like nature of the panels results in teeth protruding along cut edges and these can be used to interlock the pieces. For smaller displays, heavy-duty cable ties can be used to secure the pieces together and stabilize them. For larger structures, fiberglass angles, squares, I-beams, or threaded rod and nuts should be used.

Using fiberglass angles, square tubing, I-beams and grating, platforms can be created at various heights. Note the use of pieces of fiberglass angle, threaded rod and nuts to fasten the panels together securely. The fiberglass angle on the right side of the picture is to prevent sand from moving underneath the structure. J.C. Delbeek

Fiberglass grating panels should be assembled and tested for fit before they are placed into the exhibit. The design of the grating allows for the interlocking of panels once they are cut but still require fastening for long term stability. J.C. Delbeek

With careful placement of live rock, the fiberglass grating and supports cannot be seen as shown in this picture of the final product, the 20,900 L (5500 gallon) Barrier Reef exhibit at the Waikiki Aquarium. J.C. Delbeek

Once the fiberglass structure has been placed into the aquarium, the job of covering it with live rock begins. The smaller the display the more difficult it becomes to hide the structure with live rock. Rocks should be placed such that no grating is visible from any viewing angle, something easiest to achieve in exhibits that have only one view path or window. Various means can be used to fasten the rock to the grating and to each other such as marine epoxy, cable ties and cement, but often the rocks can be stacked in such a way that the need for fasteners is reduced. Vertical sections are the most difficult to conceal and here fasteners, cement and small *filler* rocks are best used to advantage.

Plastic screws, acrylic sheets or rods, PVC pipe

Rick Graff of the Bucks County Aquarium Society built his reef in a

The careful placement of live rock over fiberglass grating platforms and vertical sections, can lead to a very realistic and convincing display using a minimum amount of live rock. These pictures show the construction of the 1,893 L (500 gallon) Surge Coral exhibit at the Waikiki Aquarium, Honolulu, Hawaii. The fiberglass platforms also provided a means for suspending the majority of the live rock off the sand bottom in this plenum system. B. Carlson

unique way that makes it look like the rocks are floating above the bottom by some means of levitation. His trick was to use clear acrylic cubes as feet for the large bottom pieces. The feet are attached to the rocks with acrylic rods. Holes are drilled into the cubes, the lengths of acrylic rod are inserted, and then these assembled feet are inserted into the rocks. Unlike eggcrate, there is no limitation to the shape of the reef you can create with this technique.

A variation of this method could be used with sand on the bottom. Instead of using rods and cubes to make feet, the higher elevation necessary to *float* rocks above sand requires the use of cut lengths of acrylic tubing, at least 1.8 cm (3/4") diameter. With this method, it is possible to have either portions or the entire reef appearing to be suspended over the sand, with terrific caves underneath.

You can use lengths of clear, gray, or white PVC similarly to make feet, attaching them to the rocks with cable ties cinched up through holes drilled into the rock with a masonry bit. Wider pipe diameters provide greater stability. Even thick pieces of acrylic can be used, or pieces fitted together to form an *X* (a suggestion offered to us by Martin Moe). If you can find thick plastic screws, these too can be used to elevate rocks, the head serving as the foot in this case. Plastic screws or rods can also be used to position coral heads or to link rocks together. Be sure that whatever you use to support rocks above the bottom of the tank is structurally suited to this purpose, and will not break down, crumble or shift and give way.

Plastic screws and nuts can also be used to fasten massive corals such as mussids and faviids onto artificial rockwork or live rock. A hole is drilled into the bottom of the coral skeleton using a masonry bit such that the head of the screw can be inserted and glued in place using epoxy. Once the glue has hardened the other end of the

The 76 L (20 gallon) *Tubastraea* exhibit at the Waikiki Aquarium, Honolulu, Hawaii. J.C. Delbeek

The same exhibit seen from the back with the top open, showing the fiberglass insert with corals attached. The smaller colonies are the result of settled planulae. J.C. Delbeek

A nylon screw and wing nut are visible behind the insert. The screw was epoxied into the bottom of a *Tubastraea* colony and inserted through a hole in the insert, then fastened in place with a wing nut. J.C. Delbeek

Even the long plastic screw from a toilet lid has another useful function. Drill a hole in the coral, insert the screw, and the head of the screw can be inserted into a hole in the live rock. Gravity will hold it in place, but underwater epoxy can be used to form a permanent bond. J. Sprung

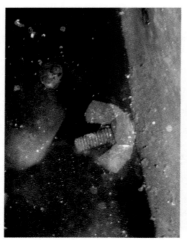

screw can be inserted and glued into a hole in the rock. When corals are mounted on thin fiberglass rockwork panels, the screws can be inserted through holes drilled into the panels and fastened with plastic nuts from behind. This technique is especially useful when mounting corals that normally grow on vertical surfaces or under overhangs e.g. *Tubastraea, Dendrophyllia*.

Underwater epoxies, hydraulic cements, and other bonding agents

Marine epoxy

There are some non-toxic (when cured) epoxy cements that are useful both for locking devices and for actually forming a bond between pieces. Two formats are commonly used, stick formats and potted (canned) formats. We caution that for the sake of safety, one should always wear rubber or latex gloves to mix or handle any epoxy, or just mix and apply the epoxy with an old knife or thin spatula.

Z-Spar® Splash Zone compound (A-788)

The following recommendations for Z-Spar®, (a canned product) was provided by Dr. Bruce Carlson, who has used it extensively. After mixing equal parts of A (yellow) and B (black) according to the directions, some heat will be generated, but not enough to really be a problem underwater. Virtually all epoxies are very sticky above water, but do not adhere well when wet. Z-Spar® loses enough stickiness to make it easy to handle if your (latex gloved) fingers are wet, but one of the unique characteristics of this compound is that it still stays relatively sticky and adheres well to rocks even underwater. With this advantage comes one minor disadvantage: it takes a long time to set up (harden).

Z-Spar® splash zone compound is a two part marine epoxy that can be purchased at boating supply stores. J.C. Delbeek

You will have to prop up the pieces of rock or coral, or hold them together by some mechanical means for at least a few hours. You can use some 20 minute underwater epoxy (which doesn't stick too well) to just hold the rocks together long enough until the Z-Spar® sets. The curing time can be increased by mixing slightly more of the black part than the yellow, as the black contains the catalyst. Do not mix in much more black or else the epoxy will get very warm and may not set properly and fail to harden completely. Once mixed, Z-Spar® has a dark green colour, but it will eventually become covered with coralline algae.

Z-Spar® is best for attaching rocks to each other, or to rocks with living coral on them. First, brush clean the surfaces that are to be bonded. Next cover both surfaces with Z-Spar® and press them together. After the surfaces are mated, spread the excess, extruded Z-

Spar® over all the adjacent surfaces to get a good set, and feather and texture it to give a natural, rock-like appearance. Sand, gravel, shells etc. can also be placed into the surface at this time if so desired. See caution about use in closed systems below.

Tip: It is important to use fresh Z-Spar®. If Z-Spar® is allowed to sit unused for long periods of time, or the cans are not sealed tightly, it loses its ability to completely harden. Fully cured Z-Spar® should be rock hard. If it is not, then not enough black was used, or the epoxy was too old.

Stick format epoxies

There are numerous clay-like two part epoxies available in the aquarium hobby, and they have the advantages of being quite easy to handle, and having a quick set up time. Simply cut off the amount you need and mix them together in your (latex gloved) fingers or with a metal spatula. You can push a piece of the mixed putty into a hole in the rock and then cover the base of the branch (it's ok even if it covers a little of the living tissue). Next, insert the base of the branch of coral into the hole, and to secure the fit push the excess epoxy firmly around the coral and the rock, filling any gaps.

Using epoxy

Some things need mentioning regarding the use of underwater epoxies. First, although they are not toxic to marinelife, they do initially leach organic compounds into the water while curing. However, once cured they do not leach anything into the water. The substances leached into the water are harmless to fish and invertebrates in a typical aquarium, but it is possible that in a small (less than 76 L/20 gallons) closed system aquarium the fish or invertebrates might be affected if a large amount of epoxy were used. For such small aquariums, we recommend that you set up a separate aquarium, bucket, or other container with seawater, for adhering rocks and corals together. The pieces can be allowed to set up in the separate container, with an airstone providing circulation and adequate gas exchange. If you need to glue pieces within the display aquarium, be careful not to use too much in one session. Another important point that is more noticeable in smaller aquariums; the organic substances leached by epoxies tend to make a protein skimmer foam more than usual, or it may produce excess *micro-bubbles* that are distracting as they get carried around in the water. For that reason we recommend turning the protein skimmer off or reducing the air input to the skimmer for at least 24 to 36 hours after using the epoxy. One may increase the use of activated carbon for a few days to remove leached substances, but it is not usually necessary to do so. This problem seems to be more of a nuisance to the aquarist, rather than harmful to the tank.

Proper use of underwater epoxy requires understanding, practice, and of course patience and planning too. Underwater epoxies are NOT superglues! Many aquarists have the impression that the epoxy will bond on contact and hold a heavy object in place, but these epoxies do not work that way. They work more like concrete than superglue. Sometimes it is possible to position the drying bond out of water until it hardens. The result is a much stronger bond than if the epoxy dried underwater (J. Brandt, pers. comm.).

The thick clay (as opposed to runny) consistency of the stick format epoxies makes them the perfect solution for attaching gorgonians. Simply find a hole to insert the gorgonian base or stem in, and then push epoxy into the hole and around the stem to secure it in place. This exercise demonstrates the best use of underwater epoxy: to surround a stem or peg, as concrete does around iron reinforcing bars. To create a natural projecting position for a large piece of coral, one should first insert a wooden or plastic rod into the base of the coral to make a peg. Insert this peg into a hole in the rockwork, using epoxy between the coral and rock to cement the piece in place. For small coral fragments, one can simply surround the base with epoxy and push the blob and coral fragment onto a rock, preferably into a depression in the rock.

Attaching corals to aquarium walls

It is also possible to attach lightweight corals to the aquarium walls with underwater epoxy. Attaching corals to glass with epoxy, however, is only a temporary possibility since glass, though hard to the touch, is a special type of liquid, and as such its molecules are in constant motion, albeit much slower than in a typical liquid. Most epoxies become rigid when they cure, and the motion of the molecules of glass gradually severs the bonds to the unmoving cured epoxy. Some epoxies are more flexible when cured, and thus adhere better to glass, but in general, the attachment of coral to glass using epoxy must be viewed as temporary. The growth of corals onto the glass may hold them in place, but here too the attachment can sever cleanly, leaving a smooth-as-glass skeleton. Some corals are able to bond better to glass than others, however, presumably due to the flexibility of the organic matrix they lay down in advance of depositing calcium carbonate. In contrast with epoxies, silicone rubber is such a superb sealer for glass aquariums because of its great flexibility when cured, and the fact that it bonds well to non-porous surfaces.

When attaching a coral to an aquarium wall such as fiberglass, epoxy coated concrete, or acrylic, two main obstacles are getting a good bond with the wall and supporting the weight of the piece until the epoxy cures. Thin, flattened pieces work best as they offer a large contact area for bonding. A flattened base on a lightweight gorgonian or other soft coral is also relatively easy to attach. The bonding site should be cleaned first with a razor blade or toothbrush to remove algal films and expose a clean bare surface. Place a sufficient quantity of epoxy on the center of the base to spread flat and cover most of it when pressed against the wall, the pressure applied squeezes out the water from between the epoxy and the wall. Hold the object steady with light pressure for about two minutes, which can seem like an eternity sometimes! If the piece is small and not heavy, it may be released after the two minutes without additional support. If it is heavy, it may need to be supported much longer, until the epoxy cures, which takes several hours. One must devise a system for holding the object in place until the epoxy cures. Two methods work well. One involves the use of a set of the magnets used to clean algae off the aquarium panes. The other method uses Styrofoam as a float. If the Styrofoam float method is used, one makes a harness from rubber bands and/or string to tie a block(s) of Styrofoam to the coral so that the coral is suspended at the proper height and angle to simply push it into place where it will be attached to the glass. Once the bond is made and the epoxy is cured (after 24 hours), the harness assembly can be cut and removed. The magnet method works for slender pieces placed flat against the glass. A magnet outside the aquarium supports the position of a magnet inside the aquarium, placed below the piece being bonded. The magnet supports the weight of the piece until the epoxy cures. In either case, a sufficient quantity of epoxy is placed as a ball or cone in the center of the piece so that when pressure is applied the spread epoxy will cover most of the base and still be about 1/4 to 1/8 inch thick. The pressure must be applied evenly (by hand usually) for about two minutes, which can seem like an excruciatingly long time if the position is an awkward one. In addition to the two methods just described, pieces of straight PVC or plastic rods can also be used to prop pieces into place and hold them there until the epoxy cures.

Suspending pieces of coral or rock from the aquarium walls affords a very natural look and opens up some creative possibilities for aquascaping. However, there are limits to the size and weight of pieces that can safely be attached to the walls. One should not attempt to attach dense pieces larger than a fist. Fragments of coral attached to the walls by epoxy will grow and form further attachments, supporting their own weight as they grow. In this way, it is possible to have an aquascape growing from the walls of the aquarium suspended over the sand bottom. Fish that live in caves

These *Montipora* colonies were originally attached to the epoxy painted fiberglass wall of this aquarium as small flat fragments using underwater epoxy. The effect creates a very natural look. J. Sprung

AquaStik is a convenient stick format two-part underwater epoxy. Photo courtesy of Two Little Fishies, Inc.

can swim in their natural upside-down position and non-photosynthetic corals that live on the undersides of ledges can be attached naturally there with epoxy.

A few solutions exist regarding the limits to the size of the structure attached to the wall of the aquarium. One is to incorporate positively buoyant sections that make the whole structure neutral (i.e. weightless). Another solution is to include a fiberglass or plastic background insert (as is done at public aquariums) and attach the reef structure to it with plastic screws or rods that pass through the insert as we mentioned previously.

Underwater epoxy is also useful to help solidify the structure of the reef made of live rock. If the rocks are fitted together with plastic rods or with cable ties, epoxy can be used in between at points of contact to give more rigidity to the structure. Underwater epoxy does not have the ability to support very heavy pieces, but it can form joints between pieces, tending to prevent movement.

There are some other uses for underwater epoxy. Peter Wilkens told us he uses it to kill *Aiptasia* anemones. He simply smothers them with it by pushing some into the crevice into which the anemones retract. Some aquarists have used underwater epoxy to halt the progression of protozoan and RTN infections in small polyped stony corals (see the descriptions of *Brown Jelly* infection in *The Reef Aquarium*, volume 1, and RTN in *The Reef Aquarium*, volume 2). The infected tissue is siphoned off and the epoxy is placed like a Band-Aid over the bare skeleton and up over a small portion (about 1.25 cm/0.5 inch) of the live healthy tissue. The technique apparently smothers the protozoans and the coral tissue grows back down over the epoxy, though sometimes the infection is not so easily halted. The epoxy can be used similarly to halt the progression of *Black Band* disease. The black bands can be siphoned off and the epoxy used to cover the exposed skeleton. Underwater naturalist Harold Hudson has used this technique for many years to *repair* afflicted coral heads on the reef tract in the Florida Keys.

There are a few types of epoxy to choose from, and there are alternatives to underwater epoxy, but each has its limitations. For attaching coral pieces underwater, right in the tank, underwater epoxy or cyanoacrylate gels work wonders. If you have the ability to make the attachment outside the aquarium, then there are some other options, such as quick setting hydraulic cements, cyanoacrylate gels with or without accelerators, UV curing dental adhesives, and hot melt glue.

Quick-setting Portland cements

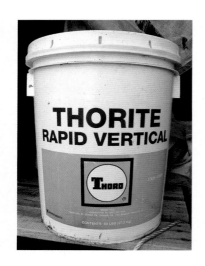

Thorite Rapid Vertical cement by Thoro® can be used to create live rock structures or to permanently attach corals to rock. J.C. Delbeek

The quick-set type of pure Portland cement is an ideal material for permanently cementing corals in place because it is very adhesive even to damp surfaces, sets in about one hour, is non-toxic, and strong (Bronikowski, 1982, 1993). These cements are most useful for building strong structures with limestone or live rock. Quick setting Portland cement can support heavy pieces, unlike epoxy. However, while the epoxy can be used in an established aquarium, the quick setting cements are best used when the aquarium is first set up, during the construction of the aquascape, as they are best applied to a dry or semi-dry surface. They can be used of course for attaching a piece of coral to a rock outside of the aquarium, which can be placed in the aquarium after the cement has cured. A temporarily lowered water level could also be employed. It is important to periodically splash the area being cemented while it hardens in order to cool it, since the reaction is exothermic (generates heat)! It can be given a rock-like texture by using a damp, large-pore sponge to shape the surface while it is still workable.

Thorite

Thorite is a cement-based product that can be used to attach live rocks together, attach corals to rock, or make plugs to aquaculture corals on. Thorite is also useful for hiding cable ties, and for attaching live rock to fiberglass grating. The product contains fibers that help it hold shape when applied to vertical surfaces. It can be used underwater but is messy; it is best used on wet rock out of the water and then submerged once it begins to set (within 20 minutes). There are several different types of Thorite available from a variety of manufacturers; the product pictured here has been used successfully at the Waikiki Aquarium for several years. Some products contain anti-fungal

Thorite can be used to cover cable ties and to thicken live rock where cable ties are attached. J.C. Delbeek

agents and are not suitable for aquarium use. Read the label carefully and always test a product before using it in a reef aquarium.

Cyanoacrylate

Cyanoacrylate glues can be used for attaching small coral fragments to substrates, including glass, and for reattaching light-weight broken branches Unless the two pieces fit together perfectly, the bond that forms is brittle, and easily broken. The value of its use is to hold a piece in place until it has the chance to grow and form a more permanent attachment. Cyanoacrylate works best if the items being attached can be partially dried, as we described for quick-setting cements. It does work underwater, but not as well. Cyanoacrylate cures quickly, and is non-toxic once cured. We recommend that the pieces be joined outside of the aquarium. The use of accelerators gives a faster and stronger bond.

The drawback to cyanoacrylate is that the bond does not have much elasticity, so it will sheer and separate if it is agitated or jarred strongly before the coral has had time to grow new tissue down over the rock. The beauty of cyanoacrylate glue is that it allows one to spot glue tiny bits of soft tissue, which is most useful for aquaculture of soft corals and zoanthid anemones (Headlee *et al.*, 1996). In our experience, the techniques work well, but sometimes the polyps or cuttings of soft bodied creatures such as soft corals or zoanthids will separate from the glue after a day, before they can grow and form a natural bond with the rock. Small stony coral fragments glued with cyanoacrylate, however, usually stay put, so the method is a good time saving technique for working with them, and it has become the standard for *fragging* SPS corals.

UV curing adhesives

Adhesives that cure upon exposure to UV, blue light and visible light are available in a number of mainly polymer-based chemical systems, such as acrylics. These are commonly used in dentistry for tooth bonding. The cure time can be rapid, some bonding instantly upon the exposure to UV light from a light wand. Others require a greater length of time to fully set. The bond formed is quite like the bond achieved with cyanoacrylate gels, but possibly requiring more effort to accomplish. The state of the art at present is cyanoacrylate gels. It remains to be seen whether a light-curing adhesive system will become as useful or cost effective as cyanoacrylate.

Hot melt glue

Hot melt glue administered by an electric heating gun is another alternative for attaching corals to rock outside of the aquarium.

Caution: Do not insert the gun or its tip underwater!

A hot glue gun and a supply of hot glue sticks are handy tools for the reef aquascaper and coral farmer alike. J.C. Delbeek

Hot melt glue is effective for attaching small stony coral fragments to rock. J. Sprung

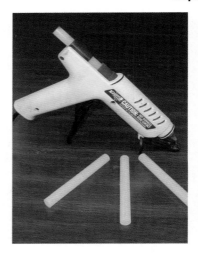

Hot melt glue works well for small coral fragments and has better elasticity than cyanoacrylate. It can also be used for attaching larger corals to rocks, but as with underwater epoxy, it is best to incorporate plastic or wooden rods to help provide a structural attachment to the rock.

The use of coral sand and other bottom media

Sometimes people think that adding coral sand to their reef tank is taboo. This notion is probably partly owing to old recommendations in aquarium literature that said, in effect, that a sand or gravel bed without an undergravel filter to pull water through it would become foul and release toxic hydrogen sulfide into the water. Gravel on the bottom has also been discouraged because it is perceived as a detritus trap that can promote the proliferation of undesirable algae. These partly factual notions resulted in a proliferation of tanks with nothing at all on the bottom! Our discussion of the biological functions of a sand bed in chapter 6 should help to clear up these notions! It is nevertheless possible to have an aesthetically interesting aquarium with no sand bed on the bottom.

The *bare-bottom* idea affords a good measure of the detritus production by the rocks, usually an astounding quantity, and it is easy to siphon this away or prevent its accumulation with bottom water jets. Such an arrangement certainly prevents the accumulation of detritus, but it does not make for a complete natural aquarium ecosystem. The sand bed, if not incorporated within the display, could be incorporated in an attached refugium, as is done in the original design proposed by Leng Sy. A substrate free aquarium gives an opportunity to place corals (e.g. *Briareum* and *Erythropodium* spp.) or zoanthids on the bottom, where they can grow into an interesting live *carpet* of polyps.

Here is the look of a bare bottom tank, common in the 1980's and early 1990's in North and South America, but rare now. J. Sprung

Corals, zoanthids, coralline algae and other marinelife quickly carpet the bottom of a bare-bottomed aquarium in well-illuminated zones with strong currents. J. Sprung

A variation on the bare bottom approach is just using a thin layer of gravel for decorative purposes, as seen here. This approach, combined with regular gravel vacuuming usually results in biological instability in the tank, and chronic problems with dinoflagellates or cyanobacteria. J. Sprung

Using sand beds for aesthetic purposes

Our discussion of sand and gravel in chapters 2 and 6 outline the types of sand/gravel available, its preparation, biological roles and effects of various sand or gravel substrata. Such focus missed the use of sand or gravel as a way to accentuate the aquascape, draw attention to a particular specimen, or provide the basis of the aquascape itself. Creative use of the different gravel substrates available can provide an enhanced appeal to any aquarium.

Black sand

Recently some aquarium industry companies that supply gravels and sand began offering dark substrates. These offer the possibility to duplicate the bottom characteristics seen by *muck divers* who visit places like the recently popularized dive sites in North Sulawesi, Indonesia. These substrates are primarily silicate in

A black sand substrate was used to recreate a habitat where flamboyant cuttlefish (*Metasepia tullbergi*) are commonly found, as seen in this exhibit at the Waikiki Aquarium. J.C. Delbeek

A clam display at the Waikiki aquarium, using black gravel to contrast the bright colours of the tridacnid clam mantles. J.C. Delbeek

nature with some calcareous material mixed in to give a *salt and pepper* appearance to the sand. As such, they do not offer much in the way of buffering but with the use of kalkwasser and calcium reactors, this should not be a major concern. A dark substrate also tends to bring out the colours in fish and corals better as it creates a stronger contrast than bright white sands. See chapter 2 for more information on using black sand.

Large gravel/rubble rock

The careful placement of large gravel pieces or small live rock pieces (rubble rock) on a sand bed can have a dramatic look and offers the creation of a distinct habitat zone where some creatures may congregate, as on wild reefs. It can also provide better *footing* for fungiid corals that might be buried when

Coralline covered rubble rock is used in this outdoor exhibit at the Waikiki Aquarium to recreate a tidepool habitat. J.C. Delbeek

placed on fine sand. Large gravel pieces are also used as structural support by fishes such as jawfish that construct burrows in the sand. In addition, many of the *Cirrhilabrus* and *Parachelinus* wrasse species popular in reef aquariums are found primarily over branching rubble rock patches, which they use for shelter. Large gravel/rubble rock can also be used in select regions of the tank where water currents might be particularly strong and the use of smaller sized sand or gravel would not be possible.

Sand beds with wave makers

The new WaveBox from Tunze (see chapter 7) that creates a real back and forth water motion in the aquarium has the ability to form ripples in a sand bed, just as in the wild. This effect has a pleasing look that contributes to the illusion of being in nature.

Sand beds and dioramas

Before the advent of reef aquariums, there was a practice of creating a so-called *diorama* behind the aquarium, which gave a sense of depth to a small display, if the aquarist kept the back glass free of algae. It is possible to utilize this old technique for special effects, a sandy bottom that leads to a backlit blue background for example. Metal halide light over the main display would cast glitter lines on the sand in the diorama. Of course, the use of a diorama requires that there be adequate space behind the tank to create it.

Foods and Feeding

During the early years of the reef keeping hobby, the emphasis on the need to create a nutrient poor reef environment, lead to the impression that reef aquariums should not be fed very much. The fact that live rock with its resident plant and animal populations provides a source of food to the fishes helped this idea. So did the fact that many zooxanthellate corals could be maintained without much food input provided they had sufficient light. Furthermore, the perception that excess feeding would lead inevitably to problems with algae made the notion stick. Thus for many years, many reef aquariums had low fish populations and low inputs of food. We tried to emphasize the need for balance in this regard in our comments on feeding in *The Reef Aquarium* volumes one and two. Aquarists should not maintain anorexic tanks, was our position, as we had seen many exhibits with fishes that looked thin and hungry!

As we have now come to a point where the methods for managing nitrogenous waste and phosphate are well known and easy to employ, the fear of feeding is outdated and the benefits of high food inputs are becoming realized. Borneman (2002a,b), Joshi (2000), Shimek (1999, 2003), Sprung (1999, 2001) and Toonen (2003) discuss feeding invertebrates heavily with various types of liquid foods, something once considered taboo by many aquarium hobbyists. When feeding any organism the key is variety. Do not get into the habit of always feeding the same food i.e. frozen brine shrimp, to your fish and invertebrates. By offering a variety of foods, you will provide a more balanced diet and complement any deficiencies in any one food type.

Joe Yaiullo really gets into feeding his big reef aquarium. T. Gardner

Fish foods

Feeding the reef aquarium involves addition of foods for both fishes and invertebrates. The foods offered to the fishes are also eaten by the invertebrates, but filter-feeding invertebrates also eat a range of specific foods. We consider first the foods for fishes. An in-depth discussion of the nutritional requirements of fishes is outside of the scope of this book. We recommend Halver and Hardy (2002), De Silva and Anderson (1995), Lovell (1998) and Guillaume *et al.* (2001) for readers who want to know more about the subject.

Flake foods

Dry flake foods are popular *staple diets* for tropical freshwater fishes. For marine aquariums, they have also gained in popularity, but they are not as universally accepted for marines as for freshwater. This should not be the case, as flake foods are very good sources of nutrition. The positive features of flake foods are the concentration of protein and fats, the ease of feeding, and the widespread acceptance by many fish species. There are also special blends made for herbivores and for carnivores. On the negative side, flake foods supply a concentrated dose of nitrogen and phosphorus—good for the fishes but not for the water quality. Flake foods are for the most part very thin and so do not hold onto the vitamins and fats very long after they hit the water. That is why the fishes may initially eat them but reject them after they have floated around for more

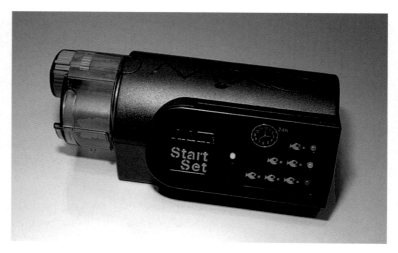

Designed by Rick Oellers, this feeding point features an acrylic feeding tube, which holds floating pellet food until it sinks, thus preventing the pellets from being drawn over the overflow. An automatic feeder is mounted on it. J. Sprung

Automatic feeder from *Hydor.*® J. Sprung

than a minute. In a short period, much of the nutritional value is dissolved in the water and the solid flakes become tasteless. It is best to feed flake food in portions small enough that they are consumed immediately. For invertebrates, flake foods are a suitable food source as well. Crabs, shrimp, hermit crabs, anemones, and corals will eagerly grab and eat flakes. It is also possible to pulverize flake foods with a mortar and pestle to make a fine powder food that can be fed to filter feeders.

Pellets

Pellet foods are denser than flake foods, so they hold onto their nutritional value better and supply a very nutrient rich morsel. Most aquaculture facilities that are interested in rapid growth feed pellet foods almost exclusively. Therefore, pellet diets have the highest vitamin concentrations and supply the greatest amount of proteins and fats. This means they are great for keeping fish healthy and making them grow, but they also supply a larger amount of phosphate and nitrogenous waste, which affects the water quality. Pellet foods are available in a wide range of sizes and formulations and thus, can be used with a wide variety of fishes. Some brands of pellet foods are appropriately sized for large polyped stony corals, corallimorphs, and some zoanthids to eat, and can be fed to them with a baster to direct the pellets directly to the tentacles or oral disc. Due to their low friability and uniform size, pellet foods lend themselves for use in automated feeders, which are useful for aquarists who cannot always be present to feed their aquariums, or for adding small amounts of food at regular intervals over the course of a day. One of the drawbacks of some pellet foods is that they tend to float and can

Scalloped fin edges like these are a symptom of nutritional deficiency, commonly associated with head and lateral line erosion in surgeonfishes and angelfishes. Often just increasing the volume of food will correct the problem. Other times offering more vegetable matter or foods high in marine lipids is helpful. J. Sprung

Herbivorous fishes need to get sufficient plant matter in their diet. Here we see a group of herbivores grazing seaweed held by a SeaVeggies™ clip. G. Schiemer

be lost to the overflow. This can be solved by using a stationary ring feeder that holds the pellets in place until they begin to sink.

Frozen foods

Frozen foods are much less concentrated compared to dry foods, so one has to feed a much larger quantity of them to match the nutritional value of dry foods. Fish like frozen foods because when thawed, they are very similar to the fresh foods that they are accustomed to eating. Frozen brine shrimp (*Artemia*) are a popular choice for many fishes, but have low nutritional value. However, some varieties are *gut loaded* to enhance their nutritional value, and in any case, fishes enjoy chasing around a large number of shrimp when feeding.

It is important to realize that in nature fishes and invertebrates spend a large amount of time feeding, while in aquariums the feeding times become centered on the times that the aquarist adds food to the aquarium. While it is not natural for them, most fishes and invertebrates easily adapt to our schedule of food inputs. In addition, many of the various feeds we offer (such as dry foods) are nutritionally dense, so that they obtain their daily needs with only one or two feedings instead of the nearly continuous grazing characteristic of the natural habitat. Shimek (2003) discusses this discrepancy, and suggests that we should consider a reverse philosophy, wherein instead of offering nutritionally dense food once or twice per day, we offer large volumes of nutritionally *light* feeds as often as possible. Frozen foods and some liquid diets offer this possibility, but a delivery apparatus must be used to assure sufficient food is added.

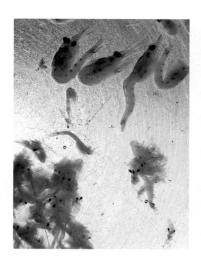

Frozen *Mysis*, above, come in a variety of sizes.
J.C. Delbeek

Several brands of frozen *Mysis* are now available, including both freshwater and marine varieties.
J.C. Delbeek

Frozen *Mysis* spp. shrimp are an excellent frozen food option, which have high levels of lipids and protein that are beneficial to fish health. The lipids have a strong odor that stimulates feeding in many fishes and invertebrates. These oils, however, make the foam temporarily collapse in a protein skimmer. Many corals will also eat *Mysis*. *Mysis* shrimp have been particularly beneficial in the husbandry of seahorses and seadragons, and other difficult to feed fishes, allowing for increased survival and improved breeding success.

The frozen food category also includes prepared diets that are blended and frozen in sheets or cube trays. They are often enriched with vitamins and are similar to dry foods nutritionally, but with much higher moisture content. Specialized herbivore, carnivore and sponge feeder diets can be easily formulated and fed in frozen form.

Binders such as gelatin can be used to formulate your own diet by mixing ingredients in a blender, adding gelatin and then freezing the mixture in small cubes or shallow trays. These can then be cut into smaller portions when needed for feeding. Moe (1982) provides formulae for making homemade frozen foods, and there are several similar recipes available online.

Live foods

Live food for marine aquaria has traditionally meant one thing: live brine shrimp, *Artemia* sp., either the newly hatched *Artemia* nauplii or adult shrimp. There are nevertheless many other live food options for marine aquariums, such as blackworms, bloodworms, mysid shrimp, grass shrimp, rotifers, copepods, *Daphnia*, and mosquito larvae, to name just a few. Live foods also include live plankton, which we discuss separately in this chapter.

Frozen *Mysis* are readily taken by corals as well as fish. J.C. Delbeek

Live brine shrimp can be easily raised and enriched to increase their nutritional value. J.C. Delbeek

A benefit of live foods is that they may contain an abundance of some types of amino acids, fatty acids, and vitamins that are depleted in frozen or prepared foods. Furthermore, live foods can also be enriched by feeding them live or preserved phytoplankton, spray-dried phytoplankton (Algemac™, PhytoPlan®), or microencapsulated feeds such as SuperSelco® or Artamac™, to increase their nutritional value. In addition, live foods also stimulate natural hunting behaviors in fishes and offer challenging activity compared to standard prepared foods. However, live foods do carry a risk of introducing pathogenic bacteria or protozoans, but this risk is quite low, with some exceptions. Bill Addison (pers. communication) found viable *Amyloodinium* in live *Artemia*, suggesting that this food has the potential to introduce this pathogen to aquariums. Some public aquariums have also experienced disease problems in seadragons, which have been traced to wild caught live *Mysis* used as food. As a result, several institutions have begun their own mysid culture programs (e.g. Toledo Zoo and Aquarium, and the Long Beach Aquarium of the Pacific, to name just a few North American aquariums). This problem does not affect frozen *Mysis*, and some brands are even gamma irradiated to make them disease free.

Invertebrate foods and feeding

Reef building corals are heterotrophic organisms that actively feed on many different types of food. They are also symbiotic organisms, which have symbiotic dinoflagellates called zooxanthellae living within their tissues that synthesize organic food utilized by the coral. Their dual mode of feeding is called mixotrophy. Studying the modes separately, it can be shown, on the one hand, that many symbiotic corals survive and grow in aquariums given sufficient light and inorganic minerals, with very little in the way of food inputs (Atkinson *et al.*, 1995; Franziskeit, 1974). Yonge and Nicholls (1931) showed, on the other hand, that many species of zooxanthellate corals could survive indefinitely in the absence of light when given adequate amounts of zooplankton. There are exceptions to this that skew the equality of the two modes of feeding. In *Pocillopora damicornis*, photosynthetic products of the zooxanthellae appear to be a more important food source according to Clayton and Lasker (1982). Ferrier-Pagès *et al.* (2003) also discuss the relative importance of zooplankton to some symbiotic corals. In general, when nutrient accumulation is managed in closed system aquariums, the benefits of feeding can be quite measurable. It has been shown, for instance, that feeding zooxanthellate corals results in calcification rates 50-75% higher than control corals that are not fed, and that feeding does not affect the light-enhancement process of photosynthesis on calcification (Witting, 1999; Fanny *et al.*, 2002; Ferrier-Pagès *et al.*, 2003).

Despite the low light level in the exhibits at Coral World, Eilat (illuminated by two standard fluorescent tubes and no reflector), the sps corals thrive. In part, the secret is the daily high input of food, combined with flushing with new seawater to remove the excess nutrients and maintain calcium and alkalinity. The other part of the secret is that these corals were collected from deep water, and were thus already adapted to low light levels. J. Sprung

Feeding corals

There is a seemingly endless variety of coral, with an equally bewildering array of polyp shapes and sizes that relate to the types of food they eat. Some corals have extremely narrow food size requirements based on their polyp size and structure, while others can feed on a wide variety of sizes. Some corals can feed on larger, meaty foods (e.g. *Catalaphyllia*, *Euphyllia*, *Trachyphyllia*, *Fungia*), others feed on tiny zooplankton (e.g. *Acropora*, *Seriatopora*), while still others include large quantities of microscopic phytoplankton in their diets (e.g. *Dendronephthya*), and finally, some appear not to actively capture any prey at all (e.g. *Xenia*). It is therefore not surprising that what to feed corals in a reef aquarium has been the subject of much debate and speculation. The subject of how to feed them is another matter. Large polyped corals such as *Plerogyra*, *Trachyphyllia*, *Caulastrea*, *Blastomussa*, and *Cynarina* can be fed

LPS corals such as *Caulastrea* can easily be fed directly by the aquarist due to the size of their polyps. J.C. Delbeek

Even sps corals such as this *Acropora* sp. actively feed on zooplankton. Their growth rates are dramatically enhanced by feeding, provided water chemistry is maintained optimally. J. Sprung

The spectacular *Tubastraea*-dominated 750 litre (approx. 200 gallon) reef aquarium of Daniella Stettler in Switzerland is managed with daily additions of 150 grams frozen brine shrimp, and twice weekly additions of 1 teaspoon dried Cyclop-eeze® with 10 drops of Sera Fishtamin. The Vodka method (see chapter 6) is used to keep nitrate levels low, and 15% weekly water changes are performed. Kalkwasser is used to maintain calcium and alkalinity, and Strontium and Iodine are added weekly. D. Stettler

flake food, pellets, chopped fish, shrimp, and worms, placed directly on the oral disc or extended tentacles, preferably at night when the feeding tentacles are extended and when the fish that might steal the food are asleep. Small-polyped corals such as *Seriatopora*, *Acropora*, and *Pocillopora* feed on zooplankton (copepods, rotifers, ciliates) or pulverized feeds, day or night, and these can be added to the water column by an automatic feeding system or manually. Following is a review of some of the various types of foods used in reef aquariums, and systems for adding them.

Zooplankton

Zooplankton are microscopic to macroscopic aquatic animals, eggs, and larvae suspended in the water column. They feed on bacteria, phytoplankton, and other zooplankton, and are in turn consumed. Some of the larvae that survive this feeding frenzy develop into fishes and invertebrates. On reefs, there is a large population of plankton called demersal or epibenthic plankton that lives in the water just above the bottom and adjacent to the reef. These creatures are produced locally and remain on-site. Pelagic plankton live higher up in the water column and are typically transported over long distances by currents and tides.

On coral reefs, demersal copepod swarms may contain between 500,000 and 1,500,000 copepods per cubic meter (Hamner and Carleton, 1979). Such densities are patchy, but they comprise a large portion of the total zooplankton availability on reefs. Nevertheless, a large quantity of pelagic zooplankton is also imported to the reef with oceanic water. Using a one meter wide trap over a fixed position on a reef crest, Hamner *et al.* (1988) collected 0.5 kg (about a pound, wet weight) of pelagic zooplankton in one day. This gives a good point of reference for reef aquariums, since the average aquarium is about a meter wide. Ignoring the additional contribution of demersal zooplankton, duplication of this amount of available food would mean adding a pound of wet feed per day per meter of tank, far greater than what most aquarists add. See our additional discussion of interpretations of this data in chapter 6.

Tidal currents carry populations of zooplankton to and from coral reefs, but the real time to see zooplankton in the coral reef environment is at night, when the life produced on the reef ascends into the water column. It is at this time especially that the creatures that feed on zooplankton unfurl their food-capturing tentacles and move out into the passing currents.

In aquariums we may use pumps and timers to duplicate the physical effect of tidal currents, but they do not bring new inputs of zooplankton. We can mimic the effect through our own inputs of food, and it is possible to automate the food inputs to be coordinated with tidal changes. The use of attached refugium aquariums boosts zooplankton production (see chapter 6) for any size aquarium and can mimic the food input offered by incoming tides.

The zooplankton produced within the reef is a feature of our aquariums, as can be witnessed at night by shining a flashlight into the aquarium; the larger the aquarium, the more plankton that will be observed. Smaller aquariums have both a higher rate of consumption of the plankton produced (higher volume of mouths per volume of water) and a lower rate of production.

The concern about damage to zooplankton by centrifugal pumps used for water circulation is, for the most part, without merit (see chapters 6, 7, and Delbeek and Sprung, 1994). Most zooplankton passes through pumps unharmed. However, they do not pass through mechanical filters, protein skimmers, and many types of plankton don't effectively escape the feeding surfaces of corals, anemones, and other filter feeders. Therefore, if these items exist in your system, the concern about pumps has a diminishing return. A system designed exclusively for the culture of zooplankton, however, would best be managed without centrifugal pumps. Such culture systems exist or can be built for home aquariums.

Rotifers

The mass culture of rotifers is a well-known procedure involving the culture of algae to feed the rotifers and careful harvest of the rotifers from their culture vessel. The procedure is used to provide a continuous supply of rotifers in aquaculture facilities raising fish larvae. In addition to cultured algae, yeast, finely pulverized flake foods, emulsified fish oil, Selco™, and spray dried algae can be used as feeds for the rotifers (see next section). In a pinch, even tomato juice, V8 (or other vegetable based juices or spray-dried powders) can be used. See Moe (1992, 1997) and Hoff and Snell (1993) for a detailed description of how to culture rotifers. It is important to note that the nutritional value of rotifers is dramatically affected by the foods given to the rotifers just before offering them as feed to the aquarium.

Artemia nauplii

Newly hatched brine shrimp, aka nauplii, are readily eaten by filter feeding invertebrates, including corals, and they can easily be hatched and fed to a reef aquarium. Regular feeding of such zooplankton has many benefits, but a distinct disadvantage is that *Aiptasia* and *Anemonia* or other stinging anemones proliferate even more rapidly when there is a regular feeding regimen of nauplii. Be sure that these anemones are not present in the aquarium before starting to feed *Artemia* on a regular basis. *Artemia* are most nutritious immediately after hatching and should be fed out no more than 24 hours later. Brine shrimp nauplii can be enriched using live phytoplankton or supplements rich in highly unsaturated omega-3 fatty acids (HUFAs), resulting in a highly nutritious feed for larval fishes, jellies and corals. Products such as Algamac™, SELCO (Self Emulsified Lipid Concentrate) and Super Selco® are commonly used to enrich not only *Artemia* but also rotifers.

There are two strains of *Artemia* cysts commonly available in North America, those collected from San Francisco Bay (SFB) and those collected from Great Salt Lake (GSL) in Utah. The GSL nauplii (300-800 microns) are larger than those from SFB (200-600 microns) but the HUFA levels are 3 to 3.5x higher in SFB nauplii. For some species of corals and jelly, the smaller SFB nauplii can be easily consumed where the larger GSL nauplii cannot.

A simple device used for feeding live *Artemia* nauplii to the reef aquarium at the Smithsonian Institution. A solenoid valve connected to a timer doses the *Artemia* nauplii by gravity feed from the hatcher vessel. The dosing hose can be seen entering the reef tank next to a strong water current that distributes the *Artemia* rapidly. J. Sprung

An in-tank or in-sump *Artemia* hatcher manufactured by *Oscar Enterprises* Inc. The *Artemia* are drawn to an illuminated exit, so that they enter the aquarium continuously, leaving the egg shells in the hatcher. J. Sprung

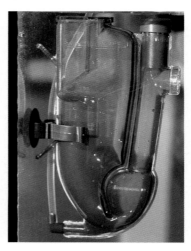

Basic *Artemia* cyst decapsulating procedure

This simple procedure removes the indigestible outer layer of the brine shrimp eggs, sterilizes them, and increases the yield of hatching.

1. Soak 1 tablespoon of brine shrimp eggs in a container with 10 oz. (300 mL) of cold freshwater for one hour to rehydrate them. Aerate gently or stir with a stirbar, trying to avoid having eggs adhering to the sides of the container.

2. After they have rehydrated, add 6 oz. of non-fragrenced household bleach (5% chlorine) and stir for 3-5 minutes. The eggs will change color, from brown to gray to orange, and will sink to the bottom. Keep stirring until the mixture turns orange.

3. Over a sink pour the mixture through a brine shrimp net or other fine mesh filter to retain the eggs, and gently rinse with cool tap water until no smell of bleach remains. Dipping the net full of decapsulated eggs for a minute or two in water with dechlorinator (sodium thiosulfate) solution or a solution made from a tablespoon of white vinegar per cup of water can be used to neutralize traces of chlorine.

4. Place the brine shrimp eggs in aerated salt water to hatch them. The decapsulated cysts can be stored in a saturated brine solution for up to 2 months in the refrigerator for later hatching. The rinsed decapsulated cysts can also be fed to fishes or invertebrates without the need to hatch them first.

With this unique and simple system, employing a venturi input of air, Jorge Gomezjurado of the National Aquarium in Baltimore separates live brine shrimp nauplii from decapsulated eggshells. The air sticks to the shells and floats them to the top. Additonal filling causes them to overflow out of the flask. J. Sprung

Copepods

The culture of copepods for larval rearing is an exploding field as the need for smaller and smaller live first food items in aquaculture increases. Not only adult copepods are used for feeds but more importantly, their nauplii stage is very important due to it's small size. In time, more species and genera of copepods will be brought into culture offering a wide size and nutritional range for aquaculture of both marine fish and invertebrates.

Zooplankton reactors

Special zooplankton culture vessels may also be incorporated in the aquarium design to supply a constant source of one or more types of zooplankton, such as rotifers, *Artemia* nauplii, *Daphnia*, copepods, or ciliates. At the time of this writing, there are few

The Zinn plankton reactor co-cultures rotifers and the microalgae they feed on. M. Haaga

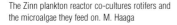

commercial models available. One such model is called a *Zinn planktonreactor*, which is used to culture both phytoplankton (*Nannochloropsis* sp.) and rotifers (*Brachionus plicatilis*) simultaneously. Once set up, it operates with very little maintenance for up to a month or two. After about a month, the reactor has to be cleaned and the cultures started again. Bingman (2002) proposed a similar system for culturing sterile algae cultures, which could then be passed directly back either to the aquarium or to a zooplankton culture vessel and then to the aquarium (see chapter 6).

Frozen zooplankton

Frozen rotifers

In 2005, Hikari introduced a frozen rotifer to its line of aquarium foods. They are available in trays with portions divided into 1 cm^3 cubes. The cubes can simply be popped out and placed in the aquarium, where they will melt and release the rotifers. Freeze-dried rotifers are also available.

Frozen *Artemia* nauplii

Some aquarium industry companies offer frozen *Artemia* nauplii, also called *baby* brine shrimp, mainly as a food for small fishes. These can be used to feed invertebrates that eat zooplankton.

Frozen oyster larvae and eggs

Living oyster trochophore larvae can be frozen, stored, and fed to aquariums as a nutritious live feed with a small size (50 microns) that is ideal for feeding fish larvae and filter feeding invertebrates. IAP TrochoFeed from Innovative Aquaculture Products, Ltd., (www.innovativeaqua.com/products/TrochoFeed.htm), was developed as a feed for raising fish larvae. It is made from trochopores of the Pacific oyster, *Crassostrea gigas*, cryopreserved with liquid nitrogen and packed in seawater in straw shaped containers. It can be stored indefinitely in liquid nitrogen or a liquid nitrogen freezer, and is alive when thawed. After thawing, it can be stored in a refrigerator at 4 to 5 °C for 24 to 48 hours, but should be used soon after thawing for optimum nutritional value.

DT's natural reef diet oyster eggs are frozen 40-50 micron sized eggs that have a high nutritional value. The eggs are concentrated so that 1 mL (1/5 teaspoon) contains approximately 3 million eggs, sufficient for feeding a 75 gallon aquarium. It can be maintained in a regular freezer. These can be obtained from your pet dealer who can contact the supplier at www.dtplankton.com.

Frozen copepods

Argent Labs (www.argent-labs.com) offers a frozen copepod by the trade name Cyclop-eeze® that is a very useful food for feeding fishes and invertebrates that feed on large swimming copepods (DiMarco, 2003; Lieberman, 2001). It is ideal for *Pseudanthias* species and some non-photosynthetic gorgonians that have big polyps, as well as juvenile fishes. Several species and sizes of frozen copepods are now available from Japan and Taiwan, where they are commonly used in aquaculture. We anticipate that such food sources will become popular with aquarists. We want to mention a caveat: feeding this food in quantity to some herbivorous fish can lead to intestinal blockages and bloating e.g. some species of *Centropyge* angelfish (F. Baensch, pers. comm.). As always, a balanced diet using a wide variety of food types and sizes is recommended. Cyclop-eeze® is also offered in a freeze-dried form, but this has the drawback of being buoyant and requiring some time soaking for it to sink when added to the aquarium.

Normally, frozen foods are thawed in a small amount of water put in a cup by the aquarist. It is nevertheless possible to devise an automatic system for feeding aquariums plankton based on a timed *washdown* of feed layers from large frozen block. From the company *AquaTech* (http://members.magnet.at/aquaculture/feeders.htm) we have seen a description for such a device designed for the professional application of frozen zooplankton as a larval diet in marine and fresh water hatcheries. A self-cleaning distributor provides homogeneous distribution of the thawed plankton to larval tanks, or a simpler model could supply just one tank. The *washdown* of food layers and thawing could be accomplished either by spraying or by flooding or by a combination of both. The remaining plankton in the block would be frozen immediately. The feed particle size can be sorted with a sieving unit. In order to avoid damaging the plankton and the resulting leaching of internal fluids from the thawed organisms, the feed is by gravity flow only. Another, less complicated system was produced by the company *Zinn Aquarientechnik*, whose website description is at this url: http://www.zinnaquarientechnik.de/Produkte/Frostfutterautomat/frostf utterautomat.html. It uses an Ice Probe TE chiller to maintain a frozen block of food in an insulated chamber that can be washed on a timed cycle and then allowed to re-freeze. Such a device can be used as an automatic feeder for both fish and invertebrates. If designed and used properly, the frozen food is not thawed and refrozen. Only a surface layer comes off and the rest remains frozen. If these devices were to thaw the food and refreeze it, the cell membranes of some types of copepods might rupture, spilling their contents into the water.

Frozen copepods, in a range of sizes from 100-400 microns, are now commercially available.
J.C. Delbeek

Preserved zooplankton

There are a few companies marketing preserved zooplankton feeds, such as preserved copepods, preserved *Daphnia*, and pulverized dried seafoods including microscopic particle sizes. These feeds are great for the same animals that feed on frozen zooplankton. The product should be refrigerated after opening to retain nutritional value. While the nutritional value of preserved products differs from live or frozen products, there is still a value to using them. Vitamins can also be added to the dried products immediately before feeding them to the tank, and they will be absorbed readily. Preserved wet zooplankton can be dosed at intervals into the aquarium using a peristaltic dosing pump.

Particulate matter

As we explained in *The Reef Aquarium* volume one, the particulate detritus that accumulates in the gravel or other bottom substrates is coated by bacteria and populated by various types of microscopic animals. It is therefore a useable food source for filter feeders if it is regularly kicked up into the water column. This stirring can be done manually, as was demonstrated to us by Peter Wilkens, who used a glass rod to stir the gravel bed in one of his aquariums that housed non-photosynthetic soft corals (Delbeek and Sprung, 1994). In addition, bottom sifting gobies or other fishes that dig in the sand provide a regular input of detritus into the water column by their digging activity. While such stirring is counter to the philosophy of maintenance in the Deep Sand Bed (DSB) method described in chapter 6, it can also be employed in attached refugia, rather than in the main display for such systems.

Pulverized foods

Finely ground flake food and the liquid fraction from whole or frozen foods (e.g. *Mysis* shrimp, brine shrimp, squid, fish blood, clams) can be used as a food for filter feeding invertebrates. These foods have the potential to pollute the water, and in the case of pulverized dry foods, are rich in phosphate. If one is careful to use filtration methods to deal with the excess input of nutrients, any of these food sources is useful in the cultivation of reef invertebrates. Various authors have produced and published their own *milkshake* recipes, see for example Borneman (2001).

Phytoplankton

Phytoplankton are microscopic plants that drift in the water column. Aquarists commonly use the term microalgae to refer to them.

Coral reefs are associated with crystal clear nutrient poor waters, which are quite unlike the phytoplankton pea-green soups of nutrient-rich water bodies. The presence of phytoplankton in these clear reef waters is nevertheless essential to the lives of numerous reef creatures that feed on it. Though the abundance of this food source seems low by appearance of the water, in fact it is not. Furthermore, tidal currents associated with reefs carry large

Large polyped gorgonian soft corals feed on zooplankton and particulate matter that they sift from strong water currents. Large volumes of zooplankton and/or pulverized feeds can be used to maintain or grow them. B. Mohr

volumes of water over the reef and this brings an abundant supply of food, including phytoplankton. Aquarists became especially interested in the use of phytoplankton to feed reef aquarium invertebrates due to several coinciding factors: 1. publications showing that soft corals of the genus *Dendronephthya* feed on phytoplankton (for example Fabricius *et al.*, 1995); 2. articles by Rob Toonen and other authors about phytoplankton as food in aquarium journals; and 3. the widespread availability of live *Nannochloropsis*, preserved strains of several phytoplankton species, and several types of spray-dried phytoplankton.

Fabricius *et al.* (1996) later reported that their initial methods for measurements of phytoplankton intake were not accurate, and needed to be corrected. In fact, they underestimated the actual rate of intake and ingestion of phytoplankton, which emphasizes that *Dendronephthya* depends on a large quantity of this food source for growth and survival.

It is apparent that *Dendronephthya* spp. feed not only on phytoplankton, but also on dissolved and microparticulate organic matter carried by the currents on reefs. J. Sprung

Widdig and Schlichter (2001) also examined the importance of phytoplankton ingestion by *Dendronephthya*. They fed 14C-labeled microalgae (diatoms, chlorophytes and dinoflagellates) and showed that digestion occurs at the point where the pharynx enters into the coelenteron of the polyps. Their data conflicts with the earlier studies, in that they calculate the digested phytoplankton on average only contributes about 30% to the daily organic carbon demand in *Dendronephthya*. Furthermore, the contribution to the daily organic carbon demand decreased with time of exposure to the feed, down to less than 5% after only a few hours. Apparently, the phytoplankton cells block the pharynx and thus prevent further ingestion. The extent of this effect may have been an artifact of flow regime, but it seems likely that their conclusions are correct. The authors concluded that the energy needs of *Dendronephthya* must be complemented by other sources of nutrition, such as dissolved and micro-particulate organic matter. We have regularly observed *Dendronephthya* and other non-photosynthetic corals respond strongly to the introduction of the juices of thawed shrimp and squid, by increasing tissue expansion and opening polyps, indicating that foods other than phytoplankton likely play a role in their diet.

Numerous marine and freshwater phytoplankton species are suitable for feeding marine invertebrates, and several are commercially available. However, there is a wide range in nutritional composition of the three main components in microalgae: protein, carbohydrates and lipids. In some cases this is due to the type of algae, in others it is due to the nutrient composition of the culture medium. Since there is such a variety in nutritional profiles between microalgae types, the best approach is to feed a mixture of two or more types in order to provide a broader nutritional profile than can be achieved by feeding just a single species.

For more information on microalgae nutrition, culturing techniques and species nutritional comparisons we recommend the web site of the Food and Agriculture Organization of the United Nations, http://www.fao.org/DOCREP/003/W3732E/w3732e03.htm#TopOfPage. We discuss here some of the common marine ones available live or in a preserved form for the marine aquarium hobby.

Nannochloropsis

Probably the most widely available and used microalgae for feeding invertebrates in marine aquariums, for shellfish culture, and rotifer culture, *Nannochloropsis* has motile, green cells with a cell size of approximately 6 microns. They are known to be a good source of the polyunsaturated fatty acid eicosapentaenoic acid (EPA). *Nannochloropsis* can be stored in a refrigerator for 3 months at -1 to 3 °C (30 to 37 °F), or it can be frozen in ice-cube trays for longer shelf life (2+ years).

Isochrysis

Isochrysis is a golden brown flagellate with a cell size of approximately 8 microns, and is a good source of the polyunsaturated fatty acid docosahexaenoic acid (DHA). *Isochrysis* is commonly used by shellfish hatcheries and some shrimp hatcheries for its high DHA content. It is also used for enrichment of rotifers, copepods, and *Artemia*. It is an ideal food for feeding clams, mussels, and scallops. *Nannochloropsis oculata* is high in EPA, but low in DHA, so pairing it with Tahitian *Isochrysis*, which is high in DHA, is a nice complement (Marini, 2002).

Pavlova

Pavlova is a golden/brown flagellate that is very similar to *Isochrysis*, but with an even higher DHA profile, and a good EPA profile. It is also used for enriching rotifers, copepods, and *Artemia*, but since it is difficult to grow, it is rarely produced. It is sometimes available from *Reed Mariculture* (www.reed-mariculture.com).

The green alga, *Tetraselmis chui*, is easily cultured in large quantities. J.C. Delbeek

Tetraselmis

Tetraselmis is a large green flagellate with a size of approximately 9-14 microns. *Tetraselmis tetrahele* produces two antibiotic-like compounds documented to increase survival of larval fish when prey items were enriched with this phytoplankton (Marini, 2002). It has a high lipid content, is a source of both EPA and DHA, and has amino acids that stimulate a feeding response in marinelife. *Tetraselmis* is often used in conjunction with *Nannochloropsis* in the culture of rotifers.

Thalassiosira

Thalassiosira weissflogii is a large diatom (5-20 microns depending on time of year) used in the shrimp and shellfish larviculture industry. Although we think of diatoms as typically having a golden brown color, the color of *Thallassiosira* may be brown, green, or yellow, depending on the chlorophyll concentration. It is a good feed for copepods and brine shrimp.

The lipids EPA and DHA mentioned in the various phytoplankton descriptions are types of omega-3 fatty acids. Omega-3 fatty acids are a necessary dietary component and a key factor in successfully raising many marine larvae. They are beneficial *good fats* for people as well. So-called *gut loading* of brine shrimp, larval shrimp, live *Mysis* or rotifers involves feeding EPA and DHA rich phytoplankton, or substitutes such as SuperSelco® or Artamac™ to them immediately before they are fed out.

Bacteria and photosynthetic bacteria

Ocean researchers have only recently recognized that bacterioplankton make up a significant amount of the carbon fixation in the sea, since they make up about 11% or more of the microbes found near the surface in seawater (Kolber *et al.*, 2003). This fact suggests that their importance as a food source for coral reefs has probably also been underestimated, though early and recent work on the subject does recognize bacteria as a food source (Sorokin, 1973a and b, Bak *et al.*, 1998).

Purple non-sulfur photosynthetic bacteria (PSB) may be a useful food for such notoriously difficult creatures as *Dendronephthya* and other filter feeders that specialize on eating microscopic plankton. Kolber *et al.* (2003) found that PSB occur from the surface down to approximately 150 meters (420 ft.), with a maximum concentration at approximately 35 meters (98 ft.). PSB are a non-taxonomic group of several different organisms that have a versatile lifestyle, being able to grow as photoheterotrophs, photoautotrophs, or chemotrophs, depending on the existing environmental conditions. PSB can switch from a metabolism based on the consumption of organic carbon to one based on its production by photosynthesis, depending on the concentration of organic matter in ocean water. In environments that are rich in dissolved organic matter, PSB stop making photosynthetic pigment and simply consume organic matter.

In the aquaculture industry, PSB are raised to help condition water and boost the health of shrimp and other aquaculture products. They can be cultured and maintained for extended periods in closed jars, so the use of them as a feed for marine invertebrates is feasible.

Photosynthetic phytoplankton reactors

Earlier in the chapter, we mentioned the Zinn plankton reactor that co-cultures algae and rotifers. There are also several companies making reactors that culture just phytoplankton. AquaMedic, for example, produces a reactor that consists of a long, vertical, transparent plastic cylinder filled with water, with a slow input of water and a slow output. The cylinder is situated next to a fluorescent lamp. We have also seen similar models, wider in diameter and shorter in height, with the lamp located in a space within the reactor.

Phytoplankton reactors without light

While photosynthetic phytoplankton are traditionally cultured with light, it is also possible to culture many types, as well as bacterioplankton such as PSB, in the absence of light, in special fermentation reactors that use an organic feed. At the time of this writing, this has not been tested for a continuous culture in connection with reef aquariums, but the possibility exists that it could prove to be a low cost, easily managed system for aquarium use. While Bingman (1998) imagined using an illuminated phytoplankton reactor as a *phytoplankton scrubber* filter as well as food source, the same can be imagined for bacterioplankton reactors. In addition, if calcium acetate could be used as a feed for bacterioplankton, then the maintenance of such a reactor might partially contribute to the calcium and alkalinity requirements of the system.

Algal film reactor

Another method of culturing phytoplankton and dosing it to an aquarium consists of a thin film of the aquarium's water flowing rapidly over a brightly illuminated surface (usually glass or acrylic) upon which various types of diatoms, green microalgae, cyanobacteria, and other algae quickly grow. A brush connected to a windshield wiper-like armature swipes across the surface at intervals during the photoperiod, thus suspending numerous algal cells in the water. This system requires little in the way of maintenance and the growth of algae on the surface is so rapid that it is capable of supplying a significant amount of food to the aquarium. Since we have no experience with this method, we cannot comment on how long the mechanical components will continue to operate.

A more natural approach, which essentially mimics the same effect, is to culture the microalgae on the surfaces of seagrass blades in an attached refugium that has a tidal system. At intervals, the refugium is exposed to extreme water flow that strips the microalgae off the grass blades, kicking it into the water column along with detritus. The suspended matter is then allowed to flow into the display tank as a source of food to filter feeders. A variation on this method could incorporate plastic seagrass blades instead of live ones, illuminated as in the algal film reactor, and positioned in a brightly illuminated chamber that is periodically flushed with a strong flow of water to blow off the attached microalgal cells. Such a system eliminates the need for a mechanical armature brush. See chapter 7 for a description of simple tidal system designs that could be used to build such a reactor.

Refugia and other algal filters

The use of refugia (described in detail in chapter 6) in which populations of algae are cultivated provides a type of phytoplankton to the aquarium. As the algae grow, they release gametes or other reproductive spores into the water. The same is true of algal turf filters in which various algae species are grown on screens and periodically harvested. The algal spores and gametes furthermore contribute to increases in the populations of various types of zooplankton that feed on them. *Mud system* refugia, such as Leng Sy's Ecosystem method also described in chapter 6, seem to promote the development of plankton, as demonstrated by the polyp extension in corals maintained with these refugia attached. However, it is also possible that the polyp expansion is due not to plankton but to some other food source, such as DOC.

Spray-dried phytoplankton

Various types of spray-dried phytoplankton (e.g. Algamac™ and PhytoPlan®) can be used as a food for filter feeding invertebrates. The spray drying process does change the nutritional value of the algae, and the size of the particles, due to clumping, may not be as ideal as live phytoplankton for raising invertebrate larvae (Toonen, 1999). However, there is still a value to using these products as a food for invertebrates, as a food to enhance the nutritional value of live zooplankton cultures, and as a supplement to enhance the nutritional value of dried, frozen, or prepared fish foods. Several commercial products are available, made from *Spirulina*, *Schizochytrium, Hematococcus*, and other species.

Preserved phytoplankton

It is possible to preserve suspensions of phytoplankton and maintain them for extended periods (months) in a refrigerator. Some varieties may even be frozen for longer storage, while in other varieties freezing breaks the cell walls. Less concentrated suspensions may be preserved and maintained in a sealed container at room temperature for extended periods (months). In addition to live phytoplankton feeds, the commercially available preserved varieties, when used with a dosing system, can be used to provide a continuous supply of food to the filter feeding invertebrates that need it.

Yeast preparations

Yeast cells are eaten by many filter-feeding invertebrates and can be used as an alternative to phytoplankton. They are easily cultured, and commercially available invertebrate foods that contain yeast cells and extracts are available. Yeast extracts are known to have the additional benefit of stimulating a physiological immune response and thus boosting immunity to disease, in fishes and invertebrates in aquaculture. Different types of yeast have different nutritional profiles. There is even a type of yeast that has been cultured for production of astaxanthin pigment; an important colouring compound used in fish feeds.

Amino acids

Dissolved amino acids, the *building blocks* of proteins, can be eaten by filter feeding invertebrates that trap the substances in mucous *molecular nets*. The amino acids are able to pass through the tissues directly into the organisms without the need to pass through an oral opening.

Corals continuously secrete an organic matrix composed largely of the amino acid aspartic acid, and this matrix serves as a framework upon which the calcium carbonate skeleton is deposited. It has not been demonstrated whether additions of this amino acid alone stimulates growth better than simply adding protein rich food to the aquarium. Ambariyanto and Hoegh-Guldberg (1999) discuss the feeding on dissolved free amino acids by the giant clam *Tridacna maxima*. They show that natural seawater concentrations of dissolved free amino acids (DFAA) could supply only up to 1% of the nutritional requirements for *T. maxima*, but they point out that *T. maxima* does effectively trap and utilize them. Furthermore, fish grazing that produces cell rupture and spillage of cytoplasm can produce local pulses of DFAA much more concentrated than the background oceanic concentrations. This is especially true in closed system aquariums, where this food source is no doubt widely available and utilized. Several aquarium industry companies now offer mixtures of dissolved amino acids as a food for reef aquariums. These products should be refrigerated, and one must remember that feeding heavily has the potential to elevate the nitrate level in the aquarium. However, with the proper use of biological denitrification, one can safely feed large quantities of such liquid foods.

Marine *snow*

A large portion of the *stuff* drifting in the sea is particulate organic matter agglomerated by the action of water currents and waves, forming a substance known as marine *snow*. It is mainly composed of carbohydrates but it attracts other living creatures such as zooplankton that land on it or phytoplankton that adhere to it and raft along in the currents. Though it is of low nutritional value, the additional creatures it carries make it more nutritious and it is an extremely abundant food source on reefs. Various particle sizes of this material literally rain down constantly on

Particulate organic matter rains down on the reef, providing an important source of food, boosting productivity, and helping to cycle nutrients. See our description of how this process works, in chapter 6. J. Sprung

reefs and other benthic communities. They are consumed directly by some invertebrates, including sponges, corals, protists, copepods, worms, and other animals. Marine *snow* is also a rich source of carbon for bacteria in bottom substrata. It therefore stimulates productivity at the base of the food web, and results in greater production of planktonic eggs and larvae from the benthos. A commercial product, MarineSnow[®], from Two Little Fishies, Inc. (http://www.twolittlefishies.com) consists of dissolved and micro-particulate organic substances (algal extracts) that agglomerate in seawater, and several types of preserved phytoplankton and zooplankton.

Microencapsulated feeds *Golden Pearls*
Brine Shrimp Direct (http://www.brineshrimpdirect.com) produces several size ranges of a larval diet called *Golden Pearls* that was initially designed as a replacement for live *Artemia* nauplii in marine fish hatcheries in Europe. A patented processing technique (agglomeration of micro-encapsulated particles) results in feed particle *clusters* that resemble raspberries under the microscope. *Golden Pearls* have tiny air pockets that keep the feed particles in the water column, not on the bottom of the tank. *Golden Pearls* are available in seven particle sizes: 5-50 microns, 50-100 microns, 100-200 microns 200-300 microns, 300-500 microns, 500-800 microns and 800-1000 microns.

Golden Pearls were developed to be a highly nutritious feed for larval fishes, so they are nutritionally dense, like pellet feeds. They are an excellent food for filter feeding marine invertebrates, but because of their concentrated nature, should be target fed rather than just dumped into the water column.

Target feeding of filter feeders

There are two ways that one can feed the filter feeders, either fill the water column with their food or administer a concentrated pulse of food directly over them, something called *target* feeding. The best way to feed them is to add a small amount of the liquid to the tank to stimulate polyp expansion, and then use a baster to *target* feed the coral with a dense cloud of particles. Afterwards some remaining food can be distributed in the water current to feed other filter feeders.

There is always a certain level of plankton available in the water on wild reefs, with increases in the evening, as we noted previously. Corals that feed on phytoplankton may do so for several hours of the day and night. For some corals such as *Dendronephthya*, it may be important to maintain a certain

A battery filler, as suggested by Terry Siegel for target feeding invertebrates. It lasts much longer than a turkey baster, and has a larger bulb. J. Sprung

Pellet food can be target fed to large polyped stony corals. J. Sprung

concentration of phytoplankton in the water as opposed to the irregular pulses that occur when fed once or twice a day. The number of cells per liter maintained in the aquarium may be more important than the total number of cells added at each feeding. Simply placing a high dosage into the tank once or twice a day may not provide enough nutrition in the long run, because it may clog the corals' feeding apparatus or get advected into the subsrata before it can be consumed by the corals. A constant drip of phytoplankton or other food source of nutritionally low value may be a better option. At this time, this hypothesis has not been tested in a closed system. See *The Reef Aquarium*, volume two for a more detailed discussion on feeding non-photosynthetic corals.

Bryozoans such as this encrusting form remain a challenge to maintain in captivity. J. Sprung

Feeding challenges

Our discussion of foods and feeding concentrates on the maintenance of corals and reef aquariums for growing corals. Many other filter feeders, such as certain sponges, feather duster worms, and certain clams also thrive with these food preparations. There are, however, some reef dwelling organisms that do not usually thrive in typical reef aquariums specifically because their food is not easily provided, or not provided in sufficient quantity. We briefly discuss these problems here.

Bryozoans

Coral reefs feature a great diversity of bryozoans, the so-called moss animals, which bear some resemblance to corals. They are commonly introduced with live rock, but rarely grow or develop new colonies in aquariums. Most species slowly die over a period of weeks or months. The principle reason for failure with bryozoans is their dietary needs. Some species can easily be grown in aquariums with daily inputs of food of the right size and type. They feed on diatoms, protozoans, and small species of zooplankton. In the absence of a controlled daily dosage of such foods for them, most species will fail to survive in a small reef aquarium. We have heard some reports of an encrusting bryozoan reproducing and growing in large systems at coral culture facilities, but have not witnessed it firsthand. It remains possible that in a large system with refugia and sand beds, the production of food could be sufficient for a type of bryozoan to thrive, but it would be exceptional.

Sponges

A large number of species of sponges thrive in reef aquariums, but some species don't. In general, the problem is related to the quantity of dissolved organic matter and phytoplankton that these species feed on, combined with a requirement for moderately strong laminar

Clathrina commonly proliferates in reef aquariums, being introduced with live rock. J. Sprung

Collospongia has symbiotic algae in its tissues, and thrives in brightly illuminated reef aquariums. J. Sprung

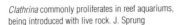

Tethya spp. come in many colours and thrive in aquariums, feeding on dissolved organic matter and bacteria. J. Sprung

This *Higginsia* sp. commonly harvested from hardbottom reefs in Florida does not usually thrive in aquariums. It normally begins losing tissue after about 4 to 6 months in captivity. It probably requires large volumes of phytoplankton, bacteriaplankton, and dissolved organic matter. J. Sprung

This *Axinella* sp. from Florida requires strong currents and a large quantity of food to survive. It is a challenge to maintain, and not recommended unless heavy feeding is planned. J. Sprung

currents. Some aquarium authors believe that silicate limitation is the cause of failure with some sponges (see for example Holmes-Farley (2003). While it seems like a logical idea, based on the use of silicate to form the skeletal material in some sponges, we think the main limiting factor is the quantity of dissolved organic food or live phytoplankton. Adding silicate as a supplement does not improve success rates with the sponge varieties that normally don't thrive in captivity. However, if the food source could be supplied to promote active growth by sponges, some would become silicate limited, and silicate additions would become necessary.

Additions of a specific food organism may not ultimately be necessary with these difficult sponges. All sponges feed on dissolved organic matter. It may be possible to feed DOC heavily to promote both sponge growth and blooms of bacteria that sponges also feed on.

Didemnum molle, which harbours photosynthetic symbionts, is common on Western Pacific reefs, but has not been collected or cultured for aquariums. J. Sprung

Not all *Didemnum* spp. have symbionts. This one would make a stunning addition to a reef aquarium, if it could be maintained with an appropriate source of food. J.C. Delbeek

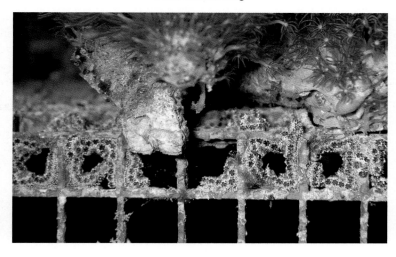

This small transparent yellow tunicate commonly proliferates in shaded areas behind rocks and in sumps of reef aquariums. J. Sprung

Some tunicates thrive in captivity. This *Botryllus* sp. is encrusting a large section of the plastic eggcrate support structure in a coral tank filtered by Leng Sy's Ecosystem aquarium® mud filter, at *Exotic Aquariums* in Miami, FL. J. Sprung

Tunicates

There are several types of colonial and solitary tunicates that thrive in reef aquariums, but many types have very short lifespans in captivity, due to insufficient available food of the right size and type. Generally, tunicates feed on dissolved organic matter, phytoplankton, and bacteria. Since DOC and bacteria are often in abundant supply in aquariums, some tunicates thrive in captivity. It is likely that the ones that don't thrive need additional phytoplankton and perhaps an even higher supply of specific dissolved organic substances, specific types of bacteria, or other picoplankton. Tunicates also concentrate certain trace elements such as vanadium, and these may be a requirement as well, though it is believed that its function is to deter predation.

Some genera of tunicate harbour green symbiotic algae such as the prochlorophyte *Prochloron* and the procyanophyte *Synechocystis*

Nephtheis is a stunning blue colonial tunicate often confused with nephtheid soft corals. It has boom and bust survival in captivity, possibly related to food availability. J. Sprung

Nephtheis is often infested with a predatory flatworm that feeds on it. J. Sprung

(Colin and Arneson, 1995). Whether these algae act like zooxanthellae and provide a significant portion of the nutrition requirements for the tunicate or are merely using the tunicate as a host, is not clear. Though it might actually thrive in reef aquariums, to our knowledge, no one has cultivated *Didemnum molle*, a photosynthetic tunicate.

Crinoids

Crinoids, a.k.a. feather stars, are conspicuous inhabitants of western Pacific reefs where they perch up high on the tips of reef projections, including the edges of large seafans, to capture plankton in the flow of water at such positions. Some species hide in the recesses of the reef during the day and only emerge to feed at night, when zooplankton also emerge from the reef in large numbers, and potential predators are scarce. A few species, mainly of the latter variety have been maintained successfully in aquariums (Yates, 1998), but the majority of them slowly disintegrate as they starve. Deepwater stalked crinoids have been successfully kept in captivity for long periods, however. The surviving ones apparently get enough to eat, while the rest, including the exquisite large yellow, red, orange, or black ones, are more specialized in their dietary requirements.

Crinoids are active feeders. Their tube feet secrete a sticky mucous that traps passing plankton and passes it to a ciliated groove in the arm, which transports the food to the mouth in the central disc. These grooves are very narrow; therefore, only small, weakly swimming plankton species can be trapped and carried to the mouth. For example, Rutman and Fishelson (1969) found that while brine shrimp naupilli could be trapped by the mucous nets, they could easily break free again. They found that the diets of the crinoids they studied were dominated by heavy, weakly swimming forms such as the semi-benthic diatom *Cocsinodiscus*, whereas the more active pelagic forms such as *Chaetoceros*, while abundant in the plankton, were rarely found to be a part of the diet.

Rutman and Fishelson (1969) examined the diets of 350 specimens of three nocturnal species of crinoids from the Red Sea. They found that nearly 85% of the diet was composed of prey items less than 300 microns in size. The average diet contained 10% phytoplankton, 50% ciliated protozoans, and 40% crustaceans and molluscs by number. Rutman and Fishelson found that the three species they studied fed predominantly on zooplankton (9:1 ratio of zooplankton to phytoplankton) where as others studying crinoids in the Caribbean found them to feed predominantly on phytoplankton.

There are differences between night active and day active, as well as crevice dwelling, gorgonian associated and reef crest perching species with respect to the way they orient their arms to the current. Species that live in strong currents tend to form a fan shape with the grooves in the arms facing downstream. Those species that feed in still waters tend to hold the arms in a radial circle around the mouth (Rutman and Fishleson, 1969). There are also differences in the length and spacing of the tube feet on each arm; those with shorter more numerous tube feet feed in strong currents while those with larger, fewer tube feet feed in slower moving waters and within crevices and caves (Meyer, 1979).

It remains a challenge to develop a suitable diet and feeding regimen for crinoids in captivity since it is clear that different species, which occupy different ecological niches on the reef, have different dietary requirements. We are hopeful that providing species specific food particles of the right size on a continuous basis is the solution to the

The tube feet along the arms of a crinoid exude a mucous net for trapping food particles, a fragment of which can be seen in the upper portion of this image. J.C. Delbeek

Night-feeding crinoids such as this one sometimes survive for long periods in reef aquariums. J. Sprung

problem. The key to this is the proper identification of crinoid species and their ecological niche, something most hobbyists are unable to provide. Until someone solves this problem, we recommend that collectors leave these delicate creatures in their natural habitat.

Stylaster and *Distichopora* spp.

These coral-like hydroids are occasionally harvested for reef aquariums, but unfortunately do not presently grow, reproduce, or survive under normal reef aquarium husbandry conditions. All hydrocorals have calcium carbonate skeletons with numerous tiny pores, from which emerge two types of polyps, the dactylozooids, which serve a defensive function, and the gastrozooids, which feed.

It appears that the missing factor is quantity of food, but that is not known definitively. These hydrocorals live in areas with swift

A closed system culture method for *Stylaster* and *Distichopora* has not yet been devised. J. Sprung

The common sea apple *Pseudocolochirus*. J. Sprung

currents and surge, and are believed to trap zooplankton exclusively. It would seem a simple matter to feed them, provide strong currents, and maintain calcium and alkalinity levels, but so far, no one has demonstrated a long-term successful cultivation technique utilizing typical crustacean planktonic organisms. It may be that they feed on protozoans or some other special component of the zooplankton found on reefs.

Sea apples

The filter-feeding sea cucumbers of the genus *Pseudocholochirus* are not suitable inhabitants of the average reef aquarium because they are potentially toxic to fishes. However, since they are among the most bizarrely beautiful creatures, and are possible to keep, a display of them without fishes is possible and worth attempting. Their main diet consists of dissolved and particulate organic matter and phytoplankton, in large quantities. Toonen (2003b) suggests that phytoplankton is their main food, but our experience with them contradicts this. We have seen them take and ingest particulate foods of many types, and even have observed them consuming algal filaments. It could be argued that not all that they stuff into their mouth is digested, but we believe they are more generalized in their diet than is widely believed. We recommend that the diet should include not only a large amount of phytoplankton, but also dissolved organic materials and a liquefied slurry of powder-sized feed. Pulverized flake food or other fine material can also be fed to them. They must have the feeding tentacles expanded to feed, and they feed best in a moderately strong current. If they don't get enough to eat the tentacles degenerate and the body size shrinks. To successfully keep them requires several daily additions of suitable food. Target feeding them by dosing food upstream of the feeding crown is possible, though the tentacles are sensitive and likely to withdraw if touched or overly disturbed.

Scallops such as the coral boring *Pedum spondyloideum*, have proven very difficult to keep long term in captivity. J.C. Delbeek

The flame scallop, *Lima scabra* seldom survives more than 6 to 8 months in captivity. It requires substantially more food than is typically offered. J. Sprung

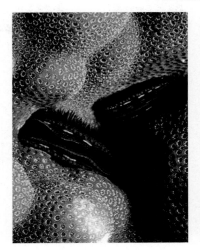 

Scallops and other difficult clams

Some species of clam thrive in aquariums, while others slowly starve. The difference probably relates to the latter's dependence on phytoplankton and or very small zooplankton as a source of food. Toonen (2002) discusses the matter. It may someday be possible to grow such species as the thorny oysters (*Spondylus* spp.) or flame scallops (*Lima* spp.), but at present members of these genera live only a few months to a year in the average reef tank, exhibiting much slower growth than in nature. High and/or frequent dosages of live or preserved phytoplankton is likely the solution to the problem, but there may be a need for the cultivation of protozoans i.e. marine infusoria, as an additional food source.

Refugia for feeding delicate organisms

At least some of the just mentioned feeding challenges could be addressed by housing the specimen in a small refugium aquarium connected with the plumbing of a larger display aquarium. The principle advantage of this technique is that the main display aquarium provides the filtration, maintenance of water quality, gas exchange, temperature maintenance, etc., while the small volume of the refugium provides the opportunity to dose high density of food without the need to pollute a larger volume of water. The water flow in the refugium is also easily adjusted to suit the particular creature, and it can be shut off or increased to meet the feeding requirements. Using such refugia would expedite the discovery of suitable feeding regimens that can be scaled up for larger displays. It is also possible that this technique will be the only practical one for the captive husbandry of certain creatures.

Maintenance, Husbandry and Disease Issues

Maintaining the health of a reef aquarium might seem like a chore to the uninitiated observer. Many people think an aquarium is complicated to maintain (clean, balance, etc). Since a reef aquarium is the ultimate aquarium, it seems logical that it could be an even bigger burden to maintain. In fact, a properly established reef aquarium may not need any attention at all on a day-to-day basis. With automated systems in place for evaporated water top-off and feeding, the maintenance can be reduced to a few weekly and monthly activities. Of course, such a hands-off approach may go against the true wishes of some aquarists. Some of us like to get our hands wet occasionally.

Keeping a log

One very helpful practice for all aquarium maintenance tasks is to keep a maintenance log. A log should be the first thing you start, even before you build your aquarium system. A log allows you to keep records of every step you make in the design and construction of your system, and every stage after that. While it might not seem like fun to have to be so organized, it offers a valuable insight into the possible causes of some of the changes that occur in the aquarium. A log may simply be a bound notebook, ruled or not. You can also print up sheets with places for the recording of water quality tests, observations, disease outbreaks and treatments, new additions, deaths, water change schedules, feeding, trace element addition, probe cleaning and calibration, and other maintenance routines that occur on a regular schedule. For those more computer oriented, there are tank maintenance log programs available for home computers as well as for Palm and PocketPC organizers.

An inside job: sometimes you really need to get into your cleaning! Here J. Charles Delbeek cleans the acrylic window of the 20,900 L (5,500 gallon) Barrier Reef exhibit at the Waikiki Aquarium using a soft hand mitt. F. Seneca

Computers for automation of maintenance and operating systems

With the advent of microprocessors that are smaller and more capable than ever, it was only a matter of time before their application to marine aquariums became commonplace. Today there are several options for automating functions of the aquarium as well as for monitoring aquarium parameters. Many of these products were originally developed for the aquaculture industry, where automation allows for increased production, labour savings and increased security. Others, such as programmable lighting systems are used in industry, homes and retail establishments.

Bill Hoffman shows a page from a maintenance logbook used for the Smithsonian coral reef exhibit in Ft. Pierce, FL. J. Sprung

Integrated controllers

There are minicomputers available today that we like to refer to as integrated controllers. These systems combine a number of functions into one device such as pump, lighting, temperature, pH and ORP controllers, as well as probes and readouts to monitor temperature, pH and ORP. In some cases the equipment all plug into the device, in others, they use satellites that plug into common electrical lines, into which the equipment is plugged e.g. a chiller, lights, water pumps etc.

X10 controllers

There are also satellite controllers available called X10 units. These are plugged into an electrical outlet and are controlled by a home computer or integrated controller. Aquarium equipment such as pumps, lights, whatever you can think of, are then plugged into these X10 units and can be switched on and off using a program on the computer. X10 satellite controllers can be used with power strips, but they don't work with surge suppressors, or when there is line noise. They also won't work when the X10 and the instrument they control are out of phase.

Automatic top-off

Topping off evaporated water automatically is a labor saving arrangement, provided it is set up with a reliable system. Many designs exist (see chapter 4), and some of them can result in costly errors that can kill the inhabitants of the aquarium and cause serious structural damage to your home. It is wise to design safety features that can prevent disasters, such as limiting the size of the dosing reservoir, limiting dosing intervals with timers, or using redundant sensing switches. It should be a part of your daily or weekly routine to observe the condition of the automated systems.

Integrated controllers such as the *Octopus*™ 3000 unit by *AquaDyne*™, can control pumps, lighting and monitor water chemistry parameters.
J.C. Delbeek

The *IKS AquaStar* controller is another popular choice for automated systems. J. Sprung

Tunze offers controllers for pumps and lighting.
J. Sprung

Dosing kalkwasser

Preparing fresh kalkwasser may involve a daily routine or biweekly at least, depending on the dosing method, the degree of automation, and the evaporation rate. As we described in chapter 5, the standard practice of mixing up a batch of supersaturated kalkwasser with excess powder has the potential to supply an overdose to an aquarium if the dosing pump remains on for too long. The result is the rapid death of all fishes, and possible injury to some invertebrates. To avoid this error, be sure to connect the dosing pump to a timer that turns it on for short intervals of fifteen or 30 minutes maximum, and then turns it off for one hour before dosing again. An alternative is to connect the dosing pump to a pH controller so that the controller will shut off the pump if the pH rises above a predetermined set point.

Maintaining calcium reactors

One of the nice features of calcium reactors is that they generally do not require daily maintenance. However, they do require some routine maintenance, and should be observed daily if possible. Sometimes the flow rate of CO_2 changes, requiring a slight turn of the valve on the CO_2 regulator. Such tweaking may or may not be necessary once a week. The aquarist should look at the flow of bubbles daily. The long-term maintenance for calcium reactors involves replacement of the consumed CO_2 and calcareous media. Depending on the size of the CO_2 cylinder and the size of the aquarium, the cylinder may need to be re-filled as often as once per month. Most home aquariums use a 10 lb. cylinder. If you choose a larger cylinder, it may only need to be refilled as infrequently as twice per year. One thing the aquarist should realize is that when CO_2 becomes compressed into a cylinder, the pressure actually turns it into a liquid. When connected to an outlet, the CO_2 is slowly released as the liquid changes to a gas. For this reason, the pressure gauge on a CO_2 cylinder will not show a change in pressure for some time. When the liquid is almost gone, the cylinder pressure will drop rapidly and it will empty in a few days. This last bit of CO_2 will also be rapidly released, causing an increase in CO_2 being injected into the calcium reactor, and lowering the pH. For this reason, when a drop in CO_2 cylinder pressure is first noted, you should install a replacement cylinder as quickly as possible. However, if a pH controller and magnetic valve are used to control CO_2 injection into the reactor, it will shut off the CO_2 supply, avoiding a sudden influx of CO_2 into the aquarium. The easiest arrangement is to have two CO_2 cylinders, so that you can quickly swap out the exhausted cylinder.

The effluent of the reactor should also be monitored daily. In some designs, the return lines are narrow or contain valves that can easily become blocked by fines coming from the reactor, bacterial slime and/or algae growth. These should be disassembled and cleaned at least once a month.

The replacement frequency for the calcareous media is variable, depending on the design of the reactor and the type of media used. Theoretically, most of the media should dissolve. In reality, the media may need to be replaced before it all dissolves due to it breaking down into a fine powder that clogs the flow through the reactor. Some reactor/media combinations may periodically need to be shut down and backwashed to flush out fines and restore uniform flow through the media. Another problem is that as the amount of media in the reactor decreases, the amount of injected CO_2 that is used also decreases, resulting in more unused CO_2 exiting the reactor, further decreasing the effluent pH. For this reason, most calcium reactor manufacturers recommend replacing all of the media when the media level in the cylinder drops below the halfway point.

Fluidized reactor designs, and reactors that use large size media, have the potential to require less maintenance of the media and utilize the media more efficiently. In any case, you will probably need to shut down the reactor to rinse and refill the media chamber with additional media about every six months. See chapter 5 for more information about the design and operation of calcium reactors.

Lighting maintenance

Cleaning light reflectors

Open topped aquariums with turbulent water motion sometimes have splashing of the water that may leave salt spray on the lamp fixture and reflector. This interferes with the reflectance and can cause corrosion of the material. It is a good idea to inspect reflectors once per week after the lights have gone off and they have cooled, and to wipe off any accumulated salt spray using a soft cloth dampened with freshwater. Of course, the best solution is to use a fixture that has a filter glass separating the lamp from the aquarium. This avoids saltwater getting onto not only the reflector but also the lamp itself. In our opinion, aquarists who do not use a protective filter glass between their lamps and the aquarium are asking for trouble.

Cleaning cover and filter glass

The cover glass over the aquarium or the filter glass on the aquarium light fixture(s) may also get salt spray buildup, and they should also be wiped clean once per week. The filter glass on the aquarium light fixture must be cool before one should attempt to clean it. A razor blade is most effective at removing baked-on salt and mineral deposits, and a damp cloth can be used to wipe clean any film that remains. Aquarium cover glass panes also develop algae films that must be scraped off, something that is easily accomplished with a blade or even an old credit card.

Salt on the lamps

Because fluorescent lamps are located so close to the water, splash results in the deposition of salt on the lamps. While this doesn't harm fluorescent lamps, it reduces the light entering the tank dramatically. A removable sheet of acrylic to protect the lamps from splash will reduce some of the light intensity (by about 15%), but makes maintenance easier; it is a simple matter to wipe the sheet down about once per week with a damp cloth. If you must wipe the lamps down, turn them off first and let them cool down.

Salt on an exposed metal halide lamp will become etched into the glass by the intense heat of the lamp. A splash of water on a hot metal halide lamp can even shatter the glass envelope. Therefore, metal halide lamps should have a cover glass to prevent splash or salt spray from reaching them.

Fluorescent fixtures

The maintenance practices we have mentioned also apply to fluorescent fixtures. In addition, fluorescent lamps rely on the contact of external pins to metal strips within the fixture to operate. For this reason, water resistant or waterproof endcap systems have been developed to isolate the pins and contacts from moisture. In fixtures that don't employ water resistant endcaps, the corrosive environment of a saltwater aquarium can corrode these metal surfaces to the point where an electrical connection becomes difficult to maintain. Every six months or so, such a fixture should be unplugged from the power source and the electrical contacts should be lightly rubbed with fine sand paper to remove any corrosion or oxidation, to insure good electrical contact. When endcaps are used on V.H.O. bulbs, however, the materials used to make them may break down over a long period due to the heat produced by these lamps. Inspect the condition of the plastic and gasket when changing the bulbs.

Lamp replacement

Our eyes are extremely poor judges of light. When looking at an aquarium day after day, it is very difficult to notice a gradual loss of intensity and change in spectrum over the course of a year. It is not until new lamps are added that you often hear, *Wow, the tank sure looks brighter*! Not only do our eyes perceive this increased brightness but the inhabitants of the tank do too. Sudden increases in brightness should be avoided because the corals can become *light shocked*, which can lead to *bleaching*, retracted polyps and/or excess mucus production (see chapter 8). For this reason, lamps need to be replaced at regular intervals to minimize the difference in light intensity when they are replaced. To decrease the chance of light shocking corals here are a few simple rules you should follow:

1) Do not replace all the lamps at once. Schedule replacements so there are at least a few weeks between each replacement. For example, if you have more than one metal halide, replace them at least a month apart. If you use combinations of fluorescent and metal halide, change the fluorescents first one month, and then change the metal halides beginning the next month.

2) After changing the most intense lights, raise the light fixture to decrease the level of light reaching the water surface. Gradually lower the lights to their original position over the course of several weeks. The use of shading material over the tank can also serve this purpose.

3) If possible, increase water motion within the tank to help the corals deal with excess oxygen free-radicals generated by photosynthesis as a result of the increased light levels. (See chapter 7, pages 405-406).

A difference in intensity is clearly visible between these two compact fluorescent lamps. The right one has been in operation for 7 months, the one on the left, 2 days. J.C. Delbeek

It is impossible to recommend a general rule for when all types of lamps should be replaced, due to differences among the large variety of lamps and ballasts on the market. Different lamps behave differently with different ballasts, showing greater efficiency and less drop-off in intensity depending on the lamp/ballast combination. Fortunately, there is a wealth of information available on the Internet that provides the important detail regarding light measurements over time of various lamp/ballast combinations. American hobbyist Sanjay Joshi has provided a website where most of these comparisons can be found and we recommend hobbyists search there for the particular lamps and ballast combination they would like information on (http://www.reeflightinginfo.arvixe.com). Unfortunately, the majority of the work on Sanjay's site involves metal halide lamps and not fluorescents.

There are a couple of strategies that can be employed when deciding when to replace lamps. The most common is to measure the light production of the lamp when first installed and then monthly after that until the lamp reduces in output by 30 or 40% at which point it is then replaced. For some lamps this can occur after only six months, for others it can take up to a year.

Replacing a lamp, every six to ten months, can be expensive, however, many lamps only show an initial drop-off in intensity over the first six months then tend to maintain intensity for quite some time after that. If how much the lamp will fall off in intensity after a certain period is known, some have suggested that buying a higher wattage version of the lamp may be more cost effective in the end. For example, in the first few months, the light fixture is raised so that the intensity at the water's surface matches the lower wattage version. Then, as the intensity of the lamp drops, the fixture is lowered in order to maintain the intensity at the water surface. The lamp is then stable in intensity and can be left in place for several more months. In this way, the lamp may not need replacing for a year or more.

The advent of electronic ballasts has increased the useful life for both fluorescent and metal halide lamps. New technologies in fluorescent lighting (e.g. T5, T6, T8 and compact fluorescent lamps, solid state ballasts) have also yielded significant improvements not only in intensity but also in spectrum stability and the useful life of the lamps.

Metal halide lamps tend to lose intensity more in the blue end of the spectrum than in the yellows and reds. Therefore, high Kelvin lamps dominated by blue light tend to look whiter as they age but also lose intensity (Joshi and Morgan, 2002). As a result, those lamps with high Kelvin values containing large amounts of blue, need to be replaced the most frequently, namely every six to eight months. Lamps with a broader spectrum (e.g. 10,000 Kelvin metal halides) may need replacement every ten to twelve months. The same general rule may also apply to fluorescent lamps.

Tank maintenance

Salt spray on the edges of the tank

Any splash of water from the aquarium leads to the buildup of salt around the aquarium perimeter. This salt can grow into substantial accumulations. If left alone, this salt creep can break off and fall back into the aquarium, landing on delicate marinelife and causing great harm.

The easiest way to remove salt creep is to use a wet/dry shop vacuum. After the major crystals have been sucked away, one can use a damp sponge to wipe the surfaces, being careful not to push any salt back into the tank.

Cleaning algae off the viewing windows

Depending on the illumination level that reaches the glass and the level of nutrients (phosphate, nitrogenous waste, organic substances) in the water, and the calcium and alkalinity, various types of algae rapidly or slowly grow on the viewing windows.

The rapid (in a few hours) coating on the viewing windows by light green or brown films of algae is a sign that the tank either has a) a high concentration of plant nutrients or b) become biologically disturbed. In the latter case, the bacteria that compete for nitrogenous plant nutrients have been set back temporarily, for example, as occur when an aquarium has been dismantled, moved, and re-established. In the former case, the concentration of dissolved phosphate is often the culprit, or there is an insufficient amount of substrate (sand, gravel, rock) for bacteria to develop populations that compete with algae for ammonia.

The installation of a thick sand or gravel bed and subsequent development of a live filter there strongly reduces the rate at which algae will grow on the viewing windows. The installation of a ferric hydroxide reactor also can also curb the growth of algae, if the problem was phosphate. See chapter 6 for more information on controlling algal growth. Despite having the nutrients controlled by these methods, it is still common for the glass to become coated by diatoms within a few days, especially in brightly illuminated aquariums. The addition of *Astraea* or *Trochus* spp. snails at a concentration of 1 per 8 L (2 gallons) to the aquarium can dramatically change the course of window cleaning required. Within a day or two the snails (if placed so that they crawl up on the windows) will eat all the diatom films and leave the viewing windows clean. A number of them will remain on the windows and maintain this clean appearance. They will also graze other types of algae off the glass, but do not prevent coralline algae and small hard green spots from growing. In home aquariums, the hard algae spots will need to be removed about once per month to maintain a clear view. Public aquariums must have the clearest view on a daily basis, so they have a daily routine of cleaning.

Tools for cleaning the viewing windows

When films of algae or coralline crusts obstruct the aquarium windows, several types of cleaning devices can be employed to clear the view, we will mention just a few here. Whatever material or method you decide to use, test it first in an inconspicuous area of the tank to make sure it does not harm the tank window. This is especially important with acrylic aquariums, since, by their softer nature, they are much more prone to scratching than glass aquariums are.

When cleaning a window, it is advised to start at the top and then, working side to side, move gradually lower using overlapping strokes until you reach the surface of the substrate. Avoid using vertical strokes as these can pick up particles from the substrate and scratch the window on the upward stroke.

Credit and hotel key cards

An old credit or hotel key card can be used like a blade to clean algal films from viewing windows. Though made of soft plastic, a credit card may still scratch acrylic surfaces so caution must be exercised. Cutting a 45-degree angled slot into the end of a short piece of

Waikiki Aquarium student aquarist, François Seneca, uses an acrylic safe cleaning pad on the end of pole to clean the window of this large coral exhibit.
J.C. Delbeek

narrow diameter PVC pipe will allow for the insertion of a credit card, this can then be used to remove spots from large windows or areas that are not easily accessed. Old cards do not work as well as new cards since their edges have often become too rounded. Considering the risk of identity theft be sure not to use a card with a valid number, or else you might find your fish ordering their own food, or worse, one-way air tickets back to the South Pacific.

Cleaning mitts

There are several soft cleaning mitts available commercially that are ideal for cleaning both acrylic and glass surfaces. The drawback to these is that one must reach into the aquarium to clean the windows with the mitt on your hand. One option is to fasten these mitts over a stiff pad attached to a short pole and use this to reach down into the tank.

Magnetic algae scrapers

Most aquarists utilize magnetic algae scrapers for weekly cleaning of the windows. There are numerous designs, all based on the system of having a magnet inside the aquarium and one outside, so that the aquarist can move the inner magnet simply by moving the one on the outside. Powerful magnets are available for aquariums with thick windows, and floating magnets, such as the *Mag-Float®*, eliminate the problem of having to retrieve a magnet that falls from the window to the bottom of the aquarium. One has to be very careful not to pick up grains of sand that would scratch the window if located between the magnets. Check also the surface of magnet that will be on the outside, since grit here will also scratch the outer surface. Magnetic cleaners are most appropriate for glass tanks. Special acrylic-safe designs can be used with acrylic aquariums, with extra caution!

A magnetic algae scraper with rubber wheels and a soft plastic edge for cleaning a curved acrylic window. J. Sprung

A magnetic algae scraper with blades helps to remove coralline algae from glass. A second magnet can be added to the outside to provide a stronger attraction. J. Sprung

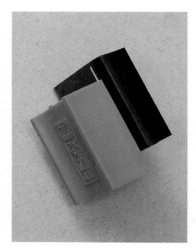

CAUTION: LARGE MAGNETIC CLEANERS ARE VERY POWERFUL AND YOU CAN EASILY CRUSH A FINGER IF IT BECOMES CAUGHT BETWEEN TWO SUCH MAGNETS. ALWAYS FOLLOW THE MANUFACTURER'S RECOMMENDATIONS FOR THEIR PROPER USE.

Razor cleaner

The use of metal razor blades to clean the viewing window is an option for glass aquariums only, since the blade would scratch an acrylic window. Even glass can be scratched by a blade, so it must be used with care. The blade must be new and without oxidation or nicks in the edge that could scratch the glass when pushed against it. Single edge safety blades are best used for cleaning aquariums.

CAUTION: Razor blades are very sharp; always use caution when using them and keep out of reach of children.

There are now commercially available plastic *razor* blades, that are much safer to use and can work well for the removal of hard spots. For large aquariums, one can also create larger plastic scrapers by cutting a small piece of 1/4 inch acrylic at a 45-degree angle creating a sharp edge. When placed on the end of a length of PVC pipe, an effective scrapper for removing tough spots from glass can be created. Placing an algae cleaning mitt over the end allows the same blade to be used on acrylic windows.

Sponge
One can use a sponge to wipe algae off the viewing window, but several caveats must be mentioned. The sponge must not have soap, fragrance, or anti-bacterial substances soaked into it. It also should not have a hard fibrous surface (used for scrubbing pots), as that will scratch glass, and certainly will scratch acrylic. Finally, any sponge can pick up grains of sand, and these will scratch a viewing window. Sponge will degrade over time and small pieces can break off and enter filters or block overflows.

Removing scratches
No matter how careful one is, scratches can and do happen in aquariums, the best you can do is to minimize how frequently they occur. For glass aquariums, there is unfortunately no easy way to remove scratches, but then they are much more difficult to scratch using normal cleaning implements. Acrylic aquariums, on the other hand, scratch much more easily due the softer nature of acrylic, but the scratches can be easily removed. Since acrylic is softer than glass, it can be easily sanded. To remove scratches from acrylic an abrasive is used to remove a thin layer of acrylic until the deepest portion of the scratch is reached. The deeper the scratch, the stronger the abrasive needs to be.

Multi-step abrasive polishes can be used to remove light scratches on the external surface of an acrylic tank. J.C. Delbeek

For external scratches that are not too deep, abrasive solutions are used that are simply applied using a soft cloth. By applying pressure as you rub across the scratch, the acrylic is gradually sanded away until the scratch is no longer visible. This is followed by a milder abrasive to remove any fine scratches caused by the first abrasive, and this is then followed by a final polish.

For deeper scratches, there are scratch removal kits available that contain various grades of abrasive cloth. By first determining the severity of the scratch, an appropriate starting abrasive grit size is selected. The cloth is wrapped around a stiff foam pad, and while kept moist, the cloth is rubbed across the scratch until it disappears. Then the next, slightly less abrasive cloth with finer grit is used and the area is rubbed in the opposite direction. This continues until the finest grit cloth has been used, and then abrasive solutions are used until the final polish is done.

A scratch removal kit for acrylic can be used above or below water. J.C. Delbeek

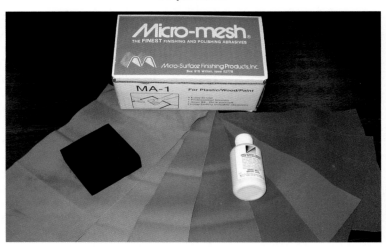

Abrasive cloth kits can also be used underwater so that internal scratches can be removed without having to drain the tank. However, the abrasive solutions are not used (for obvious reasons) and are not necessary anyway since the water will fill in the fine scratches left by the finest abrasive cloth and will not be visible.

As you can probably tell, this is a long and tedious process, but very effective. To best avoid having to go through this, be extra careful when adding or removing rocks and corals, make sure the aquascape is stable, do not rest rocks against the windows of the tank, be sure not to trap sand particles between the cleaning implement and the window, and check all cleaning implements for grit before and after using them.

Finally, keep in mind that each time you polish out a scratch in acrylic, you are removing a layer of acrylic and reducing its thickness. Therefore, although any scratch can be sanded away, deep scratches may require so much acrylic to be removed, that the window in that area may become too thin and may fail. At the very least, a distortion will be visible. In this case, you have to either live with the scratch or replace the window/tank.

Water changes

The principal reason for changing water in the old days of marine aquarium keeping was to reduce the accumulation of nitrate and refractory organic substances, and to maintain adequate pH. Natural biological processes that occur in an aquarium ecosystem such as a reef aquarium with live rock and live sand substrates, prevent the accumulation of nitrate and limit the drop in pH and accumulation of organic material. The use of protein skimming and activated carbon further remove organic substances from the water. Additions of calcium and alkalinity prevent the loss of these essential substances and help buffer the pH. With all of the *old* problems solved, it is not surprising that some aquarists have tried maintaining aquaria without water changes. Yes, it is possible to maintain a healthy aquarium for extended periods (years) without water changes, but the value of this practice appears to be more a sense of dogmatic mental satisfaction than anything else. To recommend eliminating water changes, especially to beginners who are less able to distinguish a situation that dictates the need for water change, is irresponsible, in our opinion.

We recommend that the aquarist find a comfortable water change routine and follow it. For reef aquariums, we believe the less you *get your hands in there* when things are doing well, the better. From this you can draw the conclusion that we don't recommend frequent water changes (i.e. daily or weekly ones as some aquarists perform). We recommend monthly changes of 10 to 25% of the water, all the while keeping up with the make-up water to replace evaporation, and the additions of calcium and trace supplements. When performing a water change, one can use the opportunity to siphon out detritus from between the rocks or from the sump.

Larger water changes can be performed in the event of an emergency, but for general maintenance, a change of 10 to 25% is all that is necessary and less disturbing to the aquarium. Don't forget that some saltwater is also removed by protein skimming, so the tendency over time is for the aquarium to become less salty (due to freshwater evaporation top off). A little salt mix added to the make-up reservoir on occasion can make up for the loss. The use of two-part calcium and alkalinity supplements also may effectively make up for the salt lost to protein skimmate.

Large water changes can leave some of the marinelife temporarily exposed to the air, simulating low tide on the reef flat. Though generally this is not harmful, some organisms may actually tear apart from their own sagging weight, or retain air bubbles that can cause tissue damage. Smaller water changes avoid this problem. If your sump has a volume 10 to 15% or more of the tank volume, then water changes can be performed by shutting off the pump(s) returning water to the display tank, and changing all of the sump water.

There is a way to perform a large water change without exposing the organisms to the air. Roger Bull of Tucson Arizona explained to us the technique he uses when he makes a large water change. He prepares seawater to a temperature about 2 °C (5 °F) cooler than the tank. With the circulation pumps in the display aquarium turned off, the new water is pumped into the aquarium slowly at the bottom, where it stays because it is denser than the warmer, old water. The old water at the surface flows over the surface-skimming overflow and into the sump. The sump water is simultaneously pumped out to a drain.

Trace element addition

Replenishment of the ionic forms of certain elements is required to maintain an environment ideal for the growth and reproduction of marinelife. Many organisms utilize specific elements for the formation of their tissues and skeletons, and for biological processes. In so doing they alter the composition of the water in a closed system. Chapter 4 covers this subject in detail. There are different schools of thought regarding trace element supplementation. Some aquarists add supplements; others don't, believing that feeding and water change, in addition to the use of a calcium reactor can be an effective trace element management scheme. For those who add supplements, this maintenance routine involves the weekly addition of a small volume of one or more commercially prepared or homemade liquid supplements. The sophisticated few have the supplements added by a dosing system. Until accurate means of testing for trace elements become available, trace element additions will remain a controversial topic.

Siphoning detritus

The monthly water change affords an opportunity to perform another maintenance task: siphoning of detritus. This task is not a regular routine for all styles of reef aquariums. Aquariums without sumps generally have detritus removal done less frequently, for example. Aquariums with sumps should have detritus accumulations removed with water changes. This maintenance procedure prevents the development of hydrogen sulfide pockets under piles of detritus that settle in the sump.

Cleaning mechanical filters

Mechanical filtration (see chapter 6) is not a feature of typical home reef aquariums, but some larger reef aquariums employ filter socks continuously or periodically to remove detritus from the water column. When these are used, they should be rinsed daily to prevent the biological decomposition of the trapped material. Sand filter systems that are used for mechanical filtration on large fish aquarium displays are sometimes employed on large public aquarium reef displays. These should be backwashed at least once per week to remove the accumulated detritus and to keep backpressures low.

Plumbing maintenance

The inside surfaces of the plumbing used in a reef aquarium will develop coatings of bacteria, sponges, calcareous tubeworms, vermetid snail tubes, and other life over time. These growths reduce

A build-up of biofilm inside the plumbing reduces the flow. J. Sprung

the flow through the plumbing, and they may block the intake screens of pumps. It is useful to periodically remove sections of plumbing for cleaning. In chapter 3, we described the use of union fittings that allow sections of plumbing to be removed for cleaning. We recommend performing this kind of maintenance at least once every two years or more frequently for circulation lines that carry water high in nutrients, are clear and exposed to light, or carry natural seawater.

Pump maintenance

Just as the maintenance of plumbing is important, the pumps used to circulate the water must occasionally be taken off line, opened and cleaned. Depending on the type of pump and its importance in the maintenance of the circulation in the aquarium, this maintenance chore should be done quarterly, semi-annually, or annually. As we mentioned regarding circulation lines, some pump applications may also require more frequent cleaning to maintain their performance. e.g. pumps used to pump natural seawater.

Cleaning pump openings

The intake and outflow ports on a pump can develop coatings of biofilm, and this can be brushed off when the pump is serviced. Left there it reduces the flow slightly. If an intake screen is used, be sure to check this frequently (weekly) to insure that water can always flow freely into the pump. Strainer baskets should be checked monthly and cleaned as needed.

Cleaning impellers, shafts, magnets, fans and housings

The impeller on a water pump becomes coated by carbohydrate material and bacteria biofilms. When servicing the pump, this slimy brownish substance can be brushed off the impeller with an old toothbrush. It is not critical to do this, since the pump will continue to run, but it makes a substantial difference on pump performance. The housing that holds the impeller will also develop a coating of biofilm and encrusting calcareous marinelife, and it should also be brushed clean at least once per year, preferably every six months. The magnet and the chamber where it rotates may develop a coating of bacterial biofilm as well. This can also be brushed off easily.

A more serious problem usually affects impeller magnets in reef aquariums. The heat generated by the pump's coil, the magnetic field, and the maintenance of high calcium and alkalinity levels in reef aquariums creates an ideal situation for the precipitation of calcium and magnesium carbonate. The impeller magnet, the ceramic shaft it sits on and on the walls of the chamber where it rotates can all become coated. This precipitation reduces the pump's efficiency, reduces the flow rate, and can cause the pump to stop pumping. It may be possible to affect this problem with magnetic devices inline with the pump, but that is something not fully explored at the time of this writing. For now, it is a required maintenance routine to remove the impeller and soak it in an acidic solution to dissolve away the calcium and magnesium carbonate. Simple white vinegar works fine for this purpose, but may take time (hours) to fully dissolve the material. The downtime for the pump can be resolved by having two impellers, so that there is always a clean one available to put the pump back in service. It is also possible to have a spare pump ready to put in service, allowing plenty of time to thoroughly clean and reassemble the alternate pump.

Externally mounted magnetic drive pumps usually have internal cooling fans located at the rear of the housing. In a dusty environment, this fan will accumulate dirt that will affect its ability to cool the housing of the pump. Depending on how quickly this fan

An impeller coated with calcium carbonate. J. Sprung

The submersible pump on the right has developed a thick encrustation of tubeworms that build tubes from calcium carbonate. J. Sprung

Impellers sometimes fail, such as when the magnet separates from its glued ends. In the case of the impeller shown below, a coated magnet made from a material not suitable for saltwater contact fails with long-term use in saltwater. The heat from the motor coil causes the coating to crack. Saltwater creeps inside the coating, the magnet corrodes and expands, further breaking the coating and eventually making the impeller stop when it no longer turns in its chamber within the pump housing. Avoid coated impellers or be sure to replace them frequently. Saltwater-safe magnets need no coating, but should also be inspected or replaced periodically. J. Sprung

becomes coated with dirt, it should be removed from the housing and cleaned. Some pump brands allow the rear casing to be easily removed for access to the fan, but not all pump designs allow for this.

Lubrication

Certain pump designs contain self-lubricating bearings whereas others require periodic lubrication. Those pumps that require lubrication have two or more access points where machine oil can be added for this purpose. It is best to lubricate such pumps every couple of months. Always follow the manufacturer's recommendation for the type of lubricant to use.

Noisy pumps

Sometimes a pump will suddenly make an unusual amount of noise, like a chirping, whirring, grinding, humming, or hissing. The noise may mean something is clogging the intake and restricting water entry. It could also mean low water level in the sump (in which case the presence of air bubbles spraying out of the pump is a second indicator). A broken impeller blade can make quite a racket, as can the buildup of calcium and magnesium carbonate on the impeller magnet of a magnetic drive pump. Fish gathering to feed at the water outlet in the aquarium immediately following a sudden pump noise is an indication that a fish has managed to get over the overflow, through the plumbing, past the baffles and weirs in the sump and into the pump intake whereupon it was pureed.

Bearings and seals

Split pole or non-synchronous direct drive motors have bearings or bushings that can wear out, and when they do, you'll hear it. The telltale sign of a bearing or bushing problem is increased motor noise and eventually a very loud screeching sound. At the first sign of trouble, the bearings/bushings should be replaced, however, some pump designs do not allow for this so the entire motor must then be replaced. If you wait, the pump may actually seize to a stop, or will fail to restart after it has been shut off.

Direct drive pumps contain seals that prevent water from escaping along the drive shaft. These will eventually fail and need to be replaced. It is best to have several such seals on hand to allow for rapid replacement and repairs.

As we mentioned in chapter 3, given the great deal of time and money that goes into most reef aquarium setups, having a backup main pump or motor available should not be looked on as a luxury, but a necessity.

Cleaning and calibrating probes

Not all reef aquariums use meters and controllers with continuous immersion probes, but those that do use them must have a regular maintenance of the probes to assure accurate readings and proper functioning of pH controlled dosing and calcium reactors, and ozone administration by redox control. The manuals for the controllers provide the proper time intervals and procedures for probe maintenance, calibration, and replacement. In general this is a maintenance concern that requires attention quarterly. Holmes-Farley (2003h and 2004d) provide additional information.

Changing activated carbon and other media

About every two to three months, the activated carbon should be changed to maintain its function of removing water-staining organic compounds. This maintenance chore may be as simple as removing a media bag from a flow-through chamber in the sump, and replacing it with a filled bag of fresh activated carbon. If a chemical reactor is used, replacing the carbon involves disconnecting the reactor, emptying it, and refilling it. That chore is simplified if the reactor is installed with ball valves and unions that allow it to be quickly disconnected without spilling any water.

Cleaning the protein skimmer

Protein skimmers produce stinky brownish or greenish liquid that should be discarded daily or at least biweekly if the skimmer has a collection cup. Some designs incorporate a drain that can be plumbed to a utility sink or floor drain. It is best not to connect such drains until after the skimmer has been in operation for a while. Otherwise, if the skimmer overflows after being adjusted, it could empty the tank of water overnight. Other designs have a larger collection bucket with an air filter on top plumbed to the skimmer's collection cup. These collect the

Skimmate can be the most disgusting looking and smelling material you will ever encounter in the hobby! J.C. Delbeek

skimmate and prevent foul odours from exiting. Some even have floats that rise as the skimmate fills the bucket and eventually block the exit, preventing the bucket from overflowing.

Left to sit at room temperature the skimmate can get a little funky (okay … VERY funky!). Sometimes the collection vessel develops populations of heterotrophic bacteria that lend an earthy smell to the skimmate. That is the ideal situation. Other times the skimmate becomes anaerobic, with a telltale scent of rotten eggs mixed with day old seafood, not the pleasant aroma one wants in the home. There can also be a difference in the appearance of skimmate from different skimmer designs. Some produce a watery tea-coloured skimmate while others produce an almost sludge-like material. Those that produce the sludge-like skimmate will also develop a buildup of the same material on the upper edge of the skimmer column so this must also be cleaned at least every few days.

Aside from disposing of the skimmate, there are other chores involved with protein skimmer maintenance. The inside of the skimmer cup and skimmer column develops biofilms and deposits of carbohydrate or lipid materials. The material on the cup should be brushed off with an old toothbrush under running water in a utility sink. Afterwards it should be wiped dry with a paper towel or soft cloth. The skimmer column should also be brushed and cleaned this way about every six months. Cleaning it in this way will result in a boost in the output of the skimmer. Some commercial skimmers have built-in washdown mechanisms. These are fun to watch or show your neighbours.

Designs that rely on the intake of air through a small opening (e.g. Venturi, aspirator, spray injection skimmers) may suffer from calcium carbonate or salt accumulation where the air enters. This is usually a slow buildup, the indicator of which is a reduction in foam production and a lower density of bubbles in the skimmer column. The easiest way to deal with this is to remove the air injection section and give it a thorough rinsing with freshwater or, in extreme cases, a weak acid solution. This buildup can be avoided by passing some freshwater through the air intake once a week or so. Another method is to place the pump operating the air injection device (or the skimmer if the air injection device receives water from the main skimmer pump) on a timer that shuts it off for a few minutes two or three times a day. This allows water to flood the air injector and wash away any deposits. Downdraft designs can also buildup salt deposits where the air enters the injection columns, especially if valves are used to restrict these openings. If this is a problem in your application then these will also have to be cleaned periodically (once a month or so).

Harvesting algae from a turf filter or algae refugium

The use of algae as part of a filter designed to purify the water necessitates a regular regimen of harvesting the algae to remove from the aquarium the substances the algae has taken out of the water, and to provide room for more algal growth. Algal turf filters have a screen that is periodically (once every two weeks) removed and scraped. This should be done over a utility sink to prevent ruptured algal cell contents from returning into the aquarium. Algal refugium filters usually have *Caulerpa* spp. or *Chaetomorpha*, both of which are easily harvested by hand. Simply reach in and pull out clumps of the plant. A small stainless steel scissors can also be used to trim out sections.

Controlling algae blooms

Fortunately, it is now possible to take steps on a rational basis to correct water quality issues, and add herbivores to the aquarium for limiting the growth of algae (Sprung, 2002). If an algal bloom occurs, check the alkalinity. Old-salt aquarists sometimes get comfortable in their routine of alkalinity and calcium maintenance, but forget that the demands of the aquarium increase with time as the corals grow. This often leads to a gradual decline in alkalinity; which can be enhanced if the calcium reactor is not carefully maintained.

A rise in phosphate and nitrate is another possible factor in algal blooms, with numerous possible sources. The efficiency of the biological filtration occurring in the sand or gravel depends on proper advective flow. The advective flow and efficiency of the biological filter in a sand bed is reduced over time by the buildup of detritus, and this can lead to algal blooms as the algae compete with nitrifying bacteria for ammonium. See our discussion in chapter 6.

A clean sweep- the use of a cleanup crew

Various creatures are employed (without pay) for the purpose of scavenging uneaten food, managing algae, detritus build up, and other maintenance concerns. These creatures have been dubbed the *cleanup crew.*

Herbivores

Herbivorous fishes

Herbivorous fishes have been popular in reef aquariums for several decades. At first, it was believed that these fish could subsist entirely on the growth of algae in the aquarium and did not need to be fed. Fishes that feed on algae are equivalent to cows on land in that they have very long digestive tracts compared to carnivores and spend most of the day constantly grazing on plant matter. Add to this that many of these fish are extremely active and you have a situation where a fish needs to graze on a constant basis in order to receive enough nutrition to maintain their body mass. Unfortunately, the results of minimum feedings were very skinny fish swimming in tanks devoid of algae. With the advent of more efficient and effective reef aquarium filtration methodologies, the fear of polluting the aquarium by adding too much food has all but disappeared from the hobby. This has resulted in much more healthy looking herbivores!

Blennies

Several genera of blennies are specially adapted to scrape algae from hard substrates. Their charming smile and overbite consist of a fleshy upper lip and a broad brush-like upper dentition, which they use to rasp the algae from rocks. They also leave kiss-like marks on the algal film growing on viewing windows. Their main diet seems to be algal films (diatoms and cyanobacteria), but they also consume some soft filamentous algae.

Some of the genera of blenniid algae eaters include *Atrosalarias, Cirripectes, Ecsenius, Entomacrodus, Istiblennius, Ophioblennius, Salarias* and *Scartella*. One species in the genus *Ecsenius* the midas blenny, *E. midas* feeds on zooplankton only and, though one of the most wonderful additions to any aquarium, it does not feed on algae.

Most blennies remain small, with a maximum size of under 15 cm (6 inches), so they are ideal choices for controlling algae in small reef aquaria. In larger reef tanks, several specimens may be housed together, but they may fight due to shortage of their food resource.

The Red-lipped blenny, *Ophioblennius atlanticus* is a ravenous algae eater, and occasional fin nipper. J. Sprung

Ecsenius sp. J.C. Delbeek

Sometimes these herbivores may harm corals or other sessile invertebrates. *Cirripectes, Ecsenius, Ophioblennius,* and *Scartella* are reported to occasionally bite the mantles of tridacnid clams, presumably feeding in part on the zooxanthellae. *Ecsenius* spp. (except *E. midas*) have likewise been observed eating the tissue of stony corals for the same reason. The leopard blenny, *Exallias brevis* feeds only on stony corals, mainly of the genus *Porites* and *Pocillopora*, and thus is unsuitable and should never be collected for aquariums.

Many blennies are omnivores, feeding on animal flesh in addition to algae. Some, however, are strictly herbivorous, and may starve in an aquarium if not offered sufficient algae to graze. They may also occasionally mistake soft corals for algae, nipping at the polyps of *Xenia* or *Briareum* spp. Occasionally blennies can be a bit aggressive, chasing and even nipping at other fishes. For example,

Salarias fasciata are excellent grazers on microalgae and are one of those fish that exudes personality. J.C. Delbeek

Another charming blenny, *Atrosalarias fuscus,* divides its time between grazing algae and watching you. J. Sprung

the red-lipped blenny from Florida and the Caribbean, *Ophioblennius atlanticus,* is a hardy and a very good herbivore, but it can be a fin nipper, especially at feeding time. The rock blenny, *Salarias fasciata* also referred to as jeweled rockskipper, lawnmower blenny, jeweled blenny, or sailfin/algae blenny is a good herbivore but less hardy, and very shy. *Salarias* sometimes refuse to take prepared foods and then starve in aquaria. This is a problem mainly in smaller aquaria where the algae may quickly be stripped away by its feeding. In larger aquaria, a single specimen may be able to get enough to eat whether it takes prepared foods or not.

Tangs and surgeonfishes

The most popular algae eating fishes belong to the family Acanthuridae, commonly known as *tangs* or surgeonfishes. Their popularity is due not only to their ability to eat algae, but also to their colouration and charming personality. However, many tangs are especially prone to parasitic infections, and they require large quantities of food to maintain optimal health. In a small aquarium, they may easily graze all available algae and slowly starve if not fed sufficient supplemental algae.

Furthermore, many acanthurids grow to a large size and require ample swimming room, making tangs unsuitable for very small aquariums. Several acanthurids have also been recorded to live between 30 and 45 years in the wild (Choat and Axe, 1996) and deserve the chance to do so by being kept only in systems large enough to house them comfortably (several 1000 gallons/liters and up). An excellent guide to surgeonfish and rabbitfish species identification, diet and ecology is Dr. John Randall's book *Surgeonfishes of Hawai'i and the World.*

Acanthurus

Tangs in this genus are delicate to acclimate to captivity, and they are prone to infestations with the parasites *Amyloodinium* and *Cryptocaryon*, but once acclimated they are sturdy fish. They graze all kinds of filamentous turf algae. Species such as the clown tang (*Acanthurus lineatus*) and the Red Sea tang (*Acanthurus sohal*) grow to a large size (40 cm (16 inches)) and can be extremely territorial and very aggressive to other surgeonfishes.

Paracanthurus hepatus, the blue, regal, hepatus or hippo tang is also an algae grazer, though in nature it feeds heavily on zooplankton. Nevertheless, it can be an effective grazer for a reef aquarium, and it should be offered dried seaweed to supplement its diet if it has little algae to graze. This tang often does not do well in the aquarium once it reaches adult size. They will often show

One the smaller species of acanthurid reaching only 20 cm (8 inches), *Acanthurus japonicus* is well suited to aquarium life, but does best in systems with plenty of swimming room. This species loves to eat bubble algae (*Ventricaria* and *Valonia* spp.). J.C. Delbeek

aggression towards conspecifics, especially if more than one male is kept in the aquarium. This species in unpredictable in its behaviour towards coral and has been reported to feed on *Sinularia* and other corals (B. Shepherd, pers. comm.). The spines are also venomous.

Ctenochaetus

Members of the genus *Ctenochaetus* have fleshy upper lips with brush-like dentition that they use like the blennies to scrape algae from the substrate. Their feeding behavior is a bit more delicate than the *head-pounding* blennies; *Ctenochaetus* spp. seem to *kiss* the substrate. What they feed on is detritus and algal films, including diatoms, dinoflagellates, and cyanobacteria. Some short filamentous turf algae may also be taken, but *Ctenochaetus* spp. are not as effective at eating filamentous algae as their long-snouted cousins, the *Zebrasoma* sp. tangs. *Ctenochaetus* spp. are rather prone to breaking down with *Amyloodinium*, aka velvet disease, which is actually caused by a parasitic dinoflagellate.

Naso

Members of this genus grow very large. The most popular *Naso* sp. is *Naso lituratus*, with colouring that make it appear to be wearing lipstick and eyeshadow. Due to its large size and need for plenty of swimming room, *Naso lituratus* is suitable only for larger reef aquariums (3800 L/1000 gallons or more). They take all kinds of prepared foods, including meaty foods, but are good grazers of red filamentous algae and brown seaweeds such as *Dictyota* and *Sargassum*. Some specimens may eat bubble algae, *Valonia*, *Ventricaria*, and *Borgesenia* spp. as well as *Bryopsis*, though they don't prefer the taste of these latter four algae and will choose other algae and foods first. To keep *Naso lituratus* healthy be sure to also offer it dried seaweeds, now commonly available from your pet dealer.

Right: An adult chevron tang, *Ctenochaetus hawaiiensis*. J. Sprung

Below, R to L: The yellow tang, *Zebrasoma flavescens*, purple tang, *Z. xanthurum*, and Red Sea Sailfin tang, *Z. desjardinii*. J. Sprung

Zebrasoma

The genus *Zebrasoma* contains the hardiest species in aquariums, such as the popular yellow tang from Hawaii, *Zebrasoma flavescens*, which grows to a small size of only about 20 cm (8 inches), compared to other members of the genus that may grow considerably larger. The sailfin tangs, *Z. veliferum* and *Z. desjardinii*, for example, grow twice as large.

It is possible to keep several specimens of *Zebrasoma* together in larger aquaria if they are introduced at the same time and they have plenty to graze. Otherwise, they will fight. The yellow tang and its relatives are excellent grazers of filamentous algae, *Caulerpa*, *Halimeda*, and other fleshy species. They also accept prepared commercial foods. *Spirulina* flake food and dried seaweeds are useful to keep them fat and healthy when there is not much algae to graze in the aquarium.

Siganus punctatus, above, is a stunningly beautiful rabbitfish. J. Sprung

Siganus virgatus. J. Sprung

Foxface and other rabbitfishes

The rabbitfishes, family Siganidae, are closely related to the surgeonfishes. Members of the genus *Siganus* are very good herbivores useful for controlling filamentous algae and other tough algae that other herbivores won't eat, including bubble algae. Some species grow to large size (about 20 to 50 cm/8 to 20 inches) and are therefore unsuitable for small aquariums. Rabbitfishes are venomous, having poison in their sharp dorsal spines that may inflict a painful wound. One downside to these fishes, particularly *Siganus vulpinus*, is that they may feed on soft corals.

Angelfish

All angelfish feed on algae to some extent, even though they may feed on a variety of invertebrates, including sponges and corals. The pygmy angels, genus *Centropyge*, feed on algae to a much larger

The Hawaiian endemic angelfish, *Centropyge potteri*, feeds on diatoms and microalgae in nature, but will adapt in captivity to a diet of frozen and dried foods. It prefers cooler water than most other tropical pigmy angelfish. J.C. Delbeek

extent than other angelfish genera, and some of them are fairly good herbivores for reef aquariums. The downside of including angelfish in a reef aquarium is the possibility that they will feed on corals or tridacnid clams. Corals of the genera *Cynarina*, *Trachyphyllia*, and *Lobophyllia* are most likely to be targeted by these fish. Other corals are likely to be ignored.

Centropyge spp. angels feed on detritus, diatoms, and cyanobacteria, in addition to small invertebrates found living among the algal filaments. They may take some soft varieties of turf algae, but are not very effective for the control of hair algae. *Genicanthus* spp. angels generally don't graze algae, as they feed in open water on plankton, only taking algal fragments floating in the water.

Amblyogobius

Several members of the genus *Amblyogobius* are good herbivores for a reef aquarium. *Amblyogobius phalaena*, *A. rainfordi*, and *A. hectori* are the most popular and readily available species. These fish have a downwardly turned mouth that they use to suck up sand, detritus and algal filaments. *Amblygobius phalaena* is useful for cleaning sand substrates. All three are effective for controlling filamentous algae, including *Derbesia*. In the absence of filamentous algae, these fish may starve, unless they adapt to taking prepared fish foods.

Invertebrate grazers

The simplest invertebrate grazers are microscopic protozoans. Many ciliates can be seen zipping about if one places a sample of algae under a dissecting microscope. Some of these are herbivores, and they may play a very important role in the presence or absence of some forms of algae in aquariums. One unidentified ciliate is so large

that it can be seen by the unaided eye (at least by those people with good eyes!). It is a dark reddish elongated creature that could easily be mistaken for a small worm. It occurs in large numbers on the aquarium walls, where it appears to feed on diatoms and other microalgae. Its presence is delineated on an algae-coated viewing window by a zone of cleared algae, often in a circular shape. The ciliates are located at the edge of the zone, and they proceed to graze from this front. They must also occur on live rocks and sand and surely play a role in the grazing of microalgae in these areas.

Copepods

Copepods are very small crustaceans, most being smaller than a grain of sand, though larger species exist. They are abundant in aquatic ecosystems and are an important source of food for fish larvae and planktivorous fishes. While many copepods live in the

Amblygobius phalaena is much larger than the other two species we mentioned and will construct burrows in the sand. J.C. Delbeek

The red ciliate under the microscope, seen here with diatoms. J. Sprung

A copepod living on red cyanobacteria. J. Sprung

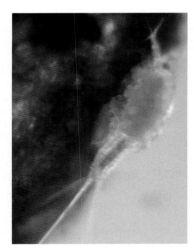

water column, feeding on phytoplankton and particulate organic material, numerous varieties of copepods also live in sediments, and especially in algal turfs and mats. These copepods may feed directly on the algae or on organic material trapped by the algal filaments. Fishes that feed heavily on copepods (e.g. mandarinfish, pipefish) may reduce their populations in a small aquarium, and this can promote the growth of algae.

When a newly imported piece of live rock has sponges and algae on it that have died in transport, the rotting mass often stimulates a prolific bloom of copepods. They swarm over the decaying areas and consume them. When they have consumed all the decaying matter, the population of copepods collapses due to the lack of available food. Many of these copepods are herbivores in addition to their affinity for decaying food. Therefore, it is possible that the

A typical amphipod. J. Sprung

availability of an organic food source that stimulates them to bloom could encourage the development of sufficient copepod populations to have an effect on undesirable algal species. Hoff and Snell (1993) provide details for how to culture copepods. It is possible that select herbivorous copepods could be isolated and cultured to be applied in aquaria as a means of controlling various algae, including cyanobacteria, diatoms, dinoflagellates, and filamentous greens.

Amphipods

Small dorso-ventrally flattened flea-like or shrimp-like creatures that scurry along the substrate are crustaceans known as amphipods (or *pods* on Internet bulletin boards, where the English language is often mutilated beyond recognition). They are among the most important grazers and scavengers in a reef aquarium. Have a look at your aquarium using a flashlight sometime after the lights have gone off. You should see a number of amphipods scurrying on the rocks and gravel. They feed on detritus and algae and make excellent food for seahorses, mandarinfish and pipefish.

Sea slugs

Various sea slugs may be used for the control of algae (Delbeek and Sprung, 1994; Sprung, 2001). The main drawback to using sea slugs for grazing algae in aquariums is the fact that they are readily drawn over surface-skimming overflows and into the suction intake strainers of pumps.

Aplysia spp. are mainly large and unsuitable for aquariums because of their ability to release a violet coloured substance when disturbed. There are some small species of *Aplysia*, however, that may be worthwhile herbivores for the control of a variety of algae, including cyanobacteria and filamentous green and red algae. The related genus *Bursatella* grows to a moderate

A Sea hare, *Aplysia* sp. J. Sprung

Dolabella sp. J. Sprung

Elysia diomedea J. Sprung

size and is a good control for red slime algae (the cyanobacteria, *Ocillatoria* sp.). It may also release a violet coloured substance when disturbed. Another related genus is *Dolabella*, which grows to enormous size. It feeds on a variety of algae, but it may starve in aquaria when the supply of algae runs out.

The lettuce slugs, *Elysia* spp. are the most popular sea slugs for controlling green filamentous algae (*Derbesia* and *Bryopsis*). These slugs incorporate in their tissues chloroplasts from their food source. They need both algae and light to grow. These sea slugs do not actually consume the algae but puncture the cell walls and extract the cellular contents.

Ercolania endophytophaga from the Indo-West Pacific is a recently named sea slug found inside the large cells of the green alga *Struvea plumosa* in Western Australia, and inside the giant cells of *Valonia* on the Great Barrier Reef. It has a single row of dark green cerata down each side of the body. *Ercolania boodleae* and *Ercolania coerulea* are reported to eat *Valonia*.

Ercolania fuscata is a small (8mm) sea slug with a transverse pattern of dark green to black pigmentation arranged in irregular bands. It occurs from Florida, the Gulf of Mexico and the East coast of North America up to Canada. *Ercolania fuscata* feeds on *Cladophora* and *Chaetomorpha*, piercing the cell wall with its radula and sucking out the cell contents. The empty cells become weak points, and the algal filaments then break off under strong water motion. When *E. fuscata* congregate and feed on algae, they cause entire algal mats to break loose.

Other sea slugs may be used for the control of filamentous green algae, *Caliphylla mediterranea* eats *Bryopsis*, as do *Placida dendritica*, *P. kingstoni*, *P. viridis*, and *Limapontia capitata*. *Stilliger* spp. may feed on filamentous green algae and possibly *Valonia* spp. *Cyerce* spp. are also known to feed on filamentous green algae. Jensen (1980, 1997) reviews the diets of sacoglossan sea slugs. She believes the evolution of the slugs' mouth and radula anatomy increased their adaptive radiation to feeding on more varieties of siphonaceous green algae that have different cell wall composition.

Snails, limpets, chitons
Numerous snails are utilized in reef aquariums for controlling the growth of algae. By far the most popular snails are *Turban* snails of the genera *Turbo*, *Astraea*, and *Trochus*. *Trochus* spp. are

being farm raised for the aquarium hobby. These snails are collected or raised in huge numbers for reef aquariums. As a rule of thumb, aquarists use one *Astraea*, *Turbo*, or *Trochus* snail per 10-15 liters (3-5 gallons). Other snails, such as ceriths, nerites, and stomatellids, are harvested incidentally or come as hitchhikers on live rock. Limpets are good herbivores, and some varieties reproduce in aquaria. Larger species have the risk of occasionally feeding on coral tissues (Sprung and Delbeek, 1997; Sprung, 2001).

Strombus alatus, the fighting conch, is now commercially raised for aquariums and distributed by Oceans, Reefs and Aquariums of Ft. Pierce, Florida. This small conch is a superb sand sifter that feeds on detritus and algal films (cyanobacteria and diatoms) on sand and gravel.

Astraea tecta. J. Sprung

Turbo fluctuosus. J. Sprung

Trochus fenestratus. J. Sprung

Nerites (*Nerita* sp.). J. Sprung

Strombus alatus from Oceans Reefs and Aquariums (ORA). T. Smoyer

Queen conch, *Strombus gigas.* J. Sprung

Stomatella varia is a beneficial *hitch-hiker* that normally finds its way into aquariums with live rock or on giant clam shells. It is another herbivore that multiplies. J. Sprung

This conch, *Strombus* sp., is commonly used in Japanese reef aquariums and is an excellent microalgae grazer; its protrusible proboscis allows it to reach between coral branches. J.C. Delbeek

This *Euplica* sp. readily reproduces in aquaria and is a very effective microalgae grazer. J.C. Delbeek

Crabs

Several crabs are useful herbivores. *Mithraculus sculptus*, the emerald crab, is popular for the control of green bubble algae (*Valonia*), and it may sometimes be coaxed to feed on the green filamentous algae *Bryopsis* and *Derbesia*. *Percnon gibbesi*, the sally lightfoot, is a good grazer of filamentous algae. Both are omnivorous and will eat meat, including fishes, given the opportunity. In the case of *Percnon*, which grows to a large size, there is a significant risk for small fishes housed in the same aquarium.

Hermit crabs

Small hermit crabs of the genera *Clibanarius*, *Calcinus*, *Phimochirus*, and *Paguristes* are very good herbivores that feed on cyanobacteria, green and red filamentous algae. They are

Mithraculus sculptus, the emerald crab, is a good herbivore. The male (above) has larger claws than the female, below. Males can control the bubble algae of the genus *Valonia*. J. Sprung

The Sally Lightfoot crab, *Percnon gibbesi* is a beautiful and nimble algea grazer, but like all crabs, poses a risk for small fishes. J. Sprung

The so-called blue-legged hermit crab, *Clibanarius tricolor*, really is red white and blue, hence its specific name. J. Sprung

The Halloween hermit is the yellow knuckled form of *Calcinus elegans*. J. Sprung

The red-legged hermit crab, *Paguristes cadenati* is a popular algae eater from the Caribbean. J. Sprung

The blue knuckled variety of *Calcinus elegans* is among the most strikingly coloured hermit crabs. J. Sprung

particularly useful for controlling filamentous algae in between coral branches, where they can reach with their pincer-like claws. *Clibanarius tricolor*, the blue-legged hermit from seagrass beds, rocky shores and tidepools in Florida and the Caribbean is also good for controlling cyanobacteria mats on sand and gravel. For an aquarium with an algal problem, adding a large number of hermit crabs as a *clean-up crew* can be effective. Once they have grazed down the algae, however, it becomes necessary to reduce the number of hermit crabs so that they don't starve.

These hermit crabs are not exclusively herbivorous. They may attack, kill and eat snails on occasion to obtain not only a bite to eat but also a new and larger shell. Sick or dying tridacnid clams will also be mobbed and consumed by hermit crabs. Nevertheless, under most circumstances these small hermit crabs serve a very useful function in a reef aquarium.

Sea urchins

Many, but not all sea urchins feed on algae. *Diadema* spp., the long-spined urchins are the most useful. The downside to them is that their spines easily (and painfully) puncture the skin, so one has to be careful around them, and they sometimes graze away coral tissue. The small globe or tuxedo urchin, *Mespilia*, is both adorable and useful for algae control. It has the added benefit of remaining small enough to be used in reef aquariums under 76 L (20 gallons). *Echinometra* spp. are commonly known as rock boring urchins and for good reason. They live in depressions they carve in the rock and venture forth at night to feed on algae. These are excellent urchins for algae removal and will remove the holdfasts of *Bryopsis*. Be sure that your corals and rocks are well fastened though, as they can easily dislodge freestanding pieces.

Echinometra mathaei, burrows holes and channels in rock and is probably the most common urchin in the Pacific. J.C. Delbeek

Collector urchins, *Tripneustes gratilla*, are excellent grazers but will remove coralline algae. J. Sprung

Mespilia globulus, the tuxedo urchin. J. Sprung

Diadema setosum, the Pacific long-spined urchin. J. Sprung

The collector urchin, *Tripneustes gratilla*, is another excellent grazer and removes *Bryopsis* once the majority of the plant has been removed. This is a large urchin, reaching up to 12.5 cm (5 inches) in diameter and is best suited for larger aquariums.

Sea urchins can knock rocks or corals over while trying to graze algae, hence their reputation as living *bulldozers. Diadema* and *Mespilia* are not particularly bad in this respect. Sea urchins also consume coralline algae, rasping it from the rock and leaving bare white areas. Under normal conditions (high calcium and alkalinity), the growth rate of coralline algae exceeds the grazing by the urchins.

Sand sifters
The bottom substrate (sand or gravel) needs a *clean-up crew* too. Fortunately, nature and the marinelife trade have joined forces to bring numerous options to your pet supplier.

Fish
One of our favorite fishes falls in this category of sand sifter, the convict blenny *Pholidichthys leucotaenia*. This eel-like fish, which is actually not a blenny, lives in a burrow it makes in the substrate. In addition, it constantly burrows through the substrate, kicking up detritus and preventing it from building up too heavily anywhere. It is thus a perfect creature for maintaining a deep gravel or sand bed in an aquarium without a plenum. The downside to this activity is that corals sitting on the bottom may be buried, and rocks not secured in position may shift due to the shifting of the sand. These things can be prevented with careful rock construction (see chapter 9) and placement of corals.

The convict or engineer goby *Pholidichthys leucotaenia*. J. Sprung

In really large reef aquariums a stingray can be an effective means of turning the surface of the sand. This one is at the Aquarium of the Americas in New Orleans. J. Sprung

Goatfish are also good at stirring up the bottom, as are a number of the small partner or watchman gobies (*Amblyeleotris* spp., *Amblygobius* spp., and *Cryptocentrus* spp.) and *Istigobius* spp. gobies (see Delbeek and Michael, 1993).

Fish of the genus *Valenciennea*, the sleeper gobies, are very good at sifting the upper layer of a sand bed but have the unfortunate habit of carrying a mouthful of sand and sifting it right over your favourite piece of coral! Bottom dwelling corals such as *Sandalolitha* and *Herpolitha* have little problem shedding this material but others such as *Heliofungia* have greater difficulty with coarse sand. Some species of *Valenciennea* such as *V. wardi* are less prone to this as they are more bottom oriented while others such as *V. strigata*, the golden-headed sleeper goby, are much more active swimmers and will deposit their load almost anywhere.

The golden-headed sleeper goby, *Valenciennea strigata*, is a wonderful sand mover, but has the undesirable habit of depositing substrate onto corals. J.C. Delbeek

A pair of *Valenciennea puellaris* working the bottom.
J. Sprung

Recently some of the best sand sifters have been bred in captivity on a commercial scale by the company ProAquatix (www.proaquatix.com). This is a very positive development for the reef aquarium hobby because these fish are now readily available, in excellent health, and feeding on all kinds of prepared foods offered. Wild caught sand sifting gobies often have intestinal worms that cause them to starve in captivity where they may not get as much food to eat as they do in the natural environment.

Tip: These gobies can only sift fine sand, as gravel may injure their gills. The sand should not be powder fine, but coarse, about the size of sugar crystals or a little larger. The most desirable and natural looking material is real coral sand, which is collected from beaches near coral reefs. A few coral fragments or small stones thrown in provide a natural appearance as well as useful building material for fortification of burrows. Pet dealers should be able to obtain coral sand for you from a number of different suppliers.

Scavengers

Sea cucumbers

Certain sea cucumbers that resemble turds (yes, we said that) are desirable for keeping the sand clean. As they move through the sand, they ingest it and digest any algae, detritus and attached bacteria, which provide them with nutrition. Their digestive acids even liberate a tiny amount of calcium to the water. Sea cucumbers are really best at mopping up detritus from between grains of gravel. Species in the genera *Actinopyga* and *Holothuria* work best as sand

The Sea star *Astropecten*, above, is a burrowing scavenger. J. Sprung

This sea cucumber is mopping up sand from the bottom to feed on diatoms, detritus and other nutritious things it contains. J. Sprung

sifters though some are strictly filter feeders. *Holothuria atra* and *H. edulis* are commonly imported from the Pacific as sand sifters.

Beware! Avoid large sea cucumbers (greater than 15 cm/6 inches) and never include a medusa worm (*Synapta* sp. sea cucumber) in your aquarium. *Synapta* sp. are toxic to fish when injured, and large sea cucumbers also can poison an aquarium if they become injured or sucked against a powerhead intake. Small sea cucumbers present no danger. The colourful sea apples (*Pseudocolochirus* sp.) and other species that are just filter feeders, are best maintained by themselves as an exhibit, as they too can be toxic to fish when injured, and their eggs are so poisonous that they are deadly candy for the fish that eat them (see chapter 10).

Sea stars

Sea stars in the genus *Astropecten* are useful for maintenance of fine sand substrates in reef aquariums. They burrow into the sand, and at times, they come out of the sand like little space ships emerging from a cloudy sky.

Serpent stars

Brittle stars, a.k.a. serpent stars are quite useful scavengers that eat fish feces or any missed food particles, and seek out and consume any organism that has died. Several of these should be included, especially in aquariums with gravel or coral fragments on the bottom. We recommend approximately one serpent star per 38 L (10 gallons), though most aquaria can easily house more than this quantity. Serpent stars come in many colours and varieties, and having many different types in the aquarium can be visually dramatic. When food is added, suddenly writhing

Serpent stars come in a variety of colour patterns and are somewhat creepy but fascinating to observe. J. Sprung

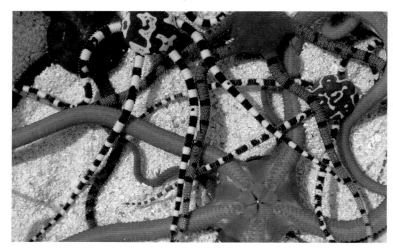

arms of many colours and patterns come out from the rocks. Some brittle stars remain beneath the rocks or between grains of sand and gravel, where they continuously move the substrate in search of edible detritus, sand grains moving along their legs as if on a conveyor belt.

Snails

We already mentioned herbivorous snails, which make up the majority of *clean-up crew* snails utilized in aquariums. Another group of snails used by aquarists includes ones that scavenge the bottom for uneaten food, feces, and dead animals. Some common snails that are commercially available in the hobby include *Nassarius* spp. and its close relatives, the peppermint snail *Hyalina albolineata*, and the bumblebee snail, *Pusiostoma mendicaria*.

Nassarius spp. above and below near right, are superb scavengers that help turn over the surface sand layers as they burrow in search of food. J. Sprung

Far right: Peppermint snails, *Hyalina albolineata*, available from Inland Marine of Terre Haute Indiana, are scavengers that multiply prolifically in large reef aquariums. M. Carl

Worms

Another useful creature is a small, harmless type of bristleworm (about 5 cm/2 inches or less and as thick as spaghetti) that multiplies prolifically in the gravel. It resembles the undesirable *Hermodice carunculata* that grows large and eats coral. The small worms often find their way into the reef tank with live rock and, though they are really benign, aquarists often worry themselves sick over the sight of them because of the generic equation that bristleworm = bad. Unlike their larger cousins, these small worms eat detritus and uneaten food, and thus help to keep the spaces between gravel grains clear. They reproduce rapidly in gravel beds without any assistance from the aquarist. Their population explosion can appear unsightly to some aquarists, and it can be checked by including a pair of banded coral shrimp, *Stenopus hispidus*. Certain fish such as *Pseudochromis springeri* and *P. aldabraensis*, and some of the small wrasses will

A spaghetti worm extending its feeding tentacles across the sand. J.C. Delbeek

also eat these bristleworms and prevent the population from becoming too large, and the commercially available worm traps may also be used to control the population.

Several other types of polychaete worms are introduced with live rock or with *live sand*, if it is available. These multiply in the aquarium both sexually and asexually, and the result is a very *live sand* bed full of worms that actively feed on detritus and prevent the sand from becoming a dirt trap. Terebellid or *spaghetti* worms live in or beneath rocks, or in gravel-lined tubes they construct in the substrate. Their tentacles stretch several centimeters to over one metre in some varieties; such as *Amphitrite* sp. Aquarists often believe the tentacles themselves are long thin worms. The tentacles *crawl* along the rocks and bottom, and trap particulate matter that passes down a thin groove running their length. Periodically the worm will defecate a large pile of detritus that it has collected and ingested. Similar to the terebellid worms are chaetopterid and spionid worms. Like terebellids, they live in rocks, beneath them, and in tubes in the sand, and they have long tentacles that collect particulate detritus. The distinguishing characteristic is that they have only two tentacles, whereas terebellids have many.

Sandy areas in coral lagoons, around seagrass beds, and intertidal mudflats often have another type of substrate dwelling worm that can be beneficial in large reef aquariums with a thick sand bottom. The lugworm, *Arenicola* spp. makes what looks like a small volcano in the sand, with the occasional plume coming out the top. It lives deep in the sand, and has two *openings* to its burrow. The volcano mound opening is the side from which the worm defecates ingested sand, and the pile created rises like a cone with a hole in the center. Water normally enters through this hole, and the worm sends a current toward the exit of its burrow, causing the sand at the surface to cave in like a sinkhole. The sinking sand from the surface is rich in detritus, bacteria, and microalgae (diatoms mainly) on which the worm feeds. When the worm defecates, the current is reversed. These worms literally turn the sand over.

Shrimp, crabs, and other crustacean scavengers

Shrimp

Various types of shrimp can be introduced to a reef aquarium for scavenging uneaten food. They include purely ornamental shrimp, cryptic species that live behind the rocks, and species that may be introduced for other purposes such as fish parasite control or control of a nuisance proliferating invertebrate such as *Aiptasia* anemones or bristle worms. A side benefit of including a shrimp population is that they will frequently breed, and their larvae are *free* live zooplankton that are readily consumed by fishes and invertebrates.

Stenopus spp. shrimp such as the coral banded shrimp and its relatives are mainly added to aquariums for their ornamental value. They also feed on bristle worms, so their presence in an aquarium can keep a booming bristleworm population under control. Generally, it is only feasible to house one specimen per aquarium unless the shrimp are purchased as a mated pair. Otherwise, they will fight until one is killed.

Lysmata spp. have ornamental appeal as well, and they have a side benefit of picking parasites off of fishes. One species in particular, *Lysmata wurdemanni*, is collected and cultured in large quantities to control *Aiptasia* anemones. When a large number of them (approximately one per gallon/3.8 L) is placed in an aquarium with an

Aiptasia infestation, the shrimp actively eat the anemones and can completely control or eliminate them. It is important to note that this size population of shrimp requires a large amount of food once the *Aiptasia* population is consumed. Therefore, it is necessary to remove most of them after they have consumed the *Aiptasia* such that approximately one shrimp per 19 L (5 gallons) remains. It is also critical to note that certain fishes consume *Lysmata* shrimp. For example, the comet or marine betta (*Calloplesiops altivelis* and *C. argus*) will rapidly eliminate these shrimp, so they are not possible to keep together. Some large hawkfish and wrasses are also adept at eating shrimp (as are we!).

Other shrimp such as small *Palaemon* spp. are cryptic and can be included in large numbers for scavenging waste and producing a copious supply of larvae. One or two shrimp per 19 L (5 gallons) is a good population size, and easily maintained.

The Peppermint shrimp, *Lysmata wurdemanni*, is useful for control of *Aiptasia* spp. and *Anemonia manjano*, small anemones that proliferate in reef aquariums, but the application requires a mob approach. Too few shrimp will have little effect. J. Sprung

Shrimp of the genus *Enoplometopus*

The lobster-like shrimp in this genus are generally safe reef inhabitants, scavenging uneaten food and fish wastes. They dig burrows in the sand, which makes them good for keeping the substrate aerated, but it comes with the risk of destabilizing the structure of the reef. Be aware that the rockwork has to be secure and supported by the bottom of the aquarium (not just resting on the sand or gravel) if you will have any burrow builders (see chapter 9).

Pistol shrimp

Alpheus and *Synalpheus* shrimp are good scavengers that actively dig a burrow in the sand. Some species live in a burrow with a partner goby, and this relationship can be a unique feature in an aquarium. Some types of pistol shrimp can harm or kill sleeping fishes, so there is a risk involved with keeping them in a reef aquarium.

Shrimp of the genus *Enoplometopus* are often mistakenly called reef lobsters. J.C. Delbeek

Crabs

A few types of crabs can be utilized as scavengers, though most run the risk of feeding on your prized fishes when they sleep at night; the ornamental arrow crab *Stenorhynchus seticornis* for example. Various crab scavengers enter the aquarium as hitchhikers on live rocks. When they grow large, they can be destructive and are a common cause for fish disappearance, or the death of small tridacnid clams.

Coral harvest/pruning

Eventually, every successful reef keeper has to get in there and chop out coral. Without this periodic activity, the stony corals grow to the surface and shade themselves, causing loss of live tissue on lower branches. The result is a ring of live tissue at the water surface that grows outward from a thick pan of dead limestone. A single micro-atoll in a big reef aquarium can be interesting (you can even make a little island on it), but a whole display like this is not attractive. Letting the corals grow too thickly not only reduces light levels below the branches, it dramatically reduces the water velocity. This reduced water flow affects the efficiency of gas exchange, reduces the efficiency of biological filtration, and promotes disease problems in corals. Soft corals also quickly crowd out other corals, necessitating the use of a large scissors.

It is wise to prune one section at a time, not the whole display, since the corals often give off excess mucus when cut, and you want to minimize this. If you are expecting guests to visit and see your reef aquarium, such pruning should be done at least two weeks beforehand. If you have visitors every week, you may end up waiting too long!

It is time to prune the corals in this tank! This top view was from a section of an aquarium at Vivarium Karlsruhe, Germany. J. Sprung

Also at Vivarium Karlsruhe, this Bali Green Slimer *Acropora* has reached the water surface and is forming microatolls that look like inverted bases. J. Sprung

Bruce Carlson demonstrates a micro-atoll of *Acropora micropthalma,* left, next to a normal-looking bushy colony, right. M. Awai.

Old tank syndrome

There is a widely held belief (based on common observation and experience) that after several years of success with growing corals, a reef aquarium may slowly or suddenly no longer support the healthy coral growth it once did. This general observation has been dubbed *old tank syndrome.* Various authors have attempted to unravel the mystery regarding the cause(s) of this decline in reef aquarium vigor, while others have pointed to reef aquariums that *keep on going and going* like the Eveready™ bunny, as proof that old tank syndrome does not really exist.

Does old tank syndrome really exist? Yes, in our opinion it does, because so many aquarists have experienced it. However, as with other syndromes, the causes are many, so it is not a simple matter

Some of the corals and fishes in Terry Siegel's aquarium have been with him for more than 20 years. J. Sprung

to say that this is just one problem since it isn't. We will examine the factors that are believed to be involved, based on the aquarium literature, and discuss their relevance to what actually happens in reef aquariums.

Slow decline in alkalinity

Beginning reef aquarists may not realize the importance of maintaining high alkalinity levels, but old time aquarists who know better also may get lazy and allow the alkalinity to slowly drift downward. This can lead to a gradual decline in the growth of corals and coralline algae, and an increase in the amount of nuisance algae such as *Derbesia*. When this decline in alkalinity is combined with a rise in phosphate level, an aquarium featuring live corals may shift to an aquarium featuring algae in a short period.

The downward drift in alkalinity occurs because of a few factors. As aquariums age, the corals and coralline algae grow, which results in an increase in the demand for calcium and carbonate alkalinity to deposit calcium carbonate skeletons, as we describe in chapter 5. If the addition of calcium and alkalinity is constant, then the trend will be for both to decline over time as calcifiers increase their mass. Eventually, the demand slows or is tempered, however, since as we just described, the lower sections of corals may die as they become shaded by their own growth.

Detritus accumulation in the substrate

In chapter 6, we outline the way biological filtration occurs in the bottom substrata, and how the advective flow of water is key to the process. With time, bottom substrata collect detritus that impedes the advective flow of water thus reducing the input of oxygen, and as the detritus decomposes, it depletes oxygen from the water within the substrata. These combined effects alter the functioning of the substrata, and may contribute to a long-term decline in the health of a reef aquarium. Despite these facts, we do not mean to imply that the aquarist should strive to eliminate detritus! On the contrary, the conditioning of a healthy aquarium involves a certain amount of detritus accumulation that promotes a healthy diversity of life within the substrata. Later on, this accumulation can become excessive, but in this chapter, we outline ways to prevent this.

Phosphate accumulation

Due to the additions of food, there is a net accumulation of phosphate in the sediment of all aquariums, and an accumulation of phosphate in the water in poorly managed aquariums. The accumulation of phosphate in the sediment is not generally a problem, since it is not very soluble. There is also an accumulation of phosphate on and within live rocks. It is hobby folklore that this long-term phosphate

The Chiton, *Stenoplax* sp., lives in the bottom substrate, attached to the undersides of rocks or to the glass. It feeds on algae and bacteria biofilms. Its movement forms channels within the sand bed, helping to keep it aerated and preventing the loss of porosity that occurs with time. It also cleans the algae off the glass along the bottom edge of the tank. J. Sprung

accumulation ultimately leads to algal blooms requiring the replacement of rocks and sand or gravel after several years. We don't agree with this replacement theory. The use of animals that turnover the sand bed is helpful in keeping it from plugging up with phosphate-rich detritus, and the use of wavemakers and other flow devices to physically force the detritus from the rockwork and sand bed can keep the substrata in a healthy condition.

Heavy metal accumulation

Shimek (2002a,b, 2003) proposes that due to artificial seawater mixes with high metal concentrations, and high inputs of food containing trace metals, our aquariums are like *toxic waste dumps*, and the result is an accumulation of heavy metals in closed systems. He recommends periodic replacement of rocks and sand as a maintenance routine. Sekha (2003) and Harker (2003b, 2004a,b) provide evidence to dispute the toxicity of metals that accumulate, as we explain in chapter 4. It is not known whether accumulation of any metal is related to long-term declines in reef aquarium vigor. If it were, one would expect all reef aquariums to suffer from the same effect after a given period. They don't, possibly due to differences in maintenance regimes, or the hypothesis is incorrect.

Accumulation of allelopathic coral metabolites

Borneman (2001, 2002d) discusses potential effects of various allelopathic metabolic products from hard and soft corals that leach into the water, and provides a list of supporting reference material from the scientific literature. This concept has been visited before (see for example, Wilkens, 1990; Delbeek and Sprung, 1994). While it is true that abundance of soft corals in an aquarium can limit the vigor of stony corals and vice versa, we don't believe that the problem is something that becomes chronically worse as an aquarium ages*. It is merely an issue of the composition of corals in the aquarium, and presents an interesting challenge when planning this composition. Borneman (2001, 2002d) hypothesizes that the effects of this chemical warfare may be the cause of periodic unexplained losses of corals. We do not dispute such an argument since there is so little known about the fate of these compounds in closed system aquariums. Measurements of these compounds at the Great Barrier Reef Marine Park Authority Aquarium (ReefHQ), however, have showed high levels of allelopathic soft coral compounds in their algae scrubber filtered system (K. Michalek-Wagner, pers. comm.). It certainly is possible that allelopathic compounds causing all kinds of problems could be an unpredictable artifact of the closed system environment, but don't let that scare you! The long-term success of reef aquariums of all sizes is evidence that this kind of problem is not the rule. Perhaps the development of bacteria populations and other fauna within the substrata helps to break down these compounds quickly, or protein skimmers, ozone,

*It is possible that a chronic problem could develop as a result of gradual failure of the biological filter within the sand bottom substrate, due to detritus accumulation, as described on the opposite page and in chapter 6 under the topic advection. In addition to the nitrification cycle, biological filtration also manages the accumulation of toxins in the environment. Various bacteria assimilate or decompose many substances that would otherwise produce harmful effects in a closed system. As the sandbed becomes less porous with time due to detritus accumulation, the efficiency of the biological filter is compromised, and allelopathic problems could become enhanced.

or activated carbon keep them in check. Why they might intermittently wreak havoc, if in fact they do, is a mystery. It is certainly possible that as the mass of the soft or stony corals increases with time, it can have a progressively stronger allelopathic effect on other stony or soft corals simply because as the mass increases it is releasing a greater quantity of compounds.

Flow reduction in pumps

The loss of water velocity in the aquarium with time due to the reduced output by the main circulatory pump(s) is universal. It has numerous causes, and is itself a cause for reduced efficiency of biological filtration within substrates (see the physical aspects of biological filtration in chapter 6) not to mention reduced gas exchange.

Greg Schiemer's 500 gallon reef in March of 2002. The *Acropora* colonies are occupying much of the space. G. Schiemer

Greg Schiemer's 500 gallon reef in July of 2003. After a major pruning and donation of corals to Joe Yaiullo's Atlantis Marine World reef (among others), Greg's fish now have more room to swim. Formerly shaded corals can now bask in the light. G. Schiemer

Flow reduction due to growth of corals

Not only do pumps lose output capacity over time, the velocity of water flow in aquariums is further reduced by the growth of corals, whose branches and polyps dampen the flow. In this case, either upsizing the main or circulation pump(s) in the aquarium or pruning coral heads is required. For this reason, creating more open aquascapes is recommended, with less rock and coral, allowing the corals to grow at a more natural density, and allowing for more flow around each colony (see chapter 9).

Light reduction by growth of corals

The coral growth not only blocks water flow, it also reduces the light reaching the substrata. This shading effect alters the rate of photosynthesis, the pH swings, the generation of oxygen, and the consumption of carbon dioxide, among other things. This can result in a decrease in health of shaded corals, as they gradually don't receive sufficient light, especially considering the gradual decrease in lamp light output over time

Water change

Old tank syndrome symptoms can be an effect of insufficient water changes. While it is true that we can manage the accumulation of nitrate and phosphate, remove water staining organic substances, and also maintain calcium and alkalinity without performing a water change, the ionic composition of the water still drifts with time in an aquarium containing so much life. Bingman (1998c; 1999g) discusses this effect, with respect to some major ions, and Fosså and Nilsen (1996) show the changes that occur with some select ions, in aquariums maintained with various water change regimes, including no water change. As we stated earlier in this chapter, we recommend water changes of approximately 10 to 25% monthly.

Disease effects?

Old tank syndrome symptoms may relate to various types of disease. See next section.

Disease

It is an ugly fact, but after you've achieved a perfect understanding of the mechanics, chemical and biological processes involved in building a reef aquarium, there is still the obstacle of disease that can eliminate any chance of having an aquarium you can sit back and enjoy. Contrary to popular belief, diseases are not caused by having imperfect water quality, though it is true that fluctuating parameters may stress fish or invertebrates and thus promote disease. If pathogens are killing your fish and invertebrates, there may be nothing you can test for to show why your multi-thousand dollar high tech aquarium can't keep any fish or corals alive. Furthermore, it is almost impossible, certainly not practical, to completely prevent

In areas with slow flow detritus settles out and can form thick accumulations. Siphoning with water change is a means of exporting it. J. Sprung

the introduction of pathogens in a reef aquarium system. This means that diseases of various sorts will affect the fish or invertebrates in an aquarium at some point. With proper care in the planning of the aquarium, careful quarantine procedures, and excellent maintenance habits, these events can be prevented to a large extent. It is a common boast made by overconfident aquarists that *fish don't get sick in a reef aquarium because it reproduces the natural conditions so closely that the fish have improved immunity against all kinds of disease causing organisms.* While there is a small amount of truth in this statement, it is not true for all kinds of diseases and so must be considered false. Occasionally some kind of disease will affect every aquarium.

Quarantine

Quarantine of fishes is the most significant step than an aquarist can take to prevent disease outbreaks that could ruin a reef aquarium. Despite this fact, the average reef aquarium hobbyist and even some professionals skip quarantine and hope for the best. Despite the persistently repeated myth that *fish don't get sick in a reef aquarium because it is a natural biotope*, the fact is that fish DO get sick in reef aquariums, and the plants and invertebrates in the aquarium severely limit the chemotherapeutic options. We direct readers to several good books about fish diseases, such as Noga (2000), for information about how to treat various fish parasites, bacterial and viral infections, and for information about quarantine procedures.

A simple quarantine procedure involving extended periods at low salinity can be quite effective for the majority of problematic fish parasites. A low salinity quarantine approach can be taken without the use of chemotherapeutic treatment unless an actual infestation is seen. However, early parasitic infections of fish are often not visible since they often occur on the gills first. The ideal level is about 1.010 S.G. (S = 10 to 14) (Tom Frakes, pers. communication). To fully eradicate *Cryptocaryon* the salinity has to be below S=15 (~1.012 S.G.). Three to six weeks is usually a sufficient quarantine period at this salinity level. The acclimation down to this salinity level does not really take long for most scaled fish, and can be accomplished in a matter of hours. Bringing them back up to natural seawater strength, you may want to take a couple days, though many fish will handle faster increases. The low salinity approach may not be good for sharks and some scale-less fishes.

Oxygen and fish health

In chapter 4, we discuss the saturation state of oxygen. In a closed aquarium full of life the oxygen level is strongly influenced by the photosynthesis and respiration of the plants and animals. For this reason, oxygen levels tend to fall below saturation at night when both plants and animals are respiring. The use of reverse daylight photosynthesis in an attached refugium aquarium counters this problem, providing oxygen to the aquarium at night. This is believed to be beneficial to fishes, as the depletion of oxygen at night is a potential stress factor that may weaken their resistance to disease.

Diet and fish health

We discuss foods and feeding in chapter 10. Nutrition is a frequently overlooked factor in the prevention and cure of fish diseases. We tend to think about water quality first for some reason, when diet may be the more significant factor in a disease outbreak. One important element in curing a sick fish is to feed it heavily (provided it is eating), as long as there is sufficient biological filtration to handle the extra food of course!

Use of ultraviolet (UV) sterilizers

Many reef-keeping aquarists avoid using a UV sterilizer because of a concern over potential harm to the bacterial and plankton population in the tank. Aside from a potential to heat the water in a small system, there is no harm from using one, and the reduction in pathogens may be beneficial.

As we discuss in chapter 6, while a UV sterilizer offers some valuable help in the reduction of water-borne pathogens, it cannot be relied on to guarantee that disease problems won't occur or spread.

Use of cleaner shrimp and fishes that pick parasites

On the natural reef, there are cleaning stations where special shrimp or fishes provide the service of removing parasites from fishes that visit. These specialized cleaners eat the parasites and bits of dead tissue. Some of these cleaner fish and shrimp can be housed in an aquarium where they offer the same service. In smaller exhibits, the cleaning fish may be too aggressive in their attempts to pick parasites, and can become a pest to other fishes. They may also not get enough to eat and slowly starve. In large reef exhibits with a large fish population, a cleaner shrimp or fish may have sufficient food and customers to survive and avoid becoming a pest to anyone. These cleaners are particularly useful for controlling parasitic trematodes. Becker and Grutter (2004) found that cleaner shrimp could reduce the presence of monogenetic trematodes on fishes in an aquarium by about 75% within just 48 hours. However, cleaner fish are not immune to all the bugs they eat, and they may become infected by doing their service. Jones *et al.* (2004) found that the cleaner wrasses, *Labroides dimidiatus* and *L. bicolour*, as well as other cleaner fishes often were infected with bucephalid trematodes (Digenea). Most cleaners are ineffective at removing protozoan parasites such as *Cryptocaryon* (ich) due to its smaller size. For this reason, we do not recommend adding these fish if the intent is to deal with a protozoan infection. Cleaner fish are best used for the

The *Ogles™ Mesoscope* is a great new *toy* for the reefkeeper, and a seriously useful instrument for observing and recording the fine details of life in the aquarium, including parasites on corals. J. Sprung See it online at: http://www.sherwoods-photo.com/ogles_mesoscope/ogles_mesoscope.htm

removal of larger parasitic organisms such as trematodes and copepods. However, these types of parasites should be taken care of during a proper quarantine procedure and really should not be present in home aquaria. We do not believe that cleaner fish can carry out their intended ecological roles in the average home aquarium, and are best left on the reef where they can do so.

TIP: Some species of cleaner wrasse are obligate feeders on fish slime and parasites e.g. *Labroides phthirophagus*, the Hawaiian cleaner wrasse. These species do not do well in home aquaria and should only be collected for use in very large exhibits housing many fish of large size.

Stony coral eatin' *varmints*

We discuss various parasites of corals and tridacnid clams, and coral diseases and infections in volumes one and two of *The Reef Aquarium*. In this new volume, we want to discuss a few new *bugs* that have been popping up in aquariums and causing much gnashing of teeth and pulling of hair among reef keepers.

Parasitic crustaceans

Red Acro bugs

Humes (1981) describes a special type of copepod, *Tegastes*, which is associated with acroporid corals. In aquariums, this *bug* has the potential to stress and kill acroporids. *Tegastes* multiplies rapidly on *Acropora* spp., so it can become a problem, especially in coral culture aquariums, and is so tiny that it then is easily overlooked and spread from the coral culture facility to stores, and display aquariums (Shimek, 2002e; Hiller, 2003b). *Tegastes* has come to be called the red Acro *bug* due to its prominent spot of red pigment.

Dustin Dorton of *Oceans, Reefs and Aquariums Inc.*, working with Jeremy Russell at *Coral Reef Aquarium* and several volunteers, reported a treatment on www.reefs.org for eradicating these red acro *bugs*. The red *bug* treatment involves the use of the dog heartworm (nematode) medication called *Interceptor*, which is only available from a veterinarian by prescription. *Interceptor* contains the active ingredient milbemycin oxime. The tablets for large dogs (23-45 kg/51-100 pounds) are just less than 1 gram each and contain 23 mg of milbemycin oxime. There are 6 tablets to a box. Milbemycin oxime is active against nematodes and certain arthropods (for example, mange in dogs). It affects marine arthropods such as shrimp, crabs, isopods, amphipods and, fortunately, the red *bugs* that affect *Acropora* spp. The official information from Novartis about the medication can be found at the following website: http://www.ah.novartis.com/products/en/cab/interceptor.shtml.

Red acro bugs on a piece of *Acropora*. J. Sprung

It is important to accurately calculate the total water volume, and to make sure that every part of the system is treated, including any refugia, the water inside the calcium reactor, and the protein skimmer. Before adding the medication to your tank, turn off the air supply to the protein skimmer, but allow water to continue to run through it. Remove and discard any mechanical filtration and any carbon if present; only add new material when the treatment is completed. Turn off UV sterilizers and ozone generators. Remove any ornamental shrimp or crabs; they will have to be maintained outside of the system for the duration of the treatment. When you add them back to your tank, there is a slight chance that you will re-introduce the *bugs* to your tank. A long quarantine period reduces that possibility.

The dosage used in an aquarium to kill the *bugs* is 25 mg (0.025 grams) of *Interceptor*/38 L (10 gallons) of actual aquarium water volume/6hrs. Note: the dosage is 25 mg of *Interceptor* tablet, not 25 mg of milbemycin oxime. Each tablet treats about 100 L (380 gallons). Use a scale capable of reading down to 0.001 grams, since the dosage is 0.025 grams per 38 L (10 gallons).

The tablets are ground with a mortar and pestle into a fine powder. The medication is dissolved into some aquarium water (it is not easily soluble, you will have to stir for a while) and spread evenly across the surface of the water. The red *bugs* can survive well into the fifth hour of the treatment, and may physically *hang on* to the coral for days even after they are dead.

Your tank should remain perfectly clear and look very normal the entire time. If anything goes wrong during treatment perform a water change immediately and add a large amount of activated carbon to your filtration system.

After six hours, perform a 25% MINIMUM water change and as much activated carbon as you can fit should be added to the filtration. Twenty four hours later, another 25 % water change should be performed and the carbon replaced.

Dustin recommends performing a MINIMUM of three treatments, since we don't know the life cycle of the bug. The goal of the second treatment is to clean up any left over adults, and any juveniles that have hatched out of eggs that might have been unaffected. The third treatment is a *just in case* treatment, its goal is to get any bugs that could have possibly survived the first two. The frequency of the treatments has yet to be fully determined. Some of the volunteers in the testing did the first two treatments seven days apart with the third treatment fourteen days after the second. Some did three treatments seven days apart. Dustin followed a treatment frequency of two treatments 24 hours apart every seven days, for four consecutive weeks, making a total of eight treatments.

Quarantine for red *bugs*

There does not appear to be an effective, quick kill dipping strength for red *bugs*. Even at 100 times the normal dosing strength, the bugs will last over 30 minutes. The best way to keep them from getting into your tank is to treat the coral for a full six hours. An increased dose for such bath treatments seems to be safe for corals. Since we don't know the life cycle of the bugs, nor the resistance of its eggs, a single treatment that kills adults may not prevent eggs from hatching later. Therefore, quarantine may require more than one treatment.

Store the medication at room temperature, in the dark in an airtight container. Do not let it get cold. Dustin found that putting it in the freezer caused it to become ineffective. Of course, KEEP OUT OF REACH OF CHILDREN.

A red *bug* predator?

It has also been proposed that pipefishes may be useful in the control of the red *bug* copepod. The yellow-line or dragonface pipefish, *Corythoichthys flavofasciatus* has been tried with reports of success (T. Vargas, pers. comm.).

Acropora flatworm

In *The Reef Aquarium* volumes one and two we discuss the relatively benign flatworms that commonly bloom in aquariums. The popularity of growing acroporid corals has brought another flatworm into the spotlight, this one not so benign. The *Acropora* flatworm feeds on *Acropora* spp., causing tissue loss and eventual loss of colonies. It lays eggs directly on the coral and quickly develops potentially devastating populations. This coral predator is probably widespread in the Indo Pacific, but is known to be common in the Marshall Islands.

The drug Levamisole, which can be obtained by prescription from a veterinarian, is a useful treatment to kill these flatworms, preferably during quarantine rather than in the display aquarium. A dose of 0.8g/100 L (26 gallons) is recommended (Mitch Carl, pers. comm.) as a dip treatment in a bucket, holding tank, or propagation system lasting up to an hour, followed by large water changes, or removal of the treated coral from the dip treatment tank. This will knock off and kill the adult flatworms, but unfortunately will not harm the eggs. Multiple treatments are needed to effect a complete eradication of this pest, and the timing of these treatments must be right to catch the newly hatched flatworms before they lay any more eggs.

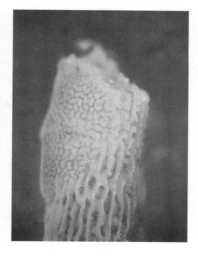

An isolated *Acropora* flatworm photographed in a plastic container. J. Sprung

A living flatworm on *Acropora* is almost invisible! F. Nosratpour

The eggs of the *Acropora* flatworm are deposited directly on the coral. J. Sprung

Levamisole harms some other invertebrates such as bristleworms and serpent stars, but does not harm corals in short dips. After the treatment of a display or propagation system, a series of water changes should be performed, and activated carbon filtration employed to remove the Levamisole. As an alternative to short treatments at high dosage, longer treatments at lower dosages (for example 0.4g/100L for 1 week) have been tried for propagating systems and display tanks, but at this duration some corals react badly, losing coloured pigments and sometimes losing basal tissue (Rob Brynda, pers. comm.). During treatment, increase aeration to insure good gas exchange. A compromise treatment of 0.6g/L for 2 hours, followed by water change and activated carbon use is another possible regimen. The flatworms normally release from the coral rapidly, so it appears that multiple short duration treatments are the better method.

Other remarks about flatworms and Levamisole

Levamisole is also very effective at eradicating the red flatworm (*Convolutriloba retrogemma*) commonly found in large numbers in some aquariums with high detrital loads (see *The Reef Aquarium*, volumes one and two). It kills them within minutes. To lessen the chance for toxin release from a large quantity of red flatworms dying at once, it is best to remove as many of them as possible by siphoning them out before adding the drug to a display tank. While most fish seem to be unaffected by the treatment, *Zebrasoma* sp. tangs may be especially sensitive to it or to the toxin released by dying red flatworms, and they may need to be removed from the aquarium to avoid stressing or killing them (Rob Brynda, pers. comm.). While Levamisole very quickly and reliably kills the red flatworm, treatments for the *Acropora* eating flatworm seem to be less effective with time, suggesting that this flatworm has some ability to develop resistance to the treatment (Rob Brynda, pers.

comm.). Not all *Acropora* species are affected by the flatworm. *Acropora millepora* and *A. valida* are strongly affected, while *A. tenuis*, *A. nobilis*, *A. yongei*, *A. gemmifera*, and *A. loripes* seem to have resistance to them (Rob Brynda, pers. comm.).

Predators

We have also had excellent success using wrasses to eradicate the red flatworm (*Convolutriloba retrogemma*). Wrasses in the genus *Halichoeres*, particularly *H. leucurus* and *H. melanurus*, have proven to be especially effective, greatly reducing red flatworm populations in a 21 m^3 (5500 gallon) reef exhibit and a 3028 L (800 gallon) seagrass/mangrove exhibit at the Waikiki Aquarium. Just one wrasse per tank is all that is needed. It is worth trying species in this genus against *Acropora* flatworms too.

Halichoeres melanurus is an effective predator of the common red flatworns that sometimes bloom in reef aquariums. C. Falkenberg

The juvenile *Halichoeres melanurus*. S. Michael

Headshield slugs of the genus *Chelidonura* are active predators of flatworms such as the red flatworm and the similar disc shaped *Waminoa* sp. that infests *Discosoma* anemones and SPS corals (Sprung and Delbeek, 1997). It is not known whether they eat the *Acropora* flatworm. The lifespan of *Chelidonura* spp. is short and though spawning is common, the larvae don't develop in typical reef aquariums, so it is doubtful that they are a practical control.

Long term puzzling problems with corals

The existence of bacteria that can produce rapid tissue necrosis (RTN) in corals is well known, though not completely understood. More recently, a related phenomenon has been observed by some aquarists, and it is at present not well understood or even widely believed to be a real phenomenon. The effect can be described this way. One or more species of coral in an old reef aquarium suddenly stop growing, after many years of rapid growth. Accompanying the growth cessation there may be reduced polyp extension, and tissue necrosis, slow or rapid. Eventually the species affected become extinct in the aquarium, though other corals in the same aquarium remain healthy and continue growing. After such an event, the aquarium may become *immune* to this one coral species. All subsequent attempts to introduce fragments of the same coral grown from cuttings of the original specimen, but housed now in other aquariums, prove futile, as the coral quickly succumbs and dies. We have no explanation for this problem, but when obvious parasites like red-acro *bugs*, protozoans, and flatworms have been ruled out, we believe such mysterious coral trouble is caused by bacteria. In time, it may affect more than one species of coral, so that the aquarium is unable to house certain species, but is able to house and grow others. While it is tempting to blame such occurrences on toxins and water quality, the use of water changes and even changing all the substrate does not make the problem go away. It really seems as if the aquarium has an *immune* response to the affected coral(s). We have no name for this situation and no recommendation. The antibiotic treatment method we published in *The Reef Aquarium* volume two may help, but so far, no one has studied that possibility.

Pocillopora damicornis suddenly loses tissue, a condition aquarists call rapid tissue necrosis (RTN), which has been shown in this coral to be caused by extracellular proteases released by the bacterium *Vibrio coralliilyticus*, that attacks zooxanthellae. J. Sprung

The recent research into pathogenic bacteria that affect stony corals lends greater credibility to the existence of this kind of phenomenon, and one day it may lead to an explanation for why this problem and similar bacteria-caused diseases sometimes occur in aquaria. For example, Ben Haim *et al.*, (2003) found that bleaching in *Pocillopora damicornis* resulted from an attack on the zooxanthellae by the bacteria *Vibrio coralliilyticus*, whereas bacterium-induced lysis and death of coral tissue are promoted by bacterial extracellular proteases.

Probiotics, predatory bacteria, and bacteria phages

Some hobbyists have been experimenting with adding cultures of non-pathogenic bacteria to their aquarium in an attempt to out compete pathogenic bacteria and reverse RTN. Probiotic application of cultured bacteria for controlling the populations of other bacteria might thus become a maintenance procedure of value for reef aquariums. In another variation of this idea, Stolp and Starr (1963), Shilo (1966), Shilo and Bruff (1965) describe the bacteriolytic effects of the bacterium *Bdellovibrio bacteriovorus*. Aquarium author Frank deGraaf (1968) proposed that this predatory bacterium might control bacterial populations in nature and it might be possible to apply this effect to aquariums to control pathogenic bacteria. We agree that this application may be invaluable in the control of pathogenic bacteria that affect corals and fishes, but it remains to be tried.

While we were going to press with this book we learned of a first-of-its-kind analysis of viruses associated with corals from an aquarium. Wilson *et al.* (2005) observed virus like particles (VLPs) in zooxanthellae and host coral tissue. They noted that tissues from heat shocked corals had abundant VLPs spread throughout the sections, while in controls that were not heat shocked the VLPs were more difficult to find. They have a working hypothesis that temperature shock induces latent viruses in zooxanthellae. Furthermore, the authors note a morphological diversity of VLPs, suggesting that a wide variety of viruses may infect corals and zooxanthellae. These observations may support our hypothesis regarding bacteriaphages, and it may also point to other viral controlled conditions affecting corals in nature and in captivity.

The aforementioned problem with stony corals being attacked as if they were a foreign body (a so-called *immune response*) may be caused by the loss of protective bacteria fauna on the coral surface due to a virus. Bacteriaphages, as such viruses are called, may target specific bacteria fauna normally living on a coral's mucus, resulting in a reduced resistance to other sorts of bacteria that can then invade the *cleaned* space. They may also be directly involved in triggering the virulence of some bacteria. Bacteriaphages are extremely abundant in the ocean. The average milliliter of seawater contains over 50 million of them (Fuhrman, 1999)! No study has been undertaken to look at what happens to them in aquaria.

Plant extracts

Numerous types of plant extracts are being studied for their antibiotic properties. The well known *tea tree oil*, an extract from a type of *Eucalyptus* tree, has been used topically to control skin infections in humans, and is now in widespread use in the pet trade,

This *Blastomussa wellsi* was saved from a rapidly progressing bacterial infection by a 3 minute therapeutic dip in seawater with 5 mL per gallon of Melafix®. J. Sprung

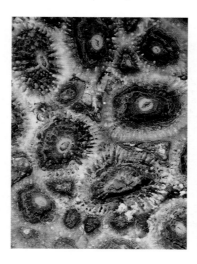
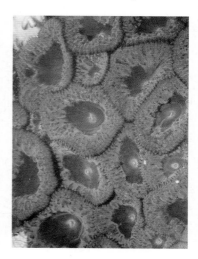

even in an emulsified liquid form for treating infections in fishes (e.g. the product Melafix® from Aquarium Pharmaceuticals). Such extracts have use for short-term therapeutic dips of LPS corals (J. Sprung, pers. obs.), though a benefit to some types of corals does not guarantee that all corals will respond positively. Treatment of whole reef displays with plant extracts is potentially risky. In time a protocol may be developed.

Future disease treatment options

It is well known among *old salt* hobbyists that certain fish always get sick while some others seldom do. Two fish, the flame hawkfish (*Neocirrhites armatus*) and the comet (*Calloplesiops altivelis*) almost never suffer from protozoan parasite infections. On the other hand, various surgeonfishes in the genus *Acanthurus* practically always break out with *Cryptocaryon* (white spot) or *Amyloodinium* (velvet) disease. They have earned the label *ich magnets* among reef keepers. Why should some fish be more susceptible to protozoan infection than others? It is likely that the answer lies in their mucus. The mucus covering the skin of fishes and frogs is known to have antibiotic properties. For example, substances extracted from the mucus of the frog *Xenopus laevis*, Magainin I and II, show antibacterial activity against a range of microbes, including both gram-positive and gram-negative bacteria. They are also effective against fungi and some protozoans. In the future, chemotherapeutic treatment of bacterial and protozoan fish and invertebrate diseases may involve administering to aquaria extracts of the mucus of resistant species.

Fish diseases are a big problem in food fish aquaculture. The high densities of fish cultured in fish farms, make them prime candidates for bacterial, viral and parasitic diseases. The potential for catastrophic, and costly, losses to disease has been the primary motivating factor in the development of fish vaccines for a number of bacterial diseases such as vibriosis and furunculosis, and viral diseases. The future may see the development of vaccines for a number of parasitic fish diseases as well. For example, *Cryptocaryon* is also a problem in aquaculture and there is ongoing research at the University of Hawaii to develop a vaccine against it. See http://www.soest.hawaii.edu/SEAGRANT/communication/kapilikai/Marine%20Ich.htm for a description of the methodology they plan to employ.

Designer corals

In recent years, genetically modified organisms have been the center of controversy in various fields, from agriculture to aquariums. Modified freshwater fishes that glow fluorescent green or orange have appeared in the aquarium trade. It seems likely that coral culture facilities will some day produce corals and anemones for the aquarium trade with pigmentation tailored by genetic manipulation.

The technology to do so already exists. What else could be done? We can imagine, for example, modified corals that don't produce sweeper tentacles and don't sting their neighbors. Other possibilities include an increase in tolerance to high or low temperature, disease resistance, or built-in senescence. Are there risks involved with such creativity? We don't doubt that there might be, and this will certainly be a subject of debate should someone actually produce genetically modified corals.

Currently, there is a trend towards using coloured dyes or food colouring to temporarily stain corals (soft and hard) and anemones. This results in bright yellow, pink, or green animals. Most of these corals have been severely bleached and lost most of their zooxanthellae and other pigments. Although it is possible for corals and anemones to survive this, often they don't, and we urge hobbyists, dealers, and wholesalers not to purchase such animals.

Sinularia dura dyed pink next to normally pigmented specimens of the same species. J. Sprung

While it is possible for some *Turbinaria* spp. to be naturally bright yellow, this *Turbinaria peltata* has been dyed yellow. A normal specimen is expanded, next to it. J. Sprung

What's next? Reef aquarium maintenance in the future

The future of reef aquarium keeping may benefit from the development of some new devices. We thought we'd take the opportunity to speculate about a few ideas here. Some of the developments in the marine aquarium hobby over the past ten years might have been predictable when we wrote *The Reef Aquarium* volume one. We wonder what the future could possibly hold in store for our hobby. From a technological point of view, there are some interesting things to imagine.

Piezoelectric pumps

Low energy consuming piezoelectric systems can be employed to pump water by causing flexible elements within the pump to expand or contract depending upon the direction of the voltage. When an alternating current is applied, one wafer expands then contracts while the other contracts then expands, causing the two elements to bend. As this cycle repeats, it generates a pumping action. Such pumps could be employed in automatic dosing systems for chemicals or live feeds, or as pumps for micro aquariums.

Wire-free electric power

The start-up company *MobileWise*, has developed a solution to the problem of multiple plugs and power supplies. Their technology makes a flat surface that transmits power to small conductive contacts on the bottom of a device. We can envision employing such a system for some electrical devices used around aquariums, thus eliminating some of the cables and plugs used to power all of the electrical devices. The devices would simply sit on the conducting surface or snap into it. The current only flows when recognized devices are in contact with the surface, and it only flows to those contacts, so there is no danger of a short circuit. In addition, the device's power requirements are communicated to the surface by its contacts, and the surface adjusts to the correct power automatically. The aquarium stand itself might incorporate such a system. Of course, the location of the surface would have to be positioned so that water would not be exposed to it, which might corrode the contacts or cause a short where a device is connected.

E-quariums

The proliferation of the World Wide Web has made it possible for computer savvy hobbyists to be able to not only observe their aquariums while traveling using web based cameras but also to control them. This technology, combined with sophisticated software and a little hardware, can be used for such things as click and feed automatic feeders, water quality monitoring (e.g. pH, temperature, ORP), water pump monitoring, click and fill top off systems, and other daily routines. Advances in electronic ballasts allow for their control via computers, which also means they can be controlled via the Internet. Recent advances in cell phone technology now make it possible to control such functions via phone. Combined with automated cell phone calling for emergency alarms and cell phones with picture screens, one need not ever worry about being disconnected from one's aquarium! For aquarium maintenance companies, such technology would allow for monitoring from a central location in much the same way that home alarm systems are monitored.

Bibliography

Achterkamp, A. 1986. De eiwitafschuimer … ja-ne? *Het Zee-Aquarium* 36(3):55-60.

Adams, G. and S. Spotte. 1985. Carbonate mineral filtrants and new surfaces reduce alkalinity in seawater and artificial seawater: preliminary findings. *Aquacultural Engineering* 4:305-311.

Adelberg, E. 1976. *The Microbial World*. Prentice-Hall Inc. New York.

Adey, W.H. 1987. Food production in low nutrient seas. *Bioscience* 37:340-348.

Adey, W.H. and J. Hackney. 1989. Harvest production of coral reef algal turfs. In *The Biology Ecology and Mariculture of Mithrax spinosissimus Utilizing Cultured Algal Turfs*. W. Adey (Ed). Mariculture Institute, Washington D.C.

Adey, W.H. and K. Loveland. 1991. *Dynamic Aquaria, Building Living Ecosystems*. Academic Press, San Diego, CA, USA, 643 pp.
———————————————. 1998. *Dynamic Aquaria, Building Living Ecosystems*. Second Edition, Academic Press, San Diego, CA, USA, 498 Pp.

Aiken, A. 2004. Use of foam fractionation for improving water quality in marine aquaria. PowerPoint presentation, 1st Aquality Symposium, Lisbon, Portugal, http://www.aqualitysymposium.org/abstracts.php.

Aiken, A. and M. Smith. 2004. Safe and effective application of ozone via applied dose, redox, and husbandry techniques. PowerPoint presentation, 1st Aquality Symposium, Lisbon, Portugal, http://www.aqualitysymposium.org/abstracts.php.

Ainsworth, J.A. 1994. A _-glucan inhibitable zymosan receptor on channel catfish neutrophils. *Veterinary Immunology and Immunopathology* 41:141-152.

Aller, R.C. 1988. Benthic fauna and biogeochemical processes in marine sediments: the role of burrow structures. In: Blackburn T.H., Sorensen, J. (eds) *Nitrogen Cycling in Coastal Marine Environments*. Wiley, Chichester, England, pp 301-338.

Ambariyanto and O. Hoegh-Guldberg. 1999. Net Uptake of dissolved free amino acids by the giant clam *Tridacna maxima*: alternative sources of energy and nitrogen. *Coral Reefs* 18:91-96.

Anonymous. 1995. Notes from the lab: Kalkwasser and phosphate. *SeaScope* 12, Winter.

Aquatic EcoSystems. *Tech Talks*, http://www.aquaticeco.com/index.cfm/fuseaction/techtalk.list

Aquatic Ecosystems 2000. *Tech Talks*. Ultraviolet (UV) sterilizers #96. http://www.aquaticeco.com/index.cfm/fuseaction/techtalk.list

Atkins, W.R.G. 1931. Note on the condition of the water in a marine aquarium. *Journal of the Marine Biological Association of the United Kingdom* 17(2):479-481.

Atkinson, M.J., Carlson, B. and G. L. Crow. 1995. Coral growth in high-nutrient, low-pH seawater: a case study of corals cultured at the Waikiki Aquarium, Honolulu, Hawaii. *Coral Reefs* 14(4):215-223.

Atkinson, M.J. and C. Bingman. 1997. Elemental composition of commercial seasalts. *Journal of Aquariculture and Aquatic Sciences* 8:39-43.
————————————and ————————————. 1999. The composition of several synthetic seawater mixes. *Aquarium Frontiers Online*, March 1999. http://www.animalnetwork.com/fish2/aqfm/1999/mar/features/1/default.asp

Atkinson, M.J, Falter, J.L and C.J. Hearn. 2001. Nutrient dynamics in the Biosphere 2 coral reef mesocosm: water velocity controls NH_4 and PO_4 uptake. *Coral Reefs* 20(4):341.

Ayukai, Y. 1991. Standing stock of microzooplankton on coral reefs: a preliminary study. *Journal of Plankton Research* 13:895-899.

Bachelor, B. and A.W. Lawrence. 1978. Stoichiometry of autotrophic denitrification using elemental sulfur. In: A.J. Rubin (Ed.) *Chemistry of Wastewater Technology*. Ann Arbor Science Publishers, Inc., Ann Arbor, Michigan, pp. 421-440.

Bak, R.P.M., Joenje, M., de Jong, I., Lambrechts, D.Y.M. and G. Nieuwland. 1998. Bacterial suspension feeding by coral reef benthic organisms. *Marine Ecology Progress Series* 175:285-288.

Baker, A.C. 2001. Reef corals bleach to survive change. *Nature* 411:765–766.
————————————. 2003. Flexibility and specificity in coral-algal symbiosis: Diversity, ecology and biogeography of *Symbiodinium*. *Annu. Rev. Ecol. Syst.* 34:661-689.
———————————— and R. Rowan. 1997. Diversity of symbiotic dinoflagellates (zooxanthellae) in scleractinian corals of the Caribbean and Eastern Pacific. *Proc. 8th Int. Coral Reef Sym.* 2:1301-6.

Barak, Y., Cytryn, E., Gelfand, I., Krom, M. and J. van Rijn 2003. Phosphorus removal in a marine prototype, recirculating aquaculture system. *Aquaculture* 220:313-316.

Barbeau, K., Rue, E.L., Bruland, K.W. and A. Butler. 2001. Photochemical cycling of iron in the surface ocean mediated by microbial iron(III)-binding ligands. *Nature* 413:409-413.

Barnes, R. D. 1980. Invertebrate Zoology. Saunders College, Philadelphia, USA.

Barnes, D.J. and B.E. Chalker. 1990. Calcification and photosynthesis in reef-building corals and algae. In: Dubinsky, Z. (ed) *Ecosystems of the World* Bd. 25; Coral Reefs; Elsevier, Amsterdam, Oxford, New York, Tokyo, pp. 109-133.

Bartelme, T. 2003. Beta glucan as a biological defense modulator: Helping fish to help themselves. *Advanced Aquarist Online*, September 2003. http://www.advancedaquarist.com/issues/sept2003/feature.htm

Bartosch, S., Wolgast, I., Spieck, E. and E. Bock. 1999. Identification of nitrite-oxidizing bacteria with monoclonal antibodies recognizing the nitrite oxidoreductase. *Applied Environmental Microbiology* 65:4126-4133.

Bassleer, G. 1997. *Diseases in marine aquarium fish: Causes, Development, Symptoms and Treatment*. Bassleer Biofish, Stationsr. 130, B-2235 Westmeerbeek, Belgium.

Becker, J.H. and A.S. Grutter. 2004. Cleaner shrimp do clean. *Coral Reefs* 23:515-520.

Ben-Haim, Y. and E. Rosenberg. 2002. A novel *Vibrio* sp. pathogen of the coral *Pocillopora damicornis*. *Marine Biology* 141:47-55.

Ben-Haim, Y., Zicherman-Keren, M. and E. Rosenberg. 2003. Temperature-regulated bleaching and lysis of the coral *Pocillopora damicornis* by the novel pathogen *Vibrio coralliilyticus*. *Applied Environmental Microbiology* 69(7):4236-4242.

Benson, A.A. 1984. Symbiosis. In: *Reader's Digest Book of the Great Barrier Reef*. Mead and Beckett Publ., Sydney, Australia.

Bibliography

Bingman, C. 1995a. Precipitation of phosphate in limewater and in the aquarium *Aquarium Frontiers, Fall*:6-9.

——————————. 1995b. The effects of activated carbon treatment on the transmission of visible and UV light through aquarium water Part 1: Time-course activated carbon treatment and biological effects. *Aquarium Frontiers* 2(3):4-8.

——————————. 1995c. Editorial. *Aquarium Frontiers*, Fall:26-27.

——————————. 1995d. Green-fluorescent protein: a model for coral host fluorescent proteins? *Aquarium Frontiers Magazine* 2(3):6-9.

——————————. 1996. Biochemistry of Reef Aquariums. Ion pairing, buffer perturbations and phosphate export in marine aquariums. *Aquarium Frontiers Magazine* 3(1):10-17.

——————————. 1997a. Biochemistry in the aquarium: How to mix a batch of synthetic seawater in under five minutes. *Aquarium Frontiers Online*, September 1997. http://www.animalnetwork.com/fish2/aqfm/1997/sep/bio/default.asp

——————————. 1997b. The halogens - Part I: Bromine in seawater and aquaria. *Aquarium Frontiers*, October 1997.

——————————. 1997c. Magnesium ion precipitation in reef aquaria: A tempest in a teapot. *Aquarium Frontiers*, July 1997. http://www.animalnetwork.com/fish2/aqfm/1997/jul/bio/default.asp

——————————. 1997d. Biochemistry in the aquarium. Defining the limits of limewater. *Aquarium Frontiers*, January/February:8-11.

——————————. 1997e. Biochemistry in the aquarium. Large-scale calcium and alkalinity maintenance. *Aquarium Frontiers, March/April*:10-13.

——————————. 1997f. Biochemistry in the aquarium. Repairing calcium and alkalinity Imbalances. *Aquarium Frontiers*, May/June:10-13.

——————————. 1997g. Calcium carbonate for $CaCO_3/CO_2$ reactors: More than meets the eye. *Aquarium Frontiers* August. http://web.archive.org/web/20010210225056/http://www.animalnetwork.com/fish2/aqfm/1997/aug/bio/default.asp

——————————. 1998a. Biochemistry of Aquaria. Reef systems of the future. *Aquarium Frontiers*. May 1998. http://webarchive.org/web/20010210225637/www.animalnetwork.com/fish2/aqfm/1998/may/bio/default.asp

——————————. 1998b. Biochemistry in the aquarium. Calculation of calcium carbonate saturation states in reef aquaria. *Aquarium Frontiers Online*, January 1998. http://www.animalnetwork.com/fish2/aqfm/1998/jan/bio/default.asp

——————————. 1998c. Biochemistry of aquaria. Simulating the effect of calcium chloride and sodium bicarbonate additions on reef systems. *Aquarium Frontiers Online*, December 1998. http://webarchive.org/web/20010210224240/www.animalnetwork.com/fish2/aqfm/1998/dec/bio/default.asp

——————————. 1998d. Biochemistry in the aquarium. Calcification rates in several tropical coral reef aquaria. *Aquarium Frontiers Online*, March 1998. http://webarchive.org/web/20010210224911/www.animalnetwork.com/fish2/aqfm/1998/mar/bio/default.asp

——————————. 1999a. Magnesium — Part I. *Aquarium Frontiers*, March 1999. http://www.animalnetwork.com/fish2/aqfm/1999/mar/bio/default.asp

——————————. 1999b. Magnesium — Part II. *Aquarium Frontiers*, April 1999. http://www.animalnetwork.com/fish2/aqfm/1999/apr/bio/default.asp

——————————. 1999c. A homemade magnesium supplement. *Aquarium Frontiers*, June 1999. http://www.animalnetwork.com/fish2/aqfm/1999/june/bio/default.asp

——————————. 1999d. Limewater, acetic acid and sand clumping. *Aquarium Frontiers Online*. http://web.archive.org/web/20010430202648/http://www.animalnetwork.com/fish/library/articleview2.asp?Section=&RecordNo=181

——————————. 1999e. Expanding the limits of limewater: Adding organic carbon sources. *Aquarium Frontiers Online*, October 1999. http://www.animalnetwork.com/fish2/aqfm/1999/oct/bio/default.asp

——————————. 1999f. Coral fluorescence: An update. *Aquarium Frontiers Online*, November 1999. http://web.archive.org/web/20001215142800/http://www.animalnetwork.com/fish2/aqfm/1999/nov/bio/default.asp

——————————. 1999g. Biochemistry of aquaria. Additional simulations: The combined effect of calcium chloride/sodium bicarbonate additions and water exchanges. *Aquarium Frontiers Online*, February 1999. http://web.archive.org/web/20010210223756/http://www.animalnetwork.com/fish2/aqfm/1999/feb/bio/default.asp

——————————. 2000. Silicon, foe or friend? *Aquarium Frontiers* February 2000. www.animalnetwork.com/fish2/aqfm/2000/feb/features/1/default.asp

——————————. 2001. Misunderstandings in the aquarium literature. A response to calcification Part 2: Are we changing natural processes? (Borneman and Small, 2000). *Aquarium Frontiers Online*. http://www.aquariumfish.com/aquariumfish/detail.aspx?aid=415&cid=124&search=

——————————. 2002. A hydrogen peroxide/UV light reactor. *Marine Fish and Reef USA Annual* 4 (2002):84-95.

Bird, K.T. and J. Jewett-Smith. 1994. Development of a medium and culture system for in vitro propagation of the seagrass *Halophila engelmanii*. *Canadian Journal of Botany* 72:1503-1510.

Bold, Harold C. & Michael J. Wynne. 1985. *Introduction to the Algae*. Prentice-Hall, NJ.

Borneman, E.H. 2000. *Coral Nutrition: Polyps not plants!*. Presentation to Western Marine Conference.

——————————. 2001. *Aquarium Corals: Selection, Husbandry, and Natural History*. Microcosm TFH Professional Series. TFH Publications, Neptune City, NJ, USA. 464 pp.

——————————. 2002a. Coralmania: Reef food. *Reefkeeping Online Magazine*, July 2002. http://www.reefkeeping.com/issues/2002-07/eb/index.htm

——————————. 2002b. Coralmania: The food of reefs. Part 3: Phytoplankton. *Reefkeeping Online Magazine*, October 2002. http://reefkeeping.com/issues/2002-10/eb/index.htm

——————————. 2002c. The Food of Reefs, Part 4: Zooplankton. *Reefkeeping Online Magazine* 1(11). http://reefkeeping.com/issues/2002-12/eb/index.htm

——————————.2002d. The Coral Whisperer. *Goniopora* revisited: If we could keep it alive, do we really want to? High levels of toxicity in *Goniopora* and other hard corals. *Advanced Aquarist Online*, November 2002. http://www.advancedaquarist.com/issues/nov2002/cw.htm

——————————. 2003a. The Food of Reefs, Part 5: Bacteria. *Reefkeeping Online Magazine* 1(12). http://reefkeeping.com/issues/2003-01/eb/index.htm

——————————. 2003b. The Food of Reefs, Part 6: Particulate Organic Matter. *Reefkeeping Online Magazine* 2(2). http://reefkeeping.com/issues/2003-03/eb/index.htm

——————————. 2003c. The Food of Reefs, Part 7: Dissolved Nutrients. *Reefkeeping Online Magazine* 2(3). http://reefkeeping.com/issues/2003-04/eb/index.htm

——————————. 2003d. Mything the point part two. Coralmania. *Reefkeeping Online Magazine*, December 2003, http://reefkeeping.com/issues/2003-12/eb/index.htm

——————————. 2004. The old becomes new yet again: sand beds and vodka, Part II. *Reefkeeping Online Magazine* 3(10). http://reefkeeping.com/issues/2004-11/eb/feature/index.htm

Breder, C.M., Jr. and T.H. Howley. 1931. The chemical control of closed circulating systems of sea water in aquaria for tropical marine fishes. *Zoologica; Scientific Contributions of the New York Zoological Society* 9(11):403-442.

Bronikowski, E.J. Jr. 1982. The collection, transportation, and maintenance of living corals. *AAZPA Conf. Proc.* 1982:65-70.

——————————. 1993a. The collection, transportation, and maintenance of living corals. Part 1. *SeaScope 10*, Spring.

——————————. 1993b. The collection, transportation, and maintenance of living corals. Part 2. *SeaScope* 10, Summer.

Brown, B. 1997. Coral bleaching: Causes and consequences. *Proc. 8th Int. Coral Reef Symp., Panama* 1:65-74.

Brown, B.E., Downs, C.A., Dunne, R.P. and S.W. Gibb. 2002. Exploring the basis of thermotolerance in the reef coral *Goniastrea aspera*. *Marine Ecology Progressive Series* 242:119-130.

Brown, E.M. 1929. Notes on the hydrogen ion concentration, excess base, and carbon-dioxide pressure of marine aquarium waters. *Proceedings of the Zoological Society of London, 1929*, No. 44, pp. 601-613.

Brown, V., Ducker, S.C. and K.S. Rowan, 1977 The effect of orthophosphate concentrations on the growth of the coralline algae (Rhodophyta). *Phycologia* 16:125-131.

Bruland, K.W. and M.C. Lohan. 2004. The control of trace metals in seawater. Chapter 2 in *The Oceans and Marine Geochemistry*, Vol. 6 (Ed. Harry Elderfield) in *Treatise on Geochemistry* (Eds. H.D. Holland and K.K. Turekian).

Buddemeier, R.W. and D.G. Fautin. 1993. Coral bleaching as an adaptive mechanism. *BioScience* 43(5):320-326.

Burleson, J. 1989. Reef tips. *Freshwater and Marine Aquarium* 12(4):120-121.

Burrell, P.C., Keller, J. and L.L. Blackall. 1998. Microbiology of a nitrite-oxidizing bioreactor. *Applied Environmental Microbiology* 64:1878-1883.
——————, Phalen, C.M. and T.A. Hovanec. 2001. Identification of bacteria responsible for ammonia oxidation in freshwater aquaria. *Applied Environmental Microbiology* 67:5791-5800.

Bythell, J.C. 1990. Nutrient uptake in the reef-building coral *Acropora palmata* at natural environmental concentrations. *Marine Ecology Progress Series* 68:65-69.
——————. 1988. A total nitrogen and carbon budget for the elkhorn coral *Acropora palmata* (Lamarck). *Proc. 6th Int. Coral Reef Symp.* 2:535-540.
——————, Thomason J.C., Heidelberg K.B. and K.P. Sebens. 2002. Is zooplankton capture an important trophic pathway in reef corals? *Proc ISRS Eur Meeting - Cambridge* 4-7th September 2002. Abstracts.

Cairns, S.D. 2000. Revision of the shallow-water azooxanthellate scleractinia of the western Atlantic. *Studies of the Natural History of the Caribbean Region* 75, 231 pp.

Calfo, A. 2003. The static on static lighting: Suggestions for better lighting applications of photosynthetic reef organisms - moving light systems. *Advanced Aquarist Online 2(10)*, October 2003. www.advancedaquarist.com/issues/oct2003/feature.htm

Capone, D.G., Dunham, S.E., Horrigan, S.G. and L. Duguay. 1992. Microbial nitrogen transformations in unconsolidated coral reef sediments. *Marine Ecology Progress Series* 80:75-88.

Carlson, B.A. 1996. How do build a powerful surge device. *SeaScope 13*, Summer, 1996. http://www.masla.com/reef/csm.html

Carpenter, K. 2000. Reverse Carlson Surge Device. *SeaScope.* Vol 17. Winter. http://www.petsforum.com/cis-fishnet/seascope/00SS1705.htm (accessed January 2005)
Case, C. 1995. *Microbiology.* Addison and Wesley Publishing Co. New York.

Chalker, B.E., Dunlap, W.C. and P.L. Jokiel. 1986. Light and corals. *Oceanus* 29:22-23.

Chandra, R.K. 1997. Nutrition and the immune system: An introduction. *American Journal of Clinical Nutrition* 66:460-638.

Chirigos, M.A. 1992. Immunomodulators: current and future development and application. *Thymus* 19(Suppl. 1):S7-20.

Clark, F.E. 1996. *Soil Microbiology and Biochemistry.* Academic Press. New York.

Claus, G. and H.J. Kuntzer 1985. Autotrophic denitrification by *Thiobacillus denitrificans* in a packed bed reactor. *Applied Microbiology and Biotechnology* 22:289-296.

Cloud, P.E. Jr. 1962. Environment of calcium carbonate deposition west of Andros Island, Bahamas. *U.S. Geological Survey Professional Paper 350*, 138 pp.

Coat, J.H. and L.M. Axe. 1996. Growth and longevity in acanthurid fishes: an analysis of otolith increments. *Marine Ecology Progress Series* 134:15-26.

Cohen, A.L and R.A. Reves-Sohn. 2004. Tidal modulation of Sr/Ca in a Pacific reef coral. *Geophysical Research Letters* 31(16): L16310.

Cohen, S. 1999. Are plenums obsolete? *Freshwater and Marine Aquarium* 2:110-116.

Coles, S.L. 1997a. Reef corals occurring in a highly fluctuating temperature environment at Fahal Island, Gulf of Oman (Indian Ocean). *Coral Reefs* 16:269-272.
——————. 1997b. Quantitative estimates of feeding and respiration for three scleractinian corals. *Limnology and Oceanography* 14:949-953.

Coles, S.L. and P.L. Jokiel. 1977. Effects of temperature on photosynthesis and respiration in hermatypic corals. *Marine Biology* 43:209-216.
—————— and ——————. 1978. Synergistic effects of temperature, salinity and light on the hermatypic coral *Montipora verrucosa. Marine Biology* 49:187-195.
—————— and B.E. Brown. 2003. Coral bleaching - capacity for acclimatization and adaptation. *Adv. Mar. Biol.* 46:183-223.

Colin, P. and C. Arneson. 1995. *Tropical Pacific Invertebrates.* Coral Reef Press, Beverly Hills, CA, 296pp.

Corredor, J.E., Wilkinson, C.R., Vincente, V.P., Morell, J.M. and E. Otero. 1988. Nitrate release by Caribbean reef sponges. *Limnology and Oceanography* 33:114-120.

Cover, D. 2004. Algae control processes for aquatic exhibits at zoos and aquariums. PowerPoint presentation, 1st Aquality Symposium, Lisbon, Portugal, http://www.aqualitysymposium.org/abstracts.php.

Crank, J. 1983. *The Mathematics of Diffusion.* Clarendon Press. Oxford.

Crossman, D.J., Choat, J.H., Clements, K.D., Hardy, T. and J. McConochie. 2001. Detritus as food for grazing fishes on coral reefs. *Limnology and Oceanography* 46(7):1596-1605.

Dai, C.D. and M.C. Lin. 1993. The effects of flow on feeding of three gorgonians from southern Taiwan. *Journal of Experimental Marine Biology and Ecology* 173:57-69.

Daims, H., Nielsen, P.H., Nielsen, J.L., Juretschko, S. and M. Wagner. 2000. Novel *Nitrospira*-like bacteria as dominant nitrite-oxidizers in biofilms from wastewater treatment plants: diversity and in situ physiology. *Water Science and Technology* 41(4-5):85–90.

Damjanovic, A., Ritz, T. and K. Schulten. 2000. Excitation transfer in the peridinin-chlorophyll-protein of *Amphidinium carterae. Biophysical Journal* 79:1695-1705.

Darley, W.M. 1982. *Algal Biology: A Physiological Approach.* Blackwell Scientific Publications, Oxford, 168 pp.

deGraaf, F. 1968. *Handboek voor Het Tropisch Zeewateraquarium.* A.J.G. Strengholt Boeken, Utrecht, The Netherlands, 362 pp.

Delaparte, S. and M. Hignette. 2000. Denitrification based on sulfur at the aquarium of MAAO. *SeaScope* 17:1,4. Fall.

Delbeek, J. C. 1990. Live rock algal succession in a reef system. *Freshwater and Marine Aquarium* 13(10):120-135,179.
—————— and S.W. Michael. 1993. Substrate-sifting gobies. *Aquarium Fish Magazine* 5(11):18-30.
—————— and J. Sprung. 1990. New trends in reefkeeping: Is it time for another change? *Freshwater and Marine Aquarium Magazine* 13(12):8-9, 11-12, 14, 16, 19-22, 180, 182, 184.
—————— and ——————. 1994. *The Reef Aquarium: A Comprehensive Guide to the Identification and Care of Tropical Marine Invertebrates.* Volume one. Ricordea Publishing, Coconut Grove, FL, USA, 544 pp.

del Negro, A.D. and L. Ungaretti. 1971. Refinement of the crystal structure of aragonite. *The American Mineralogist* 55:768-772.

den Hartog, C. 1970. *The Seagrasses of the World.* Verhandelingen der Koninklijke Nederlandse Akademie van Wetenschappen. Afdeeling Natuurkunde, Tweede Reeks. 59(1):275 +

Bibliography

plates 1-31 [also published separately by North-Holland Publishing Company, Amsterdam]

Dennison, W.C. and D.J. Barnes. 1988. Effect of water motion on coral photosynthesis and calcification. *Journal of Experimental Marine Biology and Ecology* 115:67-77.

DeSilva, S.S. and T.A. Anderson. 1995. *Fish Nutrition in Aquaculture*. Chapman and Hall, London, U.K., 319pp.

Diaz, M.C. 1997. Molecular detection and characterization of specific bacterial groups associated with tropical sponges. *Proc. 8th International Coral Reef Symposium, Panama*:1399-1402.
——————— and B.B. Ward. 1997. Sponge mediated nitrification in tropical benthic communities. *Marine Ecology Progressive Series* 156:97-107.

DiLouie, C. 2002. DALI: What's the buzz about? *Lighting Controls Association*. http://www.aboutlightingcontrols.org/education/papers/dalibuzz.shtml
———————. 2003. Controlling LED lighting systems. *Lighting Controls Association*. http://www.aboutlightingcontrols.org/education/papers/controleLED.shtml.
———————. 2004. High/low-bay applications: Fluorescent or metal halide? *Lighting Controls Association*. http://www.aboutlightingcontrols.org/education/papers/high-low-bay.shtml

DiMarco, R. 2003 What has ten legs and improves your complexion? *Freshwater and Marine Aquarium Magazine* 26(2):86-92.

DOE, 1994. *Handbook of methods for the analysis of the various parameters of the carbon dioxide system in seawater*, Version 2.0. A. G. Dickson and C. Goyet (eds.). Carbon Dioxide Information Analysis Center, Oak Ridge National Laboratory, Oak Ridge, Tenn., U.S.A. 74 pp.

Donowitz, R. 1998. Nitrate removal- A new alternative. *Aquarium Frontiers Online*, April.
http://web.archive.org/web/20010708094847/http://www.animalnetwork.com/fish2/aqfm/1998/april/features/2/default.asp

Dove, S.G., Misaki, T. and O. Hoegh-Guldberg. 1995. Isolation and partial characterization of the pink and blue pigments of pocilloporid and acroporid corals. *Biological Bulletin* 189:288-297.
———————, Hoegh-Guldberg, O. and S. Ranganathan. 2001. Major colour patterns of reef-building corals are due to a family of GFP-like proteins. *Coral Reefs* 19:197-204.

Dunlap, W.C. and B.E. Chalker. 1986. Identification and quantification of near-UV absorbing compounds (S-320) in a hermatypic scleractinian. *Coral Reefs* 5:155-159.
———————, Shick, J.M. and Y. Yamamoto. 2000. UV protection in marine organisms. I. Sunscreens, oxidative stress and antioxidants. In: T. Yoshikawa, S. Toyokuni, Y. Yamamoto, and Y. Naito (eds.) *Free Radicals in Chemistry, Biology and Medicine*. OICA International, London.

Durso, R. 2002. Disaster Readiness. *Advanced Aquarist Online 1(8)*, August 2002. http://advancedaquarist.com/issues/aug2002/feature.htm.

Dustan, P. 1982. Depth-dependent photoadaptation by zooxanthellae of the reef coral *Montastraea annularis*. *Marine Biology* 68:253-264.

Dykins, J.A. and J.M. Shick. 1984. Photobiology of the symbiotic sea anemone *Anthopleura elegantissima* defenses against photodynamic effects and seasonal photoacclimatization. *Biological. Bulletin* 167:638-697.

Dwivedy, R.C. 1973. *Removal of Dissolved Organics Through Foam Fractionation in Closed Cycle Systems for Oyster Production*. Paper No. 73-561, American Society of Agricultural Engineers. St. Joseph, MI.

Edwards, D.A., Brenner, H. and D.T. Wasan. 1991. *Interfacial Transport Processes and Rheology*. Butterworth Heinemann, Boston, 558 pp.

Emery, A.R. 1968. Preliminary observations on coral reef plankton. *Limnology and Oceanography* 13:293-303.

Eng, L.C. 1961. Nature's system of keeping marine fishes. *Tropical Fish Hobbyist* 9(6):23-30.

Engineering Handbook for Industrial Plastic Piping Systems, Harrington
Plastics Inc., Chino, CA, USA 112 pp

Engstad, R.E. and B. Robertsen. 1993. Recognition of yeast cell wall glucan by Atlantic salmon (*Salmo salar* L). Macrophages. *Development and Comparative Immunology* 17:319-330.
——————— and B. Robertsen. 1994. Specificity of a ß-glucan receptor on macrophages from Atlantic salmon (*Salmo salar* L.). *Developmental and Comparative Immunology* 18:397-408.

Erftemeijer, P.L.A. 1993. *Factors limiting growth and production of tropical seagrasses: nutrient dynamics in Indonesian seagrass beds*. Ph.D. Thesis University of Nijmegen, Netherlands. 173 p.

Escobal, P.R. 2000. *Aquatic Systems Engineering: Devices and How They Function*. Dimension Engineering Pr; 2nd edition (October 2000) 272 pp.

Fabricius, K.E., Genin, A. and Y. Benayahu. 1995. Flow-dependent herbivory and growth in zooxanthellae-free soft corals. *Limnology and Oceanography* 40(7):1290-1301.
———————, Benayahu, Y., Yahel, G. and A. Genin. 1996. Herbivory in Soft Corals: Correction. *Science* 273:293b-297.
———————, Yahel, G. and A. Genin. 1997. In situ depletion of phytoplankton by an azooxanthellate soft coral. *Limnology and Oceanography* 43:354-356.
——————— and M. Dommisse. 2000. Depletion of suspended particulate matter over coastal reef communities dominated by zooxanthellate soft corals. *Marine Ecology Progress Series* 196:157-167.
——————— and Alderslade, P. 2001. *Soft Corals and Sea Fans. A comprehensive guide to the tropical shallow-water genera of the Central-West Pacific, the Indian Ocean and the Red Sea*. AIMS and MAGNT.

Fang, L-S., Chen, Y.-W. and C.-S. Chen. 1983. Why does the white tip of stony coral grow so fast without zooxanthellae? *Marine Biology* 103:359-363.

Fanny H., Tambutte E., Ferrier-Pages C. 2002. Effect of zooplankton availability on the metabolism of the scleractinian coral *Stylophora pistillata* (Esper, 1797). *Proc ISRS Eur Meeting - Cambridge* 4-7th September 2002. Abstracts.

FDA: Federal Drug Administration, *Appendix A Food Additives, Yeast
extract (Bakers)* - FL/ADJ, GRAS, See Specs 184.1983. Washington DC.

Fenical, W. 1975. Halogenation in the rhodophyta- a review. *Journal of Phycology* 11:245-259.

Ferraris J.D. 1982. Surface zooplankton at Carrie Bow Cay, Belize. In: *The Atlantic Barrier Reef Ecosystem at Carrie Bow Cay, Belize, I. Structure and Communities* (Rutzler K, Macintyre I.G., eds.) Smithsonian Institution Press, Washington: 143-152.

Ferrier-Pagès, C., Karner, M. and F. Rassoulzadegan. 1998a. Release of dissolved amino acids by flagellates and ciliates grazing on bacteria. *Oceanologica Acta* 21(3):485-494.

Ferrier-Pagès, C., Gattuso, J.-P., Cauwet, W., Jaubert, J. and D. Allemand. 1998b. Release of dissolved organic carbon and nitrogen by the zooxanthellate coral *Galaxea fascicularis*. *Marine Ecology Progress Series* 172:265-274.
——————— and J-P. Gattuso. 1998c. Biomass, production and grazing rates of pico- and nanoplankton in coral reef waters (Miyako Island, Japan). *Microbial Ecology* 35(1):46-57.

——————, Allemand, D., Gattuso, J.-P., Jaubert, J. and F. Rassoulzadegan. 1998d. Microheterotrophy in the zooxanthellate coral *Stylophora pistillata*: effect of light and prey density. *Limnology and Oceanography* 43(7):1639-1648.

——————, Schoelzke, V., Jaubert, J., Muscatine, L. and O. Hoegh-Guldberg. 2001. Response of a scleractinian coral, *Stylophora pistillata*, to iron and nitrate enrichment. Observatoire Oceanologique Europeen, Centre Scientifique de Monaco, Monaco, Monaco. *Journal of Experimental Marine Biology and Ecology* 259(2):249-261.

——————, Witting, J., Tambutte, E. and K.P. Sebens. 2003. Effect of natural zooplankton feeding on the tissue and skeletal growth of the scleractinian coral *Stylophora pistillata*. *Coral Reefs* 22: 229-240.

Fetters, J. 2003. Applying new lighting technology. *Energy User News*. http://www.energyusernews.com/CDA/Article_Information/Fundamentals_Item/0,2637,97882,00.html

Figueras, A, Santarem, M.M. and B. Novoa. 1998. Influence of the sequence of administration of beta-glucans and a *Vibrio damsela* vaccine on the immune response of turbot (*Scophthalmus maximus* L.) *Vet. Immunol. Immunopathol.* 64(1):59-68.

Fitt, W.K. and C.B. Cook. 2001. The effects of feeding or addition of dissolved inorganic nutrients in maintaining the symbiosis between dinoflagellates and a tropical marine cnidarian. *Marine Biology* 139:507-517.

Fossà, S. and A. Nilsen. 1996. *The Modern Coral Reef Aquarium*, Vol 1. Birgit Schmettkamp Verlag, 362 pp.

Fox, J.A. 2002. Watts up with your tank: Estimating your tanks electrical costs. *Advanced Aquarist Online, March, 2002*. http://www.advancedaquarist.com/issues/mar2002/short.htm

Frakes, T.A. 1993. Red Sea reef "mesocosms" in Monaco. *SeaScope 10, Fall*.
——————. 1996. Salinity measurement in review. *Aquarium Frontiers* 3(1).
——————. 2000. Ecosystem Aquarium® comparison. *Seascope* 17.

Frankignoulle, M. 1994. A complete set of buffer factors for acid/base CO_2 system in seawater. *Journal of Marine Systems* 5:111-118.

Franziskett, L. 1974. Nitrate uptake by reef corals. *Internationale Revue Der Gesamten Hydrobiologie* 59:1-7.

Fuhrman, J.A. 1999. Marine viruses and their biogeochemical and ecological effects. *Nature* 399: 541-548.

Galitskii, N.V., Sukhareva, N. I. and T.G. Lyakhovskaya. 1993. Purification of wastewaters containing heavy metals ions. Institute of Technology, Mogilev, Belarus. *Gal'vanotekhnika i Obrabotka Poverkhnosti* 2(6):52-55.

Gattuso, J.-P. 2002. Marine biogeochemical cycles: effects on climate and response to climate change. In: Nihoul, J.C.J. (Editor), *Encyclopedia of life support systems*. Oxford: EOLSS Publishers Ltd.
——————, Reynaud-Vaganay, S., Furla, P., Romaine-Lioud, S., Jaubert, J., Bourge, I. and M. Frankignoulle. 2000. Calcification does not stimulate photosynthesis in the zooxanthellate scleractinian coral *Stylophora pistillata*. *Limnology and Oceanography* 45(1):246-250.

Genin, A., Yahel, G., Reidenbach, M.A., Monismith, S.G. and J.R. Koseff. 2002. Intense benthic grazing on phytoplankton in coral reefs revealed using the control volume approach. *Oceanography* 15:90-96.

Gil-Agudelo, D.L., Smith, G.W., Garzón-Ferreira, J., Weil, E. and D. Petersen. 2004. Dark spots disease and yellow band disease, two poorly known coral diseases with high incidence in Caribbean reefs. *In*: Rosenberg E., Loya, Y. (eds). *Coral Health and Diseases*. Springer, Heidelberg, pp 337-348.

Giovanetti, T.A. 1989. *Caulerpa* enemy of the miniature reef aquarium? *Freshwater and Marine Aquarium* 10:89.

Gratzek, J.B. and J.R. Matthews 1992. *Aquariology: The Science of Fish Health Management*. Tetra Press, NJ, USA.

Grottoli, A.G. and G.M. Wellington. 1999. Effect of light and zooplankton on skeletal C values in the eastern Pacific corals *Pavona clavus* and *Pavona gigantea*. *Coral Reefs* 18:29-41.

Guillaume, J., Kaushik, S., Bergot, P. and R. Metailler. (eds). 2001. *Nutrition and Feeding of Fish and Crustaceans*. Springer Verlag, Heidelberg, Germany, 408 pp.

Gutierrez, S. 1991. From a reef's point of view. *Freshwater and Marine Aquarium* 14(5):137-144.

Fenner, B. *The Conscientious Marine Aquarist*. Microcosm, Shelburne, VT, 432pp.

Furla, P., Orsenigo, M.N. and D. Allemand. 2000. Involvement of H+-ATPase and carbonic anhydrase in inorganic carbon absorption for endosymbiont photosynthesis. *American Journal of Physiology* 278:870-881.
——————, Galgani, I., Durand, I. and D. Allemand. 2000. Sources and mechanisms of inorganic carbon transport for coral calcification and photosynthesis. *Journal of Experimental Biology* 203:3445-3457.

Halland, B. 1983. Simple and explicit formulas for the friction factor in turbulent pipe flow. *J. Fluids Engineering* 105:89-90.

Halldal, P. 1968. Photosynthetic capacities and photosynthetic action spectra of endozoic algae of the massive coral *Favia*. *Biol. Bull.* 134:411-424.

Halver, J.E. and R.W. Hardy. 2002. *Fish Nutrition*. Third ed. Academic Press.

Hamner, W.M. and J.H. Carleton. 1979. Copepod swarms: attributes and role in coral reef ecosystems. *Limnology and Oceanography* 24(1):1-14.
——————, Jones, M.S., Carleton, J.H., Hauri, I.R. and D. McB. Williams. 1988. Zooplankton, planktivorous fish, and water currents on a windward reef face. *Bulletin of Marine Science* 42:459-479.

Harker, R.E. 1998a. Granular activated carbon: Part 1. *Aquarium Frontiers Online, May, 1998*.
http://web.archive.org/web/20010211125618/www.animalnetwork.com/fish2/aqfm/1998/may/features/1/default.asp
——————. 1998b. Granular activated carbon: Part 2. *Aquarium Frontiers Online, June, 1998*.
http://web.archive.org/web/20000918065819/http://www.animalnetwork.com/fish2/aqfm/1998/june/features/1/default.asp
——————. 1998c. Measuring turbulent flow in reef tanks. *Advanced Aquarist Online, August 1998*.
http://www.animalnetwork.com/fish2/aqfm/1998/aug/features/1/default.asp
——————. 1998d. The IceCap 175 Watt metal halide electronic ballast. *Aquarium Frontiers Magazine*, April.
http://web.archive.org/web/20010211193850/http://www.animalnetwork.com/fish2/aqfm/1998/april/product/default.asp
——————. 1998e. An inexpensive light meter and its application to reefkeeping. *Aquarium Frontiers Online, June 1998*.
http://web.archive.org/web/20000918065708/http://www.animalnetwork.com/fish2/aqfm/1998/june/product/default.asp
——————. 1999a. A quantum leap in light meters. *Aquarium Frontiers Online, June 1999*.
http://web.archive.org/web/20010420140603/http://www.animalnetwork.com/fish2/aqfm/1999/june/product/default.asp

——————. 1999b. Shedding light on the reef. *Aquarium Frontiers Online*, July 1999.
http://web.archive.org/web/20001109222100/http://www.animalnetwork.com/fish2/aqfm/1999/july/features/2/default.asp

——————. 1999c. Reflecting on lighting. *Aquarium Frontiers Online*, November 1999.
Web.archive.org/web/20011217235635/www.animalnetwork.com/fish2/aqfm/1999/nov/features/1/default.asp
——————. 2001a. The blueline metal halide electronic ballast. *Aquarium Frontiers Online*.
http://web.archive.org/web/20010905180950/http://www.animalnetwork.com/fish/library/articleview.asp?Section=Aquarium+Frontiers+—+Product+Review&RecordNo=1392
——————. 2001b. Testing for bacteria in the reef tank. *Aquarium Frontiers*.
http://web.archive.org/web/20010410005632/http://www.animalnetwork.com/fish/library/articleview.asp?Section=Aquarium+Frontiers+—+Product+Review&RecordNo=2201
——————. 2002a. Nipple nonsense. *Advanced Aquarist Online 1(1)*, January 2002. http://www.advancedaquarist.com/issues/jan2002/productreview.htm
——————. 2002b. Nipple orientation of metal halide bulbs revisited. *Advanced Aquarist Online* 1(3), March 2002.
http://www.advancedaquarist.com/issues/mar2002/product.htm
——————. 2002c. The Aqualine 150 watt metal halide bulb and fixture. *Advanced Aquarist Online* 1(8), August 2002.
http://www.advancedaquarist.com/issues/aug2002/review.htm
——————. 2002d. The Aqualine 150 watt metal halide bulb and fixture: Part 2. *Advanced Aquarist Online* 1(10):October 2002.
http://www.advancedaquarist.com/issues/oct2002/review.htm
——————. 2002e. Product Review. Propellor Pumps In The Aquarium. *Advanced Aquarist Online*. 1(6). http://advancedaquarist.com/issues/june2002/review.htm
——————. 2003a. Product Review. Eductors for water motion in reef tanks. *Advanced Aquarist Online*, September.
——————. 2003b. Is it really in the water? A critical reexamination of toxic metals in reef tanks. Part 1. *Advanced Aquarist Online, December*.
http://www.advancedaquarist.com/issues/dec2003/feature.htm
——————. 2004a. Is it really in the water? A critical reexamination of toxic metals in reef tanks. Part 2. *Advanced Aquarist Online* January, 2004.
http://www.advancedaquarist.com/issues/jan2004/feature.htm
——————. 2004b. Is it really in the water? A critical reexamination of toxic metals in reef tanks. Part 3. *Advanced Aquarist Online* February, 2004.
http://www.advancedaquarist.com/issues/feb2004/feature.htm
——————. 2004ic. Ferrous oxide phosphate removers. *Advanced Aquarist Online* 3(6), June 2004. http://www.advancedaquarist.com/issues/june2004/review.htm.

Harland, A.D. and B.E. Brown. 1989. Metal tolerance in the scleractinian coral *Porites lutea*. *Mar. Pollut. Bull.* 20(7):353-357.
Harrison, W.D., Musgrave, D., and W.S. Reeburgh. 1983. A wave-induced transport process in marine sediments. *Journal of Geophysical Research* 88: 7617-7622.
Hatcher, B. G. 1988. Coral reef primary productivity: a beggar's banquet. *TREE* 3(5):106-111.
——————, Chapman, A.R.O., and K.H. Mann. 1977. An annual carbon budget for the kelp *Laminaria longicruris*. *Marine Biology* 44:85-96.

Hebbinghaus, R. 1993. Der lobbecke-kalkreactor. *DATZ* 8:517-522.

Hentschel, U., Hopke, J., Horn, M., Friedrich, A.B., Wagner, M., Hacker, J. and B.S. Moore. 2002. Molecular evidence for a uniform microbial community in sponges from different oceans. *Applied Environmental Microbiology* 68:4431-4440.

Heslinga, G.A. 1989. Harnessing nitrogen for faster clam growth. *MMDC Bulletin* April4:1.

Hignette, M., Lamort, B., Langouet, M., Leroy, S. et G. Martin. 1997. Elimination des nitrates par filtration biologique autotrophe sur soufre en aquariologie marine. *Mém. Inst. Océano. P. Ricard pp 7-13*.

Hiller, G. 1999. Biochemistry of aquaria. Alternative calcium reactor substrates. *Aquarium Frontiers Online*.
http://web.archive.org/web/20010503191731/http://www.animalnetwork.com/fish/library/articleview2.asp?Section=Aquarium+Frontiers+—+Biochemistry+of+Aquaria&RecordNo=1571
——————. 2003a. An advanced aquarist short take: Calcium reactor substrate—phosphate levels. *Advanced Aquarist Online*, April.
http://www.advancedaquarist.com/issues/april2003/short.htm
——————. 2003b. An aquarist's experience with a species of *Acropora* parasites. *Advanced Aquarist's Online Magazine 2(6)*, June 2003.

Hoegh-Guldberg, O., Jones R.J., Ward, S. and W. Loh. 2002. "Is coral bleaching really adaptive?" *Nature* 415:601:602.

Hoff, F. and T.W. Snell, 1993. *Plankton Culture Manual*. Florida Aqua Farms, Inc. Dade City, FL, 155pp.

Hollibaugh, J.T., Bano, N. and H.W. Ducklow. 2002. Widespread distribution in polar oceans of a 16S rRNA gene sequence with affinity to *Nitrosospira*-like ammonia-oxidizing bacteria. *Applied Environmental Microbiology* 68:1478-1484.

Holmes-Farley, R. 2001. The Complete Nitrogen Cycle *Aquarium Frontiers*
http://www.animalnetwork.com/fish/library/articleview2.asp?Section=Aquarium+Frontiers+—+Biochemistry+of+Aquaria&RecordNo=3090
——————. 2002a. Specific gravity: Oh how complicated! *Advanced Aquarist Online* 1(1).
http://www.advancedaquarist.com/issues/jan2002/chemistry.htm
——————. 2002b. Iron in the reef aquarium. *Advanced Aquarist Online* 1(8). http://www.advancedaquarist.com/issues/aug2002/chem.htm
——————. 2002c. Iron: A look at organisms other than macroalgae. *Advanced Aquarist Online* 1(10): http://www.advancedaquarist.com/issues/oct2002/chem.htm
——————. 2002d. Boron in the reef tank. *Advanced Aquarist Online* 1(12). http://www.advancedaquarist.com/issues/dec2002/chem.htm
——————. 2002e. Chemistry and the aquarium: Solving calcium and alkalinity problems. *Advanced Aquarist Online* 1(11), November 2002.
http://www.advancedaquarist.com/issues/nov2002/chem.htm
——————. 2002f. Chemistry and the aquarium: The relationship between alkalinity and pH. *Advanced Aquarist Online* 1(5), May 2002
http://www.advancedaquarist.com/issues/may2002/chem.htm
——————. 2002g. Chemistry and the aquarium: Solutions to pH problems. *Advanced Aquarist Online* 1(6), June 2002.
http://www.advancedaquarist.com/issues/june2002/chem.htm
——————. 2002h. Reef alchemy: Calcium and alkalinity. *Reefkeeping* Online 2(8), April 2002. http://reefkeeping.com/issues/2002-04/rhf/feature/index.htm
——————. 2002i. Chemistry and the aquarium: The chemical and biochemical mechanisms of calcification. *Advanced Aquarist Online* 1(4), April 2002.
http://www.advancedaquarist.com/issues/apr2002/chem.htm
——————. 2003a. Strontium and the reef aquarium. *Advanced Aquarist Online* 2(11). http://www.advancedaquarist.com/issues/nov2003/chem.htm
——————. 2003b. Chemistry and the aquarium: How to select a calcium and alkalinity supplementation scheme. *Advanced Aquarist Online* 2(2), February 2003.
http://www.advancedaquarist.com/issues/feb2003/chem.htm
——————. 2003c. Chemistry and the aquarium: Metals in limewater. *Advanced Aquarist Online* 2(5). http://www.advancedaquarist.com/issues/may2003/chem.htm
——————. 2003d. Chemistry and the aquarium: Magnesium in reef aquaria. *Advanced Aquarist Online* 2(10).
http://www.advancedaquarist.com/issues/oct2003/chem.htm
——————. 2003e. Chemistry and the aquarium. Nitrate in the reef aquarium. *Advanced Aquarist Online* 2(8), August 2003.
http://www.advancedaquarist.com/issues/aug2003/chem.htm
——————. 2003f. Silica in reef aquariums. *Advanced Aquarist Online*, January 2003. http://advancedaquarist.com/issues/jan2003/feature.htm
——————. 2003g. Reef aquaria with low soluble metals. *Reefkeeping Online*. http://reefkeeping.com/issues/2003-04/rhf/feature/
——————. 2003h. ORP and the reef aquarium. Reefkeeping online. December 2003. http://reefkeeping.com/issues/2003-12/rhf/feature/index.htm
——————. 2004a. Temperature correction for hydrometers. *Reefkeeping Online*. http://reefkeeping.com/issues/2004-07/rhf/index.htm

Bibliography

——————. 2004b. Reef aquarium salinity: Homemade calibration standards. *Reefkeeping Online*. http://reefkeeping.com/issues/2004-06/rhf/index.htm

——————. 2004c. Reef alchemy: When do calcium and alkalinity demand not exactly balance? *Reefkeeping Online* 2(8), December 2004. http://reefkeeping.com/issues/2004-12/rhf/index.htm

——————. 2004d. Measuring pH with a meter. Chemistry and the aquarium. Advanced Aquarist online. http://www.advancedaquarist.com/issues/feb2004/chem.htm

——————. 2005. Reef alchemy. Electronic calcium monitoring. *Reefkeeping Online* 4(3), April 2005. http://reefkeeping.com/issues/2005-04/rhf/index.htm

Horrigan, S. G., Hagstroem, A., Koike, I. and F. Azam. 1988 Inorganic nitrogen utilization by assemblages of marine bacteria in seawater culture. *Mar. Ecol. Prog. Ser.* 50(1-2):147-150.

Houck, J.E., Buddemeier, R.W., Smith, S.V. and P. L. Jokiel. 1977. The response of coral growth and skeletal strontium content to light intensity and water temperature. Proc. 3rd Int. Symp. *Coral Reefs* 2:424-431.

Hovanec, T.A. 1998a. *Nitrospira*: not *Nitrobacter* …again! Topical science. *Aquarium Frontiers Online*. http://www.animalnetwork.com/fish2/aqfm/1998/june/science/default.asp Water Science and Technology Vol 41 No 4-5 pp 85–90 © IWA Publishing 2000

——————. 1998b. *Nitrospira*: the real nitrite-oxidizing bacteria in aquaria. Topical science. *Aquarium Frontiers Online*. http://www.animalnetwork.com/fish2/aqfm/1998/mar/science/default.asp

Hovanec, T. 2003. A comparison of coral reef filtration systems: preliminary results. *SeaScope* 20(2).

——————. and E.F. DeLong. 1996. Comparative analysis of nitrifying bacteria associated with freshwater and marine aquaria. *Applied and Environmental Microbiology*. 62:2888-2896.

——————, Talyor, L.T., Blakis, A. and E.F. DeLong. 1998. Nitrospira-like bacteria associated with nitrite oxidation in freshwater aquaria. *Applied and Environmental Microbiology* 64:258-264.

Huettel, M. and G. Gust. 1992. Impact of bioroughness on interfacial solute exchange in permeable sediments. *Marine Ecology Progress Series* 89:253-267.

——————. and A. Rusch. 2000. Transport and degradation of phytoplankton in permeable sediment. *Limnology and Oceanography* 45:534-549.

——————, Ziebis, W.S. and S. Forster. 1996. Flow-induced uptake of particulate matter in permeable sediments. *Limnology and Oceanography* 41:309-322.

——————, Ziebis, W.S., Forster, S. and G.W. Luther. 1998. Advective transport affecting metal and nutrient distributions and interfacial fluxes in permeable sediments. *Geochim Cosmochim Acta* 62(4):613-631.

Humes, A.G. 1981. A new species of *Tegastes* (Copepoda: Harpacticoida) associated with a scleractinian coral at Enewatok Atoll. *Proceedings of the Biological Society of Washington* 94:254-263.

Huntington, S. 2002. A guide to using calcium reactors. *ReefKeeping* 1(4), May 2002. http://reefkeeping.com/issues/2002-05/sh/feature/index.htm

Hutchings, P. and P. Saenger. 1987. *Ecology of Mangroves*. University of Queensland Press, Brisbane.

Iglesias-Prieto, R. 1997. Temperature-dependent inactivation of photosystem II in symbiotic dinoflagellates. *Proc. 8th Int. Coral Reef Symp., Panama*, 2:1313-1318.

Ishi, B.I. and K.J. McGlathery. 2003. Effect of ultraviolet light on dissolved nitrogen transformations in coastal lagoon water. *Limnology and Oceanography* 48(2):723–734.

Jaubert, J. 1991. System for biological purification of water containing organic materials and derivative product. United States Patent number 4,995,980.

——————. 1989. An integrated nitrifying-denitrifying biological system capable of purifying seawater in a closed circuit system. In Deuxieme Congres International d'Aquariologie (1988) Monaco. *Bulletin de l'Institut Oceanographique, Monaco, No. special* 5:101-106.

——————. and J.P. Gatusso. 1989. Changements de forme provoques par la lumier, observes, en aquarium, chez coraux (Scleractiniares a zooxanthelles). Deuxieme Congres International d'Aquariologie (1988) Monaco. *Bulletin de l'Institut Oceanographique, Monaco, No. special* 5:195-204.

——————, Pecheux, J-F., Guschemann, N. and F. Doumenge. 1992. Productivity and calcification in a coral reef mesocosm. In *Proceedings of the 7th International Coral Reef Symposium*.

——————, Chisholm, J.R.M., Minghelli-Roman, A., Marchioretti, M., Morrow, J.H., and H.T. Ripley. 2003. Re-evaluation of the extent of *Caulerpa taxifolia* development in the northern Mediterranean using airborne spectrographic sensing. *Marine Ecology Progress Series* 263:75-82.

Jensen, K.R. 1980. A review of Sacoglossan diets, with comparative notes on radular and buccal anatomy. *Malacological Review* 13:55-77.

——————. 1997. Evolution of the Sacoglossa (Mollusca, Opisthobranchia) and the ecological associations with their food plants. *Evolutionary Ecology* 11:301-335.

Jerlov, N. 1976. *Marine Optics*. Elsevier Oceanography Series, Elsevier Sci. Publ. Co., New York, 231 pp.

Johannes, R.E., Coles, S.L. and N.T. Kuenzel. 1970. The role of zooplankton in the nutrition of some scleractinian corals. *Limnology and Oceanography* 15:579-586.

Johnson, K.S. 2000. Periodic table of elements in the ocean. Monterey Bay Aquarium Research Institute, May 2000. URL: http://www.mbari.org/chemsensor/pteo.htm. Viewed: September 30, 2004.

——————, Gordon, R.M. and K.H. Coale. 1997. What controls dissolved iron concentrations in the world ocean? *Marine Chemistry* 57:137–161.

——————, Chavez, F.P. and G.E. Freiderich. 1999. Continental-shelf sediments as a primary source of iron for coastal phytoplankton. *Nature* 398:697–700.

Johnson, P.E., Borger, R. and S. Gendron. 1992. Fractionation and ozonation of large saltwater aquariums. In: *Proc. 3d Int. Symp. on the use of ozone in aquatic systems*. pp. 18-38.

Johnson, R.W., Ed. *Handbook of Fluid Dynamics*. CRC Press.

Jokiel, P.L. and R.H. York. 1982. Solar ultraviolet photobiology of the reef coral *Pocillopora damicornis*. *Bull. Mar. Sci.* 32:301-315.

Jordan, R. 2002. An advanced aquarist's short take: Indoor air quality. *Advanced Aquarist Online* 1(4), April. http://advancedaquarist.com/issues/apr2002/short.htm

Jorgensen, J.B. and G.J. Sharp. 1993. Effect of a yeast-cell-wall glucan on the bactericidal activity of rainbow trout macrophages. *Fish and Shellfish Immunology* 3:267-277.

——————. and B. Robertson. 1995. Yeast _-glucan stimulates respiratory burst activity of Atlantic salmon (*Salmo salar* L.) Macrophages. *Development and Comparative Immunology* 19(1):43-57, 1995.

Joshi, S. 2000. Feeding a coral reef. *Aquarium Marine Fish and Reef Annual 2000*. Fancy Publications.

——————. 2004. Spectral analysis of 400W double-ended lamps. *Advanced Aquarist Online* 3(10):October 2004. http://www.advancedaquarist.com/issues/oct2004/review.htm

——————. 2005a. More spectral analysis of 400W lamps and ballasts: EVC, Hamilton, Aquaconnect and Helios Lamps and EVC, Blueline, Reef Fanatic and Icecap ballasts. *Advanced Aquarist Online* 4(1), January 2005. http://www.advancedaquarist.com/issues/jan2005/feature.html

——————. 2005b. Spectral analysis of 250 Watt double ended metal halide lamps and ballasts - EVC, Happy Reefing, IceCap, AB, and CoralVue. *Advanced Aquarist Online* 4(2), February 2005. http://www.advancedaquarist.com/issues/feb2005/feature.html

——————. and T. Marks. 2002. Spectral analysis of recent metal halide lamps and ballast combinations. *Advanced Aquarist Online* 1(10), October 2002. http://www.advancedaquarist.com/issues/oct2002/feature.htm

——————. and ——————. 2003a. Analyzing reflectors: Part I. *Advanced Aquarist Online* 2(3), March 2003. http://www.advancedaquarist.com/issues/mar2003/feature.htm

Bibliography

————— and —————. 2003b. Analyzing reflectors: Part II. *Advanced Aquarist Online* 2(7), July, 2003. http://www.advancedaquarist.com/issues/July2003/feature.htm
————— and —————. 2004a. Spectral analysis of 250W double ended 10000K metal halide lamps and ballasts. *Advanced Aquarist Online* 3(2), February 2004. http://www.advancedaquarist.com/issues/feb2004/feature1.htm
————— and —————.. 2004b. Analyzing reflectors: Part III. *Advanced Aquarist Online*, March 2003. http://www.advancedaquarist.com/issues/mar2004/feature.htm
————— and —————.. 2004c. Spectral analysis of 250W mogul base metal halide lamps - Part II. *Advanced Aquarist Online* 3(8), August 2004. http://www.advancedaquarist.com/issues/aug2004/review.htm

Joshi, S. and D. Morgan. 1998. Spectral analysis of metal halide lamps used in the reef aquarium hobby Part 1: New 400-Watt lamps, *Aquarium Frontiers*, November 1998. http://www.personal.psu.edu/faculty/s/b/sbj4/aquarium/articles/MetalHalideLamps1.htm
————— and —————. 1999. Spectral analysis of metal halide lamps used in the reef aquarium hobby Part II: Used 400-watt lamps. *Aquarium Frontiers Online*, January 1999. http://web.archive.org/web/20001017172106/http://www.animalnetwork.com/fish2/aqfm/1999/jan/features/2/default.asp
————— and —————. 2001. Spectral analysis of metal halide lamps - Do ballasts make a difference. *2001 Annual Marine Fish and Reef USA*, Fancy Publications.
—————, Paden, N. and S. Graber. 2003. An engineering view of aquarium systems design: pumps and plumbing. *Advanced Aquarist Online*, January 2003. http://www.advancedaquarist.com/issues/jan2003/featurejp.htm

Juretschko, S., Timmermann, G., Schmid, M., Schleifer, K.-H., Pommerening-Röser, A., Koops, H.-P. and M. Wagner. 1998. Combined molecular and conventional analyses of nitrifying bacterium diversity in activated sludge: *Nitrosococcus mobilis* and *Nitrospira*-like bacteria as dominant populations. *Applied Environmental Microbiology* 64:3042-3051.

Kalisvaart, B.F. 2004. Photobiological effects of medium pressure ultraviolet (UV) lamps. PowerPoint presentation, 1st Aquality Symposium, Lisbon, Portugal, http://www.aqualitysymposium.org/abstracts.php.

Kallmeyer, J. 2004. Zeolite filters: A discussion of what zeolites are and how they function. www.wetwebmedia.com/ca/cav1i3/zeovit/Zeolite_Filters/Zeolite_Filters.htm

Keith, R.E. 1980. Protein skimmers in the marine aquarium. *Freshwater and Marine Aquarium Magazine* 3(9):20-21.

Kim, J.-S., Hwang, Y.-W., Kim, C.-G. and J.-H. Bae. 2003. Nitrification and denitrification using a single biofilter packed with granular sulfur. *Water Science & Technology* 47(11):153–156.

Kingsley, P. 1995. *Ancient Philosophy, Mystery and Magic: Empedocles and Pythagorean Tradition*, Oxford University Press.

Kinzie, R.A. 1993. Effects of ambient levels of solar ultraviolet radiation on zooxanthellae and photosynthesis of the reef coral *Montipora verrucosa*. *Marine Biology* 116:319-327.
—————, Jokiel, P.L. and R. York. 1984. Effects of light of altered spectral composition on coral zooxanthellae associations and on zooxanthellae in vitro. *Marine Biology* 78:239-248.
————— and T. Hunter. 1987. Effect of light quality on photosynthesis of the reef coral *Montipora verrucosa*. *Marine Biology* 94:95-109.

Kirk, J.T.O. 1994. *Light and Photosynthesis in Aquatic Ecosystems*. Cambridge University Press, Cambridge, 509 pp.

Klaus, J.S., Frias-Lopez, J., Bonheyo, G.T., Heikoop, J.M. and B.W. Fouke. 2005. Bacterial communities inhabiting the healthy tissues of two Caribbean reef corals: interspecific and spatial variation. *Coral Reefs* 24:129-137.

Kleypas, J.A., McManus, J.W. and L.A.B. Menez. 1999. Environmental limits to coral reef development: Where do we draw the line. *American Zoologist* 39:146-159.

Klostermann, A.E. 1991. The calcium question. Part II. *Freshwater and Marine Aquarium* 7: 108-110.

Knisley, J. 2003. The T5 fluorescent lamp: Coming on strong. www.ecmweb.com/ops/electric_fluorescent_lamp_coming/

Koch, E.W. 1993. Hydrodynamics of flow through seagrass canopies: biological, physical and geochemical interactions. Ph.D. dissertation, University of South Florida. ix+123 pp.

Kopp-Hoolihan L. 2001. Prophylactic and therapeutic uses of probiotics: a review. *Journal of the American Dietary Association* 101(2): 229-238.

Kuffner, I.B. 2002. Effects of ultraviolet radiation and water motion on the reef coral, *Porites compressa* Dana: a transplantation experiment. *Journal of Experimental Marine Biology and Ecology* 270:147-169.

Lang, G.T. 1993. An introduction to the biogeochemical cycling of calicum and substitutive strontium in living coral reef mesocosms. *Zoo Biology* 12:425-433.

Langdon, C., T. Takahashi, C. Sweeney, D. Chipman, J. Goddard, F. Marubini, H. Aceves, H. Barnett, and M. J. Atkinson (2000), Effect of calcium carbonate saturation state on the calcification rate of an experimental coral reef, *Global Biogeochemical Cycles, 14*(2), 639–654.

Langouet, M. 1999. La dénitratation autotrophe sur soufre. Aqua Plaisir 36.
—————. 2001. Die groBe alternative? Der Biodenitrator auf Schwefelbasis. *Der Meerwasser Aquarianer*, January 2001:12-21.

Lanyon, J. 1986. *Guide to the Identification of Seagrasses in the Great Barrier Reef Region*. (GBRMPA Special Publication Series Number 3) Great Barrier Reef Marine Park Authority, Townsville.

Largo, D.B. 1987. *Halophila spinulosa* (R. Brown) Ascherson: a new seagrass record for the Visayan waters, Cebu Province, Philippines. *The Philippine Scientist* 24.

Leclercq, N., Gattuso, J.-P. and J. Jaubert. 2000. CO_2 partial pressure controls the calcification rate of a coral community. *Global Change Biology* 6(3): 329-334.
—————, —————— and —————. 2002. Primary production, respiration, and calcification of a coral reef mesocosm under increased CO_2 partial pressure. *Limnology and Oceanography* 47(2): 558-564.

Lesser, M.P., Mazel, C.H., Gorbunov, M.Y. and P.G. Falkowski. 2004. Discovery of symbiotic nitrogen-fixing cyanobacteria in corals. *Science* 305:997-1000.

Lewis, J.B. 1974. The importance of light and food upon the early growth of the reef coral *Favia fragum* (Esper). *Journal of Experimental Marine Biology and Ecology* 13:299-304.
—————. 1976. Experimental tests of suspension feeding in Atlantic reef corals. *Marine Biology* 36:147-150.
————— and W.S. Price. 1975. Feeding mechanisms and feeding strategies of Atlantic reef corals. *Journal of the Zoological Society of London* 176:527-544.

Lewis, R.R., III. 1990. Laboratory culture methods. Chap. 4. In: *Seagrass Research Methods*. (Eds: Phillips,RC; McRoy,CP) (Monographs on Oceanographic Methodology, 9.) UNESCO, Paris, 37-41.

Lewis, E. and D.W.R. Wallace. 1998. Program developed for CO_2 system calculations. ORNL/CDIAC-105. Carbon Dioxide Information Analysis Center, Oak Ridge National Laboratory, U.S. Department of Energy, Oak Ridge, Tennessee. http://cdiac.esd.ornl.gov/oceans/co2rprt.html

Lieberman, E. 2001. CYCLOP-EEZE®: An Arctic micro-crustacean with amazing aquaculture applications. *Hatchery International*, May/June. http://www.hatcheryinternational.com/profile/pr_argent.html

Lindenberg, J. 1987. Eindelijk een goede grandkoeling. *Het Zee-Aquarium* 27(11):236-239.

Liou, C.R. 1998. Limitations and Proper Use of the Hazen-Williams Equation. ASCE vol 124. *Journal of Hydraulic Engineering*.

Lomax, K.M. 1976. *Nitrification with Waste Pretreatment on a Closed Cycle Catfish Culture System.* Unpublished Ph.D. thesis. Dept. of Agricultural Engineering, U. of Maryland, College Park.

Lovell, T. (ed.). 1998. *Nutrition and Feeding of Fish* (Second edition). Kluwer Academic Publishers, Boston, U.S.A. 267 pp.

Lowrie, J. and E.H. Borneman. 1998. Demystifying mud (sediment filtration). *Freshwater and Marine Aquarium* 20(6):96.

Macrellis, H.M., Trick, C.G., Rue, E.L., Smith, G. and K.W. Bruland. 2001. Collection and detection of natural iron-binding ligands from seawater. *Marine Chemistry* 76:175-187.

Maksin, V.I. and E.A. Valuiskaya. 1989. Precipitation of hydroxides and hydroxocarbonates of iron, nickel, and copper from wastewaters and process liquors. Inst. Kolloidn. Khim. Khim. Vody im. Dumanskogo, Kiev, USSR. *Khimiya i Tekhnologiya Vody.* 11(1):12-25.

Marini, F. 2002. The Breeder's Net. *Advanced Aquarist Online*, August 2002. http://www.advancedaquarist.com/issues/aug2002/breeder.htm

Marshal, A.T. and P. Clode. 2004. Calcification rate and the effect of temperature in a zooxanthellate and an azooxanthellate scleractinian reef coral. *Coral Reefs* 23: 218-224.

Masuda, I., Goto, M., Maruyama, T. and S. Miyachi. 1993. Photoadaptation of solitary corals, *Fungia repanda, F. echinata*, and their zooxanthellae. *Proc. 7th Int. Coral Reef Symp., Guam* 1:373-378.

Mate, J.L. 1993. Variations in chlorophyll concentration and zooxanthellae density with depth in Caribbean reef corals of Panama. *Proc. 7th Int. Coral Reef Symp., Guam* 1:382 *(abstract)*.

Mate, T. and L. Juan. 1997. Experimental responses of Panamanian reef corals to high temperature and nutrients. In: Lessions, H. A. and I. G. Macintyre. Eds. *Proceedings of the eighth international coral reef symposium, Panama, June 24-29, 1996.* Smithsonian Tropical Research Institute. Balboa, Panama. pp. 515-520.

Matthews, C. 2004. Sump improvement: For starters consider an upside-down sand bed. *Marine Fish and Reef 2005 Annual* 7:116-124.

May, F.M. and K. Guhathakurta. 1970. The precipitation of calcium carbonate from seawater by bacteria isolated from Bahama Bank sediments. *Journal of Applied Bacteriology.* 33:649-655.

Mazel, C.H. and E. Fuchs. 2003. Contribution of fluorescence to the spectral signature and perceived colour of corals. *Limnology and Oceanography* 48(1):390-401.
——————————, Lesser, M.P., Gorbunov, M.Y., Barry, T.M., Farrell, J.H., Wyman, K.D. and P.G. Falkowski. 2003. Green-fluorescent proteins in Caribbean corals. *Limnology and Oceanography* 48(1):402-411.

McCallum, M.F. and G. Kishwar. 1970. The precipitation of calcium carbonate from seawater by bacteria isolated from the Bahama Bank Sediments. *Journal of Applied Bacteriology* 33:649-655.

McConnaughey, T.A. 2000. Community and environmental influences on reef coral calcification. *Limnology and Oceanography* 45(7):1667-1671.
——————————— and J.F. Whelan. 1997. Calcification generates protons for nutrient and bicarbonate uptake. *Earth Science Review* 42:95-117.

McRoy, C.P. and H. Iizumi. 1990. Nutrient uptake. Chp. 28. In: *Seagrass Research Methods*. (Eds: Phillips,RC; McRoy,CP) (Monographs on Oceanographic Methodology, 9.) UNESCO, Paris, 163-165.

McQuillen, D. 2001. Lighting trends. *Environmental Design and Construction Magazine*. http://www.edcmag.com/CDA/ArticleInformation/coverstory/BNPCoverStoryItem/0,4118,18799,00.html

Meier, E. 2003. Notes from the trenches: Aquascaping with insulation foam. *Reefkeeping Online Magazine 2(7),* http://reefkeeping.com/issues/2003-08/nftt/index.htm.

Meinesz, A. 1999. *Killer Algae.* Translated by Daniel Simberloff. With a Foreword by David Quammen. University of Chicago Press, 360 pp.

Meñez, E.G., Phillips, R.C. and H.P. Calumpong. 1983. *Seagrasses from the Philippines.* Smithsonian Constributions to the Marine Sciences, No. 21. 40pp. 26 figures.

Meyer, K. 1991. Survey and analysis of natural and artificial aquarium seawater. *Proceedings of the American Association of Zoological Parks and Aquariums national conference.*

Michael, S.W. 1998. *Reef Fishes Vol. 1: A Guide to their Identification, Behavior, and Captive Care.* Microcosm, Shelburne, VT, 624 pp.

Michalek-Wagner, K. 2004a. Reefs "down under" turned upside down - Radical changes in the life support system of the world's largest public coral reef aquarium result in greatly improved invertebrate survival and biodiversity. Presentation at the *2004 International Aquarium Conference*, Monterey, California, December (oral presentation).
——————————— 2004b. Coral interviews Dr. Kirsten Michalek-Wagner. *Coral* 1(6):4, 6-7.
——————————— 2004c. Reefs "down under" turned upside down -
Radical changes in the life support system of the world's largest public coral reef aquarium result in greatly improved invertebrate survival and biodiversity. Presentation at the *2004 International Aquarium Conference*, Monterey, California, December (abstract).

Millero, F.J. 1996. *Chemical Oceanography,* Second Edition. CRC Press, Boca Raton, FL, 496 pp.
——————————— and M.J. Sohn. 1992. *Chemical Oceanography.* CRC Press, Boca Raton, FL.

Mills, M.M., Lipschultz, F. and K.P. Sebens. 2004. Particulate matter ingestion associated nitrogen uptake by four species of scleractinian corals. *Coral Reefs* 23:311-323.

Mizrahi, O.L., Chadwick-Furman, N.E. and Y. Achituv. 2001. Factors controlling the expansion behavior of *Favia favus* (Cnidaria: Scleractinia): Effects of light, flow and planktonic prey. *Biological Bulletin* 200:118-126.

Mizuno, Y. 2000. What the protein skimmer's dirt contains. *Marine Aquarist* 17, Autumn 2000:92. (In Japanese).

Moe, M.A. Jr. 1989. *The Marine Aquarium Reference: Systems and Invertebrates.* Green Turtle Publ. P.O. Box 17925, Plantation FL, USA, 510 pp.
——————————— 1992. *The Marine Aquarium Handbook: Beginner to Breeder.* Revised and Expanded Edition. Green Turtle Publications. Plantation, FL. USA, 320 pp.
——————————— 1997. *Breeding the Orchid Dottyback. An Aquarist's Journal.* Green Turtle Publications. Plantation, FL, USA, 288 pp.

Monismith, S.G., Genin, A., Reidenbach, M.A., Yahel, G. and J.R. Koseff. 2004. Thermally driven exchanges between a coral reef and the adjoining ocean. *Journal of Physical Oceanography* (submitted).

Bibliography

Morel, F.M.M. and N.M. Price. 2003. The biogeochemical cycles of trace metals in the oceans. *Science* 300:944-947.

Mrutzek, M. and J. Kokott. 2004. Ethanoldosierung im aquarium - neue wege zur verbesserung der lebensbedingungen. *Der Meerwasseraquarianer* 8:60-71.

Nakamura, T. and R. van Woesik. 2001. Water-flow rates and passive diffusion partially explain differential survival of corals during the 1998 bleaching event. *Marine Ecology Progress Series* 212:301-304.
——————, Yamasaki, H. and R. vanWoesik. 2003. Water flow facilitates recovery from bleaching in the coral *Stylophora pistillata*. *Marine Ecology Progress Series* 256:287-292.

Nelson, M., Burgess, T.L., Alling, A., Alvarez-Romo, N., Dempster, W.F., Walford, R.L. and J.P. Allen. 1993. Using a closed ecological system to study Earth's biosphere. *BioScience* 43:225–236.

Nelson, N.B. and D.A. Siegel. 2002. Chromophoric DOM in the open ocean, p. 547-578 *In* D.A. Hansell and C.A. Carlson [eds.], *Biogeochemistry of Marine Dissolved Organic Matter.* Academic Press.

Nilsen, A. and D. Brockmann. 1995a. A critical comparison of the most commonly used methods for dosing calcium in seawater aquariums. Part I. *Aquarium Frontiers*, Spring.
—————— and ————————. 1995b. A critical comparison of the most commonly used methods for dosing calcium in seawater aquariums. Part II. *Aquarium Frontiers*, Fall.

Noga, E.J. 2000. *Fish Disease: Diagnosis and Treatment.* Blackwell Pub Professional, 367 pp.

Nolan, C. 1994. Introduced species in European coastal waters. In: Boudouresque CF, Briand F, Nolan C. (eds) *Introduced species in European coastal waters.* Ecosystems Research Report 8, CIESM (Commission Internationale pour l'Exploration Scientifique de la Méditerranée), Monaco, p 1–3.

Nordemar, I., Nystrom, M. and R. Dizon. 2003. Effects of elevated seawater temperature and nitrate enrichment on the branching coral *Porites cylindrica* in the absence of particulate food. *Marine Biology (in press)*. (http://link.springer.de/link/service/journals/00227/contents/02/00989/)

Norton, C. 1981. *Microbiology.* Benjamin/Cummings Publishing Co. Reading, Mass.

Orlebeke, D. 2002? Lanthanum chloride heptahydrate toxicity and application data. http://www.infoecp.com/lanthanum_chloride.htm

Paletta, M. 1998. The EcoSystem revisited. *SeaScope* 15.
——————. 2000. The EcoSystem aquarium revisited: Checking in after two years. *Aquarium Fish Magazine* 12(2):66.
——————. 2001. The natural mud-filter method. *Tropical Fish* Hobbyist 49(8):94-96, 98, 100, 102, 104.
—————— and R. Hildreth. 1997. The EcoSystem filtration system. *Seascope* 14.

Paling, E.I. 1991. The relationship between nitrogen cycling and productivity in macroalgal stands and seagrass meadows. Ph.D. Thesis, University of Western Australia, Perth. 316+xii p.

Pecorelli, J.P, Sharp, A.L., Michalek-Wagner, K. and A. Schuenhoff. 2004. Refugia and the natural approach to water quality management. Part 1: Systems review and marine plant filters. PowerPoint presentation, 1st Aquality Symposium, Lisbon, Portugal, http://www.aqualitysymposium.org/abstracts.php.
——————, ——————, ——————and ——————. 2004. Refugia and the natural approach to water quality management. Part 1: Systems review and marine plant filters. (In press).

Penland, L., Kloulechad, J., Idip, D. and R. van Woesik. 2004. Coral spawning in the western Pacific Ocean is related to solar insolation: evidence of multiple spawning events in Palau. *Coral Reefs* 23:133-140.

Phillips, C.J., Smith, Z., Embley, T.M. and J.I. Prosser. 1999. Phylogenetic differences between particle-associated and planktonic ammonia-oxidizing bacteria of the beta subdivision of the class Proteobacteria in the northwestern Mediterranean Sea. *Applied Environmental Microbiology* 65:779-786.

Phillips, R.C. 1990. Transplant methods. Chp.7. In: *Seagrass Research Methods.* (Eds: Phillips, R.C.; McRoy,CP) (Monographs on Oceanographic Methodology, 9.) UNESCO, Paris, 51-54.

Pilson, M.E.Q. 1998. *An Introduction to the Chemistry of the Sea.* Prentice-Hall, Inc. Upper Saddle River, NJ, 431pp.

Porter, J.W. 1976. Autotrophy, heterotrophy and resource partitioning in Caribbean reef-building corals *American Naturalist* 110 (975):731-742.
—————— and J.G. Porter. 1977. Quantitative sampling of demersal plankton migrating from different coral reef substrate. *Limnology and Oceanography* 22:553-555.

Pro, S. 2004. Protein skimmers: A myriad of choices. *Freshwater and Marine Aquarium Magazine* 27(8):144, 146, 152, 156.

Proye, A. and J-P. Gattuso. 2003. Seacarb, an R package to calculate parameters of the seawater carbonate system. Available from: http://www.obs-vlfr.fr/~gattuso/jpg_seacarb.htm.

Purkhold, U., Pommerening-Röser, A., Juretschko, S., Schmid, M.C., Koops, H.P. and M. Wagner. 2000. Phylogeny of all recognized species of ammonia oxidizers based on comparative 16S rRNA and amoA sequence analysis: Implications for molecular diversity surveys. *Applied Environmental Microbiology* 66:5368-5382.

Quakenbush, R.C., Bunn, D. and W.E. Lingren. 1990. Phenolic compounds. Chap. 17. In: *Seagrass Research Methods.* (Eds: Phillips,RC; McRoy,CP) (Monographs on Oceanographic Methodology, 9.) UNESCO, Paris, 97-103.

Ragan, M.A. and A. Jensen 1979. Quantitative studies on brown algal phenols. III. Light-mediated exudation of polyphenols from *Ascophyllum nodosum* (L.) Le Jol. *Journal of Experimental Marine Biology and Ecology* 36:91-101.

Randall, J.E. 2001. *Surgeonfishes of Hawai'i and the World.* Mutual Publishing, Honolulu, HI, 125 pp.

Ray, A.J. and R.C. Aller. 1985. Physical irrigation of relict burrows: implications for sediment chemistry. *Marine Geology* 62: 371-379.

Redfield, A.C., Ketchum, B.H. and F.A. Richards. 1963. The influence of organisms on the composition of seawater. In: Hill, M. N. ed. *The Sea.* Volume 2: 26-87. Interscience Publishers, New York.

Regan, J.M., Harrington, G. W. and D.R. Noguera. 2002. Ammonia- and nitrite-oxidizing bacterial communities in a pilot-scale chloraminated drinking water distribution system. *Applied Environmental Microbiology* 68:73-81.

Reise, K., Gollasch, S. and W.J. Wolff. 1999. Introduced marine species of the North Sea coasts. *Helgol. Meeresunters* 52:219–234.

Rhoads, D.C. and L.F. Boyer. 1982. The effect of marine benthos on physical properties of sediments: a successional perspective. In: McCall, P.L., Tevesz, M.J.S. (eds.) *Animal-sediment relations: the biogenic alteration of sediments.* Plenum Press, New York, pp. 3-52.

Bibliography

Richter, C. and M. Wunsch. 1999. Cavity-dwelling suspension feeders in coral reefs- a new link in reef trophodynamics. *Marine Ecology Progressive Series* 188:105-116.

Riddle, D. 1996a. Water motion in the reef aquarium. *Aquarium Frontiers* 3(4):32-39.
————————. 1996b. A simple surge device. Make it yourself in 30 minutes for $30.
Marine Fish Monthly 11(7).
————————. 2003. Effects of narrow bandwidth light sources on coral host and zooxanthellae pigments. *Advance Aquarist Online* 2(11), November 2003.
http://www.advancedaquarist.com/issues/nov2003/feature.htm
————————. 2004a. PAM fluorometer experiments Part I: Effects of metal halide lamp spectral qualities on zooxanthellae photosynthesis in photoacclimated *Fungia* corals: The red light. Part II: Effects of water motion on zooxanthellae photosynthesis. *Advanced Aquarist Online*, June 2004. http://www.advancedaquarist.com/issues/june2004/feature.htm

————————. 2004b. Too much light. *Advanced Aquarist Online* 3(7), July 2004. http://www.advancedaquarist.com/issues/july2004/feature.htm
————————. 2004c. Playing with poison: Ultraviolet radiation. *Advanced Aquarist Online* 3(8), August 2004. http://www.advancedaquarist.com/issues/aug2004/feature.htm

Rindels, A.J. and J.S. Gulliver. 1989. Measurements of oxygen transfer at spillways and overfalls. *St. Anthony Falls Hydr. Lab. Project Rep. No. 266*, University of Minnesota, Minneapolis, Minn.

Riseley, R.A. 1971. *Tropical Marine Aquaria: The Natural System*. George Allen & Unwin Ltd., London, U.K.

Rittmann, B.E. and P.L. McCarty. 2001. *Environmental Biotechnology: Principles and Applications*. McGraw-Hill Book Co., New York.

Robertson, A.I. and D.M. Alongi (eds.) 1992. *Tropical Mangrove Ecosystems*. AGU Press, Washington.

Robertsen, B., Rorstad, G., Engstad, R. and J. Raa. 1990. Enhancement of non-specific resistance in Atlantic salmon, *Salmo salar* L., by a glucan from *Saccharomyces cerevisiae* cell walls. *Journal of Fish Diseases* 13:391-400.
————————, Engstad, R.E. and J.B. Jorgensen. 1994. ß-glucans as immunostimulants. Modulators of fish immune responses. J. Stolen and T. C. Fletcher. *Fair Haven, SOS* 1:83-99.

Rochelle-Newall, E.J., Fisher, T.R., Fan, C. and P.M. Glibert. 1999. Dynamics of chromophoric dissolved organic matter and dissolved organic carbon in experimental mesocosms. *International Journal of Remote Sensing* 20:627-641.
———————————————— and T.R. Fisher. 2002. Production of chromophoric dissolved organic matter in marine and estuarine environments: role of phytoplankton. *Marine Chemistry* 77:7-21.

Rougerie, F. and B. Wauthy. 1993. The endo-upwelling concept: from geothermal convection to reef construction. *Coral Reefs* 12:19-30.

Rohwer, F., Seguritan, V., Azam, F. and N. Knowlton. 2002. Scleractinian corals as microbial landscapes. *Marine Ecology Progress Series* 243:1-10.

Round, F.E. 1965. *The Biology of the Algae*. Arnold, 278 pp.

Rowan, R., and N. Knowlton. 1995. Intraspecific diversity and ecological zonation in coral-algal symbiosis. *Proceedings of the National Academy of Sciences of the United States* 92: 2850-2854.
————————, Knowlton, N., Baker, A. and J. Javier. 1997. Landscape ecology of algal symbionts creates variation in episodes of coral bleaching. *Nature* 388:265-269.

Rue, E.L. and K.W. Bruland. 1995. Complexation of iron(III) by natural organic ligands in the central north Pacific as determined by a new competitive ligand equilibration/adsorptive cathodic stripping voltammetric method. *Marine Chemistry* 50:117-138.
———————— and ————————. 2001. Domoic acid binds iron and copper: a possible role for the toxin produced by the marine diatom Pseudo-nitzchia. *Marine Chemistry* 76:127-134.

Rutgers van der Loeff, M.M. 1981. Wave effects on sediment water exchange in a submerged sand bed. *Netherlands Journal of Sea Research* 15:100-112.

Sagan, D. 1990. *Biospheres. Reproducing Planet Earth*. Bantam Books, New York.

Salih, A., Hoegh-Guldberg, O., and G. Cox. 1998. Photoprotection of Symbiotic Dinoflagellates by fluorescent pigments in reef corals. In: Greenwood, J.G. and N.J. Hall, (eds). *Proceedings of the Australian Coral Reef Society 75th Anniversary Conference*, Heron Island October 1997. School of Marine Science, The University of Queensland, Brisbane. pp. 217-230.
————————, Larkum, A., Cox, G., Kühl, M. and O. Hoegh-Guldberg. 2000. Fluorescent pigments in corals are photoprotective. *Nature* 408:850-853.

Samuel, M., Lam, T., and Y.M. Sin. 1996. Effect of laminarian [beta(1,3)-D-glucan] on the protective immunity of blue gourami, *Trichogaster trichopterus* against *Aeromonas hydrophila*. *Fish and Shellfish Immunology* 6:443-454.

Saxby, T., Dennison, W.C. and O. Hoegh-Guldberg. 2003. Photosynthetic responses of the coral *Montipora digitata* to cold temperature stress. *Marine Ecology Progress Series* 248:85–97.

Scheimer, G. 1995. What's your salinity? Product Reviews. *Aquarium Frontiers*, Spring.
————————. 2004. Product review: IceCap/150 HQI. *Advanced Aquarist Online* 3(9), September 2004. http://www.advancedaquarist.com/issues/sept2004/review.htm

Schofield, O., Prezelin, B. and G. Johnsen. 1996. Wavelength dependency of the maximum quantum yield of carbon fixation for two red tide dinoflagellates, *Heterocapsa pygmaea* and *Prorocentrum minimum* (Pyrrophyta): Implications for measuring photosynthetic rates. *Journal of Phycology* 32:574-583.

Schramm, A., de Beer, D., Wagner, M., Amann, R. 1998. Identification and Activities In Situ of *Nitrosospira* and *Nitrospira* spp. as Dominant Populations in a Nitrifying Fluidized Bed Reactor. *Applied Environmental Microbiology* 64:3480-3485.
————————, Santegoeds C.M., Nielsen, H.K., Ploug, H., Wagner, M., Pribyl, M., Wanner, J., Amann, R., de Beer D. 1999. On the occurrence of anoxic microniches, denitrification, and sulfate reduction in aerated activated sludge. *Applied Environmental Microbiology* 65(9):4189-4196.
————————, De Beer, D., Gieseke, A. and R. Amann. 2000. Microenvironments and distribution of nitrifying bacteria in a membrane-bound biofilm. *Environmental Microbiology* 2(6):680-686.

Schreiber, U. 1997. *Chlorophyll Fluorescence and Photosynthetic Energy Conversion*. Heinz Walz GmbH, Effeltrich, 73 pp.

Schuhmacher, H., van Treeck, P, Eisinger, M. and M. Paster 2000. Transplantation of coral fragments from ship groundings on electrochemically formed reef structures. *Proc. 9th Int Coral Reef Symp., Bali* 2:983-990.

Sebens, K.P. 1977. Autotrophic and heterotrophic nutrition of coral reef zoanthids. *Proc. 3rd Int. Coral Reef Symp.*:397-404.
———————— 1997. Zooplankton capture by reef corals: corals are not plants! *Reef Encounter* 21:10-15.
————————, Grace, S.P., Helmuth, B., Maney, E.J. and J.S. Miles.1998. Water flow and prey capture by three scleractinian corals, *Madracis mirabilis*, *Montastrea cavernosa*, and *Porites porites* in a field enclosure. *Marine Biology* 131:347-360.

Bibliography

Sebralla, L. and J. Kallmeyer. 2001. Miracle Mud - Der Wunderschlamm. www.lars-sebralla.de/ma_miracle.html

Seegebrecht, G.W. and S.H. Gebler. 2000. Concrete vs. shotcrete, what's the difference? http://www.concrete.com/documents/ctlshotcrete.htm

Sekha, H. 2003. Toxicity of trace elements: Truth or myth? *Advanced Aquarist Online* 2(5), May. http://www.advancedaquarist.com/issues/may2003/feature.htm

Shick, J.M. 2004. The continuity and intensity of ultraviolet radiation affect the kinetics of biosynthesis, accumulation, and conversion of mycosporine-like amino acids (MAAs) in the coral *Stylophora pistillata*. *Limnology and Oceanography* 49:442-458.
——————— and W.C. Dunlap. 2002. Mycosporine-like amino acids and related gadusols: biosynthesis, accumulation, and UV-protective function in aquatic organisms. *Annual Review of Physiology* 64:223-262.
———————, Romaine-Lioud S., Ferrier-Pagès C. and Gattuso J.-P. 1999. Ultraviolet-B radiation stimulates shikimate pathway-dependent accumulation of mycosporine-like amino acids in the coral *Stylophora pistillata* despite decreases in its population of symbiotic dinoflagellates. *Limnology and Oceanography* 44(7):1667-1682.
———————, Lesser, M.P. and P.L. Jokiel. 1996. Effects of ultraviolet radiation on corals and other coral reef organisms. *Global Change Biology* 2:527-545.
———————, Dunlap, W.C., Stochaj, W.R., Chalker, B.E. and J. Wu Won. 1995. Depth-dependent responses to solar ultraviolet radiation and oxidative stress in the zooxanthellate coral *Acropora microphthalma*. *Marine Biology* 122:41-51.

Shilo, M. 1966. Predatory bacteria. *Science Journal* 2:33-37.
——————— and B. Bruff. 1965. Lysis of gram-negative bacteria by host-independent ectoparasitic *Bdellovibrio bacteriovorus* isolates. *Journ. Gen. Microbiol.* 40:312.

Shimek, R.L. 1997. What are natural reef salinities and temperatures really and does it matter? *Aquarium Frontiers Online*, November 1997. http://www.animalnetwork.com/fish2/aqfm/1997/nov/features/1/default.asp
———————. 1998. The why's and how's of sand beds: The role of the benthos in the reef aquarium ecosystem. #Reefs Online Talk forum. http://www.reefs.org/library/talklog/r_shimek_090698.html
———————. 1999. *The Coral Reef Aquarium. An Owners Guide to A Happy Healthy Fish*. Howell Book House, New York, NY., USA. 126 pp.
———————. 2000. A beginners guide to reef aquarium ecosystems: Using nature as a model. *Aquarium Fish Magazine* 12(11):46-51.
———————. 2001a. *Sand Bed Secrets: The Common-Sense Way to Biological Filtration*. Marc Weiss Companies, Inc., 36 pp.
———————. 2001b. Necessary nutrition, foods and supplements: A preliminary investigation. *Aquarium Fish Magazine* 13:42-53.
———————. 2001c. Beginner's guide to reef aquarium ecosystems: The importance of deep sand. *Aquarium Fish Magazine* 13(3):50-57.
———————. 2002a. It's (in) the water. *Reefkeeping Online Magazine* 1(1), February 2002. http://reefkeeping.com/issues/2002-02/rs/feature/index.htm
———————. 2002b. It's still in the water. *Reefkeeping.com* 1(2), March 2002. http://reefkeeping.com/issues/2002-03/rs/feature/index.htm
———————. 2002c. What we put in the water. *Reefkeeping Online Magazine* 1(3), April 2002. http://reefkeeping.com/issues/2002-04/rs/feature/index.htm
———————. 2002d. Our coral reef aquaria – Our own personal experiments in the effects of trace element toxicity. *Reefkeeping Online Magazine* 1(7), August, 2002. http://reefkeeping.com/issues/2002-08/rs/feature/index.htm
———————. 2002e. Bitty Bugs: Copepods in the reef aquarium. *Reefkeeping Online Magazine* 10. http://reefkeeping.com/issues/2002-10/rs/index.htm
———————. 2003a. The toxicity of some freshly mixed artificial seawater: A bad beginning for a reef aquarium. *Reefkeeping Online Magazine* 2(2). http://reefkeeping.com/issues/2003-03/rs/feature/index.htm
———————. 2003b. Feeding the reef aquarium, a new paradigm. *Reefkeeping Online Magazine*. http://reefkeeping.com/issues/2003-02/rs/feature/index.htm

Shinn, E.A., Steinen, R.P., Lidz, B.H. and P.K. Swart. 1989. Whitings, a sedimentologic dilemma. *Journal of Sedimentary Petrology* 59:147-161.

Siddall, S.E. 1977. Some design ideas. *Marine Aquarist* 8(5):5-57.

Simkiss, K. 1964. Phosphates as crystal poisons of calcification. *Biological Review* 39:487-505.

Small, A.M. and Adey W.H. 2001. Reef corals, zooxanthellae and free-living algae: a microcosm study that demonstrates synergy between calcification and primary production. *Ecological Engineering* 16:443-457.

Smit, G. 1986. Marine aquariums. Part one. Is it time for a change? *Freshwater and Marine Aquarium Magazine* 9(1):35.

Sonnenchein, L. 2004. Lowering nitrate levels in closed saltwater ecosystems. *Coral* 1(5): 90-94.

Sorokin, Y.I. 1973a. Trophical role of bacteria in the ecosystem of the coral reef. *Nature* 242:415-417.
———————. 1973b. On the feeding of some scleractinian corals with bacteria and dissolved organic matter. *Limnology and Oceanography* 18:380-385.
———————. 1980. Experimental investigation of heterotrophic nutrition of abundant species of reef building corals. *Dokl. Biol. Sci.* 246 (1-6):1323-1325.
———————. 1981a. Aspects of the biomass, feeding, and metabolism of common corals of the Great Barrier Reef, Australia. *Proceedings 4th International Coral Reef Symposium* 2:27-31.
———————. 1981b. Microheterotrophic organisms in marine ecosystems. In: *Analysis of Marine Ecosystems*, (A.R. Longhurst, ed.) Academic Press, New York. pp. 293-311.
———————. 1995. *Coral Reef Ecology*. 2nd Edition, Springer Verlag, New York, USA.

Spotte, S. 1979. *Seawater Aquariums: The Captive Environment*. Wiley-Interscience, John Wiley and Sons, New York, 413 pp.
———————. 1985. *Standard Methods For The Examination Of Water And Wastewater, 16th Edition*. American Public Health Association, Washington DC.
———————. 1992. *Captive Seawater Fishes. Science and Technology*. Wiley-Interscience, John Wiley and Sons, New York, 942 pp.
——————— and G. Adams 1981. Pathogen reduction in closed aquaculture systems by UV radiation: fact or artifact? *Marine Ecology Progress Series* 6:295-298.

Sprung, J. 1993. Reef notes. *Freshwater and Marine Aquarium* 16(6):155.
——————— and J.C. Delbeek. 1997. *The Reef Aquarium: A Comprehensive Guide to the Identification and Care of Tropical Marine Invertebrates*. Volume two. Ricordea Publishing, Coconut Grove, FL. USA. 544 pp.
———————. 1999. *Corals: A Quick Reference Guide*. Ricordea Publishing, Miami, FL, USA. 240 pp.
———————. 2001a. *Invertebrates: A Quick Reference Guide*. Ricordea Publishing, Coconut Grove, FL, 240 pp.
———————. 2001b. Coral bleaching. *Marine Fish and Reef USA Annual 2001*.
———————. 2001c. Sifting the waters - filter feeders. *Marine Fish and Reef USA*, 76-87.
———————. 2002a. Captive husbandry of *Goniopora*, spp. with remarks about the similar genus *Alveopora*. *Advanced Aquarist Online* 1(12). http://advancedaquarist.com/issues/dec2002/invert.htm
———————. 2002b. *Algae. A Problem Solver Guide*. Ricordea Publishing. Coconut Grove, FL USA. 80 pp.
———————. 2002c. Jaubert's method, the "Monaco System," defined and refined. *Advanced Aquarist Online Magazine* 1(9), September. http://www.advancedaquarist.com/issues/sept2002/feature.htm

Stapel, J. 1997. Nutrient dynamics in Indonesian seagrass beds: factors determining conservation and loss of nitrogen and phosphorus. Ph.D. Thesis University of Nijmegen, Netherlands. 127 p. http://helikon.ubn.kun.nl/mono/s/stapel_j/nutrdyini.pdf

Stark, B. 1995. Editorial. *Aquarium Frontiers*, Fall.
———————. 1998. Reef aquaria compromises: Live sand. *Aquarium Frontiers Online* 10, October. http://web.archive.org/web/20010211125328/http://www.animalnetwork.com/fish2/aqfm/1998/oct/features/2/default.asp

Stewart, J.R. and R.M. Brown. 1969. Cytophage that kills or lyses algae. *Science* 164:1523-1524.

Stolp, H. and M. Starr. 1963. *Bdellovibrio bacteriovorus* sp.n. a predatory ectoparasite and bacteriolytic microorganism. In: *Antonie van Leeuwenhoek International Journal of General and Molecular Microbiology* 29:212.

Straughan, R.P.L. 1961. Experiments with living coral in home aquariums. *Tropical Fish Hobbyist* 9(10):69-71.

Stryer, L. 1981. *Biochemistry.* W. H. Freeman and Company, San Francisco.

Studt, R. and T.A. Frakes. 1995. Lab Notes: Phosphate from Gravel. *SeaScope, 12,* Fall.

Stumm, W. and J.J. Morgan. 1981. *Aquatic Chemistry.* Wiley-Interscience, New York.
——————— and J.J. Morgan. 1996. *Aquatic Chemistry, Chemical Equilibria and Rates in Natural Waters,* 3rd Ed. John Wiley and Sons, Inc. New York. 1022pp.

Sunda, W., Kieber, D.J, Kiene, R.P. and S. Huntsman. 2002. An antioxidant function for DMSP in marine algae. *Nature* 418:317-320.

Swamee P.K. and Jain, A.K. 1976. Explicit equations for pipe flow problems. *J. of Hydraulics Engineering.* ASCE 102(5), pp 657-664.

Swart, P.K. 1981. The strontium, magnesium and sodium composition of recent scleractinian coral skeletons as standards for paleoenvironmental analysis. *Palaeogeogrraphy, Paleoclimatololy, Paleoecology* 34:115-136.

Tal, Y., Watts, J.E.M., Schreier, S.B., Sowers, K.R. and H.J. Schreier. 2003. Characterization of the microbial community and nitrogen transformation processes associated with moving bed bioreactors in a closed recirculated mariculture system. *Aquaculture* 215(1-4):187-202.

Tambutte, E., Allemand, D., Mueller, E. and J. Jaubert. 1996. A compartmental approach to the mechanism of calcification in hermatypic corals. *Journal of Experimental Biology* 199:1029-1041.

Teske, A., Alm, E., Regan, J.M., Toze, S., Rittmann, B.E. and D.A. Stahl. 1994. Evolutionary relationships among ammonia- and nitrite-oxidizing bacteria. *Journal of Bacteriology* 176(21):6623-6630.

Thackry, P. 2005. Light emitting diodes in PAR applications: Aquarium lighting. (submitted for publication).

Theodoropoulos, D. 2003. *Invasion Biology: Critique of a Pseudoscience.* Avvar Books, 256 pp.

Thiel, A. 1988. *The Marine Fish and Invert Aquarium.* Aardvark Press, Bridgeport, CT, 320 pp.

Timmons, M.B. 1994, Use of foam fractionators in aquaculture. *Developments in Aquaculture and Fisheries Sciences 27.* Elsevier

Titlyanov, E.A., Shaposhnikova, M.G. and V.I. Zvalinskii. 1980. Photosynthesis and adaptation of corals to irradiance. I. Contents and native state of photosynthetic pigments in symbiotic microalga. *Photosynthetica* 14(3):413-421.

Tombácz, E. Csanaki, Cs. Márk, Cs. and M. Szekeres. 2000. Particle interactions in complex aquatic systems, In: *Entering the Third Millenium with a common approach to Humic Substances and Organic Matter in Water, Soil and Sediments* (Ed. J.P.Croue) PROGEP, Toulouse. Vol.1. pp. 457-460.

Toonen, R.J. 1998-99. What exactly is a "sand bed" anyway? A brief introduction to the ecology of marine sediments, Parts 1-3. J. *MaquaCulture, the Journal of the Breeders Registry.* Part 1, 6(3):42-48; Part 2, 6(4):62-79; Part 3, 7(1):2-11.
——————. 1999. Spray dried phytoplankton. Article Posted to Reefkeepers emailing list, Friday 17th September 1999. http://www.reefs.org/library/article/r_toonen15.html
——————. 2000a. Are plenums obsolete? Another viewpoint. Part 1. *Freshwater and Marine Aquarium* 23(1):44-46, 48, 50, 52, 56, 58, 60, 62, 66. http://www.seabay.org/art_plenums_part1.htm
——————. 2000b. Are plenums obsolete? Another viewpoint. Part 2. *Freshwater and Marine Aquarium* 23(2):44-45, 48, 52-54, 56, 58-60, 64, 66, 68. http://www.seabay.org/art_plenums_part2.htm
——————. 2002. Aquarium Invertebrates: Flame scallops. *Advanced Aquarists Online Magazine,* 1(7). http://www.advancedaquarist.com/issues/july2002/toonen.htm
——————. 2003 Live Foods for Reef Aquariums: If you want animals to thrive, offer them these foods. *Aquarium Fish* 15(11):50-56.
——————. 2003b. Aquarium Invertebrates: Sea Cucumbers - Part III: Sea Apples. *Advanced Aquarists Online Magazine* 2(3). http://www.advancedaquarist.com/issues/mar2003/invert.htm
——————. and C.B. Wee. 2005. An experimental comparison of sediment-based biological filtration designs for recirculating aquarium systems (submitted for publication).

Tullock, J.H. 1995. *The Reef Tank Owner Manual.* Energy Savers Ltd., Harbor City, CA.
——————. 1997. *Natural Reef Aquariums. Simplified Approaches to Creating Living Saltwater Microcosms.* Microcosm Ltd. Shelburne, VT, 336 pp.

Tyree, S. 1998. *The Porifera (Living Sponges) Their Biology, Physiology and Natural Filtration Integration.* DE Publishing. Murrieta, CA USA, 204 pp.
——————. 2000. *The Environmental Gradient. Cryptic Sponge and Sea Squirt Filtration Models.* DE Publishing. Rancho Cucamonga, CA USA, 288 pp.

van Keulen, M. 1998. Water flow in seagrass ecosystems. Ph.D. Thesis, Murdoch University, Perth. ix+220 p. Abstract available on-line (text - 6kb) at: http://possum.murdoch.edu.au/~keulen/phd_abstract.html

Verwey, J. 1930. Coral reef studies. I. The symbiosis between damselfishes and sea anemones in Batavia Bay. *Treubia* 12:305-366.

Wabnitz, C., Taylor, M., Green, E. and T. Razak. 2003. *From Ocean to Aquarium: The global trade in marine ornamental species.* (UNEP World Conservation Monitoring Centre. 219 Huntington Rd. Cambridge, CB3 0DL. UK. 2003.) www.unep-wcmc.org/resources/publications/WCMC_Aquarium.pdf

Wafar, M., Wafar, S. and J.D. David. 1990. Nitrification in coral reefs. *Limnology and Oceanography* 35:725-730.

Walter, L.M. and E.A. Burton. 1990. Dissolution of recent platform carbonate sediments in marine pore fluids. *American Journal of Science* 290:601-643.

Ward, B. B., Martino, D. P., Diaz, M. C. and S.B Joye. 2000. Analysis of ammonia-oxidizing bacteria from hypersaline Mono Lake, California, on the basis of 16S rRNA sequences. *Applied Environmental Microbiology* 66:2873-2881.

Warner, M., Fitt, M. and G. Schmidt. 1999. Damage to photosystem II in symbiotic dinoflagellates: A determinate of coral bleaching. *Proceedings of the National Academy of Sciences* 96:8007-8012.

Bibliography

Webb, J.E. and J. Theodor. 1968. Irrigation of submerged marine sands through wave action. *Nature* 220:682-683.

Webb, K.L. and W.J. Wiebe. 1975. Nitrification on a coral reef. *Canadian Journal of Microbiology* 21:1427-1431.
——————, Dupaul, W.D., Wiebe, W., Sottile, W., and R.E. Johannes. 1975. Enewetak (Eniwetok) Atoll: Aspects of the nitrogen cycle on a coral reef. *Limnology and Oceanography* 20:198-210.

Wellington, G.M. 1982. An experimental analysis of the effects of light and zooplankton on coral zonation. *Oecologia* (Berl) 52: 311-320.

Wells, M.L. and K.W. Bruland. 1998. An improved method for rapid preconcentration and determination of bioactive trace metals in seawater using solid phase extraction and high resolution inductivity coupled plasma mass spectrometry. *Marine Chemistry* 63:145-153.

Wheaton, F.W. 1977. *Aquacultural Engineering.* Robert E. Krieger Publishing Co., Malabarm Florida, USA.

White, F.M. 1986. *Fluid Mechanics.* 2nd Edition, McGraw Hill Book Company.

Whitfield, P.E., Gardner, T., Vives, S.P., Gilligan, M.R., Courtenay, W.R., Carleton-Ray, G. and J.A. Hare. 2002 Biological invasion of the Indo-Pacific lionfish *Pterois volitans* along the Atlantic coast of North America. *Marine Ecology Progress Series* 235:289-297.

Widdig, A. and D. Schlichter. 2001. Phytoplankton: a significant trophic source for soft corals? *Helgol. Mar. Res.* 55:198-211.

Wilkens, P. 1973. *The Saltwater Aquarium for Tropical Marine Invertebrates.* Engelbert Pfriem Verlag, Wuppertal, Germany, 216 pp.
—————— 1990. *Marine Invertebrates: Stone and False Corals, Colonial Anemones.* Dähne Verlag, 136pp.
—————— and J. Birkholz. 1986. *Invertebrates – Tube-, Soft- and Branching Corals.* Engelbert Pfriem Verlag, Wuppertal, Germany, 134 pp.

Wilkinson, C.R. 1986. The nutritional spectrum of coral reef benthos; or sponging off one another for dinner. *Oceanus* 29(2):68-75.

Wilson, D.P. 1952. The aquarium and sea-water circulation system at the Plymouth laboratory. *Journal of the Marine Biological Association of the United Kingdom* 31(1):193-212.
—————— . 1960. The new aquarium and new sea-water circulation systems at the Plymouth laboratory. *Journal of the Marine Biological Association of the United Kingdom* 39(2):391-412.

Wilson, W.H., Dale, A.L., Davy, J.E. and S.K. Davy. 2005. An enemy within? Observations of virus-like particles in reef corals. *Coral Reefs* 24:145-148.

Winogradsky, S. 1890. Sur les orgasnismes de la nitrofication. *C.R. Acad. Sci.* 110:1013-101.

* Witting, J.H. 1999. Zooplankton capture and coral growth: the role of heterotrophy in Caribbean reef corals. PhD Dissertation, Northeastern University, Boston, USA, 285 pp.

Woodhead, J.L., and K.T. Bird. 1998. Efficient rooting and acclimation of micropropagated *Ruppia maritima* Loisel. *J. Mar. Biotechnology* 6:152-156.

Wotton, R.S. 1988. Dissolved organic material and trophic dynamics. *Bioscience* 38(3):172-178.
Yahel, G. 1998. Suspension feeding in coral reefs - what about dissolved matter? *Israeli Journal of Zoology* 44:90-91.
——————, Post, A.F., Fabricius, K.E., Marie, D., Vaulot, D. and A. Genin. 1998. Phytoplankton distribution and grazing near coral reefs. *Limnology and Oceanography* 43:551-563.
——————, Yahel, G. and A. Genin. 2002. Daily Cycles of Suspended Sand at Coral Reefs: A Biological Control. *Limnology and Oceanography* 47:1071-1083.
——————, Zalogin, T., Yahel, R. and A. Genin. 2003. Phytoplankton grazing in coral-reef "bare" rocks. http://web.uvic.ca/~yahel/gyhp.htm.
——————, Sharp, J.H., Marie, D., Häse, C. and A. Genin. 2003. *In situ* feeding and element removal in the coral-reef sponge *Theonella swinhoei:* Bulk DOC is the major source for carbon. *Limnology and Oceanography* 48:141-149.
——————, Marie, D. and A. Genin. (submitted). "InEx" – an *in situ* method to measure rates of element intake and excretion by active suspension feeders. Submitted to *Coral Reefs.*
——————, Zalogin, T., Yahel, R. and A. Genin. (in press). Phytoplankton grazing in coral- reef "bare" rocks. *Coral Reefs.*

Yahel, R., Yahel, G. and A. Genin. (in press). Near-bottom depletion of zooplankton over coral reefs: I. Diurnal dynamics and size distribution. *Coral Reefs.*
——————, Yahel, G. and A. Genin. (submitted). Diel pattern with abrupt crepuscular changes of zooplankton over a coral reef. *Limnology and Oceanography.*

Yates, K.R. 1998. Lilies of the sea: Challenges and success in crinoid husbandry. *1998 AZA Annual Conference.* 58-61.

Yonge, C.M. and A.G. Nicholls. 1931. Studies on the physiology of corals. V. The effects of starvation in light and darkness on the relationship between corals and zooxanthellae. *Scientific Report Great Barrier Reef Expedition 1928-1929* 1:177-211.

Zeebe, R.E. and D.A. Wolf-Gladrow. 2001. *CO$_2$ in seawater: equilibrium, kinetics, isotopes.* Amsterdam: Elsevier, 346 pp.

Zehr, J.P. and B.B. Ward. 2002. Nitrogen cycling in the ocean: New perspectives on processes and paradigms. *Applied Environmental Microbiology* 68:1015-1024.

Index

Index

You should be able to find this book in your local library, book store, aquarium shop, pet store, or public aquarium. If you cannot find it locally, please contact:

Two Little Fishies, Inc.
d.b.a. Ricordea Publishing
4016 El Prado Blvd., Coconut Grove
Florida, 33133 USA
eMail: info@twolittlefishies.com
Website: www.twolittlefishies.com

Although numerous products are mentioned by name and pictured in The Reef Aquarium Volume Three, this should not be taken as any form of endorsement of these products nor any assurance as to their safety or performance by the authors or publisher. Concurrently, the omission of any product should not be taken as a form of criticism or lack of confidence in that product by the authors or publisher.

Internet URLs are frequently mentioned in *The Reef Aquarium*, Volume Three. These are included for convenience, and often the Internet is the only source for the citation mentioned. However, we recognize that the Internet is constantly changing, and websites come and go. Therefore, if a URL mentioned in this book is no longer valid, please use a search engine to search for the topic, author's name, and/or product name to locate it. We would also appreciate hearing from readers who find URLs that are no longer valid and can provide the new URLs, so that we may update future editions of volume three when possible.